THE WORLD : Political

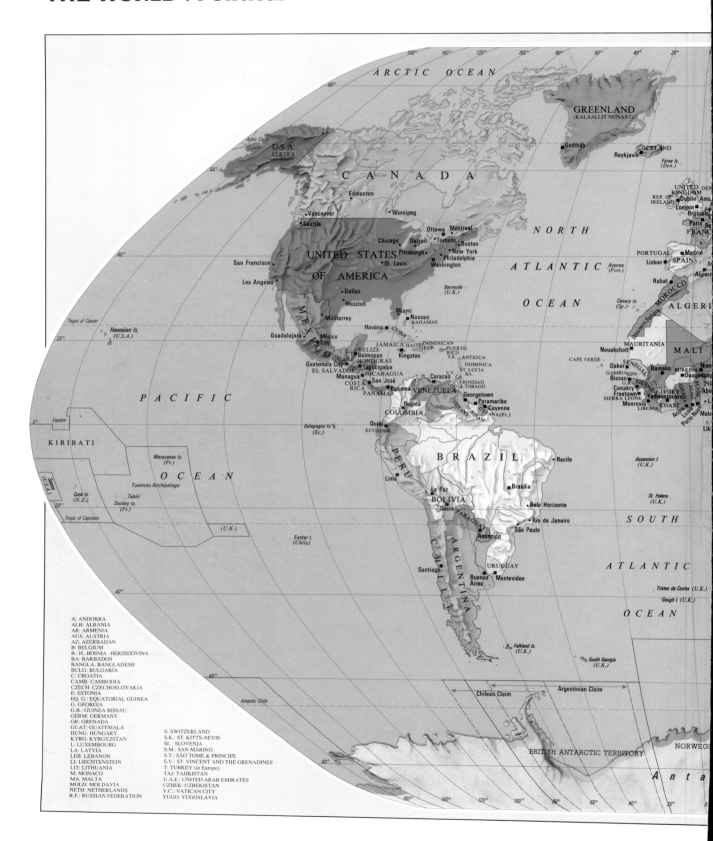

ARCTIC OCEAN

GREENLAND
(KALAALLIT NUNAAT)

Godthåb

ICELAND
Reykjavík

Faroe Is.
(Den.)

Arctic Circle

U.S.A.
ALASKA

C A N A D A

Edmonton

Vancouver
Seattle
Winnipeg
Ottawa Montreal
Chicago Detroit Toronto Boston
San Francisco Pittsburgh New York
UNITED STATES St. Louis Philadelphia
OF AMERICA Washington
Los Angeles
Dallas
Houston
Monterrey Miami Nassau
Havana BAHAMAS
Guadalajara Mexico CUBA
City JAMAICA HAITI DOMINICAN
BELIZE Kingston REP. PUERTO
Belmopan RICO
Guatemala City HONDURAS ST. LUCIA
EL SALVADOR Tegucigalpa
Managua NICARAGUA
San José Caracas
COSTA Panama VENEZUELA Georgetown
RICA PANAMA Paramaribo
Bogotá Cayenne
COLOMBIA GUYANA (Fr.)
Quito SURINAM
ECUADOR

Galapagos Is.
(Ec.)

PERU
Lima
B R A Z I L Recife

La Paz Brasília
BOLIVIA
Sucre Belo Horizonte
PARAGUAY Río de Janeiro
São Paulo
Asunción
A R G E N T I N A
URUGUAY
Santiago Buenos Montevideo
Aires

Falkland Is.
(U.K.)

South Georgia
(U.K.)

Chilean Claim Argentinian Claim

BRITISH ANTARCTIC TERRITORY NORWEGI

P A C I F I C

O C E A N

KIRIBATI

Samoa
(U.S.A.)

Marquesas Is.
(Fr.)

Tuamotu Archipelago

Tahiti
Cook Is. Society Is.
(N.Z.) (Fr.)

Tropic of Capricorn

Easter I.
(Chile)

(U.K.)

Equator

N O R T H

A T L A N T I C

O C E A N

Bermuda
(U.K.)

Azores
(Port.)

PORTUGAL Madrid
Lisbon SPAIN
Rabat MOROCCO
Canary Is.
(Sp.) ALGERIA

UNITED DEN
KINGDOM
REP. OF Dublin Ams
IRELAND London
Brussels
Paris
FRANC

Algiers

Western Sahara

Nouakchott MAURITANIA MALI

CAPE VERDE Dakar SENEGAL Bamako BURKINA Nian
GAMBIA Ouagadoug
Bissau GUINEA
Conakry G.B. IVORY Ab
Freetown Yamoussoukro NI
SIERRA LEONE COAST Acc
Monrovia LIBERIA Lomé Porto Nov Mala
Porto-Novo Lib

Ascension I.
(U.K.)

St. Helena
(U.K.)

S O U T H

A T L A N T I C

O C E A N

Tristan da Cunha (U.K.)
Gough I. (U.K.)

Tropic of Cancer

Hawaiian Is.
(U.S.A.)

Antarctic Circle

Anta

A: ANDORRA
ALB: ALBANIA
AR: ARMENIA
AUS: AUSTRIA
AZ: AZERBAIJAN
B: BELGIUM
B.-H.: BOSNIA - HERZEGOVINA
BA: BARBADOS
BANGLA: BANGLADESH
BULG: BULGARIA
C: CROATIA
CAMB: CAMBODIA
CZECH: CZECHOSLOVAKIA
E: ESTONIA
EQ. G.: EQUATORIAL GUINEA
G: GEORGIA
G.B.: GUINEA BISSAU
GERM: GERMANY
GR: GRENADA
GUAT: GUATEMALA
HUNG: HUNGARY
KYRG: KYRGYZSTAN
L: LUXEMBOURG
LA: LATVIA
LEB: LEBANON
LI: LIECHTENSTEIN
LIT: LITHUANIA
M: MONACO
MA: MALTA
MOLD: MOLDAVIA
NETH: NETHERLANDS
R.F.: RUSSIAN FEDERATION

S: SWITZERLAND
S.K.: ST. KITTS-NEVIS
SL: SLOVENIA
S.M.: SAN MARINO
S.T.: SÃO TOME & PRINCIPE
S.V.: ST. VINCENT AND THE GRENADINES
T: TURKEY (in Europe)
TAJ: TAJIKISTAN
U.A.E.: UNITED ARAB EMIRATES
UZBEK: UZBEKISTAN
V.C.: VATICAN CITY
YUGO: YUGOSLAVIA

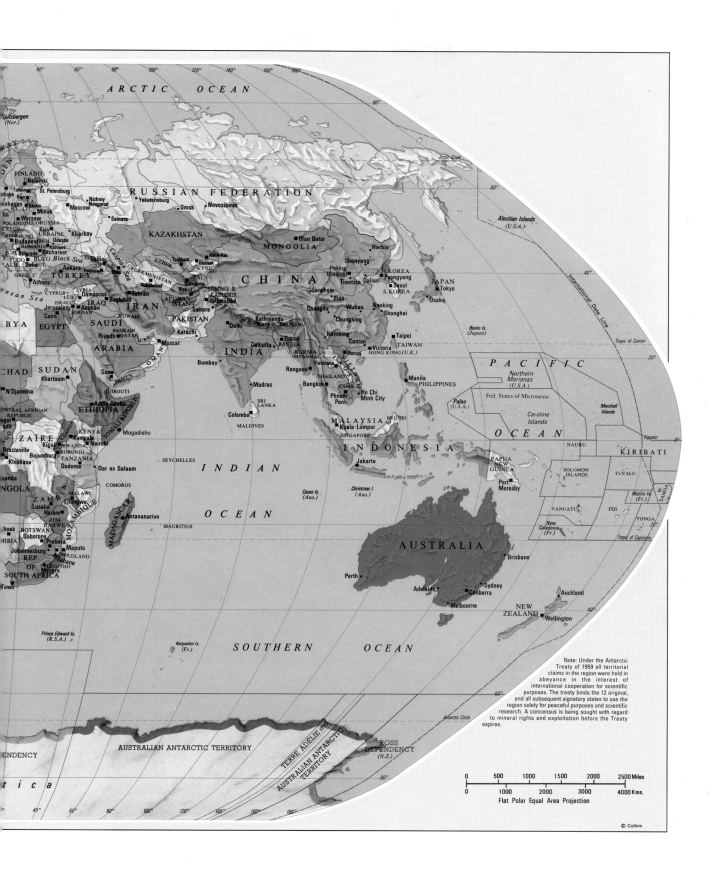

ARCTIC OCEAN

Spitsbergen
(Nor.)

FINLAND
Helsinki
Tallinn St. Petersburg
enhagen Riga
Minsk
Vilnius Nizhniy Moscow
Warsaw BELORUSSIA Novgorod
CZECH Kiev UKRAINE Samara
Budapest MOL. Kharkov
ROMANIA Kishinev
B.-H Belgrade Bucharest
YUGO. BULG. Black Sea
ALB. Sofia
GREECE
TURKEY Tbilisi
Athens Ankara Yerevan
CYPRUS SYRIA
LEB. Damascus IRAQ
ISRAEL Baghdad
Jerusalem JORDAN Amman
Cairo KUWAIT
EGYPT SAUDI BAHRAIN
Riyadh QATAR
ARABIA U.A.E.
Muscat

RUSSIAN FEDERATION

Yekaterinburg
Omsk Novosibirsk

KAZAKHSTAN

Ulan Bator
MONGOLIA

Tashkent Alma-Ata
UZBEK. Bishkek
TURKMENISTAN KYRG.

Ashkhabad
Kabul
Tehran AFGHAN- JAMMU &
ISTAN KASHMIR
Islamabad
Lahore
PAKISTAN Delhi

Harbin

Shenyang
N.KOREA
Peking Pyongyang
(Beijing) Dalian
CHINA Tientsin Seoul
Lanchow S.KOREA

CHAD SUDAN
N'Djamena Khartoum
DJIBOUTI
CENTRAL Addis Ababa
AFRICAN ETHIOPIA
REPUBLIC YEMEN
ugui Mogadishu
ndé
ZAIRE KENYA
Brazzaville Kampala
Kinshasa Bujumbura BURUNDI
uanda Dodoma TANZANIA

Sana
OMAN

SOMALI
REPUBLIC
Nairobi

SEYCHELLES
Dar es Salaam

COMOROS

INDIAN

OCEAN

MADAGASCAR
Antananarivo

MAURITIUS

NGOLA

ZAMBIA MALAWI
Lusaka Lilongwe
ZIM-
Harare BABWE
hoek BOTSWANA MOZAMBIQUE
Gaborone Pretoria Maputo
MIBIA Johannesburg SWAZILAND
REP. Mbabane
OF LESOTHO
SOUTH AFRICA Maseru
Town

Kathmandu
NEPAL BHUTAN
Delhi
Karachi

INDIA
Bombay

Madras
SRI
LANKA
Colombo
MALDIVES

Calcutta
Dacca BANGLA.
BURMA
(MYANMA)

Rangoon

THAILAND
Bangkok

Changdu
Sian Wuhan Nanking
Chungking Shanghai
Kunming Canton
Hanoi Taipei
Victoria TAIWAN
HONG KONG (U.K.)

Vientiane

CAMB.
Phnom Ho Chi
Penh Minh City

MALAYSIA BRUNEI
Kuala Lumpur
SINGAPORE

INDONESIA

Jakarta

Christmas I.
(Aus.)

JAPAN
Tokyo
Osaka

PACIFIC

Bonin Is.
(Japan)

Tropic of Cancer

Manila
PHILIPPINES

Northern
Marianas
(U.S.A.)
Palau Fed. States of Micronesia
(U.S.A.)
Caroline
Islands

OCEAN

PAPUA
NEW
GUINEA
Port
Moresby

NAURU

SOLOMON
ISLANDS

VANUATU

New
Caledonia
(Fr.)

Aleutian Islands
(U.S.A.)

International Date Line

Marshall
Islands

KIRIBATI

Equator

TUVALU

FIJI

Wallis Is.
(Fr.)

W.
SAMOA

TONGA

Tropic of Capricorn

Cocos Is.
(Aus.)

OCEAN

AUSTRALIA

Perth

Adelaide

Melbourne

Brisbane

Sydney
Canberra

Auckland

NEW
ZEALAND Wellington

Prince Edward Is.
(R.S.A.)

Kerguelen Is.
(Fr.)

SOUTHERN OCEAN

Antarctic Circle

Note: Under the Antarctic
Treaty of 1959 all territorial
claims in the region were held in
abeyance in the interest of
international cooperation for scientific
purposes. The treaty binds the 12 original,
and all subsequent signatory states to use the
region solely for peaceful purposes and scientific
research. A concensus is being sought with regard
to mineral rights and exploitation before the Treaty
expires.

ENDENCY

tica

AUSTRALIAN ANTARCTIC TERRITORY

TERRE ADÉLIE (Fr.)
AUSTRALIAN ANTARCTIC
TERRITORY

ROSS
DEPENDENCY
(N.Z.)

| 0 | 500 | 1000 | 1500 | 2000 | 2500 Miles |
| 0 | 1000 | 2000 | 3000 | 4000 Kms. |

Flat Polar Equal Area Projection

© Collins

COLLINS

PAPERBACK
ATLAS
OF THE WORLD

HarperCollins*Publishers*

Collins Paperback Atlas of the World
first published 1988 by William Collins Sons & Co. Ltd.

New Edition 1992
Maps © Collins and Collins-Longman Atlases
Illustrated section and statistics © Bartholomew

Collins is an imprint of Bartholomew,
a division of HarperCollins *Publishers*

12 Duncan Street
Edinburgh
EH9 1TA

Printed in Scotland by HarperCollins Manufacturing, Glasgow

The contents of this edition of the Collins Paperback Atlas of the World are believed to be correct at the time of printing. Nevertheless, the publishers can accept no responsibility for errors, or for omissions, or for changes in detail given.

ISBN 0 00 448023 6

Photograph Credits
Credits read from top to bottom and left to right on each page.
XI Space Frontiers. VIII Lockheed Solar Laboratory. XV NASA. XVI Robert Harding; Zefa; Grisewood & Dempsey. XVII Pat Morris; Robert Harding; Zefa. XIX M. Borland. XX National Coal Board; Grisewood & Dempsey (2). XXI Nasou; Atomic Energy Authority. XXII Photo Library International; Zefa; Daily Telegraph Library. XXIII Picturepoint; U.S. Environmental Protection Society.
XXIV NASA.

CONTENTS

GUIDE TO THE ATLAS

COLLINS PAPERBACK ATLAS OF THE WORLD consists of three self-contained but interrelated sections, as is clearly indicated in the preceding list of contents.

OUR PLANET EARTH

This concise encyclopaedia section, by use of stimulating illustration and informative text, brings together many of the latest scientific discoveries and conclusions about our world, our place in the universe, our neighbours in space, the origin, structure and dynamics of our planet, the distribution of peoples and resources, and the increasingly significant effects of man on his environment. Each double-page opening has been carefully designed to highlight an important facet of our world as we know it today. As a special feature, every subject presentation includes a factfinder panel, to which quick and easy reference can be made in order to find out particularly notable facts. All statistics quoted in this section are presented in metric terms in accordance with the System International d'Unites (S.I. units).

WORLD ATLAS

The main section of 64 pages of maps has been carefully planned and designed to meet the contemporary needs of the atlas user. Full recognition has been given to the many different purposes that currently call for map reference.

Map coverage Map coverage extends to every part of the world in a balanced scheme that avoids any individual country or regional bias. Map areas are chosen to reflect the social, economic, cultural or historical importance of a particular region. Each double spread or single page map has been planned deliberately to cover an entire physical or political unit. Generous map overlaps are included to maintain continuity. Each of the continents is treated systematically in a subsection of its own. As an aid to the reader in locating the required area, a postage stamp key map is incorporated into the title margin of each map page.

Map projections have been chosen to reflect the different requirements of particular areas. No map can be absolutely true on account of the impossibility of representing a spheroid accurately on a flat surface without some distortion in either area, distance, direction or shape. In a general world atlas it is the equal area property that is most important to retain for comparative map studies and feature size evaluation and this principle has been followed wherever possible in this map section. As a special feature of this atlas, the Global View projections used for each continental political map have been specially devised to allow for a realistic area comparison between the land areas of each continent and also between land and sea.

Map scales, as expressions of the relationship which the distance between any two points of the map bears to the corresponding distance on the ground, are in the context of this atlas grouped into three distinct categories.

Large scales, of between 1:2 000 000 (1 centimetre to 20 kilometres or 1 inch to 32 miles) and 1:3 000 000 (1 centimetre to 30 kilometres or 1 inch to 48 miles), are used to cover particularly dense populated areas of Western Europe and Japan.

Medium scales of between 1:3 000 000 and 1:10 000 000 are used for maps of important parts of Europe, North America, Australasia, etc.

Small scales of less than 1:10 000 000 (1 centimetre to 100 kilometres or 1 inch to 160 miles), are selected for maps of the complete world, continents, polar regions and many of the larger countries.

The actual scale at which a particular area is mapped therefore reflects its shape, size and density of detail, and as a basic principle the more detail required to be shown of an area, the greater its scale. However, throughout this atlas, map scales have been limited in number, as far as possible, in order to facilitate comparison between maps.

Map measurements give preference to the metric system which is now used in nearly every country throughout the world. All spot heights and ocean depths are shown in metres and the relief and submarine layer delineation is based on metric contour levels. However, all linear scalebar and height reference column figures are given in metric and Imperial equivalents to facilitate conversion of measurements for the non-metric reader.

Map symbols used are fully explained in the legend to be found on the first page of the World Atlas section. Careful study and frequent reference to this legend will aid in the reader's ability to extract maximum information.

Topography is shown by the combined means of precise spot heights, contouring, layer tinting and three-dimensional hill shading. Similar techniques are also used to depict the sea bed on the World Physical map and those of the oceans and polar regions.

Hydrographic features such as coastlines, rivers, lakes, swamps and canals are clearly differentiated.

Communications are particularly well represented with the contemporary importance of airports and road networks duly emphasized.

International boundaries and national capitals are fully documented and internal administrative divisions are shown with the maximum detail that the scale will allow. Boundary delineation reflects the 'de facto' rather than the 'de jure' political interpretation and where relevant an undefined or disputed boundary is distinguished. However there is no intended implication that the publishers necessarily endorse or accept the status of any political entity recorded on the maps.

Settlements are shown by a series of graded town stamps from major cities down to tiny villages.

Other features, such as notable ancient monuments, oases, national parks, oil and gas fields, are selectively included on particular maps that merit their identification.

Lettering styles used in the maps have been chosen with great care to ensure maximum legibility and clear distinction of named feature categories. The size and weight of the various typefaces reflect the relative importance of the features. Town names are graded to correspond with the appropriate town stamp.

Map place names have been selected in accordance with maintaining legibility at a given scale and at the same time striking an appropriate balance between natural and man-made features worthy of note. Name forms have been standardized according to the widely accepted principle, now well established in international reference atlases, of including place names and geographical terms in the local language of the country in question. In the case of non-Roman scripts (e.g. Arabic), transliteration and transcription have either been based on the rules recommended by the Permanent Committee on Geographical Names and the United States Board of Geographical Names, or as in the case of the adopted Pinyin transcription of Chinese names, a system officially proposed by the country concerned. The diacritical signs used in each language or transliteration have been retained on all the maps and throughout the index. However the English language reader's requirements have also been recognised in that the names of all countries, oceans, major seas and land features as well as familiar alternative name versions of important towns are presented in English.

Map sources used in the compilation of this atlas were many and varied, but always of the latest available information. At each stage of their preparation the maps were submitted to a thorough process of research and continual revision to ensure that on publication all data would be as accurate as practicable. A well-documented data bank was created to ensure consistency and validity of all information represented on the maps.

WORLD DATA

This detailed data section forms an appropriate complement to the preceding maps and illustrated texts. There are three parts, each providing a different type of essential geographical information.

World Facts and Figures Drawn from the latest available official sources, these tables present an easy reference profile of significant world physical, political and demographic as well as national data.

World Index This concluding part of the atlas lists in alphabetical order all individual place names to be found on the maps, which total about 20,000. Each entry in the index is referenced to the appropriate map page number, the country or region in which the name is located and the position of the name on the map, given by its co-ordinates of latitude and longitude. A full explanation of how to use the index is to be found on page 71.

World Maps Finally two summary maps giving separate coverage of the main political and physical features of the world are to be found on the front and back endpapers.

OUR PLANET EARTH

While the earth formed about 4500 million years ago, life as we know it today has only evolved gradually over the last 45 million years. Human beings have inhabited the earth for less than half a million years, and a couple of hundred generations takes us back to the dawn of history. Within this time people have conquered the animal kingdom, learnt how to harness the forces of nature, and proliferated in such numbers that they have colonised nearly every corner of the earth. Even more stunning are the changes which have taken place within living memory. The use of electricity, nuclear fission and modern technology have now given us the power to alter the balance of life on earth.

The first astronauts reported that the earth hangs "like a blue pearl in space". Their experience has helped dispel the dangerous notion that the world is boundless in extent, with limitless resources. Ecologists have also shown that the earth is a self enclosed system in which all forms of life are interconnected. Disruption in one part of the ecosystem can have serious consequences elsewhere. It follows that all human activity has an effect on the natural environment, and that we misuse this fragile planet at our peril.

In recent years people have been putting the environment under increasing stress. Raw materials such as timber, water and minerals are beginning to run short. Pollution and the disposal of wastes are becoming critical issues, and global warming has highlighted the dangers that we face. Environmental problems have been compounded by inequalities of wealth, where rich nations control and exploit the bulk of available resources in a world in which large numbers of people are struggling for survival. Decisive and concerted action will be needed to confront the growing ecological crisis.

Despite these threats there are encouraging signs. Over the past few decades food production has more than matched the growth in population. In industry there is scope for much greater efficiency and more careful use of resources. Sustainable development holds one of the keys to the future. Improvements in social justice also offer great possibilities.

These are exciting times in which we live. In the next decade the state of the environment is set to become the most pressing issue confronting us all. The way we respond to the challenge will have a profound effect on the earth and its life support systems. We will only make balanced decisions on the basis of detailed and careful research. This illustrated encyclopaedia seeks to provide up-to-date information on the issues that confront us all.

THE SOLAR SYSTEM

The Solar System rotates once around the centre of the Milky Way galaxy every 200 million years. The Solar System consists principally of the Sun and the nine planets that orbit around it, but it also includes moons and much debris, such as the spectacular rings of Saturn, and asteroids, which are called minor planets because they measure up to about 1000 km across. Other rocky matter and frozen gas form comets, which are even more numerous than asteroids. Comets have extremely elongated orbits, the farthest point of which may be in the vicinity of the outer planets. The path of one is shown by the red line in the diagram below. As the comets near the Sun, the frozen matter vaporizes to form a tail that is millions of kilometres long. If the orbit of a comet crosses that of the Earth, loose particles may be ejected into the atmosphere. There, they burn up in meteor showers. Fragments large enough to reach Earth are called meteorites.

Many solar systems probably exist in the Universe. In 1982 Russian astronomers

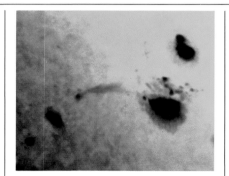

Groups of sunspots are dark areas on the Sun's surface that are around 1000° cooler than surrounding areas. The largest recorded sunspot covered 10,000 million km². Sunspots probably result from magnetic fields that cause local cooling. Sunspots may last for months, but small ones vanish after a few days.

estimated that 130 solar systems similar to our own lie within the observable part of the Milky Way galaxy. But their presence can only be inferred.

Our Sun probably began to form about 4600 million years ago from the solar nebula, a huge cloud of dust and gas. The planets formed somewhat later from the debris that was left over. The Sun consists mainly of hydrogen that is being turned into a central core of helium. The reactions involved in this process generate energy, giving the Sun a surface temperature of 6000°C. Prominences, eruptions of gas from the surface, may reach 50,000°C or more. They are often associated with sunspots, cooler patches possibly caused by strong magnetic fields that block the outward flow of heat. The Sun is surrounded by a thin atmosphere, the corona, which can be seen during a total eclipse. Eventually, the Sun, like all stars, will use up most of its hydrogen and will become a red giant star, engulfing the Solar System. But this will not occur for another 5000 million years.

The Inner Planets

The planets differ in many ways in their makeup, appearance, size and temperature. The four inner planets are the cratered Mercury, whose surface resembles that of our Moon; Venus, which is swathed by a cloudy atmosphere containing much carbon dioxide; Earth; and Mars, which also has a cratered surface. These four, comparatively small, rocky bodies are called terrestrial planets.

The Outer Planets

Most of the asteroids in the Solar System lie between Mars, the outermost of the terrestrial planets, and Jupiter, the innermost of the outer planets. The outer planets include three others – the ringed Saturn, Uranus and Neptune – which, like Jupiter, are huge balls of gas, mainly hydrogen and its compounds, with nitrogen (giving ammonia), carbon (giving methane) and helium. Rocky cores may exist beneath the gases. Pluto, which was discovered in 1930, is probably a rocky body with a methane-type atmosphere.

FACTFINDER

		Mean distance from the Sun (millions of km)	Equatorial diameter (km)	Period of rotation on axis	Surface °C temp- erature	Mass (Earth = 1)	Sidereal Period
1	Sun	—	1,392,000	25d 9h	6000°	333,434.00	—
2	Mercury	58	4,850	58d 14h	350/−170°	0·04	88d
3	Venus	108	12,104	243d	480°	0·83	225d
4	Earth	149·5	12,756	23h56m	22°	1·00	1y
5	Mars	228	6,790	24h 37m	−50°	0·11	1y 322d
6	Jupiter	778·5	142,600	9h 50m	−150°	318.00	11y 315d
7	Saturn	1427	120,000	10h 14m	−180°	95.00	29y 167d
8	Uranus	2870	52,300	15h 30m	−210°	15.00	84y 6d
9	Neptune	4497	49,500	15h 50m	−220°	17.00	164y 288d
10	Pluto	5900	3,000?	6d 9h	−230°?	0·06	247y 255d

Number of satellites: Mercury and Venus – 0; Earth – 1; Mars – 2; Jupiter – 14?; Saturn – 17?; Uranus – 5; Neptune – 2; Pluto – 1.
Orbital inclination: Mercury – 7°; Venus – 3°24'; Mars – 1°51'; Jupiter – 1°18'; Saturn – 2°29'; Uranus – 0°46'; Neptune – 1°46'; Pluto – 17°06'.

THE WHIRLING EARTH

The Earth moves in three ways: it spins on its axis; it orbits the Sun; and it moves around the Milky Way galaxy with the rest of the Solar System. As it spins on its axis, the Sun appears to move around the sky once every 24 hours. This, the mean solar day, is slightly longer than the sidereal day of 23 hours, 56 minutes and 4 seconds. The difference between the two is explained by the fact that the Earth is orbiting the Sun while it spins on its axis, with the effect that it must rotate 1/365th of a revolution more than a sidereal day in order that the same meridian exactly faces the Sun again.

As the Earth spins on its axis, the time at any point on the surface is calculated from the position of the Sun in the sky. This is called the local or apparent time. Because the Earth rotates 360° in 24 hours, local time changes by one hour for every 15° of longitude or 4 minutes for every 1° of longitude. For practical purposes, however, we use standard or zone time, so that the times are fixed over extensive north-south zones that also take account of national boundaries. By an international agreement in 1884, time zones are measured east and west of the prime meridian (0° longitude) which passes through Greenwich, London. Because clocks are advanced by 12 hours 180° east of Greenwich, but put back by 12 hours 180° west of Greenwich, there is a time difference of 24 hours at the International Date Line. This is approximately 180°W or E, although internationally agreed deviations prevent confusion of dates in island groups and land areas.

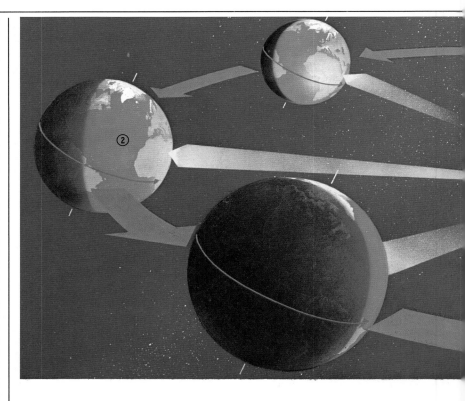

People crossing the International Date Line from west to east gain a day. Those going from east to west lose a day.

The Seasons

Because the Earth's axis is tilted by 23½°, the Sun appears to travel in a higher or lower path across the sky at various times of the year, giving differing lengths of daylight. The diagram at the top of the page shows that, at the spring equinox in the northern hemisphere (March 21), the Sun is overhead at the Equator. After March 21, the overhead Sun moves northwards as the northern hemisphere tilts towards the Sun. On June 21, the summer solstice in the northern hemisphere, the Sun is overhead at the Tropic of Cancer (latitude 23½° North). By September 23, the Sun is again overhead at the Equator. By about December 21, the Sun is overhead at the Tropic of Capricorn (23½° S). This is the winter solstice in the northern hemisphere. The seasons are reversed in the southern hemisphere.

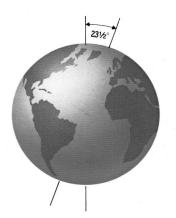

Above: The Earth's axis (joining the North and South poles via the centre of the Earth) is tilted by 23½°. The Earth rotates on its axis once every 23 hours, 56 minutes and 4 seconds. The tilt of the axis remains constant as the Earth orbits the Sun.

Right: The path of the Sun across the sky is highest on Midsummer Day, the longest day, and lowest at midwinter (December 21), the shortest day. The total variation in altitude is 47°, which is twice the angle by which the Earth's axis is tilted.

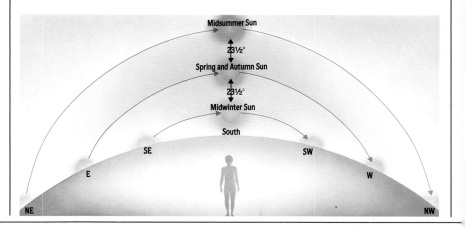

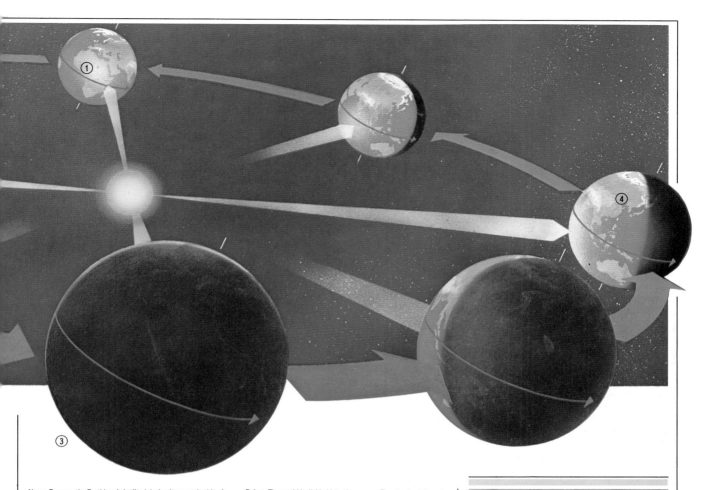

Above: Because the Earth's axis is tilted during its annual orbit of the Sun, there are variations in solar radiation that cause seasons. On March 21, the spring or vernal equinox in the northern hemisphere, the Sun is overhead at the Equator (1). On June 21, it is overhead at the Tropic of Cancer, the summer solstice (2). On September 23, it is overhead at the Equator, the autumn equinox (3). On December 21, it is overhead at the Tropic of Capricorn, the winter solstice (4).

Below: The world is divided into time zones. The standard time at Greenwich (0° longitude) on the map is 12.00 Greenwich Mean Time (not British Summer Time). East of Greenwich, standard times are ahead of GMT, while west of Greenwich, they are behind it. Ideally, time zones should be longitudinal bands of 15° or 7½° (representing time differences of 1 hour or 30 minutes). But time zones are irregular in shape to prevent small countries having two standard times.

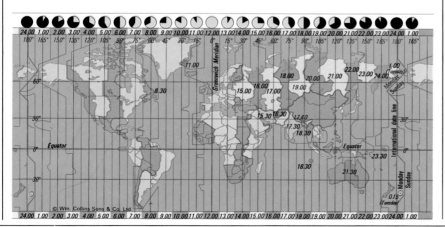

FACTFINDER

Length of day: Mean solar day, 24 hours. Sidereal day (measured against fixed stars) 23·93 hours.

Speed of the Earth's rotation on its axis: At the Equator, it is rotating at 1660 km/h. It is less away from the Equator: at 30°N and S, it is 1438 km/h; at 60° N and S, it is 990 km/h.

Equinoxes: The vernal equinox is on March 21, and the autumn equinox on September 23 in the northern hemisphere. The equinoxes are reversed in the southern hemisphere.

Solstices: In the northern hemisphere, the summer solstice is on June 21 and the winter solstice on December 21. The reverse applies in the southern hemisphere.

THE EARTH'S STRUCTURE

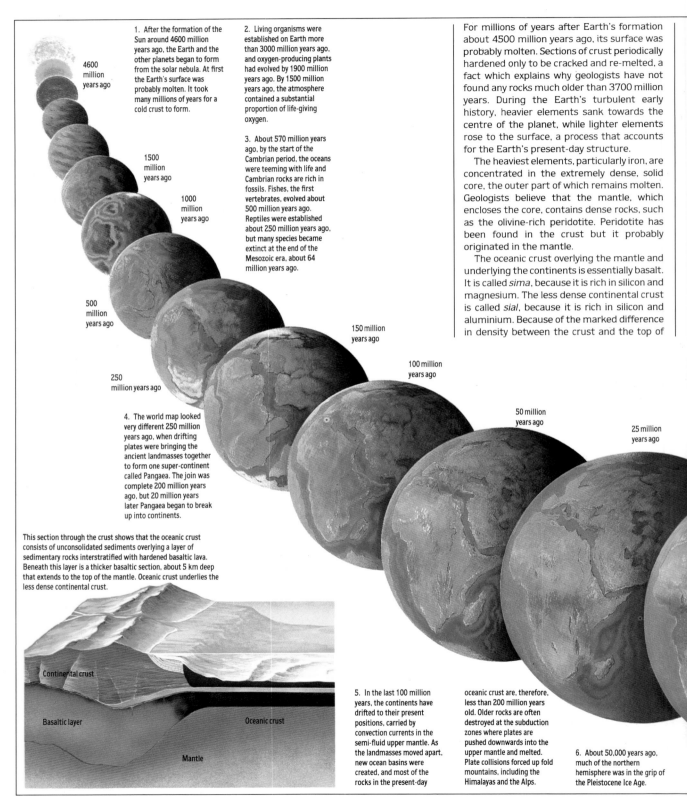

1. After the formation of the Sun around 4600 million years ago, the Earth and the other planets began to form from the solar nebula. At first the Earth's surface was probably molten. It took many millions of years for a cold crust to form.

2. Living organisms were established on Earth more than 3000 million years ago, and oxygen-producing plants had evolved by 1900 million years ago. By 1500 million years ago, the atmosphere contained a substantial proportion of life-giving oxygen.

3. About 570 million years ago, by the start of the Cambrian period, the oceans were teeming with life and Cambrian rocks are rich in fossils. Fishes, the first vertebrates, evolved about 500 million years ago. Reptiles were established about 250 million years ago, but many species became extinct at the end of the Mesozoic era, about 64 million years ago.

For millions of years after Earth's formation about 4500 million years ago, its surface was probably molten. Sections of crust periodically hardened only to be cracked and re-melted, a fact which explains why geologists have not found any rocks much older than 3700 million years. During the Earth's turbulent early history, heavier elements sank towards the centre of the planet, while lighter elements rose to the surface, a process that accounts for the Earth's present-day structure.

The heaviest elements, particularly iron, are concentrated in the extremely dense, solid core, the outer part of which remains molten. Geologists believe that the mantle, which encloses the core, contains dense rocks, such as the olivine-rich peridotite. Peridotite has been found in the crust but it probably originated in the mantle.

The oceanic crust overlying the mantle and underlying the continents is essentially basalt. It is called *sima*, because it is rich in silicon and magnesium. The less dense continental crust is called *sial*, because it is rich in silicon and aluminium. Because of the marked difference in density between the crust and the top of

4600 million years ago

1500 million years ago

1000 million years ago

500 million years ago

250 million years ago

150 million years ago

100 million years ago

50 million years ago

25 million years ago

4. The world map looked very different 250 million years ago, when drifting plates were bringing the ancient landmasses together to form one super-continent called Pangaea. The join was complete 200 million years ago, but 20 million years later Pangaea began to break up into continents.

This section through the crust shows that the oceanic crust consists of unconsolidated sediments overlying a layer of sedimentary rocks interstratified with hardened basaltic lava. Beneath this layer is a thicker basaltic section, about 5 km deep that extends to the top of the mantle. Oceanic crust underlies the less dense continental crust.

Continental crust

Basaltic layer

Oceanic crust

Mantle

5. In the last 100 million years, the continents have drifted to their present positions, carried by convection currents in the semi-fluid upper mantle. As the landmasses moved apart, new ocean basins were created, and most of the rocks in the present-day

oceanic crust are, therefore, less than 200 million years old. Older rocks are often destroyed at the subduction zones where plates are pushed downwards into the upper mantle and melted. Plate collisions forced up fold mountains, including the Himalayas and the Alps.

6. About 50,000 years ago, much of the northern hemisphere was in the grip of the Pleistocene Ice Age.

FACTFINDER

The Earth's crust: The oceanic crust averages 6 km thick; density, 3·0 g/cm³. The continental crust averages 35—40 km, reaching 60—70 km under high mountains; density 2·7 g/cm³.

Mantle: About 2900 km thick; density, 3·4—4·5 g/cm³.

Core: Diameter 6740 km. Outer core 2000 km thick, molten iron and nickel. Inner core, a solid metal ball, 1370 km thick. Density of core, 10—13 g/cm³. Temperature at 2700°C, under pressure of 3800 tonnes per sq cm.

Surface area of the Earth: 510,066,000 km². About 148,326,000 km², or just over 29 per cent of the Earth's surface, is land.

Mass: 5976 million million million tonnes.

Shape and size: Oblate spheroid, slightly flattened at the poles and bulging at the Equator. So, at sea level, the diameter of the Earth between the poles is 12,713 km, as compared with a diameter of 12,756 km. across the plane of the Equator. Similarly, the equatorial circumference of 40,075 km is greater than the polar circumference of 40,007 km.

the mantle, the crust cannot sink. It is split into large, rigid plates that 'float' on the denser mantle. Plate movements cause earthquakes, mountain building and volcanic activity – occurrences that remind us of the restless nature of our world.

About 85 per cent of the top 16 km of the crust are either igneous rocks (rocks formed from molten magma) or metamorphic rocks (igneous or sedimentary rocks that have been changed by heat, pressure or, sometimes, chemical action). However, sedimentary rocks cover 75 per cent of the surface of landmasses. Many sedimentary rocks are clastic (formed from eroded rock fragments), some, such as coal, are organic, and some are formed by chemical action, such as rock salt precipitated from water.

Below are eight rocks found in the Earth's crust. There are three main kinds of rocks: igneous, sedimentary and metamorphic. Igneous rocks, including obsidian and granite, are forms of hardened magma. Many sedimentary rocks, such as sandstone and conglomorate, are composed of worn fragments of other rocks, while coal is compressed plant remains. Metamorphic rocks, such as marble and slate, are formed when great heat and pressure alter igneous or sedimentary rocks.

Obsidian is a glassy, extrusive igneous rock, formed on the surface.

Granite is a coarse-grained, intrusive igneous rock, which forms in huge underground masses.

Marble is formed by the action of great heat and pressure on limestone.

Slate is usually formed by the metamorphism of shale.

Coal is a fossil fuel formed in ancient swamps.

Limestones are sedimentary rocks composed mainly of calcium carbonate.

Sandstone contains grains of quartz and other minerals bound together by tough mineral cements.

Conglomerates contain pebbles cemented in a fine silt or sand matrix.

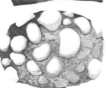

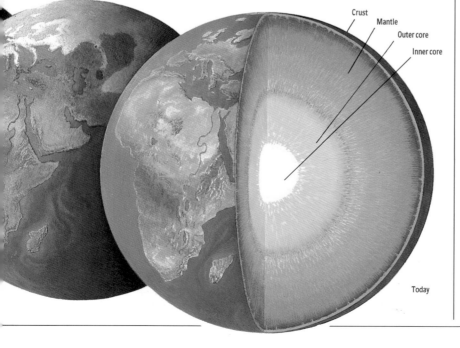

50,000 years ago

Crust
Mantle
Outer core
Inner core

Today

THE ATMOSPHERE AND CLOUDS

The atmosphere is a thin skin of gases, chiefly nitrogen and life-giving oxygen, that encircles and protects the Earth. It moderates temperatures, preventing enormous diurnal changes in heating that would destroy life on Earth. And, in the stratosphere, one of the five main layers of the atmosphere, is a belt of ozone that absorbs most of the Sun's dangerous ultraviolet radiation. The depth of the atmosphere cannot be defined precisely, because it becomes increasingly rarefied with height. But more than 99 per cent of its mass is within 40 km of the surface.

Air Pressure

Air has weight and the total weight of the atmosphere is about 5000 million million tonnes. However, we do not feel the constant pressure of about one tonne of air on our shoulders, because there is an equal air pressure inside our bodies. Air pressure varies, a major factor in weather. Generally, pressures are lower in warm, expanding air which tends to rise, as at the doldrums. It is higher in cold, dense air which sinks downwards, as at the high pressure horse latitudes.

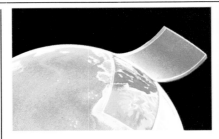

The Earth is surrounded by a thin layer of gases, known as the atmosphere.

This section through the atmosphere shows its five main layers.

EXOSPHERE, which begins at about 500 km above the surface, is extremely rarefied and composed mainly of hydrogen and helium. The exosphere merges into space.

IONOSPHERE, between 80 and 500 km, contains gas molecules that are ionized, or electrically charged, by cosmic or solar rays. Disturbances in the ionosphere cause glowing lights, called aurorae. Temperatures rise steadily with height from –92°C at 80 km to 2200°C at 400 km.

MESOSPHERE, between 50 and 80 km, is marked by a fall in temperature from 10°C at 50 km to –92°C. at 80 km. (Temperatures as low as –170°C have been recorded in this layer in the presence of noctilucent clouds, thought to be composed of ice-covered meteoric dust.)

STRATOSPHERE, stretches above the tropopause (the name for the upper boundary of the troposphere) to 50 km height. It has a layer of ozone (oxygen with three rather than two atoms) that filters out most of the Sun's ultraviolet rays. Temperatures rise from –55°C to 10°C at 50 km.

TROPOSPHERE is the lowest 18km of the atmosphere over the Equator, the lowest 10 to 11 km in the middle latitudes, and the lowest 8 km over the poles. It contains most of the atmosphere's mass. Temperatures fall with height, but stabilize at the tropopause.

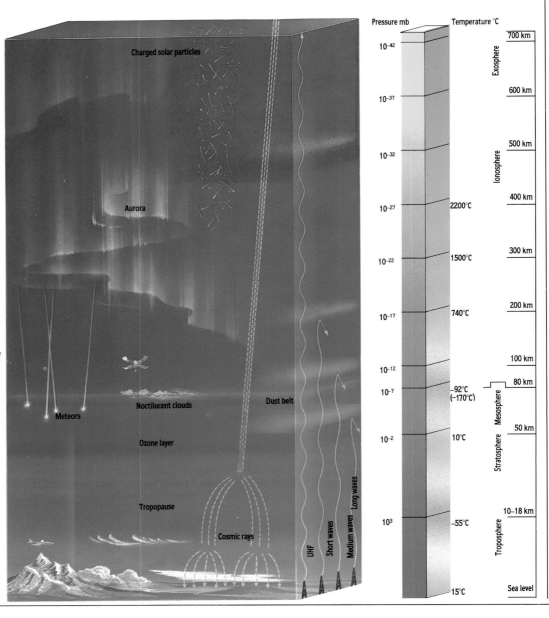

Charged solar particles

Aurora

Meteors

Noctilucent clouds

Dust belt

Ozone layer

Tropopause

Cosmic rays

UHF

Short waves

Medium waves

Long waves

Pressure mb	Temperature °C	
10^{-42}		700 km
		Exosphere
10^{-37}		600 km
		500 km
10^{-32}		Ionosphere
		400 km
10^{-27}	2200°C	
10^{-22}	1500°C	300 km
10^{-17}	740°C	200 km
		100 km
10^{-12}		80 km
10^{-7}	–92°C (–170°C)	Mesosphere
		50 km
10^{-2}	10°C	Stratosphere
		10–18 km
10^3	–55°C	Troposphere
	15°C	Sea level

The clouds on this photograph reveal a hurricane, a rotating low pressure air system.

FACTFINDER

Composition of the air: Nitrogen (78·09 per cent); oxygen (20·95 per cent); argon (0·93 per cent). Other gases include carbon dioxide, helium, hydrogen, krypton, methane, neon, ozone, and xenon. **Average surface pressure**: 1013 mb.	**Atmospheric level reached by radio waves** (frequency in kilohertz) Long waves (below 500 kHz) : 50 km; Medium waves (500 – 1500 kHz) : 95 km; Short (1500 – 30,000 kHz by day) :200 km; waves (1500 – 30,000 kHz by night) :280 km; Very short wavelengths (UHF) penetrate all layers.

Cloud Formation

All air contains water vapour, but warm air holds much more than cold air. When air is cooled it can hold less water vapour. At dew point, it is saturated, containing all the water vapour it can at that temperature. Further cooling causes water vapour to condense around specks of dust or salt in the air to form tiny, visible water droplets or ice crystals, masses of which form clouds.

Circulation of Air

Air is invisible but, powered by energy from the Sun, it is always moving. Generally, winds blow from areas of high air pressure, such as the horse latitudes, towards areas of low pressure, such as the doldrums. Winds are deflected by the Coriolis effect, which is caused by the Earth's rotation. Local factors, such as mountains, also affect winds. Monsoons are seasonal reversals of winds. For example, over northern India in winter, cold, dense air masses develop, from which winds blow outwards. But heating in summer creates low air pressure and moist winds are sucked on to the land.

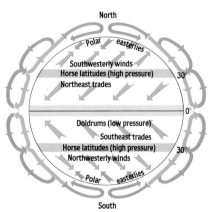

Above: The diagram shows the main movements of air in the atmosphere and across the surface in the prevailing wind systems. Winds generally blow towards low pressure regions, such as the doldrums, and outwards from high pressure systems at the horse latitudes and the poles.

Cloud Types

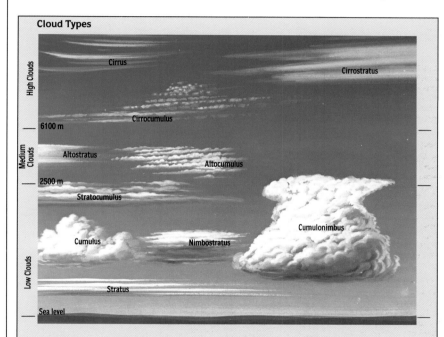

High Clouds
High clouds form above 6100 metres above ground level, as follows:
CIRRUS is a delicate feathery cloud, sometimes called mares' tails or ice banners. It is often the first sign of an approaching depression.
CIRROSTRATUS is a thin layer cloud, with ripples and rounded masses. It veils but does not block out the Sun.
CIRROCUMULUS is a patchy cloud composed of small white balls. Formed from ice crystals, it is often called mackerel sky.

Medium Clouds
Medium clouds occur between about 2500 and 6100 metres, as follows:
ALTOSTRATUS is a greyish or bluish layer cloud that may become so thick that it blocks out the Sun. It is a sign of an advancing depression.
ALTOCUMULUS resembles a mass of tiny clouds. It indicates unsettled weather.

Low Clouds
Low clouds form below 2500 metres above ground level as follows:
STRATOCUMULUS is a greyish-white cloud, consisting of rounded masses.
NIMBOSTRATUS is a dark cloud, associated with rain and snow, which often occurs along the warm fronts of depressions.
CUMULUS is a white, heap cloud, usually with a flat base and a dome-shaped top. In summer, fluffy cumulus is a feature of fine weather. Heavy cumulus can develop into cumulonimbus cloud.
STRATUS is a grey layer cloud that often forms ahead of warm fronts in depressions where warm air is rising fairly slowly over cold air. Such clouds bring drizzle, rain and snow.
CUMULONIMBUS is a dark, heavy cloud. It may rise 4500 metres or more from its ragged base to its often anvil-shaped top. It is associated with thunder, lightning, rain and snow.

Cloud Classification. There are three main types of cloud shapes: feathery cirrus; heap or cumuliform clouds; and layer or stratiform clouds.

THE WATER OF LIFE

In some countries, people take their regular supply of fresh water for granted, while elsewhere, in desert lands, it is a prized commodity. Water reaches us, in one way or another, through the hydrological, or water, cycle, whereby land areas are supplied with precipitation that originates in the saline oceans, where more than 97 per cent of the world's water is found.

Another vital resource, also taken for granted in many places, is the soil, the character of which is largely determined by the climate. The delicate balance between climate, water, and plant life is something that we disturb at our peril.

Soil is the thin layer of loose material derived from and overlying the bedrock. Soils vary in thickness. Mineral grains, the product of weathering, make up more than 90 per cent of most dry soils. Soil also contains humus, including the remains of dead plants and animals. About 40 per cent of moist soils is made up of spaces, occupied by air or water. Soils vary according to the climate, for example, soils in tropical rainy regions are leached by heavy rain. By contrast, some soils in arid regions contain mineral salts deposited by water rising *upwards* towards the surface.

Plant life shows remarkable adaptations to a vast variety of environments. The main vegetation zones are largely determined by climate. But, like climatic regions, vegetation zones have no marked boundaries; they merge imperceptibly with one another.

Vegetation zones usually refer to the original plant cover, or optimum growth, before it was altered by human activity. Human interference with nature can be disastrous. For example, semi-arid grasslands have been ploughed up. Prolonged droughts have reduced the exposed soil to a powdery dust which is removed by the wind, creating dust bowls and encouraging the spread of deserts. The destruction of tropical forests, such as in Brazil, is a matter of concern today. Plants that have never been identified are being destroyed for ever, when they might be sources of new drugs. A massive forest clearance might change world climates.

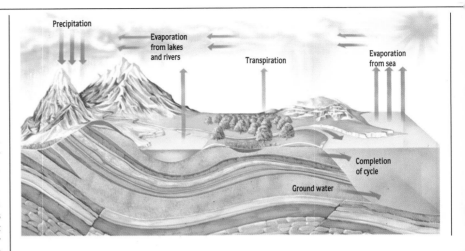

Above: The water cycle provides landmasses with fresh water. The water comes mainly from moisture evaporated from the oceans, to which the water eventually returns.

Right: The map shows the world's chief vegetation zones.

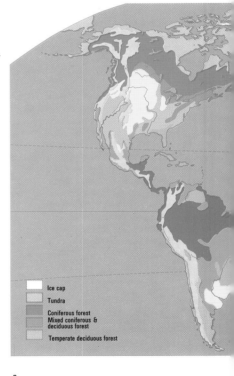

Ice cap
Tundra
Coniferous forest
Mixed coniferous & deciduous forest
Temperate deciduous forest

Below: The photographs show major vegetation regions:
1. Tundra is the name for treeless regions near the poles and near the tops of high mountains that are snow-covered for most of the year. But mosses, lichens and some flowering plants flourish in the short summer.
2. Coniferous forests, or taiga, cover a broad belt south of the tundra in the northern hemisphere. The shapes of conifers prevent their being overloaded by snow. The needle-like leaves reduce transpiration, while the thick bark and pitch-like sap reduce evaporation.
3. Broadleaf, or deciduous, forests grow in warm temperate regions. By shedding their leaves, deciduous trees are better able to survive the winter.
4. Scrub and semi-arid grasslands cover large areas of the world. They are highly susceptible to soil erosion if the vegetation cover is removed. Scrub, called maquis, fynbos, chaparral and mallee scrub, are typical of Mediterranean lands where the original forest cover has been destroyed.
5. Tropical grassland includes the llanos of Venezuela. The palm trees in the photograph are growing in a swamp. Tropical grassland is also called campos or savanna.
6. Evergreen tropical rain forest flourishes in regions which are hot and have ample rain throughout the year.

1

2

3

FACTFINDER

Water distribution: 97·2% is in the oceans (about 1360 million km³); 2·15% is frozen in bodies of ice; 0·625% is ground water; 0·171% is in rivers and lakes; 0·001 is water vapour in the atmosphere.

Average daily water consumption: In the United States: about 200 litres (flushing toilet, washing and bathing, 78%; kitchen use, 6%; drinking, 5%; other, 11%). In many hot countries, the daily per capita water consumption is less than 4 litres.

Common soils: Laterites (leached soils in tropical rainy regions); grey marginal soils (deserts); chestnut-brown soils (arid grasslands); brown forest earths (Mediteranean lands); podsols (cold temperate regions).

Vegetation: Ice covers about 10% of the world's land surfaces and hot deserts 20%. The largest forest is the coniferous forest of Northern Asia, which covers 1100 million hectares – 27% of the world's total forests.

Right: Prairie soils occur in regions that are wet enough in places to support woodland. The A horizon contains much humus, but it is also much leached by seeping water.

A

B

C

Woodland and mixed grasses

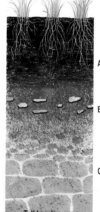

A

B

C

Tall bunch grass

Chernozem soils, sometimes called black earths, contain much humus (mainly decomposed grass). They occur in steppelands which have less rainfall than prairies.

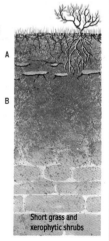

A

B

Short grass and xerophytic shrubs

Chestnut-brown soils are typical of particularly arid grasslands. They occur south of the Russian steppes and in the drier parts of Argentina, South Africa and the United States.

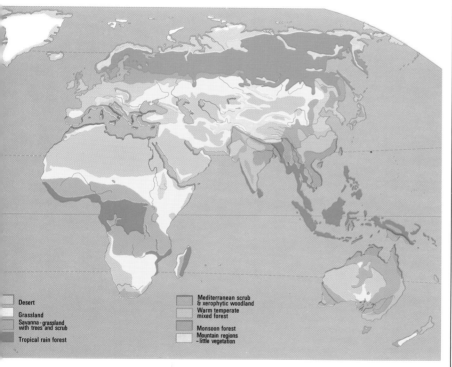

Desert

Grassland

Savanna - grassland with trees and scrub

Tropical rain forest

Mediterranean scrub & xerophytic woodland

Warm temperate mixed forest

Monsoon forest

Mountain regions – little vegetation

4

5

6

THE POPULATION EXPLOSION

One of the world's most serious problems is the population explosion and the difficulties that can be foreseen in feeding the people of the world in the future. Assuming present growth rates of 1.8 per cent continue, the UN estimates that total world population will increase from 5 321 million in 1990 to around 6 260 million by the turn of the century. The problems arising from the population explosion are most marked in the developing world and least in the industrial nations where people see advantages in population control.

Population explosions occur when average birth rates far exceed death rates. In recent years, death rates have everywhere declined mainly because of improved medical care. In industrial countries, birth rates have also fallen so that a growing proportion of people is in the senior age groups. But while such countries must finance retirement pensions, developing nations have the highest expenditures on health and other children's services, because 40 per cent or more of their population is under 15. This contrast between developing and developed nations is also illustrated by the average life expectancies of 41 years in Sierra Leone and 79 years in Japan.

The distribution of people throughout the world is uneven, because few people live in the vast hot and cold deserts, mountain regions and rain forests. In the world's most densely populated areas, the proportions of urban dwellers is increasing quickly. Urban growth is also a problem in developing nations where unqualified youngsters flock to the cities only to become unemployed occupants of unhealthy shanty towns.

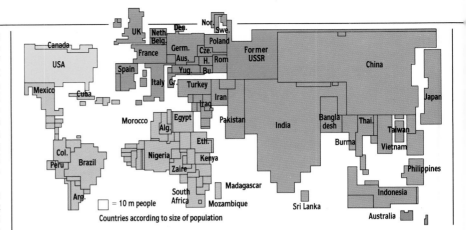

Countries according to size of population

☐ = 10 m people

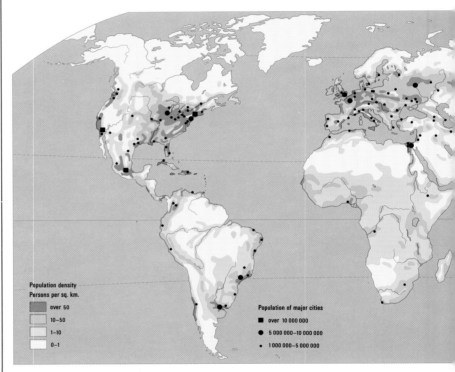

Population density
Persons per sq. km.
■ over 50
☐ 10–50
☐ 1–10
☐ 0–1

Population of major cities
■ over 10 000 000
● 5 000 000–10 000 000
• 1 000 000–5 000 000

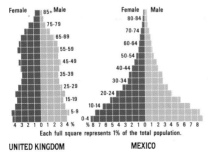

Each full square represents 1% of the total population.

UNITED KINGDOM   MEXICO

Left: The graphs depict the population structures of two nations according to sex and age. Developed nations, such as the United Kingdom (left), have a high proportion of older people, while developing nations such as Mexico (right) have a young population, with as many as 40 per cent of the people being under 15 years of age.

Above: The map shows the uneven distribution of the world's population, a feature that is emphasized by the cartogram, top, which represents the size of nations by their populations rather than by their areas.

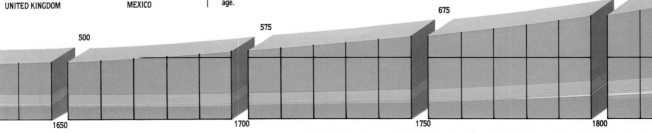

FACTFINDER

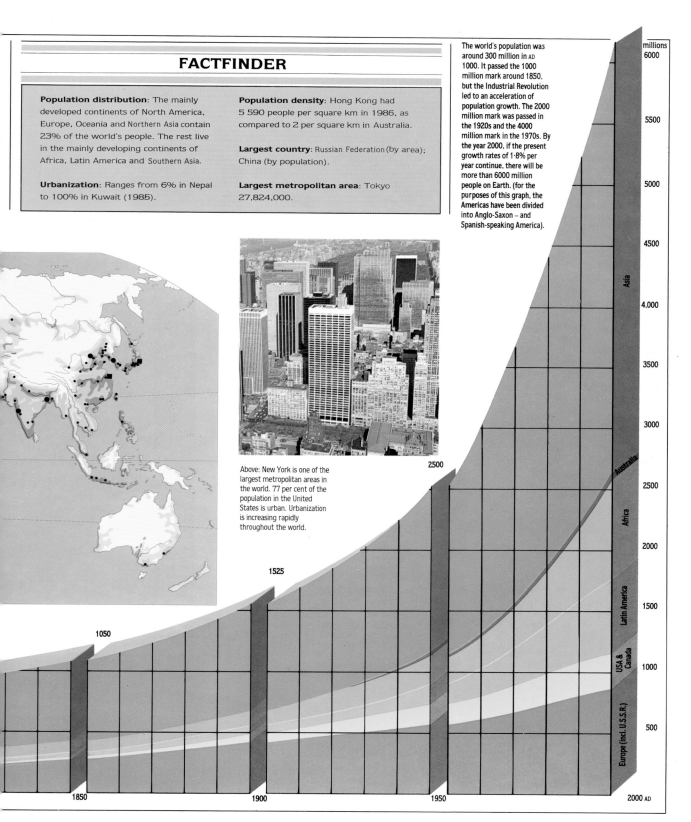

Population distribution: The mainly developed continents of North America, Europe, Oceania and Northern Asia contain 23% of the world's people. The rest live in the mainly developing continents of Africa, Latin America and Southern Asia.

Urbanization: Ranges from 6% in Nepal to 100% in Kuwait (1985).

Population density: Hong Kong had 5 590 people per square km in 1986, as compared to 2 per square km in Australia.

Largest country: Russian Federation (by area); China (by population).

Largest metropolitan area: Tokyo 27,824,000.

The world's population was around 300 million in AD 1000. It passed the 1000 million mark around 1850, but the Industrial Revolution led to an acceleration of population growth. The 2000 million mark was passed in the 1920s and the 4000 million mark in the 1970s. By the year 2000, if the present growth rates of 1·8% per year continue, there will be more than 6000 million people on Earth. (for the purposes of this graph, the Americas have been divided into Anglo-Saxon – and Spanish-speaking America).

Above: New York is one of the largest metropolitan areas in the world. 77 per cent of the population in the United States is urban. Urbanization is increasing rapidly throughout the world.

millions
6000
5500
5000
4500
4,000
3500
3000
2500
2000
1500
1000
500

Asia
Australia
Africa
Latin America
USA & Canada
Europe (incl. U.S.S.R.)

2500
1525
1050
2000 AD
1850
1900
1950

ALTERNATIVE ENERGY

All forms of energy come directly or indirectly from the Sun. Prehistoric people had only their own labour, but as life styles changed and technology developed, draught animals, the burning of wood, windmills, waterwheels and sails to propel ships were all employed. With the onset of the Industrial Revolution, another abundant source of energy, the fossil fuel coal, was used to power 'the age of steam'. And recently, oil and natural gas have become the main fossil fuels, chiefly because they are fairly cheap to extract, easy to transport, and weight for weight they are more heat-efficient than coal. In consequence, world coal production has remained roughly stable over the last thirty years, although in some industrial nations, such as France, West Germany and the United Kingdom, it has declined. And yet coal may again become important if the existing reserves of oil start to run out, as predicted on current levels of consumption, in the early 21st century.

Despite the recent pre-eminence of oil and natural gas, alternative forms of energy that could replace fossil fuels have been successfully developed, notably hydro-electricity and, in the last thirty years, nuclear power. Hydro-electricity is now the chief form of electrical energy in such countries as Norway, where it supplies 100 per cent of the nation's electrical supply, Brazil (93 per cent), Switzerland (61 per cent) and Canada (61 per cent). But hydro-electricity is clearly unsuited to flat nations, such as the Netherlands.

Nuclear power, using the heat of nuclear fission, can be generated anywhere and, in several Western nations, including the United States and the United Kingdom, it already supplies more than one tenth of the total electrical supply. Uranium, the raw material used in nuclear fission, is generally abundant, and is produced in the West by the United States, South Africa and Canada.

But nuclear power is surrounded by controversy, particularly concerning the disposal of radioactive nuclear wastes. This factor, together with the finite nature of fossil fuel reserves, have led conservationists to explore many other possible forms of energy, employing the latest modern technology. The diagram, right, summarizes the main possibilities that are currently under investigation, including the harnessing of solar radiation, the power of winds and moving water, and the exploitation of the heat that exists not far beneath the Earth's surface.

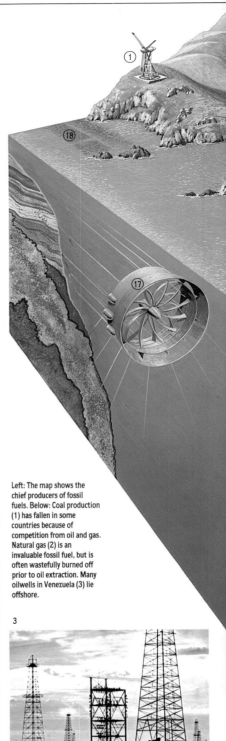

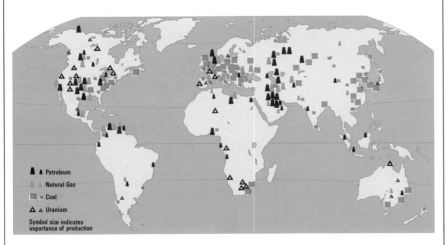

Left: The map shows the chief producers of fossil fuels. Below: Coal production (1) has fallen in some countries because of competition from oil and gas. Natural gas (2) is an invaluable fossil fuel, but is often wastefully burned off prior to oil extraction. Many oilwells in Venezuela (3) lie offshore.

▲ ▲ Petroleum
△ □ Natural Gas
■ □ Coal
△ △ Uranium
Symbol size indicates importance of production

1

2

3

Energy consumption (per capita, in equivalents of kg of coal, 1986): Africa 429; South America 1041; Middle East 1601; Western Europe 4027; Oceania 6006; North America 7146.

Largest oil producers (1988): Former USSR (20 per cent of world production); United States (14 per cent); Saudi Arabia (9 per cent); China (5 per cent); Iraq (5 per cent); Mexico (4 per cent); Iran (4 per cent); United Kingdom (4 per cent).

Oil reserves (1990): Saudi Arabia (28 per cent); Iraq (11 per cent); Kuwait (11 per cent); Iran (7 per cent); Mexico, United Arab Emirates, Former USSR and Venezuela (6 per cent each).

Nuclear power: France (70 per cent of its electrical energy production in 1988); Belgium (67 per cent); Sweden (48 per cent); Hungary (46 per cent); United Kingdom (21 per cent).

Left: Alternative energy sources include improved windmills (1) and pump storage reservoirs (2), into which water is pumped when energy is abundant and then used to drive turbine generators. Hydro-electric stations (3) are important in many countries, while solar power stations, powered by concentrated sunlight, could get microwave energy beamed from a satellite (4) or from banks of angled mirrors or heliostats (5). Decaying waste (6) is a source of heat, as are geysers (7) in volcanic areas. Mud (8) can be used to store heat, while greenhouses (9) are familiar ways of utilizing solar energy. Shallow solar ponds (10) produce heated water to drive generators, and solar houses (11) are self-supporting. Geothermal energy (12) comes from heat inside the Earth. Tidal power stations (13) have much potential, and wave power (14) could be harnessed by moving floats ('bobbing ducks'). Ordinary powered ships might use aluminium sails (15) as an extra form of energy. Floating thermal stations (16) could tap heat under the sea, while huge underwater turbines (17) could be driven by ocean currents. Even kelp (18), a seaweed, could be cultivated as a plant fuel. Solar furnaces (19) can produce temperatures of 4000°C by concentrating the Sun's rays with a paraboloid mirror.

Below: Hydro-electricity is a major alternative to fossil fuels in upland areas with abundant rivers that can be dammed (4). Nuclear power stations (5), a recent development, now supply a substantial proportion of the total electrical energy in several developed nations.

4

5

ENVIRONMENT IN DANGER

Because of the population explosion and the industrial and technological developments of the last 200 years, great damage has been done to the environment in many areas by the disruption of the balance of nature.

Pollution has become a major problem particularly in modern industrial societies. For example, air pollution in the form of smog has made cities unpleasant and unhealthy. It causes bronchitis and various other respiratory diseases – the London smog of 1952 killed an estimated 4000 people.

Water pollution by sewage and industrial wastes has fouled rivers, lakes and even seas, notably parts of the almost tideless Mediterranean. The flora and fauna have been destroyed and people's health has been directly affected as at Minamata in Japan in the 1950s. Here perhaps as many as 10,000 people suffered death, deformity or acute illness after eating fish poisoned by acetaldehyde waste pumped into the sea by a chemical company.

The land, too, has been polluted in many ways. For example, the pesticide DDT was once regarded as a means of raising food production. But it has also wiped out large populations of birds and, because of its persistence, it has damaged the fragile ecology of soils by weakening the micro-organisms in it.

Steps have been taken in many places to control the dangers of smog, Minamata disease and DDT. But many other, perhaps even more serious, problems lie ahead if the balance of nature is disturbed. For example, if jet airliners and rocket discharges damage the ozone layer in the stratosphere, it could expose the Earth to the Sun's broiling ultraviolet rays. And no one is sure of the consequences of the rising content in the air of carbon dioxide, which increased by nine per cent between 1958 and 1990. One estimate is that it could double by the year 2030. The atmosphere would then increasingly block long-wave radiation from the Earth, like the glass roof of a greenhouse, and temperatures would rise by an average of 3°C. Climatic zones would change and ice sheets would melt, submerging coastal plains and cities.

Radioactive fallout from nuclear weapons' tests (1) pollutes the air, as do kerosene combustion products, soot and unburned fuel expelled by aircraft (2). The build-up of carbon dioxide in the air (3), caused mainly by the burning of fossil fuels and the cutting down of forests may have a greenhouse effect, causing the atmosphere to overheat.

Aerial crop spraying (4) can introduce poisons into the soil that can disturb its ecology for years, while nuclear power stations (5) may discharge radioactive coolants, and thermal power stations (6) and city air conditioning systems may cause thermal and chemical pollution.

Below: Rubbish dumps for cars (1), open-cast mines (2) and oil spillages (3) that foul beaches are all examples of pollution.

1

2

3

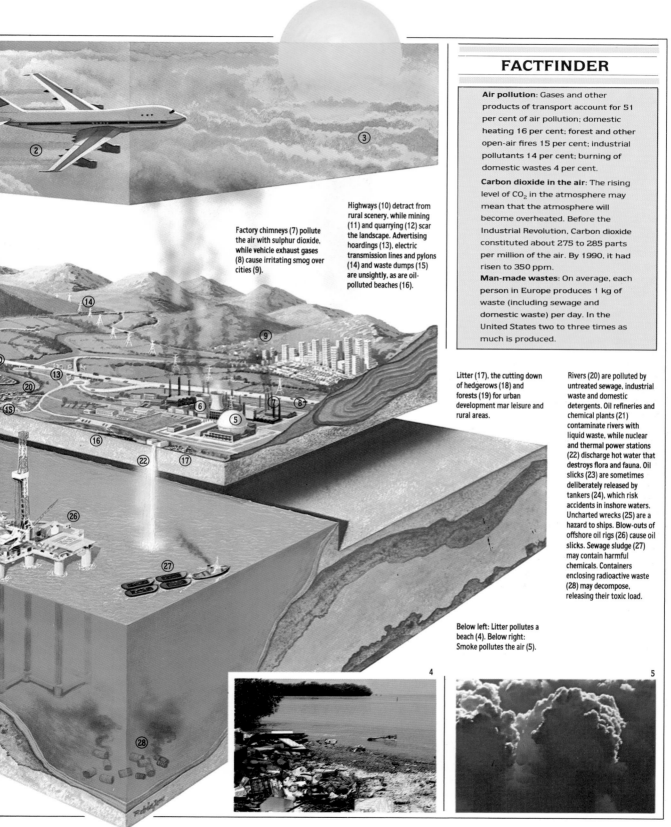

Air pollution: Gases and other products of transport account for 51 per cent of air pollution; domestic heating 16 per cent; forest and other open-air fires 15 per cent; industrial pollutants 14 per cent; burning of domestic wastes 4 per cent.

Carbon dioxide in the air: The rising level of CO_2 in the atmosphere may mean that the atmosphere will become overheated. Before the Industrial Revolution, Carbon dioxide constituted about 275 to 285 parts per million of the air. By 1990, it had risen to 350 ppm.

Man-made wastes: On average, each person in Europe produces 1 kg of waste (including sewage and domestic waste) per day. In the United States two to three times as much is produced.

Factory chimneys (7) pollute the air with sulphur dioxide, while vehicle exhaust gases (8) cause irritating smog over cities (9).

Highways (10) detract from rural scenery, while mining (11) and quarrying (12) scar the landscape. Advertising hoardings (13), electric transmission lines and pylons (14) and waste dumps (15) are unsightly, as are oil-polluted beaches (16).

Litter (17), the cutting down of hedgerows (18) and forests (19) for urban development mar leisure and rural areas.

Rivers (20) are polluted by untreated sewage, industrial waste and domestic detergents. Oil refineries and chemical plants (21) contaminate rivers with liquid waste, while nuclear and thermal power stations (22) discharge hot water that destroys flora and fauna. Oil slicks (23) are sometimes deliberately released by tankers (24), which risk accidents in inshore waters. Uncharted wrecks (25) are a hazard to ships. Blow-outs of offshore oil rigs (26) cause oil slicks. Sewage sludge (27) may contain harmful chemicals. Containers enclosing radioactive waste (28) may decompose, releasing their toxic load.

Below left: Litter pollutes a beach (4). Below right: Smoke pollutes the air (5).

The problems that face mankind are truly monumental. According to the United Nations Environment Programme (UNEP), a recently established agency, soil erosion and soil degradation were still widespread in the early 1990s, and one third of the world's arable land was at risk of becoming desert because of human misuse. Tropical forests were disappearing at an estimated rate of 50 hectares a minute – a rate that, if it continues, will eliminate all tropical forests in forty years. One plant or animal species was also being lost per day – a rate that was accelerating. And in human terms, UNEP estimated that every day some 40,000 infants and young children were dying from hunger or from pollution-related disease.

Disease and malnutrition are features of everyday life in the developing world and, despite all the aid that goes to developing nations, the economic gap between them and the developed world is enormous and increasing. In 1988, the per capita gross national products of the United Kingdom, United States and Switzerland were, respectively, US $12,800, $19,780 and $27,260. By contrast, the per capita GNPs of Chad, Burma and India were $160, $200 and $330. A world split into two sectors – one rich and one poor – is a world fraught with danger. And the population explosion, which is most marked in the poorest countries, could cause global chaos.

The world's problems must be tackled with a real understanding of all the factors involved. People once talked of 'taming' Nature, as if Nature were hostile towards and separate from them. However, in recent years, we have begun to realize that the key to our future lies not in 'taming' but in comprehending Nature, particularly the highly complex ecological relationships that exist between us, the Earth and the millions of animals and plant species that the Earth supports. A view from space has made us realize that damage has been and is still being done. But hopefully it is not too late for us to heal the wounds we have inflicted.

WORLD ATLAS

SYMBOLS

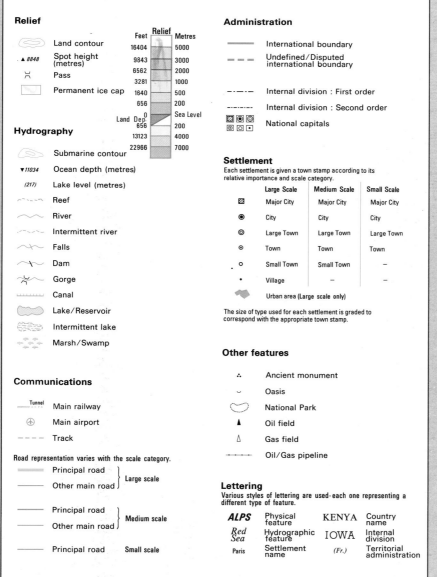

Relief

- Land contour
- ▲ 8848 Spot height (metres)
- Pass
- Permanent ice cap

	Relief	
Feet		Metres
16404		5000
9843		3000
6562		2000
3281		1000
1640		500
656		200
Land Dep. 0		Sea Level
656		200
13123		4000
22966		7000

Hydrography

- Submarine contour
- ▼11034 Ocean depth (metres)
- (217) Lake level (metres)
- Reef
- River
- Intermittent river
- Falls
- Dam
- Gorge
- Canal
- Lake/Reservoir
- Intermittent lake
- Marsh/Swamp

Communications

- Tunnel — Main railway
- ⊕ Main airport
- - - - - Track

Road representation varies with the scale category.

- Principal road
- Other main road } Large scale
- Principal road
- Other main road } Medium scale
- Principal road — Small scale

Administration

- International boundary
- Undefined/Disputed international boundary
- Internal division : First order
- Internal division : Second order
- National capitals

Settlement

Each settlement is given a town stamp according to its relative importance and scale category.

		Large Scale	Medium Scale	Small Scale
▨	Major City	Major City	Major City	Major City
◉	City	City	City	City
◎	Large Town	Large Town	Large Town	Large Town
⊙	Town	Town	Town	Town
○	Small Town	Small Town	Small Town	–
•	Village	Village	–	–
⬟	Urban area (Large scale only)			

The size of type used for each settlement is graded to correspond with the appropriate town stamp.

Other features

- ∴ Ancient monument
- ⌣ Oasis
- National Park
- ▲ Oil field
- △ Gas field
- Oil/Gas pipeline

Lettering

Various styles of lettering are used - each one representing a different type of feature.

ALPS	Physical feature	KENYA	Country name
Red Sea	Hydrographic feature	IOWA	Internal division
Paris	Settlement name	*(Fr.)*	Territorial administration

© Collins

1

EUROPE

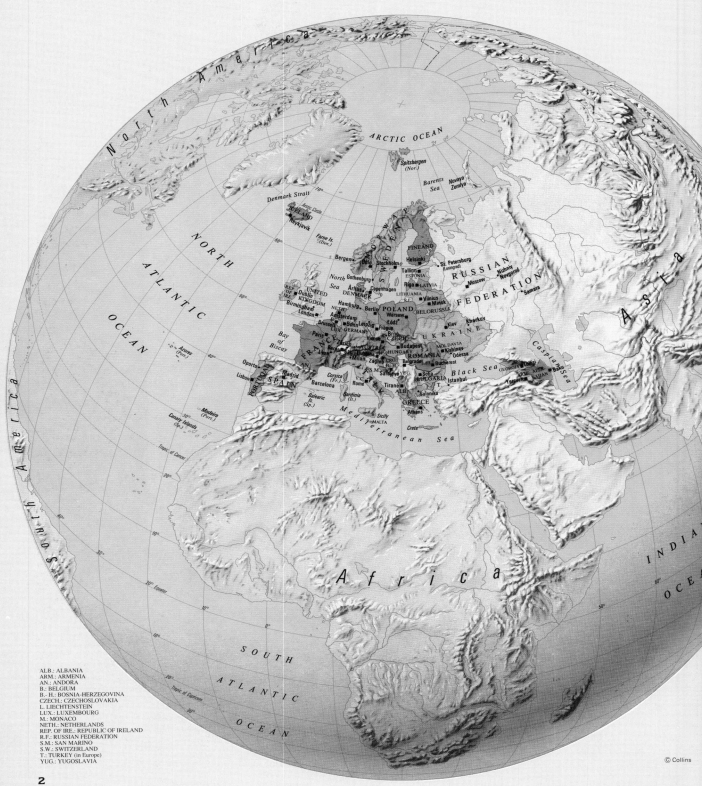

ALB.: ALBANIA
ARM.: ARMENIA
AN.: ANDORA
B.: BELGIUM
B.-H.: BOSNIA-HERZEGOVINA
CZECH: CZECHOSLOVAKIA
L. LIECHTENSTEIN
LUX.: LUXEMBOURG
M.: MONACO
NETH.: NETHERLANDS
REP. OF IRE.: REPUBLIC OF IRELAND
R.F.: RUSSIAN FEDERATION
S.M.: SAN MARINO
S.W.: SWITZERLAND
T.: TURKEY (in Europe)
YUG.: YUGOSLAVIA

© Collins

BRITISH ISLES

ATLANTIC OCEAN

1788

1633

159

Shetland Islands
Clair
Lerwick

Magnus
Tern
Cormorant
Dunlin
Heather
Columba
Hutton
Brent
Ninian
Alwyn
Hild
Odin
Frigg N.E.
Frigg E.
Frigg
Murchison
Thistle
Statfjord
Gullfaks
Troll
Oseberg
Brage
Sotra
Bergen

NORWAY

Hardanger Vidda
Ringerike
Oslo
Drammen
Kongsberg
Skien

Bruce
Beryl
Heimdal
Haugesund
Karmøy
Bokn
Stavanger
Larvik
Risør

Crawford
Balder
Gudrun
Brae
S. Brae
Thelma
Dagny
Sleipner
Piper
Tartan
Maureen
Balmoral
Andrew
143
Claymore
Egersund
Arendal
Kristiansand

Lindesnes
Mandal

Buchan
Glenn
Forties

Skagerrak

Orkney Islands
Kirkwall
Cape Wrath
Thurso
Wick
Pentland Firth
Stornoway
Lewis
The Minch
Beatrice
Montrose
Gannet
Lomond
Ula
Cod
Albuskjell
Josephine
Auk
Clyde
Fulmar
Argyll
Tor
Ekofisk
Edda
Eldfisk
Valhall
Duncan
Roar
Adda
Germ
Tyra
Ruth
Anna
Dan

NORTH SEA

DENMARK
Thisted
Jylland (Jutland)
Viborg
Holstebro
Ringkøbing
Silkeborg
Varde
Esbjerg

Outer Hebrides
Skye
Moray Firth
Elgin
Inverness
Peterhead
Aviemore
Spey
Dee
Aberdeen
Esmond
Forbes
Gordon

Inner Hebrides
Mull
Oban
Ben Nevis
Fort William
Perth
Dundee
Furfar
Stirling
Kirkcaldy
Dunfermline
Edinburgh
Firth of Forth
Berwick-upon-Tweed
Rough
West Sole
Ann
Viking
Amethyst
Indefatigable
Placid
Noordwinning
Den Helder
Helm

SCOTLAND
Jura
Islay
Lomond
Greenock
Glasgow
Motherwell
Galashiels
Hawick
Tweed

North Channel
Firth of Clyde
Arran
Ayr
Southern Uplands
Dumfries
Carlisle
Esmond
Gannet

Malin Hd.
Londonderry
Ballymena
Larne
Stranraer
UNITED

Newcastle upon Tyne
Sunderland
Middlesbrough
Darlington
Scarborough

Donegal Bay
NORTHERN IRELAND
Lough Neagh
Armagh
Belfast
Mourne Mts
852
Dundalk
Isle of Man
Solway Firth
Workington
978
Barrow-in-Furness
Morecambe
Lancaster
KINGDOM
York

Sligo
Achill Island
Westport
Lough Mask
REPUBLIC
Athlone
Mullingar
OF
IRELAND
Drogheda
Dublin
Dun Laoghaire
IRISH SEA
Anglesey
Holyhead
Blackpool
Preston
Southport
Bolton
Bradford
Huddersfield
Leeds
Manchester
Sheffield
Stockport
Lincoln
Grimsby
Kingston upon Hull
Humber
West Sole
Ann
Audrey
Viking
Amethyst
Indefatigable
Valiant
Dotty
Sean
Leman Bank
Hewett
Scram

Galway
Galway Bay
Shannon
Limerick
Ennis
Tralee
Tipperary
Suir
WALES
1085
Snowdon
Chester
Crewe
Stoke-on-Trent
Derby
Nottingham
Mansfield
Leicester
King's Lynn
The Wash
Norwich
Great Yarmouth

Killarney
Carrauntoohil
Macgillycuddy
113
Cardigan Bay
Aberystwyth
Shrewsbury
Birmingham
Coventry
Rugby
Northampton
Cambridge
Ipswich

Cape Clear
Kinsale Head
Wexford
Waterford
St. George's Channel
Fishguard
Worcester
Cheltenham
Gloucester
Cotswold Hills
Oxford
Luton
Stevenage
Bedford
Harwich
Colchester
ENGLAND

Celtic Sea
Swansea
Newport
Cardiff
Bristol
Bristol Channel
Barnstaple
Exmoor
Taunton
Salisbury
Swindon
Reading
Basingstoke
London
Crawley
Maidstone
Southend-on-Sea
Margate
Dover
Strait of Dover
Folkestone
Open 1993
Calais
Boulogne
Dunkerque
Gent
Brugge
Oostende
BELGIUM

Cape Clear
Land's End
Penzance
Isles of Scilly
Truro
Plymouth
Torquay
Exeter
Dartmoor
624
Bournemouth
Weymouth
Southampton
Portsmouth
Brighton
Hastings
Isle of Wight

English Channel
C. de la Hague
Cherbourg
Guernsey
122
Channel Islands
Jersey
Berck
Abbeville
Somme
St. Quentin
Arras
Douai
Valenciennes

Relief

Feet	Metres
16 404	5000
9843	3000
6562	2000
3281	1000
1640	500
656	200
0	Sea Level

Land Dep.	
656	200
13 123	4000
22 966	7000

Dieppe
Le Havre
Bolbec
Rouen
Beauvais
Amiens
Laon
Charleville-Mézières
Sedan

Morlaix
Brest
St. Brieuc
Dinan
St. Malo
Golfe de St. Malo
Granville
Bayeux
Caen
Lisieux
Elbeuf
Evreux
Dreux
Creil
Compiègne
Senlis
Meaux
Épernay
Reims
Vitry-le-François
Châlons-sur-Marne
Verdun
Metz

I. d'Ouessant
Douarnenez
Quimper
Pont-l'Abbé
Quimperlé
Lorient
Vannes
Rennes
Vitré
Laval
Le Mans
Château-Gontier
Châteaubriant
Mayenne
Alençon
Argentan
Flers
Chartres
Fontainebleau
Malesherbes
Montargis
Troyes
Chaumont
Épinal

FRANCE

0   50   100   150 Miles
0   50   100   150   200   250 Kms.
Conic Projection

© Collins ◇ Longman Atlases Cbii

Belle Île
St. Nazaire
Nantes
Cholet
La Roche-sur-Yon
Niort
Angers
Trélazé
Loire
Saumur
Tours
Blois
Vierzon
Orléans
Auxerre
Gien
Bourges
Nevers
Le Creusot
Châlon-sur-Saône
Mâcon

Châtellerault
Poitiers
Châteauroux
Moulins
Montluçon
Parthenay

3

ENGLAND AND WALES

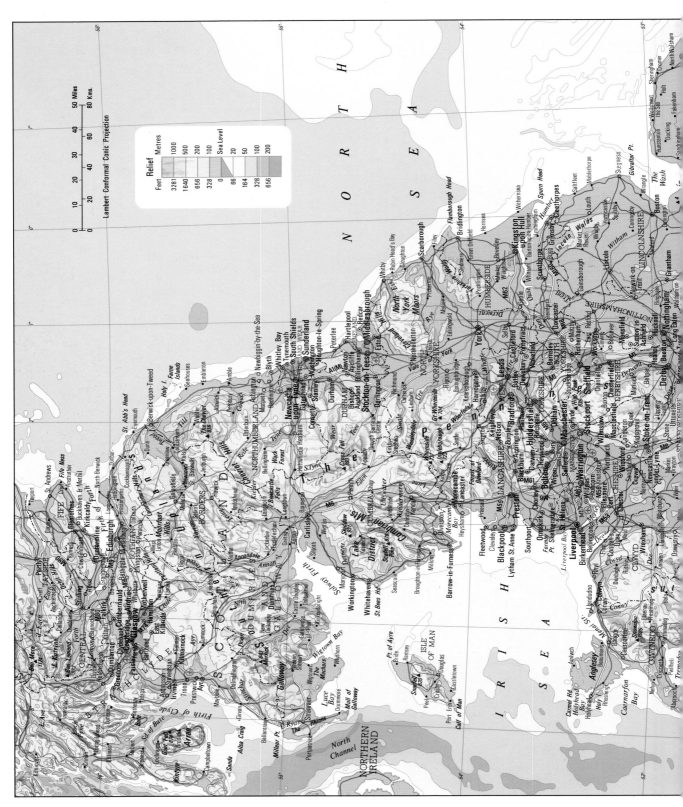

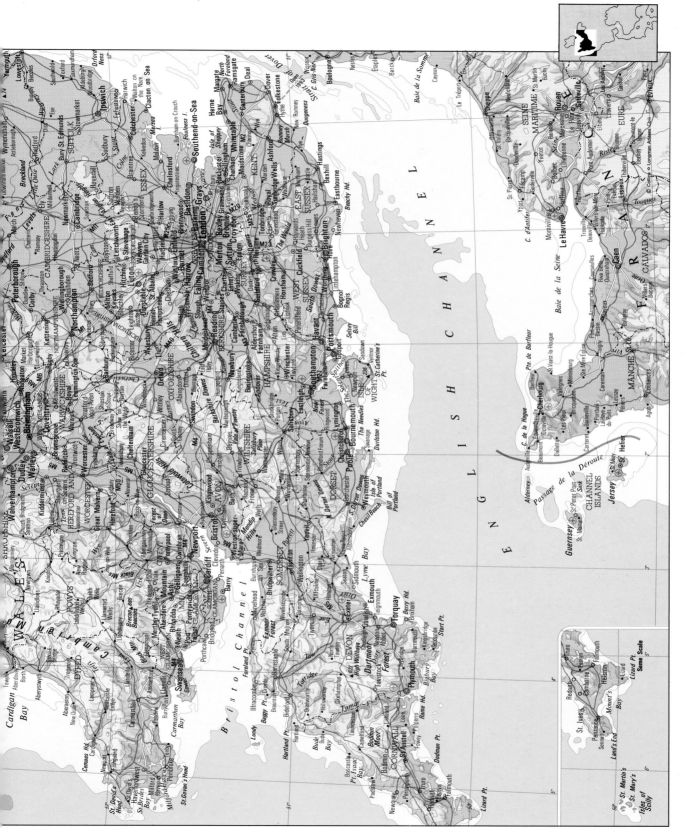

SCOTLAND

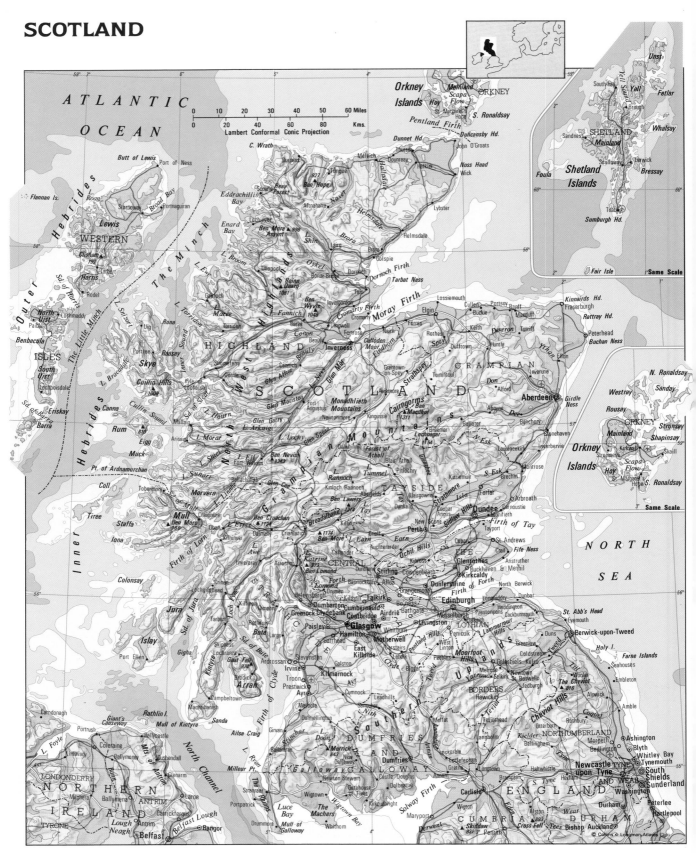

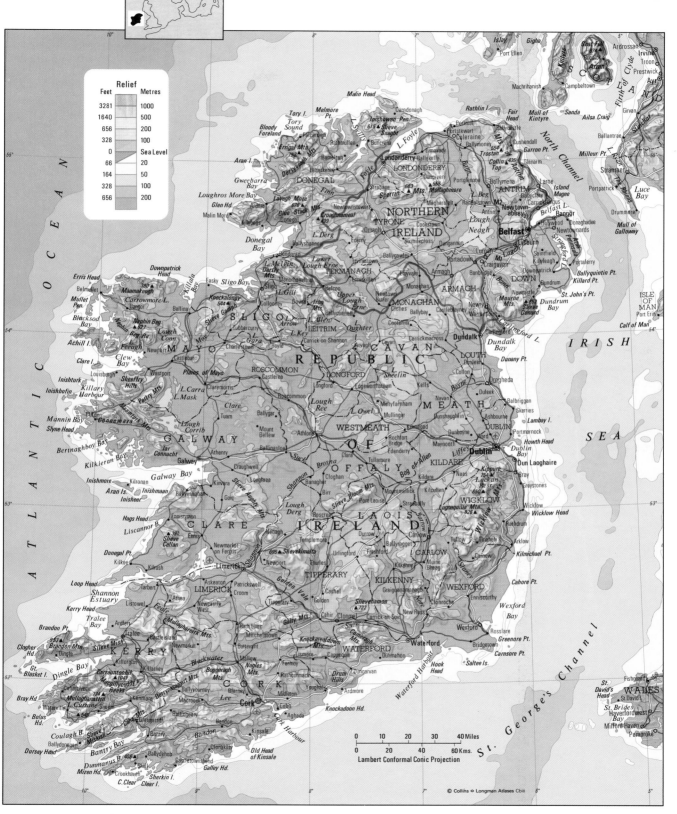

IRELAND

THE LOW COUNTRIES

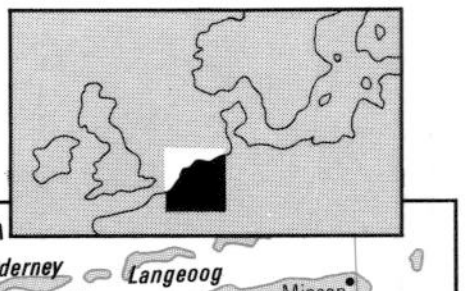

Scale / Legend

0 10 20 30 40 50 60 Miles
0 20 40 60 80 Kms.
Conic Projection

Relief

Feet	Metres
16 404	5000
9843	3000
6562	2000
3281	1000
1640	500
656	200
0	Sea Level

Land Dep.

656	200
13 123	4000
22 966	7000

Major regions and countries

NORTH SEA

NETHERLANDS

BELGIUM

GERMANY

LUXEMBOURG

FRANCE

NIEDERSACHSEN

NORDRHEIN WESTFALEN

RHEINLAND-PFALZ

SAARLAND

FRIESLAND · GRONINGEN · DRENTHE · OVERIJSSEL · FLEVOLAND · GELDERLAND · UTRECHT · NOORD HOLLAND · ZUID HOLLAND · ZEELAND · NOORD BRABANT · LIMBURG

VLAANDEREN · WEST VLAANDEREN · OOST VLAANDEREN · BRABANT · LIMBURG · HAINAUT · NAMUR · LIÈGE · LUXEMBOURG

NORD · PICARDIE · ARTOIS · FLANDRE · CHAMPAGNE · ARDENNE

Waddeneilanden · Waddenzee · IJsselmeer · Markerwaard (U.C.) · Veluwe · De Peel · Ostfriesische Inseln

Selected place names

Amsterdam · 's Gravenhage (The Hague) · Rotterdam · Haarlem · Leiden · Utrecht · Arnhem · Nijmegen · Eindhoven · Tilburg · Breda · Den Helder · Alkmaar · Hoorn · Zwolle · Groningen · Leeuwarden · Assen · Meppel · Enschede · Almelo · Hengelo · Deventer · Apeldoorn · Amersfoort · Middelburg · Vlissingen (Flushing) · Bergen op Zoom · Roosendaal · 's-Hertogenbosch · Helmond · Venlo · Roermond · Maastricht · Heerlen · Sittard

Antwerpen · Bruxelles (Brussel) · Brugge (Bruges) · Gent · Oostende (Ostend) · Mechelen · Leuven · Hasselt · Namur · Charleroi · Liège · Verviers · Mons · Tournai · Aalst · Kortrijk (Courtrai) · Roeselare

Dunkerque (Dunkirk) · Lille · Roubaix · Tourcoing · Valenciennes · Douai · Lens · Béthune · Arras · Cambrai · St. Quentin · Laon · Sedan · Charleville-Mézières

Luxembourg · Esch · Diekirch · Echternach

Wilhelmshaven · Oldenburg · Emden · Leer · Papenburg · Lingen · Osnabrück · Münster · Rheine · Nordhorn · Gronau · Bocholt · Wesel · Duisburg · Essen · Oberhausen · Mülheim · Düsseldorf · Mönchen Gladbach · Krefeld · Neuss · Köln (Cologne) · Leverkusen · Bonn · Aachen · Düren · Koblenz · Trier · Wuppertal · Solingen · Remscheid · Dortmund · Bochum · Hagen · Gelsenkirchen · Recklinghausen · Herne · Bottrop · Siegen

North Sea · Dollard · Westerschelde · Oosterschelde · Jadebusen

Collins · Longman Atlases

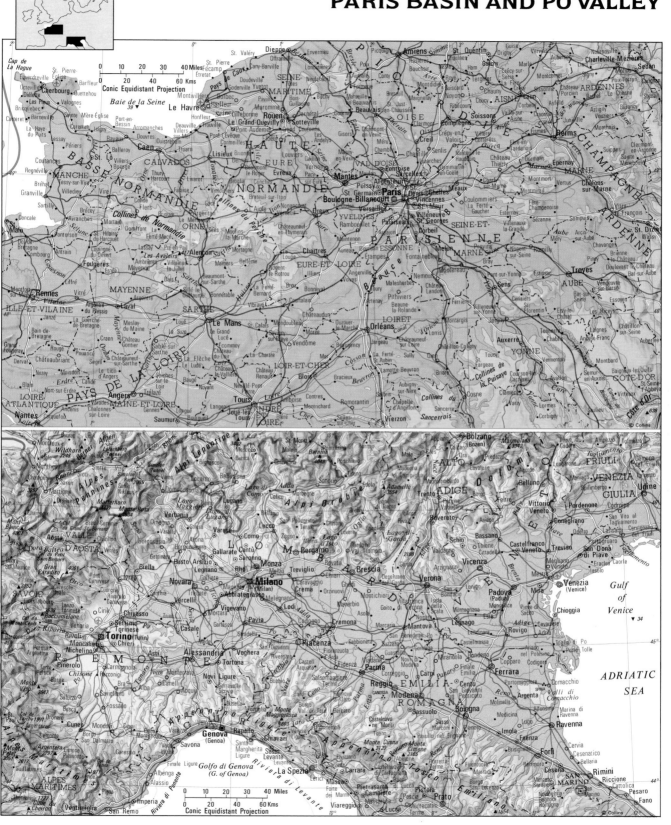

SPAIN AND PORTUGAL

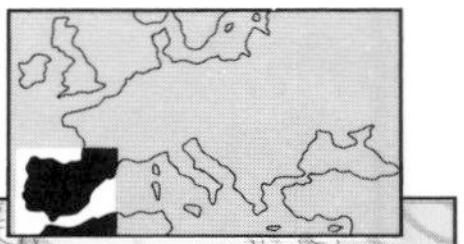

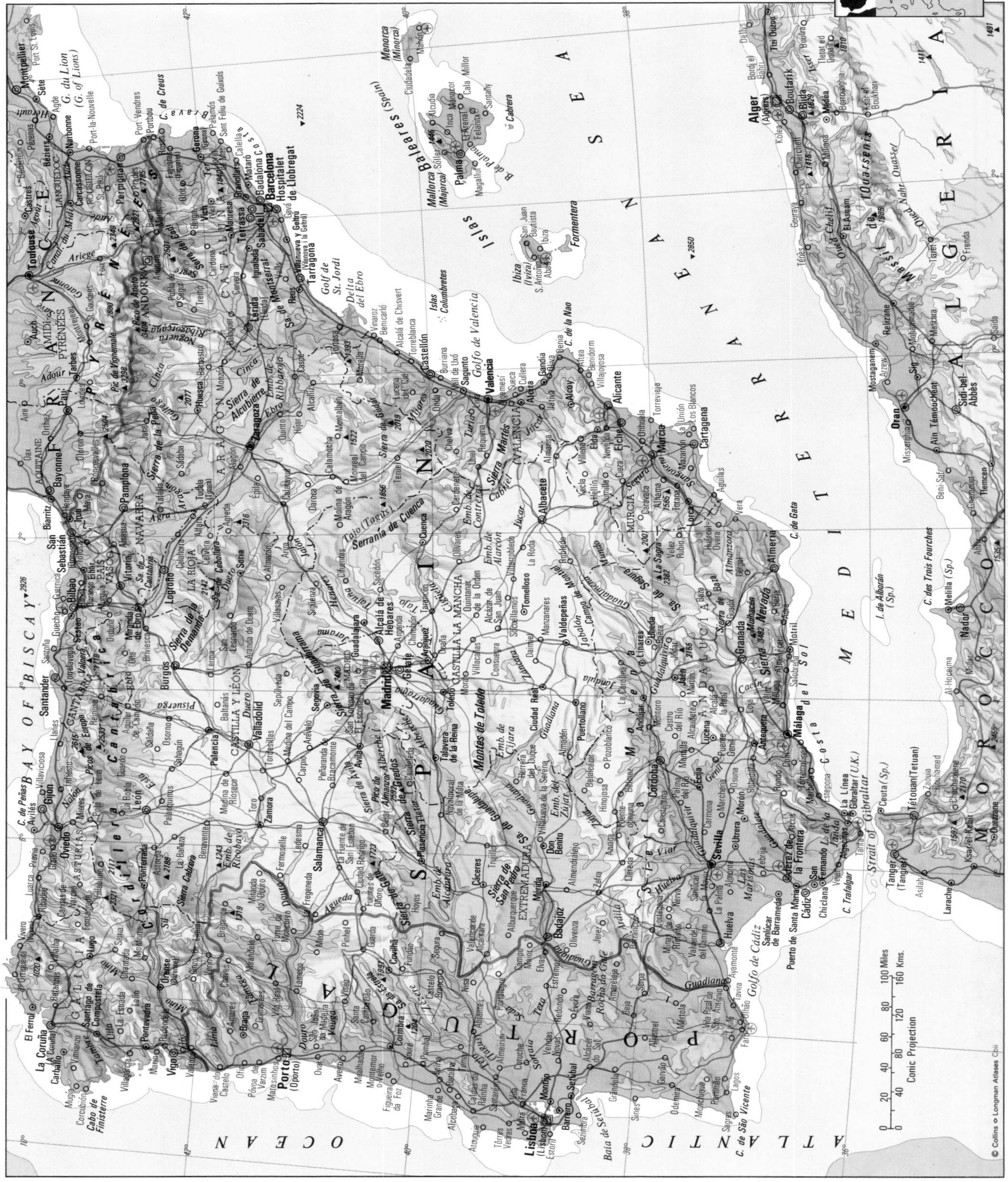

ALGERIA

MOROCCO

BAY OF BISCAY

ATLANTIC OCEAN

MEDITERRANEAN SEA

Islas Baleares (Spain)

Mallorca (Majorca)

Menorca (Minorca)

Ibiza (Iviza)

Formentera

PYRÉNÉES

AQUITAINE

ARAGÓN

NAVARRA

LA RIOJA

PAÍS VASCO

CATALUÑA

VALENCIA

MURCIA

ANDALUCÍA

CASTILLA Y LEÓN

CASTILLA-LA MANCHA

EXTREMADURA

GALICIA

P O R T U G A L

S P A I N

Cordillera Cantábrica

Sierra Morena

Sierra Nevada

Costa del Sol

Strait of Gibraltar

Golfo de Cádiz

Golfo de Valencia

Madrid · **Barcelona** · **Valencia** · **Sevilla** · **Zaragoza** · **Málaga** · **Bilbao** · **Lisboa (Lisbon)** · **Porto (Oporto)** · **Murcia** · **Alicante** · **Granada** · **Córdoba** · **Valladolid** · **Palencia** · **Salamanca** · **Oviedo** · **Gijón** · **La Coruña** · **Vigo** · **San Sebastián** · **Pamplona** · **Logroño** · **Santander** · **Alger** · **Oran**

| 0 | 20 | 40 | 60 | 80 | 100 Miles |

| 0 | 40 | 80 | 120 | 160 Kms. |

Conic Projection

© Collins ○ Longman Atlases Chii

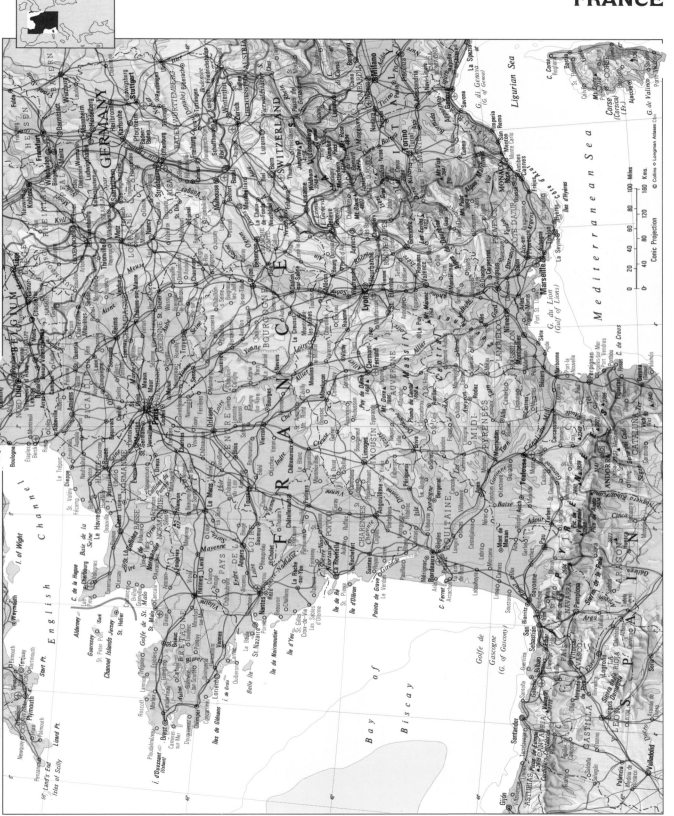

ITALY AND THE BALKANS

CENTRAL EUROPE

SCANDINAVIA AND BALTIC LANDS

ICELAND
on the same scale

© Collins

FAROE IS.
(Denmark)
on the same scale

Relief

Feet	Metres							Sea Level		

100 Miles
160 Kms.

Conic Projection

A T L A N T I C   O C E A N

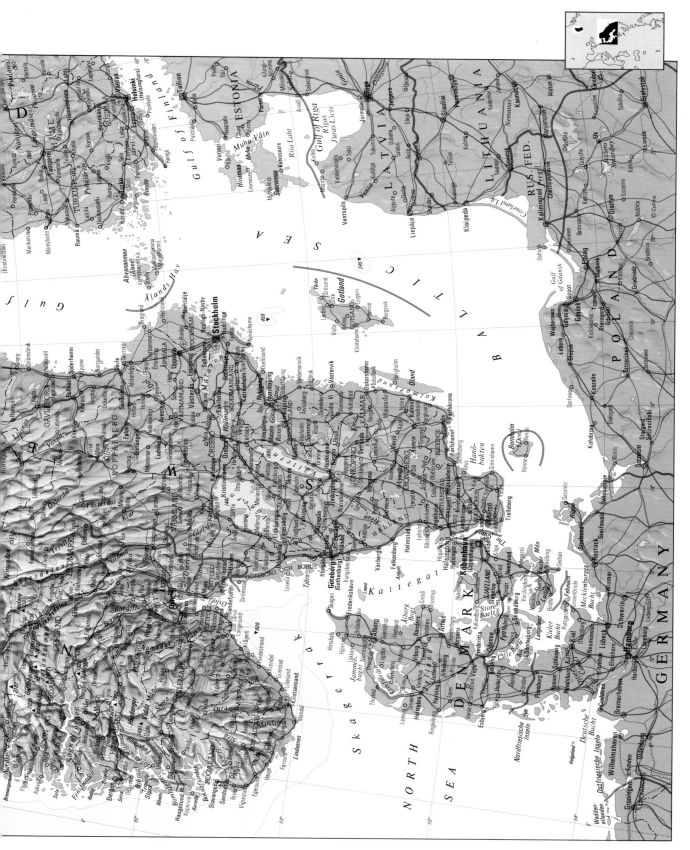

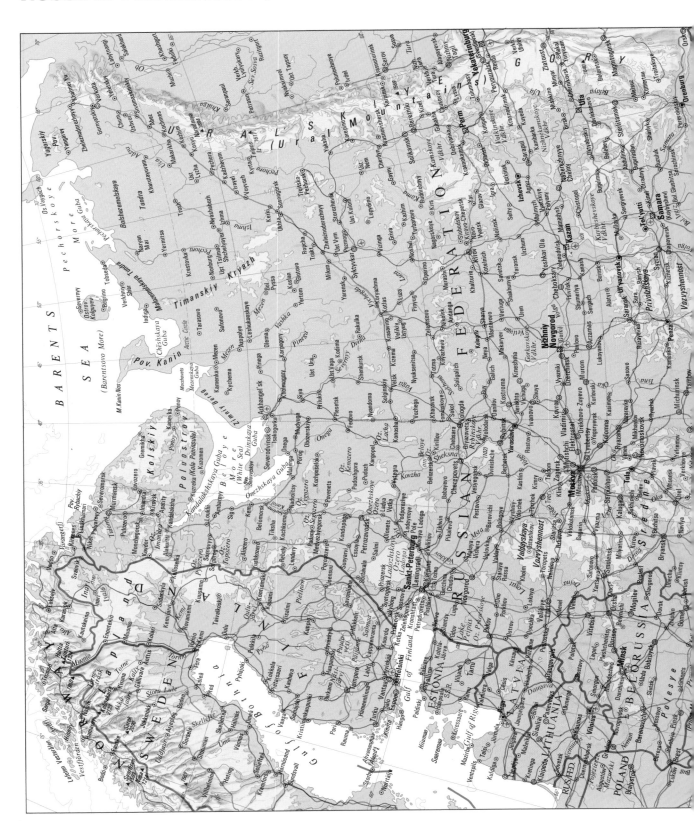

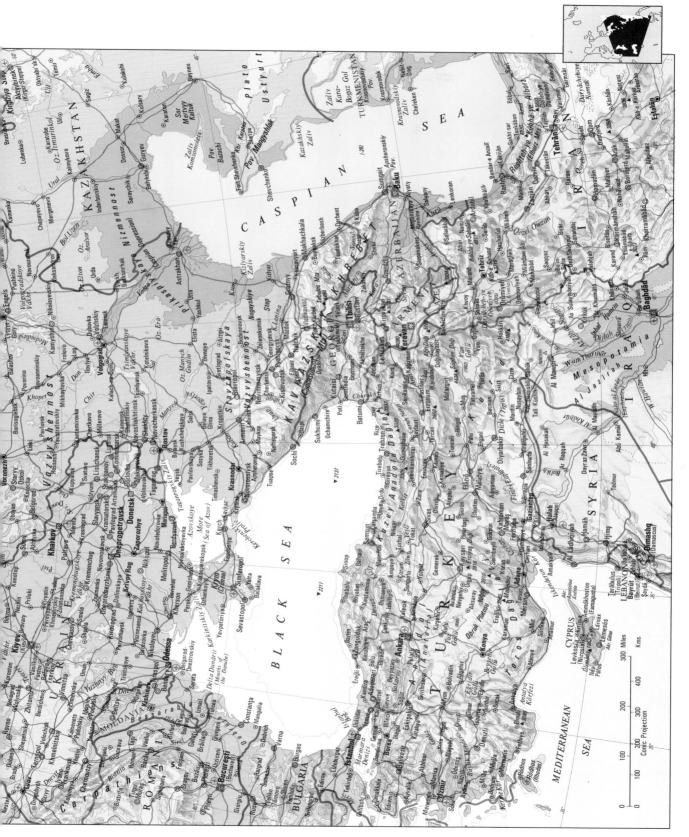

19

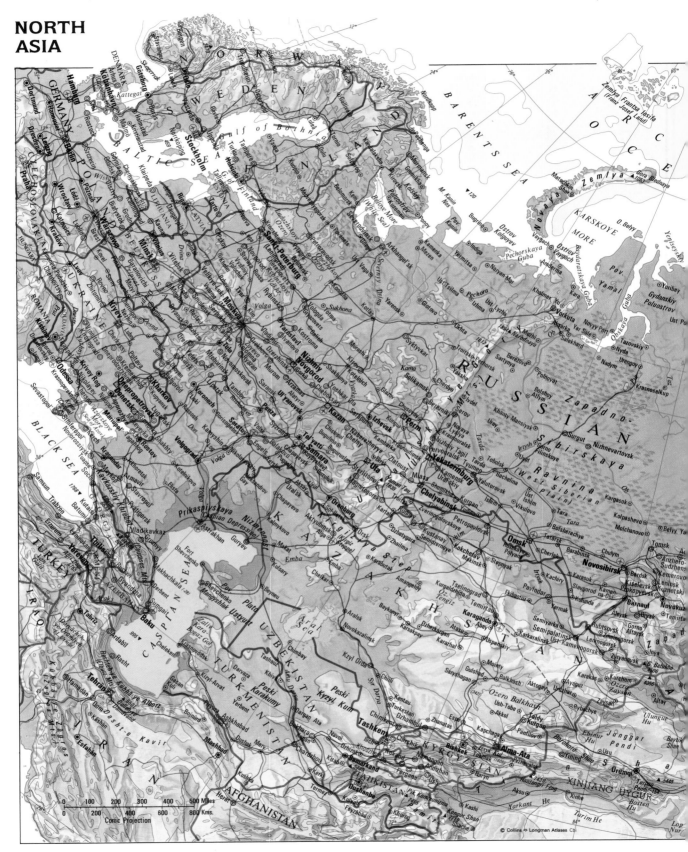

NORTH
ASIA

ASIA

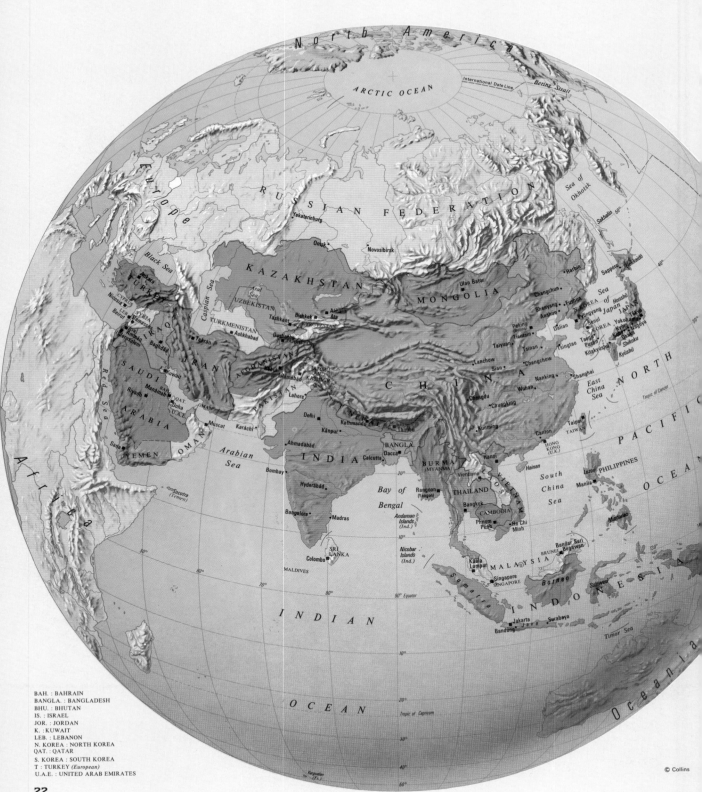

North America

ARCTIC OCEAN

International Date Line

Bering Strait

Europe

RUSSIAN FEDERATION

Yekaterinburg

Omsk

Novosibirsk

Sea of Okhotsk

Sakhalin

Black Sea

Ankara

TURKEY

KAZAKHSTAN

MONGOLIA

Ulan Bator

Harbin

Sapporo

Hokkaidō

CYPRUS

Aral Sea

UZBEKISTAN

Alma Ata

Changchun

Shenyang

Sea of Japan

Honshū

JAPAN

Nicosia

LEB.

SYRIA

Beirut

Damascus

Tashkent

Bishkek

Anshan

N. KOREA

Pyongyang

KOREA

Seoul

Yokohama

Caspian Sea

TURKMENISTAN

Ashkhabad

Dushanbe

Peking (Beijing)

Tientsin

Dalian

S. KOREA

Pusan

Kitakyūshū

Kyōto

Shikoku

Tōkyō

Nagoya

Amman

Baghdad

IRAQ

Jerusalem

Tehran

IRAN

AFGHANISTAN

Taiyuan

Tsingtao

Kyūshū

K.

Kuwait

JAMMU AND KASHMIR

Lanchow

Sian

C H I N A

Nanking

Shanghai

East China Sea

NORTH

SAUDI

Manamah

BAH.

QAT.

Doha

Riyadh

OMAN

U.A.E.

PAKISTAN

Lahore

Chengdu

Chungking

Chengchow

Wuhan

Muscat

Karāchi

Delhi

NEPAL

Kathmandu

Kunming

Canton

Taipei

TAIWAN

HONG KONG (U.K.)

PACIFIC

ARABIA

Sana

YEMEN

OMAN

Red Sea

Arabian Sea

Socotra (Yemen)

Ahmadābād

Bombay

INDIA

Kānpur

BHU.

Thimbu

BANGLA.

Dacca

Calcutta

BURMA (MYANMA)

Hanoi

Hainan

South China Sea

OCEAN

Luzon

PHILIPPINES

Manila

Africa

Hyderābād

Bay of Bengal

Rangoon (Yangon)

THAILAND

LAOS

Vientiane

VIETNAM

Bangalore

Madras

Andaman Islands (Ind.)

Bangkok

CAMBODIA

Phnom Penh

Ho Chi Minh

Mindanao

Colombo

SRI LANKA

Nicobar Islands (Ind.)

BRUNEI

Bandar Seri Begawan

MALDIVES

Kuala Lumpur

MALAYSIA

Singapore

SINGAPORE

Borneo

Sulawesi

I N D O N E S I A

INDIAN

Sumatra

Jakarta

Java

Surabaya

Timor Sea

O C E A N

Bandung

Oceania

Tropic of Cancer

Tropic of Capricorn

Equator

Kerguelen (Fr.)

© Collins

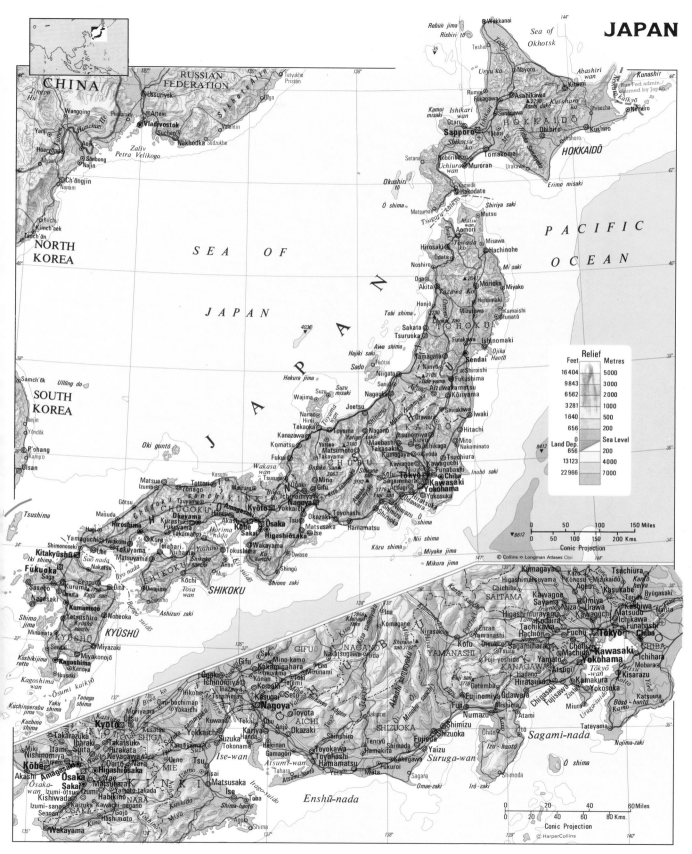

JAPAN

EAST ASIA

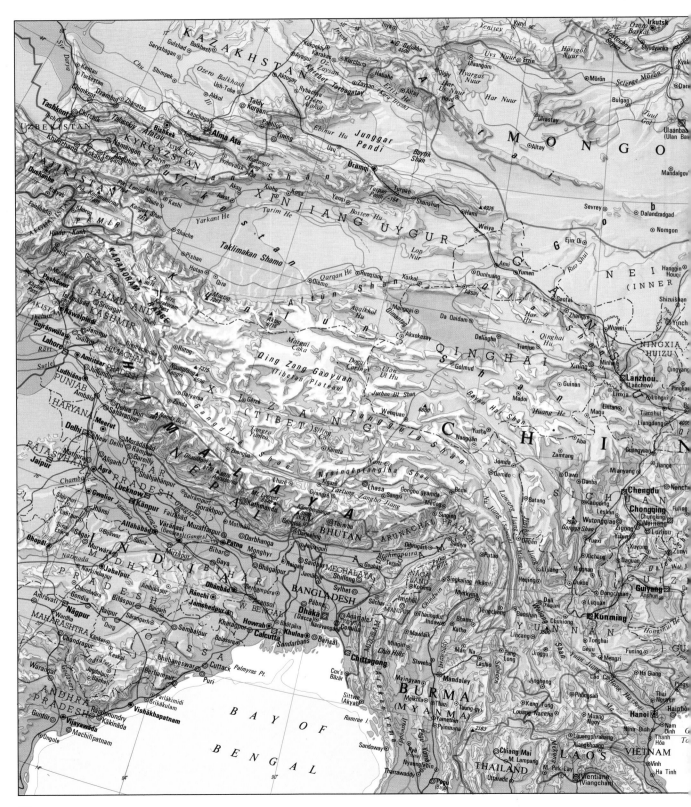

SOUTHEAST ASIA

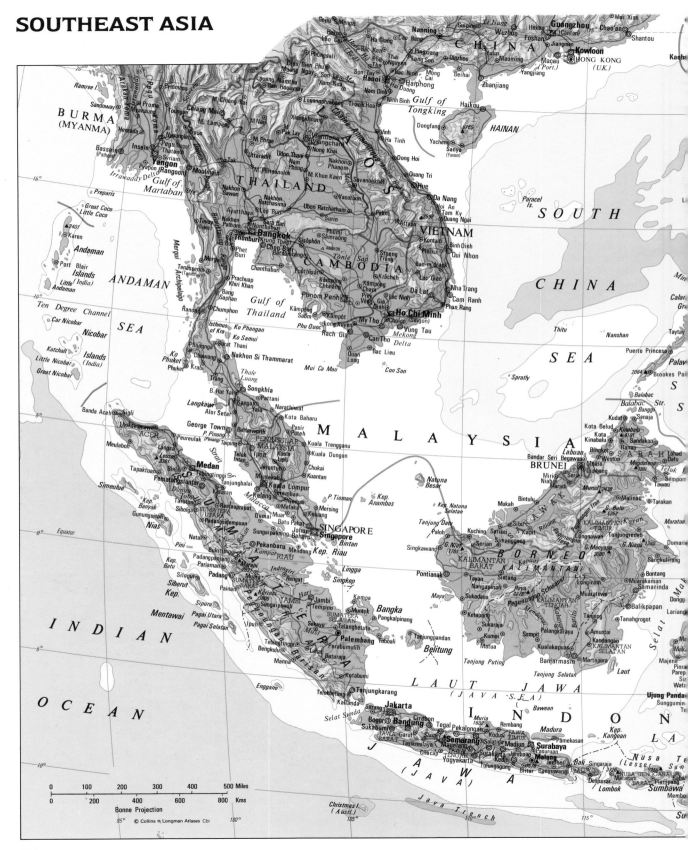

TAIWAN
(FORMOSA)

Batan Is.

uzon Strait

Babuyan Is.

ngtung

C. Engaño

Aparri

Tuguegarao

anap

llagan

n Fernando
Bayombong
gupan

an Carlos

Cabanatuan

LUZON

Quezon City
Manila

San Pablo   Daet

Lucena   Naga   Catanduanes
Virac

Legazpi

Burias   Sorsogon

Iindoro   Catarman

Sablayan   Bulan   Oras

Looc   Masbate   Catbalogan   Samar

Roxas   Guiuan

Panay   Pototan   Visayan   Sea

Iloilo   Cadiz

Bacolod   Ormoc   Leyte

Negros   Tacloban

Tanay   Tagbilaran   Dinagat   Siargao

Dumaguete   Bohol   Surigao

Mindanao   Butuan

Liloy   Sea   San Juan

Dipolog   Cagayan de Oro   Tagum
Ozamiz   Iligan

Siocon   Davao   Mati

Zamboanga   Cotabato   Moro   Pikit

Basilan   Datu Mabita   Piang

Basilan   Lebak   Gulf

Jolo   General
Jolo   Santos

Sulu
Arch.

PHILIPPINES

Philippine   Trench

Cape Johnson
Depth 10497

MINDANAO

LEBES

SEA

Karakelong
Bulu
Kep.
Talaud

Tahuna
Sangihe

Siau   Kep.
Sangihe

Manado

Kema
Tondano

Paleleh   Belang
Buol   2267

omini   Kuandang
Gorontalo   1970

Kep. Togian

Poso   Tokala
Tolii   2630
St

Teluk   Peleng   Taliabu
Tolo

Kep.   Kep. Sula
Banggai

ombola   Mekongga
AN   2790
luk

Kolaka   Kendari

Raha   Wowoni

Muna   Buton
abaena   Baubau   Kep.
Tukangbesi

elayar

S   I   A

F   L   O   R   E   S

ORES SEA)
ands)
ng   Maumere   Wetar   Kalabahi
Endeh   Atapupu   Alor   Dili
NUSA   TIMOR
apu   TENGGARA   TIMUR   Vikeke
Sawu   TIMUR   2066
Roti   Kupang   Timor

Laut Sawu
(Savu Sea)

M   O   L   U   C   C   A   S

Laut Maluku
(Molucca Sea)

Sopi
Morotai

Tobelo
Akelamo

Jailolo   Halmahera

Ternate   Weda
Soasiu

Wosi   Gebe   Laluaha
Bacan
Sesepe

Lenmalu   Misoöl

Kep. Sula

LAUT SERAM
(CERAM SEA)

Binaiya   Wahai
3055
Wamsasi   Namlea   Seram   Bula
Buru   Ambon   (Ceram)   Tum

MALUKU   Banda
Besar

LAUT BANDA
(BANDA SEA)

Kep.
Kai

Nila   Dobo   Wokam
Damar   Teun   Kep.   Kobroor
Aru
Rebi

Wasiri   Yamdena   Trangan
Romang   Tepa
Babar

Tutuala   Kep.   Saumlaki   Kep.
Leti   Sermata   Tanimbar

PACIFIC

OCEAN

FEDERATED STATES OF MICRONESIA

Yap

Ifalik
Faraulep

Sorol

Ngulu

Palau
(U.S.A.)   Koror

Sonsorol

Merir

Tobi

Helen Reef

Waigeo   Wakre

Selat Dampier   Kwoka
Sorong   Klamono   Artak
Jazirah Doberai   2939
(Vogelkop)   Inanwatan   Wasian

Misoöl   Teluk Berau

Kokas   Fakfak   Weri

Adi   Kaimana

Wanapoi   Karufa

Pulau Yos
Sudarsa
(Kolepom)   Kimaan
Okaba
Meraike

Tanjung
Vals

Sebidiro

Challenger Depth
11034

Gaferut

Pigailoe
Lamotrek

Eauripik

Caroline   Islands

Kep.
Mapia

Kep.
Schouten

Manokwari   Korim   Biak   Bosnik
Warkapi   Mokmer
Serui   Yapen

Teluk
Cenderawasih   Sarmi   Ansudu

Pegunungan
1340   Jayapura   Vanimo

IRIAN   Pegunungan   Maoke
JAYA   Sudirman   Puncak Jaya   Mendi
Puncak Jaya   8030   Pk. Mandala

NEW   GUINEA

Tanahmerah

Kepi

Mepi

Digul

Kokenau

Lake
Murray   Kikori
Fly
Aramia

Gulf of
Papua

Mulgrave I.

Torres Str.
Thursday I.
Prince of Wales I.   C. York

ARAFURA   SEA

Nero Deep
9631

Manus
Lorengau
Admiralty Is.

Bismarck
Sea

Karkar I.

Madang

PAPUA NEW
GUINEA

Mt. Hagen
Mt. Wilhelm   Wabag
4694

Mendi

Laiagam

JAYA   Mindiptana

Kimaan   Daru   Sebidiro   Port Moresby
Kila Kila

Wewak   Maprik   Anguram
Angoram   Bogia

Sepik

Ramu   Bismarck

Saidor   Huon Pen.
Finschhafen

Lae   Wau
3993

Marobe

Kerema   Popondetta

Kila Kila

Coral
Sea

Banks I.

Laut Bali
(Bali Sea)

Kep.
Kangean

Relief

Feet		Metres
16404		5000
9843		3000
6562		2000
3281		1000
1640		500
656		200
0		Sea Level
Land Dep.		
656		200
13123		4000
22966		7000

Equator

SOUTH ASIA

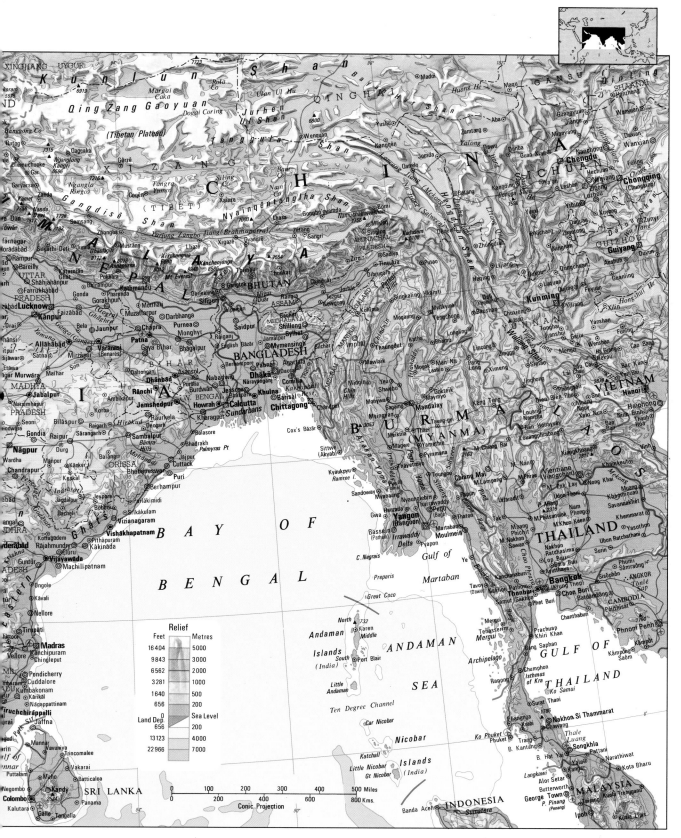

XINGJIANG   UYGUR

Kunlun Shan
6919   Rola Co
Margai Caka   Ulan Ul Hu   QINGHAI
Qing Zang Gaoyuan   Jurhen Ul Shan
Dogai Coring
(Tibetan Plateau)   6800   Zamtang
Tänggula   Shan   Nanggen
Wenquan   Yushu
Qamdo
XIZANG   C H I N A
7315   Nganglong   Siling Co
Kangri
6596   Tangra   Co   Nam   Bomi
Gar   Yumco   Ringco   Co   Namuchabawa Shan
Gangdisê   Shan   7756
(TIBET)   Xainza   Gonbo gyamda
Yarlung Zangbo Jiang (Brahmaputra)   Sangri   ARUNACHAL
Zhongba   Xigazê   Gyangze   Zêtang   Sadiya   PRADESH
Dhaulagiri   Xixabangma   Kanchenjunga   Thimbu   Ziro   Tinsukia
Annapurna   8586   Gangtok   BHUTAN   Changla   Dibrugarh
Mt Everest   Darjeeling   Rangia   Tezpur   NAGALAND
NEPAL   Pokhara   Siliguri   Paro   ASSAM   Kohima
Kathmandu   Jalpaiguri   Duar   Newgong   Putao
Pharenda   Sikkim   MEGHALAYA   Mokokchung   Myitkyina
Gorakhpur   Morihari   Saukai   Shillong   Imphal   Tengchong
Gonda   Darbhanga   Purnea   Saidpur   Silchar   Thaungdut   Katha   Baoshan
Jaunpur   Chapra   Monghyr   Raiganj   Jamalpur   Sylhet   Lincang   YUNNAN
Patna   Gaya Bihar   Bhagalpur   Pabna   Agartala   Mawlaik   Mogok   Mandalay   KUNMING
Varanasi   BIHAR   BANGLADESH   Comilla   Chin Hills   Shwebo   Goktei   Kunming
Dhanbad   Asansol   Nabadwip   Dhaka   Barisal   Minbin   Yeu   Monywa   Sagaing   Keng Tung   VIETNAM
INDIA   Ranchi   Burdwan   Jessore   Narayanganj   Khulna   Chittagong   Maymyo   Louangnamtha   Hanoi
Jamshedpur   Howrah   Calcutta   Sundarbans   Mandalay   BURMA   LAOS
W. BENGAL   Kharagpur   Cox's Bazar   Meiktila   MYANMA
Raurkela   Balasore   Sittwe   Magwe   Yamethin   Chiang Rai
ORISSA   Cuttack   (Akyab)   Pye   THAILAND
Nagpur   Bhubaneswar   Puri   Kyaukpyu   Chiang Mai
Berhampur   Ramree I.   Nyaunglebin   Vientiane
Vishakhapatnam   Sandoway   Henzada   Pegu   Bangkok
Gwa   Yangon (Rangoon)   CAMBODIA
BAY   OF   Bassein (Pathein)   Moulmein   Phnom Penh
Irrawaddy   Pyapon
Delta   Ye
BENGAL   C. Negrais   Gulf of   GULF   OF
Preparis   Martaban   THAILAND
Great Coco   Tavoy   Isthmus
North   732   Mergui   of Kra
Andaman   Karen   Tenasserim   Ko Samui
Islands   Middle   ANDAMAN   Archipelago   Surat Thani
South   Port Blair   Ranong   Songkhla
(India)   SEA   Phangnga   Nakhon Si Thammarat
Little   Ko Phuket   Krabi
Andaman   Phuket   Trang   MALAYSIA
Ten Degree Channel   George Town
Car Nicobar   INDONESIA   Ipoh
Madras   Nicobar   Sumatera
SRI LANKA   Islands
Colombo   Kandy   (India)

SOUTHWEST ASIA

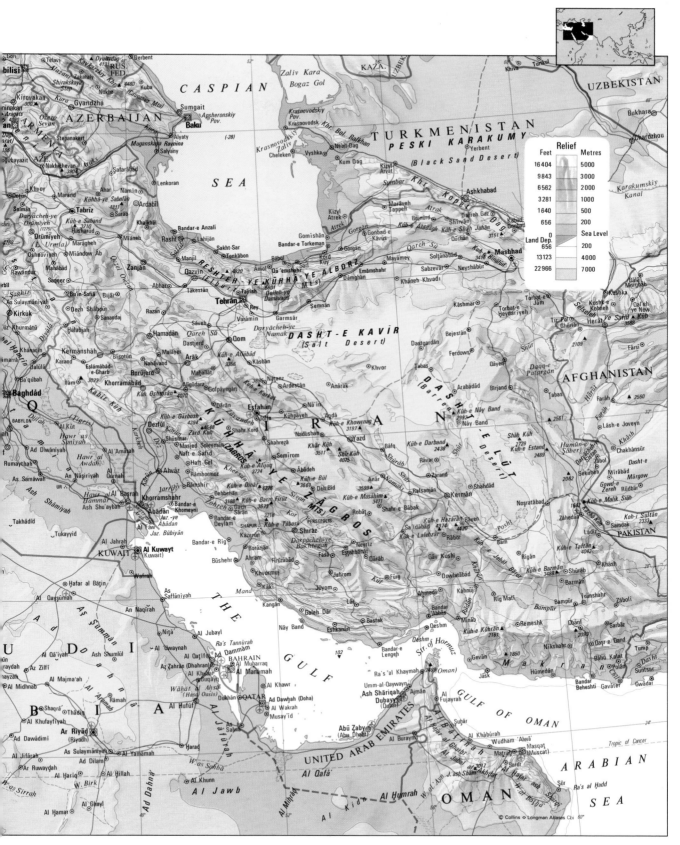

THE LEVANT

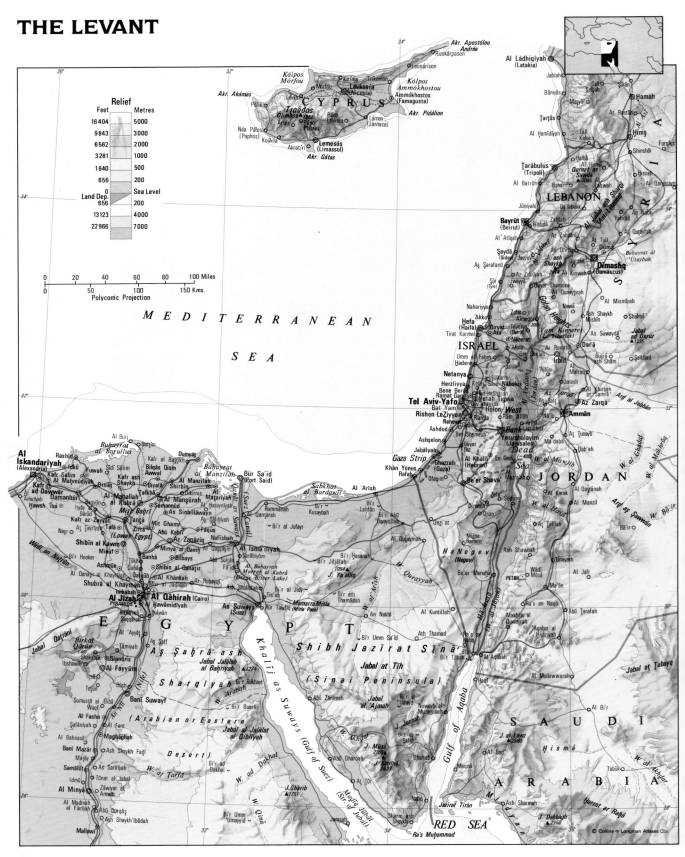

AFRICA

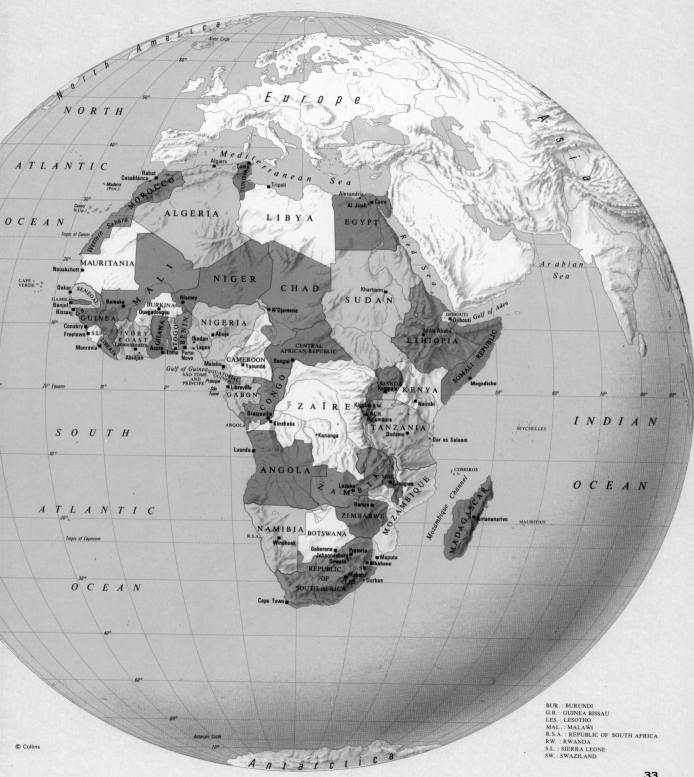

BUR. : BURUNDI
G.B. : GUINEA BISSAU
LES. : LESOTHO
MAL. : MALAWI
R.S.A. : REPUBLIC OF SOUTH AFRICA
RW. : RWANDA
S.L. : SIERRA LEONE
SW. : SWAZILAND

© Collins

33

NORTHERN AFRICA

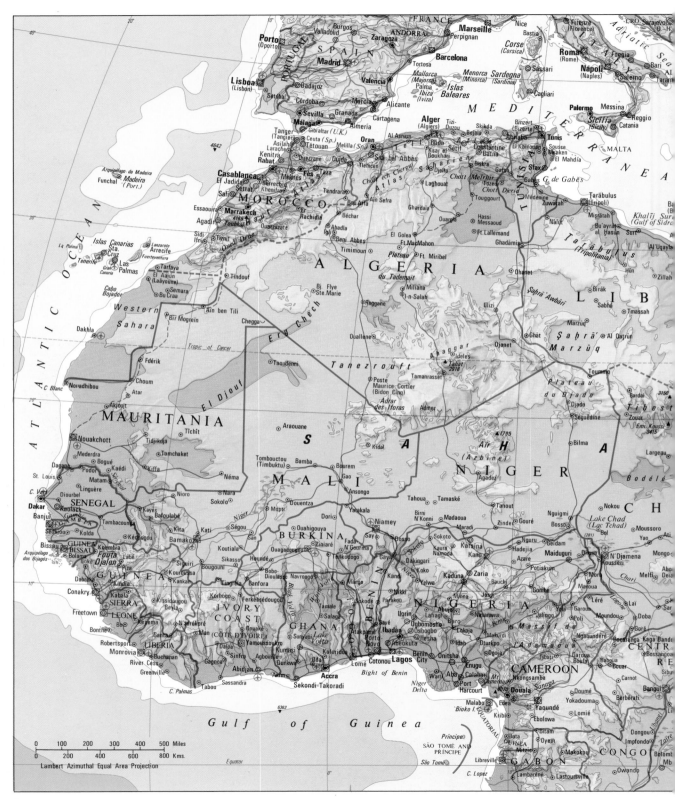

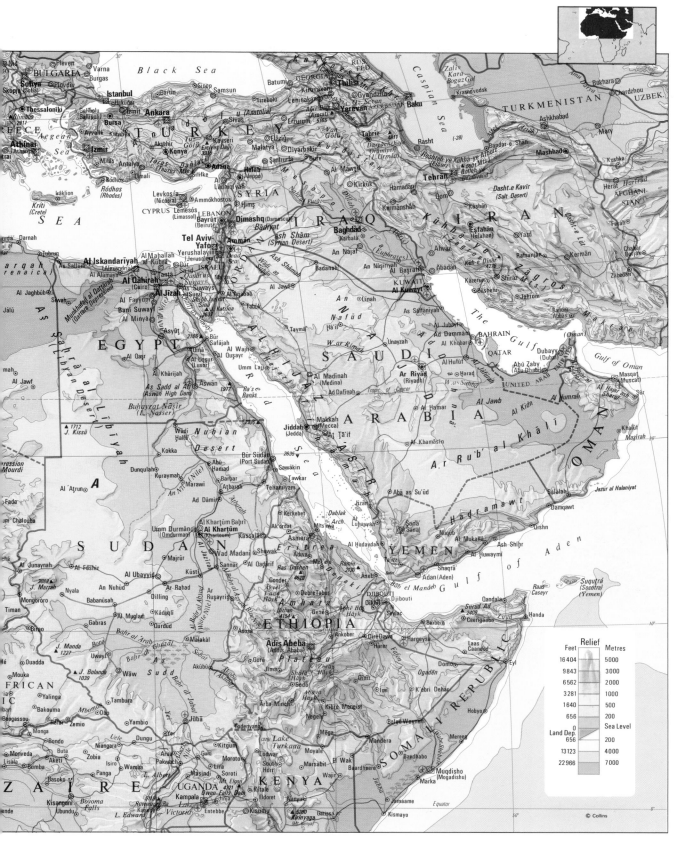

35

CENTRAL AND SOUTHERN AFRICA

Relief

Feet	Metres
16 404	5000
9843	3000
6562	2000
3281	1000
1640	500
656	200
0	Sea Level
656	200
13 123	4000

ATLANTIC OCEAN

INDIAN OCEAN

Mozambique Channel

0 100 200 300 400 500 Miles
0 200 400 600 800 Kms.
Lambert Azimuthal Equal Area Projection

© Collins ● Longman Atlases Cbi

NIGERIA   CHAD   SUDAN   ETHIOPIA   SOMALI REPUBLIC

CAMEROON   CENTRAL AFRICAN REPUBLIC   UGANDA   KENYA

EQUATORIAL GUINEA   GABON   CONGO   ZAÏRE   RWANDA   BURUNDI   TANZANIA

ANGOLA   ZAMBIA   MALAWI   MOZAMBIQUE   COMOROS

NAMIBIA   BOTSWANA   ZIMBABWE

REPUBLIC OF SOUTH AFRICA   SWAZILAND   LESOTHO

MADAGASCAR

Tropic of Capricorn

Namib Desert   Kalahari Desert

Lake Victoria   Lake Tanganyika   Lake Malawi   L. Kariba   Etosha Pan   Okavango Basin

Cape of Good Hope   C. Agulhas

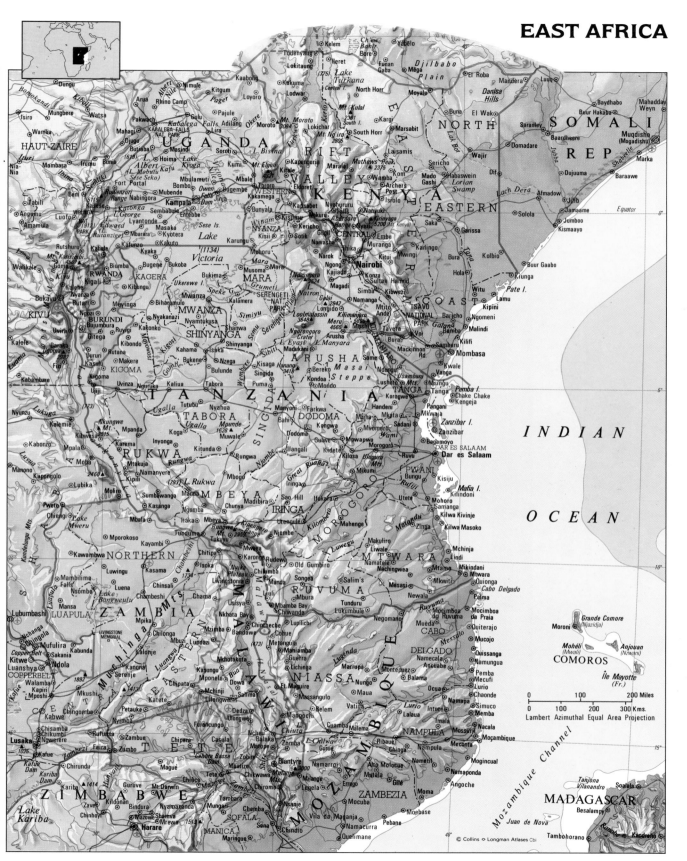

WEST AFRICA – EAST

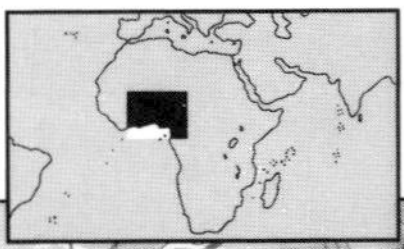

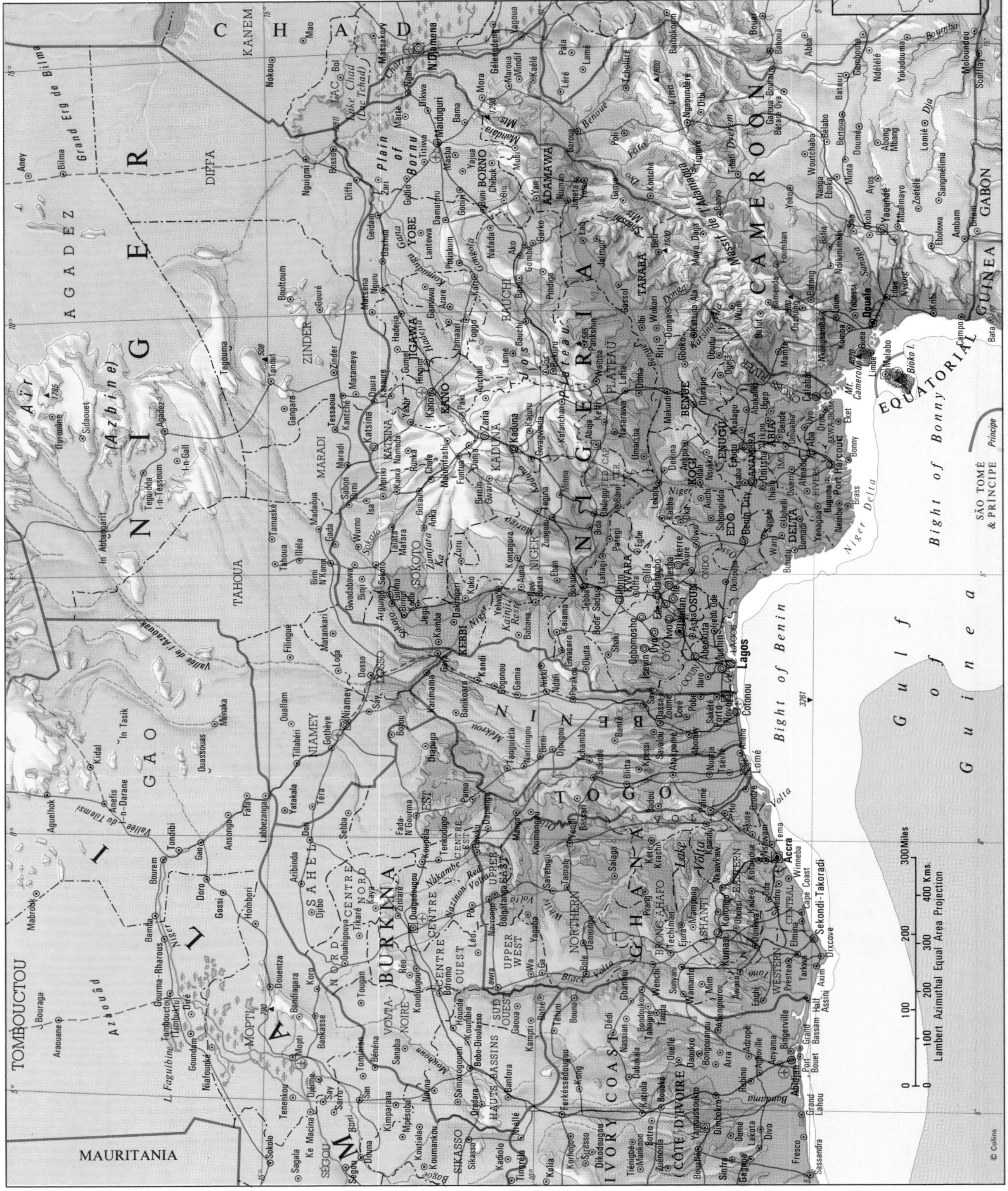
CHAD
NIGER
MALI
BURKINA
NIGERIA
CAMEROON
GHANA
TOGO
BENIN
IVORY COAST
CÔTE D'IVOIRE
MAURITANIA
GABON
EQUATORIAL GUINEA
SÃO TOMÉ & PRÍNCIPE
Gulf of Guinea
Bight of Benin
Bight of Bonny
Niger Delta
Lake Chad (Lac Tchad)
Aïr (Azbine)
Grand Erg de Bilma
Plain of Bornu
Jos Plateau
N'Djamena
Niamey
Lagos
Accra
Kano
Kaduna
Abidjan
Douala
Yaoundé
Lomé
Cotonou
300 Miles
400 Kms.
Lambert Azimuthal Equal Area Projection
© Collins

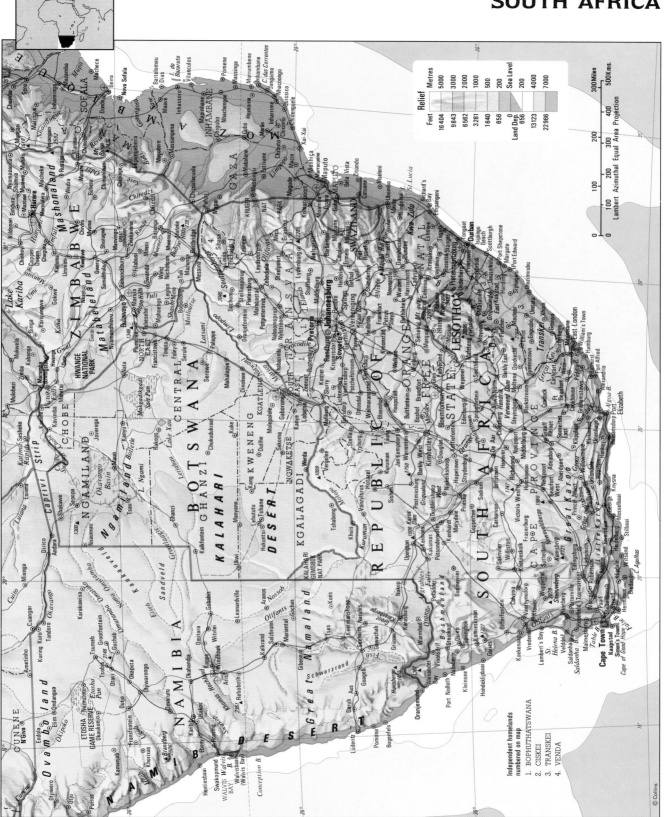

OCEANIA

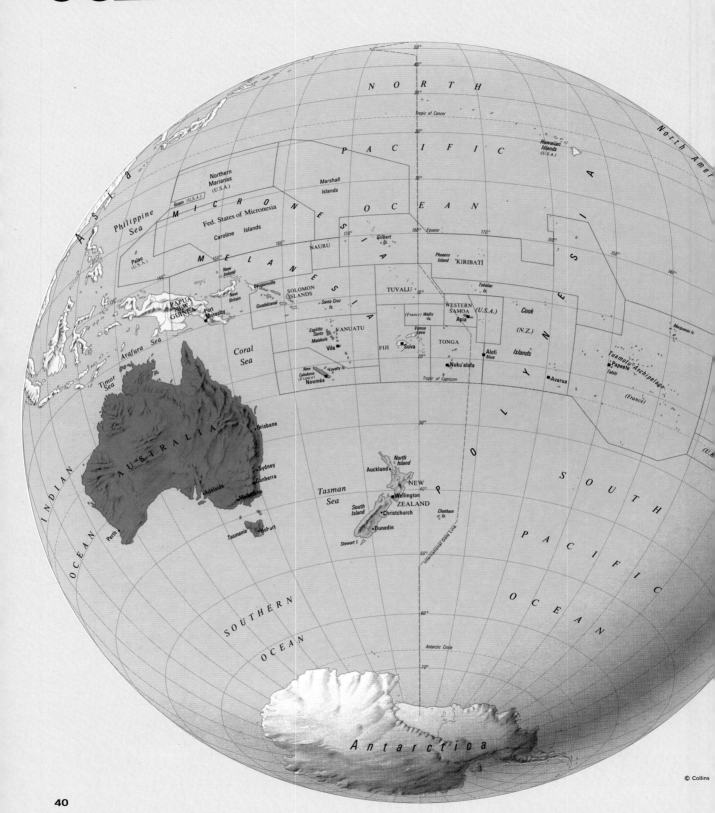

NORTH

PACIFIC

OCEAN

Tropic of Cancer

Hawaiian
Islands
(U.S.A.)

North Ameri

ASIA

Philippine
Sea

MICRONESIA

Northern
Marianas
(U.S.A.)

Guam (U.S.A.)

Marshall
Islands

Fed. States of Micronesia

Caroline Islands

NAURU

Gilbert
Is.

Equator

Phoenix
Island

KIRIBATI

Palau
(U.S.A.)

MELANESIA

New
Ireland

Bougainville

New
Britain

SOLOMON
ISLANDS

Guadalcanal

Santa Cruz
Is.

TUVALU

Tokelau
Is.

WESTERN
SAMOA

(U.S.A.)

Cook

POLYNESIA

Marquesas Is.

PAPUA
NEW
GUINEA

Port
Moresby

Arafura Sea

Espiritu
Santo

Malakula

VANUATU

Vila

(France) Wallis
Is.

Vanua
Levu

FIJI

Suva

Apia

TONGA

Alofi
Niue

Islands

(N.Z.)

Tuamotu Archipelago

Papeete

Tahiti

Coral
Sea

New
Caledonia
(France)

Nouméa

Loyalty Is.

Nuku'alofa

Tropic of Capricorn

Avarua

(France)

Timor
Sea

AUSTRALIA

Brisbane

Sydney

Canberra

Melbourne

Adelaide

Perth

Tasmania

Hobart

Tasman
Sea

North
Island

Auckland

NEW
Wellington

ZEALAND

South
Island

Christchurch

Chatham
Is.

Dunedin

Stewart I.

SOUTH

PACIFIC

OCEAN

(U.

INDIAN

OCEAN

International Date Line

SOUTHERN

OCEAN

Antarctic Circle

Antarctica

© Collins

AUSTRALIA

WESTERN AUSTRALIA

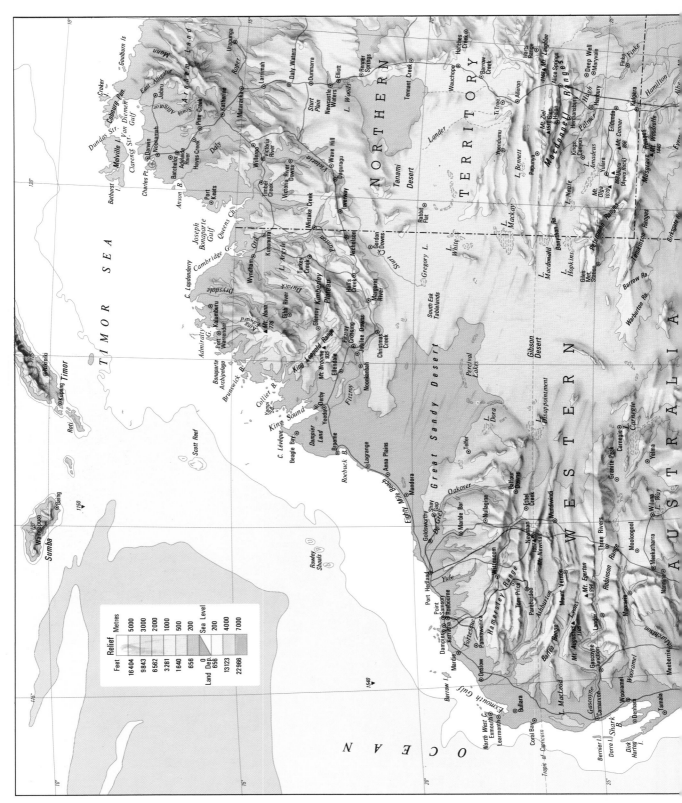

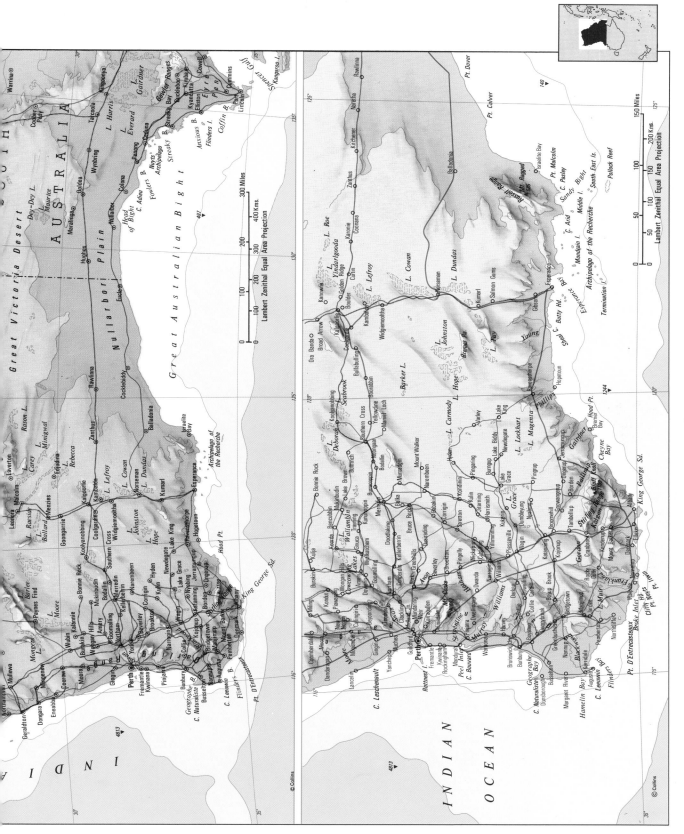

EASTERN AUSTRALIA

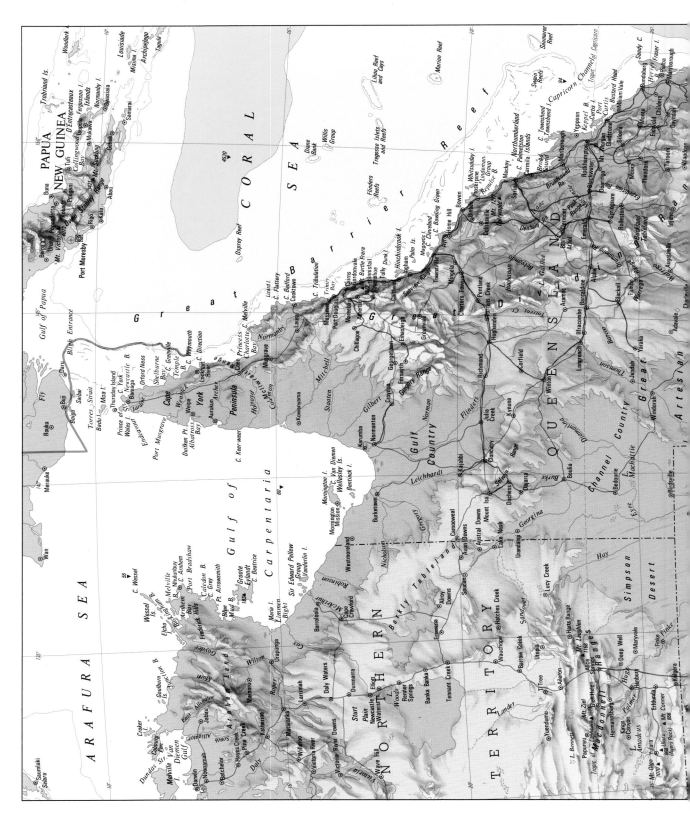

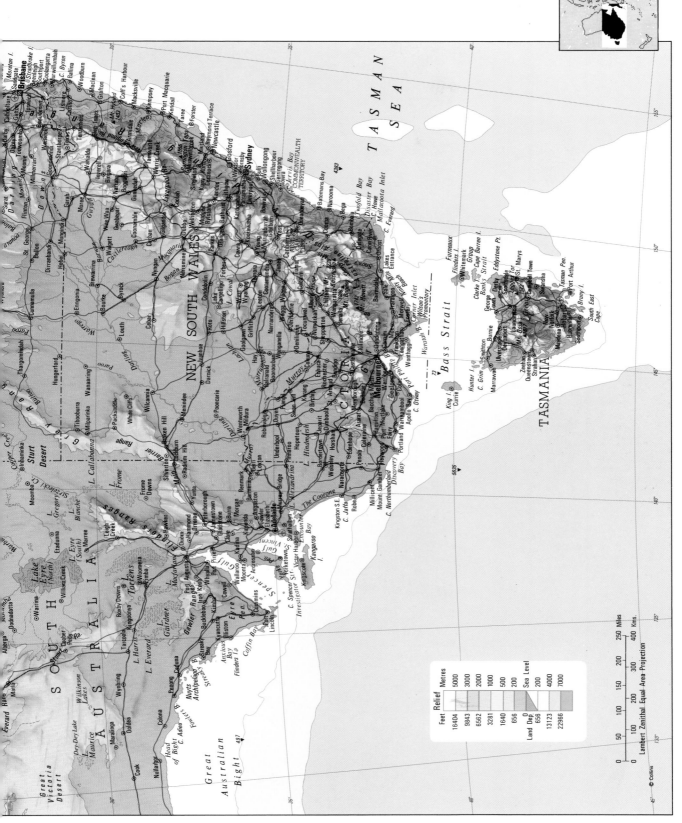

45

SOUTHEAST AUSTRALIA

NEW ZEALAND

Relief

Feet	Metres
16404	5000
9843	3000
6562	2000
3281	1000
1640	500
656	200
0	Sea Level

Land Dep.

656	200
13123	4000
22966	7000

NORTH ISLAND

SOUTH ISLAND

TASMAN SEA

PACIFIC OCEAN

NORTHLAND

North Cape
Ninety Mile Beach
Mangonui
Doubless Bay
Kaitaia
Rawene
Paihia
Bay of Islands
C. Brett
Kaikohe
Hikurangi
Whangarei
Dargaville
Waihi
Bream Bay
Gt. Barrier I.
Warkworth
Hauraki Gulf
Helensville
Kaipara Harbour
Takapuna
Auckland
Manukau
AUCKLAND
Coromandel
Coromandel Peninsula
Whitianga
Waiuku
Pukekohe
Thames
Manukau Harbour
Mayor I.
Waikato
Huntly
Morrinsville
Waihi
Bay of Plenty
Ngaruawahia
Waihi
Tauranga
Hamilton
Matakana I.
Te Kaha
Hicks Bay
Cambridge
Tokoroa
Whakatane
East Cape
Te Awamutu
Putaruru
Rotorua
Hikurangi 1754
Te Aratua
Kawhia
WAIKATO
Te Kuiti
Kaweraub
BAY OF PLENTY
Opotiki
Tikitiki
Rotorua
Lake
Mokau
Dennevyidale
Matawai
Waipiro
North Taranaki Bight
Taupo
Murupara
Tolaga Bay
New Plymouth
Waitara
Ruatoria
GISBORNE
Mt. Egmont
Inglewood
Ngauruhoe 2291
Turangi
Huiarau Ra.
Gisborne
2518
Stratford
Ruapehu 2797
Waikokopu
Opunake
Normanby
Waiparoa
Mahia Peninsula
TARANAKI
Hawera
HAWKES BAY
Wairoa
Patea
Taihape
Hawke Bay
MANAWATU
Waipawa
Bay View
Wanganui
Taname
Napier
WANGANUI
Mangaweka
Hastings
Marton
Feilding
Waipukurau
Palmerston North
Dannevirke
Foxton
Levin
Kapiti I.
Paraparaumu
Pahiatua
WELLINGTON
Masterton
Porirua
Carterton
Upper Hutt
WELLINGTON
Lower Hutt
Wellington
Blenheim
C. Palliser

Cape Farewell
Golden Bay
Collingwood
Takaka
D'Urville I.
Tasman Mts.
Tasman Bay
Karamea Bight
Motueka
Nelson
Picton
Karamea
Richmond
Havelock
Granity
Tadmor
Wairau
Westport
Buller
Murchison
NELSON
Cape Foulwind
Inangahua
Seddon
MARLBOROUGH
Junction
Kaikoura Ra.
Cape Campbell
Reefton
Mt. Travers 2338
Clarence
Akaroa
Hanmer Springs
Greymouth
Lewis Pass
Kaikoura
Kumara
Brunner
Waiau
Hokitika
Ross
Hurunui
Cheviot
Arthur's Pass
Waipara
Whataroa
Pegasus Bay
Okarito
Rangiora
Kaiapoi
SOUTHERN ALPS
Fox Glacier
Amberley
SOUTH ISLAND
Springfield
Darfield
Christchurch
Mt. Cook 3764
Rakaia
Banks Peninsula
Cascade Pt.
Lincoln
Leeston
Akaroa
Okuru
Oakaki
Ashburton
Timaru
L. Tekapo
Fairlie
Mt. Aspiring 3027
Canterbury Bight
Wanaka
Geraldine
Hawea
Twizel
Timaru
Milford Sound
Homer Tunnel
Omarama
Waimate
Arrowtown
Cromwell
Queenstown
Clyde
Oamaru
Te Anau
Wakatipu
Kingston
Alexandra
Palmerston
Anau
Naseby
Pukeuri
SOUTHLAND
Mossburn
Ranfurly
Waikouaiti
Lumsden
Roxburgh
Port Chalmers
Resolution I.
Otautau
Tapanui
Otago Peninsula
Ohai
Nightcaps
Lawrence
Mosgiel
Dunedin
Puysegur Pt.
Winton
Gore
Clinton
Balclutha
Riverton
Edendale
Owaka
Foveaux
Invercargill
Fortrose
Bluff
Ruapuke I.
Stewart I.
Strait
Halfmoon Bay
Southwest Cape

0   50   100   150 Miles
0   50   100   150   200 Kms.
Conic Projection

© Collins © Longman Atlases Cbii

NORTH AMERICA

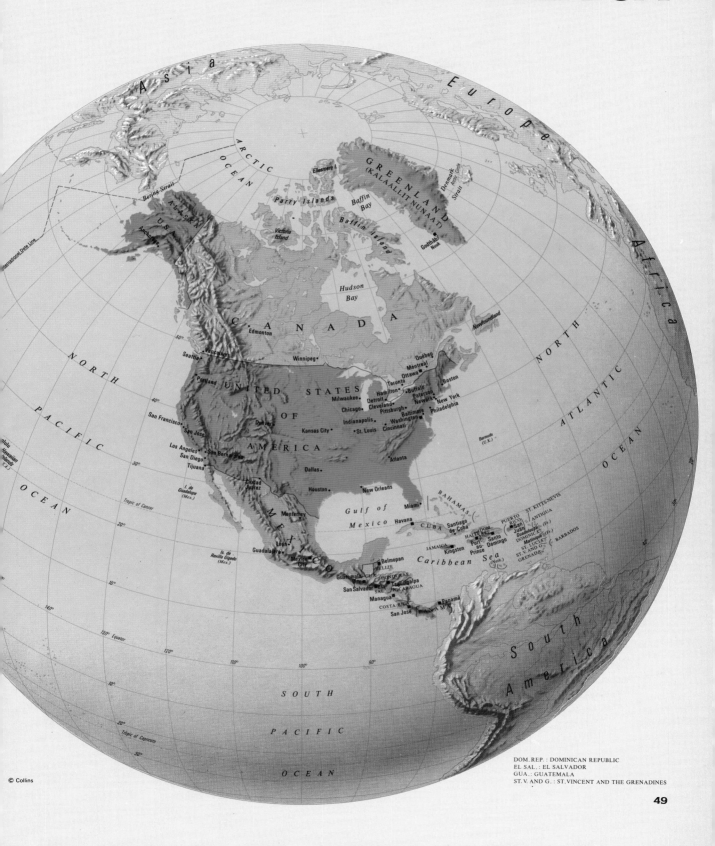

DOM. REP. : DOMINICAN REPUBLIC
EL SAL. : EL SALVADOR
GUA. : GUATEMALA
ST. V. AND G. : ST. VINCENT AND THE GRENADINES

© Collins

CANADA AND ALASKA

Relief

Feet	Metres
16 404	5000
9843	3000
6562	2000
3281	1000
1640	500
656	200
0	Sea Level
Land Dep.	
656	200
13 123	4000
22 966	7000

0	100	200	300	400	500	Miles
0	100 200 300 400 500 600 700 800					Kms.

Bonne Projection

51

UNITED STATES

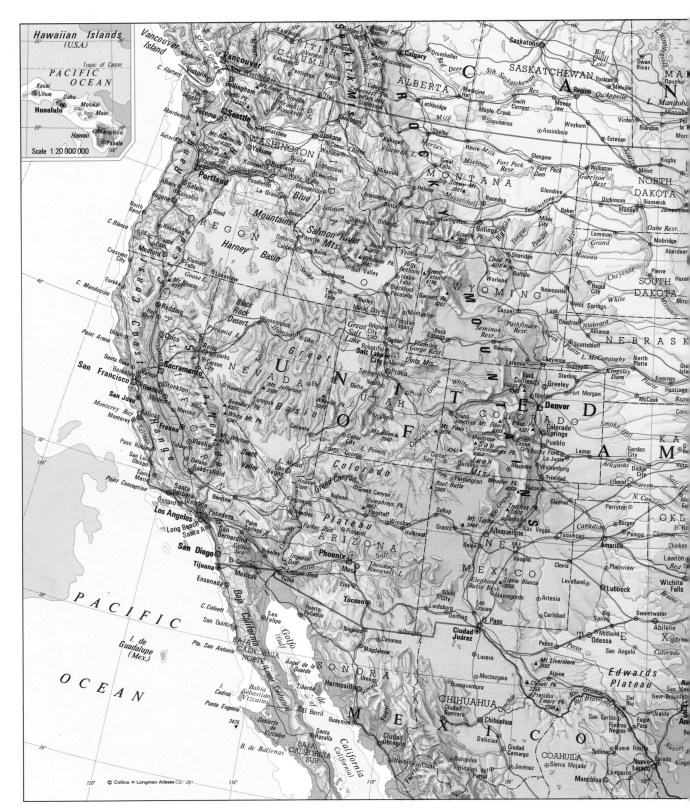

Hawaiian Islands
(U.S.A.)

PACIFIC
OCEAN

Scale 1:20 000 000

Honolulu

PACIFIC

OCEAN

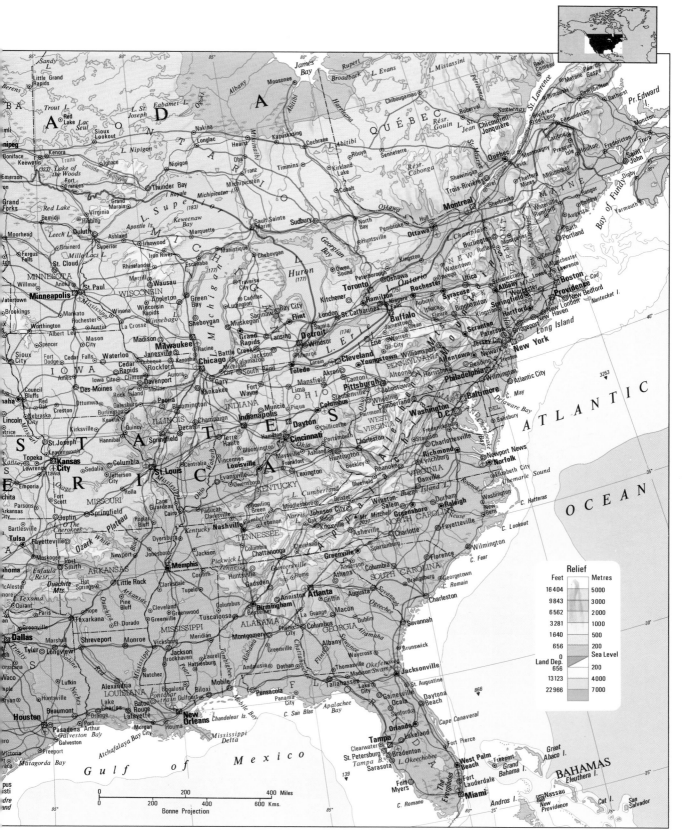

WESTERN UNITED STATES

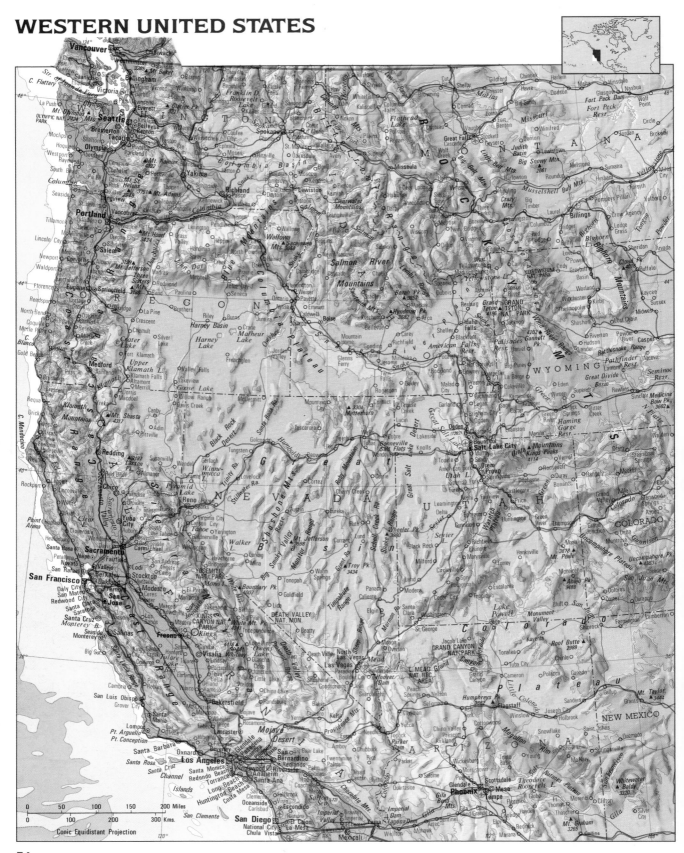

Relief

Metres	Feet
5000	16404
3000	9843
2000	6562
1000	3281
500	1640
200	656
Sea Level	0
Land Dep.	656
200	13123
4000	22966
7000	

200 Miles
300 Kms.

Conic Equidistant Projection

© Collins

CENTRAL AMERICA AND THE CARIBBEAN

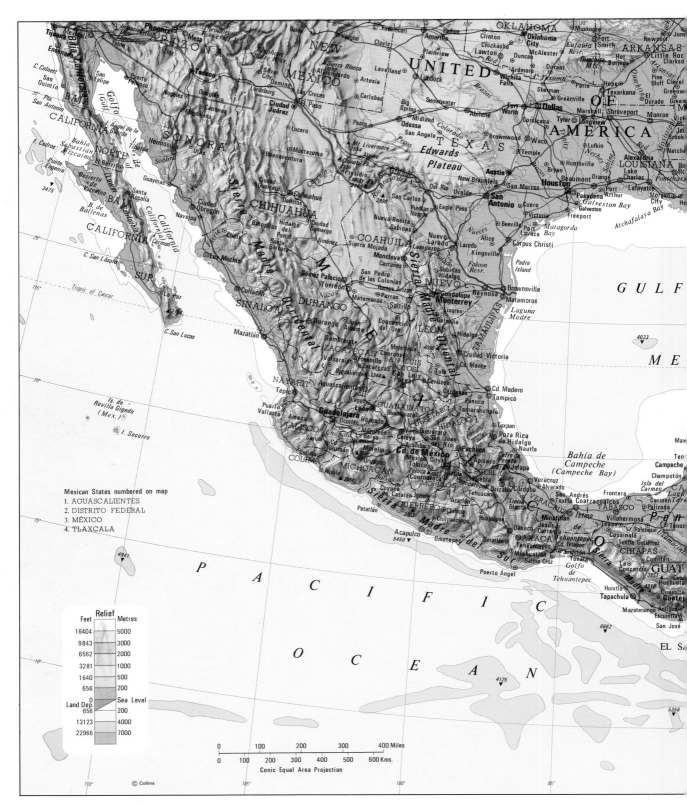

Mexican States numbered on map
1. AGUASCALIENTES
2. DISTRITO FEDERAL
3. MÉXICO
4. TLAXCALA

Relief

Feet	Metres
16404	5000
9843	3000
6562	2000
3281	1000
1640	500
656	200
0	Sea Level
Land Dep.	200
656	4000
13123	7000
22966	

0   100   200   300   400 Miles

0   100   200   300   400   500   600 Kms.

Conic Equal Area Projection

© Collins

TENNESSEE
Jackson
Columbia
Asheville
NORTH
Charlotte
Fayetteville
New Bern
C. Lookout
75°
Pickwick L.
Chattanooga
Cleveland
Greenville
SOUTH
Spartanburg
Wilmington
mphis
Huntsville
Gadsden
Tennessee
Gaffney
Anderson
CAROLINA
Corinth
Rome
Athens
CAROLINA
Columbia
Florence
upelo
Guntersville
Columbus
Orangeburg
C. Fear
STATES
Anniston
Atlanta
Griffin
Augusta
Georgetown
C. Romain
SIPPI
Birmingham
Bessemer
Phenix
City
Macon
Dublin
Charleston
ALABAMA
Montgomery
GEORGIA
Savannah
rel
Greenville
Andalusia
Dothan
Altamaha
ATLANTIC
iesburg
Mobile
Pensacola
Thomasville
Madison
Waycross
Brunswick
OCEAN
Biloxi
Panama
City
Tallahassee
Lake City
Okefenokee
Swamp
Jacksonville
30°
eans
Chandeleur
Is.
C. San Blas
Apalachee
Bay
Gainesville
Ocala
St. Augustine
Mississippi
Delta
Daytona Beach
Sanford
866
Cape Canaveral
Orlando
1137
OF
Clearwater
St. Petersburg
Tampa
Lakeland
Fort Pierce
Tampa B.
Bradenton
Lake
Okeechobee
West
Palm
Beach
Freeport
Great
Abaco I.
BAHAMAS
Sarasota
The Everglades
Fort
Lauderdale
Grand
Bahama I.
Fort Myers
C. Romano
Miami
New
Providence
Eleuthera I.
CO
C. Sable
Nicolls
Town
Nassau
Rock Sound
Cat I.
San
Salvador
Tropic of Cancer
Key West
Florida Keys
of Florida
Andros I.
Andros
Town
The Bight
Rolleville
Rum Cay
Straits
Gt.
Exuma
Long I.
Samana Cay
MAS
Cárdenas
Archo. de Sabana
Crooked I.
Plana Cays
Mayaguana I.
La Habana
(Havana)
Matanzas
Archo. de Camagüey
Acklin's I.
Little
Turks and Caicos Is.
(U.K.)
Marianao
Güines
La Grande
Sagua
Caibarién
Inagua
Caicos Is.
Turks Is.
Pinar del Río
Santa Clara
Morón
20°
Guane
Golfo de
Batabanó
Cienfuegos
Sancti
Spíritus
Ciego de Ávila
Nuevitas
Great
Inagua
Matthew
Town
Île de
la Tortue
8528
Puerto Rico Trench
Nueva
Gerona
Archo. de los
Canarreos
Trinidad
CUBA
Camagüey
Holguín
Banes
Baracoa
Cap-Haïtien
Port-de-Paix
Puerto Plata
San Francisco
de Macoris
Samaná
San Juan
Bayamón
Isla de
Pinos
Jardines de la
Reina
Victoria de
las Tunas
Manzanillo
Bayamo
S. Luis
Guantánamo
G. de la
Gonâve
Môle St.
Nicolas
Gonaïves
Valverde
La Vega
Santiago
DOMINICAN
REP.
La Romana
Arecibo
Mayagüez
Ponce
Caguas
Turquino
Santiago
de Cuba
1971
S. de la
Maestra
Île de la
Gonâve
HAÏTI
Azua
Santo
Domingo
S. Pedro
Saona
Mona
PUERTO
RICO
(U.S.A.)
C. Cruz
Windward
Passage
Jérémie
Port-au-
Prince
2680
San Cristóbal
Barahona
Little
Cayman
Cayman Brac
474
Les
Cayes
Hispaniola
4647
Grand Cayman
Georgetown
Cayman Is.
(U.K.)
C
Greater
Antilles
4297
A
Montego Bay
St. Ann's Bay
Port
Antonio
R
Black River
May Pen
Kingston
I
JAMAICA
B
B
E
A
N
S
E
A
Chetumal
Bay
Gulf of Honduras
Is.
de la Bahía
C. Camarón
15°
Netherlands
Antilles
Chetumal
Corozal
Ambergris
Cay
BELIZE
Belize
Turneffe Is.
Aruba
(Neth.)
Curaçao (Neth.)
Bonaire
Mts.
Dangriga
Punta
Gorda
Pto.
Barrios
Pto. Cortés
Tela
Laguna de
Caratasca
Willemstad
Pta. Gallinas
Pen. de
la Guajira
Golfo
de
Ulúa
S. Pedro Sula
Trujillo
Mosquitia
C. Gracias á Dios
Pta.
Pen. de
Paraguaná
Punto
Fijo
La Vela
Coro
Tucacas
Puerto
Cabello
ta. Ana
Yoro
HONDURAS
Juticalpa
Costa de Mosquitia
Santa
Marta
Sa. Nevada de
Santa Marta
Castilletes
Venezuela
La
Guaira
Maracaibo
San Felipe
Valencia
San Salvador
2489
Comayagua
Tegucigalpa
Danlí
Pto. Cabezas
5775
Riohacha
Uribia
Golfo de
Venezuela
Cabimas
Ciudad Ojeda
Barquisimeto
Yaritagua
OR
S. Miguel
Ampala
Ocotal
2400
I. de
Providencia
(Col.)
Barranquilla
Barranca
Concepción
L. de
Maracaibo
Mene
Grande
Trujillo
Guanare
Chinandega
NICARAGUA
León
Lago de
Managua
Escondido
Prinzapolca
Río
San Andrés
(Col.)
Cartagena
Turbaco
Sabanalarga
Calamar
Valledupar
Machiques
San Carlos
del Zulia
Valera
Barinas
VENEZUELA
Managua
Granada
Rama
Bluefields
Agustín
Arjona
Sincelejo
Apure
Jinotepe
L. de
Nicaragua
San Carlos
Magangué
Guanarito
Rivas
S. Juan del Norte
Carmen
Mompós
Barinas
Apure
Pen. de
Nicoya
Liberia
COSTA
Laguna de Chiriquí
Golfo del
Darién
Cereté
Montería
San
José
Limón
Golfo de
los
Mosquitos
Colón
San Miguelito
PANAMA
CITY
G. de Urabá
Turbo
Puerto Rey
COLOMBIA
C. Blanco
RICA
Cartago
Chirrio
Lake
Gatún
Balboa
Ocaña
Cúcuta
San Cristóbal
Pto. Quepos
David
Penonomé
Golfo
Archo. de
las Perlas
El Real
Barrancabermeja
4200
Bucaramanga
Pamplona
Pto. Cortés
Pen. de Osa
Pta. S. Osa
Santiago
de Coiba
Isla de
Coiba
Pen. de
Azuero
de Panamá
Jurado
Ríosucio
Yarumal
San
Socorro
COLOMBIA
Meta
Arauca

SOUTH AMERICA

North America

NORTH ATLANTIC OCEAN

Tropic of Cancer

Africa

Caribbean Sea

Barranquilla

Maracaibo • Caracas • TRINIDAD AND TOBAGO

VENEZUELA

Medellín

Bogotá

Georgetown Paramaribo

GUYANA SURINAM GUIANA Cayenne

Cali

COLOMBIA

Quito

ECUADOR

Guayaquil

PERU

Galapagos Is. (Ec.)

Belém

Equator

Fortaleza

Lima

Recife

La Paz

BOLIVIA

Brasília

Sucre

Salvador

Belo Horizonte

San Félix (Chile)

San Ambrosio

B R A Z I L

PARAGUAY

Asunción

Rio de Janeiro

São Paulo Santo André

Curitiba

Tropic of Capricorn

Islas Juan Fernández (Chile)

Córdoba

URUGUAY

Pôrto Alegre

Valparaíso

Santiago

Rosario

ARGENTINA

CHILE

Buenos Aires

La Plata

Montevideo

SOUTH PACIFIC OCEAN

SOUTH ATLANTIC OCEAN

Falkland Is. (U.K.)

Tierra del Fuego

South Georgia (U.K.)

International Date Line

Antarctic Circle

Antarctica

© Collins

58

Relief

Feet		Metres
16404		5000
9843		3000
6562		2000
3281		1000
1640		500
656		200
0	Land Dep.	Sea Level
656		200
13123		4000

0   100   200   300   400 Miles
0 100 200 300 400 500 600 Kms.
Lambert Azimuthal Equal Area Projection

© Collins ○ Longman Atlases Cbi

0   40   80 Miles
0   40   80   120 Kms.

© Collins

60

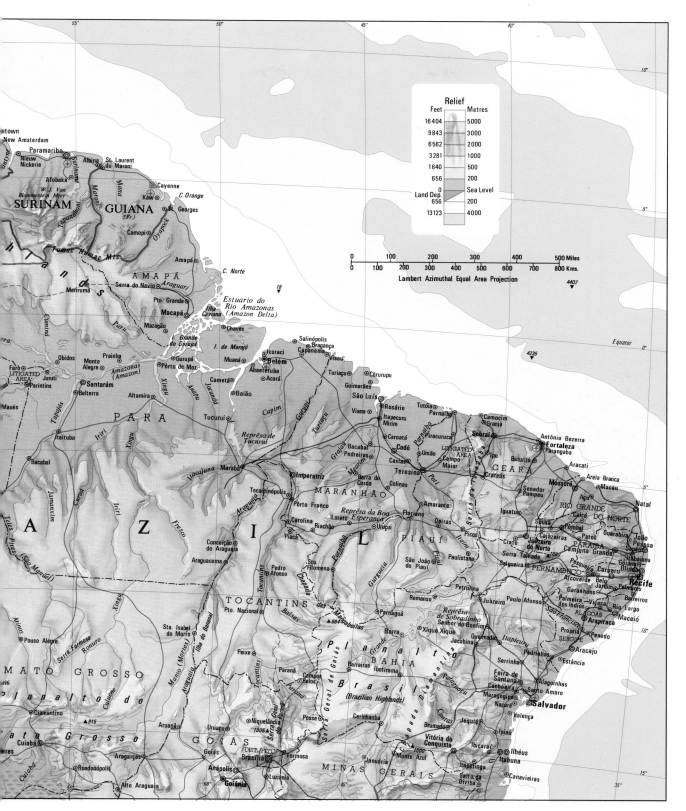

Relief

Feet		Metres
16 404		5000
9 843		3000
6 562		2000
3 281		1000
1 640		500
656		200
0		Sea Level
Land Dep.		
656		200
13 123		4000

0	100		200		300		400		500 Miles
0	100	200	300	400	500	600	700	800 Kms.

Lambert Azimuthal Equal Area Projection

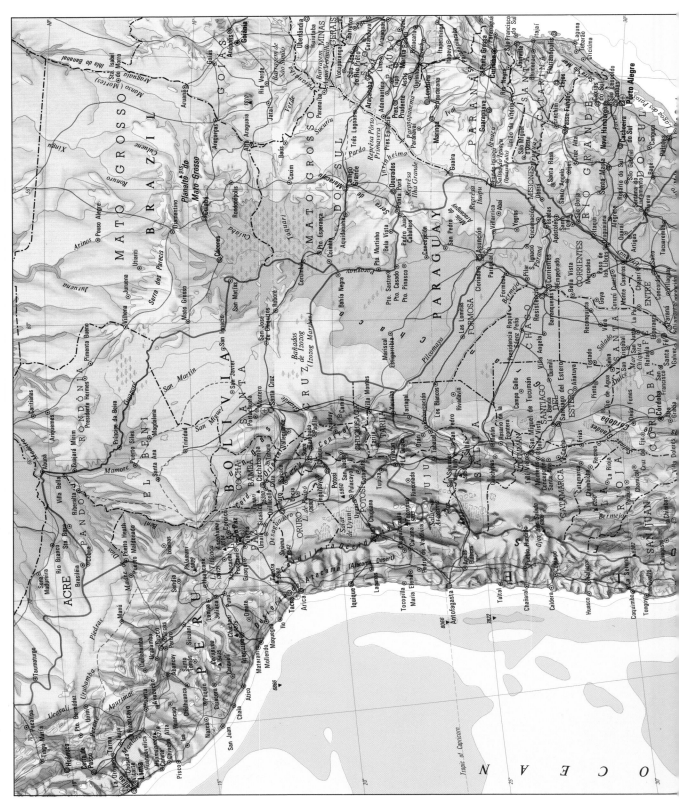

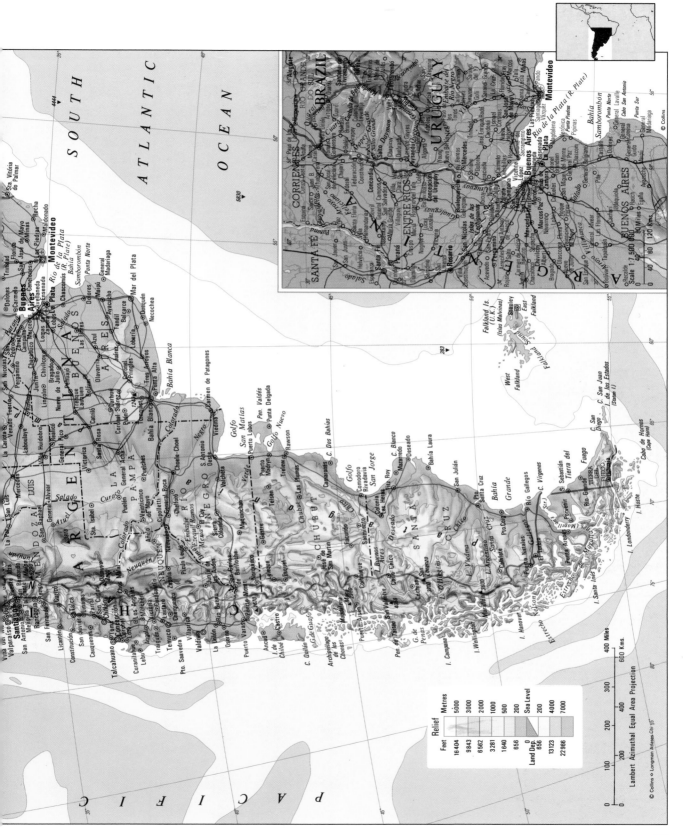

SOUTH

ATLANTIC

OCEAN

S O U T H

A T L A N T I C

O C E A N

P A C I F I C

P A C I F I C

BRAZIL

URUGUAY

Montevideo

CORRIENTES

SANTA FE

ENTRE RIOS

BUENOS AIRES

Buenos Aires

Río de la Plata (R. Plate)

A R G E N T I N A

Scale 1:7 500 000

0   40   80   Miles
0   40   80   120 Kms.

© Collins

ARGENTINA

MENDOZA

SAN LUIS

LA PAMPA

BUENOS AIRES

Buenos Aires

Montevideo

Río de la Plata (R. Plate)

Mar del Plata

Bahía Blanca

RIO NEGRO

NEUQUEN

Golfo San Matías

Pen. Valdés

Golfo Nuevo

C. Dos Bahías

Golfo San Jorge

Comodoro Rivadavia

C. Blanco

Bahía Laura

San Julián

CHUBUT

SANTA CRUZ

Bahía Grande

Río Gallegos

C. San Diego

C. San Juan I. de los Estados (Staten I)

TIERRA DEL FUEGO

Cabo de Hornos (Cape Horn)

Falkland Is. (U.K.) (Islas Malvinas)

Stanley

East Falkland

West Falkland

Falkland Sound

Santiago

Valparaíso

Talcahuano

CHILE

Relief

Feet	Metres
16 404	5000
9843	3000
6562	2000
3281	1000
1640	500
656	200
0	Sea Level 0
Land Dep. 656	200
13 123	4000
22 966	7000

0   100   200   300   400 Miles
0   200   400   600 Kms.

Lambert Azimuthal Equal Area Projection

© Collins · Longman Atlases Chr. 95

63

POLAR REGIONS

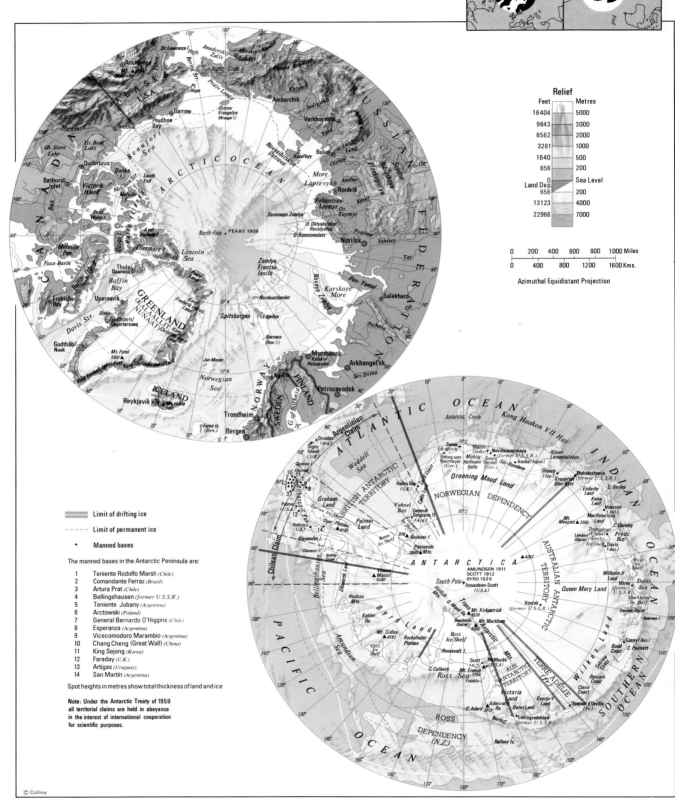

Relief

Feet	Metres
16404	5000
9843	3000
6562	2000
3281	1000
1640	500
656	200
0	Sea Level
Land Dep.	
656	200
13123	4000
22966	7000

0 200 400 600 800 1000 Miles
0 400 800 1200 1600 Kms.

Azimuthal Equidistant Projection

Limit of drifting ice

Limit of permanent ice

• Manned bases

The manned bases in the Antarctic Peninsula are:

1 Teniente Rodolfo Marsh (Chile)
2 Comandante Ferraz (Brazil)
3 Artura Prat (Chile)
4 Bellingshausen (former U.S.S.R.)
5 Teniente Jubany (Argentina)
6 Arctowski (Poland)
7 General Bernardo O'Higgins (Chile)
8 Esperanza (Argentina)
9 Vicecomodoro Marambio (Argentina)
10 Chang Cheng (Great Wall) (China)
11 King Sejong (Korea)
12 Faraday (U.K.)
13 Artigas (Uruguay)
14 San Martín (Argentina)

Spot heights in metres show total thickness of land and ice

Note: Under the Antarctic Treaty of 1959 all territorial claims are held in abeyance in the interest of international cooperation for scientific purposes.

© Collins

64

WORLD DATA

Part 1

WORLD FACTS AND FIGURES 66-70

Part 2

WORLD INDEX 71-112

Part 3

WORLD MAPS–ENDPAPERS

WORLD PHYSICAL DATA

Earth's Dimensions

Superficial area	510 066 000 km²
Land surface	148 326 000 km²
Water surface	361 740 000 km²
Equatorial circumference	40 075 km
Meridional circumference	40 007 km
Volume	1 083 230x10⁶ km³
Mass	5.976x10²¹ tonnes

The Continents

Asia	43 608 000 km²
Africa	30 355 000 km²
North America	25 349 000 km²
South America	17 611 000 km²
Antarctica	13 338 500 km²
Europe	10 498 000 km²
Oceania	8 547 000 km²

Oceans and Sea Areas

Pacific Ocean	165 384 000 km²
Atlantic Ocean	82 217 000 km²
Indian Ocean	73 481 000 km²
Arctic Ocean	14 056 000 km²
Mediterranean Sea	2 505 000 km²
South China Sea	2 318 000 km²
Bering Sea	2 269 000 km²
Caribbean Sea	1 943 000 km²
Gulf of Mexico	1 544 000 km²
Okhotskoye More (Sea of Okhotsk)	1 528 000 km²
East China Sea	1 248 000 km²
Hudson Bay	1 233 000 km²
Sea of Japan	1 008 000 km²
North Sea	575 000 km²
Black Sea	461 000 km²

Island Areas

Greenland; Arctic / Atlantic Ocean	2 175 597 km²
New Guinea; Indonesia / Papua New Guinea	808 510 km²
Borneo; Malaysia / Indonesia / Brunei	757 050 km²
Madagascar; Indian Ocean	594 180 km²
Sumatera (Sumatra) ; Indonesia	524 100 km²
Baffin Island; Canada	476 068 km²
Honshū; Japan	230 455 km²
Great Britain; United Kingdom	229 867 km²
Ellesmere Island; Canada	212 688 km²
Victoria Island; Canada	212 199 km²
Sulawesi (Celebes) ; Indonesia	189 040 km²
South Island; New Zealand	150 461 km²
Jawa (Java) ; Indonesia	134 045 km²
North Island; New Zealand	114 688 km²
Cuba; Caribbean Sea	114 525 km²

River Lengths

An Nīl (Nile) ; Africa	6695 km
Amazonas (Amazon) ; South America	6516 km
Chang Jiang (Yangtze) ; Asia	6380 km
Mississippi - Missouri; North America	6020 krn
Ob-Irtysh; Asia	5570 km
Huang He (Hwang Ho) ; Asia	5464 km
Zaïre; Africa	4667 km
Mekong; Asia	4425 km
Amur; Asia	4416 km
Lena; Asia	4400 km
Mackenzie; North America	4250 km
Yenisey; Asia	4090 km
Niger; Africa	4030 km
Murray - Darling; Oceania	3750 km
Volga; Europe	3688 km

Mountain Heights (Selected)

Everest; Nepal / China	8848 m
K2; Jammu & Kashmir / China	8611 m
Kānchenjunga; Nepal / India	8586 m
Dhaulāgiri; Nepal	8167 m
Annapurna; Nepal	8091 m
Aconcagua; Argentina	6960 m
Ojos del Salado; Argentina / Chile	6908 m
McKinley; Alaska U.S.A.	6194 m
Logan; Canada	5951 m
Kilimanjaro; Tanzania	5895 m
Elbrus; Russian Federation	5642 m
Kenya; Kenya	5200 m
Vinson Massif; Antarctica	5139 m
Puncak Jaya; Indonesia	5030 m
Blanc; France / Italy	4807 m

Lake and Inland Sea Areas

Some areas are subject to seasonal variations.

Caspian Sea; Central Asia	371 795 km²
Lake Superior; U.S.A. / Canada	83 270 km²
Lake Victoria; East Africa	69 485 km²
Lake Huron; U.S.A. / Canada	60 700 km²
Lake Michigan; U.S.A.	58 016 km²
Aralskoye More (Aral Sea) ; Central Asia	36 500 km²
Lake Tanganyika; East Africa	32 893 km²
Great Bear Lake; Canada	31 792 km²
Ozero Baykal (Lake Baikal) ; Russian Federation	30 510 km²
Great Slave Lake; Canada	28 930 km²
Lake Erie; U.S.A. / Canada	25 667 km²
Lake Winnipeg; Canada	24 514 km²
Lake Malaŵi; Malaŵi / Mozambique	22 490 km²
Lake Ontario; U.S.A. / Canada	19 529 km²
Ladozhskoye Ozero (Lake Ladoga) ; Russian Federation	18 390 km²

Volcanoes (Selected)

	Last Eruption	Height
Cameroun; Cameroon	1922	4070 m
Cotopaxi; Ecuador	1975	5897 m
Elbrus; Russian Federation	extinct	5642 m
Erebus; Antarctica	1979	3794 m
Etna; Sicilia, Italy	1983	3340 m
Fuji san (Fujiyama) ; Japan	extinct	3776 m
Hekla; Iceland	1981	1491 m
Kilimanjaro; Tanzania	extinct	5895 m
Mauna Loa; Hawaii	1978	4171 m
Ngauruhoe; New Zealand	1975	2291 m
Popocatépetl; Mexico	1920	5452 m
St. Helens; U.S.A.	1981	2949 m
Stromboli; Italy	1975	926 m
Tristan da Cunha; Atlantic Ocean	1962	2160 m
Vesuvio (Vesuvius) ; Italy	1944	1277 m

WORLD POLITICAL DATA

National Areas

Russian Federation; Asia / Europe	17 075 000 km²
Canada; North America	9 922 385 km²
China; Asia	9 596 961 km²
United States; North America	9 363 123 km²
Brazil; South America	8 511 965 km²
Australia; Oceania	7 686 848 km²
India; Asia	3 166 830 km²
Argentina; South America	2 766 889 km²
Sudan; Africa	2 505 813 km²
Saudi Arabia; Asia	2 400 900 km²
Algeria; Africa	2 381 741 km²
Zaïre; Africa	2 345 409 km²
Greenland; North America	2 175 600 km²
Mexico; North America	1 972 547 km²
Indonesia; Asia	1 919 445 km²
Libya; Africa	1 759 540 km²
Iran; Asia	1 648 000 km²
Mongolia; Asia	1 565 000 km²
Peru; South America	1 285 216 km²
Chad; Africa	1 284 000 km²

National Populations

China; Asia	1 118 760 000
India; Asia	853 094 000
United States; North America	249 224 000
Indonesia; Asia	185 020 000
Brazil; South America	150 368 000
Russian Federation; Asia / Europe	147 386 000
Japan; Asia	123 460 000
Pakistan; Asia	122 626 000
Bangladesh; Asia	115 593 000
Nigeria; Africa	108 542 000
Mexico; North America	107 233 000
Germany; Europe	79 070 000
Vietnam; Asia	66 693 000
Philippines; Asia	62 413 000
United Kingdom; Europe	57 237 000
Italy; Europe	57 061 000
France; Europe	56 138 000
Turkey; Asia / Europe	55 868 000
Thailand; Asia	55 702 000
Iran; Asia	54 607 000

World Cities

Ciudad de México (Mexico City) ; Mexico	20 200 000
Tōkyō; Japan	18 100 000
São Paulo; Brazil	17 400 000
New York; United States	16 200 000
Shanghai; China	13 400 000
Chicago; United States	11 900 000
Calcutta; India	11 800 000
Buenos Aires; Argentina	11 500 000
Bombay; India	11 200 000
Sŏul (Seoul) ; South Korea	11 000 000
Beijing (Peking) ; China	10 800 000
Rio de Janeiro; Brazil	10 700 000
Tianjin; China	9 400 000
Jakarta; Indonesia	9 300 000
Al Qāhirah (Cairo); Egypt	9 000 000

Major International Organisations

United Nations - On December 1990 the United Nations had 160 members. Independent States not represented include Liechtenstein, Monaco, Nauru, North Korea, San Marino, South Korea, Switzerland, Taiwan, Tonga.

Commonwealth

Antigua	Australia	Bahamas	Bangladesh
Barbados	Belize	Botswana	Brunei
Canada	Cyprus	Dominica	Fiji
Gambia	Ghana	Grenada	Guyana
Hong Kong	India	Jamaica	Kenya
Kiribati	Lesotho	Malaẁi	Malaysia
Maldives	Malta	Mauritius	Nauru
New Zealand	Nigeria	Pakistan	Papua New Guinea
St. Kitts & Nevis	St. Lucia	St. Vincent	Seychelles
Sierra Leone	Singapore	Solomon Islands	Sri Lanka
Swaziland	Tanzania	Tonga	Trinidad & Tobago
Tuvalu	Uganda	United Kingdom	Vanuatu
Western Samoa	Zambia	Zimbabwe	

OAU - Organisation of African Unity

Algeria	Angola	Benin	Botswana
Burkina	Burundi	Cameroon	Cape Verde
Central African Rep.	Chad	Comoros	Congo
Djibouti	Egypt	Equatorial Guinea	Ethiopia
Gabon	Gambia	Ghana	Guinea
Guinea Bissau	Ivory Coast	Kenya	Lesotho
Liberia	Libya	Madagascar	Malaẁi
Mali	Mauritania	Mauritius	Mozambique
Namibia	Niger	Nigeria	Rwanda
São Tomé & Príncipe	Senegal	Seychelles	Sierra Leone
Somali Rep.	Sudan	Swaziland	Tanzania
Togo	Tunisia	Uganda	Western Sahara
Zaïre	Zambia	Zimbabwe	

OAS - Organisation of American States

Antigua	Argentina	Bahamas	Barbados
Bolivia	Brazil	Chile	Colombia
Costa Rica	Dominica	Dominican Rep.	Ecuador
El Salvador	Grenada	Guatemala	Haiti
Honduras	Jamaica	Mexico	Nicaragua
Panama	Paraguay	Peru	St. Kitts & Nevis
St. Lucia	St. Vincent	Surinam	Trinidad & Tobago
United States	Uruguay	Venezuela	

EEC - European Economic Community

Belgium	Denmark	France	Germany
Greece	Ireland	Italy	Luxembourg
Netherlands	Portugal	Spain	United Kingdom

EFTA - European Free Trade Association

Austria	Finland (assoc.)	Iceland	Norway
Sweden	Switzerland		

ASEAN - Association of Southeast Asian Nations

Brunei	Indonesia	Malaysia	Philippines
Singapore	Thailand		

ECOWAS - Economic Community of West African States

Benin	Burkina	Cape Verde	Gambia
Ghana	Guinea	Guinea Bissau	Ivory Coast
Liberia	Mali	Mauritania	Niger
Nigeria	Senegal	Sierra Leone	Togo

CARICOM - Caribbean Community and Common Market

Antigua	Bahamas	Barbados	Belize
Dominica	Grenada	Guyana	Jamaica
Montserrat	St. Kitts & Nevis	St. Lucia	St. Vincent
Trindad & Tobago			

NATIONS OF THE WORLD

COUNTRY	AREA sq. km.	POPULATION total	POPULATION per sq. km.	FORM OF GOVERNMENT	CAPITAL CITY	MAIN LANGUAGES	CURRENCY
AFGHANISTAN	652,225	16,557,000	25	republic	Kābol	Pushtu, Dari (Persian)	afghani
ALBANIA	28,750	3,245,000	113	socialist republic	Tiranë	Albanian	lek
ALGERIA	2,381,745	24,960,000	10	republic	Alger (Algiers)	Arabic	dinar
ANDORRA	465	50,000	108	principality	Andorra	Catalan	French franc, Spanish peseta
ANGOLA	1,246,700	10,020,000	8	people's republic	Luanda	Portuguese	kwanza
ANTIGUA AND BARBUDA	442	76,000	172	constitutional monarchy	St John's	English	East Caribbean dollar
ARGENTINA	2,777,815	32,322,000	12	federal republic	Buenos Aires	Spanish	austral
ARMENIA	30,000	3,283,000	109	republic	Yerevan	Armenian, Russian	rouble
AUSTRALIA	7,682,300	16,873,000	2	monarchy (federal)	Canberra	English	dollar
AUSTRIA	83,855	7,583,000	90	federal republic	Wien (Vienna)	German	schilling
AZERBAIJAN	87,000	7,029,000	81	republic	Baku	Azerbaijan, Russian	rouble
BAHAMAS	13,865	253,000	18	constitutional monarchy	Nassau	English	dollar
BAHRAIN	661	516,000	781	emirate	Al Manāmah	Arabic	dinar
BANGLADESH	144,000	115,593,000	803	republic	Dhaka	Bengali	taka
BARBADOS	430	255,000	593	constitutional monarchy	Bridgetown	English	dollar
BELGIUM	30,520	9,845,000	323	constitutional monarchy	Bruxelles/Brussel (Brussels)	French, Dutch, German	franc
BELIZE	22,965	187,000	8	constitutional monarchy	Belmopan	English	dollar
BELORUSSIA	208,000	10,200,000	49	republic	Minsk	Belorussian	rouble
BENIN	112,620	4,630,000	41	republic	Porto-Novo	French	CFA franc
BHUTAN	46,620	1,516,000	33	monarchy (Indian protection)	Thimbu	Dzongkha	Indian rupee, nguitrum
BOLIVIA	1,098,575	7,314,000	7	republic	La Paz/Sucre	Spanish	bolivano
BOSNIA-HERZEGOVINA	51,130	4,363,911	85	republic	Sarajevo	Serbo-Croat	dinar
BOTSWANA	575,000	1,304,000	2	republic	Gaborone	English, Tswana	pula
BRAZIL	8,511,965	150,368,000	18	federal republic	Brasília	Portuguese	cruzado
BRUNEI	5,765	266,000	46	sultanate	Bander Seri Begawan	Malay	dollar
BULGARIA	110,910	9,010,000	81	people's republic	Sofiya (Sofia)	Bulgarian	lev
BURKINA	274,200	8,996,000	33	republic	Ouagadougou	French	CFA franc
BURMA (MYANMA)	678,030	41,675,000	61	federal republic	Rangoon	Burmese	kyat
BURUNDI	27,835	5,472,000	197	republic	Bujumbura	French, Kirundi	franc
CAMBODIA	181,000	8,246,000	45	republic	Phnom Penh	Cambodian, Khmer	riel
CAMEROON	475,500	11,833,000	25	republic	Yaoundé	French, English	CFA franc
CANADA	9,922,385	26,521,000	3	monarchy (federal)	Ottawa	English, French	dollar
CAPE VERDE	4,035	370,000	92	republic	Praia	Portuguese, Creole	escudo
CENTRAL AFRICAN REPUBLIC	624,975	3,039,000	5	republic	Bangui	French, Sango	CFA franc
CHAD	1,284,000	5,678,000	4	republic	N'Djamena	French	CFA franc
CHILE	751,625	13,173,000	18	republic	Santiago	Spanish	peso
CHINA	9,597,000	1,118,760,000	117	people's republic	Beijing (Peking)	Mandarin	yuan
COLOMBIA	1,138,915	32,978,000	29	republic	Bogotá	Spanish	peso
COMOROS	1,860	550,000	296	federal republic	Moroni	Comoran, Arabic, French	CFA franc
CONGO	342,000	2,271,000	7	republic	Brazzaville	French	CFA franc
COSTA RICA	50,900	3,015,000	59	republic	San José	Spanish	colon
CROATIA	56,540	4,601,000	81	republic	Zagreb	Serbo-Croat	dinar
CUBA	114,525	10,608,000	93	people's republic	La Habana (Havana)	Spanish	peso
CYPRUS	9,250	701,000	76	republic	Levkosía (Nicosia)	Greek	pound
CZECHOSLOVAKIA	127,870	15,667,000	123	federal republic	Praha (Prague)	Czech, Slovak	koruna
DENMARK	43,075	5,143,000	119	constitutional monarchy	København (Copenhagen)	Danish	krone
DJIBOUTI	23,000	409,000	18	republic	Djibouti	French, Somali, Afar	franc
DOMINICA	751	82,000	109	republic	Roseau	English, French	East Caribbean dollar
DOMINICAN REPUBLIC	48,440	7,170,000	148	republic	Santo Dominigo	Spanish	peso
ECUADOR	461,475	10,587,000	23	republic	Quito	Spanish	sucre
EGYPT	1,000,250	52,426,000	52	republic	Al Qāhirah (Cairo)	Arabic	pound
EL SALVADOR	21,395	5,252,000	245	republic	San Salvador	Spanish	colón
EQUATORIAL GUINEA	28,050	352,000	13	republic	Malabo	Spanish	CFA franc
ESTONIA	45,100	1,573,000	35	republic	Tallinn	Estonian, Russian	rouble, kroon prop.
ETHIOPIA	1,221,900	49,240,000	40	people's republic	Ādīs Ābeba (Addis Ababa)	Amharic	birr
FEDERATED STATES OF MICRONESIA	1,300	99,000	76	federal republic	Kolonia	Kosrean, Yapese, Pohnpeian, Trukese, English	US dollar
FIJI	18,330	764,000	42	republic	Suva	English, Fijian, Hindustani	dollar
FINLAND	337,030	4,975,000	15	republic	Helsinki	Finnish, Swedish	markka
FRANCE	543,965	56,138,000	103	republic	Paris	French	franc
GABON	267,665	1,172,000	4	republic	Libreville	French	CFA franc
GAMBIA	10,690	861,000	81	republic	Banjul	English	dalasi

COUNTRY	AREA sq. km.	POPULATION total	per sq. km.	FORM OF GOVERNMENT	CAPITAL CITY	MAIN LANGUAGES	CURRENCY
GEORGIA	69,700	5,449,000	78	republic	Tbilisi	Georgian, Russian	rouble
GERMANY	357,868	79,070,000	221	federal republic	Berlin/Bonn	German	mark
GHANA	238,305	15,028,000	63	republic	Accra	English	cedi
GREECE	131,985	10,047,000	76	republic	Athínai (Athens)	Greek	drachma
GRENADA	345	85,000	246	constitutional monarchy	St George's	English	East Caribbean dollar
GUATEMALA	108,890	9,197,000	84	republic	Guatemala	Spanish	quetzal
GUINEA	245,855	5,755,000	23	republic	Conakry	French	franc
GUINEA BISSAU	36,125	964,000	27	republic	Bissau	Portuguese	peso
GUYANA	214,970	796,000	4	republic	Georgetown	English	dollar
HAITI	27,750	6,513,000	235	republic	Port-au-Prince	French, Creole	goude
HONDURAS	112,085	5,138,000	46	republic	Tegucigalpa	Spanish	lempira
HUNGARY	93,030	10,552,000	113	republic	Budapest	Magyar	forint
ICELAND	102,820	253,000	2	republic	Reykjavik	Icelandic	króna
INDIA	3,166,830	853,093,000	269	republic	New Delhi	Hindi	rupee
INDONESIA	1,919,445	185,020,000	96	republic	Jakarta	Bahasa Indonesia	rupiah
IRAN	1,648,000	54,607,000	33	Islamic republic	Tehrān	Persian	rial
IRAQ	438,445	18,920,000	43	republic	Baghdād	Arabic	dinar
IRELAND, REPUBLIC OF	68,895	3,720,000	54	republic	Dublin	English, Irish	punt
ISRAEL	20,770	4,600,000	221	republic	Yerushalayim (Jerusalem)	Hebrew	shekel
ITALY	301,245	57,061,000	189	republic	Roma (Rome)	Italian	lira
IVORY COAST (COTE D'IVOIRE)	322,465	11,997,000	37	republic	Yamoussoukro	French	CFA franc
JAMAICA	11,425	2,456,000	215	constitutional monarchy	Kingston	English	dollar
JAPAN	369,700	123,460,000	334	monarchy	Tōkyō	Japanese	yen
JORDAN	96,000	4,009,000	42	monarchy	'Ammān	Arabic	dinar
KAZAKHSTAN	2,717,300	16,538,000	6	republic	Alma-Ata	Kazakh, Russian	rouble
KENYA	582,645	24,031,000	41	republic	Nairobi	Swahili, English	shilling
KIRIBATI	684	66,000	96	republic	Tarawa	English, Gilbertese (I-Kiribati)	Australian dollar
KUWAIT	24,280	2,039,000	84	emirate	Al Kuwayt (Kuwait)	Arabic	dinar
KYRGYZSTAN	198,500	4,291,000	22	republic	Bishkek	Kirgiz, Russian	rouble
LAOS	236,725	4,139,000	17	people's republic	Vientiane (Viangchan)	Lao	new kip
LATVIA	63,700	2,681,000	42	republic	Riga	Latvian, Russian	rouble, Lat prop.
LEBANON	10,400	2,701,000	260	republic	Bayrūt (Beirut)	Arabic	pound
LESOTHO	30,345	1,774,000	58	monarchy	Maseru	English, Sesotho	maluti
LIBERIA	111,370	2,575,000	23	republic	Monrovia	English	dollar
LIBYA	1,759,540	4,545,000	3	republic (jamahiriya)	Tarābulus (Tripoli)	Arabic	dinar
LIECHTENSTEIN	160	28,000	175	constitutional monarchy	Vaduz	German	Swiss franc
LITHUANIA	65,200	3,690,000	56	republic	Vilnius	Lithuanian	rouble, Litas prop.
LUXEMBOURG	2,585	373,000	144	constitutional monarchy	Luxembourg	Letzeburgish, French, German	franc
MADAGASCAR	594,180	12,004,000	20	republic	Antananarivo	Malagasy	Malagasy franc
MALAWI	94,080	8,754,000	93	republic	Lilongwe	English, Chichewa	kwacha
MALAYSIA	332,965	17,891,000	54	constitutional monarchy	Kuala Lumpur	Malay	ringgit
MALDIVES	298	215,000	721	republic	Malé	Divehi	rufiya
MALI	1,240,140	9,214,000	7	republic	Bamako	French, Bambara	CFA franc
MALTA	316	353,000	1117	republic	Valletta	Maltese, English	pound
MARSHALL ISLANDS	180	41,000	228	republic	Majuro	English	US dollar
MAURITANIA	1,030,700	2,024,000	2	republic	Nouakchott	French, Arabic	ouguiya
MAURITIUS	1,865	1,082,000	580	constitutional monarchy	Port-Louis	English, Creole	rupee
MEXICO	1,972,545	107,233,000	54	federal republic	Ciudad de México (Mexico City)	Spanish	peso
MOLDAVIA	33,700	4,341,000	129	republic	Kishinev	Romanian, Russian	rouble
MONACO	2	28,000	18667	constitutional monarchy	Monaco	French	French franc
MONGOLIA	1,565,000	2,190,000	1	people's republic	Ulaanbaatar (Ulan Bator)	Mongol	tugrik
MOROCCO	710,850	25,061,000	35	monarchy	Rabat	Arabic	dirham
MOZAMBIQUE	784,755	15,656,000	20	people's republic	Maputo	Portuguese	metical
NAMIBIA	824,295	1,781,000	2	republic	Windhoek	Afrikaans, English	Namibian dollar
NAURU	21	9,000	429	republic	Nauru	Nauruan, English	Australian dollar
NEPAL	141,415	19,143,000	135	monarchy	Kātmāndu	Nepali	rupee
NETHERLANDS	41,160	14,951,000	363	constitutional monarchy	Amsterdam	Dutch	guilder
NEW ZEALAND	265,150	3,392,000	13	constitutional monarchy	Wellington	English	dollar
NICARAGUA	148,000	3,871,000	26	republic	Managua	Spanish	córdoba
NIGER	1,186,410	7,731,000	7	republic	Niamey	French	CFA franc
NIGERIA	923,850	108,542,000	117	federal republic	Abuja	English	naira
NORTH KOREA	122,310	21,773,000	178	people's republic	Pyŏngyang	Korean	won
NORWAY	323,895	4,212,000	13	constitutional monarchy	Oslo	Norwegian	krone
OMAN	271,950	1,502,000	6	sultanate	Masqaṭ (Muscat)	Arabic	rial

NATIONS OF THE WORLD

COUNTRY	AREA sq. km.	POPULATION total	POPULATION per sq. km.	FORM OF GOVERNMENT	CAPITAL CITY	MAIN LANGUAGES	CURRENCY
PAKISTAN	803,940	122,626,000	152	federal republic	Islāmābād	Urdu, Punjabi, English	rupee
PANAMA	78,515	2,418,000	31	republic	Panamá	Spanish	balboa
PAPUA NEW GUINEA	462,840	3,874,000	8	constitutional monarchy	Port Moresby	English, Pidgin, Motu	kina
PARAGUAY	406,750	4,277,000	11	republic	Asunción	Spanish, Guaraní	guaraní
PERU	1,285,215	21,550,000	17	republic	Lima	Spanish	inti
PHILIPPINES	300,000	62,413,000	208	republic	Manila	Pilipino	peso
POLAND	312,685	38,423,000	123	republic	Warszawa (Warsaw)	Polish	zloty
PORTUGAL	91,630	10,285,000	112	republic	Lisboa (Lisbon)	Portugese	escudo
QATAR	11,435	368,000	32	emirate	Ad Dawhah (Doha)	Arabic	riyal
ROMANIA	237,500	23,272,000	98	republic	Bucuresti (Bucharest)	Romanian	leu
RUSSIAN FEDERATION	17,078,000	147,386,000	9	republic	Moskva	Russian	rouble
RWANDA	26,330	7,237,000	275	republic	Kigali	Kinyarwanda, French	franc
ST KITTS-NEVIS	261	44,000	169	constitutional monarchy	Basseterre	English	East Caribbean dollar
ST LUCIA	616	150,000	244	constitutional monarchy	Castries	English, French	East Caribbean dollar
ST VINCENT AND THE GRENADINES	389	116,000	298	constitutional monarchy	Kingstown	English	East Caribbean dollar
SAN MARINO	61	23,000	377	republic	San Marino	Italian	Italian lira
SÃO TOMÉ AND PRINCIPE	964	121,000	126	republic	São Tomé	Portuguese, Creole	dobra
SAUDI ARABIA	2,400,900	14,134,000	6	monarchy	Ar Riyād (Riyadh)	Arabic	riyal
SENEGAL	196,720	7,327,000	37	republic	Dakar	French	CFA franc
SEYCHELLES	404	69,000	156	republic	Victoria	English, French	rupee
SIERRA LEONE	72,325	4,151,000	58	republic	Freetown	English	leone
SINGAPORE	616	2,723,000	4420	republic	Singapore	Malay, English, Chinese, Tamil	dollar
SLOVENIA	20,250	1,940,000	93	republic	Ljubljana	Slovene	dinar
SOLOMON ISLANDS	29,790	320,000	11	constitutional monarchy	Honiara	English	dollar
SOMALI REPUBLIC	630,000	7,497,000	12	republic	Muqdisho	Arabic, Italian, English, Somali	shilling
SOUTH AFRICA, REPUBLIC OF	1,184,825	35,282,000	30	federal republic	Cape Town (Kaapstad)/Pretoria	Afrikaans, English	rand
SOUTH KOREA	98,445	42,793,000	435	republic	Sŏul (Seoul)	Korean	won
SPAIN	504,880	39,187,000	78	constitutional monarchy	Madrid	Spanish	peseta
SRI LANKA	65,610	17,217,000	262	republic	Colombo	Sinhala, Tamil	rupee
SUDAN	2,505,815	25,203,000	10	republic	Al Kharṭūm (Khartoum)	Arabic	pound
SURINAM	163,820	422,000	3	republic	Paramaribo	Dutch, English	guilder
SWAZILAND	17,365	788,000	45	monarchy	Mbabane	English, Siswati	lilangeni
SWEDEN	449,790	8,444,000	19	constitutional monarchy	Stockholm	Swedish	krona
SWITZERLAND	41,285	6,609,000	160	federal republic	Bern (Berne)	German, French, Italian, Romansh	franc
SYRIA	185,680	12,530,000	67	republic	Dimashq (Damascus)	Arabic	pound
TAIWAN	35,990	20,300,000	564	republic	Taipei	Mandarin	dollar
TAJIKISTAN	143,100	5,112,000	36	republic	Dushanbe	Tajik, Russian	rouble
TANZANIA	939,760	27,318,000	29	republic	Dodoma	Swahili	shilling
THAILAND	514,000	55,702,000	108	monarchy	Bangkok (Krung Thep)	Thai	baht
TOGO	56,785	3,531,000	62	republic	Lomé	French	CFA franc
TONGA	699	95,000	136	monarchy	Nuku'alofa	Tongan, English	pa anga
TRINIDAD AND TOBAGO	5,130	1,281,000	250	republic	Port of Spain	English	dollar
TUNISIA	164,150	8,180,000	50	republic	Tunis	Arabic	dinar
TURKEY	779,450	55,868,000	72	republic	Ankara	Turkish	lira
TURKMENISTAN	488,100	3,534,000	7	republic	Ashkhabad	Turkmen, Russian	rouble
TUVALU	25	9,000	360	constitutional monarchy	Funafuti	Tuvalu, English	Australian dollar
UGANDA	236,580	18,794,000	79	republic	Kampala	English	new shilling
UKRAINE	603,700	51,704,000	86	republic	Kiyev	Ukrainian, Russian	rouble
UNITED ARAB EMIRATES	75,150	1,589,000	21	self-governing union		Arabic	dirham
UNITED KINGDOM	244,755	57,237,000	234	constitutional monarchy	London	English	pound
UNITED STATES OF AMERICA	9,363,614	249,224,000	27	federal republic	Washington	English	dollar
URUGUAY	186,925	3,094,000	17	republic	Montevideo	Spanish	peso
UZBEKISTAN	447,400	19,906,000	44	republic	Tashkent	Uzbek, Russian	rouble
VANUATU	14,765	158,000	11	republic	Vila	English, French	vatu
VATICAN CITY	1	1,000	1,000	ecclesiastical state	Vatican City	Italian	Vatican City Lira
VENEZUELA	912,045	19,735,000	22	federal republic	Caracas	Spanish	bolivar
VIETNAM	329,565	66,693,000	202	people's republic	Hanoi	Vietnamese	dong
WESTERN SAMOA	2,840	168,000	59	constitutional monarchy	Apia	Samoan, English	tala
YEMEN	481,155	11,687,000	24	republic	San'ā	Arabic	rial
YUGOSLAVIA	127,885	13,047,000	102	socialist federal republic	Beograd (Belgrade)	Serbo-Croat, Macedonian, Slovene	dinar
ZAÏRE	2,345,410	35,568,000	15	republic	Kinshasa	French, Lingala	zaïre
ZAMBIA	752,615	8,452,000	11	republic	Lusaka	English	kwacha
ZIMBABWE	390,310	9,709,000	25	republic	Harare	English	dollar

Introduction to World Index

The index includes an alphabetical list of all names appearing on the maps in the World Atlas section. Each entry indicates the country or region of the world in which the name is located. This is followed by a page reference and finally the name's location on the map, given by latitude and longitude co-ordinates. Most features are indexed to the largest scale map on which they appear, however when the name applies to countries or other extensive features it is generally indexed to the map on which it appears in its entirety. Areal features are generally indexed using co-ordinates which indicate

the centre of the feature. The latitude and longitude indicated for a point feature gives the location of the point on the map. In the case of rivers the mouth or confluence is always taken as the point of reference.

Names in the index are generally in the local language and where a conventional English version exists, this is cross referenced to the entry in the local language. Names of features which extend across the boundaries of more than one country are usually named in English if no single official name exists. Names in languages not

written in the Roman alphabet have been transliterated using the official system of the country if one exists, e.g. Pinyin system for China, otherwise the systems recognised by the United States Board on Geographical Names have been used.

Names abbreviated on the maps are given in full in the Index. Abbreviations are used for both geographical terms and administrative names in the Index. All abbreviations used in the Index are listed below.

Abbreviations of Geographical Terms

b., B.	bay, Bay	**f.**	physical feature e.g. valley, plain, geographic district or region	**mts., Mts.**	mountains, Mountains
c., C.	cape, Cape			**pen., Pen.**	peninsula, Peninsula
d.	internal division e.g county, region, state	**g., G.**	gulf, Gulf	Pt.	Point
des.	desert	**i., I., is., Is.**	island, Island, islands, Islands	**r.**	river
est.	estuary	**l., L.**	lake, Lake	**resr., Resr.**	reservoir, Reservoir
		mtn., Mtn.	mountain, Mountain	Sd.	Sound
				str., Str.	strait, Strait

Abbreviations of Country / Administrative Names

Afghan.	Afghanistan	Madhya P.	Madhya Pradesh	Que.	Québec
A.H. Prov.	Alpes de Haut Provence	Man.	Manitoba	Raj.	Rājasthān
Ala.	Alabama	Mass.	Massachusetts	Rep. of Ire.	Republic of Ireland
Alas.	Alaska	Md.	Maryland	Rhein.-Pfalz	Rheinland-Pfalz
Alta.	Alberta	Mich.	Michigan	R.I.	Rhode Island
Ariz.	Arizona	Minn.	Minnesota	R.S.A.	Republic of South Africa
Ark.	Arkansas	Miss.	Mississippi	Russian Fed.	Russian Federation
Baja Calif. Norte	Baja California Norte	Mo.	Missouri	S.A.	South Australia
Baja Calif. Sur	Baja California Sur	Mont.	Montana	Sask.	Saskatchewan
Bangla.	Bangladesh	M.-Pyr.	Midi-Pyrénées	S.C.	South Carolina
B.C.	British Columbia	N.B.	New Brunswick	Sch.-Hol.	Schleswig-Holstein
Bos.-Her.	Bosnia-Herzegovina	N.C.	North Carolina	S. Dak.	South Dakota
B.-Würt	Baden-Württemberg	N. Dak.	North Dakota	S. Korea	South Korea
Calif.	California	Nebr.	Nebraska	S. Mar.	Seine Maritime
C.A.R.	Central African Republic	Neth.	Netherlands	Sogn og Fj.	Sogn og Fjordane
Char. Mar.	Charente Maritime	Nev.	Nevada	Somali Rep.	Somali Republic
Colo.	Colorado	Nfld.	Newfoundland	Switz.	Switzerland
Conn.	Connecticut	N.H.	New Hampshire	Tas.	Tasmania
C.P.	Cape Province	N. Ireland	Northern Ireland	Tenn.	Tennessee
Czech.	Czechoslovakia	N.J.	New Jersey	Tex.	Texas
D.C.	District of Colombia	N. Korea	North Korea	T.G.	Tarn-et-Garonne
Del.	Delaware	N. Mex	New Mexico	Trans.	Transvaal
Dom. Rep.	Dominican Republic	Nschn.	Niedersachsen	U.A.E.	United Arab Emirates
Equat. Guinea	Equatorial Guinea	N.S.W.	New South Wales	U.K.	United Kingdom
Eth.	Ethiopia	N. Trönd.	North Tröndelag	U.S.A.	United States of America
Fla.	Florida	N.T.	Northern Territory	Uttar P.	Uttar Pradesh
Ga.	Georgia	N.-Westfalen	Nordrhein-Westfalen	Va.	Virginia
Guang. Zhuang	Guangxi Zhuangzu	N.W.T.	Northwest Territories	Vic.	Victoria
H.-Gar.	Haute Garonne	N.Y.	New York State	Vt.	Vermont
Himachal P.	Himachal Pradesh	O.F.S.	Orange Free State	W.A.	Western Australia
H. Zaïre	Haut Zaïre	Okla.	Oklahoma	Wash.	Washington
Ill.	Illinois	Ont.	Ontario	W. Bengal	West Bengal
Ind.	Indiana	Oreg.	Oregon	Wisc.	Wisconsin
Kans.	Kansas	P.E.I.	Prince Edward Island	W. Sahara	Western Sahara
K. Occidental	Kasai Occidental	Penn.	Pennsylvania	W. Va.	West Virginia
K. Oriental	Kasai Oriental	Phil.	Philippines	Wyo.	Wyoming
Ky.	Kentucky	P.N.G.	Papua New Guinea	Xin Uygur	Xinjiang Uygur
La.	Louisiana	Poit.-Char.	Poitou-Charente	Yugo.	Yugoslavia
Liech.	Liechtenstein	Pyr. Or.	Pyrénées Orientales		
Lux.	Luxembourg	Qld.	Queensland		

A

Aachen Germany 8 50.46N 6.06E
Aalsmeer Neth. 8 52.17N 4.46E
Aalst Belgium 8 50.57N 4.03E
Äänekoski Finland 16 62.36N 25.44E
Aarau Switz. 14 47.24N 8.04E
Aardenburg Neth. 8 51.16N 3.26E
Aare *r.* Switz. 14 47.37N 8.13E
Aarschot Belgium 8 50.59N 4.50E
Aba China 29 32.55N101.42E
Aba Nigeria 38 5.06N 7.21E
Abā as Su'ūd Saudi Arabia 35 17.28N 44.06E
Ābādān Iran 31 30.21N 48.15E
Abadan, Jazīreh-ye *i.* Iran 31 30.10N 48.30E
Ābādeh Iran 31 31.10N 52.40E
Abadla Algeria 34 31.01N 2.45W
Abaetetuba Brazil 61 1.45S 48.54W
Abaí Paraguay 62 26.01S 55.57W
Abajo Peak *mtn.* U.S.A. 54 37.51N109.28W
Abakaliki Nigeria 38 6.17N 8.04E
Abakan Russian Fed. 21 53.43N 91.25E
Abancay Peru 62 13.35S 72.55W
Abau P.N.G. 44 10.10S148.40E
Abay Kazakhstan 20 49.40N 72.47E
Ābaya Hāyk' *l.* Ethiopia 35 6.20N 38.00E
Abayḑ, Al Baḩr al *r.* Sudan 35 15.45N 32.25E
Abba C.A.R. 38 5.20N 15.11E
Abbeville France 11 50.06N 1.51E
Abbiategrasso Italy 9 45.24N 8.54E
Abbotsbury U.K. 5 50.40N 2.36W
Abdulino Russian Fed. 18 53.42N 53.40E
Abéché Chad 35 13.49N 20.49E
Abengourou Ivory Coast 38 6.42N 3.27W
Åbenrå Denmark 17 55.02N 9.26E
Abeokuta Nigeria 38 7.10N 3.26E
Aberayron U.K. 5 52.15N 4.16W
Abercrombie *r.* Australia 47 33.50S149.10E
Aberdare U.K. 5 51.43N 3.27W
Aberdare Range *mts.* Kenya 37 0.20S 36.40E
Aberdeen Australia 47 32.10S150.54E
Aberdeen R.S.A. 39 32.28S 24.03E
Aberdeen U.K. 6 57.08N 2.07W
Aberdeen Md. U.S.A. 55 39.30N 76.10W
Aberdeen Ohio U.S.A. 55 38.39N 83.46W
Aberdeen S. Dak. U.S.A. 52 45.28N 98.30W
Aberdeen Wash. U.S.A. 54 46.59N123.50W
Aberdovey U.K. 5 52.33N 4.03W
Aberfeldy U.K. 6 56.37N 3.54W
Abergavenny U.K. 5 51.49N 3.01W
Abersoch U.K. 4 52.50N 4.31W
Aberystwyth U.K. 5 52.25N 4.06W
Abetone Italy 9 44.08N 10.40E
Abez Russian Fed. 18 66.33N 61.51E
Abhar Iran 31 36.09N 49.13E
Ābhē Bid Hāyk' *l.* Ethiopia 35 11.06N 41.50E
Abia *d.* Nigeria 38 5.45N 7.40E
Abidjan Ivory Coast 38 5.19N 4.01W
Abilene Tex. U.S.A. 52 32.27N 99.45W
Abingdon U.K. 5 51.40N 1.17W
Abisko Sweden 16 68.20N 18.51E
Abitibi *r.* Canada 55 51.03N 80.55W
Abitibi, L. Canada 55 48.42N 79.45W
Abnūb Egypt 30 27.16N 31.09E
Åbo *see* Turku Finland 17
Abomey Benin 38 7.14N 2.00E
Abong Mbang Cameroon 38 3.59N 13.12E
Abou Deïa Chad 34 11.20N 19.20E
Aboyne U.K. 6 57.05N 2.48W
Abrantes Portugal 10 39.28N 8.12W
Abrud Romania 15 46.17N 23.04E
Abruzzi *d.* Italy 12 42.05N 13.45E
Absaroka Range *mts.* U.S.A. 54 44.45N109.50W
Abu Dhabi *see* Abū Ẓaby U.A.E. 31
Abū Dharbah Egypt 32 28.29N 33.20E
Abū Ḩamad Sudan 35 19.32N 33.20E
Abuja Nigeria 38 9.12N 7.11E
Abū Kabīr Egypt 32 30.44N 31.40E
Abū Kamāl Syria 30 34.27N 40.55E
Abū Madd, Ra's *c.* Saudi Arabia 30 24.50N 37.07E
Abunã Brazil 60 9.41S 65.20W
Abū Qurqāṣ Egypt 32 27.56N 30.50E
Abū Sulṭān Egypt 32 30.25N 32.19E
Abū Sunbul Egypt 30 22.18N 31.40E
Abū Ṭarafah Jordan 32 30.00N 35.56E
Abū Tīj Egypt 32 27.06N 31.17E
Abū Ẓaby U.A.E. 31 24.27N 54.23E
Abū Zanīmah Egypt 32 29.03N 33.06E
Åby Sweden 17 58.40N 16.11E
Acámbaro Mexico 56 20.01N101.42W
Acapulco Mexico 56 16.51N 99.56W
Acará Brazil 61 1.57S 48.11W
Acarigua Venezuela 60 9.35N 69.12W
Acatlán Mexico 56 18.12N 98.02W
Accra Ghana 38 5.33N 0.15W
Accrington U.K. 4 53.46N 2.22W
Aceh *d.* Indonesia 26 4.00N 97.30E
Acevedo Argentina 63 33.46S 60.27W
Achacachi Bolivia 62 16.03S 68.43W
Achar Uruguay 63 32.25S 56.10W
Acheng China 25 45.32N126.59E
Achill I. Rep. of Ire. 7 53.57N 10.00W
Achinsk Russian Fed. 20 56.10N 90.10E
Acklin's I. Bahamas 57 22.30N 74.10W
Aconcagua *mtn.* Argentina 62 32.39S 70.00W
A Coruña *see* La Coruña Spain 10
Acqui Italy 9 44.41N 8.28E
Acraman, L. Australia 46 32.02S135.26E
Acre *d.* Brazil 60 8.50S 71.30W
Acuña Argentina 63 29.54S 57.57W
Açu Brazil 61 5.35S 36.57W
Adair, C. Canada 51 71.24N 71.13W
Adamantina Brazil 59 21.42S 51.04W
Adamaoua, Massif de l' *mts.* Cameroon / Nigeria 38 7.05N 12.00E
Adamawa *d.* Nigeria 38 9.55N 12.30E
Adamello *mtn.* Italy 9 46.10N 10.35E
Adaminaby Australia 47 36.04S148.42E
Adamintina Brazil 62 21.42S 51.04W
Adams N.Y. U.S.A. 55 43.49N 76.01W
Adams, Mt. U.S.A. 54 46.12N121.28W
'Adan Yemen 35 12.50N 45.00E
Adana Turkey 30 37.00N 35.19E
Adapazari Turkey 30 40.45N 30.23E
Adare, C. Antarctica 64 71.30S171.00E
Adavale Australia 44 25.55S144.36E
Adda *r.* Italy 9 45.08N 9.55E
Ad Ḑab'ah Egypt 30 31.02N 28.26E
Ad Dafīnah Saudi Arabia 30 23.18N 41.58E
Ad Dahnā' *des.* Saudi Arabia 31 26.00N 47.00E
Ad Dāmir Sudan 35 17.37N 33.59E
Ad Dammām Saudi Arabia 31 26.23N 50.08E
Ad Dawādimī Saudi Arabia 31 24.29N 44.23E
Ad Dawḩah Qatar 31 25.15N 51.34E
Ad Ḑiffah *f.* Africa 30 30.45N 26.00E
Ad Dilam Saudi Arabia 31 23.59N 47.10E
Ad Dimās Syria 32 33.35N 36.05E
Addis Ababa *see* Ādīs Ābeba Ethiopia 35
Ad Dīwānīyah Iraq 31 31.59N 44.57E
Adelaide Australia 46 34.56S138.36E
Adelaide Pen. Canada 51 68.09N 97.45W
Adelaide River *town* Australia 42 13.14S131.06E
Adelong Australia 47 35.21S148.04E
Aden *see* 'Adan Yemen 35
Aden, G. of Indian Oc. 35 13.00N 50.00E
Adendorp R.S.A. 39 32.18S 24.31E
Adi *i.* Indonesia 27 4.10S133.10E
Adieu, C. Australia 43 31.59S132.09E
Adige *r.* Italy 9 45.10N 12.20E
Adilang Uganda 37 2.44N 33.28E
Adin U.S.A. 54 41.12N120.57W
Adirondack Mts. U.S.A. 55 44.00N 74.00W
Ādīs Ābeba Ethiopia 35 9.03N 38.42E
Adiyaman Turkey 30 37.46N 38.15E
Adjud Romania 15 46.04N 27.11E
Admer *well* Algeria 34 20.23N 5.27E
Admiralty G. Australia 42 14.20S125.50E
Admiralty Is. P.N.G. 27 2.30S147.20E
Admiralty Range *mts.* Antarctica 64 72.00S164.00E
Adour *r.* France 11 43.28N 1.35W
Adra Spain 10 36.43N 3.03W
Adrano Italy 12 37.39N 14.49E
Adrar des Iforas *mts.* Algeria / Mali 34 20.00N 2.30E
Adria Italy 9 45.03N 12.03E
Adrian Mich. U.S.A. 55 41.55N 84.01W
Adriatic Sea Med. Sea 12 42.30N 16.00E
Ādwa Ethiopia 35 14.12N 38.56E
Adzopé Ivory Coast 38 6.07N 3.49W
Adzva *r.* Russian Fed 18 66.30N 59.30E
Aegean Sea Med. Sea 13 39.00N 25.00E
Afghanistan Asia 28 34.00N 65.30E
'Afīf Saudi Arabia 30 23.53N 42.59E
Afikpo Nigeria 38 5.53N 7.55E
Afjord Norway 16 63.57N 10.12E
Afmadow Somali Rep. 37 0.27N 42.05E
Afobaka Surinam 61 5.00N 55.05W
Afognak I. U.S.A. 50 58.15N152.30W
Afonso Cláudio Brazil 59 20.05S 41.06W
Afsluitdijk *f.* Neth. 8 53.04N 5.11E
'Afula Israel 32 32.36N 35.17E
Afyon Turkey 30 38.46N 30.32E
Agadez Niger 38 17.00N 7.56E
Agadez *d.* Niger 38 19.25N 11.00E
Agadir Morocco 34 30.26N 9.36W
Agapa Russian Fed. 21 71.29N 86.16E
Agartala India 29 23.49N 91.15E
Agboville Ivory Coast 38 5.55N 4.15W
Agde France 11 43.19N 3.28E
Agen France 11 44.12N 0.38E
Ageo Japan 23 35.58N139.36E
Agger *r.* Germany 8 50.45N 7.06E
Aghada Rep. of Ire. 7 51.50N 8.13W
Aginskoye Russian Fed. 21 51.10N114.32E
Agnew Australia 43 28.01S120.30E
Ago Japan 23 34.17N136.48E
Agordo Italy 9 46.17N 12.02E
Āgra India 29 27.09N 78.00E
Agra *r.* Spain 10 42.12N 1.43W
Agraciada Uruguay 63 33.48S 58.15W
Agreda Spain 10 41.51N 1.55W
Agri *r.* Italy 13 40.13N 16.45E
Agri Turkey 30 39.44N 43.04E
Agri Daği *mtn.* Turkey 31 39.45N 44.15E
Agrigento Italy 12 37.19N 13.36E
Agropoli Italy 12 40.21N 15.00E
Agryz Russian Fed. 18 56.30N 53.00E
Aguas Blancas Chile 62 24.13S 69.50W
Aguascalientes Mexico 56 21.51N102.18W
Aguascalientes *d.* Mexico 56 22.00N102.00W
Agudos Brazil 59 22.27S 49.03W
Agueda *r.* Spain 10 41.00N 6.56W
Aguelhok Mali 38 19.28N 0.52E
Aguilar de Campóo Spain 10 42.47N 4.15W
Aguilas Spain 10 37.25N 1.35W
Agulhas, C. R.S.A. 39 34.50S 20.00E
Agulhas Negras *mtn.* Brazil 59 22.20S 44.43W
Ahaggar *mts.* Algeria 34 24.00N 5.50E
Ahar Iran 31 38.25N 47.07E
Ahaura New Zealand 48 42.21S171.33E
Ahaus Germany 8 52.04N 7.01E
Ahklun Mts. U.S.A. 50 59.15N161.00W
Ahlen Germany 8 51.47N 7.52E
Ahmadābād India 28 23.03N 72.40E
Aḩmadī Iran 31 27.56N 56.42E
Ahmadnagar India 28 19.08N 74.48E
Ahoada Nigeria 38 5.06N 6.39E
Ahr *r.* Germany 8 50.34N 7.16E
Ahram Iran 31 28.52N 51.16E
Aḩsā', Wāḩat al *oasis* Saudi Arabia 31 25.37N 49.40E
Ähtäri Finland 16 62.34N 24.06E
Åhus Sweden 17 55.55N 14.17E
Ahvāz Iran 31 31.17N 48.44E
Ahvenanmaa *d.* Finland 17 60.15N 20.00E
Ahvenanmaa *is.* Finland 17 60.15N 20.00E
Aichi *d.* Japan 23 35.02N137.15E
Aigle Switz. 9 46.19N 6.58E
Aigues-Mortes France 11 43.34N 4.11E
Aileron Australia 44 22.38S133.20E
Ailette *r.* France 8 49.35N 3.09E
Ailsa Craig *i.* U.K. 6 55.15N 5.07W
Aim Russian Fed. 21 58.50N134.15E
Aimorés Brazil 59 19.30S 41.04W
Ain *r.* France 11 45.47N 5.12E
Ainaži Estonia 17 57.52N 24.21E
Aïn ben Tili Mauritania 34 26.00N 9.32W
Aïn Sefra Algeria 34 32.45N 0.35W
Aïr *mts.* Niger 38 18.30N 8.30E
Airdrie U.K. 6 55.52N 3.59W
Aire France 11 43.39N 0.15W
Aire *r.* France 9 49.19N 4.49E
Aire *r.* U.K. 4 53.42N 0.54W
Aisne *d.* France 9 49.30N 3.30E
Aisne *r.* France 9 49.27N 2.51E
Aitape P.N.G. 27 3.10S142.17E
Aiud Romania 15 46.19N 23.44E
Aix-en-Provence France 11 43.31N 5.27E
Aix-les-Bains France 11 45.42N 5.55E
Aíyina *i.* Greece 13 37.43N 23.30E
Aíyion Greece 13 38.15N 22.05E
Aizpute Latvia 17 56.43N 21.38E
Ajaccio France 11 41.55N 8.43E
Ajdābiyā Libya 34 30.48N 20.15E
'Ajlūn Jordan 32 32.20N 35.45E
'Ajmah, Jabal al *f.* Egypt 32 29.12N 33.58E
'Ajmān U.A.E. 31 25.23N 55.26E
Ajmer India 28 26.29N 74.40E
Akaishi sammyaku *mts.* Japan 23 35.20N138.10E
Akámas, Akrotírion *c.* Cyprus 32 35.06N 32.17E
Akaroa New Zealand 48 43.50S172.59E
Akashi Japan 23 34.38N134.59E
Akbulak Russian Fed. 19 51.00N 55.40E
Akelamo Indonesia 27 1.35N129.40E
Akershus *d.* Norway 17 60.00N 11.10E
Aketi Zaïre 36 2.46N 23.51E
Akhaltsikhe Georgia 30 41.37N 42.59E
Akhḑar, Al Jabal al *mts.* Libya 35 32.10N 22.00E
Akhḑar, Al Jabal al *mts.* Oman 31 23.10N 57.25E
Akhḑar, Wādī *r.* Egypt 32 28.42N 33.41E
Akhḑar, Wādī al *r.* Saudi Arabia 32 28.30N 36.48E
Akhelóös Greece 13 38.20N 21.04E
Akhisar Turkey 13 38.54N 27.49E
Akhmīm Egypt 30 26.34N 31.44E
Akhtyrka Ukraine 19 50.19N 34.54E
Akimiski I. Canada 51 53.00N 81.20W
Akita Japan 25 39.44N140.05E
Akjoujt Mauritania 34 19.44N 14.26W
Akkajaure *l.* Sweden 16 67.40N 17.30E
'Akko Israel 32 32.55N 35.04E
Akkol Kazakhstan 24 45.04N 75.39E
Aklavik Canada 50 68.12N135.00W
Ako Nigeria 38 10.19N 10.48E
Ākobo *r.* Ethiopia 35 8.30N 33.15E
Akola India 28 20.44N 77.00E
Āk'ordat Ethiopia 35 15.35N 37.55E
Akpatok I. Canada 51 60.30N 68.30W
Akranes Iceland 16 64.19N 22.05W
Akron Ohio U.S.A. 55 41.04N 81.31W
Akrotíri Cyprus 32 34.36N 32.57E
Aksaray Turkey 30 38.22N 34.02E
Aksarka Russian Fed. 20 66.31N 67.50E
Aksay China 24 39.28N 94.15E
Aksay Kazakhstan 19 51.24N 52.11E
Aksu China 24 42.10N 80.00E
Āksum Ethiopia 35 14.08N 38.48E
Aktag *mtn.* China 24 36.45N 84.40E
Aktogay Kazakhstan 24 46.59N 79.42E
Aktyubinsk Kazakhstan 19 50.16N 57.13E
Akūbū Sudan 36 7.47N 33.01E
Akūbū *r. see* Ākobo *r.* Sudan 36
Akure Nigeria 38 7.14N 5.08E
Akureyri Iceland 16 65.41N 18.04W
Akuse Ghana 38 6.04N 0.12E
Akwa-Ibom *d.* Nigeria 38 4.45N 7.50E
Akxokesay China 24 36.48N 91.06E
Akyab *see* Sittwe Burma 29
Ål Norway 17 60.38N 8.34E
Alabama *d.* U.S.A. 53 33.00N 87.00W
Alabama *r.* U.S.A. 53 31.05N 87.55W
Alādāgh, Kūh-e *mts.* Iran 31 37.15N 57.30E
Alagoas *d.* Brazil 61 9.30S 37.00W
Alagoinhas Brazil 61 12.09S 38.21W
Alagón Spain 10 41.46N 1.12W
Alakol, Ozero *l.* Kazakhstan 24 46.00N 81.40E
Alakurtti Russian Fed. 18 67.00N 30.23E
Al 'Alamayn Egypt 30 30.49N 28.57E
Al 'Amārah Iraq 31 31.52N 47.50E
Al 'Āmirīyah Egypt 32 31.01N 29.48E
Alamogordo U.S.A. 52 32.54N105.57W
Alamosa U.S.A. 52 37.28N105.52W
Åland *is. see* Ahvenanmaa *is.* Finland 17
Ålands Hav *sea* Finland 17 60.00N 19.30E
Alanya Turkey 30 36.32N 32.02E
Alapayevsk Russian Fed. 18 57.55N 61.42E
Alappuzha India 28 9.30N 76.22E
Al 'Aqabah Jordan 32 29.32N 35.00E
Al 'Aramah *f.* Saudi Arabia 31 25.30N 46.30E
Alarcón, Embalse de *resr.* Spain 10 39.36N 2.10W
Al 'Arīsh Egypt 32 31.08N 33.48E
Alaska *d.* U.S.A. 50 65.00N153.00W
Alaska, G. of U.S.A. 50 58.45N145.00W
Alaska Pen. U.S.A. 50 56.00N160.00W
Alaska Range *mts.* U.S.A. 50 62.10N152.00W
Alassio Italy 9 44.00N 8.10E
Alaşehir Turkey 13 38.22N 28.29E
Al 'Aṭīqah Lebanon 32 33.42N 35.27E
Al 'Aṭrun Sudan 35 18.11N 26.36E
Alatyr Russian Fed. 18 54.51N 46.35E
Alausí Ecuador 60 2.00S 78.50W
Alavus Finland 16 62.35N 23.37E
Alawoona Australia 46 34.44S140.33E
Al 'Ayyāṭ Egypt 32 29.37N 31.15E
Alazani *r.* Georgia 31 41.06N 46.40E
Alba Italy 9 44.42N 8.02E
Albacete Spain 10 39.00N 1.52W
Al Bad' Saudi Arabia 32 28.29N 35.02E
Al Badārī Egypt 30 26.59N 31.25E
Al Bahnasā Egypt 32 28.32N 30.39E
Alba-Iulia Romania 15 46.04N 23.33E
Albania Europe 13 41.00N 20.00E
Albany Australia 43 34.57S117.54E
Albany *r.* Canada 51 52.10N 82.00W
Albany Ga. U.S.A. 53 31.37N 84.10W
Albany N.Y. U.S.A. 55 42.39N 73.45W
Albany Oreg. U.S.A. 54 44.38N123.06W
Al Başrah Iraq 31 30.33N 47.50E
Al Bāṭinah *f.* Oman 31 24.25N 56.50E
Albatross B. Australia 44 12.45S141.43E
Al Batrūn Lebanon 32 34.16N 35.40E
Al Bawīṭī Egypt 30 28.21N 25.52E
Al Bayḑā' Libya 35 32.50N 21.50E
Albemarle Sd. U.S.A. 53 36.10N 76.00W
Albenga Italy 9 44.03N 8.13E
Alberche *r.* Spain 10 40.00N 4.45W
Alberga Australia 45 27.12S135.28E
Alberga *r.* Australia 45 27.12S135.28E
Albert Australia 47 32.21S147.33E
Albert France 8 50.02N 2.38E
Albert, L. Australia 46 35.38S139.17E
Albert, L. Uganda / Zaïre 37 1.45N 31.00E
Alberta *d.* Canada 50 55.00N115.00W
Alberti Argentina 63 35.01S 60.16W
Albertirsa Hungary 15 47.15N 19.38E
Albert Kanaal *canal* Belgium 8 51.00N 5.15E
Albert Lea U.S.A. 53 43.38N 93.16W
Albert Nile *r.* Uganda 37 3.30N 32.00E
Albi France 11 43.56N 2.08E
Albina Surinam 61 5.30N 54.03W
Albino Italy 9 45.46N 9.47E
Albion Mich. U.S.A. 55 42.14N 84.45W
Albion Penn. U.S.A. 55 41.53N 80.22W
Al Bi'r Saudi Arabia 32 28.52N 36.15E
Alborán, Isla de *i.* Spain 10 35.55N 3.10W
Ålborg Denmark 17 57.03N 9.56E
Ålborg Bugt *b.* Denmark 17 56.45N 10.30E
Alborz, Reshteh-ye Kūhhā-ye *mts.* Iran 31 36.00N 52.30E
Albuquerque U.S.A. 52 35.05N106.40W
Al Buraymī U.A.E. 31 24.15N 55.45E
Al Burj Egypt 32 31.35N 30.59E
Alburquerque Spain 10 39.13N 6.59W
Albury Australia 47 36.03S146.53E
Alby Sweden 16 62.30N 15.25E
Alcácer do Sal Portugal 10 38.22N 8.30W
Alcalá de Chisvert Spain 10 40.19N 0.13E
Alcalá de Henares Spain 10 40.28N 3.22W
Alcalá la Real Spain 10 37.28N 3.55W
Alcamo Italy 12 37.59N 12.58E
Alcañiz Spain 10 41.03N 0.09W
Alcántara, Embalse de *resr.* Spain 10 39.45N 6.25W
Alcaudete Spain 10 37.35N 4.05W
Alcázar de San Juan Spain 10 39.24N 3.12W
Alcira Spain 10 39.10N 0.27W
Alcobaça Portugal 10 39.33N 8.59W
Alcova U.S.A. 54 42.35N106.34W
Alcoy Spain 10 38.42N 0.29W
Alcubierre, Sierra de *mts.* Spain 10 41.40N 0.20W
Alcudia Spain 10 39.51N 3.09E
Aldan Russian Fed. 21 58.44N125.22E
Aldan *r.* Russian Fed. 21 63.30N130.00E
Aldeburgh U.K. 5 52.09N 1.35E
Alderney *i.* U.K. 5 49.42N 2.11W
Aldershot U.K. 5 51.15N 0.47W
Aldridge U.K. 5 52.36N 1.55W
Alegre Brazil 59 20.44S 41.30W
Alegrete Brazil 63 29.46S 55.46W
Aleksandrov Gay Russian Fed. 19 50.08N 48.34E
Aleksandrovsk Sakhalinskiy Russian Fed. 21 50.55N142.12E
Além Paraíba Brazil 59 21.49S 42.36W
Alençon France 9 48.25N 0.05E
Aleppo *see* Ḩalab Syria 30
Aléria France 11 42.05N 9.30E
Alès France 11 44.08N 4.05E
Alessandria Italy 9 44.54N 8.37E
Ålesund Norway 16 62.28N 6.11E
Aleutian Range *mts.* U.S.A. 50 58.00N156.00W
Alexander Archipelago *is.* U.S.A. 50 56.30N134.30W
Alexander Bay *town* R.S.A. 39 28.36S 16.26E
Alexander I. Antarctica 64 72.00S 70.00W
Alexandra Australia 47 37.12S145.14E
Alexandra New Zealand 48 45.14S169.26E
Alexandria B.C. Canada 50 52.38N122.27W
Alexandria Ont. Canada 55 45.18N 74.39W
Alexandria *see* Al Iskandarīyah Egypt 32
Alexandria Romania 15 43.58N 25.20E
Alexandria R.S.A. 39 33.39S 26.24E
Alexandria La. U.S.A. 53 31.19N 92.29W
Alexandria Va. U.S.A. 55 38.48N 77.03W
Alexandrina, L. Australia 46 35.26S139.10E
Alexandroúpolis Greece 13 40.50N 25.53E
Aleysk Russian Fed. 20 52.32N 82.45E
Al Fant Egypt 32 28.46N 30.53E
Alfaro Spain 10 42.11N 1.45W
Al Fāshir Sudan 35 13.37N 25.22E
Al Fashn Egypt 32 28.49N 30.54E
Al Fāw Iraq 31 29.57N 48.30E
Al Fayyūm Egypt 32 29.19N 30.50E
Alfeld Germany 14 51.59N 9.50E
Alfenas Brazil 59 21.28S 45.48W
Alfiós *r.* Greece 13 37.37N 21.27E
Alfonsine Italy 9 44.30N 12.03E
Alford U.K. 6 57.14N 2.42W
Al Fujayrah U.A.E. 31 25.10N 56.20E
Alga Kazakhstan 20 49.49N 57.16E
Ålgård Norway 17 58.46N 5.51E
Algeciras Spain 10 36.08N 5.27W
Algemesí Spain 10 39.11N 0.27W
Alger Algeria 34 36.50N 3.00E
Algeria Africa 34 28.00N 2.00E
Al Ghayl Saudi Arabia 31 22.36N 46.19E
Alghero Italy 12 40.33N 8.20E
Al Ghurdaqah Egypt 30 27.14N 33.50E
Algiers *see* Alger Algeria 34
Algoa B. R.S.A. 39 33.50S 26.00E
Algonquin Prov. Park Canada 55 45.27N 78.26W
Algorta Uruguay 63 32.25S 57.23W
Al Ḩajar al Gharbī *mts.* Oman 31 24.00N 56.30E
Al Ḩajar ash Sharqī *mts.* Oman 31 22.45N 58.45E
Alhama Spain 10 37.51N 1.25W
Al Ḩamād *des.* Saudi Arabia 30 31.45N 39.00E
Al Ḩamar Saudi Arabia 31 22.26N 46.12E
Alhambra U.S.A. 54 34.06N118.08W
Al Ḩamīdīyah Syria 32 34.43N 35.56E
Al Ḩanākīyah Saudi Arabia 30 24.53N 40.30E
Al Ḩarīq Saudi Arabia 31 23.37N 46.31E
Al Ḩasakah Syria 30 36.29N 40.45E
Al Ḩawāmidīyah Egypt 32 29.54N 31.15E
Al Ḩayz Egypt 30 28.02N 28.39E
Al Ḩijāz *f.* Saudi Arabia 30 26.00N 37.30E
Al Ḩillah Iraq 31 32.28N 44.29E
Al Ḩillah Saudi Arabia 31 23.30N 46.51E
Al Hirmil Lebanon 32 34.25N 36.23E
Al Ḩudaydah Yemen 35 14.50N 42.58E
Al Hufūf Saudi Arabia 31 25.20N 49.34E
Al Ḩumrah *des.* U.A.E. 31 22.45N 55.10E
Al Ḩusaynīyah Egypt 32 30.52N 31.55E
Al Ḩuwaymī Yemen 35 14.05N 47.44E
Alīābād, Kūh-e *mtn.* Iran 31 34.09N 50.48E
Aliákmon *r.* Greece 13 40.30N 22.38E
Alicante Spain 10 38.21N 0.29W
Alice R.S.A. 39 32.47S 26.49E
Alice U.S.A. 52 27.45N 98.06W
Alice Springs *town* Australia 44 23.42S133.52E
Alīgarh India 29 27.54N 78.04E
Alīgūdarz Iran 31 33.25N 49.38E
'Alījūq, Kūh-e *mtn.* Iran 31 31.27N 51.43E
Alingsås Sweden 17 57.56N 12.31E
Alīpur Duār India 29 26.29N 89.44E
Aliquippa U.S.A. 55 40.38N 80.16W
Al Iskandarīyah Egypt 32 31.13N 29.55E
Al Ismā'īlīyah Egypt 32 30.36N 32.15E
Aliwal North R.S.A. 39 30.41S 26.41E
Al Jafr Jordan 32 30.16N 36.11E
Al Jāfūrah *des.* Saudi Arabia 31 24.40N 50.20E
Al Jaghbūb Libya 35 29.42N 24.38E
Al Jahrah Kuwait 31 29.20N 47.41E
Al Jawārah Oman 28 18.55N 57.17E
Al Jawb *f.* Saudi Arabia 31 23.00N 50.00E
Al Jawf Libya 35 24.09N 23.19E
Al Jawf Saudi Arabia 30 29.49N 39.52E
Al Jazīrah *f.* Iraq 30 35.00N 41.00E
Al Jazīrah *f.* Sudan 35 14.30N 33.00E
Al Jifārah Saudi Arabia 31 23.59N 45.11E
Al Jīzah Egypt 32 30.01N 31.12E
Al Jubayl Saudi Arabia 31 27.59N 49.40E
Al Junaynah Sudan 35 13.27N 22.30E
Aljustrel Portugal 10 37.55N 8.10W
Al Karak Jordan 32 31.11N 35.42E
Al Khābūr *r.* Syria 30 35.07N 40.30E
Al Khābūrah Oman 31 23.58N 57.10E
Al Khalīl Jordan 32 31.32N 35.06E
Al Khamāsīn Saudi Arabia 35 20.29N 44.49E
Al Khānkah Egypt 32 30.12N 31.21E
Al Khārijah Egypt 30 25.26N 30.33E
Al Kharṭūm Sudan 35 15.33N 32.35E
Al Kharṭūm Baḩrī Sudan 35 15.39N 32.34E
Al Khawr Qatar 31 25.39N 51.32E
Al Khirbah as Samrā' Jordan 32 32.11N 36.10E
Al Khubar Saudi Arabia 31 26.18N 50.06E
Al Khufayfīyah Saudi Arabia 31 24.55N 44.42E
Al Khunn Saudi Arabia 31 23.18N 49.15E
Al Kidn *des.* Saudi Arabia 35 22.30N 54.00E
Al Kiswah Syria 32 33.21N 36.14E
Alkmaar Neth. 8 52.37N 4.44E
Al Kuntillah Egypt 32 30.00N 34.41E
Al Kūt Iraq 31 32.30N 45.51E
Al Kuwayt Kuwait 31 29.20N 48.00E
Al Labwah Lebanon 32 34.11N 36.21E
Al Lādhiqīyah Syria 32 35.31N 35.47E
Allāhābād India 29 25.57N 81.50E
Allakaket U.S.A. 50 66.30N152.45W
Allanche France 11 45.14N 2.56E
'Allāqī, Wādī al *r.* Egypt 30 22.55N 33.02E
Allegheny *r.* U.S.A. 55 40.27N 80.00W
Allegheny Mts. U.S.A. 53 38.30N 80.00W
Allen, Lough Rep. of Ire. 7 54.07N 8.04W
Allentown U.S.A. 55 40.37N 75.30W
Aller *r.* Germany 14 52.57N 9.11E
Alliance Nebr. U.S.A. 52 42.06N102.52W
Allier *r.* France 11 46.58N 3.04E
Al Līṭānī *r.* Lebanon 32 33.22N 35.14E
Alloa U.K. 6 56.07N 3.49W
Allos France 11 44.14N 6.38E
Al Luḩayyah Yemen 35 15.43N 42.42E
Alluitsup-Paa *see* Sydpröven Greenland 51
Alma Canada 55 48.32N 71.40W
Alma Mich. U.S.A. 55 43.23N 84.40W
Al Ma'ānīyah *well* Iraq 30 30.44N 43.00E
Alma-Ata Kazakhstan 24 43.19N 76.55E
Almadén Spain 10 38.47N 4.50W
Al Madīnah Saudi Arabia 30 24.30N 39.35E
Al Madīnah al Fikrīyah Egypt 32 27.56N 30.49E
Al Mafraq Jordan 32 32.20N 36.12E
Al Maghrah *well* Egypt 30 30.14N 28.56E
Almagor Israel 32 32.55N 35.36E
Al Maḩallah al Kubrá Egypt 32 30.59N 31.12E
Al Maḩārīq Egypt 30 25.37N 30.39E
Al Maḩmūdīyah Egypt 32 31.10N 30.30E
Al Majma'ah Saudi Arabia 31 25.52N 45.25E
Al Manāmah Bahrain 31 26.12N 50.36E
Almanor U.S.A. 54 40.15N121.08W
Almansa Spain 10 38.52N 1.06W

Al Manshâh Egypt 30 26.28N 31.48E
Al Manşûrah Egypt 32 31.03N 31.23E
Al Manzil Jordan 32 31.03N 36.01E
Al Manzilah Egypt 32 31.10N 31.56E
Almanzor, Pico de mtn. Spain 10 40.20N 5.22W
Almanzora r. Spain 10 37.16N 1.49W
Al Maţarīyah Egypt 32 31.12N 32.02E
Al Mawşil Iraq 30 36.21N 43.08E
Al Mayâdīn Syria 30 35.01N 40.28E
Almazán Spain 10 41.29N 2.31W
Al Mazra'ah Jordan 32 31.16N 35.31E
Almeirim Portugal 10 39.12N 8.37W
Almelo Neth. 8 52.21N 6.40E
Almendralejo Spain 10 38.41N 6.26W
Almería Spain 10 36.50N 2.26W
Älmhult Sweden 17 56.33N 14.08E
Al Midhnab Saudi Arabia 31 25.52N 44.15E
Al Miḩrāḑ des. Saudi Arabia 31 20.00N 52.30E
Al Minyâ Egypt 32 28.06N 30.45E
Al Mismīyah Syria 32 33.08N 36.24E
Almonte Spain 10 37.16N 6.31W
Al Mudawwarah Jordan 32 29.20N 36.00E
Al Muglad Sudan 35 11.01N 27.50E
Al Muḩarraq Bahrain 31 26.16N 50.38E
Al Mukallâ Yemen 35 14.34N 49.09E
Almuñécar Spain 10 36.44N 3.41W
Al Muwayh Saudi Arabia 30 22.41N 41.37E
Alnwick U.K. 4 55.25N 1.41W
Alofi Niue 40 19.03S169.55W
Alónnisos i. Greece 13 39.08N 23.50E
Alor i. Indonesia 27 8.20S124.30E
Alor Setar Malaysia 26 6.06N100.23E
Alozero Russian Fed. 18 65.02N 31.10E
Alpena U.S.A. 55 45.04N 83.27W
Alpes Maritimes mts. France 11 44.07N 7.08E
Alpha Australia 44 23.39S146.38E
Alphen Neth. 8 52.08N 4.40E
Alpine U.S.A. 52 30.22N103.40W
Alps mts. Europe 11 46.00N 7.30E
Al Qaḑārif Sudan 35 14.02N 35.24E
Al Qafā' des. U.A.E. 31 23.30N 53.30E
Al Qâhirah Egypt 32 30.03N 31.15E
Al Qā'īyah Saudi Arabia 30 24.18N 43.30E
Al Qā'īyah well Saudi Arabia 31 26.27N 45.35E
Al Qalībah Saudi Arabia 30 28.24N 37.42E
Al Qanāţir al Khayrīyah Egypt 32 30.12N 31.08E
Al Qanţarah Egypt 32 30.52N 32.20E
Al Qaryatayn Syria 32 34.13N 37.13E
Al Qaşr Egypt 30 25.43N 28.54E
Al Qaşşāşīn Egypt 32 30.34N 31.56E
Al Qaţīf Saudi Arabia 31 26.31N 50.00E
Al Qaţrānah Jordan 32 31.15N 36.03E
Al Qaţrūn Libya 34 24.55N 14.38E
Al Qayşūmah Saudi Arabia 31 28.20N 46.07E
Al Qunayţirah Syria 32 33.08N 35.49E
Al Qurnah Iraq 31 31.00N 47.26E
Al Quşaymah Egypt 32 30.40N 34.22E
Al Quşayr Egypt 30 26.06N 34.17E
Al Qūşīyah Egypt 30 27.26N 30.49E
Al Quţayfah Syria 32 33.44N 36.36E
Alroy Downs town Australia 44 19.18S136.04E
Als i. Denmark 17 54.59N 9.55E
Alsace d. France 11 48.25N 7.40E
Alsask Canada 50 51.23N109.59W
Alsasua Spain 10 42.54N 2.10W
Älsborg d. Sweden 17 58.00N 12.20E
Alsfeld Germany 14 50.45N 9.16E
Alsten i. Norway 16 65.55N 12.35E
Alston U.K. 6 54.48N 2.26W
Alta Norway 16 70.00N 23.15E
Alta r. Norway 16 69.50N 23.30E
Altafjorden est. Norway 16 70.10N 23.00E
Alta Gracia Argentina 62 31.40S 64.26W
Altagracia de Orituco Venezuela 60 9.54N 66.24W
Altai mts. Mongolia 24 46.30N 93.30E
Altamaha r. U.S.A. 53 31.15N 81.23W
Altamira Brazil 61 3.12S 52.12W
Altamont Oreg. U.S.A. 54 42.12N121.44W
Altamura Italy 13 40.50N 16.32E
Altay China 24 47.48N 88.07E
Altay Mongolia 24 46.20N 97.00E
Altea Spain 10 38.37N 0.03W
Altenburg Germany 14 50.59N 12.27E
Altenkirchen Germany 8 50.41N 7.40E
Altnaharra U.K. 6 58.16N 4.26W
Alto Araguaia Brazil 61 17.19S 53.10W
Alto Molocue Mozambique 37 15.38S 37.42E
Alton U.K. 5 51.08N 0.59W
Altona Germany 14 53.32N 9.56E
Altoona U.S.A. 55 40.30N 78.24W
Altun Shan mts. China 24 38.10N 87.50E
Al Ubayyiḑ Sudan 35 13.11N 30.10E
Al 'Ulá Saudi Arabia 30 26.39N 37.58E
Al' Uqaylah Libya 34 30.15N 19.12E
Al Uqşur Egypt 30 25.41N 32.24E
Al Urduun r. Asia 32 31.47N 35.31E
Al 'Uwaynah well Saudi Arabia 31 26.46N 48.13E
Al 'Uyūn Saudi Arabia 31 26.32N 43.41E
Alva U.S.A. 52 36.48N 98.40W
Alvarado Mexico 56 18.49N 95.46W
Älvdalen Sweden 17 61.14N 14.02E
Alvesta Sweden 17 56.54N 14.33E
Älvho Sweden 17 61.30N 14.46E
Älvkarleby Sweden 17 60.34N 17.27E
Älvsbyn Sweden 16 65.39N 20.59E
Al Wajh Saudi Arabia 30 26.16N 36.28E
Al Wakrah Qatar 31 25.09N 51.36E
Alwar India 28 27.32N 76.35E
Al Yamâmah Saudi Arabia 31 24.11N 47.21E
Alyaty Azerbaijan 31 39.59N 49.20E
Alytus Lithuania 15 54.24N 24.03E
Alzette r. Lux. 8 49.52N 6.07E
Amadeus, L. Australia 42 24.50S130.45E
Amadjuak Canada 51 64.00N 72.50W
Amadjuak L. Canada 51 65.00N 71.00W
Amagasaki Japan 23 34.43N135.25E
Åmål Sweden 17 59.03N 12.42E
Amaliás Greece 13 37.48N 21.21E
Amami ō shima i. Japan 25 28.20N129.30E
Amamula Zaïre 37 0.17S 27.49E
Amanã, L. Brazil 60 2.35S 64.40W
Amangeldy Kazakhstan 20 50.12N 65.11E
Amapá Brazil 61 2.00N 50.50W
Amapá d. Brazil 61 2.00N 52.00W
Amarante Brazil 61 6.14S 42.51W
Amareleja Portugal 10 38.12N 7.13W
Amares Portugal 10 41.38N 8.21W
Amarillo U.S.A. 52 35.14N101.50W
Amaro, Monte mtn. Italy 12 42.06N 14.04E
Amasya Turkey 30 40.37N 35.50E
Amazon r. see Amazonas r. Brazil 61
Amazonas d. Brazil 60 4.50S 64.00W
Amazonas r. Brazil 61 2.00S 52.00W
Amazonas, Estuario do Rio f. Brazil 61 0.00 50.30W
Amazon Delta see Amazonas, Estuario do Rio f. Brazil 61
Ambâla India 28 30.19N 76.49E
Ambam Cameroon 38 2.25N 11.16E
Ambarchik Russian Fed. 21 69.39N162.27E
Ambarnyy Russian Fed. 18 65.59N 33.53E
Ambato Ecuador 60 1.18S 78.36W
Ambato-Boeni Madagascar 36 16.28S 46.43E
Ambatondrazaka Madagascar 36 17.50S 48.25E
Amberg Germany 14 49.27N 11.52E
Ambergris Cay i. Belize 57 18.00N 87.58W
Ambikāpur India 29 23.07N 83.12E
Ambilobe Madagascar 36 13.12S 49.04E
Amble U.K. 4 55.20N 1.34W
Ambleside U.K. 4 54.26N 2.58W
Amboise France 9 47.25N 1.00E
Ambon Indonesia 27 4.50S128.10E
Ambovombe Madagascar 36 25.11S 46.05E
Amboy U.S.A. 54 34.33N115.44W
Ambrières France 9 48.24N 0.38W
Ambriz Angola 36 7.54S 13.12E
Amderma Russian Fed. 20 69.44N 61.35E
Ameca Mexico 56 20.33N104.02W
Ameland i. Neth. 8 53.28N 5.48E
Americana Brazil 59 22.44S 47.19W
American Falls Resr. U.S.A. 54 43.00N113.00W
American Fork U.S.A. 54 40.23N111.48W
Amersfoort Neth. 8 52.10N 5.23E
Amery Australia 43 31.09S117.05E
Ames U.S.A. 53 42.02N 93.39W
Ameson Canada 55 49.49N 84.34W
Ametinho Angola 39 17.20S 17.20E
Amga Russian Fed. 21 60.51N131.59E
Amga r. Russian Fed. 21 62.40N135.20E
Amgu Russian Fed. 25 45.48N137.36E
Amgun r. Russian Fed. 21 53.10N139.47E
Amhara Plateau f. Ethiopia 35 10.00N 37.00E
Amiata mtn. Italy 12 42.53N 11.37E
Amiens France 9 49.54N 2.18E
Åmli Norway 17 58.47N 8.30E
Amlwch U.K. 4 53.24N 4.21W
'Ammān Jordan 32 31.57N 35.56E
Ammanford U.K. 5 51.48N 4.00W
Ammassalik Greenland 51 65.40N 38.00W
Ammókhostos Cyprus 32 35.07N 33.57E
Ammókhostou, Kólpos b. Cyprus 32 35.12N 34.05E
Āmol Iran 31 36.26N 52.24E
Amorgós i. Greece 13 36.50N 25.55E
Amos Canada 55 48.34N 78.07W
Amoy see Xiamen China 25
Ampala Honduras 57 13.16N 87.39W
Amparo Brazil 59 22.44S 46.44W
Ampezzo Italy 9 46.25N 12.48E
Ampotaka Madagascar 36 25.03S 44.41E
Amqui Canada 55 48.28N 67.27W
Amrāvati India 28 20.58N 77.50E
Amritsar India 28 31.35N 74.56E
Amstelveen Neth. 8 52.18N 4.51E
Amsterdam Neth. 8 52.22N 4.54E
Amsterdam N.Y. U.S.A. 55 42.57N 74.11W
Am Timan Chad 35 11.02N 20.17E
Amu Darya r. Uzbekistan 20 43.50N 59.00E
Amundsen G. Canada 50 70.30N122.00W
Amundsen Sea Antarctica 64 72.00S120.00W
Amuntai Indonesia 26 2.24S115.14E
Amur r. Russian Fed. 21 53.17N140.00E
Amurzet Russian Fed. 25 47.50N131.05E
Anabar r. Russian Fed. 21 72.40N113.30E
Anabranch r. Australia 46 34.08S141.46E
Anaco Venezuela 60 9.27N 64.28W
Anaconda U.S.A. 54 46.08N112.57W
Anadolu f. Turkey 30 38.00N 35.00E
Anadyr Russian Fed. 21 64.40N177.32E
Anadyr r. Russian Fed. 21 65.00N176.00E
Anadyrskiy Zaliv g. Russian Fed. 21 64.30N177.50W
Anáfi i. Greece 13 36.21N 25.50E
Anaheim U.S.A. 54 33.51N117.57W
Analalava Madagascar 36 14.38S 47.45E
Anambas, Kepulauan is. Indonesia 26 3.00N106.10E
Anambra d. Nigeria 38 6.20N 7.25E
Anamur Turkey 30 36.06N 32.49E
Anantapur India 28 14.41N 77.36E
Anápolis Brazil 61 16.19S 48.58W
Anapú r. Brazil 61 1.53S 50.53W
Anār Iran 31 30.54N 55.18E
Anārak Iran 31 33.20N 53.42E
Anatolia f. see Anadolu f. Turkey 30
Anatone U.S.A. 54 46.08N117.09W
Añatuya Argentina 62 28.26S 62.48W
Ancenis France 9 47.21N 1.10W
Anchau Nigeria 38 11.00N 8.23E
Anchorage U.S.A. 50 61.10N150.00W
Ancohuma mtn. Bolivia 62 16.05S 68.36W
Ancón Peru 60 11.50S 77.10W
Ancona Italy 12 43.37N 13.33E
Ancuabe Mozambique 37 13.00S 39.50E
Ancud Chile 63 41.05S 73.50W
Ancy-le-Franc France 9 47.46N 4.10E
Anda China 25 46.25N125.20E
Andalsnes Norway 16 62.33N 7.43E
Andalucía d. Spain 10 37.36N 4.30W
Andalusia U.S.A. 53 31.20N 86.30W
Andaman Is. India 29 12.00N 93.00E
Andaman Sea Indian Oc. 29 11.15N 95.30E
Andamooka Australia 46 30.27S137.12E
Andanga Russian Fed. 18 59.11N 45.44E
Andara Namibia 39 18.04S 21.26E
Andelot France 11 48.15N 5.18E
Andenes Norway 16 69.18N 16.10E
Andenne Belgium 8 50.29N 5.04E
Anderlecht Belgium 8 50.51N 4.18E
Andernach Germany 8 50.25N 7.24E
Anderson r. Canada 50 69.45N129.00W
Anderson Ind. U.S.A. 55 40.05N 85.41W
Anderson S.C. U.S.A. 53 34.30N 82.39W
Andes mts. S. America 63 32.40S 70.00W
Andevoranto Madagascar 36 18.57S 49.06E
Andfjorden est. Norway 16 68.55N 16.00E
Andhra Pradesh d. India 29 17.00N 79.00E
Andikíthira i. Greece 13 35.52N 23.18E
Andizhan Uzbekistan 24 40.48N 72.23E
Andong S. Korea 25 36.37N128.44E
Andorra town Andorra 11 42.30N 1.31E
Andorra Europe 11 42.30N 1.32E
Andover U.K. 5 51.13N 1.29W
Andöy i. Norway 16 69.05N 15.40E
Andreyevo-Ivanovka Ukraine 15 47.28N 30.29E
Andria Italy 12 41.13N 16.18E
Ándros Greece 13 37.50N 24.57E
Ándros i. Greece 13 37.50N 24.50E
Andros I. Bahamas 57 24.30N 78.00W
Andros Town Bahamas 57 24.43N 77.47W
Andrushevka Ukraine 15 50.00N 28.59E
Andújar Spain 10 38.02N 4.03W
Anefis I-n-Darane Mali 38 17.57N 0.35E
Anegada i. B.V.Is. 57 18.46N 64.24W
Anécho Togo 38 6.17N 1.40E
Añelo Argentina 63 38.20S 68.45W
Aneto, Pico de mtn. Spain 10 42.40N 0.19E
Aney Niger 38 19.24N 12.56E
Angara r. Russian Fed. 21 58.00N 93.00E
Angarsk Russian Fed. 21 52.31N103.55E
Angaston Australia 45 34.30S139.03E
Angatuba Brazil 59 23.27S 48.25W
Ånge Sweden 16 62.31N 15.40E
Ángel de la Guarda, Isla i. Mexico 56 29.20N113.25W
Angel Falls f. Venezuela 60 5.55N 62.30W
Ängelholm Sweden 17 56.15N 12.50E
Angels Camp U.S.A. 54 38.04N120.32W
Ångerman r. Sweden 16 63.00N 17.43E
Angermünde Germany 14 53.01N 14.00E
Angers France 9 47.29N 0.32W
Angerville France 9 48.19N 2.00E
Ångesån r. Sweden 16 66.22N 22.58E
Angkor ruins Cambodia 26 13.26N103.50E
Anglesey i. U.K. 4 53.16N 4.25W
Angoche Mozambique 37 16.10S 39.57E
Angol Chile 63 37.48S 72.43W
Angola Africa 36 12.00S 18.00E
Angola Ind. U.S.A. 55 41.38N 85.01W
Angola N.Y. U.S.A. 55 42.39N 79.02W
Angoram P.N.G. 27 4.04S144.04E
Angoulême France 11 45.40N 0.10E
Angra dos Reis Brazil 59 22.59S 44.17W
Anguilla i. Leeward Is. 57 18.14N 63.05W
Angumu Zaïre 37 0.10S 27.38E
Anholt i. Denmark 17 56.42N 11.34E
Anholt Germany 8 51.51N 6.26E
Anhui d. China 25 31.30N116.45E
Aniak U.S.A. 50 61.32N159.40W
Anina Romania 15 45.05N 21.51E
Anjō Japan 23 34.57N137.05E
Anjouan i. Comoros 37 12.12S 44.28E
Anju N. Korea 25 39.36N125.42E
Anka Nigeria 38 12.06N 5.56E
Ankara Turkey 30 39.55N 32.50E
Anklam Germany 14 53.51N 13.41E
Ānkober Ethiopia 35 9.32N 39.43E
Ankpa Nigeria 38 7.26N 7.38E
Annaba Algeria 34 36.55N 7.47E
An Nabk Syria 32 34.02N 36.43E
Anna Creek town Australia 46 28.50S136.07E
An Nafūd des. Saudi Arabia 30 28.40N 41.30E
An Najaf Iraq 31 31.59N 44.19E
An Nakhl Egypt 32 29.55N 33.45E
Annam Highlands see Annamitique, Chaîne mts. Laos / Vietnam 26
Annamitique, Chaîne mts. Laos / Vietnam 26 17.40N105.30E
Annan U.K. 6 54.59N 3.16W
Annan r. U.K. 6 54.58N 3.16W
Annandale f. U.K. 6 55.12N 3.25W
Anna Plains Australia 42 19.18S121.34E
Annapolis U.S.A. 55 38.59N 76.30W
Annapurna mtn. Nepal 29 28.34N 83.50E
An Naqīrah well Saudi Arabia 31 27.53N 48.15E
Ann Arbor U.S.A. 55 42.18N 83.43W
An Nāşirīyah Iraq 31 31.04N 46.16E
Annecy France 11 45.54N 6.07E
Anniston U.S.A. 53 33.58N 85.50W
Annonay France 11 45.15N 4.40E
Annuello Australia 46 34.52S142.54E
An Nuhūd Sudan 35 12.41N 28.28E
Anoka U.S.A. 53 45.11N 93.20W
Anqing China 25 30.20N116.50E
Ansbach Germany 14 49.18N 10.36E
Anshan China 25 41.05N122.58E
Anshun China 29 26.02N105.57E
Anson B. Australia 42 13.10S130.00E
Ansongo Mali 38 15.40N 0.30E
Anstruther U.K. 6 56.14N 2.42W
Ansudu Indonesia 27 2.11S139.22E
Antakya Turkey 30 36.12N 36.10E
Antalya Turkey 30 36.53N 30.42E
Antalya Körfezi g. Turkey 30 36.38N 31.00E
Antananarivo Madagascar 36 18.55S 47.31E
Antarctica 64
Antas Brazil 61 10.20S 38.20W
Antequera Spain 10 37.01N 4.34W
Antibes France 11 43.35N 7.07E
Anticosti, Île d' i. Canada 51 49.20N 63.00W
Antifer, Cap d' c. France 9 49.41N 0.10E
Antigua Guatemala 56 14.33N 90.42W
Antigua i. Leeward Is. 57 17.09N 61.49W
Anti-Lebanon mts. see Sharqī, Al Jabal ash mts. Lebanon 32
Antofagasta Chile 62 23.39S 70.24W
Antônio Bezerra Brazil 61 3.44S 38.35W
Antônio Carlos Brazil 59 21.18S 43.48W
Antrain France 9 48.28N 1.30W
Antrim U.K. 7 54.43N 6.14W
Antrim d. U.K. 7 54.58N 6.20W
Antrim, Mts. of U.K. 7 55.00N 6.10W
Antsiranana Madagascar 36 12.16S 49.17E
Anttis Sweden 16 67.16N 22.52E
Antwerp see Antwerpen Belgium 8
Antwerpen Belgium 8 51.13N 4.25E
Antwerpen d. Belgium 8 51.16N 4.45E
Anvik U.S.A. 50 62.38N160.20W
Anxi Gansu China 24 40.32N 95.57E
Anxious B. Australia 46 33.25S134.35E
Anyama Ivory Coast 38 5.30N 4.03W
Anyang China 25 36.04N114.20E
Anzhero-Sudzhensk Russian Fed. 20 56.10N 86.10E
Anzio Italy 12 41.27N 12.37E
Aohan Qi China 25 42.23N119.59E
Aomori Japan 25 40.50N140.43E
Aosta Italy 9 45.43N 7.19E
Apalachee B. U.S.A. 53 29.30N 84.00W
Apaporis r. Colombia 60 1.40S 69.20W
Aparri Phil. 27 18.22N121.40E
Apatin Yugo. 13 45.40N 18.59E
Apatity Russian Fed. 18 67.32N 33.21E
Apeldoorn Neth. 8 52.13N 5.57E
Apia W. Samoa 40 13.48S171.45W
Apizaco Mexico 56 19.25N 98.09W
Apollo Bay town Australia 46 38.45S143.40E
Apostle Is. U.S.A. 53 47.00N 90.30W
Apóstoles Argentina 62 27.55S 55.45W
Apostólou Andréa, Akrotírion c. Cyprus 32 35.40N 34.35E
Apoteri Guyana 60 4.02N 58.32W
Appalachian Mts. U.S.A. 53 39.30N 78.00W
Appennino mts. Italy 12 42.00N 13.30E
Appennino Ligure mts. Italy 9 44.30N 9.00E
Appennino Tosco-Emiliano mts. Italy 9 44.05N 11.00E
Appiano Italy 9 46.28N 11.15E
Appingedam Neth. 8 53.18N 6.52E
Appleby U.K. 4 54.35N 2.29W
Appleton U.S.A. 53 44.17N 88.24W
Apsheronsk Russian Fed. 19 44.26N 39.45E
Apsheronskiy Poluostrov pen. Azerbaijan 31 40.28N 50.00E
Apsley Australia 46 36.58S141.08E
Apsley Canada 55 44.45N 78.06W
Apucarana Brazil 59 23.34S 51.28W
Apure r. Venezuela 60 7.40N 66.30W
Apurimac r. Peru 60 10.43S 73.55W
Aqaba, G. of Asia 32 28.45N 34.45E
Aqabat al Ḩijāzīyah Jordan 32 29.40N 35.55E
'Aqdā Iran 31 32.25N 33.38E
Aqqikkol Hu l. China 24 35.44N 81.34E
Aquidauana Brazil 62 20.27S 55.45W
Aquila Mexico 56 18.30N103.50W
Aquitaine d. France 11 44.40N 0.00
'Arab, Baḩr al r. Sudan 35 9.02N 29.28E
Arabādād Iran 31 33.02N 57.41E
'Arabah, Wādī r. Egypt 32 29.07N 32.40E
Arabian Sea Asia 28 16.00N 65.00E
Aracaju Brazil 61 10.54S 37.07W
Aracanguy, Montañas de mts. Paraguay 62 24.00S 55.50W
Aracati Brazil 61 4.32S 37.45W
Araç Turkey 30 41.14N 33.20E
Araçatuba Brazil 59 21.12S 50.24W
Arad Romania 15 46.12N 21.19E
Arafura Sea Austa. 44 9.00S133.00E
Aragarças Brazil 61 15.55S 52.12W
Aragats mtn. Armenia 31 40.32N 44.11E
Aragón d. Spain 10 41.25N 1.00W
Aragón r. Spain 10 42.20N 1.45W
Araguacema Brazil 61 8.50S 49.34W
Araguaia r. Brazil 61 5.20S 48.30W
Araguari Brazil 59 18.38S 48.13W
Araguari r. Brazil 61 1.15N 50.05W
Arāk Iran 31 34.05N 49.44E
Arakan Yoma mts. Burma 29 20.00N 94.00E
Araks r. Azerbaijan 31 40.00N 48.28E
Aral Sea Asia 20 45.00N 60.00E
Aralsk Kazakhstan 20 46.56N 61.43E
Aralsor, Ozero l. Kazakhstan 19 49.00N 48.40E
Aramac Australia 44 22.59S145.14E
Aramia r. P.N.G. 27 8.00S143.20E
Aranda de Duero Spain 10 41.40N 3.41W
Aran I. Rep. of Ire. 7 53.07N 9.38W
Aran Is. Rep. of Ire. 7 53.07N 9.38W
Aranjuez Spain 10 40.02N 3.37W
Aranos Namibia 39 24.09S 19.09E
Araouane Mali 38 18.53N 3.31W
Arapey Uruguay 63 30.58S 57.30W
Arapey Grande r. Uruguay 63 30.55S 57.49W
Arapiraca Brazil 61 9.45S 36.40W
Arapkir Turkey 30 39.03N 38.29E
'Ar'ar, Wādī r. Iraq 30 32.00N 42.30E
Araraquara Brazil 59 21.46S 48.08W
Araras Brazil 59 22.20S 47.23W
Ararat Australia 46 37.20S143.00E
Ararat mtn. see Ağri Daği mtn. Turkey 31
Aras r. see Araks r. Turkey 30
Arauca Colombia 60 7.04N 70.41W
Arauca r. Venezuela 60 7.05N 70.45W
Araure Venezuela 60 9.36N 69.15W
Araxá Brazil 59 19.37S 46.50W
Araxes r. Iran see Araks r. Iran 31
Ārba Minch' Ethiopia 35 6.02N 37.40E
Arbatax Italy 12 39.56N 9.41E
Arboga Sweden 17 59.24N 15.50E
Arbroath U.K. 6 56.34N 2.35W
Arcachon France 11 44.40N 1.11W
Arcata U.S.A. 54 40.52N124.05W
Archer r. Australia 44 13.28S141.41E
Archers Post Kenya 37 0.42N 37.40E
Arcis-sur-Aube France 9 48.32N 4.08E
Arckaringa r. Australia 46 27.56S134.45E
Arco Italy 9 45.55N 10.53E
Arco U.S.A. 54 43.38N113.18W
Arcoona Australia 46 31.06S137.19E
Arcos Brazil 59 20.12S 45.30W
Arcos Spain 10 36.45N 5.45W
Arcoverde Brazil 61 8.23S 37.00W
Arctic Bay town Canada 51 73.05N 85.20W
Arctic Ocean 64
Arctic Red r. Canada 50 67.26N133.48W
Arctic Red River town Canada 50 67.27N133.46W
Arda r. Greece 13 41.39N 26.30E
Ardabīl Iran 31 38.15N 48.18E
Ardahan Turkey 30 41.08N 42.41E
Årdalstangen Norway 17 61.14N 7.43E
Ardara Rep. of Ire. 7 54.46N 8.25W
Arḑ aş Şawwān f. Jordan 32 30.45N 37.15E
Ardèche r. France 11 44.31N 4.40E
Ardennes mts. Belgium 8 50.10N 5.30E
Ardennes d. France 9 49.40N 4.40E
Ardennes, Canal des France 9 49.26N 4.02E
Ardestān Iran 31 33.22N 52.25E
Ardfert Rep. of Ire. 7 52.20N 9.48W
Ardila r. Portugal 10 38.10N 7.30W
Ardlethan Australia 47 34.20S146.53E
Ardmore Rep. of Ire. 7 51.58N 7.43W
Ardmore Okla. U.S.A. 53 34.11N 97.08W
Ardnamurchan, Pt. of U.K. 6 56.44N 6.14W
Ardrossan Australia 46 34.25S137.55E
Ardrossan U.K. 6 55.38N 4.49W
Ards Pen. U.K. 7 54.30N 5.30W
Åre Sweden 16 63.25N 13.05E
Arecibo Puerto Rico 57 18.29N 66.44W
Areia Branca Brazil 61 4.56S 37.07W
Arena, Pt. U.S.A. 52 38.58N123.44W
Arendal Norway 17 58.27N 8.48E
Arequipa Peru 60 16.25S 71.32W
Arès France 11 44.47N 1.08W
Arévalo Spain 10 41.03N 4.43W
Arezzo Italy 12 43.27N 11.52E
Arfak mtn. Indonesia 27 1.30S133.50E
Arganda Spain 10 40.19N 3.26W
Argelès-sur-Mer France 11 42.33N 3.01E
Argens r. France 11 43.10N 6.45E
Argenta Italy 9 44.37N 11.50E
Argentan France 9 48.45N 0.01W
Argentera Italy 9 44.24N 6.57E
Argentera mtn. Italy 9 44.10N 7.18E
Argenteuil France 9 48.57N 2.15E
Argentina S. America 63 36.00S 63.00W
Argentino, L. Argentina 63 50.15S 72.25W
Argenton France 11 46.36N 1.30E
Argentré France 9 48.05N 0.39W
Argentré du Plessis France 9 48.03N 1.08W
Argeş r. Romania 13 44.13N 26.22E
Árgos Greece 13 37.37N 22.45E
Argostólion Greece 13 38.10N 20.30E
Arguello, Pt. U.S.A. 54 34.35N120.39W
Argun r. Russian Fed. 25 53.30N121.48E
Argungu Nigeria 38 12.45N 4.35E
Århus Denmark 17 56.09N 10.13E
Ariah Park town Australia 47 34.20S147.10E
Ariano Italy 12 41.04N 15.00E
Ariano nel Polesine Italy 9 44.56N 12.07E
Aribinda Burkina 38 14.17N 0.52W
Arica Chile 62 18.29S 70.20W
Arica Colombia 60 2.07S 71.46W
Arid, C. Australia 43 33.58S123.05E
Arieş r. Romania 15 46.26N 23.59E
Arīḩā Al Quds Jordan 32 31.51N 35.27E
Arima Trinidad 60 10.38N 61.17W
Arinos r. Brazil 61 10.20S 57.35W
Aripuanã Brazil 60 9.10S 60.38W
Aripuanã r. Brazil 60 5.05S 60.30W
Ariquemes Brazil 60 9.56S 63.04W
Aris Namibia 39 22.48S 17.10E
Arisaig U.K. 6 56.55N 5.51W
'Arīsh, Wādī al r. Egypt 32 31.09N 33.49E
Ariza Spain 10 41.19N 2.03W
Arizona d. U.S.A. 52 34.00N112.00W
Årjäng Sweden 17 59.23N 12.08E
Arjeplog Sweden 16 66.00N 17.58E
Arjona Colombia 60 10.14N 75.22W
Arkaig, Loch U.K. 6 56.58N 5.08W
Arkansas d. U.S.A. 53 35.00N 92.00W
Arkansas r. U.S.A. 53 33.50N 91.00W
Arkansas City U.S.A. 53 37.03N 97.02W
Arkhangel'sk Russian Fed. 18 64.32N 41.10E
Árki i. Greece 13 37.22N 26.45E
Arklow Rep. of Ire. 7 52.47N 6.10W
Arkville U.S.A. 55 42.09N 74.37W
Arlberg Pass Austria 14 47.00N 10.05E
Arles France 11 43.41N 4.38E
Arlington Oreg. U.S.A. 54 45.16N120.13W
Arlington Va. U.S.A. 55 38.52N 77.05W
Arlon Belgium 8 49.41N 5.49E
Armadale Australia 43 32.10S115.57E
Armagh U.K. 7 54.21N 6.41W
Armagh d. U.K. 7 54.16N 6.35W
Armançon r. France 9 47.57N 3.30E
Armavir Russian Fed. 19 44.59N 41.10E
Armenia Colombia 60 4.32N 75.40W
Armenia Europe 31 40.00N 45.00E
Armenia f. Iran / Turkey / Armenia 31 40.00N 44.30E
Armeniş Romania 15 45.12N 22.19E
Armentières France 8 50.41N 2.53E
Armidale Australia 47 30.32S151.40E
Arnaud r. Canada 51 60.00N 69.45W

B

Ballyconnell Rep. of Ire. **7** 54.06N 7.37W
Ballydehob Rep. of Ire. **7** 51.34N 9.28W
Ballydonegan Rep. of Ire. **7** 51.38N 10.04W
Ballygar Rep. of Ire. **7** 53.32N 8.20W
Ballygawley U.K. **7** 54.28N 7.03W
Ballykelly U.K. **7** 55.03N 7.00W
Ballymena U.K. **7** 54.52N 6.17W
Ballymoney U.K. **7** 55.04N 6.31W
Ballyquintin Pt. U.K. **7** 54.40N 5.30W
Ballyragget Rep. of Ire. **7** 52.47N 7.21W
Ballyshannon Rep. of Ire. **7** 54.30N 8.11W
Ballyvaughan Rep. of Ire. **7** 53.06N 9.09W
Ballyvourney Rep. of Ire. **7** 51.57N 9.10W
Balmoral Australia **46** 37.17S141.50E
Balochistan *f.* Pakistan **28** 28.00N 66.00E
Balonne *r.* Australia **47** 28.30S148.20E
Balrâmpur India **29** 27.26N 82.11E
Balranald Australia **46** 34.37S143.37E
Balş Romania **15** 44.21N 24.06E
Balsas *r.* Brazil **61** 9.00S 48.10W
Balsas *r.* Mexico **56** 18.10N102.05W
Balta Ukraine **15** 47.58N 29.39E
Baltanás Spain **10** 41.56N 4.15W
Baltasar Brum Uruguay **63** 30.44S 57.19W
Baltic Sea Europe **17** 57.00N 20.00E
Balţîm Egypt **32** 31.34N 31.05E
Baltimore Md. U.S.A. **55** 39.17N 76.37W
Baltiysk Russian Fed. **17** 54.39N 19.55E
Balumbah Australia **46** 33.16S136.14E
Balygychan Russian Fed. **21** 63.55N154.12E
Balykshi Kazakhstan **19** 47.04N 51.55E
Bām Iran **31** 29.07N 58.20E
Bama Nigeria **38** 11.35N 13.40E
Bamaga Australia **44** 10.52S142.23E
Bamako Mali **34** 12.40N 7.59W
Bamba Kenya **37** 3.33S 39.32E
Bamba Mali **38** 17.05N 1.23W
Bambari C.A.R. **36** 5.40N 20.37E
Bamberg Germany **14** 49.54N 10.53E
Bambuí Brazil **59** 20.01S 45.59W
Bam Co *l.* China **29** 31.30N 91.10E
Bamenda Cameroon **38** 5.55N 10.09E
Bampton Devon U.K. **5** 51.00N 3.29W
Bampūr Iran **31** 27.13N 60.29E
Bampūr *r.* Iran **31** 27.18N 59.02E
Bāmra Hills India **29** 21.30N 84.30E
Banagher Rep. of Ire. **7** 53.12N 8.00W
Bananal, Ilha do *f.* Brazil **61** 11.30S 50.15W
Banâs, Ra's *c.* Egypt **30** 23.54N 35.48E
Ban Ban Laos **29** 19.38N103.34E
Banbridge U.K. **7** 54.21N 6.17W
Banbury U.K. **5** 52.04N 1.21W
Banchory U.K. **6** 57.03N 2.30W
Bancroft Canada **55** 45.03N 77.51W
Banda Gabon **36** 3.47S 11.04E
Banda, Laut *sea* Indonesia **27** 5.00S128.00E
Banda Aceh Indonesia **26** 5.35N 95.20E
Banda Besar *i.* Indonesia **27** 4.30S129.55E
Bandama *r.* Ivory Coast **38** 5.10N 4.59W
Bandar 'Abbās Iran **31** 27.10N 56.15E
Bandar Beheshtī Iran **31** 25.17N 60.41E
Bandar-e Anzalī Iran **31** 37.26N 49.29E
Bandar-e Deylam Iran **31** 30.05N 50.11E
Bandar-e Khomeynī Iran **31** 30.26N 49.03E
Bandar-e-Lengeh Iran **31** 26.34N 54.53E
Bandar-e Rīg Iran **31** 29.30N 50.40E
Bandar-e Torkeman Iran **31** 36.55N 54.05E
Bandar Seri Begawan Brunei **26** 4.56N114.58E
Banda Sea *see* Banda, Laut *sea* Indonesia **27**
Bandawe Malaŵi **37** 11.57S 34.11E
Bandeira *mtn.* Brazil **59** 20.25S 41.45W
Bandiagara Mali **38** 14.12N 3.29W
Bandirma Turkey **13** 40.22N 28.00E
Bandon Rep. of Ire. **7** 51.45N 8.45W
Bandon *r.* Rep. of Ire. **7** 51.43N 8.38W
Bandundu Zaïre **36** 3.20S 17.24E
Bandung Indonesia **26** 6.57S107.34E
Banes Cuba **57** 20.59N 75.24W
Banff Canada **50** 51.10N115.34W
Banff U.K. **6** 57.40N 2.31W
Banfora Burkina **38** 10.36N 4.45W
Bangalore India **28** 12.58N 77.35E
Bangassou C.A.R. **35** 4.41N 22.48E
Banggai, Kepulauan *is.* Indonesia **27** 1.30S123.10E
Banggi *i.* Malaysia **26** 7.17N117.12E
Bangong Co *l.* China **29** 33.45N 79.15E
Banghāzī Libya **34** 32.07N 20.05E
Bangka *i.* Indonesia **26** 2.20S106.10E
Bangkok Thailand **29** 13.45N100.35E
Bangladesh Asia **29** 24.00N 90.00E
Bangor Rep. of Ire. **7** 54.09N 9.44W
Bangor U.K. **4** 53.13N 4.09W
Bangor U.K. **7** 54.40N 5.41W
Bangor Maine U.S.A. **55** 44.49N 68.47W
Bang Saphan Thailand **29** 11.14N 99.31E
Bangui C.A.R. **36** 4.23N 18.37E
Bangweulu, L. Zambia **37** 11.15S 29.45E
Banhâ Egypt **32** 30.28N 31.11E
Ban Hat Yai Thailand **26** 7.00N100.28E
Ban Houayxay Laos **29** 20.21N100.26E
Bani *r.* Mali **38** 14.30N 4.15W
Banikoara Benin **38** 11.21N 2.25E
Banī Mazār Egypt **32** 28.29N 30.48E
Banī Suwayf Egypt **32** 29.05N 31.05E
Bāniyās Syria **32** 35.09N 35.58E
Banja Luka Bosnia-Herzegovina **13** 44.47N 17.10E
Banjarmasin Indonesia **26** 3.22S114.36E
Banjul Gambia **34** 13.28N 16.39W
Banka Banka Australia **44** 18.48S134.01E
Ban Kantang Thailand **29** 7.25N 99.30E
Bankasse Mali **38** 14.01N 3.29W
Banks I. N.W.T. Canada **50** 73.00N122.00W
Banks Pen. New Zealand **48** 43.45S173.10E
Banks Str. Australia **45** 40.37S148.07E
Ban-m'drack Vietnam **26** 12.42N108.47E
Bann *r.* U.K. **7** 55.10N 6.46W
Bannockburn U.K. **6** 56.06N 3.55W
Bannockburn Zimbabwe **39** 20.16S 29.51E
Banská Bystrica Czech. **15** 48.44N 19.07E
Bantaeng Indonesia **26** 5.32S119.58E
Banté Benin **38** 8.26N 1.54E
Bantry Rep. of Ire. **7** 51.41N 9.27W
Bantry B. Rep. of Ire. **7** 51.40N 9.40W
Banyak, Kepulauan *is.* Indonesia **26** 2.15N 97.10E
Banyo Cameroon **38** 6.47N 11.50E
Banyuwangi Indonesia **26** 8.12S114.22E
Banzare Coast *f.* Antarctica **64** 66.30S125.00E
Baoding China **25** 38.54N115.26E
Baoji China **24** 34.23N107.16E
Baoshan China **29** 25.07N 99.08E
Baotou China **25** 40.38N109.59E
Bapaume France **8** 50.07N 2.51E
Ba'qūbah Iraq **31** 33.45N 44.38E
Bar Albania **13** 42.05N 19.06E
Bar Ukraine **15** 49.05N 27.40E
Bara Nigeria **38** 10.24N 10.43E
Baraawe Somali Rep. **37** 1.02N 44.02E
Barabinsk Russian Fed. **20** 55.20N 78.18E
Baracoa Cuba **57** 20.23N 74.31W
Baradero Argentina **63** 33.50S 59.30W
Baradine Australia **47** 30.56S149.05E
Baradine *r.* Australia **47** 30.17S148.27E
Barahona Dom. Rep. **57** 18.13N 71.07W
Baraka Zaïre **37** 4.09S 29.05E
Bārāmūla Jammu & Kashmir **28** 34.12N 74.21E
Baranoa Colombia **60** 10.50N 74.55W
Baranof I. U.S.A. **50** 57.05N135.00W
Baranovichi Belorussia **15** 53.09N 26.00E
Baratta Australia **46** 32.01S139.10E
Barbacena Brazil **59** 21.13S 43.47W
Barbados Lesser Antilles **57** 13.20N 59.40W
Barbar Sudan **35** 18.01N 33.59E
Barbastro Spain **10** 42.02N 0.07E
Barberton R.S.A. **39** 25.46S 31.02E
Barbezieux France **11** 45.28N 0.09W
Barbuda *i.* Leeward Is. **57** 17.41N 61.48W
Barcaldine Australia **44** 23.31S145.15E
Barcellona Italy **12** 38.10N 15.13E
Barcelona Spain **10** 41.25N 2.10E
Barcelona Venezuela **60** 10.08N 64.43W
Barcelos Brazil **60** 0.59S 62.58W
Barcoo *r.* Australia **44** 25.30S142.50E
Barcs Hungary **13** 45.58N 17.28E
Barcs Hungary **15** 45.58N 17.28E
Bardai Chad **34** 21.21N 16.56E
Bardejov Czech. **15** 49.18N 21.16E
Bardi Italy **9** 44.38N 9.44E
Bardsey *i.* U.K. **4** 52.45N 4.48W
Bardu Norway **16** 68.54N 18.20E
Bardufoss Norway **16** 69.00N 18.30E
Bareilly India **29** 28.20N 79.24E
Barellan Australia **47** 34.17S146.34E
Barentsovo More *see* Barents Sea Arctic Oc. **18**
Barents Sea Arctic Oc. **18** 73.00N 40.00E
Barfleur France **9** 49.40N 1.15W
Barge Italy **9** 44.43N 7.20E
Barguzin Russian Fed. **21** 53.40N109.35E
Barham Australia **46** 35.37S144.10E
Bari Italy **13** 41.08N 16.52E
Baricho Kenya **37** 3.07S 39.47E
Barīm *i.* Yemen **35** 12.40N 43.24E
Barinas Venezuela **60** 8.36N 70.15W
Bariri Brazil **59** 22.04S 48.41W
Bâris Egypt **30** 24.40N 30.36E
Barisāl Bangla. **29** 22.41N 90.20E
Barisan, Pegunungan *mts.* Indonesia **26** 3.30S102.30E
Barito *r.* Indonesia **26** 3.35S114.35E
Barker L. Australia **43** 31.45S120.05E
Barking U.K. **5** 51.32N 0.05E
Barkly East R.S.A. **39** 30.58S 27.33E
Barkly Tableland *f.* Australia **42** 19.00S136.40E
Barkly West R.S.A. **39** 28.32S 24.29E
Bar-le-Duc France **11** 48.46N 5.10E
Barlee, L. Australia **43** 29.30S119.30E
Barlee Range *mts.* Australia **42** 23.40S116.00E
Barletta Italy **12** 41.20N 16.15E
Barmedman Australia **47** 34.08S147.25E
Barmera Australia **46** 34.15S140.31E
Barm Fīrūz, Kūh-e *mtn.* Iran **31** 30.21N 52.00E
Barmouth U.K. **4** 52.44N 4.03W
Barnard Castle *town* U.K. **4** 54.33N 1.55W
Barnato Australia **47** 31.38S144.59E
Barnaul Russian Fed. **20** 53.21N 83.15E
Barnet U.K. **5** 51.39N 0.11W
Barneveld Neth. **8** 52.10N 5.39E
Barneville France **9** 49.23N 1.45W
Barneys L. Australia **46** 33.16S144.13E
Barnsley U.K. **4** 53.33N 1.29W
Barnstaple U.K. **5** 51.05N 4.03W
Baro Nigeria **38** 8.37N 6.19E
Barqah *f.* Libya **35** 31.00N 22.10E
Barquisimeto Venezuela **60** 10.03N 69.18W
Barra Brazil **61** 11.06S 43.15W
Barra *i.* U.K. **6** 56.59N 7.28W
Barra, Sd. of U.K. **6** 57.04N 7.20W
Barraba Australia **47** 30.24S152.36E
Barra do Corda Brazil **61** 5.30S 45.15W
Barra do Piraí Brazil **59** 22.28S 43.49W
Barragem Agua Vermelha *resr* Brazil **59** 19.50S 50.00W
Barragem de Sáo Simão *resr* Brazil **59** 18.35S 50.00W
Barra Mansa Brazil **59** 22.35S 44.12W
Barranca Peru **60** 4.50S 76.40W
Barrancabermeja Colombia **60** 7.06N 73.54W
Barrancas Venezuela **60** 8.45N 62.13W
Barrancos Portugal **10** 38.10N 7.01W
Barranqueras Argentina **59** 27.30S 58.55W
Barranquilla Colombia **60** 11.10N 74.50W
Barraute Canada **55** 48.26N 77.39W
Barre U.S.A. **55** 44.12N 72.30W
Barreiras Brazil **61** 12.09S 44.58W
Barreiro Portugal **10** 38.40N 9.05W
Barreiros Brazil **61** 8.49S 35.12W
Barrême France **14** 43.57N 6.22E
Barretos Brazil **59** 20.37S 48.38W
Barrhead U.K. **6** 55.47N 4.24W
Barrie Canada **55** 44.24N 79.40W
Barrier Range *mts.* Australia **46** 31.25S141.25E
Barrington Tops *mts.* Australia **47** 32.30S151.28E
Barringun Australia **47** 29.01S145.43E
Barron U.S.A. **54** 48.44N120.43W
Barrow *r.* Rep. of Ire. **7** 52.17N 7.00W
Barrow U.S.A. **50** 71.16N156.50W
Barrow Creek *town* Australia **44** 21.32S133.53E
Barrow I. Australia **42** 21.40S115.27E
Barrow-in-Furness U.K. **4** 54.08N 3.15W
Barrow Range *mts.* Australia **42** 26.04S127.28E
Barry U.K. **5** 51.23N 3.19W
Barstow U.S.A. **54** 34.54N117.01W
Bar-sur-Aube France **9** 48.14N 4.43E
Bar-sur-Seine France **9** 48.07N 4.22E
Bartica Guyana **60** 6.24N 58.38W
Bartin Turkey **30** 41.37N 32.20E
Bartle Frere, Mt. Australia **44** 17.23S145.49E
Bartlesville U.S.A. **53** 36.44N 95.59W
Bartolomeu Dias Mozambique **39** 21.10S 35.09E
Barton-upon-Humber U.K. **4** 53.41N 0.27W
Bartoszyce Poland **15** 54.16N 20.49E
Barwon *r.* Australia **47** 30.00S148.05E
Barysh Russian Fed. **18** 53.40N 47.09E
Basavilbaso Argentina **63** 32.20S 58.52W
Basel Switz. **14** 47.33N 7.36E
Bashi Channel Phil. / Taiwan **25** 21.40N121.20E
Basilan Phil. **27** 6.40N121.59E
Basilan *i.* Phil. **27** 6.40N122.10E
Basildon U.K. **5** 51.34N 0.25E
Basilicata *d.* Italy **12** 40.30N 16.20E
Basin U.S.A. **54** 44.23N108.02W
Basingstoke U.K. **5** 51.15N 1.05W
Baskatong, Résr. Canada **55** 46.48N 75.50W
Basoko Zaïre **36** 1.20N 23.36E
Bassano Canada **50** 50.47N112.28W
Bassano Italy **9** 45.46N 11.44E
Bassari Togo **38** 9.12N 0.18E
Bassein Burma **29** 16.45N 94.30E
Basse Normandie *d.* France **9** 49.00N 0.00
Basse-Terre Guadeloupe **57** 16.00N 61.43W
Bass Str. Australia **45** 39.45S146.00E
Bassum Germany **14** 52.51N 8.43E
Båstad Sweden **17** 56.26N 12.51E
Bastak Iran **31** 27.15N 54.26E
Bastelica France **11** 42.00N 9.03E
Bastia France **11** 42.41N 9.26E
Bastogne Belgium **8** 50.00N 5.43E
Basyûn Egypt **32** 30.57N 30.49E
Bata Equat. Guinea **38** 1.51N 9.49E
Batabanó, Golfo de *g.* Cuba **57** 23.15N 82.30W
Batalha Portugal **10** 39.39N 8.50W
Batang China **29** 30.02N 99.01E
Batangas Phil. **27** 13.46N121.01E
Batan Is. Phil. **27** 20.50N121.55E
Bátaszék Hungary **15** 46.12N 18.44E
Batatais Brazil **59** 20.54S 47.37W
Bataysk Russian Fed. **19** 47.09N 39.46E
Batchelor Australia **44** 13.04S131.01E
Bătdâmbâng Cambodia **26** 13.06N103.13E
Batemans Bay *town* Australia **47** 35.55S150.09E
Bath Canada **55** 46.30N 67.36W
Bath U.K. **5** 51.22N 2.22W
Bath Maine U.S.A. **55** 43.55N 69.49W
Bath N.Y. U.S.A. **55** 42.20N 77.19W
Baṭḥā, Wādī al *r.* Oman **31** 20.01N 59.39E
Bathgate U.K. **6** 55.44N 3.38W
Bathurst Australia **47** 33.27S149.35E
Bathurst Canada **55** 47.37N 65.40W
Bathurst R.S.A. **39** 33.30S 26.48E
Bathurst, C. Canada **50** 70.30N128.00W
Bathurst I. Australia **42** 11.45S130.15E
Bathurst I. Canada **51** 76.00N100.00W
Bathurst Inlet *town* Canada **50** 66.48N108.00W
Batié Burkina **38** 9.42N 2.53W
Batina Croatia **15** 45.51N 18.51E
Batley U.K. **4** 53.43N 1.38W
Batlow Australia **47** 35.32S148.10E
Batman Turkey **30** 37.52N 41.07E
Batna Algeria **34** 35.34N 6.11E
Baton Rouge U.S.A. **53** 30.30N 91.10W
Batopilas Mexico **56** 27.00N107.45W
Batouri Cameroon **38** 4.26N 14.27E
Batticaloa Sri Lanka **29** 7.43N 81.42E
Battle U.K. **5** 50.55N 0.30E
Battle Creek *town* U.S.A. **55** 42.20N 85.11W
Battle Harbour Canada **51** 52.16N 55.36W
Batu, Kepulauan *is.* Indonesia **26** 0.30S 98.20E
Batumi Georgia **30** 41.37N 41.36E
Batu Pahat Malaysia **26** 1.50N102.48E
Baturaja Indonesia **26** 4.10S104.10E
Baturité Brazil **61** 4.20S 38.53W
Bat Yam Israel **32** 32.01N 34.45E
Baubau Indonesia **27** 5.30S122.37E
Bauchi Nigeria **38** 10.16N 9.50E
Bauchi *d.* Nigeria **38** 10.40N 10.00E
Baugé France **9** 47.33N 0.06W
Bauld, C. Canada **51** 51.30N 55.45W
Bauru Brazil **59** 22.19S 49.07W
Baús Brazil **59** 18.19S 53.10W
Bauska Latvia **17** 56.24N 24.14E
Bautzen Germany **14** 51.11N 14.29E
Bavay France **8** 50.18N 3.48E
Bawean *i.* Indonesia **26** 5.50S112.35E
Bawku Ghana **38** 11.05N 0.13W
Bayamo Cuba **57** 20.23N 76.39W
Bayamón Puerto Rico **57** 18.24N 66.10W
Bayan Har Shan *mts.* China **24** 34.00N 97.20E
Bayburt Turkey **30** 40.15N 40.16E
Bay City Mich. U.S.A. **55** 43.35N 83.52W
Baydaratskaya Guba *b.* Russian Fed. **20** 70.00N 66.00E
Baydhabo Somali Rep. **37** 3.08N 43.34E
Bayern *d.* Germany **14** 48.30N 11.30E
Bayeux France **9** 49.16N 0.42W
Baykal, Ozero *l.* Russian Fed. **24** 53.30N100.00E
Baykit Russian Fed. **21** 61.45N 96.22E
Baykonyr Kazakhstan **20** 47.50N 66.03E
Bay of Plenty *d.* New Zealand **48** 38.00S177.10E
Bayombong Phil. **27** 16.27N121.10E
Bayonne France **11** 43.30N 1.28W
Bayovar Peru **60** 5.50S 81.03W
Bayreuth Germany **14** 49.56N 11.35E
Bayrūt Lebanon **32** 33.52N 35.30E
Baytik Shan *mts.* China **24** 45.15N 90.50E
Bay View New Zealand **48** 39.26S176.52E
Baza Spain **10** 37.30N 2.45W
Baza, Sierra de *mts.* Spain **10** 37.15N 2.45W
Bazaliya Ukraine **15** 49.42N 26.29E
Bazaruto, Ilha do *i.* Mozambique **39** 21.40S 35.28E
Bazas France **11** 44.26N 0.13W
Bazmān Iran **31** 27.48N 60.12E
Bazmān, Kūh-e *mtn.* Iran **31** 28.06N 60.00E
Beachport Australia **46** 37.29S140.01E
Beachy Head U.K. **5** 50.43N 0.15E
Beagle Bay Australia **42** 16.58S122.40E
Bear I. *see* Bjørnøya *i.* Arctic Oc. **64**
Bear L. U.S.A. **54** 42.00N111.20W
Beatrice U.S.A. **53** 40.17N 96.45W
Beatrice, C. Australia **44** 14.15S136.59E
Beatty U.S.A. **54** 36.54N116.46W
Beattyville Canada **55** 48.53N 77.10W
Beauce *f.* France **9** 48.22N 1.50E
Beaudesert Australia **47** 27.58S153.01E
Beaufort Australia **46** 37.28S143.28E
Beaufort Sea N. America **50** 72.00N141.00W
Beaufort West R.S.A. **39** 32.20S 22.34E
Beaugency France **9** 47.47N 1.38E
Beauly U.K. **6** 57.29N 4.29W
Beauly *r.* U.K. **6** 57.29N 4.25W
Beaumaris U.K. **4** 53.16N 4.07W
Beaumetz-lès-Loges France **8** 50.15N 2.36E
Beaumont Belgium **8** 50.14N 4.16E
Beaumont Tex. U.S.A. **53** 30.04N 94.06W
Beaumont-le-Roger France **9** 49.05N 0.47E
Beaumont-sur-Sarthe France **9** 48.13N 0.07E
Beaune France **11** 47.02N 4.50E
Beaune-la-Rolande France **9** 48.04N 2.26E
Beaupréau France **11** 47.12N 0.59W
Beauvais France **9** 49.26N 2.05E
Beauval Canada **50** 55.09N107.35W
Beauvoir France **11** 46.55N 2.01W
Beaver Alaska U.S.A. **50** 66.22N147.24W
Beaver I. U.S.A. **55** 45.42N 85.28W
Beāwar India **28** 26.02N 74.20E
Bebedouro Brazil **59** 20.54S 48.31W
Bebington U.K. **4** 53.23N 3.01W
Beccles U.K. **5** 52.27N 1.33E
Bečej Yugo. **15** 45.37N 20.03E
Béchar Algeria **34** 31.35N 2.17W
Beckley U.S.A. **53** 37.46N 81.12W
Beckum Germany **8** 51.45N 8.02E
Beclean Romania **15** 47.11N 24.10E
Bédarieux France **11** 43.35N 3.10E
Bedford U.K. **5** 52.08N 0.29W
Bedford U.S.A. **55** 38.51N 86.30W
Bedford, C. Australia **44** 15.14S145.21E
Bedford Levels *f.* U.K. **5** 52.35N 0.08W
Bedfordshire *d.* U.K. **5** 52.04N 0.28W
Bedlington U.K. **4** 55.08N 1.34W
Bedourie Australia **44** 24.21S139.28E
Beech Grove U.S.A. **55** 39.42N 86.06W
Beechworth Australia **47** 36.23S146.42E
Beenleigh Australia **47** 27.43S153.09E
Be'er Menuha Israel **32** 30.19N 35.08E
Be'er Sheva' Israel **32** 31.15N 34.47E
Beerta Neth. **8** 53.12N 7.07E
Beeston U.K. **4** 52.55N 1.11W
Beeville U.S.A. **52** 28.25N 97.47W
Beg, Lough U.K. **7** 54.47N 6.29W
Bega Australia **47** 36.41S149.50E
Bègles France **11** 44.48N 0.32W
Begna *r.* Norway **17** 60.32N 10.00E
Behbehān Iran **31** 30.35N 50.17E
Bei'an China **25** 48.17N126.33E
Beihai China **25** 21.29N109.10E
Beijing China **25** 39.55N116.25E
Beijing Shi *d.* China **25** 40.15N116.30E
Beilen Neth. **8** 52.51N 6.31E
Beinn Dearg *mtn.* U.K. **6** 57.47N 4.55W
Beipa'a P.N.G. **44** 8.30S146.35E
Beira Mozambique **39** 19.49S 34.52E
Beirut *see* Bayrūt Lebanon **32**
Beitbridge Zimbabwe **39** 22.10S 30.01E
Beiuş Romania **15** 46.40N 22.21E
Beja Portugal **10** 38.01N 7.52W
Bejaïa Algeria **34** 36.45N 5.05E
Béjar Spain **10** 40.24N 5.45W
Bejestān Iran **31** 34.32N 58.08E
Bejoording Australia **43** 31.22S116.30E
Békés Hungary **15** 46.46N 21.08E
Békéscsaba Hungary **15** 46.41N 21.06E
Bela India **29** 25.55N 82.00E
Bela Pakistan **28** 26.12N 66.20E
Bélabo Cameroon **38** 5.00N 13.20E
Bela Crkva Yugo. **15** 44.54N 21.26E
Bel Air U.S.A. **55** 39.32N 76.21W
Belalcázar Spain **10** 38.35N 5.10W
Belang Indonesia **27** 0.58N124.56E
Bela Vista Brazil **62** 22.05S 56.22W
Bela Vista Mozambique **39** 26.20S 32.41E
Belaya *r.* Russian Fed. **20** 55.40N 52.30E
Belaya Glina Russian Fed. **19** 46.04N 40.54E
Belaya Tserkov Ukraine **15** 49.49N 30.10E
Belcher Is. Canada **51** 56.00N 79.00W
Belcoo U.K. **7** 54.18N 7.53W
Belebey Russian Fed. **18** 54.05N 54.07E
Beled Weyne Somali Rep. **35** 4.47N 45.12E
Belém Brazil **61** 1.27S 48.29W
Belem Mozambique **37** 14.11S 35.59E
Belén Uruguay **63** 30.47S 57.47W
Belen U.S.A. **52** 34.40N106.46W
Belén, Cuchilla de *mts.* Uruguay **63** 30.49S 56.28W
Belev Russian Fed. **18** 53.50N 36.08E
Belfast U.K. **7** 54.36N 5.57W
Belfast Maine U.S.A. **55** 44.27N 69.01W
Belfast Lough U.K. **7** 54.42N 5.45W
Belfort France **11** 47.38N 6.52E
Belfry U.S.A. **54** 45.09N109.01W
Belgaum India **28** 15.54N 74.36E
Belgium Europe **8** 51.00N 4.30E
Belgorod Russian Fed. **19** 50.38N 36.36E
Belgorod-Dnestrovskiy Ukraine **15** 46.10N 30.19E
Belgrade *see* Beograd Yugo. **15**
Beli Nigeria **38** 7.53N 10.59E
Belitung *i.* Indonesia **26** 3.00S108.00E
Belize Belize **57** 17.29N 88.20W
Belize C. America **57** 17.00N 88.30W
Belka Australia **43** 31.45S118.09E
Bellac France **11** 46.07N 1.04E
Bella Coola Canada **50** 52.22N126.46W
Bellagio Italy **9** 45.59N 9.15E
Bellaria Italy **9** 44.09N 12.28E
Bellary India **28** 15.11N 76.54E
Bellata Australia **47** 29.55S149.50E
Bella Unión Uruguay **63** 30.15S 57.35W
Bella Vista Corrientes Argentina **62** 28.30S 59.00W
Bella Vista Tucuman Argentina **62** 27.02S 65.19W
Bellbrook Australia **47** 30.48S152.30E
Bellefontaine U.S.A. **55** 40.22N 83.45W
Belle Île France **11** 47.20N 3.10W
Belle Isle, Str. of Canada **51** 51.35N 56.30W
Bellême France **9** 48.22N 0.34E
Belleville Canada **55** 44.10N 77.23W
Bellevue Idaho U.S.A. **54** 43.28N114.16W
Bellevue Penn. U.S.A. **55** 40.32N 80.08W
Bellevue Wash. U.S.A. **54** 47.37N122.12W
Bellingen Australia **47** 30.28S152.43E
Bellingham U.K. **4** 55.09N 2.16W
Bellingham U.S.A. **54** 48.46N122.29W
Bellingshausen Sea Antarctica **64** 70.00S 88.00W
Bellinzona Switz. **9** 46.11N 9.02E
Bello Colombia **60** 6.20N 75.41W
Belluno Italy **9** 46.09N 12.13E
Bell Ville Argentina **63** 32.35S 62.41W
Bélmez Spain **10** 38.17N 5.17W
Belmont Australia **47** 33.02S151.40E
Belmopan Belize **57** 17.25N 88.46W
Belmullet Rep. of Ire. **7** 54.14N 10.00W
Belogradchik Bulgaria **15** 43.38N 22.41E
Belo Horizonte Brazil **59** 19.45S 43.54W
Belo Jardim Brazil **61** 8.22S 36.22W
Belokorovichi Ukraine **15** 51.04N 28.00E
Belomorsk Russian Fed. **18** 64.34N 34.45E
Beloretsk Russian Fed. **18** 53.59N 58.20E
Belorussia Europe **15** 53.30N 28.00E
Beloye More *sea* Russian Fed. **18** 65.30N 38.00E
Beloye Ozero *l.* Russian Fed. **18** 60.12N 37.45E
Belozersk Russian Fed. **18** 60.00N 37.49E
Belper U.K. **4** 53.02N 1.29W
Beltana Australia **46** 30.40S138.27E
Belterra Brazil **61** 2.38S 54.57W
Belton Australia **46** 32.12S138.45E
Beltsy Moldavia **15** 47.45N 27.59E
Belukha, Gora *mtn.* Russian Fed. **24** 49.48N 86.40E
Belyando *r.* Australia **44** 21.38S146.50E
Belyayevka Ukraine **15** 46.30N 30.12E
Belynichi Belorussia **15** 54.00N 29.42E
Belyy, Ostrov Russian Fed. **20** 73.10N 70.45E
Belyy Yar Russian Fed. **20** 58.28N 85.03E
Belzec Poland **15** 50.24N 23.26E
Bemidji U.S.A. **53** 47.29N 94.52W
Benagerie Australia **46** 31.30S140.21E
Benalla Australia **47** 36.35S145.58E
Benanee Australia **46** 34.32S142.56E
Benares *see* Vārānasi India **29**
Benavente Spain **10** 42.00N 5.40W
Benbecula *i.* U.K. **6** 57.26N 7.18W
Ben Cruachan *mtn.* U.K. **6** 56.26N 5.18W
Bencubbin Australia **43** 30.48S117.52E
Bend U.S.A. **54** 44.03N121.19W
Bende Nigeria **38** 5.34N 7.37E
Bendemeer Australia **47** 30.52S151.10E
Bendery Moldavia **15** 46.50N 29.29E
Bendigo Australia **46** 36.48S144.21E
Bendoc Australia **47** 37.10S148.55E
Bendorf Germany **8** 50.26N 7.34E
Bénéna Mali **38** 13.09N 4.17W
Benešov Czech. **14** 49.45N 14.22E
Benevento Italy **12** 41.07N 14.46E
Bengal, B. of Indian Oc. **29** 17.00N 89.00E
Bengbu China **25** 32.56N117.27E
Benghazi *see* Banghāzī Libya **34**
Bengkulu Indonesia **26** 3.46S102.16E
Benguela Angola **36** 12.34S 13.24E
Ben Hope *mtn.* U.K. **6** 58.24N 4.36W
Beni *r.* Bolivia **62** 10.23S 65.24W
Beni Zaïre **37** 0.29N 29.27E
Beni Abbes Algeria **34** 30.08N 2.10W
Benicarló Spain **10** 40.25N 0.25E
Benidorm Spain **10** 38.33N 0.09W
Benin Africa **38** 9.00N 2.30E
Benin, Bight of Africa **38** 5.30N 3.00E
Benin City Nigeria **38** 6.19N 5.41E
Benjamin Constant Brazil **60** 4.22S 70.02W
Ben Lawers *mtn.* U.K. **6** 56.33N 4.14W
Ben Lomond *mtn.* U.K. **6** 56.12N 4.38W
Ben Macdhui *mtn.* U.K. **6** 57.04N 3.40W
Ben More *mtn.* Central U.K. **6** 56.23N 4.31W
Ben More *mtn.* Strath. U.K. **6** 56.26N 6.02W
Ben More Assynt *mtn.* U.K. **6** 58.07N 4.52W
Bennett Canada **50** 59.49N135.01W
Bennett, L. Australia **44** 22.50S131.01E
Ben Nevis *mtn.* U.K. **6** 56.48N 5.00W
Benneydale New Zealand **48** 38.31S175.21E

76

Borgomanero Italy 9 45.42N 8.28E
Borgo San Dalmazzo Italy 9 44.20N 7.30E
Borgo San Lorenzo Italy 9 43.57N 11.23E
Borgosesia Italy 9 45.43N 8.16E
Borgo Val di Taro Italy 9 44.29N 9.46E
Borgund Norway 17 61.03N 7.49E
Borislav Ukraine 15 49.18N 23.28E
Borisoglebsk Russian Fed. 19 51.23N 42.02E
Borisov Belorussia 15 54.09N 28.30E
Borispol Ukraine 15 50.21N 30.59E
Borja Peru 60 4.20S 77.40W
Borken Germany 8 51.50N 6.52E
Borkum Germany 8 53.34N 6.41E
Borkum *i.* Germany 8 53.35N 6.45E
Borlänge Sweden 17 60.29N 15.25E
Borley, C. Antarctica 64 66.15S 55.00E
Bormio Italy 9 46.28N 10.22E
Borndiep *g.* Neth. 8 53.28N 5.35E
Borneo *i.* Asia 26 1.00N 114.00E
Bornheim Germany 8 50.45N 7.00E
Bornholm *i.* Denmark 17 55.10N 15.00E
Borno *d.* Nigeria 38 11.20N 12.40E
Bornu, Plain of *f.* Nigeria 38 12.30N 13.00E
Boro *r.* Sudan 35 8.50N 28.00E
Borodyanka Ukraine 15 50.38N 29.59E
Boromo Burkina 38 11.43N 2.53W
Boroughbridge U.K. 4 54.06N 1.23W
Borovichi Russian Fed. 18 58.22N 34.00E
Borrika Australia 46 35.00S 140.05E
Borroloola Australia 44 16.04S 136.17E
Borşa Romania 15 46.56N 23.40E
Borşa Romania 15 47.39N 24.40E
Borth U.K. 5 52.29N 4.03W
Borūjerd Iran 31 33.54N 48.47E
Bory Tucholskie *f.* Poland 15 53.45N 17.30E
Borzhomi Georgia 19 41.49N 43.23E
Borzna Ukraine 19 51.15N 32.25E
Borzya Russian Fed. 21 50.24N 116.35E
Bosa Italy 12 40.18N 8.29E
Bosanska Gradiška Croatia 13 45.09N 17.15E
Bosanski Novi Bosnia-Herzegovina 14 45.03N 16.23E
Boscastle U.K. 5 50.42N 4.42W
Boshof R.S.A. 39 28.32S 25.12E
Bosna *r.* Bosnia-Herzegovina 13 45.04N 18.27E
Bosnia-Herzegovina Europe 13 44.00N 18.10E
Bosnik Indonesia 27 1.09S 136.14E
Bōsō-hantō *pen.* Japan 23 35.08N 140.00E
Bosporus *str. see* Istanbul Bogazi *str.* Turkey 13
Bossangoa C.A.R. 36 6.27N 17.21E
Bosso Niger 38 13.43N 13.19E
Bosten Hu *l.* China 24 42.00N 87.00E
Boston U.K. 4 52.59N 0.02W
Boston U.S.A. 55 42.21N 71.04W
Botany B. Australia 47 34.04S 151.08E
Botev *mtn.* Bulgaria 13 42.43N 24.55E
Botevgrad Bulgaria 13 42.55N 23.57E
Bothnia, G. of Europe 16 63.30N 20.30E
Botletle *r.* Botswana 39 21.06S 24.47E
Botoşani Romania 15 47.44N 26.41E
Botou Burkina 38 12.47N 2.02E
Botrange *mtn.* Belgium 8 50.30N 6.04E
Botro Ivory Coast 38 7.51N 5.19W
Botswana Africa 39 22.00S 24.15E
Bottrop Germany 8 51.31N 6.55E
Botucatu Brazil 59 22.52S 48.30W
Bouaflé Ivory Coast 38 7.01N 5.47W
Bouaké Ivory Coast 38 7.42N 5.00W
Bouar C.A.R. 38 5.58N 15.35E
Bou Arfa Morocco 34 32.30N 1.59W
Bouchoir France 9 49.45N 2.41E
Bougainville *i.* Pacific Oc. 40 6.00S 155.00E
Bougouni Mali 34 11.25N 7.28W
Bouillon Belgium 8 49.48N 5.03E
Boulder Australia 43 30.55S 121.32E
Boulder U.S.A. 52 40.01N 105.17W
Boulder City U.S.A. 54 35.59N 114.50W
Boulia Australia 44 22.54S 139.54E
Boulogne France 11 50.43N 1.37E
Boulogne-Billancourt France 9 48.50N 2.15E
Boultoum Niger 38 14.45N 10.25E
Boumba *r.* Cameroon 38 2.00N 15.10E
Bouna Ivory Coast 38 9.19N 2.53W
Boundary Peak *mtn.* U.S.A. 54 37.51N 118.21W
Bountiful U.S.A. 54 40.53N 111.53W
Bouraga *well* Mali 38 19.00N 3.36W
Bourem Mali 38 16.59N 0.20W
Bourg France 11 46.12N 5.13E
Bourganeuf France 11 45.57N 1.44E
Bourges France 11 47.05N 2.23E
Bourg Madame France 11 42.26N 1.55E
Bourgogne *d.* France 11 47.10N 4.20E
Bourgogne, Canal de France 9 47.58N 3.30E
Bourgoin France 11 45.35N 5.17E
Bourgueil France 9 47.17N 0.10E
Bourke Australia 47 30.09S 145.59E
Bournemouth U.K. 5 50.43N 1.53W
Boussac France 11 46.22N 2.13E
Bouvard, C. Australia 43 32.40S 115.34E
Bovill U.S.A. 54 46.51N 116.24W
Bovril Argentina 63 31.22S 59.25W
Bowelling Australia 43 33.25S 116.27E
Bowen Australia 44 20.00S 148.15E
Bowen, Mt. Australia 47 37.11S 148.34E
Bowling Green U.S.A. 53 37.00N 86.29W
Bowling Green, C. Australia 44 19.19S 146.25E
Bowman I. Antarctica 64 65.00S 104.00E
Bowral Australia 47 34.30S 150.24E
Bowser Australia 47 36.19S 146.23E
Boxholm Sweden 17 58.12N 15.03E
Bo Xian China 25 33.40N 115.50E
Box Tank Australia 46 32.13S 142.17E
Boxtel Neth. 8 51.36N 5.20E
Boyabat Turkey 30 41.27N 34.45E
Boyanup Australia 43 33.29S 115.40E
Boyarka Ukraine 15 50.20N 30.26E
Boyd *r.* Australia 47 29.51S 152.25E
Boyle Rep. of Ire. 7 53.58N 8.19W
Boyne *r.* Rep. of Ire. 7 53.43N 6.17W
Boyoma Falls *f.* Zaïre 36 0.18N 25.30E
Boyup Brook Australia 43 33.50S 116.22E
Bozca Ada *i.* Turkey 13 39.49N 26.03E
Bozeman U.S.A. 54 45.41N 111.02W
Bozen *see* Bolzano Italy 9
Bö Nordland Norway 16 68.38N 14.35E
Bö Telemark Norway 17 59.25N 9.04E
Böhmerwald *mts.* Germany 14 49.20N 13.10E
Bömlafjorden *est.* Norway 17 59.39N 5.20E
Bömlo *i.* Norway 17 59.46N 5.13E
Börgefjell *mtn.* Norway 16 65.20N 13.45E
Börgefjell Nat. Park Norway 16 65.00N 13.58E
Bra Italy 9 44.42N 7.51E
Brabant *d.* Belgium 8 50.47N 4.30E
Brač *i.* Croatia 13 43.20N 16.38E
Bracadale, Loch U.K. 6 57.22N 6.30W
Bracebridge Canada 55 45.02N 79.19W
Bracieux France 9 47.33N 1.33E
Bräcke Sweden 16 62.44N 15.30E
Brad Romania 13 46.06N 22.48E
Bradano *r.* Italy 13 40.23N 16.52E
Bradenton U.S.A. 53 27.29N 82.33W
Bradford Canada 55 44.07N 79.34W
Bradford U.K. 4 53.47N 1.45W
Bradford Penn. U.S.A. 55 41.58N 78.39W
Bradworthy U.K. 5 50.54N 4.22W
Braemar U.K. 6 57.01N 3.24W
Braga Portugal 10 41.32N 8.26W
Bragado Argentina 63 35.10S 60.30W
Bragança Brazil 61 1.03S 46.46W
Bragança Portugal 10 41.47N 6.46W
Bragança Paulista Brazil 59 22.59S 46.32W
Bragin Belorussia 15 51.49N 30.16E
Brahmaputra *r.* Asia 29 23.50N 89.45E
Braidwood Australia 47 35.27S 149.50E
Brăila Romania 15 45.18N 27.58E
Brainerd U.S.A. 53 46.20N 94.10W
Braintree U.K. 5 51.53N 0.32E
Brålanda Sweden 17 58.34N 12.22E
Bramfield Australia 46 33.37S 134.59E
Brampton Canada 55 43.41N 79.46W
Brampton U.K. 4 54.56N 2.43W
Bramsche Germany 8 52.26N 7.59E
Branco *r.* Brazil 60 1.00S 62.00W
Brandberg *mtn.* Namibia 39 21.08S 14.35E
Brandbu Norway 17 60.28N 10.30E
Brande Denmark 17 55.57N 9.07E
Brandenburg Germany 14 52.25N 12.34E
Brandenburg *d.* Germany 14 52.15N 13.10E
Brandfort R.S.A. 39 28.41S 26.27E
Brandon Canada 51 49.50N 99.57W
Brandon Mtn. Rep. of Ire. 7 52.14N 10.15W
Brandon Pt. Rep. of Ire. 7 52.17N 10.11W
Braniewo Poland 15 54.24N 19.50E
Bransby Australia 46 28.40S 142.00E
Brasil, Planalto *mts.* Brazil 61 17.02S 50.00W
Brasiléia Brazil 60 11.00S 68.44W
Brasília Brazil 61 15.45S 47.57W
Brass Nigeria 38 4.20N 6.15E
Brasschaat Belgium 8 51.18N 4.28E
Braşov Romania 15 45.40N 25.35E
Bratislava Czech. 15 48.10N 17.10E
Bratsk Russian Fed. 21 56.20N 101.15E
Bratsk Vodokhranilishche *resr.* Russian Fed. 21 54.40N 103.00E
Bratslav Ukraine 15 48.49N 28.51E
Braunau Austria 14 48.15N 13.02E
Braunschweig Germany 14 52.15N 10.30E
Braunton U.K. 5 51.06N 4.09W
Bravo del Norte, Rio *r.* Mexico *see* Rio Grande *r.* Mexico / U.S.A. 56
Brawley U.S.A. 54 32.59N 115.31W
Bray France 9 48.25N 3.14E
Bray Rep. of Ire. 7 53.12N 6.07W
Bray Head Kerry Rep. of Ire. 7 51.53N 10.26W
Brazilian Highlands *see* Brasil, Planalto *mts.* Brazil 61
Brazos *r.* U.S.A. 53 28.55N 95.20W
Brazzaville Congo 36 4.14S 15.14E
Brčko Bosnia-Herzegovina 15 44.53N 18.48E
Brda *r.* Poland 15 53.07N 18.08E
Breadalbane *f.* U.K. 6 56.30N 4.20W
Bream B. New Zealand 48 36.00S 174.30E
Brécey France 9 48.44N 1.10W
Brechin U.K. 6 56.44N 2.40W
Breckland *f.* U.K. 5 52.28N 0.40E
Břeclav Czech. 14 48.46N 16.53E
Brecon U.K. 5 51.57N 3.23W
Brecon Beacons *mts.* U.K. 5 51.53N 3.27W
Breda Neth. 8 51.35N 4.46E
Bredasdorp R.S.A. 39 34.31S 20.03E
Bredbo Australia 47 35.57S 149.10E
Bregenz Austria 14 47.31N 9.46E
Bregovo Bulgaria 13 44.08N 22.39E
Bréhal France 9 48.53N 1.30W
Breidhafjördhur *est.* Iceland 16 65.15N 23.00W
Breim Norway 17 61.44N 6.25E
Brekstad Norway 16 63.42N 9.40E
Bremangerland *i.* Norway 17 61.51N 5.02E
Bremen Germany 14 53.05N 8.48E
Bremer Bay *town* Australia 43 34.21S 119.20E
Bremerhaven Germany 14 53.33N 8.35E
Bremer Range *mts.* Australia 43 32.40S 120.55E
Bremerton U.S.A. 54 47.34N 122.38W
Brenner Pass Italy / Austria 14 47.00N 11.30E
Breno Italy 9 45.57N 10.18E
Brent Canada 55 46.02N 78.29W
Brenta *r.* Italy 9 45.25N 12.15E
Brentwood U.K. 5 51.38N 0.18E
Brescia Italy 9 45.33N 10.12E
Breskens Neth. 8 51.24N 3.34E
Bressay *i.* U.K. 6 60.08N 1.05W
Bressuire France 11 46.50N 0.28W
Brest Belorussia 15 52.08N 23.40E
Brest France 11 48.23N 4.30W
Bretagne *d.* France 11 48.15N 2.30W
Breteuil France 9 49.38N 2.18E
Breteuil-sur-Iton France 9 48.50N 0.55E
Brett, C. New Zealand 48 35.15S 174.20E
Breuil-Cervinia Italy 9 45.56N 7.38E
Brevik Norway 17 59.04N 9.42E
Brewarrina Australia 47 29.57S 147.54E
Brewer U.S.A. 55 44.48N 68.46W
Brezovo Bulgaria 13 42.20N 25.06E
Bria C.A.R. 35 6.32N 21.59E
Briançon France 11 44.53N 6.39E
Briare France 9 47.38N 2.44E
Bribbaree Australia 47 34.07S 147.51E
Brichany Moldavia 15 48.20N 27.01E
Bricquebec France 9 49.28N 1.38W
Bride I.o.M Europe 4 54.23N 4.24W
Bridgend U.K. 5 51.30N 3.35W
Bridgeport Calif. U.S.A. 54 38.10N 119.13W
Bridgeport Conn. U.S.A. 55 41.12N 73.12W
Bridger U.S.A. 54 45.18N 108.55W
Bridgetown Australia 43 33.57S 116.08E
Bridgetown Barbados 57 13.06N 59.37W
Bridgetown Rep. of Ire. 7 52.14N 6.33W
Bridgewater Canada 51 44.23N 64.31W
Bridgewater, C. Australia 46 38.25S 141.28E
Bridgnorth U.K. 5 52.33N 2.25W
Bridgwater U.K. 5 51.08N 3.00W
Bridlington U.K. 4 54.06N 0.11W
Brie *f.* France 9 48.40N 3.20E
Brienne-le-Château France 9 48.24N 4.32E
Brig Switz. 9 46.19N 8.00E
Brigg U.K. 4 53.33N 0.30W
Brigham City U.S.A. 54 41.31N 112.01W
Bright Australia 47 36.42S 146.58E
Brighton U.K. 5 50.50N 0.09W
Brindisi Italy 13 40.38N 17.57E
Brinkworth Australia 46 33.42S 138.24E
Brionne France 9 49.12N 0.43E
Briouze France 9 48.42N 0.22W
Brisbane Australia 47 27.30S 153.00E
Brisighella Italy 9 44.13N 11.46E
Bristol U.K. 5 51.26N 2.35W
Bristol Tenn. U.S.A. 53 36.35N 82.12W
Bristol B. U.S.A. 50 58.00N 158.50W
Bristol Channel U.K. 5 51.17N 3.20W
British Antarctic Territory Antarctica 64 70.00S 50.00W
British Columbia *d.* Canada 50 55.00N 125.00W
British Mts. Canada 50 69.00N 140.20W
British Virgin Is. C. America 57 18.30N 64.30W
Britstown R.S.A. 39 30.34S 23.30E
Britt Canada 55 45.46N 80.35W
Brive France 11 45.09N 1.32E
Briviesca Spain 10 42.33N 3.19W
Brixham U.K. 5 50.24N 3.31W
Brno Czech. 14 49.11N 16.39E
Broach India 28 21.42N 72.58E
Broad Arrow Australia 43 30.32S 121.20E
Broad B. U.K. 6 58.15N 6.15W
Broadback *r.* Canada 55 51.20N 78.50W
Broadford Australia 47 37.16S 145.03E
Broadmere Australia 44 25.30S 149.30E
Broad Sd. Australia 44 22.20S 149.50E
Broadsound Range *mts.* Australia 44 22.30S 149.30E
Broadway U.K. 5 52.02N 1.51W
Brochet Canada 51 57.53N 101.40W
Brockton U.S.A. 55 42.05N 71.01W
Brockville Canada 55 44.35N 75.41W
Brockway Mont. U.S.A. 54 47.15N 105.45W
Brod Croatia 15 45.09N 18.02E
Brodeur Pen. Canada 51 73.00N 88.00W
Brodick U.K. 6 55.34N 5.09W
Brodnica Poland 15 53.16N 19.23E
Brody Ukraine 15 50.05N 25.08E
Broglie France 9 49.01N 0.32E
Broke Inlet Australia 43 34.55S 116.25E
Broken B. Australia 47 33.34S 151.18E
Broken Hill *town* Australia 46 31.57S 141.30E
Bromley U.K. 5 51.24N 0.02E
Bromsgrove U.K. 5 52.20N 2.03W
Brong-Ahafo *d.* Ghana 38 7.45N 1.30W
Brooke's Point *town* Phil. 26 8.50N 117.52E
Brookhaven U.S.A. 53 31.36N 90.28W
Brookings Oreg. U.S.A. 54 42.03N 124.17W
Brookings S.Dak. U.S.A. 53 44.19N 96.47W
Brooks Canada 50 50.35N 111.53W
Brooks Range *mts.* U.S.A. 50 68.50N 152.00W
Brookton Australia 43 32.22S 117.01E
Broom, Loch U.K. 6 57.52N 5.07W
Broome Australia 42 17.58S 122.15E
Broome, Mt. Australia 42 17.21S 125.23E
Broomehill *town* Australia 43 33.50S 117.35E
Brora U.K. 6 58.01N 3.52W
Brora *r.* U.K. 6 58.00N 3.51W
Brosna *r.* Rep. of Ire. 7 53.13N 7.58W
Brothers U.S.A. 54 43.49N 120.36W
Brou France 9 48.13N 1.11E
Brough England U.K. 4 54.32N 2.19W
Brough Scotland U.K. 6 60.29N 1.12W
Broughton *r.* Australia 46 33.21S 137.46E
Broughton in Furness U.K. 4 54.17N 3.12W
Brouwershaven Neth. 8 51.44N 3.53E
Brovary Ukraine 15 50.30N 30.45E
Brovst Denmark 17 57.06N 9.32E
Brown, Mt. Australia 46 32.33S 138.02E
Browning U.S.A. 54 48.34N 113.01W
Brownwood U.S.A. 52 31.42N 98.59W
Brönderslev Denmark 17 57.16N 9.58E
Brönnöysund Norway 16 65.30N 12.10E
Bruay-en-Artois France 8 50.29N 2.36E
Bruce Pen. Canada 55 44.50N 81.20W
Bruce Rock *town* Australia 43 31.52S 118.09E
Bruges *see* Brugge Belgium 8
Brugge Belgium 8 51.13N 3.14E
Brumadinho Brazil 59 20.09S 44.11W
Brumado Brazil 61 14.13S 41.40W
Brunei Asia 26 4.56N 114.58E
Brunflo Sweden 16 63.04N 14.50E
Brunner New Zealand 48 42.28S 171.12E
Brunsbüttel Germany 14 53.44N 9.05E
Brunssum Neth. 8 50.57N 5.59E
Brunswick Ga. U.S.A. 53 31.09N 81.21W
Brunswick Maine U.S.A. 55 43.55N 69.58W
Brunswick B. Australia 42 15.05S 125.00E
Brunswick Junction Australia 43 33.15S 115.45E
Bruny I. Australia 45 43.15S 147.16E
Brusilovka Kazakhstan 19 50.39N 54.59E
Brussel *see* Bruxelles Belgium 8
Brussels *see* Bruxelles Belgium 8
Bruthen Australia 47 37.44S 147.49E
Bruton U.K. 5 51.06N 2.28W
Bruxelles Belgium 8 50.50N 4.23E
Brühl Germany 8 50.50N 6.55E
Brünen Germany 8 51.45N 6.41E
Bryan Ohio U.S.A. 55 41.30N 84.34W
Bryan Tex. U.S.A. 53 30.41N 96.24W
Bryan, Mt. Australia 46 33.26S 138.27E
Bryansk Russian Fed. 18 53.15N 34.09E
Bryne Norway 17 58.44N 5.39E
Bryson Canada 55 45.41N 76.37W
Bryson, Lac *l.* Canada 55 46.19N 77.27W
Brzeg Poland 15 50.52N 17.27E
Bsharrī Lebanon 32 34.15N 36.00E
Bua *r.* Malaŵi 37 12.42S 34.15E
Bu'ayrāt al Ḥasūn Libya 34 31.24N 15.44E
Būbiyān, Jazīrat *i.* Kuwait 31 29.45N 48.15E
Bubye *r.* Zimbabwe 39 22.18S 31.00E
Bucak Turkey 30 37.28N 30.36E
Bucaramanga Colombia 60 7.08N 73.10W
Buchach Ukraine 15 49.09N 25.20E
Buchanan Liberia 34 5.57N 10.02W
Buchanan, L. Australia 44 21.28S 145.52E
Buchan Ness *c.* U.K. 6 57.28N 1.47W
Buchans Canada 51 48.49N 56.52W
Bucharest *see* Bucureşti Romania 15
Buchloe Germany 14 48.02N 10.44E
Buchy France 9 49.35N 1.22E
Buckambool Mt. Australia 47 31.55S 145.40E
Buckhaven and Methil U.K. 4 56.11N 3.03W
Buckie U.K. 6 57.40N 2.58W
Buckingham U.K. 5 52.00N 0.59W
Buckingham B. Australia 44 12.10S 135.46E
Buckinghamshire *d.* U.K. 5 51.50N 0.48W
Buckland Tableland *f.* Australia 44 25.00S 148.00E
Buckleboo Australia 46 32.55S 136.12E
Bucquoy France 8 50.09N 2.43E
Bu Craa W. Sahara 34 26.21N 12.57W
Bucureşti Romania 15 44.25N 26.06E
Bucyrus U.S.A. 55 40.47N 82.57W
Bud Norway 16 62.54N 6.56E
Budapest Hungary 15 47.30N 19.03E
Budaun India 29 28.02N 79.07E
Budda Australia 46 31.12S 144.16E
Budd Coast *f.* Antarctica 64 67.00S 112.00E
Bude U.K. 5 50.49N 4.33W
Bude B. U.K. 5 50.50N 4.40W
Budennovsk Russian Fed. 19 44.50N 44.10E
Buea Cameroon 38 4.09N 9.13E
Buenaventura Colombia 60 3.54N 77.02W
Buenaventura Mexico 56 29.51N 107.29W
Buenos Aires Argentina 63 34.40S 58.25W
Buenos Aires *d.* Argentina 63 36.30S 59.00W
Buenos Aires, L. Argentina / Chile 63 46.35S 72.00W
Buffalo N.Y. U.S.A. 55 42.52N 78.55W
Buffalo Wyo. U.S.A. 54 44.21N 106.42W
Bug *r.* Poland 15 52.29N 21.11E
Buga Colombia 60 3.53N 76.17W
Bugaldie Australia 47 31.02S 149.08E
Bugembe Uganda 37 0.26N 33.16E
Bugene Tanzania 37 1.34S 31.07E
Buggs Island *l.* U.S.A. 53 36.35N 78.20W
Bugrino Russian Fed. 18 68.45N 49.15E
Bugt China 25 48.45N 121.58E
Bugulma Russian Fed. 18 54.32N 52.46E
Buguma Nigeria 38 4.43N 6.53E
Buguruslan Russian Fed. 18 53.36N 52.30E
Buhera Zimbabwe 39 19.21S 31.25E
Buhuşi Romania 15 46.43N 26.41E
Builth Wells U.K. 5 52.09N 3.24W
Buinsk Russian Fed. 18 54.58N 48.15E
Bu'in-Sofiā Iran 31 35.51N 46.02E
Buitenpost Neth. 8 53.15N 6.09E
Buji P.N.G. 44 9.07S 142.26E
Bujumbura Burundi 37 3.22S 29.21E
Bukavu Zaïre 37 2.30S 28.49E
Bukene Tanzania 37 4.13S 32.52E
Bukhara Uzbekistan 31 39.47N 64.26E
Buki Ukraine 15 49.02N 30.29E
Bukima Tanzania 37 1.48S 33.25E
Bukittinggi Indonesia 26 0.18S 100.20E
Bukoba Tanzania 37 1.20S 31.49E
Bukuru Nigeria 38 9.48N 8.52E
Būl, Kūh-e *mtn.* Iran 31 30.48N 52.45E
Bula Indonesia 27 3.07S 130.27E
Bulahdelah Australia 47 32.25S 152.13E
Bulan Phil. 27 12.40N 123.53E
Bulawayo Zimbabwe 39 20.10S 28.43E
Buldern Germany 8 51.52N 7.21E
Bulgan Mongolia 24 48.34N 103.12E
Bulgaria Europe 13 42.30N 25.00E
Bullabulling Australia 43 31.05S 120.52E
Bullara Australia 42 22.40S 114.03E
Buller *r.* New Zealand 48 41.45S 171.35E
Buller, Mt. Australia 47 37.11S 146.26E
Bullfinch Australia 43 30.59S 119.06E
Bulli Australia 47 34.20S 150.55E
Bull Mts. U.S.A. 54 46.05N 109.00W
Bulloo *r.* Australia 46 28.43S 142.27E
Bulloo Downs *town* Australia 46 28.30S 142.45E
Bulolo P.N.G. 27 7.13S 146.35E
Bultfontein R.S.A. 39 28.17S 26.09E
Bulu Indonesia 27 4.34N 126.45E
Bulu, Gunung *mtn.* Indonesia 26 3.00N 116.00E
Bulun Russian Fed. 21 70.50N 127.20E
Bulunde Tanzania 37 4.19S 32.57E
Bumba Zaïre 35 2.15N 22.32E
Buna Kenya 37 2.49N 39.27E
Buna P.N.G. 44 8.40S 148.25E
Bunbury Australia 43 33.20S 115.34E
Buncrana Rep. of Ire. 7 55.08N 7.27W
Bundaberg Australia 44 24.50S 152.21E
Bundaleer Australia 47 28.39S 146.31E
Bundarra Australia 47 30.11S 151.04E
Bunde Germany 8 53.12N 7.16E
Bundella Australia 47 31.35S 149.59E
Bundoran Rep. of Ire. 7 54.28N 8.17W
Bungay U.K. 5 52.27N 1.26E
Bungu Tanzania 37 7.37S 39.07E
Buni Nigeria 38 11.20N 11.59E
Bunia Zaïre 37 1.30N 30.10E
Buninyong Australia 46 37.41S 143.58E
Bunyan Australia 47 36.11S 149.09E
Buol Indonesia 27 1.12N 121.28E
Buqayq Saudi Arabia 31 25.55N 49.40E
Bura Coast Kenya 37 3.30S 38.19E
Bura Coast Kenya 37 1.09S 39.55E
Burakin Australia 43 30.30S 117.08E
Buraydah Saudi Arabia 31 26.18N 43.58E
Burcher Australia 47 33.32S 147.18E
Burdur Turkey 30 37.44N 30.17E
Burdwān India 29 23.15N 87.52E
Burg Germany 14 52.17N 11.51E
Burgas Bulgaria 13 42.30N 27.29E
Burgenland *d.* Austria 14 47.30N 16.20E
Burgess Hill U.K. 5 50.57N 0.07W
Burgos Spain 10 42.21N 3.41W
Burgsteinfurt Germany 8 52.09N 7.21E
Burgsvik Sweden 17 57.03N 18.16E
Burhānpur India 28 21.18N 76.08E
Buri Brazil 59 23.46S 48.39W
Burias *i.* Phil. 27 12.50N 123.10E
Burica, Punta *c.* Panama 57 8.05N 82.50W
Burke *r.* Australia 44 23.12S 139.33E
Burketown Australia 44 17.44S 139.22E
Burkina Africa 38 12.30N 2.00W
Burley U.S.A. 54 42.32N 113.48W
Burlington Canada 55 43.19N 79.48W
Burlington Iowa U.S.A. 53 40.50N 91.07W
Burlington Vt. U.S.A. 55 44.29N 73.13W
Burma Asia 29 21.00N 96.30E
Burngup Australia 43 33.00S 118.39E
Burnham-on-Crouch U.K. 5 51.37N 0.50E
Burnham-on-Sea U.K. 5 51.15N 3.00W
Burnie Australia 45 41.03S 145.55E
Burnley U.K. 4 53.47N 2.15W
Burns Oreg. U.S.A. 54 43.35N 119.03W
Burnside *r.* Canada 50 66.51N 108.04W
Buronga Australia 46 34.08S 142.11E
Burra Australia 46 33.40S 138.57E
Burracoppin Australia 43 31.22S 118.30E
Burragorang, L. Australia 47 33.58S 150.27E
Burren Junction Australia 47 30.08S 148.59E
Burrewarra Pt. Australia 47 35.56S 150.12E
Burriana Spain 10 39.54N 0.05W
Burrinjuck Australia 47 35.01S 148.33E
Burrinjuck Resr. Australia 47 35.00S 148.40E
Burry Port U.K. 5 51.41N 4.17W
Bursa Turkey 13 40.11N 29.04E
Būr Safājah Egypt 30 26.44N 33.56E
Būr Sa'īd Egypt 32 31.17N 32.18E
Būr Sūdān Sudan 35 19.39N 37.01E
Burta Australia 46 32.30S 141.05E
Būr Tawfīq Egypt 32 29.57N 32.34E
Burton upon Trent U.K. 4 52.58N 1.39W
Burundy Australia 46 33.45S 142.22E
Buru *i.* Indonesia 27 3.30S 126.30E
Burullus, Buḥayrat al *l.* Egypt 32 31.30N 30.45E
Burundi Africa 37 3.00S 30.00E
Bururi Burundi 37 3.58S 29.35E
Burutu Nigeria 38 5.20N 5.31E
Bury G.M. U.K. 4 53.36N 2.19W
Bury St. Edmunds U.K. 5 52.15N 0.42E
Busalla Italy 9 44.34N 8.57E
Busca Italy 9 44.31N 7.29E
Būsh Egypt 32 29.09N 31.07E
Būshehr Iran 31 28.57N 50.52E
Bushmanland *f.* R.S.A. 39 29.25S 19.40E
Busigny France 8 50.03N 3.29E
Buskerud Norway 17 60.20N 9.00E
Busselton Australia 43 33.43S 115.15E
Bussum Neth. 8 52.17N 5.10E
Bustard Head *c.* Australia 44 24.02S 151.48E
Busto Arsizio Italy 9 45.37N 8.51E
Buşrá ash Shām Syria 32 32.30N 36.29E
Buta Zaïre 35 2.49N 24.50E
Butari Rwanda 37 2.38S 29.43E
Bute Australia 46 33.24S 138.01E
Bute *i.* U.K. 6 55.51N 5.07W
Bute, Sd. of U.K. 6 55.44N 5.10W
Butiaba Uganda 37 1.48N 31.15E
Buton *i.* Indonesia 27 5.00S 122.50E
Butte Mont. U.S.A. 54 46.00N 112.32W
Butterworth Malaysia 26 5.24N 100.22E
Buttevant Rep. of Ire. 7 52.14N 8.41W
Butt of Lewis *c.* U.K. 6 58.31N 6.15W
Butty Head Australia 43 33.52S 121.35E
Butuan Phil. 27 8.56N 125.31E
Buur Gaabo Somali Rep. 37 1.10S 41.50E
Buur Hakaba Somali Rep. 37 2.43N 44.10E
Buxton U.K. 4 53.16N 1.54W
Buy Russian Fed. 18 58.23N 41.27E
Buyaga Russian Fed. 21 59.42N 126.59E
Buynaksk Russian Fed. 19 42.48N 47.07E
Buzachi, Poluostrov *pen.* Kazakhstan 19 45.00N 51.55E
Buzancy France 9 49.30N 4.59E
Buzău Romania 15 45.10N 26.49E
Buzău *r.* Romania 15 45.24N 27.48E
Buzaymah Libya 35 24.55N 22.02E
Buzi *r.* Mozambique 39 19.52S 34.00E
Buzuluk Russian Fed. 18 52.49N 52.19E
Büyük Menderes *r.* Turkey 13 37.30N 27.05E
Bwasiaia P.N.G. 44 10.06S 150.48E
Byala Bulgaria 13 42.53N 27.55E
Byam Martin I. Canada 50 75.15N 104.00W
Bydgoszcz Poland 15 53.16N 17.33E
Bygland Norway 17 58.48N 7.50E
Bykhov Belorussia 15 53.30N 30.15E

Bykle Norway 17 59.21N 7.20E
Bylot I. Canada 51 73.00N 78.30W
Byrd Land f. Antarctica 64 79.30S125.00W
Byrock Australia 47 30.40S146.25E
Byron, C. Australia 47 28.37S153.40E
Byron Bay town Australia 47 28.43S153.34E
Byrranga, Gory mts. Russian Fed. 21 74.50N101.00E
Byske Sweden 16 64.57N 21.12E
Byske r. Sweden 16 64.57N 21.13E
Byten Belorussia 15 52.50N 25.28E
Bytom Poland 15 50.22N 18.54E
Bzipi Georgia 19 43.15N 40.24E

C

Cabanatuan Phil. 27 15.30N120.58E
Cabimas Venezuela 60 10.26N 71.27W
Cabinda Angola 36 5.34S 12.12E
Cabinet Mts. U.S.A. 54 48.08N115.46W
Cabo Delgado d. Mozambique 37 12.30S 39.00E
Cabo Frio town Brazil 59 22.51S 42.03W
Cabonga, Résr. Canada 55 47.35N 76.35W
Caboolture Australia 45 27.05S152.57E
Cabo Pantoja Peru 60 1.00S 75.10W
Cabot Str. Canada 51 47.00N 59.00W
Cabras Italy 12 39.56N 8.32E
Cabrera i. Spain 10 39.08N 2.56E
Cabrera, Sierra mts. Spain 10 42.10N 6.30W
Cabriel r. Spain 10 39.13N 1.07W
Cabruta Venezuela 60 7.40N 66.16W
Čačak Yugo. 15 43.53N 20.21E
Cáceres Brazil 61 16.05S 57.40W
Cáceres Spain 10 39.29N 6.23W
Cacharí Argentina 63 36.23S 59.29W
Cachoeira Brazil 61 12.35S 38.59W
Cachoeira do Sul Brazil 59 30.03S 52.52W
Cachoeiro de Itapemirim Brazil 59 20.51S 41.07W
Cacín r. Spain 10 37.10N 4.01W
Caconda Angola 36 13.46S 15.06E
Caçapava Brazil 59 23.05S 45.40W
Čadca Czech. 15 49.26N 18.48E
Cader Idris mtn. U.K. 5 52.40N 3.55W
Cadí, Serra del mts. Spain 10 42.12N 1.35E
Cadibarrawirracanna, L. Australia 46 28.52S135.27E
Cadillac U.S.A. 55 44.15N 85.23W
Cadiz Phil. 27 10.57N123.18E
Cádiz Spain 10 36.32N 6.18W
Cádiz, Golfo de g. Spain 10 37.00N 7.10W
Cadoux Australia 43 30.47S117.05E
Caen France 9 49.11N 0.22W
Caernarfon U.K. 4 53.08N 4.17W
Caernarfon B. U.K. 4 53.05N 4.25W
Caerphilly U.K. 5 51.34N 3.13W
Caeté Brazil 59 19.54S 43.37W
Cagayan de Oro Phil. 27 8.29N124.40E
Cagliari Italy 12 39.14N 9.07E
Cagliari, Golfo di g. Italy 12 39.07N 9.15E
Cagnes France 9 43.40N 7.09E
Caguán r. Colombia 60 0.08S 74.18W
Caguas Puerto Rico 57 18.08N 66.00W
Caha Mts. Rep. of Ire. 7 51.44N 9.45W
Caherciveen Rep. of Ire. 7 51.51N 10.14W
Cahir Rep. of Ire. 7 52.23N 7.56W
Cahora Bassa Dam Mozambique 37 15.36S 32.41E
Cahore Pt. Rep. of Ire. 7 52.34N 6.12W
Cahors France 11 44.28N 0.26E
Cahuapanas Peru 60 5.15S 77.00W
Caianda Angola 36 11.02S 23.29E
Caibarién Cuba 57 22.31N 79.28W
Caicó Brazil 61 6.25S 37.04W
Caicos Is. Turks & Caicos Is. 57 21.30N 72.00W
Caird Coast f. Antarctica 64 75.00S 20.00W
Cairngorms mts. U.K. 6 57.04N 3.30W
Cairns Australia 44 16.51S145.43E
Cairo see Al Qāhirah Egypt 32
Cairo Ill. U.S.A. 53 37.02N 89.02W
Cairo Montenotte Italy 9 44.24N 8.16E
Caiwarro Australia 47 28.38S144.45E
Cajamarca Peru 60 7.09S 78.32W
Cajàzeiras Brazil 61 6.52S 38.31W
Cajuru Brazil 59 21.15S 47.18W
Čakovec Croatia 14 46.23N 16.26E
Calabar Nigeria 38 4.56N 8.22E
Calabozo Venezuela 60 8.58N 67.28W
Calabria d. Italy 13 39.00N 16.30E
Calafat Romania 15 43.59N 22.57E
Calafate Argentina 63 50.20S 72.16W
Calahorra Spain 10 42.18N 1.58W
Calais France 3 50.57N 1.52E
Calama Brazil 60 8.03S 62.53W
Calama Chile 62 22.30S 68.55W
Calamar Colombia 60 10.15N 74.55W
Calamian Group is. Phil. 27 12.00N120.05E
Cala Millor Spain 10 39.35N 3.22E
Calamocha Spain 10 40.54N 1.18W
Calapan Phil. 27 13.23N121.10E
Călăraşi Romania 15 44.11N 27.21E
Calatayud Spain 10 41.21N 1.39W
Calau Germany 14 51.45N 13.56E
Calbayog Phil. 27 12.04N124.58E
Calcutta India 29 22.35N 88.21E
Caldaro Italy 9 46.25N 11.14E
Caldas Colombia 60 6.05N 75.36W
Caldas da Rainha Portugal 10 39.24N 9.08W
Caldera Chile 62 27.04S 70.50W
Caldwell Idaho U.S.A. 54 43.40N116.41W
Caldwell Ohio U.S.A. 55 39.44N 81.32W
Caledon r. R.S.A. 39 30.27S 26.12E
Caledon B. Australia 44 12.58S136.52E
Calella Spain 10 41.37N 2.40E
Calexico Mexico 54 32.40N115.30W
Calf of Man i. I.o.M Europe 4 54.03N 4.49W
Calgary Canada 50 51.05N114.05W
Cali Colombia 60 3.24N 76.30W
Caliente U.S.A. 54 37.37N114.31W
California d. U.S.A. 54 37.29N119.58W
California, G. of see California, Golfo de g. Mexico 56
California, Golfo de g. Mexico 56 28.00N112.00W
Calingasta Argentina 62 31.15S 69.30W
Calingiri Australia 43 31.07S116.27E
Callabonna, L. Australia 46 29.47S140.07E
Callabonna Creek r. Australia 46 29.37S140.08E
Callander U.K. 6 56.15N 4.13W
Callao Peru 62 12.05S 77.08W
Caloocan Phil. 27 14.38N120.58E
Caloundra Australia 45 26.47S153.08E
Caltagirone Italy 12 37.14N 14.30E
Caltanissetta Italy 12 37.30N 14.05E
Calulo Angola 36 10.05S 14.56E
Calvados d. France 9 49.10N 0.30W
Calvi France 11 42.34N 8.44E
Calvinia R.S.A. 39 31.29S 19.44E
Cam r. U.K. 5 52.34N 0.21E
Camacupa Angola 36 12.01S 17.22E
Camagüey Cuba 57 21.25N 77.55W
Camagüey, Archipiélago de Cuba 57 22.30N 78.00W
Camaiore Italy 9 43.56N 10.18E
Camarès France 11 43.49N 2.53E
Camaret-sur-Mer France 11 48.16N 4.37W
Camarón, C. Honduras 57 15.59N 85.00W
Camarones Argentina 63 44.45S 65.40W
Camas U.S.A. 54 45.35N122.24W
Cambay India 28 22.18N 72.37E
Camberley U.K. 5 51.21N 0.45W
Cambodia Asia 26 12.00N105.00E
Camborne U.K. 5 50.12N 5.19W
Cambrai Australia 46 34.39S139.17E
Cambrai France 11 50.10N 3.14E
Cambria U.S.A. 54 35.34N121.05W
Cambrian Mts. U.K. 5 52.33N 3.33W
Cambridge New Zealand 48 37.53S175.29E
Cambridge U.K. 5 52.13N 0.08E
Cambridge Idaho U.S.A. 54 44.34N116.41W
Cambridge Mass. U.S.A. 55 42.22N 71.06W
Cambridge Md. U.S.A. 55 38.34N 76.04W
Cambridge Bay town Canada 50 69.09N105.00W
Cambridge G. Australia 42 15.00S128.05E
Cambridgeshire d. U.K. 5 52.15N 0.05E
Cambundi-Catembo Angola 36 10.09S 17.35E
Camden U.K. 5 51.33N 0.10W
Camden N.J. U.S.A. 55 39.57N 75.07W
Camelford U.K. 5 50.37N 4.41W
Cameron Ariz. U.S.A. 54 35.51N111.25W
Cameron Hills Canada 50 59.48N118.00W
Cameron Mts. New Zealand 48 45.50S167.00E
Cameroon Africa 34 6.00N 12.30E
Cameroun, Mont mtn. Cameroon 38 4.20N 9.05E
Cametá Brazil 61 2.12S 49.30W
Camiri Bolivia 62 20.03S 63.31W
Camocim Brazil 61 2.55S 40.50W
Camooweal Australia 44 19.55S138.07E
Camopi Guiana 61 3.12N 52.15W
Campana Argentina 63 34.10S 58.57W
Campana, Isla i. Chile 63 48.25S 75.20W
Campania d. Italy 12 41.00N 14.30E
Campbell, C. New Zealand 48 41.45S174.15E
Campbellton Canada 55 48.00N 66.41W
Campbell Town Australia 47 41.55S147.30E
Campbelltown Australia 47 34.04S150.49E
Campbeltown U.K. 6 55.25N 5.36W
Campeche Mexico 56 19.50N 90.30W
Campeche d. Mexico 56 19.00N 90.00W
Campeche, Bahía de b. Mexico 56 19.30N 94.00W
Campeche B. see Campeche, Bahía de b. Mexico 56
Camperdown Australia 46 38.15S143.14E
Campina Grande Brazil 61 7.15S 35.50W
Campinas Brazil 59 22.54S 47.06W
Campo Cameroon 38 2.22N 9.50E
Campobasso Italy 12 41.34N 14.39E
Campo Belo Brazil 59 20.52S 45.16W
Campo Gallo Argentina 62 26.35S 62.50W
Campo Grande Brazil 62 20.24S 54.35W
Campo Maior Brazil 61 4.50S 42.12W
Campo Maior Portugal 10 39.01N 7.04W
Campos Brazil 59 21.45S 41.18W
Campos Belos Brazil 61 13.09S 47.03W
Campos do Jordão Brazil 59 23.28S 46.10W
Cam Ranh Vietnam 26 11.54N109.14E
Camrose Canada 50 53.01N112.48W
Canada N. America 50 60.00N105.00W
Cañada de Gómez Argentina 62 32.49S 61.25W
Canadian r. U.S.A. 53 35.20N 95.40W
Canal du Midi France 11 43.18N 2.00E
Cananea Mexico 56 30.57N110.18W
Canarias, Islas is. Atlantic Oc. 34 29.00N 15.00W
Canastra, Serra da mts. Brazil 59 20.05S 46.30W
Canaveral, C. U.S.A. 53 28.28N 80.28W
Canavieiras Brazil 61 15.44S 38.58W
Canbelego Australia 47 31.33S146.19E
Canberra Australia 47 35.18S149.08E
Canby Calif. U.S.A. 54 41.27N120.52W
Cancale France 9 48.40N 1.50W
Cancon France 11 44.32N 0.38E
Candé France 9 47.34N 1.02W
Candeias Brazil 59 20.44S 45.18W
Candeleda Spain 10 40.10N 5.14W
Canelli Italy 9 44.43N 8.17E
Canelones Uruguay 63 34.32S 56.17W
Cañete Peru 60 13.00S 76.30W
Cangas de Narcea Spain 10 43.11N 6.33W
Canguçu Brazil 62 31.24S 52.41W
Caniapiscau, Résr l. Canada 51 54.10N 69.55W
Canna i. U.K. 6 57.03N 6.30W
Cannes France 11 43.33N 7.00E
Cannich U.K. 6 57.20N 4.45W
Cannock U.K. 5 52.42N 2.02W
Cann River town Australia 47 37.35S149.06E
Canôas Brazil 59 29.55S 51.10W
Canonba Australia 47 31.19S147.22E
Canon City U.S.A. 52 38.27N105.14W
Canopus Australia 46 33.30S140.57E
Canossa site Italy 9 44.35N 10.27E
Canowindra Australia 47 33.34S148.30E
Cantabria d. Spain 10 43.10N 4.15W
Cantabria, Sierra de mts. Spain 10 42.40N 2.30W
Cantábrica, Cordillera mts. Spain 10 42.55N 5.10W
Cantagalo Brazil 59 21.59S 42.22W
Cantaura Venezuela 60 9.22N 64.24W
Canterbury d. New Zealand 48 43.30S172.00E
Canterbury U.K. 5 51.17N 1.05E
Canterbury Bight New Zealand 48 44.15S172.00E
Can Tho Vietnam 26 10.03N105.46E
Canton see Guangzhou China 25
Canton Ohio U.S.A. 55 40.48N 81.23W
Cantù Italy 9 45.44N 9.08E
Cantua Creek town U.S.A. 54 36.30N120.19W
Cañuelas Argentina 63 35.03S 58.44W
Canumã r. Brazil 60 3.55S 59.10W
Canutama Brazil 60 6.32S 64.20W
Cany-Barville France 9 49.47N 0.38E
Canyon Wyo. U.S.A. 54 44.43N110.32W
Cao Bang Vietnam 26 22.40N106.16E
Caorle Italy 9 45.36N 12.53E
Capanema Brazil 61 1.08S 47.07W
Cap-Chat Canada 55 48.56N 66.53W
Cap-de-la-Madeleine town Canada 55 46.22N 72.31W
Cape Barren I. Australia 45 40.25S148.15E
Cape Borda Australia 46 35.44S136.37E
Cape Breton I. Canada 51 46.00N 61.00W
Cape Coast town Ghana 38 5.10N 1.13W
Cape Cod B. U.S.A. 55 41.50N 70.17W
Cape Crawford town Australia 44 16.38S135.43E
Cape Dyer town Canada 51 66.30N 61.20W
Cape Girardeau town U.S.A. 53 37.19N 89.31W
Cape Johnson Depth Pacific Oc. 27 10.20N127.20E
Capellen Lux. 8 49.39N 5.59E
Cape Province d. R.S.A. 39 31.30S 23.30E
Cape Town R.S.A. 39 33.55S 18.27E
Cape York Pen. Australia 44 12.40S142.20E
Cap-Haïtien town Haiti 57 19.47N 72.17W
Capim r. Brazil 61 1.40S 47.47W
Capoompeta, Mt. Australia 47 29.22S151.59E
Cappoquin Rep. of Ire. 7 52.09N 7.52W
Capraia i. Italy 12 43.03N 9.50E
Caprera i. Italy 12 41.48N 9.27E
Capri i. Italy 12 40.33N 14.13E
Caprivi Strip f. Namibia 39 17.50S 23.10E
Captains Flat Australia 47 35.34S149.28E
Caqueta r. Colombia 60 1.20S 70.50W
Caracal Romania 15 44.08N 24.18E
Caracas Venezuela 60 10.35N 66.56W
Caragabal Australia 47 33.49S147.46E
Caraguatatuba Brazil 59 23.39S 45.26W
Carandaí Brazil 59 20.55S 43.46W
Carangola Brazil 59 20.44S 42.03W
Caransebeş Romania 15 45.25N 22.13E
Caratasca, Laguna de b. Honduras 57 15.10N 84.00W
Caratinga Brazil 59 19.50S 42.06W
Caravaca Spain 10 38.06N 1.51W
Caravaggio Italy 9 45.30N 9.38E
Caravelí Peru 60 15.45S 73.25W
Carballo Spain 10 43.13N 8.41W
Carbenyabba Creek r. Australia 46 29.02S143.28E
Carbonara, Capo c. Italy 12 39.06N 9.32E
Carbondale Penn. U.S.A. 55 41.35N 75.30W
Carbonear Canada 51 47.45N 53.13W
Carbonia Italy 12 39.11N 8.32E
Carcassonne France 11 43.13N 2.21E
Carcross Canada 50 60.11N134.41W
Cárdenas Cuba 57 23.02N 81.12W
Cárdenas Mexico 56 22.00N 99.40W
Cardenete Spain 10 39.46N 1.42W
Cardiff U.K. 5 51.28N 3.11W
Cardigan U.K. 5 52.06N 4.41W
Cardigan B. U.K. 5 52.30N 4.30W
Cardona Spain 10 41.56N 1.40E
Cardona Uruguay 63 33.53S 57.23W
Cardwell Australia 44 18.21S146.04E
Carei Romania 15 47.42N 22.28E
Carentan France 9 49.18N 1.14W
Carey U.S.A. 54 43.18N113.56W
Carey, L. Australia 43 29.05S122.15E
Carhaix France 11 48.16N 3.35W
Carhué Argentina 63 37.11S 62.45W
Caribbean Sea C. America 57 15.00N 75.00W
Caribou U.S.A. 55 46.52N 68.01W
Caribou Mts. Canada 50 58.30N115.00W
Carignan France 9 49.38N 5.10E
Carinda Australia 47 30.29S147.45E
Carinhanha Brazil 61 14.18S 43.47W
Carini Italy 12 38.08N 13.11E
Caritianas Brazil 60 9.25S 63.06W
Carleton Place Canada 55 45.08N 76.09W
Carlingford Rep. of Ire. 7 54.03N 6.12W
Carlingford Lough Rep. of Ire. 7 54.03N 6.09W
Carlisle U.K. 4 54.54N 2.55W
Carlos Reyles Uruguay 63 33.03S 56.29W
Carlow Rep. of Ire. 7 52.50N 6.46W
Carlow d. Rep. of Ire. 7 52.43N 6.50W
Carlsbad Calif. U.S.A. 54 33.10N117.21W
Carlsbad N.Mex. U.S.A. 52 32.25N104.14W
Carmacks Canada 50 62.04N136.21W
Carmagnola Italy 9 44.51N 7.43E
Carmarthen U.K. 5 51.52N 4.20W
Carmarthen B. U.K. 5 52.30N 4.30W
Carmaux France 11 44.03N 2.09E
Carmel Head U.K. 4 53.24N 4.35W
Carmelo Uruguay 63 34.00S 58.17W
Carmen Colombia 60 9.46N 75.06W
Carmen Mexico 56 18.38N 91.50W
Carmen Uruguay 63 33.15S 56.01W
Carmen, Isla i. Mexico 56 25.55N111.10W
Carmen, Isla del i. Mexico 56 18.35N 91.40W
Carmen de Areco Argentina 63 34.20S 59.50W
Carmen de Patagones Argentina 63 40.48S 63.00W
Carmichael U.S.A. 54 38.38N121.19W
Carmila Australia 44 21.55S149.25E
Carmo Brazil 59 21.56S 42.37W
Carmody, L. Australia 43 32.27S119.20E
Carmona Spain 10 37.28N 5.38W
Carnac France 11 47.35N 3.05W
Carnarvon Australia 42 24.53S113.40E
Carnarvon R.S.A. 39 30.58S 22.07E
Carndonagh Rep. of Ire. 7 55.15N 7.15W
Carnegie Australia 42 25.43S122.59E
Carnegie, L. Australia 42 26.15S123.00E
Carnew Rep. of Ire. 7 52.43N 6.31W
Carniche, Alpi mts. Austria / Italy 12 46.40N 12.48E
Car Nicobar i. India 29 9.06N 92.57E
Carnot C.A.R. 36 4.59N 15.56E
Carnot, C. Australia 46 34.57S135.38E
Carnoustie U.K. 6 56.30N 2.44W
Carnsore Pt. Rep. of Ire. 7 52.10N 6.21W
Carolina Brazil 61 7.20S 47.25W
Carolina Puerto Rico 57 18.23N 65.57W
Carolina R.S.A. 39 26.04S 30.07E
Caroline Is. Pacific Oc. 40 7.50N145.00E
Caroni r. Venezuela 60 8.20N 62.42W
Carora Venezuela 60 10.12N 70.07W
Carpathians mts. Europe 15 48.45N 23.45E
Carpaţii Meridionali mts. Romania 15 45.35N 24.40E
Carpentaria, G. of Australia 44 14.00S139.00E
Carpentras France 11 44.03N 5.03E
Carpi Italy 9 44.47N 10.53E
Carpio Spain 10 41.13N 5.07W
Carquefou France 9 47.18N 1.30W
Carra, Lough Rep. of Ire. 7 53.41N 9.15W
Carrara Italy 9 44.04N 10.06E
Carrathool Australia 47 34.25S145.24E
Carrauntoohil mtn. Rep. of Ire. 7 52.00N 9.45W
Carrickfergus U.K. 7 54.43N 5.49W
Carrickmacross Rep. of Ire. 7 53.58N 6.43W
Carrick-on-Shannon Rep. of Ire. 7 53.57N 8.06W
Carrick-on-Suir Rep. of Ire. 7 52.21N 7.26W
Carrieton Australia 46 32.28S138.34E
Carrowmore Lough Rep. of Ire. 7 54.11N 9.47W
Carrum Australia 47 38.05S145.08E
Carson City U.S.A. 54 39.10N119.46W
Carstairs U.K. 6 55.42N 3.41W
Cartagena Colombia 60 10.24N 75.33W
Cartagena Spain 10 37.36N 0.59W
Cartago Colombia 60 4.45N 75.55W
Cartago Costa Rica 57 9.50N 83.52W
Carter U.S.A. 54 41.27N110.25W
Carteret France 9 49.22N 1.48W
Carterton New Zealand 48 41.01S175.31E
Cartwright Canada 51 53.42N 57.01W
Caruarú Brazil 61 8.15S 35.55W
Carúpano Venezuela 60 10.39N 63.14W
Carvin France 8 50.30N 2.58E
Carvoeiro Brazil 60 1.24S 61.59W
Caryapundy Swamp Australia 46 29.00S142.36E
Casablanca Morocco 34 33.39N 7.35W
Casa Branca Brazil 59 21.45S 47.06W
Casa Grande U.S.A. 54 32.53N111.45W
Casale Italy 9 45.08N 8.27E
Casarano Italy 13 40.00N 18.10E
Cascade Idaho U.S.A. 54 44.31N116.02W
Cascade Mont. U.S.A. 54 47.16N111.42W
Cascade Pt. New Zealand 48 44.01S168.22E
Cascade Range mts. U.S.A. 52 46.15N121.00W
Caserta Italy 12 41.06N 14.21E
Cashel Tipperary Rep. of Ire. 7 52.31N 7.54W
Casilda Argentina 63 33.03S 61.10W
Casimiro de Abreu Brazil 59 22.28S 42.12W
Casino Australia 47 28.50S153.02E
Casma Peru 60 9.30S 78.20W
Caspe Spain 10 41.14N 0.03W
Casper U.S.A. 54 42.51N106.19W
Caspian Depression see Prikaspiyskaya Nizmennost ost Russian Fed. / Kazakhstan 19
Caspian Sea Europe / Asia 19 42.00N 51.00E
Cassano allo Ionio Italy 13 39.47N 16.20E
Cass City U.S.A. 55 43.37N 83.11W
Cassilis Australia 47 32.01S149.59E
Castaños Mexico 56 26.48N101.26W
Castelfranco Veneto Italy 9 45.40N 11.55E
Casteljaloux France 11 44.19N 0.06W
Castell' Arquato Italy 9 44.51N 9.52E
Castelli Argentina 63 36.07S 57.50W
Castellón Spain 10 39.59N 0.03W
Castelmassa Italy 9 45.01N 11.18E
Castelnovo ne'Monti Italy 9 44.26N 10.24E
Castelnuovo di Garfagnana Italy 9 44.06N 10.24E
Castelo Brazil 59 20.33S 41.14W
Castelo Branco Portugal 10 39.50N 7.30W
Castel San Giovanni Italy 9 45.04N 9.26E
Castelvetrano Italy 12 37.41N 12.47E
Casterton Australia 46 37.35S141.25E
Castets France 11 43.53N 1.09W
Castilla Peru 60 5.16S 80.36W
Castilla la Mancha d. Spain 10 40.00N 3.45W
Castilla y León d. Spain 10 41.50N 4.15W
Castilletes Colombia 60 11.55N 71.20W
Castlebar Rep. of Ire. 7 53.52N 9.19W
Castleblayney Rep. of Ire. 7 54.08N 6.46W
Castle Douglas U.K. 6 54.56N 3.56W
Castleford U.K. 4 53.43N 1.21W
Castlegate U.S.A. 54 39.44N110.52W
Castleisland Rep. of Ire. 7 52.13N 9.28W
Castlemaine Australia 46 37.05S144.19E
Castlerea Rep. of Ire. 7 53.45N 8.30W
Castlereagh r. Australia 47 30.12S147.32E
Castle Rock town Wash. U.S.A. 54 46.17N122.54W
Castletown I.o.M Europe 4 54.04N 4.38W
Castletownshend Rep. of Ire. 7 51.32N 9.12W
Castres France 11 43.36N 2.14E
Castries St. Lucia 57 14.01N 60.59W
Castro Chile 63 42.30S 73.46W
Castro del Río Spain 10 37.41N 4.29W
Casula Mozambique 37 15.26S 33.32E
Cataguases Brazil 59 21.23S 42.39W
Cataluña d. Spain 10 42.00N 2.00E
Catamarca Argentina 62 28.30S 65.45W
Catamarca d. Argentina 62 27.45S 67.00W
Catanduanes i. Phil. 27 13.45N124.20E
Catanduva Brazil 59 21.03S 49.00W
Catania Italy 12 37.31N 15.05E
Catanzaro Italy 13 38.55N 16.35E
Catarman Phil. 27 12.28N124.50E
Catbalogan Phil. 27 11.46N124.55E
Catete Angola 36 9.09S 13.40E
Cathcart Australia 47 36.49S149.25E
Cathcart R.S.A. 39 32.17S 27.08E
Cat I. Bahamas 57 24.30N 75.30W
Catoche, C. Mexico 57 21.38N 87.08W
Catonsville U.S.A. 55 39.16N 76.44W
Catriló Argentina 63 36.23S 63.24W
Catterick U.K. 4 54.23N 1.38W
Cattolica Italy 9 43.58N 12.44E
Catuane Mozambique 39 26.49S 32.17E
Cauca r. Colombia 60 8.57N 74.30W
Caucasus Mts. see Kavkazskiy Khrebet mts. Europe 19
Caudry France 11 50.07N 3.22E
Cauquenes Chile 63 35.58S 72.21W
Caura r. Venezuela 60 7.38N 64.53W
Cavaillon France 11 43.50N 5.02E
Cavalese Italy 9 46.17N 11.26E
Cavan Rep. of Ire. 7 54.00N 7.22W
Cavan d. Rep. of Ire. 7 53.58N 7.10W
Cavarzere Italy 9 45.08N 12.05E
Caviana, Ilha i. Brazil 61 0.10N 50.00W
Cawndilla L. Australia 46 32.30S142.18E
Caxambu Brazil 59 21.59S 44.54W
Caxias Brazil 61 4.53S 43.20W
Caxias do Sul Brazil 59 29.14S 51.10W
Caxito Angola 36 8.32S 13.38E
Cayambe Ecuador 60 0.03N 78.08W
Cayenne Guiana 61 4.55N 52.18W
Cayman Brac i. Cayman Is. 57 19.44N 79.48W
Cayman Is. C. America 57 19.00N 81.00W
Cazères France 11 43.13N 1.05E
Ceara d. Brazil 61 4.50S 39.00W
Cebollera, Sierra de mts. Spain 10 41.58N 2.30W
Cebu Phil. 27 10.17N123.56E
Cebu i. Phil. 27 10.15N123.45E
Cecina Italy 12 43.18N 10.30E
Cedar City U.S.A. 52 37.40N113.04W
Cedar Falls town U.S.A. 53 42.34N 92.26W
Cedar Rapids town U.S.A. 53 41.59N 91.31W
Cedros, Isla i. Mexico 56 28.10N115.15W
Ceduna Australia 46 32.07S133.42E
Ceerigaabo Somali Rep. 35 10.40N 47.20E
Cefalù Italy 12 38.01N 14.03E
Cegléd Hungary 15 47.10N 19.48E
Celaya Mexico 56 20.32N100.48W
Celebes i. see Sulawesi i. Indonesia 27
Celebes Sea Indonesia 27 3.00N122.00E
Celina U.S.A. 55 40.34N 84.35W
Celje Slovenia 12 46.15N 15.16E
Celle Germany 14 52.37N 10.05E
Celtic Sea Europe 3 50.00N 8.00W
Cemaes Head U.K. 5 52.08N 4.42W
Cenderawasih, Teluk b. Indonesia 27 2.20S135.50E
Ceno r. Italy 9 44.41N 10.05E
Cento Italy 9 44.43N 11.17E
Central d. Botswana 39 21.45S 26.15E
Central d. Ghana 38 5.30N 1.10W
Central d. Kenya 37 0.30S 37.00E
Central d. U.K. 6 56.10N 4.20W
Central d. Zambia 37 14.30S 29.30E
Central, Cordillera mts. Bolivia 62 18.30S 65.00W
Central, Cordillera mts. Colombia 60 5.00N 75.20W
Central African Republic Africa 34 6.30N 20.00E
Central I. Kenya 37 3.30N 36.02E
Centralia Ill. U.S.A. 53 38.32N 89.08W
Centralia Wash. U.S.A. 54 46.43N122.58W
Central Makran Range mts. Pakistan 28 26.40N 64.30E
Central Siberian Plateau see Sredne Sibirskoye Ploskogor'ye f. Russian Fed. 21
Centre d. Burkina 38 11.50N 1.10W
Centre d. France 11 47.40N 1.45E
Centre Est d. Burkina 38 11.20N 0.10W
Centre Nord d. Burkina 38 13.30N 1.00W
Centre Ouest d. Burkina 38 12.00N 2.20W
Ceram i. see Seram i. Indonesia 27
Ceram Sea see Seram, Laut sea Pacific Oc. 27
Ceres U.S.A. 54 37.35N120.57W
Ceresole Reale Italy 9 45.26N 7.15E
Cereté Colombia 60 8.54N 75.51W
Cerignola Italy 12 41.17N 15.53E
Cérilly France 11 46.37N 2.50E
Cerisiers France 9 48.08N 3.29E
Cerknica Slovenia 12 45.48N 14.22E
Cernavodă Romania 15 44.20N 28.02E
Cerritos Mexico 56 22.26N100.17W
Cerro de Pasco Peru 60 10.43S 76.15W
Cervera Lérida Spain 10 41.40N 1.16E
Cervia Italy 9 44.15N 12.22E
Cervignano del Friuli Italy 9 45.49N 13.20E
Cesena Italy 9 44.08N 12.15E
Cesenatico Italy 9 44.12N 12.24E
Cēsis Latvia 18 57.18N 25.18E
České Budějovice Czech. 14 49.00N 14.30E

Česke Zemé d. Czech. 14 49.50N 15.50E
Český Krumlov Czech. 14 48.49N 14.19E
Cessnock Australia 47 32.51S151.21E
Cetinje Yugo. 13 42.24N 18.55E
Ceuta Spain 10 35.53N 5.19W
Ceva Italy 9 44.23N 8.01E
Cévennes mts. France 11 44.25N 4.05E
Ceyhan Turkey 30 37.02N 35.48E
Ceyhan r. Turkey 30 36.54N 34.58E
Chablis France 9 47.47N 3.48E
Chacabuco Argentina 63 34.38S 60.29W
Chachani mtn. Peru 60 16.12S 71.32W
Chachapoyas Peru 60 6.13S 77.54W
Chaco d. Argentina 62 26.30S 60.00W
Chad Africa 34 13.00N 19.00E
Chad, L. Africa 38 13.30N 14.00E
Chadron U.S.A. 52 42.50N103.02W
Chafe Nigeria 38 11.56N 6.55E
Chagda Russian Fed. 21 58.44N130.38E
Chahār Borjak Afghan. 28 30.17N 62.03E
Chajarí Argentina 63 30.45S 57.59W
Chake Chake Tanzania 37 5.13S 39.46E
Chakhānsūr Afghan. 31 31.10N 62.02E
Chala Peru 60 15.48S 74.20W
Chaleur B. Canada 55 48.00N 65.45W
Chalhuanca Peru 60 14.20S 73.10W
Challans France 11 46.51N 1.52W
Challenger Depth Pacific Oc. 27 11.19N142.15E
Challis U.S.A. 54 44.30N114.14W
Chalonnes-sur-Loire France 9 47.21N 0.46W
Châlons-sur-Marne France 9 48.58N 4.22E
Chalon-sur-Saône France 11 46.47N 4.51E
Cham Germany 14 49.13N 12.41E
Chama Zambia 37 11.09S 33.10E
Chambal r. India 29 26.30N 79.20E
Chambersburg U.S.A. 55 39.56N 77.39W
Chambéry France 11 45.34N 5.55E
Chambeshi Zambia 37 10.57S 31.04E
Chambeshi r. Zambia 37 11.15S 30.37E
Chambly France 9 49.10N 2.15E
Chamical Argentina 62 30.22S 66.19W
Chamonix France 11 45.55N 6.52E
Champagne-Ardenne d. France 8 49.42N 4.30E
Champaign U.S.A. 53 40.07N 88.14W
Champéry Switz. 9 46.10N 6.52E
Champlain, L. U.S.A. 55 44.45N 73.15W
Champotón Mexico 56 19.21N 90.43W
Chañaral Chile 62 26.21S 70.37W
Chandeleur Is. U.S.A. 53 29.50N 88.50W
Chandīgarh India 28 30.44N 76.54E
Chāndpur Bangla. 29 22.08N 91.55E
Chandrapur India 29 19.58N 79.21E
Chānf Iran 31 26.40N 60.31E
Changchun China 25 43.50N125.20E
Changde China 25 29.03N111.35E
Chang Jiang r. China 25 31.40N121.15E
Changjin N. Korea 25 40.21N127.20E
Changning China 25 26.24N112.24E
Changping China 25 40.12N116.12E
Changsha China 25 28.10N113.00E
Changting China 25 25.47N116.17E
Changzhi China 25 36.09N113.12E
Changzhou China 25 31.45N119.57E
Channel Is. Europe 5 49.28N 2.13W
Channel Is. U.S.A. 54 34.00N120.00W
Channel-Port-aux-Basques town Canada 51 47.35N 59.10W
Channing Mich. U.S.A. 55 46.08N 88.06W
Chantada Spain 10 42.36N 7.46W
Chanthaburi Thailand 29 12.38N102.12E
Chantilly France 9 49.12N 2.28E
Chao'an China 25 23.43N116.35E
Chaonde Mozambique 37 13.43S 40.31E
Chao Phraya r. Thailand 29 13.30N100.25E
Chaoyang Guangdong China 25 23.17N116.33E
Chapada das Mangabeiras mts. Brazil 61 10.00S 46.30W
Chapada Diamantina Brazil 59 13.30S 42.30W
Chapala, Lago de l. Mexico 56 20.00N103.00W
Chapayevo Kazakhstan 19 50.12N 51.09E
Chapayevsk Russian Fed. 18 52.58N 49.44E
Chapelle-d'Angillon France 9 47.22N 2.26E
Chapicuy Uruguay 63 31.39S 57.54W
Chapleau Canada 55 47.50N 83.24W
Chāpra India 29 25.46N 84.45E
Chaqui Bolivia 62 19.36S 65.32W
Characot I. Antarctica 64 70.00S 75.00W
Charcas Mexico 56 23.08N101.07W
Chard U.K. 5 50.52N 2.59W
Charduār India 29 26.52N 92.46E
Chardzhou Turkmenistan 31 39.09N 63.34E
Charente r. France 11 45.57N 1.00W
Chari r. Chad 38 13.00N 14.30E
Chārīkār Afghan. 28 35.02N 69.13E
Charing U.K. 5 51.12N 0.49E
Charleroi Belgium 8 50.25N 4.27E
Charlesbourg Canada 55 46.53N 71.16W
Charles Pt. Australia 42 12.23S130.37E
Charleston S.C. U.S.A. 53 32.48N 79.58W
Charleston W.Va. U.S.A. 55 38.23N 81.40W
Charlestown Rep. of Ire. 7 53.57N 8.48W
Charlestown Ind. U.S.A. 55 38.28N 85.40W
Charleville Australia 44 26.25S146.13E
Charleville-Mézières France 9 49.46N 4.43E
Charlieu France 11 46.10N 4.10E
Charlotte N.C. U.S.A. 53 35.05N 80.50W
Charlottesville U.S.A. 53 38.02N 78.29W
Charlottetown Canada 51 46.14N 63.09W
Charlton Australia 46 36.18S143.27E
Charly-sur-Marne France 9 48.58N 3.17E
Charolles France 11 46.26N 4.17E
Charters Towers Australia 44 20.05S146.16E
Chartres France 9 48.27N 1.30E
Chascomús Argentina 63 35.35S 58.00W
Châteaubriant France 9 47.43N 1.22W
Château-du-Loir France 9 47.42N 0.25E
Châteaudun France 9 48.04N 1.20E
Château Gontier France 9 47.50N 0.42W
Château Landon France 9 48.09N 2.42E
Château-la-Vallière France 9 47.33N 0.19E
Châteauneuf-en-Thymerais France 9 48.35N 1.15E
Châteauneuf-sur-Loire France 9 47.52N 2.14E
Chateauneuf-sur-Sarthe France 9 47.41N 0.30W
Château-Porcien France 9 49.32N 4.15E
Château Renault France 9 47.35N 0.55E
Châteauroux France 11 46.49N 1.41E
Château-Thierry France 9 49.03N 3.24E
Châtelet Belgium 8 50.24N 4.32E
Châtellerault France 11 46.49N 0.33E
Chatham N.B. Canada 55 47.02N 65.30W
Chatham Ont. Canada 55 42.24N 82.11W
Chatham U.K. 5 51.23N 0.32E
Chatham Is. Pacific Oc. 40 44.00S176.35W
Châtillon Italy 9 45.45N 7.37E
Châtillon-Coligny France 9 47.50N 2.51E
Châtillon-sur-Seine France 9 47.52N 4.35E
Chattahoochee r. U.S.A. 53 30.52N 84.57W
Chattanooga U.S.A. 53 35.01N 85.18W
Chatteris U.K. 5 52.27N 0.03E
Chaulnes France 9 49.49N 2.48E
Chaumont France 11 48.07N 5.08E
Chaumont-en-Vexin France 9 49.16N 1.53E
Chauny France 9 49.37N 3.13E
Chausy Belorussia 15 53.49N 30.57E
Chavanges France 9 48.31N 4.34E
Chaves Brazil 61 0.10S 49.55W
Chaves Portugal 10 41.44N 7.28W
Chawang Thailand 29 8.25N 99.32E
Cheb Czech. 14 50.04N 12.20E
Cheboksary Russian Fed. 18 56.08N 47.12E
Cheboygan U.S.A. 55 45.40N 84.28W
Chebsara Russian Fed. 18 59.14N 38.59E
Chech, Erg des. Africa 34 25.00N 2.15W
Chechersk Belorussia 15 52.54N 30.54E
Checiny Poland 15 50.48N 20.28E
Chegdomyn Russian Fed. 21 51.09N133.01E
Chegga well Mauritania 34 25.30N 5.46W
Chegutu Zimbabwe 39 18.09S 30.07E
Chehalis U.S.A. 54 46.40N122.58W
Cheiron, Cime du mtn. France 9 43.49N 6.58E
Cheju S. Korea 25 33.31N126.29E
Cheju do i. S. Korea 25 33.20N126.30E
Cheleken Turkmenistan 31 39.26N 53.11E
Chelforó Argentina 63 39.04S 66.33W
Chelkar Kazakhstan 20 47.48N 59.39E
Chelles France 9 48.53N 2.36E
Chełm Poland 15 51.10N 23.28E
Chelmsford U.K. 5 51.44N 0.28E
Chełmża Poland 15 53.12N 18.37E
Cheltenham U.K. 5 51.53N 2.07W
Chelva Spain 10 39.45N 1.00W
Chelyabinsk Russian Fed. 20 55.10N 61.25E
Chelyuskin, Mys c. Russian Fed. 21 77.20N106.00E
Chemainus Canada 54 48.55N123.48W
Chemba Mozambique 37 17.11S 34.53E
Chemnitz Germany 14 50.50N 12.55E
Chemult U.S.A. 54 43.13N121.47W
Chën, Gora mtn. Russian Fed. 21 65.30N141.20E
Chenāb r. Asia 28 29.26N 71.09E
Cheney U.S.A. 54 47.29N117.34W
Chengde China 25 40.48N118.06E
Chengdu China 29 30.37N104.06E
Chen Xian China 25 25.48N113.02E
Chepen Peru 60 7.15S 79.20W
Chepstow U.K. 5 51.38N 2.40W
Cher r. France 9 47.12N 2.04E
Cherbourg France 9 49.38N 1.37W
Cherdyn Russian Fed. 18 60.25N 55.22E
Cheremkhovo Russian Fed. 21 53.08N103.01E
Cherepovets Russian Fed. 18 59.05N 37.55E
Cherikov Belorussia 15 53.35N 31.23E
Cherkassy Ukraine 19 49.27N 32.04E
Cherkessk Russian Fed. 19 44.14N 42.05E
Cherkovitsa Bulgaria 13 43.41N 24.49E
Cherlak Russian Fed. 20 54.10N 74.52E
Chernigov Ukraine 15 51.30N 31.18E
Chernikovsk Russian Fed. 18 54.51N 56.06E
Chernobyl Ukraine 15 51.17N 30.15E
Chernovtsy Ukraine 15 48.19N 25.52E
Chernyakhov Ukraine 15 50.30N 28.38E
Chernyakhovsk Russian Fed. 17 54.38N 21.49E
Cherquenco Chile 63 38.41S 72.00W
Cherry Creek town Nev. U.S.A. 54 39.54N113.53W
Cherskogo, Khrebet mts. Russian Fed. 21 65.50N143.00E
Chertkovo Russian Fed. 19 49.22N 40.12E
Chertsey U.K. 5 51.23N 0.27W
Chervonograd Ukraine 15 50.25N 24.10E
Cherwell r. U.K. 5 51.44N 1.15W
Chesapeake B. U.S.A. 53 38.40N 76.25W
Chesham U.K. 5 51.43N 0.38W
Cheshire d. U.K. 4 53.14N 2.30W
Chëshskaya Guba g. Russian Fed. 18 67.20N 46.30E
Chesil Beach f. U.K. 5 50.37N 2.33W
Chester U.K. 4 53.12N 2.53W
Chester Mont. U.S.A. 54 48.31N110.58W
Chester Penn. U.S.A. 55 39.51N 75.21W
Chesterfield U.K. 4 53.14N 1.26W
Chesterfield Inlet town Canada 51 63.00N 91.00W
Chesuncook L. U.S.A. 55 46.00N 69.20W
Chetumal Mexico 57 18.30N 88.17W
Chetumal B. Mexico 57 18.30N 88.00W
Cheviot New Zealand 48 42.49S173.16E
Cheviot U.S.A. 55 39.10N 84.32W
Cheyenne r. U.S.A. 52 44.40N101.15W
Cheyenne Wyo. U.S.A. 52 41.08N104.49W
Cheyne B. Australia 43 34.35S118.50E
Chhindwāra India 29 22.04N 78.58E
Chiang Mai Thailand 29 18.48N 98.59E
Chiapas d. Mexico 56 16.30N 93.00W
Chiari Italy 9 45.32N 9.56E
Chiavari Italy 9 44.19N 9.19E
Chiavenna Italy 9 46.19N 9.24E
Chiba Japan 23 35.36N140.07E
Chiba d. Japan 23 35.10N140.00E
Chibemba Angola 36 15.43S 14.07E
Chibougamau Canada 55 49.53N 74.24W
Chibougamau Lac l. Canada 55 49.50N 74.19W
Chibougamau Prov. Park Canada 55 49.24N 73.48W
Chibuk Nigeria 38 10.52N 12.50E
Chibuto Mozambique 39 24.41S 33.32E
Chicago U.S.A. 53 41.50N 87.45W
Chichagof I. U.S.A. 50 57.55N135.45W
Chichester U.K. 5 50.50N 0.47W
Chichibu Japan 23 35.59N139.05E
Chickasha U.S.A. 52 35.03N 97.57W
Chiclana Spain 10 36.26N 6.09W
Chiclayo Peru 60 6.47S 79.47W
Chico r. Chubut Argentina 63 43.45S 66.10W
Chico r. Santa Cruz Argentina 63 50.03W 68.35W
Chico U.S.A. 54 39.44N121.50W
Chicomo Mozambique 39 24.33S 34.11E
Chicoutimi-Jonquière Canada 55 48.26N 71.04W
Chicualacuala Mozambique 39 22.06S 31.42E
Chidambaram India 29 11.24N 79.42E
Chidenguele Mozambique 39 24.54S 34.13E
Chidley, C. Canada 51 60.30N 65.00W
Chiemsee l. Germany 14 47.55N 12.30E
Chiengi Zambia 37 8.42S 29.07E
Chieri Italy 9 45.01N 7.49E
Chieti Italy 12 42.22N 14.12E
Chifeng China 25 41.17N118.56E
Chigasaki Japan 23 35.19N139.24E
Chiguana Bolivia 62 21.05S 67.58W
Chigubo Mozambique 39 22.38S 33.18E
Chihuahua Mexico 56 28.38N106.05W
Chihuahua d. Mexico 56 28.40N106.00W
Chiili Kazakhstan 20 44.10N 66.37E
Chikumbi Zambia 37 15.14S 28.21E
Chikwawa Malaŵi 37 16.00S 34.54E
Chil r. Iran 31 25.12N 61.30E
Chilapa Mexico 56 17.38N 99.11W
Chilcoot U.S.A. 54 39.49N120.08W
Childers Australia 44 25.14S152.17E
Chile S. America 62 32.30S 71.00W
Chile Chico Chile 63 46.33S 71.44W
Chilko L. Canada 50 51.20N124.05W
Chillagoe Australia 44 17.09S144.32E
Chillán Chile 63 36.36S 72.07W
Chillicothe Ohio U.S.A. 55 39.20N 82.59W
Chilliwack Canada 54 49.10N122.00W
Chiloé, Isla de i. Chile 63 43.00S 73.00W
Chilonga Zambia 37 12.02S 31.17E
Chilpancingo Mexico 56 17.33N 99.30W
Chiltern Australia 47 36.11S146.36E
Chiltern Hills U.K. 5 51.40N 0.53W
Chilumba Malaŵi 37 10.25S 34.18E
Chilwa, L. Malaŵi 37 15.15S 35.45E
Chimanimani Zimbabwe 39 19.48S 32.52E
Chimay Belgium 8 50.03N 4.20E
Chimbas Argentina 62 31.28S 68.30W
Chimbay Uzbekistan 20 42.56N 59.46E
Chimborazo mtn. Ecuador 60 1.29S 78.52W
Chimbote Peru 60 9.04S 78.34W
Chimishliya Moldavia 15 46.30N 28.50E
Chimkent Kazakhstan 24 42.16N 69.05E
Chimoio Mozambique 39 19.04S 33.29E
China Asia 24 33.00N103.00E
China Lake town U.S.A. 54 35.46N117.39W
Chinandega Nicaragua 57 12.35N 87.10W
Chinati Peak U.S.A. 52 29.57N104.29W
Chincha Alta Peru 60 13.25S 76.07W
Chinchilla Australia 45 26.44S150.39E
Chinchón Spain 10 40.09N 3.26W
Chindio Mozambique 37 17.46S 35.23E
Chindwin r. Burma 24 21.30N 95.12E
Chinga Mozambique 37 15.14S 38.40E
Chingleput India 29 12.42N 79.59E
Chingola Zambia 37 12.29S 27.53E
Chingombe Zambia 37 14.25S 29.56E
Chin Hills Burma 29 22.40N 93.30E
Chinhoyi Zimbabwe 39 17.22S 30.10E
Chinkapook Australia 46 35.11S142.57E
Chinle U.S.A. 54 36.09N109.33W
Chinon France 11 47.10N 0.15E
Chinook U.S.A. 54 48.35N109.14W
Chino Valley town U.S.A. 54 34.45N112.27W
Chinsali Zambia 37 10.33S 32.05E
Chintheche Malaŵi 37 11.50S 34.13E
Chiny Belgium 8 49.45N 5.20E
Chiôco Mozambique 37 16.27S 32.49E
Chioggia Italy 9 45.13N 12.17E
Chipata Zambia 37 13.37S 32.40E
Chipera Mozambique 37 15.20S 32.35E
Chipie r. Canada 55 51.30N 83.16W
Chipinge Zimbabwe 39 20.12S 32.38E
Chippenham U.K. 5 51.27N 2.07W
Chipping Norton U.K. 5 51.56N 1.32W
Chiquian Peru 60 10.10S 77.00W
Chiquinquirá Colombia 60 5.37N 73.50W
Chir r. Russian Fed. 19 48.34N 42.53E
Chirchik Uzbekistan 24 41.28N 69.31E
Chiredzi Zimbabwe 39 21.03S 31.39E
Chiredzi r. Zimbabwe 39 21.10S 31.50E
Chiriquí mtn. Panama 57 8.49N 82.38W
Chiriquí, Laguna de b. Panama 57 9.00N 82.00W
Chiromo Malaŵi 37 16.28S 35.10E
Chirripó mtn. Costa Rica 57 9.31N 83.30W
Chirundu Zimbabwe 37 16.04S 28.51E
Chisamba Zambia 37 14.58S 28.23E
Chisasibi Canada 51 53.50N 79.01W
Chisone r. Italy 9 44.49N 7.25E
Chistopol Russian Fed. 18 55.25N 50.38E
Chita Russian Fed. 25 52.03N113.35E
Chitipa Malaŵi 37 9.41S 33.19E
Chitorgarh India 28 24.53N 74.38E
Chitrāl Pakistan 28 35.52N 71.58E
Chittagong Bangla. 29 22.20N 91.48E
Chittoor India 29 13.13N 79.06E
Chiuta, L. Malaŵi/Mozambique 37 14.45S 35.50E
Chivasso Italy 9 45.11N 7.53E
Chivhu Zimbabwe 39 19.01S 30.53E
Chivilcoy Argentina 63 34.52S 60.02W
Chiwanda Tanzania 37 11.21S 34.55E
Chobe d. Botswana 39 18.30S 25.15E
Chobe r. Namibia/Botswana 39 17.48S 25.12E
Chobe Swamp f. Namibia 39 18.20S 23.40E
Chocolate Mts. U.S.A. 54 33.20N115.15W
Chocope Peru 60 7.47S 79.12W
Choele-Choel Argentina 63 39.15S 65.30W
Chōfu Japan 23 35.39N139.33E
Choix Mexico 56 26.43N108.17W
Chojnice Poland 15 53.42N 17.32E
Cholet France 11 47.04N 0.53W
Cholon Vietnam 26 10.45N106.39E
Choluteca Honduras 57 13.16N 87.11W
Choma Zambia 36 16.51S 27.04E
Chomutov Czech. 14 50.28N 13.25E
Chon Buri Thailand 29 13.21N101.01E
Chone Ecuador 60 0.44S 80.04W
Ch'ŏngjin N. Korea 25 41.55N129.50E
Ch'ŏngju S. Korea 25 36.39N127.31E
Chongqing China 29 29.31N106.35E
Chŏnju S. Korea 25 35.50N127.05E
Chonos, Archipelago de los is. Chile 63 45.00S 74.00W
Chorley U.K. 4 53.39N 2.39W
Chorokh r. Georgia 19 41.36N 41.35E
Chortkov Ukraine 15 49.01N 25.42E
Chorzów Poland 15 50.19N 18.56E
Chosica Peru 60 11.55S 76.38W
Chos Malal Argentina 63 37.20S 70.15W
Choszczno Poland 14 53.10N 15.26E
Choteau U.S.A. 54 47.49N112.11W
Chott Djerid f. Tunisia 34 33.30N 8.30E
Chott ech Chergui f. Algeria 34 34.00N 0.30E
Chott Melrhir f. Algeria 34 34.15N 7.00E
Choum Mauritania 34 21.10N 13.00W
Chowchilla U.S.A. 54 37.07N120.16W
Christchurch New Zealand 48 43.33S172.40E
Christchurch U.K. 5 50.44N 1.47W
Christianshåb Greenland 51 68.50N 51.00W
Christmas Creek town Australia 42 18.55S125.56E
Christmas I. Indian Oc. 26 10.30S105.40E
Chrudim Czech. 14 49.57N 15.48E
Chu r. Kazakhstan 24 42.30N 76.10E
Chubbuck U.S.A. 54 34.22N115.20W
Chūbu d. Japan 23 35.25N137.40E
Chubut d. Argentina 63 44.00S 68.00W
Chubut r. Argentina 63 43.18S 65.06W
Chudleigh U.K. 5 50.35N 3.36W
Chudnov Ukraine 15 50.05N 28.01E
Chudovo Russian Fed. 18 59.10N 31.41E
Chuiquimula Guatemala 57 15.52N 89.50W
Chukai Malaysia 26 4.16N103.24E
Chukotskiy Poluostrov pen. Russian Fed. 21 66.00N174.30W
Chukudukraal Botswana 39 22.30S 23.22E
Chula Vista U.S.A. 54 32.39N117.05W
Chulman Russian Fed. 21 56.54N124.55E
Chulucanas Peru 60 5.08S 80.00W
Chulym Russian Fed. 20 55.09N 80.59E
Chum Russian Fed. 18 67.05N 63.15E
Chumbicha Argentina 62 28.50S 66.18W
Chumikan Russian Fed. 21 54.40N135.15E
Chumphon Thailand 29 10.35N 99.14E
Chuna r. Russian Fed. 21 58.00N 94.00E
Ch'unch'ŏn S. Korea 25 37.53N127.45E
Chungking see Chongqing China 29
Chunya Tanzania 37 8.31S 33.28E
Chuquicamata Chile 62 22.20S 68.56W
Chuquisaca d. Bolivia 62 21.00S 64.00W
Chur Switz. 11 46.52N 9.32E
Churchill Canada 51 58.45N 94.00W
Churchill r. Man. Canada 51 58.20N 94.15W
Churchill r. Nfld. Canada 51 53.20N 60.00W
Churchill, C. Canada 51 58.50N 93.00W
Churchill L. Canada 50 56.00N108.00W
Churchill Peak mtn. Canada 50 58.10N125.00W
Church Stretton U.K. 5 52.32N 2.49W
Chusovoy Russian Fed. 18 58.18N 57.50E
Chuxiong China 29 25.03N101.33E
Ciechanów Poland 15 52.53N 20.38E
Ciego de Avila Cuba 57 21.51N 78.47W
Ciénaga Colombia 60 11.11N 74.15W
Cienfuegos Cuba 57 22.10N 80.27W
Cieszyn Poland 15 49.45N 18.38E
Cieza Spain 10 38.14N 1.25W
Cifuentes Spain 10 40.47N 2.37W
Cigüela r. Spain 10 39.47N 3.00W
Cijara, Embalse de resr. Spain 10 39.20N 4.50W
Cilacap Indonesia 26 7.44S109.00E
Cimarron r. U.S.A. 53 36.15N 96.55W
Cimone, Monte mtn. Italy 9 44.12N 10.42E
Cîmpina Romania 13 45.08N 25.44E
Cîmpulung Romania 13 45.16N 25.03E
Cinca r. Spain 10 41.22N 0.20E
Cincinnati U.S.A. 55 39.10N 84.30W
Ciney Belgium 8 50.17N 5.06E
Cinto, Monte mtn. France 11 42.23N 8.57E
Cipolletti Argentina 63 38.56S 67.59W
Circle U.S.A. 54 47.25N105.35W
Circleville Ohio U.S.A. 55 39.36N 82.57W
Circleville Utah U.S.A. 54 38.10N112.16W
Cirebon Indonesia 26 6.46S108.33E
Cirencester U.K. 5 51.43N 1.59W
Ciriè Italy 9 45.14N 7.36E
Cirò Marina Italy 13 39.22N 17.08E
Ciskei Africa 39 32.45S 27.00E
Cittadella Italy 9 45.39N 11.47E
Cittanova Italy 12 38.21N 16.05E
Ciudad Bolívar Venezuela 60 8.06N 63.36W
Ciudad Camargo Mexico 56 27.40N105.10W
Ciudad de México Mexico 56 19.25N 99.10W
Ciudadela Spain 10 40.00N 3.50E
Ciudad Guayana Venezuela 60 8.22N 62.40W
Ciudad Guerrero Mexico 56 28.33N107.28W
Ciudad Guzmán Mexico 56 19.41N103.29W
Ciudad Ixtepec Mexico 56 16.32N 95.10W
Ciudad Jiménez Mexico 56 27.08N104.55W
Ciudad Juárez Mexico 56 31.44N106.29W
Ciudad Madero Mexico 56 22.19N 97.50W
Ciudad Mante Mexico 56 22.44N 98.57W
Ciudad Obregón Mexico 56 27.29N109.56W
Ciudad Ojeda Venezuela 60 10.05N 71.17W
Ciudad Piar Venezuela 60 7.27N 63.19W
Ciudad Real Spain 10 38.59N 3.55W
Ciudad Rodrigo Spain 10 40.36N 6.33W
Ciudad Victoria Mexico 56 23.43N 99.10W
Civitanova Italy 12 43.19N 13.40E
Civitavecchia Italy 12 42.06N 11.48E
Civray France 11 46.09N 0.18E
Cizre Turkey 30 37.21N 42.11E
Clackline Australia 43 31.43S116.31E
Clacton on Sea U.K. 5 51.47N 1.10E
Claire, L. Canada 50 58.30N112.00W
Clamecy France 9 47.27N 3.31E
Clara Rep. of Ire. 7 53.21N 7.37W
Clare N.S.W. Australia 46 33.27S143.55E
Clare S.A. Australia 46 33.50S138.38E
Clare d. Rep. of Ire. 7 52.52N 8.55W
Clare r. Rep. of Ire. 7 53.17N 9.04W
Clare U.S.A. 55 43.49N 84.47W
Clare I. Rep. of Ire. 7 53.48N 10.00W
Claremorris Rep. of Ire. 7 53.44N 9.00W
Clarence r. Australia 47 29.25S153.02E
Clarence r. New Zealand 48 42.10S173.55E
Clarence I. Antarctica 64 61.30S 53.50W
Clarence Str. Australia 42 12.00S131.00E
Clarie Coast f. Antarctica 64 67.00S133.00E
Clark, L. U.S.A. 50 60.15N154.15W
Clarke I. Australia 45 40.30S148.10E
Clark Fork r. U.S.A. 54 48.09N116.15W
Clarksburg U.S.A. 55 39.16N 80.22W
Clarksdale U.S.A. 53 34.12N 90.33W
Clarkston U.S.A. 54 46.26N117.02W
Clarksville Tenn. U.S.A. 53 36.31N 87.21W
Clary France 8 50.05N 3.21E
Clayton r. Australia 46 29.06S137.59E
Clayton Idaho U.S.A. 54 44.16N114.25W
Clayton N.Mex. U.S.A. 52 36.27N103.12W
Clear, C. Rep. of Ire. 3 51.25N 9.32W
Clearfield Utah U.S.A. 54 41.07N112.01W
Clear I. Rep. of Ire. 7 51.26N 9.30W
Clear L. U.S.A. 54 39.02N122.50W
Clearwater U.S.A. 53 27.57N 82.48W
Clearwater Mts. U.S.A. 54 46.00N115.30W
Cle Elum U.S.A. 54 47.12N120.56W
Cleethorpes U.K. 4 53.33N 0.02W
Clermont Australia 44 22.49S147.39E
Clermont France 9 49.23N 2.24E
Clermont-en-Argonne France 9 49.05N 5.05E
Clermont-Ferrand France 11 45.47N 3.05E
Clervaux Lux. 8 50.04N 6.01E
Cles Italy 9 46.22N 11.02E
Cleve Australia 46 33.37S136.32E
Clevedon U.K. 5 51.26N 2.52W
Cleveland d. U.K. 4 54.37N 1.08W
Cleveland Miss. U.S.A. 53 33.43N 90.46W
Cleveland Ohio U.S.A. 55 41.30N 81.41W
Cleveland Tenn. U.S.A. 53 35.10N 84.51W
Cleveland, C. Australia 44 19.11S147.01E
Cleveland Heights town U.S.A. 55 41.30N 81.34W
Cleveland Hills U.K. 4 54.25N 1.10W
Cleveleys U.K. 4 53.52N 3.01W
Clew B. Rep. of Ire. 7 53.50N 9.47W
Clifden Rep. of Ire. 7 53.29N 10.02W
Cliffy Head Australia 43 34.58S116.24E
Clifton Ariz. U.S.A. 54 33.03N109.18W
Clinton B.C. Canada 50 51.05N121.35W
Clinton New Zealand 48 46.13S169.23E
Clinton Iowa U.S.A. 53 41.51N 90.12W
Clinton Okla. U.S.A. 52 35.32N 98.59W
Clisham mtn. U.K. 6 57.58N 6.50W
Cliza Bolivia 62 17.36S 65.56W
Cloghan Offaly Rep. of Ire. 7 53.13N 7.54W
Clogher Head Kerry Rep. of Ire. 7 52.09N 10.28W
Clonakilty Rep. of Ire. 7 51.37N 8.54W
Cloncurry Australia 44 20.42S140.30E
Clones Rep. of Ire. 7 54.11N 7.16W
Clonmel Rep. of Ire. 7 52.21N 7.44W
Clonroche Rep. of Ire. 7 52.27N 6.45W
Cloppenburg Germany 8 52.52N 8.02E
Clorinda Argentina 62 25.20S 57.40W
Cloud Peak mtn. U.S.A. 54 44.25N107.10W
Cloughton U.K. 4 54.20N 0.27W
Cloverdale U.S.A. 54 38.48N123.01W
Clovis Calif. U.S.A. 54 36.49N119.42W
Clovis N.Mex. U.S.A. 52 34.14N103.13W
Clowne U.K. 4 53.18N 1.16W
Cluj-Napoca Romania 15 46.47N 23.37E
Clunes Australia 46 37.16S143.47E
Cluny France 11 46.26N 4.39E
Clusone Italy 9 45.53N 9.57E
Clutha r. New Zealand 48 46.18S169.05E
Clwyd d. U.K. 4 53.07N 3.20W
Clwyd r. U.K. 4 53.19N 3.30W
Clyde Canada 51 70.30N 68.30W
Clyde New Zealand 48 45.11S169.19E
Clyde r. U.K. 6 55.58N 4.53W
Clydebank U.K. 6 55.53N 4.23W
Coachella U.S.A. 54 33.41N116.10W
Coahuila d. Mexico 56 27.00N103.00W
Coalinga U.S.A. 54 36.09N120.21W
Coalville U.K. 5 52.43N 1.21W
Coast d. Kenya 37 3.00S 39.30E
Coast Mts. Canada 50 55.30N128.00W
Coast Range mts. U.S.A. 54 42.40N123.30W
Coatbridge U.K. 6 55.52N 4.02W
Coats I. Canada 51 62.30N 83.00W
Coats Land f. Antarctica 64 77.00S 25.00W
Coatzacoalcos Mexico 56 18.10N 94.25W
Cobalt Canada 55 47.24N 79.41W

80

Épinal France 11 48.10N 6.28E
Epping U.K. 5 51.42N 0.07E
Epsom U.K. 5 51.20N 0.16W
Epte r. France 9 49.04N 1.37E
Equatorial Guinea Africa 34 1.30N 10.30E
Equerdreville France 9 49.40N 1.40W
Era, Ozero l. Russian Fed. 19 47.38N 45.18E
Eraclea Italy 9 45.35N 12.40E
Erciyaş Daği mtn. Turkey 30 38.33N 35.25E
Erdre r. France 9 47.27N 1.34W
Erebus, Mt. Antarctica 64 77.40S167.20E
Erechim Brazil 59 27.35S 52.15W
Eregli Konya Turkey 30 37.30N 34.02E
Eregli Zonguldak Turkey 30 41.17N 31.26E
Erenhot China 25 43.50N112.00E
Erft r. Germany 8 51.12N 6.45E
Erfurt Germany 14 50.58N 11.02E
Ergani Turkey 30 38.17N 39.44E
Ergene r. Turkey 13 41.02N 26.22E
Erica Neth. 8 52.44N 6.56E
Erie U.S.A. 55 42.07N 80.05W
Erie, L. Canada/U.S.A. 55 42.15N 81.00W
Eriskay i. U.K. 6 57.04N 7.17W
Eritrea f. Ethiopia 35 15.30N 38.00E
Erkelenz Germany 8 51.05N 6.18E
Erlangen Germany 14 49.36N 11.02E
Erldunda Australia 44 25.14S133.12E
Ermelo Neth. 8 52.19N 5.38E
Ermelo R.S.A. 39 26.30S 29.59E
Ernée France 9 48.18N 0.56W
Erode India 28 11.21N 77.43E
Er Rachidia Morocco 34 31.58N 4.25W
Errego Mozambique 37 16.02S 37.11E
Errigal Mtn. Rep. of Ire. 7 55.02N 8.08W
Erris Head Rep. of Ire. 7 54.19N 10.00W
Ertix He r. Kazakhstan 24 48.00N 84.20E
Erudina Australia 46 31.30S139.23E
Ervy-le-Châtel France 9 48.02N 3.55E
Erzgebirge mts. Germany 14 50.30N 12.50E
Erzin Russian Fed. 24 50.16N 95.14E
Erzincan Turkey 30 39.44N 39.30E
Erzurum Turkey 30 39.57N 41.17E
Esbjerg Denmark 17 55.28N 8.27E
Esbo see Espoo Finland 17
Escalante U.S.A. 54 37.47N111.36W
Escanaba U.S.A. 55 45.47N 87.04W
Esch Lux. 8 49.31N 5.59E
Eschweiler Germany 8 50.49N 6.16E
Escondido r. Nicaragua 57 11.58N 83.45W
Escondido U.S.A. 54 33.07N117.05W
Escuintla Guatemala 56 14.18N 90.47W
Esens Germany 8 53.40N 7.40E
Esher U.K. 5 51.23N 0.22W
Eshkanān Iran 31 27.10N 53.38E
Eshowe R.S.A. 39 28.53S 31.29E
Esk r. N. Yorks. U.K. 4 54.29N 0.37W
Eskifjördhur town Iceland 16 65.05N 14.00W
Eskilstuna Sweden 17 59.22N 16.30E
Eskimo Point town Canada 51 61.10N 94.15W
Eskişehir Turkey 30 39.46N 30.30E
Esla r. Spain 10 41.29N 6.03W
Eslāmābād-e-Gharb Iran 31 34.08N 46.35E
Eslöv Sweden 17 55.50N 13.20E
Esmeraldas Ecuador 60 0.56N 79.40W
Espanola Canada 55 46.15N 81.46W
Espe Kazakhstan 20 43.50N 74.10E
Esperance Australia 43 33.49S121.52E
Esperance B. Australia 43 33.51S121.53E
Esperanza Argentina 63 31.30S 61.00W
Espinal Colombia 60 4.08N 75.00W
Espinhaço, Serra do mts. Brazil 59 17.15S 43.10W
Espírito Santo d. Brazil 59 20.00S 40.30W
Espíritu Santo i. Vanuatu 40 15.50S166.50E
Espoo Finland 17 60.13N 24.40E
Espungabera Mozambique 39 20.28S 32.48E
Esquel Argentina 63 42.55S 71.20W
Esquimalt Canada 54 48.30N123.23W
Esquina Argentina 63 30.00S 59.30W
Essaouira Morocco 34 31.30N 9.47W
Essen Germany 8 51.27N 6.57E
Essequibo r. Guyana 60 6.30N 58.40W
Essex d. U.K. 5 51.46N 0.30E
Essex U.S.A. 54 34.45N115.15W
Essonne d. France 9 48.36N 2.20E
Essoyes France 9 48.04N 4.32E
Essoyla Russian Fed. 18 61.47N 33.11E
Est d. Burkina 38 12.45N 0.25E
Est, Pointe de l' c. Canada 51 49.08N 61.41W
Estados, Isla de los i. Argentina 63 54.45S 64.00W
Estância Brazil 61 11.15S 37.28W
Estand, Kūh-e mtn. Iran 31 31.18N 60.03E
Este Italy 9 45.14N 11.39E
Estepona Spain 10 36.26N 5.09W
Esternay France 9 48.44N 3.34E
Estevan Canada 50 49.09N103.00W
Estissac France 9 48.16N 3.49E
Estivane Mozambique 39 24.07S 32.38E
Eston U.K. 4 54.34N 1.07W
Estonia Europe 18 59.00N 25.00E
Estoril Portugal 10 38.42N 9.23W
Estrela, Serra da mts. Portugal 10 40.20N 7.40W
Estremoz Portugal 10 38.50N 7.35W
Esztergom Hungary 15 47.48N 18.45E
Eşfahān Iran 31 32.42N 51.40E
Eştahbānāt Iran 31 29.05N 54.03E
Étables France 11 48.37N 2.50W
Etadunna Australia 46 28.43S138.38E
Étampes France 9 48.26N 2.10E
Étaples France 11 50.31N 1.39E
Ethel Creek town Australia 42 23.05S120.14E
Ethiopia Africa 35 10.00N 39.00E
Etive, Loch U.K. 6 56.27N 5.15W
Etna, Monte mtn. Italy 12 37.43N 14.59E
Etosha Game Res. Namibia 39 18.50S 15.40E
Etosha Pan f. Namibia 39 18.50S 16.20E
Étretat France 9 49.42N 0.12E
Ettelbrück Lux. 8 49.51N 6.06E
Euabalong Australia 47 33.07S146.28E
Euboea see Évvoia i. Greece 13
Eucla Australia 43 31.40S128.51E
Euclid U.S.A. 55 41.34N 81.33W
Eucumbene, L. Australia 47 36.05S148.45E
Eudunda Australia 46 34.09S139.04E
Eufaula Resr. U.S.A. 53 35.15N 95.35W
Eugene U.S.A. 54 44.02N123.05W
Eugenia, Punta c. Mexico 56 27.50N115.03W
Eugowra Australia 47 33.24S148.25E
Eupen Belgium 8 50.38N 6.04E
Euphrates r. see Nahr al Furāt r. Asia 31
Eure d. France 9 49.10N 1.00E
Eure r. France 9 48.18N 1.12E
Eure et Loire d. France 9 48.30N 1.30E
Eureka Calif. U.S.A. 54 40.47N124.09W
Eureka Nev. U.S.A. 54 39.31N115.58W
Eureka Utah U.S.A. 54 39.57N112.07W
Eurinilla r. Australia 46 30.50S140.01E
Euriowie Australia 46 31.22S141.42E
Euroa Australia 47 36.46S145.35E
Europa, Picos de mts. Spain 10 43.10N 4.40W
Euskirchen Germany 8 50.40N 6.47E
Euston Australia 46 34.34S142.49E
Evans, Lac l. Canada 55 50.50N 77.00W
Evans Head c. Australia 47 29.06S153.25E
Evanston Wyo. U.S.A. 54 41.16N110.58W
Evansville U.S.A. 55 38.00N 87.33W
Evelyn Creek r. Australia 46 28.20S134.50E
Everard, C. Australia 47 37.50S149.16E
Everard, L. Australia 46 31.25S135.05E
Everard Range mts. Australia 45 27.05S132.28E
Everest, Mt. Asia 29 27.59N 86.56E
Everett Wash. U.S.A. 54 47.59N122.13W
Evesham U.K. 5 52.06N 1.57W
Evijärvi Finland 16 63.22N 23.29E
Evje Norway 17 58.36N 7.51E
Évora Portugal 10 38.34N 7.54W
Évreux France 9 49.03N 1.11E
Évry France 9 48.38N 2.27E
Évvoia i. Greece 13 38.30N 23.50E
Ewe, Loch U.K. 6 57.48N 5.38W
Exe r. U.K. 5 50.40N 3.28W
Exeter U.K. 5 50.43N 3.31W
Exmoor Forest hills U.K. 5 51.08N 3.45W
Exmouth Australia 42 21.54S114.10E
Exmouth U.K. 5 50.37N 3.24W
Exmouth G. Australia 42 22.00S114.20E
Expedition Range mts. Australia 44 24.30S149.05E
Extremadura d. Spain 10 39.00N 6.00W
Exuma Is. Bahamas 57 24.00N 76.00W
Eyasi, L. Tanzania 37 3.40S 35.00E
Eye U.K. 5 52.19N 1.09E
Eyemouth U.K. 6 55.52N 2.05W
Eygurande France 11 45.40N 2.26E
Eyjafjördhur est. Iceland 16 65.54N 18.15W
Eyl Somali Rep. 35 8.00N 49.51E
Eyrarbakki Iceland 16 63.52N 21.09W
Eyre r. Australia 44 26.40S139.00E
Eyre, L. Australia 46 28.30S137.25E
Eyre Pen. Australia 46 34.00S135.45E
Ezequil Ramos Mexia, Embalse resr. Argentina 63 39.20S 69.00W

F

Fåberg Norway 17 61.10N 10.22E
Fåborg Denmark 17 55.06N 10.15E
Fabriano Italy 12 43.20N 12.54E
Facatativá Colombia 60 4.48N 74.32W
Facundo Argentina 63 45.19S 69.59W
Fada Chad 35 17.13N 21.30E
Fada-N'Gourma Burkina 38 12.03N 0.22E
Faenza Italy 9 44.17N 11.52E
Fafa Mali 38 15.20N 0.43E
Fafen r. Ethiopia 35 6.07N 44.20E
Făgăraş Romania 15 45.51N 24.58E
Fagernes Norway 17 60.59N 9.17E
Fagersta Sweden 17 60.00N 15.47E
Faguibine, Lac l. Mali 38 16.45N 3.54W
Fagus Egypt 32 30.44N 31.47E
Fā'id Egypt 32 30.19N 32.19E
Fairbanks U.S.A. 50 64.50N147.50W
Fairborn U.S.A. 55 39.48N 84.03W
Fairfield Calif. U.S.A. 54 38.15N122.03W
Fair Head U.K. 7 55.13N 6.09W
Fair Isle U.K. 6 59.32N 1.38W
Fairlie New Zealand 48 44.06S170.50E
Fairmont W.Va. U.S.A. 55 39.28N 80.08W
Fairview Utah U.S.A. 54 39.38N111.26W
Fairweather, Mt. U.S.A. 50 59.00N137.30W
Faisalābād Pakistan 28 31.25N 73.09E
Faizābād India 29 26.46N 82.08E
Fajr, Wādī r. Saudi Arabia 30 30.00N 38.25E
Fakenham U.K. 4 52.50N 0.51E
Fakfak Indonesia 27 2.55S132.17E
Falaise France 9 48.54N 0.11W
Falcarragh Rep. of Ire. 7 55.08N 8.06W
Falcone, Capo del c. Italy 12 40.57N 8.12E
Faleshty Moldavia 15 47.30N 27.45E
Falkenberg Sweden 17 56.54N 12.28E
Falkirk U.K. 6 56.00N 3.48W
Falkland Is. Atlantic Oc. 63 51.45W 59.00W
Falkland Sd. str. Falkland Is. 63 51.45W 59.25W
Falköping Sweden 17 58.10N 13.31E
Fallbrook U.S.A. 54 33.23N117.15W
Fall River town U.S.A. 55 41.43N 71.08W
Falmouth U.K. 5 50.09N 5.05W
False B. R.S.A. 39 34.10S 18.40E
Falster i. Denmark 17 54.48N 11.58E
Fălticeni Romania 15 47.28N 26.18E
Falun Sweden 17 60.36N 15.38E
Famagusta see Ammókhostos Cyprus 32
Famoso U.S.A. 54 35.36N119.14W
Fannich, Loch U.K. 6 57.38N 5.00W
Fano Italy 9 43.50N 13.01E
Faradje Zaïre 37 3.45N 29.43E
Faradofay Madagascar 36 25.02S 47.00E
Farāfirah, Wāḥāt al oasis Egypt 30 27.15N 28.10E
Farāh Afghan. 31 32.23N 62.07E
Farāh r. Afghan. 31 31.25N 61.30E
Faraulep is. Federated States of Micronesia 27 8.36N144.33E
Fareham U.K. 5 50.52N 1.11W
Farewell, C. see Farvel, Kap c. Greenland 51
Farewell, C. New Zealand 48 40.30S172.35E
Fargo U.S.A. 53 46.52N 96.59W
Farina Australia 46 30.05S138.20E
Farkwa Tanzania 37 5.26S 35.15E
Farmington N.Mex. U.S.A. 54 36.44N108.12W
Farnborough U.K. 5 51.17N 0.46W
Farne Is. U.K. 4 55.38N 1.36W
Farnham U.K. 5 51.13N 0.49W
Faro Brazil 61 2.11S 56.44W
Faro Portugal 10 37.01N 7.56W
Faroe Is. Europe 16 62.00N 7.00W
Fårön i. Sweden 17 57.56N 19.08E
Fårösund Sweden 17 57.52N 19.03E
Farrell U.S.A. 55 41.13N 80.31W
Farrukhābād India 29 27.23N 79.35E
Fársala Greece 13 39.17N 22.22E
Fārsī Afghan. 31 33.47N 63.12E
Farsund Norway 17 58.05N 6.48E
Farvel, Kap c. Greenland 51 60.00N 44.20W
Fasā Iran 31 28.55N 53.38E
Fastov Ukraine 15 50.08N 29.59E
Făurei Romania 15 45.04N 27.15E
Fauske Norway 16 67.17N 15.25E
Favara Italy 12 37.19N 13.40E
Favignana i. Italy 12 37.57N 12.19E
Faxaflói b. Iceland 16 64.30N 22.50W
Faxe r. Sweden 16 63.15N 17.15E
Fayetteville Ark. U.S.A. 53 36.03N 94.10W
Fayetteville N.C. U.S.A. 53 35.03N 78.53W
Fdérik Mauritania 34 22.35N 12.30W
Feale r. Rep. of Ire. 7 52.28N 9.37W
Fear, C. U.S.A. 53 33.51N 77.59W
Fécamp France 9 49.45N 0.23E
Federación Argentina 63 31.00S 57.55W
Federal Argentina 63 30.55S 58.45W
Federal Capital Territory d. Nigeria 38 8.50N 7.00E
Federated States of Micronesia Pacific Oc. 40 10.00N155.00E
Fedovo Russian Fed. 18 62.22N 39.21E
Fedulki Russian Fed. 18 65.00N 66.10E
Feeagh, Lough Rep. of Ire. 7 53.56N 9.35W
Fehmarn i. Germany 14 54.30N 11.05E
Feia, Lagoa l. Brazil 59 22.00S 41.20W
Feijó Brazil 60 8.09S 70.21W
Feilding New Zealand 48 40.10S175.25E
Feira Zambia 37 15.30S 30.27E
Feira de Santana Brazil 61 12.17S 38.53W
Felanitx Spain 10 39.27N 3.08E
Feldkirch Austria 14 47.15N 9.38E
Felixstowe U.K. 5 51.58N 1.20E
Feltre Italy 9 46.01N 11.54E
Femunden l. Norway 17 62.12N 11.52E
Femundsenden Norway 17 61.55N 11.55E
Fengfeng China 25 36.34N114.19E
Fengjie China 25 31.00N109.30E
Fensfjorden est. Norway 17 60.51N 4.50E
Fenton U.S.A. 55 42.48N 83.42W
Fenyang China 25 37.14N111.43E
Feodosiya Ukraine 19 45.03N 35.23E
Ferdows Iran 31 34.00N 58.10E
Fère-Champenoise France 9 48.45N 3.59E
Fère-en-Tardenois France 9 48.12N 3.31E
Fergana Uzbekistan 24 40.23N 71.19E
Fergus Falls town U.S.A. 53 46.18N 96.00W
Fergusson I. P.N.G. 44 9.30S150.40E
Ferkéssédougou Ivory Coast 38 9.30N 5.10W
Fermanagh d. U.K. 7 54.21N 7.40W
Fermo Italy 12 43.09N 13.43E
Fermoselle Spain 10 41.19N 6.24W
Fermoy Rep. of Ire. 7 52.08N 8.17W
Fernlee Australia 47 28.12S147.05E
Ferrara Italy 9 44.49N 11.38E
Ferreñafe Peru 60 6.42S 79.45W
Ferret, Cap c. France 11 44.42N 1.16W
Ferrières France 9 48.05N 2.48E
Fès Morocco 34 34.05N 5.00W
Feshi Zaïre 36 6.08S 18.12E
Festubert Canada 55 47.12N 72.40W
Feteşti Romania 15 44.23N 27.50E
Fethiye Turkey 30 36.37N 29.06E
Fetlar i. U.K. 6 60.37N 0.52W
Feuilles, Rivière aux r. Canada 51 58.47N 70.06W
Fevzipaşa Turkey 30 37.07N 36.38E
Fianarantsoa Madagascar 36 21.26S 47.05E
Fidenza Italy 9 44.52N 10.03E
Fier Albania 13 40.43N 19.34E
Fife d. U.K. 6 56.10N 3.10W
Fife Ness c. U.K. 6 56.17N 2.36W
Figeac France 11 44.32N 2.01E
Figueira da Foz Portugal 10 40.09N 8.51W
Figueras Spain 10 42.16N 2.57E
Figueres see Figueras Spain 10
Fiji Pacific Oc. 40 18.00S178.00E
Filabusi Zimbabwe 39 20.34S 29.20E
Filey U.K. 4 54.13N 0.18W
Filiaşi Romania 15 44.33N 23.31E
Filiatrá Greece 13 37.09N 21.35E
Filingué Niger 38 14.21N 3.22E
Filipstad Sweden 17 59.43N 14.10E
Fillmore Calif. U.S.A. 54 34.24N118.55W
Finale Emilia Italy 9 44.50N 11.17E
Finale Ligure Italy 9 44.10N 8.20E
Findhorn r. U.K. 6 57.38N 3.37W
Findlay U.S.A. 55 41.02N 83.40W
Finisterre, Cabo de c. Spain 10 42.54N 9.16W
Finke Australia 44 25.35S134.34E
Finke r. Australia 45 27.00S136.10E
Finland Europe 18 64.30N 27.00E
Finland, G. of Finland/Estonia 17 59.30N 24.00E
Finlay r. Canada 50 56.30N124.40W
Finley Australia 47 35.40S145.34E
Finmark Canada 55 48.36N 89.44W
Finn r. Rep. of Ire. 7 54.50N 7.30W
Finnmark d. Norway 16 70.10N 26.00E
Finschhafen P.N.G. 27 6.35S147.51E
Finse Norway 17 60.36N 7.30E
Finspång Sweden 17 58.43N 15.47E
Fiorenzuola d'Arda Italy 9 44.56N 9.55E
Firat r. Turkey see Al Furāt r. Asia 30
Firenze Italy 12 43.46N 11.15E
Firenzuola Italy 9 44.07N 11.23E
Firozābād India 29 27.09N 78.24E
Firozpur India 28 30.55N 74.38E
Firth of Clyde est. U.K. 6 55.35N 4.53W
Firth of Forth est. U.K. 6 56.05N 3.00W
Firth of Lorn est. U.K. 6 56.20N 5.40W
Firth of Tay est. U.K. 6 56.24N 3.08W
Firūzābād Iran 31 28.50N 52.35E
Firyuza Turkmenistan 20 37.55N 58.03E
Fish r. Namibia 39 28.07S 17.45E
Fisher Str. Canada 51 63.00N 84.00W
Fishguard U.K. 5 51.59N 4.59W
Fiskenaesset Greenland 51 63.05N 50.40W
Fiskivötn f. Iceland 16 64.50N 20.45W
Fismes France 9 49.18N 3.41E
Fitz Roy Argentina 63 47.00S 67.15W
Fitzroy r. Australia 42 17.31S123.35E
Fitzroy Crossing Australia 42 18.13S125.33E
Fivizzano Italy 9 44.14N 10.08E
Fizi Zaïre 37 4.18S 28.56E
Fjällåsen Sweden 16 67.29N 20.10E
Fjällsjo r. Sweden 16 63.27N 17.06E
Flå Norway 17 60.25N 9.26E
Flagstaff U.S.A. 54 35.12N111.39W
Flåm Norway 17 60.50N 7.07E
Flamborough Head U.K. 4 54.06N 0.05W
Flaming Gorge Resr. U.S.A. 54 41.15N109.30W
Flandre f. Belgium 8 50.52N 3.00E
Flannan Is. U.K. 6 58.16N 7.40W
Flåsjön l. Sweden 16 64.06N 15.51E
Flathead L. U.S.A. 54 47.52N114.08W
Flattery, C. Australia 44 14.58S145.21E
Flattery, C. U.S.A. 52 48.23N124.43W
Fleetwood U.K. 4 53.55N 3.01W
Flekkefjord town Norway 17 58.17N 6.41E
Flen Sweden 17 59.04N 16.35E
Flensburg Germany 14 54.47N 9.27E
Flers France 9 48.45N 0.34W
Flevoland d. Neth. 8 52.25N 5.30E
Flinders r. Australia 44 17.30S140.45E
Flinders B. Australia 43 34.23S115.19E
Flinders I. S.A. Australia 46 33.44S134.30E
Flinders I. Tas. Australia 45 40.00S148.00E
Flinders Ranges mts. Australia 46 31.25S138.45E
Flinders Reefs Australia 44 17.37S148.31E
Flin Flon Canada 51 54.47N101.51W
Flint U.K. 4 53.15N 3.07W
Flint U.S.A. 55 43.03N 83.40W
Flint r. Ga. U.S.A. 53 30.52N 84.35W
Flinton Australia 45 27.54S149.34E
Flisa Norway 17 60.34N 12.06E
Florac France 11 44.19N 3.36E
Florence see Firenze Italy 12
Florence Ariz. U.S.A. 54 33.02N111.23W
Florence Oreg. U.S.A. 54 43.58N124.07W
Florence S.C. U.S.A. 53 34.12N 79.44W
Florence, L. Australia 46 28.52S138.08E
Florencia Colombia 60 1.37N 75.37W
Florennes Belgium 8 50.14N 4.35E
Florenville Belgium 8 49.42N 5.19E
Flores i. Indonesia 27 8.40S121.20E
Flores, Laut sea Indonesia 27 7.00S121.00E
Floreshty Moldavia 15 47.52N 28.12E
Flores Sea see Flores, Laut sea Indonesia 27
Floriano Brazil 61 6.45S 43.00W
Florianópolis Brazil 59 27.35S 48.34W
Florida Uruguay 63 34.06S 56.13W
Florida d. U.S.A. 53 29.00N 82.00W
Florina Australia 46 32.23S139.58E
Flórina Greece 13 40.48N 21.25E
Florö Norway 17 61.36N 5.00E
Fluessen l. Neth. 8 52.58N 5.23E
Flushing see Vlissingen Neth. 8
Fly r. P.N.G. 44 8.22S142.23E
Focşani Romania 15 45.40N 27.12E
Foggia Italy 12 41.28N 15.33E
Foggo Nigeria 38 11.21N 9.57E
Foix France 11 42.57N 1.35E
Folda est. Nordland Norway 16 67.36N 14.50E
Folda est. N. Trönd. Norway 16 64.45N 11.20E
Folégandros i. Greece 13 36.35N 24.55E
Foley Botswana 39 21.34S 27.21E
Foleyet Canada 55 48.05N 82.26W
Folgefonna glacier Norway 17 60.00N 6.20E
Foligno Italy 12 42.56N 12.43E
Folkestone U.K. 5 51.05N 1.11E
Folsom U.S.A. 54 38.41N121.15W
Fominskoye Russian Fed. 18 59.45N 42.03E
Fond du Lac Canada 50 59.20N107.09W
Fonsagrada Spain 10 43.08N 7.04W
Fonseca, Golfo de g. Honduras 57 13.10N 87.30W
Fontainebleau France 9 48.24N 2.42E
Fonte Boa Brazil 60 2.33S 65.59W
Fontenay France 11 46.28N 0.48W
Foochow see Fuzhou China 25
Forbach France 11 49.11N 6.54E
Forbes Australia 47 33.24S148.03E
Forchheim Germany 14 49.43N 11.04E
Ford's Bridge Australia 47 29.46S145.25E
Forel, Mt. Greenland 51 67.00N 37.00W
Foreland Pt. U.K. 5 51.15N 3.47W
Forest of Bowland hills U.K. 4 53.57N 2.30W
Forest of Dean f. U.K. 5 51.48N 2.32W
Forfar U.K. 6 56.38N 2.54W
Forlì Italy 9 44.13N 12.02E
Formby Pt. U.K. 4 53.34N 3.07W
Formentera i. Spain 10 38.41N 1.30E
Formerie France 9 49.39N 1.44E
Formiga Brazil 59 20.30S 45.27W
Formosa Argentina 62 26.06S 58.14W
Formosa d. Argentina 62 25.00S 60.00W
Formosa see Taiwan Asia 25
Formosa Brazil 61 15.30S 47.22W
Formosa, Serra mts. Brazil 61 12.00S 55.20W
Fornovo di Taro Italy 9 44.42N 10.06E
Forres U.K. 6 57.37N 3.38W
Fors Sweden 17 60.13N 16.18E
Forsayth Australia 44 18.35S143.36E
Forssa Finland 17 60.49N 23.38E
Forst Germany 14 51.46N 14.39E
Forster Australia 47 32.12S152.30E
Forsyth U.S.A. 54 46.16N106.41W
Fort Albany Canada 51 52.15N 81.35W
Fortaleza Brazil 61 3.45S 38.35W
Fort Augustus U.K. 6 57.09N 4.41W
Fort Beaufort R.S.A. 39 32.46S 26.36E
Fort Benton U.S.A. 54 47.49N110.40W
Fort Chipewyan Canada 50 58.46N111.09W
Fort Collins U.S.A. 52 40.35N105.05W
Fort Coulonge Canada 55 45.51N 76.44W
Fort-de-France Martinique 57 14.36N 61.05W
Fort Dodge U.S.A. 53 42.31N 94.10W
Forte dei Marmi Italy 9 43.57N 10.10E
Fortescue r. Australia 42 21.00S116.06E
Fort Frances Canada 51 48.37N 93.23W
Fort Franklin Canada 50 65.11N123.45W
Fort Good Hope Canada 50 66.16N128.37W
Fort Grahame Canada 50 56.30N124.35W
Forth r. U.K. 6 56.06N 3.48W
Fort Klamath U.S.A. 54 42.42N122.00W
Fort Lallemand Algeria 34 31.13N 6.17E
Fort Lauderdale U.S.A. 53 26.08N 80.08W
Fort Liard Canada 50 60.14N123.28W
Fort MacKay Canada 50 57.12N111.41W
Fort MacMahon Algeria 34 29.51N 1.45E
Fort Maguire Malaŵi 37 13.38S 34.59E
Fort McMurray Canada 50 56.45N111.27W
Fort McPherson Canada 50 67.29N134.50W
Fort Miribel Algeria 34 29.31N 2.55E
Fort Morgan U.S.A. 52 40.15N103.48W
Fort Myers U.S.A. 53 26.39N 81.51W
Fort Nelson Canada 50 58.48N122.44W
Fort Norman Canada 50 64.55N125.29W
Fort Peck Dam U.S.A. 54 47.52N106.38W
Fort Peck Resr. U.S.A. 54 47.45N106.50W
Fort Pierce U.S.A. 53 27.28N 80.20W
Fort Portal Uganda 37 0.40N 30.17E
Fort Providence Canada 50 61.21N117.39W
Fort Randall U.S.A. 50 55.10N162.47W
Fort Reliance Canada 50 62.45N109.08W
Fort Resolution Canada 50 61.10N113.39W
Fortrose New Zealand 48 46.34S168.48E
Fortrose U.K. 6 57.34N 4.09W
Fort Rousset Congo 36 0.30S 15.48E
Fort St. John Canada 50 56.14N120.55W
Fort Scott U.S.A. 53 37.52N 94.43W
Fort Severn Canada 51 56.00N 87.40W
Fort Shevchenko Kazakhstan 19 44.31N 50.15E
Fort Simpson Canada 50 61.46N121.15W
Fort Smith Canada 50 60.00N111.53W
Fort Smith d. Canada 50 63.30N118.00W
Fort Smith U.S.A. 53 35.22N 94.27W
Fort Thomas U.S.A. 54 33.02N109.58W
Fortuna Calif. U.S.A. 54 40.36N124.09W
Fort Vermilion Canada 50 58.22N115.59W
Fort Wayne U.S.A. 55 41.05N 85.08W
Fort William U.K. 6 56.49N 5.07W
Fort Worth U.S.A. 53 32.45N 97.20W
Forty Mile town Canada 50 64.24N140.31W
Fort Yukon U.S.A. 50 66.35N145.20W
Foshan China 25 23.03N113.08E
Fossano Italy 9 44.33N 7.43E
Foster Australia 47 38.39S146.12E
Fostoria U.S.A. 55 41.10N 83.25W
Fougères France 9 48.21N 1.12W
Foula i. U.K. 6 60.08N 2.05W
Foulness I. U.K. 5 51.35N 0.55E
Foulwind, C. New Zealand 48 41.45S171.30E
Foumban Cameroon 38 5.43N 10.50E
Fourmies France 8 50.01N 4.02E
Foúrnoi i. Greece 13 37.34N 26.30E
Fouta Djalon f. Guinea 34 11.30N 12.30W
Foveaux Str. New Zealand 48 46.40S168.00E
Fowey U.K. 5 50.20N 4.39W
Fowlers B. Australia 45 31.59S132.27E
Foxe Basin b. Canada 51 67.30N 79.00W
Foxe Channel Canada 51 65.00N 80.00W
Foxe Pen. Canada 51 65.00N 76.00W
Fox Glacier town New Zealand 48 43.28S170.01E
Foxton New Zealand 48 40.27S175.18E
Foyle r. U.K. 7 55.00N 7.20W
Foyle, Lough U.K. 7 55.05N 7.10W
Foz do Iguaçu Brazil 59 25.33S 54.31W
Förde Norway 17 61.27N 5.52E
Franca Brazil 59 20.33S 47.27W
Francavilla Fontana Italy 13 40.31N 17.35E
France Europe 11 47.00N 2.00E
Frances Australia 46 36.41S140.59E
Frances L. Canada 50 61.25N129.30W
Francesville U.S.A. 55 40.59N 86.54W
Franche-Comté d. France 11 47.10N 6.00E
Francia Uruguay 63 32.33S 56.37W
Francistown Botswana 39 21.12S 27.29E
Franeker Neth. 8 53.13N 5.31E
Frankfort R.S.A. 39 27.15S 28.30E
Frankfort Ky. U.S.A. 55 38.11N 84.53W
Frankfurt Brandenburg Germany 14 52.20N 14.32E
Frankfurt Hessen Germany 14 50.06N 8.41E
Frankland r. Australia 43 34.58S116.49E
Franklin N.H. U.S.A. 55 43.27N 71.39W
Franklin W.Va. U.S.A. 55 38.39N 79.20W
Franklin B. Canada 50 70.00N126.30W

84

Goiana Brazil 61 7.30S 35.00W
Goiânia Brazil 61 16.43S 49.18W
Goiás Brazil 61 15.57S 50.07W
Goiás d. Brazil 61 15.00S 48.00W
Goito Italy 9 45.15N 10.40E
Gojō Japan 23 34.21N135.42E
Gokteik Burma 29 22.26N 97.00E
Gokwe Zimbabwe 39 18.14S 28.54E
Gol Norway 17 60.42N 8.57E
Golan Heights mts. Syria 32 32.55N 35.42E
Golconda U.S.A. 54 40.57N117.30W
Goldap Poland 15 54.19N 22.19E
Gold Beach town U.S.A. 54 42.25N124.25W
Golden Rep. of Ire. 7 52.30N 7.59W
Golden B. New Zealand 48 40.45S172.50E
Goldendale U.S.A. 54 45.49N120.50W
Golden Ridge town Australia 43 30.51S121.42E
Golden Vale f. Rep. of Ire. 7 52.30N 8.07W
Goldfield U.S.A. 54 37.42N117.14W
Goldsworthy Australia 42 20.20S119.30E
Goleniów Poland 14 53.36N 14.50E
Golets Skalisty mtn. Russian Fed. 21 56.00N130.40E
Golfito Costa Rica 57 8.42N 83.10W
Golfo degli Aranci town Italy 12 41.00N 9.38E
Golling Austria 14 47.36N 13.10E
Golmud China 24 36.22N 94.55E
Golovanevsk Ukraine 15 48.25N 30.30E
Golpāyegān Iran 31 33.23N 50.18E
Golspie U.K. 6 57.58N 3.58W
Goma Zaïre 37 1.37S 29.10E
Gombe Nigeria 38 10.17N 11.20E
Gombe r. Tanzania 37 4.43S 31.30E
Gomel Belorussia 15 52.25N 31.00E
Gómez Palacio Mexico 56 25.39N103.30W
Gomishān Iran 31 37.04N 54.06E
Gonaïves Haiti 57 19.29N 72.42W
Gonâve, Golfe de la g. Haiti 57 19.20N 73.00W
Gonâve, Île de la i. Haiti 57 18.50N 73.00W
Gonbad-e Kāvūs Iran 31 37.15N 55.11E
Gonda India 29 27.08N 81.58E
Gonder Ethiopia 35 12.39N 37.29E
Gondia India 29 21.27N 80.12E
Gongbo'gyamda China 29 29.56N 93.23E
Gongga Shan mtn. China 24 29.30N101.30E
Gongola r. Nigeria 38 9.30N 12.06E
Gongolgon Australia 47 30.22S146.56E
Goñi Uruguay 63 33.31S 56.24W
Goniri Nigeria 38 11.30N 12.15E
Gonzaga Italy 9 44.57N 10.49E
Good Hope, C. of R.S.A. 39 34.21S 18.28E
Gooding U.S.A. 54 42.56N114.43W
Goodooga Australia 47 29.08S147.30E
Goodsprings U.S.A. 54 35.50N115.26W
Goole U.K. 4 53.42N 0.52W
Goolgowi Australia 47 33.59S145.42E
Goolma Australia 47 32.21S149.20E
Gooloogong Australia 47 33.36S148.27E
Goolwa Australia 46 35.31S138.45E
Goomalling Australia 43 31.19S116.49E
Goombalie Australia 47 29.59S145.24E
Goondiwindi Australia 47 28.30S150.17E
Goongarrie Australia 43 30.03S121.09E
Goor Neth. 8 52.16N 6.33E
Goose L. U.S.A. 54 41.57N120.25W
Gorakhpur India 29 26.45N 83.23E
Gordon r. Australia 43 34.12S117.00E
Gordon Downs town Australia 42 18.43S128.33E
Gordonvale Australia 44 17.05S145.47E
Goré Chad 34 7.57N 16.31E
Gorē Ethiopia 35 8.08N 35.33E
Gore New Zealand 48 46.06S168.58E
Gorgān Iran 31 36.50N 54.29E
Gorgān r. Iran 31 37.00N 54.00E
Gori Georgia 31 41.59N 44.05E
Gorinchem Neth. 8 51.50N 4.59E
Gorizia Italy 12 45.58N 13.37E
Gorki see Nizhniy Novgorod Russian Fed 18
Gorkovskoye Vodokhranilishche resr. Russian Fed. 18 56.49N 43.00E
Gorlovka Ukraine 19 48.17N 38.05E
Gorna Oryakhovitsa Bulgaria 13 43.07N 25.40E
Gorno Altaysk Russian Fed. 20 51.59N 85.56E
Gorno Filinskoye Russian Fed. 20 60.06N 69.58E
Gornyatskiy Russian Fed. 18 67.30N 64.03E
Gorodenka Ukraine 15 48.40N 25.30E
Gorodishche Belorussia 15 53.18N 26.00E
Gorodishche Belorussia 15 53.45N 29.45E
Gorodnitsa Ukraine 15 50.50N 27.19E
Gorodnya Ukraine 15 51.54N 31.37E
Gorodok Ukraine 15 49.48N 23.39E
Goroka P.N.G. 27 6.02S145.22E
Goroke Australia 46 36.43S141.30E
Gorokhov Ukraine 15 50.30N 24.46E
Gorongosa r. Mozambique 39 20.29S 34.36E
Gorontalo Indonesia 27 0.33N123.05E
Gort Rep. of Ire. 7 53.04N 8.49W
Goryn r. Ukraine 15 52.08N 27.17E
Gorzów Wielkopolski Poland 14 52.42N 15.12E
Gosford Australia 47 33.25S151.18E
Goslar Germany 14 51.54N 10.25E
Gospić Croatia 14 44.34N 15.23E
Gosport U.K. 5 50.48N 1.08W
Gossi Mali 38 15.49N 1.17W
Gostivar Yugo. 13 41.47N 20.24E
Gostynin Poland 15 52.26N 19.29E
Gotemba Japan 23 35.18N138.56E
Gotha Germany 14 50.57N 10.43E
Gothenburg see Göteborg Sweden 17
Gothèye Niger 38 13.51N 1.31E
Gotland d. Sweden 17 57.30N 18.30E
Gotland i. Sweden 17 57.30N 18.33E
Gouda Neth. 8 52.01N 4.43E
Gouin, Résr. Canada 55 48.38N 74.50W
Goulburn Australia 47 34.47S149.43E
Goulburn r. Australia 47 36.08S144.30E
Goulburn Is. Australia 44 11.33S133.26E
Goundam Mali 38 17.27N 3.39W
Gourdon France 11 44.45N 1.22E
Gouré Niger 38 13.59N 10.15E
Gourma-Rharous Mali 38 16.58N 1.50W
Gournay France 9 49.29N 1.44E
Governador Valadares Brazil 59 18.51S 42.00W
Gowanda U.S.A. 55 42.28N 78.57W
Gowd-e Zereh des. Afghan. 31 30.00N 62.00E
Gower pen. U.K. 5 51.37N 4.10W
Goya Argentina 62 29.10S 59.20W
Goyder r. Australia 44 12.38S135.11E
Gozo i. Malta 12 36.03N 14.16E
Gökçeada i. Turkey 13 40.10N 25.51E
Göksun Turkey 30 38.03N 36.30E
Göppingen Germany 14 48.43N 9.39E
Görlitz Germany 14 51.09N 15.00E
Göta r. Sweden 17 57.42N 11.52E
Göta Kanal Sweden 17 58.50N 13.58E
Göteborg Sweden 17 57.43N 11.58E
Göteborg och Bohus d. Sweden 17 58.30N 11.30E
Götene Sweden 17 58.32N 13.29E
Göttingen Germany 14 51.32N 9.57E
Graaff Reinet R.S.A. 39 32.15S 24.31E
Gračac Croatia 14 44.18N 15.51E
Grace, L. Australia 43 33.18S118.15E
Gracias á Dios, Cabo c. Honduras/Nicaragua 57 15.00N 83.10W
Grado Italy 9 45.40N 13.23E
Grado Spain 10 43.23N 6.04W
Grafton Australia 47 29.40S152.56E
Grafton N.Dak. U.S.A. 53 48.28N 97.25W
Grafton W.Va. U.S.A. 55 39.21N 80.03W
Graham, Mt. U.S.A. 54 32.42N109.52W
Graham Land f. Antarctica 64 67.00S 60.00W
Grahamstown R.S.A. 39 33.18S 26.30E
Graiguenamanagh Rep. of Ire. 7 52.33N 6.57W
Grajaú r. Brazil 61 3.41S 44.48W
Grampian d. U.K. 6 57.22N 2.35W
Grampian Mts. U.K. 6 56.55N 4.00W
Grampians mts. Australia 46 37.12S142.34E
Granada Nicaragua 57 11.58N 85.59W
Granada Spain 10 37.10N 3.35W
Granby Canada 55 45.23N 72.44W
Gran Canaria i. Canary Is. 34 28.00N 15.30W
Gran Chaco f. S. America 62 22.00S 60.00W
Grand r. S.Dak. U.S.A. 52 45.40N100.32W
Grand Bahama I. Bahamas 57 26.35N 78.00W
Grand Bassam Ivory Coast 38 5.14N 3.45W
Grand Canyon f. U.S.A. 54 36.10N112.45W
Grand Canyon town U.S.A. 54 36.03N112.09W
Grand Canyon Nat. Park U.S.A. 54 36.15N112.58W
Grand Cayman i. Cayman Is. 57 19.20N 81.30W
Grand Couronne France 9 49.21N 1.00E
Grande r. Bolivia 62 15.10S 64.55W
Grande r. Bahia Brazil 61 11.05S 43.09W
Grande r. Minas Gerais Brazil 62 20.00S 51.00W
Grande, Bahía b. Argentina 63 51.30S 67.30W
Grande, Ilha i. Brazil 59 23.07S 44.16W
Grande Cascapédia Canada 55 48.21N 65.52W
Grande Comore i. Comoros 37 11.35S 43.20E
Grande do Gurupá, Ilha i. Brazil 61 1.00S 51.30W
Grande Prairie town Canada 50 55.10N118.52W
Grand Erg de Bilma des. Niger 38 18.30N 14.00E
Grandes, Salinas f. Argentina 62 29.37S 64.56W
Grandes Bergeronnes Canada 55 48.16N 69.35W
Grand Falls town Nfld. Canada 51 48.57N 55.40W
Grand Falls town N.B. Canada 55 46.55N 67.45W
Grand Forks U.S.A. 53 47.57N 97.05W
Grand Fougeray France 9 47.44N 1.44W
Grand Island town U.S.A. 52 40.56N 98.21W
Grand Junction U.S.A. 54 39.05N108.33W
Grand L. N.B. Canada 55 45.38N 67.38W
Grand L. U.S.A. 55 45.15N 67.50W
Grand Lahou Ivory Coast 38 5.09N 5.01W
Grand Manan I. Canada 55 44.38N 66.50W
Grand Marais U.S.A. 53 47.55N 90.15W
Grand' Mère Canada 55 46.37N 72.41W
Grândola Portugal 10 38.10N 8.34W
Grand Rapids town Canada 51 53.08N 99.20W
Grand Rapids town Mich. U.S.A. 55 42.57N 85.40W
Grand St. Bernard, Col du pass Italy/Switz. 9 45.52N 7.11E
Grand Teton mtn. U.S.A. 54 43.44N110.48W
Grand Teton Nat. Park U.S.A. 54 43.30N110.37W
Grand Traverse B. U.S.A. 55 45.02N 85.30W
Grand Valley town U.S.A. 54 39.27N108.03W
Grandville U.S.A. 55 42.54N 85.48W
Grangemouth U.K. 6 56.01N 3.44W
Granger U.S.A. 54 41.35N109.58W
Grängesberg Sweden 17 60.05N 14.59E
Grangeville U.S.A. 54 45.56N116.07W
Granite Peak town Australia 42 25.38S121.21E
Granite Peak mtn. U.S.A. 52 45.10N109.50W
Granity New Zealand 48 41.38S171.51E
Granja Brazil 61 3.06S 40.50W
Gränna Sweden 17 58.01N 14.28E
Granollers Spain 10 41.37N 2.18E
Granön Sweden 16 64.15N 19.19E
Gran Paradiso mtn. Italy 9 45.31N 7.15E
Grant Mich. U.S.A. 55 43.20N 85.49W
Grantham U.K. 4 52.55N 0.39W
Grantown-on-Spey U.K. 6 57.20N 3.38W
Grant Range mts. U.S.A. 54 38.25N115.30W
Grants U.S.A. 54 35.09N107.52W
Grants Pass town U.S.A. 54 42.26N123.19W
Grantsville U.S.A. 55 38.55N 81.07W
Granville France 9 48.50N 1.35W
Gras, Lac de l. Canada 50 64.30N110.30W
Graskop R.S.A. 39 24.55S 30.50E
Grasse France 11 43.40N 6.56E
Grasset, L. Canada 55 49.53N 78.07W
Grass Valley town Calif. U.S.A. 54 39.13N121.04W
Grass Valley town Oreg. U.S.A. 54 45.22N120.47W
Grave Neth. 8 51.45N 5.45E
Grave, Pointe de c. France 11 45.35N 1.04W
Gravenhurst Canada 55 44.55N 79.22W
Gravesend Australia 47 29.35S150.20E
Gravesend U.K. 5 51.27N 0.24E
Gray France 11 47.27N 5.35E
Grayling U.S.A. 55 44.40N 84.43W
Grays U.K. 5 51.29N 0.20E
Graz Austria 14 47.05N 15.22E
Grdelica Yugo. 13 42.54N 22.04E
Great Abaco I. Bahamas 57 26.30N 77.00W
Great Artesian Basin f. Australia 44 26.30S143.02E
Great Australian Bight Australia 43 33.10S129.30E
Great Barrier I. New Zealand 48 36.15S175.30E
Great Barrier Reef f. Australia 44 16.30S146.30E
Great Basin f. U.S.A. 54 40.35N116.00W
Great Bear L. Canada 50 66.00N120.00W
Great Bend town U.S.A. 52 38.22N 98.46W
Great Bitter L. see Murrah al Kubrá, Al Buḩayrah al h5ayrah al Egypt 32
Great Blasket I. Rep. of Ire. 7 52.05N 10.32W
Great Coco i. Burma 29 14.10N 93.25E
Great Divide Basin f. U.S.A. 54 42.00N108.10W
Great Dividing Range mts. Australia 47 29.00S152.00E
Great Driffield U.K. 4 54.01N 0.26W
Greater Antilles is. C. America 57 17.00N 70.00W
Greater London d. U.K. 5 51.31N 0.06W
Greater Manchester d. U.K. 4 53.30N 2.18W
Great Exuma i. Bahamas 57 23.00N 76.00W
Great Falls town U.S.A. 54 47.30N111.17W
Great Inagua I. Bahamas 57 21.00N 73.20W
Great Indian Desert see Thar Desert India/Pakistan 28
Great Karoo f. R.S.A. 39 32.40S 22.20E
Great Kei r. R.S.A. 39 32.39S 28.23E
Great L. Australia 45 41.50S146.43E
Great Malvern U.K. 5 52.07N 2.19W
Great Namaland f. Namibia 39 25.30S 17.20E
Great Nicobar i. India 29 7.00N 93.50E
Great Ouse r. U.K. 4 52.47N 0.23E
Great Ruaha r. Tanzania 37 7.55S 37.52E
Great Salt L. U.S.A. 54 41.10N112.30W
Great Salt Lake Desert U.S.A. 54 40.40N113.30W
Great Sandy Desert Australia 42 20.30S123.35E
Great Sandy Desert see An Nafūd des. Saudi Arabia 30
Great Slave L. Canada 50 61.30N114.20W
Great Victoria Desert Australia 43 29.00S127.30E
Great Whernside mtn. U.K. 4 54.09N 1.59W
Great Yarmouth U.K. 5 52.40N 1.45E
Great Zimbabwe ruins Zimbabwe 39 20.30S 30.30E
Gréboun, Mont mtn. Niger 38 20.01N 8.35E
Gredos, Sierra de mts. Spain 10 40.18N 5.20W
Greece Europe 13 39.00N 22.00E
Greeley U.S.A. 52 40.25N104.42W
Green r. U.S.A. 54 38.11N109.53W
Green Bay town U.S.A. 53 44.32N 88.00W
Greenbushes Australia 43 33.50S116.00E
Greencastle Ind. U.S.A. 55 39.39N 86.51W
Greene U.S.A. 55 42.20N 75.46W
Greenhills Australia 43 31.58S117.01E
Greening Canada 55 48.07N 74.55W
Greenland N. America 51 68.00N 45.00W
Greenlaw U.K. 6 55.43N 2.28W
Greenock U.K. 6 55.57N 4.45W
Greenore Pt. Rep. of Ire. 7 52.14N 6.19W
Greenough r. Australia 43 29.22S114.34E
Green River town Utah U.S.A. 54 38.59N110.10W
Green River town Wyo. U.S.A. 54 41.32N109.28W
Greensboro N.C. U.S.A. 53 36.03N 79.50W
Greensburg Ind. U.S.A. 55 39.20N 85.29W
Greenvale Australia 44 18.57S144.53E
Greenville Liberia 34 5.01N 9.03W
Greenville Ala. U.S.A. 53 31.50N 86.40W
Greenville Mich. U.S.A. 55 43.11N 85.13W
Greenville Miss. U.S.A. 53 33.23N 91.03W
Greenville S.C. U.S.A. 53 34.52N 82.25W
Greenville Tex. U.S.A. 53 33.09N 96.07W
Greenwood Miss. U.S.A. 53 33.31N 90.10W
Gregory r. Australia 44 17.53S139.17E
Gregory, L. S.A. Australia 46 28.55S139.00E
Gregory, L. W.A. Australia 42 20.10S127.20E
Gregory Range mts. Australia 44 19.00S143.05E
Greifswald Germany 14 54.06N 13.24E
Gremikha Russian Fed. 18 68.03N 39.38E
Grenå Denmark 17 56.25N 10.53E
Grenada C. America 57 12.07N 61.40W
Grenade France 11 43.47N 1.10E
Grenfell Australia 47 33.53S148.11E
Grenoble France 11 45.11N 5.43E
Grenville, C. Australia 44 12.00S143.13E
Gretna U.K. 6 55.00N 3.04W
Greven Germany 8 52.07N 7.38E
Grevenbroich Germany 8 51.07N 6.33E
Grevesmühlen Germany 14 53.51N 11.10E
Grey r. New Zealand 48 42.28S171.13E
Grey, C. Australia 44 13.00S136.40E
Greybull U.S.A. 54 44.30N108.03W
Greymouth New Zealand 48 42.28S171.12E
Grey Range mts. Australia 45 27.30S143.59E
Greystones Rep. of Ire. 7 53.09N 6.04W
Greytown R.S.A. 39 29.04S 30.36E
Griffin U.S.A. 53 33.15N 84.17W
Griffith Australia 47 34.18S146.04E
Grignan France 11 44.25N 4.54E
Grigoriopol Moldavia 15 47.08N 29.18E
Grim, C. Australia 45 40.45S144.45E
Grimsby U.K. 4 53.35N 0.05W
Grimstad Norway 17 58.20N 8.36E
Grimsvötn mtn. Iceland 16 64.30N 17.10W
Grindavik Iceland 16 63.50N 22.27W
Grindsted Denmark 17 55.45N 8.56E
Griqualand East f. R.S.A. 39 30.40S 29.10E
Griqualand West f. R.S.A. 39 28.50S 23.30E
Griva Russian Fed. 18 60.35N 50.58E
Grobina Latvia 17 56.33N 21.10E
Groblershoop R.S.A. 39 28.55S 20.59E
Grodno Belorussia 15 53.40N 23.50E
Grodzisk Poland 14 52.14N 16.22E
Grodzyanka Belorussia 15 53.30N 28.41E
Groenlo Neth. 8 52.02N 6.36E
Groix, Île de i. France 11 47.38N 3.26W
Gronau Germany 8 52.14N 7.02E
Grong Norway 16 64.27N 12.19E
Groningen Neth. 8 53.13N 6.35E
Groningen d. Neth. 8 53.15N 6.45E
Groot r. C.P. r. R.S.A. 39 33.58S 25.03E
Groote Eylandt i. Australia 44 14.00S136.40E
Grootfontein Namibia 39 19.32S 18.07E
Groot Karasberge mts. Namibia 39 27.20S 18.50E
Grootlaagte r. Botswana 39 20.58S 21.42E
Groot Swartberge mts. R.S.A. 39 33.20S 22.00E
Grossenbrode Germany 14 54.23N 11.07E
Grossenhain Germany 14 51.17N 13.31E
Grosseto Italy 12 42.46N 11.08E
Gross Glockner mtn. Austria 14 47.05N 12.50E
Grote Nete r. Belgium 8 51.07N 4.20E
Groundhog r. Canada 55 49.43N 81.58W
Grouse Creek town U.S.A. 54 41.22N113.53W
Grover City U.S.A. 54 35.07N120.37W
Groznyy Russian Fed. 19 43.21N 45.42E
Grudziądz Poland 15 53.29N 18.45E
Grumeti r. Tanzania 37 2.05S 33.45E
Grundarfjördhur town Iceland 16 64.55N 23.20W
Grungedal Norway 17 59.44N 7.43E
Grünau Namibia 39 27.44S 18.18E
Gryazovets Russian Fed. 18 58.52N 40.12E
Gryfice Poland 14 53.56N 15.12E
Guachipas Argentina 62 25.31S 65.31W
Guacuí Brazil 59 20.44S 41.40W
Guadalajara Mexico 56 20.30N103.20W
Guadalajara Spain 10 40.37N 3.10W
Guadalcanal i. Solomon Is. 40 9.32S160.12E
Guadalete r. Spain 10 36.37N 6.15W
Guadalmena r. Spain 10 38.00N 3.50W
Guadalquivir r. Spain 10 36.50N 6.20W
Guadalupe Mexico 56 25.41N100.15W
Guadalupe, Isla de i. Mexico 52 29.00N118.16W
Guadalupe, Sierra de mts. Spain 10 39.30N 5.25W
Guadarrama r. Spain 10 39.55N 4.10W
Guadarrama, Sierra de mts. Spain 10 41.00N 3.50W
Guadeloupe i. Leeward Is. 57 16.20N 61.40W
Guadiana r. Portugal 10 37.10N 7.36W
Guadix Spain 10 37.19N 3.08W
Guafo, Golfo de g. Chile 63 43.35S 74.15W
Guainía r. Colombia 60 2.01N 67.07W
Guaíra Brazil 62 24.04S 54.15W
Guajará Mirim Brazil 60 10.48S 65.22W
Guajira, Península de la pen. Colombia 60 12.00N 72.00W
Gualeguay Argentina 63 33.10S 59.20W
Gualeguay r. Argentina 63 33.18S 59.38W
Gualeguaychu Argentina 63 33.00S 58.30W
Guam i. Mariana Is. 40 13.30N144.40E
Guamal Colombia 60 9.10N 74.15W
Guanajuato Mexico 56 21.00N101.16W
Guanajuato d. Mexico 56 21.00N101.00W
Guanare Venezuela 60 9.04N 69.45W
Guanarito Venezuela 60 8.43N 69.12W
Guane Cuba 57 22.13N 84.07W
Guangdong d. China 25 23.00N113.00E
Guanghua China 25 32.30N111.50E
Guangxi Zhuangzu d. China 25 23.50N109.00E
Guangyuan China 29 32.26N105.52E
Guangzhou China 25 23.20N113.30E
Guanling China 29 25.57N105.38E
Guantánamo Cuba 57 20.09N 75.14W
Guan Xian Sichuan China 29 30.59N103.40E
Guaporé r. Bolivia/Brazil 62 12.00S 65.15W
Guaqui Bolivia 62 16.35S 68.51W
Guarabira Brazil 61 6.46S 35.25W
Guarapuava Brazil 59 25.22S 51.28W
Guaratinguetá Brazil 59 22.49S 45.09W
Guarda Portugal 10 40.32N 7.17W
Guardavalle Italy 13 38.30N 16.30E
Guardo Spain 10 42.47N 4.50W
Guareim r. Uruguay see Quarí r. Brazil 63
Guasipati Venezuela 60 7.28N 61.54W
Guastalla Italy 9 44.55N 10.39E
Guatemala C. America 57 15.40N 90.00W
Guatemala town Guatemala 56 14.38N 90.22W
Guatire Venezuela 60 10.28N 66.32W
Guaviare r. Colombia 60 4.00N 67.35W
Guaxupé Brazil 59 21.17S 46.44W
Guayaquil Ecuador 60 2.13S 79.54W
Guayaquil, Golfo de g. Ecuador 60 3.00S 80.35W
Guaymallén Argentina 63 32.54S 68.47W
Guaymas Mexico 56 27.56N110.54W
Guayquiraró r. Argentina 63 30.25S 59.36W
Gubakha Russian Fed. 18 58.55N 57.30E
Gubeikou China 25 40.41N117.09E
Gubin Poland 14 51.59N 14.42E
Gubio Nigeria 38 12.31N 12.44E
Guchab Namibia 39 19.40S 17.47E
Gúdar, Sierra de mts. Spain 10 40.27N 0.42W
Gudbrandsdalen f. Norway 17 61.30N 10.00E
Gudvangen Norway 17 60.52N 6.50E
Guecho Spain 10 43.21N 3.01W
Guelph Canada 55 43.33N 80.15W
Guéméné-sur-Scorff France 11 48.04N 3.13W
Guéret France 11 46.10N 1.52E
Guernica Spain 10 43.19N 2.40W
Guernsey i. U.K. 5 49.27N 2.35W
Guerra Mozambique 37 13.05S 35.12E
Guerrero d. Mexico 56 18.00N100.00W
Guiana S. America 61 3.40N 53.00W
Guiana Highlands S. America 60 4.00N 59.00W
Guichón Uruguay 63 32.21S 57.12W
Guildford Australia 43 31.55S115.55E
Guildford U.K. 5 51.14N 0.35W
Guilin China 25 25.21N110.11E
Guimarães Brazil 61 2.08S 44.36W
Guimarães Portugal 10 41.27N 8.18W
Guinan China 24 35.20N100.50E
Guinea Africa 34 10.30N 11.30W
Guinea, G. of Africa 38 3.00N 3.00E
Guinea Bissau Africa 34 11.30N 15.00W
Guingamp France 11 48.34N 3.09W
Guiping China 25 23.20N110.04E
Guiscard France 8 49.39N 3.01E
Guiscard France 9 49.39N 3.03E
Guise France 9 49.54N 3.38E
Guiuan Phil. 27 11.02N125.44E
Guiyang China 24 26.35N106.40E
Guizhou d. China 24 27.00N106.30E
Gujarat d. India 28 22.45N 71.30E
Gujrānwāla Pakistan 28 32.06N 74.11E
Gujrāt Pakistan 28 32.35N 74.06E
Gulargambone Australia 47 31.21S148.32E
Gulbarga India 28 17.22N 76.47E
Gulfport U.S.A. 53 30.21N 89.08W
Gulgong Australia 47 32.20S149.49E
Gulma Nigeria 38 12.41N 4.24E
Gulshad Kazakhstan 24 46.37N 74.22E
Gulu Uganda 37 2.46N 32.21E
Gulwe Tanzania 37 6.27S 36.27E
Gumel Nigeria 38 12.39N 9.23E
Gummersbach Germany 8 51.03N 7.32E
Guna India 28 24.39N 77.18E
Gunbar Australia 47 34.04S145.25E
Gundagai Australia 47 35.07S148.05E
Gundlupet India 28 11.48N 76.41E
Gungu Zaïre 36 5.43S 19.20E
Gunnedah Australia 47 30.59S150.15E
Gunning Australia 47 34.46S149.17E
Gunnison r. U.S.A. 54 39.03N108.35W
Gunnison Utah U.S.A. 54 39.09N111.49W
Guntersville L. U.S.A. 53 34.35N 86.00W
Guntūr India 29 16.20N 80.27E
Gunungsitoli Indonesia 26 1.17N 97.37E
Gura Portiței f. Romania 15 44.40N 29.00E
Gurgueia r. Brazil 61 6.45S 43.35W
Gursköy i. Norway 16 62.16N 5.42E
Gurué Mozambique 37 15.30S 36.58E
Gurupá Brazil 61 1.25S 51.39W
Gurupi r. Brazil 61 1.13S 46.06W
Guruve Zimbabwe 37 16.42S 30.40E
Guryev Kazakhstan 19 47.08N 51.59E
Gusau Nigeria 38 12.12N 6.40E
Gusev Russian Fed. 15 54.32N 22.12E
Guspini Italy 12 39.32N 8.38E
Gustav Holm, Kap c. Greenland 51 67.00N 34.00W
Guyana S. America 60 4.40N 59.00W
Guyra Australia 47 30.14S151.40E
Guzhen Anhui China 25 33.19N117.19E
Güines Cuba 57 22.50N 82.02W
Gümüşhane Turkey 30 40.26N 39.26E
Günzburg Germany 14 48.27N 10.16E
Gürün Turkey 30 38.44N 37.15E
Güstrow Germany 14 53.48N 12.11E
Gütersloh Germany 14 51.54N 8.22E
Gwa Burma 29 17.36N 94.35E
Gwabegar Australia 47 30.34S149.00E
Gwadabawa Nigeria 38 13.23N 5.15E
Gwādar Pakistan 28 25.09N 62.21E
Gwagwada Nigeria 38 10.15N 7.15E
Gwai Zimbabwe 39 19.15S 27.42E
Gwai r. Zimbabwe 39 17.59S 26.55E
Gwalior India 29 26.12N 78.09E
Gwanda Zimbabwe 39 20.59S 29.00E
Gwasero Nigeria 38 9.30N 8.30E
Gweebarra B. Rep. of Ire. 7 54.52N 8.28W
Gwent d. U.K. 5 51.44N 3.00W
Gweru Zimbabwe 39 19.25S 29.50E
Gwydir r. Australia 47 29.35S148.45E
Gwynedd d. U.K. 4 53.00N 4.00W
Gyandzha Azerbaijan 31 40.39N 46.20E
Gyangzê China 29 29.00N 89.40E
Gydanskiy Poluostrov pen. Russian Fed. 20 70.00N 78.30E
Gympie Australia 44 26.11S152.40E
Gyöngyös Hungary 15 47.47N 19.56E
Györ Hungary 15 47.41N 17.40E
Gypsumville Canada 51 51.45N 98.35W

H

Haan Germany 8 51.10N 7.02E
Haapajärvi Finland 16 63.45N 25.20E
Haapamäki Finland 16 62.15N 24.28E
Haapavesi Finland 16 64.08N 25.22E
Haapsalu Estonia 17 58.56N 23.33E
Hā Arava r. Israel/Jordan 32 30.30N 35.10E
Haarlem Neth. 8 52.22N 4.38E
Haarlem R.S.A. 39 33.46S 23.28E
Habahe China 24 47.53N 86.12E
Ḩabarūt Yemen 28 17.18N 52.44E
Habaswein Kenya 37 1.06N 39.26E
Habay-la-Neuve Belgium 8 49.45N 5.38E
Habikino Japan 23 34.33N135.37E
Habo Sweden 17 57.55N 14.04E
Hachinohe Japan 25 40.30N141.30E
Hachiōji Japan 23 35.39N139.20E
Hack, Mt. Australia 46 30.44S138.45E
Hadano Japan 23 35.22N139.14E
Ḩadd, Ra's al c. Oman 31 22.32N 59.49E
Haddington U.K. 6 55.57N 2.47W
Hadejia Nigeria 38 12.30N 10.03E
Hadejia r. Nigeria 38 12.47N 10.44E

Izumi Japan **23** 34.29N135.26E
Izumi-ōtsu Japan **23** 34.30N135.24E
Izumi-sano Japan **23** 34.25N135.19E
Izumo *r.* Japan **23** 34.38N136.33E
Izyaslav Ukraine **15** 50.10N 26.46E
Izyum Ukraine **19** 49.12N 37.19E

J

Jabal, Baḩr al *r.* Sudan **35** 9.30N 30.20E
Jabalón *r.* Spain **10** 38.55N 4.07W
Jabalpur India **29** 23.10N 79.59E
Jabālyah Egypt **32** 31.32N 34.29E
Jabbān, Arḑ al *f.* Jordan **32** 32.08N 36.35E
Jabiru Australia **44** 12.39S132.55E
Jablah Syria **32** 35.22N 35.56E
Jablonec nad Nisou Czech. **14** 50.44N 15.10E
Jaboticabal Brazil **59** 21.15S 48.17W
Jaca Spain **10** 42.34N 0.33W
Jacareí Brazil **59** 23.17S 45.57W
Jackman U.S.A. **55** 45.38N 70.16W
Jackson Mich. U.S.A. **55** 42.15N 84.24W
Jackson Miss. U.S.A. **53** 32.20N 90.11W
Jackson Ohio U.S.A. **55** 39.03N 82.40W
Jackson Tenn. U.S.A. **53** 35.37N 88.50W
Jackson Wyo. U.S.A. **54** 43.29N110.38W
Jacksonville Fla. U.S.A. **53** 30.20N 81.40W
Jacobābād Pakistan **28** 28.16N 68.30E
Jacobina Brazil **61** 11.13S 40.30W
Jacob Lake *town* U.S.A. **54** 36.41N112.14W
Jacques Cartier, Mt. Canada **55** 49.00N 65.55W
Jacuí *r.* Brazil **59** 29.56S 51.13W
Jacundá *r.* Brazil **61** 1.57S 50.26W
Jade Germany **8** 53.21N 8.11E
Jadebusen *b.* Germany **8** 53.30N 8.12E
Jaén Peru **60** 5.21S 78.28W
Jaén Spain **10** 37.46N 3.48W
Jaffa *see* Tel Aviv-Yafo Israel **32**
Jaffa, C. Australia **46** 36.58S139.39E
Jaffna Sri Lanka **29** 9.38N 80.02E
Jagdalpur India **29** 19.04N 82.05E
Jaguarão Brazil **59** 32.30S 53.25W
Jahrom Iran **31** 28.30N 53.30E
Jailolo Indonesia **27** 1.05N127.29E
Jaipur India **28** 26.53N 75.50E
Jajawijaya Mts. Asia **27** 4.20S139.10E
Jājpur India **29** 20.50N 86.20E
Jakarta Indonesia **26** 6.08S106.45E
Jäkkvik Sweden **16** 66.23N 17.00E
Jakobstad *see* Pietarsaari Finland **16**
Jalālah al Baḩrīyah, Jabal *mts.* Egypt **32** 29.20N 32.12E
Jalālat al Qiblīyah, Jabal al *mts.* Egypt **32** 28.42N 32.23E
Jalapa Mexico **56** 19.45N 96.48W
Jalgaon India **28** 21.01N 75.39E
Jalingo Nigeria **38** 8.54N 11.21E
Jalisco *d.* Mexico **56** 21.00N103.00W
Jālna India **28** 19.50N 75.58E
Jalón *r.* Spain **10** 41.47N 1.02W
Jālor India **28** 25.21N 72.37E
Jalpaiguri India **29** 26.30N 88.50E
Jālū Libya **35** 29.00N 21.30E
Jalūlā Iraq **31** 34.16N 45.10E
Jamaame Somali Rep. **37** 0.04N 42.46E
Jamaari Nigeria **38** 11.44N 9.53E
Jamaica C. America **57** 18.00N 77.00W
Jamālpur Bangla. **29** 24.54N 89.57E
Jamanxim *r.* Brazil **61** 4.43S 56.18W
Jambes Belgium **8** 50.28N 4.52E
Jambi Indonesia **26** 1.36S103.39E
Jambi *d.* Indonesia **26** 2.00S102.30E
James *r.* S.Dak. U.S.A. **53** 42.50N 97.15W
James B. Canada **51** 53.00N 80.00W
James Bay Prov. Park Canada **55** 51.24N 79.00W
Jamestown Australia **46** 33.12S138.38E
Jamestown N.Dak. U.S.A. **52** 46.54N 98.42W
Jamestown N.Y. U.S.A. **55** 42.06N 79.14W
Jammerbught *b.* Denmark **17** 57.20N 9.30E
Jammu Jammu & Kashmir **28** 32.44N 74.52E
Jammu & Kashmir Asia **28** 33.30N 76.00E
Jāmnagar India **28** 22.28N 70.06E
Jamsah Egypt **32** 27.39N 33.35E
Jämsänkoski Finland **17** 61.55N 25.11E
Jamshedpur India **29** 22.47N 86.12E
Jämtland *d.* Sweden **16** 63.00N 14.30E
Janda, Laguna de la *l.* Spain **10** 36.15N 5.50W
Jándula *r.* Spain **10** 38.08N 4.08W
Janesville U.S.A. **53** 42.42N 89.02W
Jangamo Mozambique **39** 24.06S 35.21E
Janin Jordan **32** 32.28N 35.18E
Jan Kempdorp R.S.A. **39** 27.55S 24.48E
Jan Mayen *i.* Arctic Oc. **64** 71.00N 9.00W
Januária Brazil **59** 15.28S 44.23W
Janzé France **9** 47.58N 1.30W
Japan Asia **25** 36.00N136.00E
Japan, Sea of Asia **25** 40.00N135.00E
Japurá *r.* Brazil **60** 3.00S 64.50W
Jarama *r.* Spain **10** 40.27N 3.32W
Jarash Jordan **32** 32.17N 35.54E
Jardee Australia **43** 34.18S116.04E
Jardine *r.* Australia **44** 11.07S142.30E
Jardines de la Reina *is.* Cuba **57** 20.30N 79.00W
Jardinópolis Brazil **59** 20.59S 47.48W
Jargeau France **9** 47.52N 2.07E
Jarocin Poland **15** 51.59N 17.31E
Jarosław Poland **15** 50.02N 22.42E
Jarrāḩi *r.* Iran **31** 30.40N 48.23E
Järvenpää Finland **17** 60.28N 25.06E
Jāsk Iran **31** 25.40N 57.45E
Jasło Poland **15** 49.45N 21.29E
Jasper Canada **50** 52.55N118.05W
Jastrebarsko Croatia **14** 45.40N 15.39E
Jastrowie Poland **14** 53.26N 16.49E
Jászberény Hungary **15** 47.30N 19.55E
Jataí Brazil **59** 17.58S 51.45W
Játiva Spain **10** 39.00N 0.32W
Jaú Brazil **59** 22.11S 48.35W
Jauja Peru **60** 11.50S 75.15W
Jaunjelgava Latvia **18** 56.34N 25.02E
Jaunpur India **29** 25.44N 82.41E
Java *i. see* Jawa *i.* Indonesia **26**
Javari *r.* Peru **60** 4.30S 71.20W
Java Sea *see* Jawa, Laut *sea* Indonesia **26**
Java Trench *f.* Indonesia **26** 10.00S110.00E
Jawa *i.* Indonesia **26** 7.30S110.00E
Jawa, Laut *sea* Indonesia **26** 5.00S111.00E
Jawa Barat *d.* Indonesia **26** 7.15S107.00E
Jawa Tengah *d.* Indonesia **26** 7.40S109.40E
Jawa Timur *d.* Indonesia **26** 7.00S112.00E
Jayah, Wādī al *see* Hā 'Arava Jordan / Israel **32**
Jayapura Indonesia **27** 2.28S140.38E
Jazirah Doberai *f.* Indonesia **27** 1.10S132.30E
Jazzin Lebanon **32** 33.32N 35.34E
Jean U.S.A. **54** 35.46N115.20W
Jean Marie River *town* Canada **50** 61.32N120.40W
Jebāl Bārez, Kūh-e *mts.* Iran **31** 28.40N 58.10E
Jebba Nigeria **38** 9.11N 4.49E
Jedburgh U.K. **6** 55.29N 2.33W
Jedda *see* Jiddah Saudi Arabia **35**
Jedrzejów Poland **15** 50.39N 20.18E
Jefferson, Mt. Nev. U.S.A. **54** 38.46N116.55W
Jefferson, Mt. Oreg. U.S.A. **54** 44.40N121.47W
Jefferson City U.S.A. **53** 38.33N 92.10W
Jeffersonville U.S.A. **55** 38.16N 85.45W
Jega Nigeria **38** 12.12N 4.23E
Jēkabpils Latvia **18** 56.28N 25.58E
Jelenia Góra Poland **14** 50.55N 15.45E
Jelgava Latvia **17** 56.39N 23.42E
Jember Indonesia **26** 8.07S113.45E
Jena Germany **14** 50.56N 11.35E
Jenbach Austria **14** 47.24N 11.47E
Jenolan Caves *town* Australia **47** 33.53S150.03E
Jeparit Australia **46** 36.09S141.59E
Jeppo Finland **16** 63.24N 22.37E
Jequié Brazil **61** 13.52S 40.06W
Jequitinhonha *r.* Brazil **59** 16.46S 39.45W
Jerantut Malaysia **26** 3.56N102.22E
Jérémie Haiti **57** 18.40N 74.09W
Jerez Spain **10** 38.20N 6.45W
Jerez de la Frontera Spain **10** 36.41N 6.08W
Jericho *see* Arīḩā Jordan **32**
Jerilderie Australia **47** 35.23S145.41E
Jerome U.S.A. **54** 42.43N114.31W
Jerramungup Australia **43** 33.57S118.53E
Jersey *i.* U.K. **5** 49.13N 2.08W
Jersey City U.S.A. **55** 40.44N 74.04W
Jerusalem *see* Yerushalayim Israel / Jordan **32**
Jervis B. Australia **47** 35.05S150.44E
Jesenice Slovenia **12** 46.27N 14.04E
Jessore Bangla. **29** 23.10N 89.12E
Jesús Carranza Mexico **56** 17.26N 95.02W
Jever Germany **8** 53.34N 7.54E
Jevnaker Norway **17** 60.15N 10.28E
Jeypore India **29** 18.51N 82.41E
Jeziorak, Jezioro *l.* Poland **15** 53.40N 19.04E
Jhang Sadar Pakistan **28** 31.16N 72.19E
Jhānsi India **29** 25.27N 78.34E
Jhelum *r.* Pakistan **28** 31.04N 72.10E
Jialing Jiang *r.* China **29** 29.33N106.30E
Jiamusi China **25** 46.50N130.21E
Ji'an China **25** 27.08N115.00E
Jiange China **29** 32.04N105.26E
Jiangling China **25** 30.20N112.20E
Jiangsu *d.* China **25** 34.00N119.00E
Jiangxi *d.* China **25** 27.25N115.20E
Jianyang Fujian China **25** 27.20N117.50E
Jiaohe China **25** 43.42N127.19E
Jiashan China **25** 32.47N117.59E
Jiaxian China **25** 38.02N110.29E
Jiaxing China **25** 30.40N120.50E
Jiayi Taiwan **25** 23.38N120.27E
Jiddah Saudi Arabia **35** 21.30N 39.10E
Jigawa *d.* Nigeria **38** 12.30N 9.30E
Jihlava Czech. **14** 49.24N 15.35E
Jilib Somali Rep. **37** 0.28N 42.50E
Jilin China **25** 43.53N126.35E
Jilin *d.* China **25** 44.50N125.00E
Jilong Taiwan **25** 25.10N121.43E
Jima Ethiopia **35** 7.39N 36.47E
Jiménez Mexico **56** 27.08N104.55W
Jimeta Nigeria **38** 9.19N 12.25E
Jinan China **25** 36.50N117.00E
Jindabyne Australia **47** 36.24S148.37E
Jingdezhen China **25** 29.16N117.11E
Jingellic Australia **47** 35.54S147.44E
Jinggu Yunnan China **29** 23.29N100.19E
Jinghong China **24** 21.59N100.49E
Jing Xian China **25** 26.35N109.41E
Jinhua China **25** 29.06N119.40E
Jining Nei Monggol China **25** 40.56N113.00E
Jining Shantung China **25** 35.25N116.40E
Jinja Uganda **37** 0.27N 33.10E
Jinotepe Nicaragua **57** 11.50N 86.10W
Jinsha Jiang *r.* China **29** 26.30N101.40E
Jinxi Liaoning China **25** 40.54N120.36E
Jin Xian Liaoning China **25** 39.04N121.45E
Jinzhou China **25** 41.07N121.06E
Jipijapa Ecuador **60** 1.23S 80.35W
Jirjā Egypt **30** 26.20N 31.53E
Jitarning Australia **43** 32.48S117.57E
Jiu *r.* Romania **13** 43.44N 23.52E
Jiujiang China **25** 29.41N116.03E
Jixi China **25** 45.17N131.00E
Jizān Saudi Arabia **35** 16.56N 42.33E
Jizl, Wādī al *r.* Saudi Arabia **30** 25.37N 38.20E
João Pessoa Brazil **61** 7.06S 34.53W
Jódar Spain **10** 37.50N 3.21W
Jodhpur India **28** 26.18N 73.08E
Jodoigne Belgium **8** 50.45N 4.52E
Joensuu Finland **18** 62.35N 29.46E
Joetsu Japan **23** 37.07N138.15E
Johannesburg R.S.A. **39** 26.11S 28.04E
John Day U.S.A. **54** 44.25N118.57W
John Day *r.* U.S.A. **54** 45.44N120.39W
John O'Groats U.K. **6** 58.39N 3.02W
Johnson City Tenn. U.S.A. **53** 36.20N 82.23W
Johnston, L. Australia **43** 32.25S120.30E
Johnstown Penn. U.S.A. **55** 40.20N 78.55W
Johor Baharu Malaysia **26** 1.29N103.40E
Joigny France **9** 48.00N 3.20E
Joinville Brazil **59** 26.20S 48.49W
Joinville France **11** 48.27N 5.08E
Jokkmokk Sweden **16** 66.37N 19.50E
Jolfa Iran **31** 32.40N 51.39E
Joliette Canada **55** 46.02N 73.27W
Jolo *i.* Phil. **27** 5.55N121.20E
Jolo *town* Phil. **27** 6.03N121.00E
Jombang Indonesia **26** 7.30S112.21E
Jomda China **29** 31.30N 98.16E
Jonava Lithuania **17** 55.05N 24.17E
Jonesboro Ark. U.S.A. **53** 35.50N 90.41W
Jones Sd. Canada **51** 76.00N 85.00W
Joplin U.S.A. **53** 37.04N 94.31W
Jordan Asia **30** 31.00N 36.00E
Jordan *r. see* Al Urdunn *r.* Asia **32**
Jordan Mont. U.S.A. **54** 47.19N106.55W
Jordan Valley *town* U.S.A. **54** 42.58N117.03W
Jorhāt India **29** 26.45N 94.13E
Jos Nigeria **38** 9.54N 8.53E
José de San Martín Argentina **63** 44.04S 70.26W
José Enrique Rodó Uruguay **63** 33.41S 57.34W
Joseph Bonaparte G. Australia **42** 14.00S128.30E
Joseph City U.S.A. **54** 34.57N110.20W
Jos Plateau *f.* Nigeria **38** 10.00N 9.00E
Jotunheimen *mts.* Norway **17** 61.38N 8.18E
Joué-lès-Tours France **9** 47.21N 0.40E
Joure Neth. **8** 52.59N 5.49E
Joverega Botswana **39** 19.08S 24.15E
Jökulsá á Brú *r.* Iceland **16** 65.33N 14.23W
Jökulsá á Fjöllum *r.* Iceland **16** 66.05N 16.32W
Jönköping Sweden **17** 57.47N 14.11E
Jönköping *d.* Sweden **17** 57.30N 14.30E
Jörn Sweden **16** 65.04N 20.02E
Juan Aldama Mexico **56** 24.19N103.21W
Juan B. Arruabarrena Argentina **63** 30.25S 58.15W
Juan de Fuca, Str. of Canada / U.S.A. **54** 48.15N124.00W
Juan de Nova *i.* Madagascar **37** 17.03S 42.45E
Juárez Argentina **63** 37.40S 59.48W
Juàzeiro Brazil **61** 9.25S 40.30W
Juàzeiro do Norte Brazil **61** 7.10S 39.18W
Jūbā Sudan **35** 4.50N 31.35E
Jūbāl, Maḑīq *str.* Egypt **32** 27.40N 33.55E
Jubal, Str. of *see* Jūbāl, Maḑīq *str.* Egypt **32**
Jubba *r.* Somali Rep. **37** 0.20S 42.40E
Jubilee Downs *town* Australia **42** 18.22S125.17E
Júcar *r.* Spain **10** 39.10N 0.15W
Juchitán Mexico **56** 16.27N 95.05W
Judenburg Austria **14** 47.10N 14.40E
Judith Basin *f.* U.S.A. **54** 47.10N109.58W
Juist Germany **8** 53.41N 7.01E
Juist *i.* Germany **8** 53.43N 7.00E
Juiz de Fora Brazil **59** 21.47S 43.23W
Jujuy *d.* Argentina **62** 23.00S 66.00W
Juklegga *mtn.* Norway **17** 61.03N 8.13E
Juliaca Peru **60** 15.29S 70.09W
Julia Creek *town* Australia **44** 20.39S141.45E
Juliana Kanaal *canal* Neth. **8** 51.00N 5.48E
Julianehåb Greenland **51** 60.45N 46.00W
Jullundur India **28** 31.18N 75.40E
Jumboo Somali Rep. **37** 0.12S 42.38E
Jumet Belgium **8** 50.27N 4.27E
Jumilla Spain **10** 38.28N 1.19W
Jumla Nepal **29** 29.17N 82.10E
Jumna *r. see* Yamuna India **28**
Junāgadh India **28** 21.32N 70.32E
Junan China **25** 35.11N118.50E
Junction B. Australia **44** 11.50S134.15E
Junction City Kans. U.S.A. **53** 39.02N 96.51W
Junction City Oreg. U.S.A. **54** 44.13N123.12W
Jundah Australia **44** 24.50S143.02E
Jundiaí Brazil **59** 23.10S 46.54W
Juneau U.S.A. **50** 58.20N134.20W
Junee Australia **47** 34.51S147.40E
Jungfrau *mtn.* Switz. **11** 46.30N 8.00E
Junggar Pendi *f.* Asia **24** 44.20N 86.30E
Junglinster Lux. **8** 49.41N 6.13E
Junín Argentina **63** 34.35S 60.58W
Junín de los Andes Argentina **63** 39.57S 71.05W
Juniville France **9** 49.24N 4.23E
Jūnīyah Lebanon **32** 33.59N 35.38E
Junnah, Jabal *mts.* Egypt **32** 28.52N 34.15E
Junsele Sweden **16** 63.40N 16.55E
Juntura U.S.A. **54** 43.46N118.05W
Jura *mts.* Europe **11** 46.55N 6.45E
Jura *i.* U.K. **6** 55.58N 5.55W
Jura, Sd. of U.K. **6** 56.00N 5.45W
Jurado Colombia **60** 7.07N 77.46W
Jura Krakowska *mts.* Poland **15** 50.30N 19.30E
Jurhen Ul Shan *mts.* China **29** 34.00N 91.00E
Jūrmala Latvia **17** 56.58N 23.42E
Juruá *r.* Brazil **60** 2.33S 65.50W
Juruena Brazil **62** 12.50S 58.58W
Juruena *r.* Brazil **61** 7.20S 57.30W
Juruti Brazil **61** 2.09S 56.04W
Jussey France **11** 47.49N 5.54E
Jutaí *r.* Brazil **60** 2.35S 67.00W
Juticalpa Honduras **57** 14.45N 86.12W
Jutland *pen. see* Jylland *pen.* Denmark **17**
Jūyom Iran **31** 26.10N 53.52E
Juzur al Ḩalaniyat *is.* Oman **28** 17.30N 56.00E
Jülich Germany **8** 50.55N 6.21E
Jwayyā Lebanon **32** 33.14N 35.20E
Jylland *pen.* Denmark **17** 56.00N 9.15E
Jyväskylä Finland **16** 62.14N 25.44E

K

K2 *mtn.* Asia **24** 35.53N 76.32E
Ka *r.* Nigeria **38** 11.35N 4.10E
Kaabong Uganda **37** 3.28N 34.08E
Kaapstad *see* Cape Town R.S.A. **39**
Kabaena *i.* Indonesia **27** 5.25S122.00E
Kabala Sierra Leone **34** 9.40N 11.36W
Kabale Uganda **37** 1.13S 30.00E
Kabalega Falls *f.* Uganda **37** 2.17N 31.46E
Kabalega Falls Nat. Park Uganda **37** 2.15N 31.45E
Kabalo Zaïre **36** 6.02S 27.00E
Kabambare Zaïre **37** 4.40S 27.41E
Kabanga Zambia **39** 17.36S 26.45E
Kabba Nigeria **38** 7.50N 6.07E
Kabinakagami *r.* Canada **55** 50.20N 84.20W
Kabīr Kūh *mts.* Iran **31** 33.00N 47.00E
Kābol Afghan. **28** 34.30N 69.10E
Kabongo Zaïre **36** 7.22S 25.34E
Kabonzo Zaïre **37** 6.41S 27.49E
Kabūd Gonbad Iran **31** 37.02N 59.46E
Kabul *see* Kābol Afghan. **28**
Kabunda Zaïre **37** 12.27S 29.15E
Kabwe Zambia **37** 14.27S 28.25E
Kāchā Kūh *mts.* Iran **31** 29.30N 61.20E
Kachchh, G. of India **28** 22.30N 69.30E
Kachiry Kazakhstan **20** 53.07N 76.08E
Kade Ghana **38** 6.08N 0.51W
Kadina Australia **46** 33.58S137.14E
Kadioli Mali **38** 10.38N 5.45W
Kadoma Zimbabwe **39** 18.23S 29.52E
Kaduna Nigeria **38** 10.28N 7.25E
Kaduna *d.* Nigeria **38** 11.00N 7.35E
Kaduna *r.* Nigeria **38** 8.45N 5.45E
Kāduqlī Sudan **35** 11.01N 29.43E
Kadusam *mtn.* China **29** 28.30N 96.45E
Kadzherom Russian Fed. **18** 64.42N 55.59E
Kaédi Mauritania **34** 16.12N 13.32W
Kaélé Cameroon **38** 10.05N 14.28E
Kaesŏng N. Korea **25** 37.59N126.30E
Kafanchan Nigeria **38** 9.38N 8.20E
Kafirévs, Ákra *c.* Greece **13** 38.11N 24.30E
Kafr ad Dawwār Egypt **32** 31.08N 30.08E
Kafr al Baţţīkh Egypt **32** 31.24N 31.44E
Kafr ash Shaykh Egypt **32** 31.07N 30.56E
Kafr az Zayyāt Egypt **32** 30.50N 30.49E
Kafr Salīm Egypt **32** 31.09N 30.07E
Kafu *r.* Uganda **37** 1.40N 32.07E
Kafue Zambia **37** 15.40S 28.13E
Kafue *r.* Zambia **36** 15.53S 28.55E
Kafue Dam Zambia **37** 15.40S 27.10E
Kafunzo Uganda **37** 1.05S 30.26E
Kaga Bandoro C.A.R. **36** 7.00N 19.10E
Kagan Uzbekistan **20** 39.45N 64.32E
Kagarlyk Ukraine **15** 49.50N 30.50E
Kagera *d.* Tanzania **37** 2.00S 31.20E
Kağizman Turkey **30** 40.08N 43.07E
Kagoshima Japan **25** 31.37N130.32E
Kagul Moldavia **15** 45.54N 28.11E
Kahama Tanzania **37** 3.48S 32.38E
Kahayan *r.* Indonesia **26** 3.20S114.04E
Kahnūj Iran **31** 27.55N 57.45E
Kahraman Maraş Turkey **30** 37.34N 36.54E
Kai, Kepulauan *is.* Indonesia **27** 5.45S132.55E
Kaiama Nigeria **38** 9.37N 4.03E
Kaiapoi New Zealand **48** 43.23S172.39E
Kaifeng China **25** 34.47N114.20E
Kaikohe New Zealand **48** 35.25S173.49E
Kaikoura New Zealand **48** 42.24S173.41E
Kaikoura Range *mts.* New Zealand **48** 42.00S173.40E
Kaimana Indonesia **27** 3.39S133.44E
Kaimanawa Mts. New Zealand **48** 39.10S176.15E
Kainantu P.N.G. **27** 6.16S145.50E
Kainji Resr. Nigeria **38** 10.00N 4.35E
Kaipara Harbour New Zealand **48** 36.30S174.00E
Kaiserslautern Germany **8** 49.27N 7.47E
Kaitaia New Zealand **48** 35.08S173.18E
Kaitum *r.* Sweden **16** 67.30N 21.05E
Kaizuka Japan **23** 34.27N135.21E
Kajaani Finland **16** 64.14N 27.41E
Kajabbi Australia **44** 20.02S140.02E
Kajiado Kenya **37** 1.50S 36.48E
Kajuru Nigeria **38** 10.19N 7.40E
Kakamas R.S.A. **39** 28.44S 20.35E
Kakamega Kenya **37** 0.21N 34.47E
Kakamigahara Japan **23** 35.28N136.48E
Kakegawa Japan **23** 34.46N138.01E
Kakhovskoye Vodokhranilishche *resr.* Ukraine **19** 47.33N 34.40E
Kākī Iran **31** 28.19N 51.34E
Kākināda India **29** 16.59N 82.20E
Kakonko Tanzania **37** 3.19S 30.54E
Kakuma Kenya **37** 3.38N 34.48E
Kakuto Uganda **37** 0.54S 31.26E
Kala *r.* Finland **16** 64.17N 23.55E
Kalaallit Nunaat *see* Greenland N.America **51**
Kalabahi Indonesia **27** 8.13S124.31E
Kalabáka Greece **13** 39.42N 21.43E
Kalabity Australia **46** 31.53S140.18E
Kalach-na-Donu Russian Fed. **19** 48.43N 43.31E
Kalahari Desert Botswana **39** 23.30S 22.00E
Kalahari Gemsbok Nat. Park R.S.A. **39** 25.45S 20.25E
Kalajoki Finland **16** 64.15N 23.57E
Kalakan Russian Fed. **21** 55.10N116.45E
Kalámai Greece **13** 37.02N 22.05E
Kalamazoo U.S.A. **55** 42.17N 85.36W
Kalamera Tanzania **37** 2.07S 33.43E
Kalamurra, L. Australia **46** 28.00S138.00E
Kalannie Australia **43** 30.21S117.04E
Kalarash Moldavia **15** 47.18N 28.16E
Kalāt Pakistan **28** 29.01N 66.38E
Kalbarri Australia **43** 27.40S114.12E
Kalecik Turkey **30** 40.06N 33.22E
Kalehe Zaïre **37** 2.05S 28.53E
Kalemie Zaïre **37** 5.57S 29.10E
Kalgan *r.* Australia **43** 34.55S117.58E
Kalgoorlie Australia **43** 30.49S121.29E
Kaliakra, Nos *c.* Bulgaria **13** 43.23N 28.29E
Kalianda Indonesia **26** 5.50S105.45E
Kalimantan *d.* Indonesia **26** 1.00S113.00E
Kalimantan *f.* Indonesia **26** 0.05N112.30E
Kalimantan Barat *d.* Indonesia **26** 0.30N110.00E
Kalimantan Selatan *d.* Indonesia **26** 2.30S115.30E
Kalimantan Tengah *d.* Indonesia **26** 2.00S113.30E
Kalimantan Timur *d.* Indonesia **26** 2.20N116.30E
Kálimnos *i.* Greece **13** 37.00N 27.00E
Kaliningrad Russian Fed. **17** 54.43N 20.30E
Kalinkovichi Belorussia **15** 52.10N 29.13E
Kalinovka Ukraine **15** 49.29N 28.30E
Kalispell U.S.A. **54** 48.12N114.19W
Kalisz Poland **15** 51.46N 18.02E
Kaliua Tanzania **37** 5.08S 31.50E
Kalix *r.* Sweden **16** 65.50N 23.11E
Kalkar Germany **8** 51.45N 6.17E
Kalkfontein Botswana **39** 22.08S 20.54E
Kalkrand Namibia **39** 24.05S 17.34E
Kallsjön *l.* Sweden **16** 63.35N 13.00E
Kalmar Sweden **17** 56.40N 16.22E
Kalmar *d.* Sweden **17** 57.20N 16.00E
Kalmarsund *str.* Sweden **17** 56.40N 16.25E
Kalmthout Belgium **8** 51.23N 4.28E
Kalmykovo Kazakhstan **19** 49.02N 51.55E
Kalo P.N.G. **44** 10.05S147.45E
Kalocsa Hungary **15** 46.32N 18.59E
Kalole Zaïre **37** 3.40S 27.22E
Kalomo Zambia **36** 17.03S 26.29E
Kalonje Zambia **37** 12.21S 31.06E
Kaltag U.S.A. **50** 64.20N158.44W
Kaluga Russian Fed. **18** 54.31N 36.16E
Kalumburu Australia **42** 14.14S126.38E
Kalundborg Denmark **17** 55.41N 11.06E
Kalush Ukraine **15** 49.02N 24.20E
Kalutara Sri Lanka **29** 6.35N 79.58E
Kama *r.* Russian Fed. **18** 55.30N 52.00E
Kamakura Japan **23** 35.19N139.33E
Kamanashi *r.* Japan **23** 35.33N138.28E
Kamanjab Namibia **39** 19.39S 14.50E
Kamba Nigeria **38** 11.52N 3.42E
Kambalda Australia **43** 31.12S121.40E
Kambarka Russian Fed. **18** 56.18N 54.13E
Kamchatka, Poluostrov *pen.* Russian Fed. **21** 56.00N160.00E
Kamen *mtn.* Russian Fed. **21** 68.40N 94.20E
Kamenets Podolskiy Ukraine **15** 48.40N 26.36E
Kamenka Russian Fed. **18** 53.10N 44.05E
Kamenka Russian Fed. **18** 65.55N 44.02E
Kamenka Bugskaya Ukraine **15** 50.07N 24.30E
Kamen Kashirskiy Ukraine **15** 51.32N 24.59E
Kamen-na-Obi Russian Fed. **20** 53.46N 81.18E
Kamenskoye Russian Fed. **21** 62.31N165.15E
Kamensk-Shakhtinskiy Russian Fed. **19** 48.20N 40.16E
Kamensk-Ural'skiy Russian Fed. **20** 56.29N 61.49E
Kāmet *mtn.* China **29** 31.03N 79.25E
Kameyama Japan **23** 34.51N136.27E
Kamiah U.S.A. **54** 46.14N116.02W
Kamieskroon R.S.A. **39** 30.12S 17.53E
Kamina Zaïre **36** 8.46S 25.00E
Kamloops Canada **50** 50.39N120.24W
Kamo *r.* Japan **23** 35.00N139.52E
Kamp Germany **8** 50.14N 7.37E
Kampa Indonesia **26** 1.46S105.26E
Kampala Uganda **37** 0.19N 32.35E
Kampar *r.* Indonesia **26** 0.20N102.55E
Kampen Neth. **8** 52.33N 5.55E
Kamp-Lintfort Germany **8** 51.34N 6.38E
Kâmpóng Cham Cambodia **26** 11.59N105.26E
Kâmpóng Chhnăng Cambodia **26** 12.16N104.39E
Kâmpóng Saôm Cambodia **26** 10.38N103.30E
Kâmpôt Cambodia **26** 10.37N104.11E
Kampti Burkina **38** 10.07N 3.22W
Kamsack Canada **51** 51.34N101.54W
Kamskoye Vodokhranilishche *resr.* Russian Fed. **18** 58.55N 56.20E
Kamyshin Russian Fed. **19** 50.05N 45.24E
Kana *r.* Zimbabwe **39** 18.30S 26.50E
Kanagawa *d.* Japan **23** 35.25N139.10E
Kananga Zaïre **36** 5.53S 22.26E
Kanash Russian Fed. **18** 55.30N 47.27E
Kanawha *r.* U.S.A. **55** 38.50N 82.08W
Kanazawa Japan **25** 36.35N136.38E
Kanchanaburi Thailand **29** 14.08N 99.31E
Kānchenjunga *mtn.* Asia **29** 27.44N 88.11E
Kānchipuram India **29** 12.50N 79.44E
Kandalaksha Russian Fed. **18** 67.09N 32.31E
Kandalakshskaya Guba *g.* Russian Fed. **18** 66.30N 34.00E
Kandangan Indonesia **26** 2.50S115.15E
Kandi Benin **38** 11.05N 2.59E
Kandira Turkey **30** 41.05N 30.08E
Kandos Australia **47** 32.53S149.59E
Kandrāch Pakistan **28** 25.29N 65.29E
Kandreho Madagascar **37** 17.29S 46.06E
Kandy Sri Lanka **29** 7.18N 80.43E
Kane U.S.A. **55** 41.40N 78.49W
Kanem *d.* Chad **38** 15.10N 15.30E
Kanevka Russian Fed. **18** 67.08N 39.50E
Kang Botswana **39** 23.43S 22.51E
Kangaarsussuaq *see* Parry, Kap Greenland **51**
Kangān Iran **31** 27.50N 52.07E
Kangar Malaysia **26** 6.28N100.10E
Kangaroo I. Australia **46** 35.50S137.06E
Kangding China **24** 30.05N102.04E
Kangean, Kepulauan *is.* Indonesia **26** 7.00S115.45E
Kangerlussuaq *see* Söndreströmfjord Greenland **51**
Kangiqsualujjuaq Canada **51** 58.35N 65.59W
Kangiqsujuaq Canada **51** 61.30N 72.00W
Kangirsuk Canada **51** 60.01N 70.01W
Kanin, Poluostrov *pen.* Russian Fed. **18** 68.00N 45.00E
Kaningo Kenya **37** 0.52S 38.31E
Kanin Nos, Mys *c.* Russian Fed. **18** 68.38N 43.20E

Kaniva Australia 46 36.33S141.17E
Kanjiža Yugo. 15 46.04N 20.04E
Kankakee U.S.A. 53 41.08N 87.52W
Kankan Guinea 34 10.22N 9.11W
Kānker India 29 20.17N 81.30E
Kano r. Japan 23 35.05N138.52E
Kano Nigeria 38 12.00N 8.31E
Kano d. Nigeria 38 11.45N 8.30E
Kanona Zambia 37 13.03S 30.37E
Kanowna Australia 43 30.36S121.36E
Kānpur India 29 26.27N 80.14E
Kansas d. U.S.A. 52 38.00N 99.00W
Kansas r. U.S.A. 53 39.07N 94.36W
Kansas City Mo. U.S.A. 53 39.02N 94.33W
Kansk Russian Fed. 21 56.11N 95.20E
Kansŏng S. Korea 25 38.20N128.28E
Kantché Niger 38 13.31N 8.30E
Kantemirovka Russian Fed. 19 49.40N 39.52E
Kantō d. Japan 23 35.35N139.30E
Kantōheiya f. Japan 23 36.02N140.10E
Kantō-sanchi mts. Japan 23 36.00N138.35E
Kanye Botswana 39 24.58S 25.17E
Kanyu Botswana 39 20.05S 24.39E
Kaolack Senegal 34 14.09N 16.08W
Kapchagay Kazakhstan 24 43.51N 77.14E
Kapenguria Kenya 37 1.13N 35.07E
Kapfenberg Austria 14 47.27N 15.18E
Kapiri Mposhi Zambia 37 13.59S 28.40E
Kapit Malaysia 26 2.01N112.56E
Kapiti I. New Zealand 48 40.50S174.50E
Kapongolo Zaïre 37 7.51S 28.12E
Kaposvár Hungary 13 46.22N 17.47E
Kapps Namibia 39 22.22S 17.52E
Kapsabet Kenya 37 0.12N 35.05E
Kapuas r. Indonesia 26 0.13S109.12E
Kapunda Australia 46 34.21S138.54E
Kapuskasing Canada 55 49.25N 82.26W
Kaputar, Mt. Australia 47 30.20S150.10E
Kapuvár Hungary 15 47.36N 17.02E
Kara Russian Fed. 20 69.12N 65.00E
Kara-Bogaz Gol, Zaliv b. Turkmenistan 31 41.20N 53.40E
Karabutak Kazakhstan 20 49.55N 60.05E
Karabük Turkey 30 41.12N 32.36E
Karāchi Pakistan 28 24.51N 67.02E
Karād India 28 17.17N 74.12E
Karaganda Kazakhstan 20 49.53N 73.07E
Karaginskiy, Ostrov i. Russian Fed. 21 59.00N165.00E
Karakas Kazakhstan 24 48.20N 83.30E
Karakelong i. Indonesia 27 4.20N126.50E
Karakoram Pass Asia 29 35.33N 77.51E
Karakoram Range mts. Jammu & Kashmir 28 35.30N 76.30E
Karaköse see Ağri Turkey 19
Karakumskiy Kanal canal Turkmenistan 31 37.30N 65.48E
Karakumy, Peski f. Turkmenistan 31 37.45N 60.00E
Karakuwisa Namibia 39 18.56S 19.43E
Karaman Turkey 30 37.11N 33.13E
Karamay China 24 45.48N 84.30E
Karamea New Zealand 48 41.15S172.07E
Karamea Bight b. New Zealand 48 41.15S171.30E
Karamürsel Turkey 30 40.42N 29.37E
Karand Iran 31 34.16N 46.15E
Karasburg Namibia 39 28.00S 18.46E
Karasjok Norway 16 69.27N 25.30E
Karasuk Russian Fed. 20 53.45N 78.01E
Karatau, Khrebet mts. Kazakhstan 19 44.15N 52.10E
Karatobe Kazakhstan 19 49.44N 53.30E
Karaton Kazakhstan 19 46.26N 53.32E
Karazhal Kazakhstan 20 48.00N 70.55E
Karbalā' Iraq 31 32.37N 44.03E
Karcag Hungary 15 47.19N 20.56E
Kardhitsa Greece 13 39.22N 21.59E
Kärdla Estonia 17 59.00N 22.42E
Karema Tanzania 37 6.50S 30.25E
Karen India 29 12.50N 92.55E
Karepino Russian Fed. 18 61.05N 58.02E
Karesuando Finland 16 68.25N 22.30E
Kargasok Russian Fed. 20 59.07N 80.58E
Kargi Kenya 37 2.31N 37.34E
Kargil Jammu & Kashmir 28 34.32N 76.12E
Kargopol Russian Fed. 18 61.32N 38.59E
Kari Nigeria 38 11.17N 10.35E
Kariba Zimbabwe 37 16.32S 28.50E
Kariba, L. Zimbabwe / Zambia 37 16.50S 28.00E
Kariba Dam Zimbabwe / Zambia 37 16.15S 28.55E
Karibib Namibia 39 21.56S 15.52E
Kārikāl India 29 10.58N 79.50E
Karimama Benin 38 12.02N 3.15E
Karis Finland 17 60.05N 23.40E
Karisimbi, Mt. Zaïre / Rwanda 37 1.31S 29.25E
Kariya Japan 23 34.59N136.59E
Kariyangwe Zimbabwe 39 17.57S 27.30E
Karkaralinsk Kazakhstan 20 49.21N 75.27E
Karkar I. P.N.G. 27 4.40S146.00E
Karkas, Kūh-e mtn. Iran 31 33.25N 51.40E
Karkheh r. Iran 31 31.45N 47.52E
Karkinitskiy Zaliv g. Ukraine 19 45.50N 32.45E
Karkoo Australia 46 34.02S135.44E
Karlino Poland 14 54.03N 15.51E
Karl-Marx-Stadt see Chemnitz Germany 14
Karlovac Croatia 12 45.30N 15.34E
Karlovy Vary Czech. 14 50.14N 12.53E
Karlsborg Sweden 17 58.32N 14.31E
Karlshamn Sweden 17 56.10N 14.51E
Karlskoga Sweden 17 59.20N 14.31E
Karlskrona Sweden 17 56.10N 15.35E
Karlsruhe Germany 14 49.00N 8.24E
Karlstad Sweden 17 59.22N 13.30E
Karmöy i. Norway 17 59.15N 5.15E
Karnafuli Resr. Bangla. 29 22.40N 92.05E
Karnataka d. India 28 14.45N 76.00E
Karnobat Bulgaria 13 42.40N 27.00E
Kärnten d. Austria 14 46.50N 13.50E
Karonga Malaŵi 37 9.54S 33.55E
Karonie Australia 43 30.58S122.32E
Karoonda Australia 46 35.09S139.54E
Karos Dam R.S.A. 39 28.27S 21.39E
Karpach Moldavia 15 48.00N 27.10E
Kárpathos Greece 13 35.30N 27.14E
Kárpathos i. Greece 13 35.35N 27.08E
Karpineny Moldavia 15 46.46N 28.18E
Karpinsk Russian Fed. 18 59.48N 59.59E
Karpogory Russian Fed. 18 64.01N 44.30E
Karragullen Australia 43 32.05S116.03E
Karratha Australia 42 20.44S116.50E
Karridale Australia 43 34.12S115.04E
Kars Turkey 30 40.35N 43.05E
Karsakpay Kazakhstan 20 47.47N 66.43E
Kärsämaki Finland 16 63.58N 25.46E
Kārsava Russian Fed. 18 56.45N 27.40E
Karskoye More sea Russian Fed. 20 73.00N 65.00E
Kartaly Russian Fed. 20 53.06N 60.37E
Karufa Indonesia 27 3.50S133.27E
Karumba Australia 44 17.28S140.50E
Kārūn r. Iran 31 30.25N 48.12E
Karungi Sweden 16 66.03N 23.55E
Karungu Kenya 37 0.50S 34.09E
Karviná Czech. 15 49.50N 18.30E
Kasai r. Zaïre 36 3.10S 16.13E
Kasama Zambia 37 10.10S 31.11E
Kasane Botswana 39 17.48S 25.09E
Kasanga Tanzania 37 8.27S 31.10E
Kāsaragod India 28 12.30N 75.00E
Kasba L. Canada 51 60.18N102.07W
Kasese Uganda 37 0.07N 30.06E
Kāshān Iran 31 33.59N 51.31E
Kashi China 24 39.29N 76.02E
Kashin Russian Fed. 18 57.22N 37.39E
Kashiwa Japan 23 35.52N139.59E
Kāshmar Iran 31 35.12N 58.26E
Kasimov Russian Fed. 18 54.55N 41.25E
Kaskinen Finland 16 62.23N 21.13E
Kaskö see Kaskinen Finland 16
Kásos i. Greece 13 35.22N 26.56E
Kassalā Sudan 35 15.24N 36.30E
Kassel Germany 14 51.18N 9.30E
Kastamonu Turkey 30 41.22N 33.47E
Kastoría Greece 13 40.32N 21.15E
Kasugai Japan 23 35.14N136.58E
Kasukabe Japan 23 35.58N139.45E
Kasulu Tanzania 37 4.34S 30.06E
Kasungu Malaŵi 37 13.04S 33.29E
Kasūr Pakistan 28 31.07N 74.30E
Katanning Australia 43 33.42S117.33E
Katarniān Ghāt India 29 28.20N 81.09E
Katchall i. India 29 7.57N 93.22E
Katete Zambia 37 14.08S 31.50E
Katha Burma 29 24.11N 96.20E
Katherine Australia 44 14.29S132.20E
Kathmandu Nepal 29 27.42N 85.19E
Kati Mali 34 12.41N 8.04W
Katima Rapids f. Zambia 39 17.27S 24.13E
Katiola Ivory Coast 38 8.10N 5.10W
Katonga r. Uganda 37 0.03N 30.15E
Katoomba Australia 47 33.42S150.23E
Katowice Poland 15 50.15N 18.59E
Kātrīnā, Jabal mtn. Egypt 32 28.30N 33.57E
Katrine, Loch U.K. 6 56.15N 4.30W
Katrineholm Sweden 17 59.00N 16.12E
Katsina Nigeria 38 13.00N 7.32E
Katsina d. Nigeria 38 12.25N 7.55E
Katsina Ala Nigeria 38 7.10N 9.30E
Katsina Ala r. Nigeria 38 7.50N 8.58E
Katsura r. Japan 23 34.53N135.42E
Katsuura Japan 23 35.08N140.18E
Kattegat str. Denmark / Sweden 17 57.00N 11.20E
Katwijk aan Zee Neth. 8 52.13N 4.27E
Kauai i. Hawaii U.S.A. 52 22.05N159.30W
Kaub Germany 8 50.07N 7.50E
Kaufbeuren Germany 14 47.53N 10.37E
Kauhajoki Finland 16 62.26N 22.11E
Kauhava Finland 16 63.06N 23.05E
Kaukauveld mts. Namibia 39 20.00S 20.15E
Kauliranta Finland 16 66.26N 23.40E
Kaunas Lithuania 17 54.54N 23.54E
Kaura Namoda Nigeria 38 12.39N 6.38E
Kautokeino Norway 16 69.00N 23.02E
Kavála Greece 13 40.56N 24.24E
Kāvali India 29 14.55N 80.01E
Kavarna Bulgaria 13 43.26N 28.22E
Kavimba Botswana 39 18.05S 24.34E
Kavkaz Russian Fed. 19 45.20N 36.39E
Kavkazskiy Khrebet mts. Europe 19 43.00N 44.00E
Kaw Guiana 61 4.29N 52.02W
Kawachi-nagano Japan 23 34.25N135.32E
Kawagoe Japan 23 35.55N139.29E
Kawaguchi Japan 23 35.48N139.43E
Kawambwa Zambia 37 9.47S 29.10E
Kawasaki Japan 23 35.32N139.43E
Kawerau New Zealand 48 38.05S176.42E
Kawhia New Zealand 48 38.04S174.49E
Kaya Burkina 38 13.04N 1.04W
Kayambi Zambia 37 9.26S 32.01E
Kayan r. Indonesia 26 2.47N117.46E
Kaycee U.S.A. 54 43.43N106.38W
Kayenta U.S.A. 54 36.44N110.17W
Kayes Mali 34 14.26N 11.28W
Kayseri Turkey 30 38.42N 35.28E
Kaysville U.S.A. 54 41.02N111.56W
Kazachye Russian Fed. 21 70.46N136.15E
Kazakhskiy Zaliv b. Kazakhstan 19 42.43N 52.30E
Kazakhstan Asia 19 48.00N 52.30E
Kazan Russian Fed. 18 55.45N 49.10E
Kazanlŭk Bulgaria 13 42.38N 25.26E
Kazatin Ukraine 15 49.41N 28.49E
Kazaure Nigeria 38 12.40N 8.25E
Kazbek mtn. Russian Fed. 19 42.42N 44.30E
Kāzerūn Iran 31 29.35N 51.39E
Kazhim Russian Fed. 18 60.18N 51.34E
Kazincbarcika Hungary 15 48.16N 20.37E
Kazo Japan 23 36.07N139.36E
Kéa i. Greece 13 37.36N 24.20E
Kearney U.S.A. 52 40.42N 99.04W
Keban Turkey 30 38.48N 38.45E
Kebbi d. Nigeria 38 11.30N 3.45E
Kebnekaise mtn. Sweden 16 67.53N 18.33E
K'ebri Dehar Ethiopia 35 6.47N 44.17E
Kecskemét Hungary 15 46.54N 19.42E
Kedainiai Lithuania 17 55.17N 24.00E
Kedgwick Canada 55 47.38N 67.21W
Kediri Indonesia 26 7.55S112.01E
Kédougou Senegal 34 12.35N 12.09W
Keele Peak mtn. Canada 50 63.15N129.50W
Keene U.S.A. 55 42.56N 72.17W
Keepit, L. Australia 47 30.52S150.30E
Keer-Weer, C. Australia 44 13.58S141.30E
Keetmanshoop Namibia 39 26.34S 18.07E
Keewatin d. Canada 51 65.00N 90.00W
Kefallinía i. Greece 13 38.15N 20.33E
Kefar Sava Israel 32 32.11N 34.54E
Keffi Nigeria 38 8.52N 7.53E
Keflavík Iceland 16 64.01N 22.35W
Keighley U.K. 4 53.52N 1.54W
Keila Estonia 17 59.18N 24.29E
Keimoes R.S.A. 39 28.41S 20.58E
Keitele l. Finland 16 62.55N 26.00E
Keith Australia 46 36.06S140.22E
Keith U.K. 6 57.32N 2.57W
Keith Arm b. Canada 50 65.20N122.15W
Kelang Malaysia 26 2.57N101.24E
Kelberg Germany 8 50.17N 6.56E
Kelkit r. Turkey 30 40.46N 36.32E
Keller U.S.A. 54 48.03N118.40W
Kellerberrin Australia 43 31.38S117.43E
Kellet, C. Canada 50 71.59N125.34W
Kelloselkä Finland 16 66.55N 28.50E
Kells Meath Rep. of Ire. 7 53.44N 6.53W
Kelme Lithuania 17 55.38N 22.56E
Kelowna Canada 50 49.50N119.29W
Kelso U.K. 6 55.36N 2.26W
Kelso Calif. U.S.A. 54 35.01N115.39W
Kelso Wash. U.S.A. 54 46.09N122.54W
Keluang Malaysia 26 2.01N103.18E
Kelvedon U.K. 5 51.50N 0.43E
Kem Russian Fed. 18 64.58N 34.39E
Kema Indonesia 27 1.22N125.08E
Ke Macina Mali 38 14.05N 5.20W
Kemah Turkey 30 39.35N 39.02E
Kemaliye Turkey 30 39.16N 38.29E
Kemerovo Russian Fed. 20 55.25N 86.10E
Kemi Finland 16 65.49N 24.32E
Kemi r. Finland 16 65.47N 24.30E
Kemijärvi Finland 16 66.36N 27.24E
Kemmerer U.S.A. 54 41.48N110.32W
Kempen f. Belgium 8 51.05N 5.00E
Kemp Land f. Antarctica 64 69.00S 57.00E
Kempsey Australia 47 31.05S152.50E
Kempt, Lac l. Canada 55 47.26N 74.30W
Kempten Germany 14 47.44N 10.19E
Kenai U.S.A. 50 60.33N151.15W
Kendal U.K. 4 54.19N 2.44W
Kendall Australia 47 31.28S152.40E
Kendari Indonesia 27 3.57S122.36E
Kendenup Australia 43 34.28S117.35E
Kendrick U.S.A. 54 46.37N116.39W
Kenebri Australia 47 30.45S149.02E
Kenema Sierra Leone 34 7.57N 11.11W
Kengeja Tanzania 37 5.24S 39.45E
Keng Tung Burma 29 21.16N 99.39E
Kenhardt R.S.A. 39 29.21S 21.08E
Kenilworth U.K. 5 52.22N 1.35W
Kenitra Morocco 34 34.20N 6.34W
Kenmare Rep. of Ire. 7 51.53N 9.36W
Kennebec r. U.S.A. 55 44.00N 69.50W
Kennet r. U.K. 5 51.28N 0.57W
Kennewick U.S.A. 54 46.12N119.07W
Kenogami r. Canada 55 50.24N 84.20W
Keno Hill town Canada 50 63.58N135.22W
Kenora Canada 51 49.47N 94.26W
Kenosha U.S.A. 53 42.34N 87.50W
Kenozero, Ozero l. Russian Fed. 18 62.20N 37.00E
Kent d. U.K. 5 51.12N 0.40E
Kent Ohio U.S.A. 55 41.10N 81.20W
Kent Wash. U.S.A. 54 47.23N122.14W
Kentau Kazakhstan 24 43.28N 68.36E
Kentland U.S.A. 55 40.46N 87.26W
Kenton U.S.A. 55 40.38N 83.38W
Kent Pen. Canada 50 68.30N107.00W
Kentucky d. U.S.A. 53 38.00N 85.00W
Kentucky L. U.S.A. 53 36.15N 88.00W
Kenya Africa 37 1.00N 38.00E
Kenya, Mt. see Kirinyaga Kenya 37
Keokuk U.S.A. 53 40.23N 91.25W
Kepi Indonesia 27 6.32S139.19E
Kepno Poland 15 51.17N 17.59E
Keppel B. Australia 44 23.21S150.55E
Kerala d. India 28 10.30N 76.30E
Kerang Australia 46 35.42S143.59E
Kerch Ukraine 19 45.22N 36.27E
Kerchenskiy Proliv str. Ukraine / Russian Fed. 19 45.15N 36.35E
Kerema P.N.G. 27 7.59S145.46E
Kericho Kenya 37 0.22S 35.19E
Kerinci, Gunung mtn. Indonesia 26 1.45S101.20E
Kerio r. Kenya 37 3.00N 36.14E
Kerkebet Ethiopia 35 16.13N 37.30E
Kerki Russian Fed 18 63.40N 54.00E
Kerki Turkmenistan 20 37.53N 65.10E
Kérkira Greece 13 39.37N 19.50E
Kérkira i. Greece 13 39.35N 19.50E
Kerkrade Neth. 8 50.52N 6.02E
Kermān Iran 31 30.18N 57.05E
Kermānshāh Iran 31 34.19N 47.04E
Kerme Körfezi g. Turkey 13 36.52N 27.53E
Kerpen Germany 8 50.52N 6.42E
Kerry d. Rep. of Ire. 7 52.07N 9.35W
Kerry Head Rep. of Ire. 7 52.24N 9.56W
Kerulen r. Mongolia 25 48.45N117.00E
Kesagami L. Canada 55 50.23N 80.15W
Keşan Turkey 13 40.50N 26.39E
Keshod India 28 21.18N 70.15E
Keskal India 29 20.05N 81.35E
Keski-Suomi d. Finland 16 62.30N 25.30E
Keswick U.K. 4 54.35N 3.09W
Keszthely Hungary 15 46.46N 17.15E
Ketapang Kalimantan Indonesia 26 1.50S110.02E
Ketchikan U.S.A. 50 55.25N131.40W
Ketchum U.S.A. 54 43.41N114.22W
Kete Krachi Ghana 38 7.50N 0.03W
Ketrzyn Poland 15 54.06N 21.23E
Kettering U.K. 5 52.24N 0.44W
Kettering U.S.A. 55 39.41N 84.10W
Kettle Falls town U.S.A. 54 48.36N118.03W
Keweenaw B. U.S.A. 55 46.46N 88.26W
Keweenaw Pen. U.S.A. 55 47.10N 88.30W
Key, Lough Rep. of Ire. 7 54.00N 8.15W
Key Harbour Canada 55 45.52N 80.48W
Keynsham U.K. 5 51.25N 2.30W
Kezhma Russian Fed. 21 58.58N101.08E
Kežmarok Czech. 15 49.08N 20.25E
Kgalagadi d. Botswana 39 25.00S 21.30E
Kgatleng d. Botswana 39 24.20S 26.20E
Khabarovsk Russian Fed. 25 48.32N135.08E
Khairpur Sind Pakistan 28 27.30N 68.50E
Khalkhāl Iran 31 37.36N 48.36E
Khalkis Greece 13 38.27N 23.36E
Khalmer Yu Russian Fed. 18 67.58N 64.48E
Khalturin Russian Fed. 18 58.38N 48.50E
Khalūf Oman 28 20.31N 58.04E
Khambhāt, G. of India 28 20.30N 72.00E
Khamkeut Laos 29 18.14N104.44E
Khānaqīn Iraq 31 34.22N 45.22E
Khandwa India 28 21.49N 76.23E
Khāneh Khvodī Iran 31 36.05N 56.04E
Khaniá Greece 13 35.30N 24.02E
Khanka, Ozero l. Russian Fed. 25 45.00N132.30E
Khanty-Mansiysk Russian Fed. 20 61.00N 69.00E
Khān Yūnus Egypt 32 31.21N 34.18E
Khapcheranga Russian Fed. 25 49.46N112.20E
Kharagpur India 29 22.23N 87.22E
Khārān r. Iran 31 27.37N 58.48E
Khārijah, Al Wāḥāt al oasis Egypt 30 24.55N 30.35E
Kharkov Ukraine 19 50.00N 36.15E
Khār Kūh mtn. Iran 31 31.37N 53.47E
Kharovsk Russian Fed. 18 59.67N 40.07E
Khartoum see Al Kharṭūm Sudan 35
Kharutayuvam Russian Fed. 18 66.51N 59.31E
Khasavyurt Russian Fed. 19 43.16N 46.36E
Khāsh r. Afghan. 31 31.12N 62.00E
Khāsh Iran 31 28.14N 61.15E
Khashgort Russian Fed. 18 65.25N 65.40E
Khaskovo Bulgaria 13 41.57N 25.33E
Khatanga Russian Fed. 21 71.50N102.31E
Khatangskiy Zaliv g. Russian Fed. 21 75.00N112.10E
Khemmarat Thailand 29 16.04N105.10E
Khenifra Morocco 34 33.00N 5.40W
Khersān r. Iran 31 31.29N 48.53E
Kherson Ukraine 19 46.39N 32.38E
Khios Greece 13 38.23N 26.07E
Khios i. Greece 13 38.23N 26.04E
Khiva Uzbekistan 31 41.25N 60.49E
Khmelnik Ukraine 15 49.36N 27.59E
Khmelnitskiy Ukraine 15 49.25N 26.49E
Khodorov Ukraine 15 49.20N 24.19E
Kholm Russian Fed. 18 57.10N 31.11E
Kholmogory Russian Fed. 18 63.51N 41.46E
Khomas-Hochland mts. Namibia 39 22.50S 16.25E
Khonu Russian Fed. 21 66.29N143.12E
Khoper r. Russian Fed. 19 49.35N 42.17E
Khorixas Namibia 39 20.24S 14.58E
Khorog Tajikistan 24 37.32N 71.32E
Khorramābād Iran 31 33.29N 48.21E
Khorramshahr Iran 31 30.26N 48.09E
Khotimsk Belorussia 15 53.24N 32.36E
Khotin Ukraine 15 48.30N 26.31E
Khowrnag, Kūh-e mtn. Iran 31 32.10N 54.38E
Khoyniki Belorussia 15 51.54N 30.00E
Khudzhand Tajikistan 24 40.14N 69.40E
Khuis Botswana 39 26.37S 21.45E
Khulga r. Russian Fed. 18 63.33N 61.53E
Khulna Bangla. 29 22.49N 89.34E
Khurra Bārīk r. Iraq 30 32.00N 44.15E
Khust Ukraine 15 48.11N 23.19E
Khvor Iran 31 33.47N 55.06E
Khvormuj Iran 31 28.40N 51.20E
Khvoy Iran 31 38.32N 45.02E
Khyber Pass Asia 28 34.06N 71.05E
Kiama Australia 47 34.41S150.49E
Kibali r. Zaïre 37 3.37N 28.38E
Kibombo Zaïre 36 3.58S 25.57E
Kibondo Tanzania 37 3.35S 30.41E
Kibre Mengist Ethiopia 35 5.52N 39.00E
Kibungu Rwanda 37 2.10S 30.31E
Kibwesa Tanzania 37 6.30S 29.57E
Kibwezi Kenya 37 2.28S 37.57E
Kichiga Russian Fed. 21 59.50N163.27E
Kicking Horse Pass Canada 50 51.28N116.23W
Kidal Mali 38 18.27N 1.25E
Kidderminster U.K. 5 52.24N 2.13W
Kidete Morogoro Tanzania 37 6.39S 36.42E
Kidsgrove U.K. 4 53.06N 2.15W
Kiel Germany 14 54.20N 10.08E
Kielce Poland 15 50.52N 20.37E
Kielder resr. U.K. 4 55.12N 2.30W
Kieler Bucht b. Germany 14 54.30N 10.30E
Kiev see Kiyev Ukraine 15
Kiffa Mauritania 34 16.38N 11.28W
Kigali Rwanda 37 1.59S 30.05E
Kigoma Tanzania 37 4.52S 29.36E
Kigoma d. Tanzania 37 4.45S 30.00E
Kigosi r. Tanzania 37 4.37S 31.29E
Kiiminkin r. Finland 16 65.12N 25.18E
Kikinda Yugo. 15 45.51N 20.30E
Kikládhes is. Greece 13 37.00N 25.00E
Kikori P.N.G. 27 7.25S144.13E
Kikori r. P.N.G. 27 7.10S144.05E
Kikwit Zaïre 36 5.02S 18.51E
Kil Sweden 17 59.30N 13.19E
Kilafors Sweden 17 61.14N 16.34E
Kila Kila P.N.G. 27 9.31S147.10E
Kilchu N. Korea 25 40.55N129.21E
Kilcoy Australia 45 26.57S152.33E
Kilcullen Rep. of Ire. 7 53.08N 6.46W
Kildare Rep. of Ire. 7 53.10N 6.55W
Kildare d. Rep. of Ire. 7 53.10N 6.50W
Kildonan Zimbabwe 39 17.22S 30.33E
Kilfinan U.K. 6 55.58N 5.18W
Kilifi Kenya 37 3.30S 39.50E
Kilimanjaro d. Tanzania 37 3.45S 37.40E
Kilimanjaro mtn. Tanzania 37 3.02S 37.20E
Kilindoni Tanzania 37 7.55S 39.39E
Kilingi-Nõmme Estonia 17 58.09N 24.58E
Kilis Turkey 30 36.43N 37.07E
Kiliya Ukraine 15 45.30N 29.16E
Kilkee Rep. of Ire. 7 52.41N 9.40W
Kilkenny Rep. of Ire. 7 52.39N 7.16W
Kilkenny d. Rep. of Ire. 7 52.35N 7.15W
Kilkieran B. Rep. of Ire. 7 53.20N 9.42W
Kilkis Greece 13 40.59N 22.51E
Killala B. Rep. of Ire. 7 54.15N 9.10W
Killard Pt. U.K. 7 54.19N 5.31W
Killarney Australia 47 28.18S152.15E
Killarney Rep. of Ire. 7 52.04N 9.32W
Killary Harbour est. Rep. of Ire. 7 53.38N 9.56W
Killin U.K. 6 56.29N 4.19W
Killini mtn. Greece 13 37.56N 22.22E
Killorglin Rep. of Ire. 7 52.07N 9.45W
Killybegs Rep. of Ire. 7 54.38N 8.27W
Killyleagh U.K. 7 54.24N 5.39W
Kilmarnock U.K. 6 55.37N 4.30W
Kilmichael Pt. Rep. of Ire. 7 52.44N 6.09W
Kilmore Australia 47 37.18S144.58E
Kilninver U.K. 6 56.21N 5.30W
Kilombero r. Tanzania 37 8.30S 37.28E
Kilosa Tanzania 37 6.49S 37.00E
Kilronan Rep. of Ire. 7 53.08N 9.41W
Kilrush Rep. of Ire. 7 52.39N 9.30W
Kilsyth U.K. 6 55.59N 4.04W
Kilvo Sweden 16 66.50N 21.04E
Kilwa Kivinje Tanzania 37 8.45S 39.21E
Kilwa Masoko Tanzania 37 8.55S 39.31E
Kimaan Indonesia 27 7.54S138.51E
Kimba Australia 46 33.09S136.25E
Kimberley R.S.A. 39 28.44S 24.44E
Kimberley Plateau Australia 42 17.20S127.20E
Kimito i. Finland 17 60.10N 22.30E
Kimparana Mali 38 12.52N 4.59W
Kimry Russian Fed. 18 56.51N 37.20E
Kinabalu mtn. Malaysia 26 6.10N116.40E
Kincardine Canada 55 44.11N 81.38W
Kindia Guinea 34 10.03N 12.49W
Kindu Zaïre 36 3.00S 25.56E
Kinel Russian Fed. 18 53.17N 50.42E
Kineshma Russian Fed. 18 57.28N 42.08E
Kingaroy Australia 44 26.33S151.50E
King City U.S.A. 54 36.13N121.08W
King Edward r. Australia 42 14.12S126.34E
King George Is. Canada 51 57.20N 78.25W
King George Sd. Australia 43 35.03S117.57E
King I. Australia 45 39.50S144.00E
King Leopold Range mts. Australia 42 17.00S125.30E
Kingman Ariz. U.S.A. 54 35.12N114.04W
Kingoonya Australia 46 30.54S135.18E
Kings r. U.S.A. 54 36.03N119.49W
Kingsbridge U.K. 5 50.17N 3.46W
Kings Canyon Australia 44 24.15S131.33E
Kings Canyon Nat. Park U.S.A. 54 36.48N118.30W
Kingsclere U.K. 5 51.20N 1.14W
Kingscote Australia 46 35.40S137.38E
King Sd. Australia 42 17.00S123.30E
Kingsdown Kent U.K. 5 51.21N 0.17E
Kingsley Dam U.S.A. 52 41.15N101.30W
King's Lynn U.K. 4 52.45N 0.25E
Kings Peaks mts. U.S.A. 54 40.46N110.23W
Kingston Canada 55 44.14N 76.30W
Kingston Jamaica 57 17.58N 76.48W
Kingston New Zealand 48 45.20S168.43E
Kingston N.Y. U.S.A. 55 41.55N 74.00W
Kingston S.E. Australia 46 36.50S139.50E
Kingston upon Hull U.K. 4 53.45N 0.20W
Kingstown St. Vincent 57 13.12N 61.14W
Kingsville U.S.A. 52 27.32N 97.53W
Kingswood Avon U.K. 5 51.27N 2.29W
Kings Worthy U.K. 5 51.06N 1.18W
Kington U.K. 5 52.12N 3.02W
Kingussie U.K. 6 57.05N 4.04W
King William I. Canada 51 69.00N 97.30W
King William's Town R.S.A. 39 32.52S 27.23E
Kinloch Rannoch U.K. 6 56.42N 4.11W
Kinna Sweden 17 57.30N 12.41E
Kinnairds Head U.K. 6 57.42N 2.00W
Kinnegad Rep. of Ire. 7 53.28N 7.08W
Kino r. Japan 23 34.13N135.09E
Kinross U.K. 6 56.13N 3.27W
Kinsale Rep. of Ire. 7 51.42N 8.32W
Kinshasa Zaïre 36 4.18S 15.18E
Kintyre pen. U.K. 6 55.35N 5.35W
Kinvara Rep. of Ire. 7 53.08N 8.56W
Kiparissía Greece 13 37.15N 21.40E
Kipawa, Lac l. Canada 55 46.55N 79.00W
Kipengere Range mts. Tanzania 37 9.15S 34.15E
Kipili Tanzania 37 7.30S 30.39E
Kipini Kenya 37 2.31S 40.32E
Kippure mtn. Rep. of Ire. 7 53.11N 6.20W
Kirby U.S.A. 54 43.49N108.10W

Kvaenangen *est.* Norway **16** 69.50N 21.30E
Kwale Kenya **37** 4.20S 39.25E
Kwangju S. Korea **25** 35.07N126.52E
Kwango *r.* Zaïre **36** 3.20S 17.23E
Kwara *d.* Nigeria **38** 8.20N 5.35E
Kwatisore Indonesia **27** 3.18S134.50E
Kwa Zulu *f.* R.S.A. **39** 27.30S 32.00E
Kwekwe Zimbabwe **39** 18.59S 29.46E
Kweneng *d.* Botswana **39** 24.30S 25.40E
Kwethluk U.S.A. **50** 60.49N161.27W
Kwidzyn Poland **15** 53.45N 18.56E
Kwigillingok U.S.A. **50** 59.51N163.08W
Kwiguk U.S.A. **50** 62.45N164.28W
Kwinana Australia **43** 32.15S115.48E
Kwoka *mtn.* Indonesia **27** 1.30S132.30E
Kyabé Chad **34** 9.28N 18.54E
Kyabram Australia **47** 36.18S145.05E
Kyaka Tanzania **37** 1.16S 31.27E
Kyakhta Russian Fed. **24** 50.22N106.30E
Kyalite Australia **46** 34.57S143.31E
Kyancutta Australia **46** 33.08S135.34E
Kyaukpyu Burma **29** 19.28N 93.30E
Kybybolite Australia **46** 36.54S140.58E
Kychema Russian Fed. **18** 65.32N 42.42E
Kyle of Lochalsh *town* U.K. **6** 57.17N 5.43W
Kyll *r.* Germany **8** 49.48N 6.42E
Kyllburg Germany **8** 50.03N 6.36E
Kyluchevskaya *mtn.* Russian Fed. **21** 56.00N160.30E
Kyneton Australia **46** 37.14S144.28E
Kynuna Australia **44** 21.35S141.55E
Kyoga, L. Uganda **37** 1.30N 33.00E
Kyogle Australia **47** 28.36S152.59E
Kyotera Uganda **37** 0.40S 31.31E
Kyōto Japan **23** 35.00N135.45E
Kyōto *d.* Japan **23** 34.55N135.35E
Kyrgyzstan Asia **24** 41.30N 75.00E
Kyrta Russian Fed. **18** 64.02N 57.40E
Kyūshū *i.* Japan **25** 32.50N130.50E
Kyustendil Bulgaria **13** 42.18N 22.39E
Kywong Australia **47** 35.01S146.45E
Kyyjärvi Finland **16** 63.02N 24.34E
Kyzyl Russian Fed. **24** 51.42N 94.28E
Kyzyl Kum, Peski *f.* Uzbekistan **20** 42.00N 64.30E
Kzyl Orda Kazakhstan **20** 44.52N 65.28E

L

Laas Caanood Somali Rep. **35** 8.26N 47.24E
La Asunción Venezuela **60** 11.06N 63.53W
Laâyoune *see* El Aaiún W. Sahara **34**
La Baleine *r.* Canada **51** 58.00N 57.50W
La Banda Argentina **62** 27.44S 64.15W
La Bañeza Spain **10** 42.17N 5.55W
Labao Indonesia **27** 8.12S122.49E
La Barca Mexico **56** 20.20N102.33W
La Barge U.S.A. **54** 42.16N110.12W
La Bassée France **8** 50.32N 2.49E
La Baule France **11** 47.18N 2.23W
Labbezanga Mali **38** 14.57N 0.42E
Labe *r.* Czech. *see* Elbe *r.* Germany **14**
Labé Guinea **34** 11.17N 12.11W
Labinsk Russian Fed. **19** 44.39N 40.44E
La Blanquilla *i.* Venezuela **57** 11.53N 64.38W
Labouheyre France **11** 44.13N 0.55W
Laboulaye Argentina **63** 34.05S 63.25W
Labrador *f.* Canada **51** 54.00N 61.30W
Labrador City Canada **51** 52.54N 66.50W
Labrador Sea Canada/Greenland **51** 57.00N 53.00W
Lábrea Brazil **60** 7.16S 64.47W
Labrit France **11** 44.07N 0.33W
Labuan *i.* Malaysia **26** 5.20N115.15E
Labuha Indonesia **27** 0.37S127.29E
Labyrinth, L. Australia **46** 30.43S135.07E
Lac *d.* Chad **38** 13.30N 14.35E
La Calera Chile **63** 32.47S 71.12W
La Capelle France **8** 49.59N 3.57E
La Carlota Argentina **63** 33.25S 63.18W
La Carolina Spain **10** 38.16N 3.36W
Lacaune France **11** 43.42N 2.41E
La Ceiba Honduras **57** 15.45N 86.45W
Lacepede B. Australia **46** 36.47S139.45E
Lac Giao Vietnam **26** 12.41N108.02E
Lacha, Ozero *l.* Russian Fed. **18** 61.25N 39.00E
La Charité France **11** 47.11N 3.01E
La Chartre France **9** 47.44N 0.35E
La Chaux-de-Fonds Switz. **14** 47.07N 6.51E
Lach Dera *r.* Somali Rep. **37** 0.01S 42.45E
Lachlan *r.* Australia **46** 34.21S143.58E
Lackan Resr. Rep. of Ire. **7** 53.09N 6.31W
Lackawanna U.S.A. **55** 42.49N 78.49W
Lac la Biche *town* Canada **50** 54.46N111.58W
La Cocha Argentina **62** 27.45S 65.35W
Lacombe Canada **50** 52.28N113.44W
La Concepción Venezuela **60** 10.25N 71.41W
La Concordia Mexico **56** 16.05N 92.38W
La Coruña Spain **10** 43.22N 8.24W
La Crosse Wisc. U.S.A. **53** 43.48N 91.15W
La Cruz Uruguay **63** 33.56S 56.15W
La Demanda, Sierra de *mts.* Spain **10** 42.10N 3.20W
Ladismith R.S.A. **39** 33.29S 21.15E
Ladispoli Italy **12** 41.56N 12.05E
Lādīz Iran **31** 28.57N 61.18E
Ladoga *l. see* Ladozhskoye Ozero *l.* Russian Fed. **18**
La Dorada Colombia **60** 5.27N 74.40W
Ladozhskoye Ozero *l.* Russian Fed. **18** 61.00N 32.00E
Ladushkin Russian Fed. **15** 54.30N 20.05E
Ladva Vetka Russian Fed. **18** 61.16N 34.23E
Ladybrand R.S.A. **39** 29.11S 27.26E
Ladysmith Canada **50** 48.58N123.49W
Ladysmith R.S.A. **39** 28.32S 29.47E
Lae P.N.G. **27** 6.45S146.30E
Laesö *i.* Denmark **17** 57.16N 11.01E
La Estrada Spain **10** 42.40N 8.30W
Lafayette Ind. U.S.A. **55** 40.25N 86.54W
Lafayette La. U.S.A. **53** 30.12N 92.18W
La Fère France **9** 49.40N 3.22E
La Ferté-Bernard France **9** 48.11N 0.40E
La Ferté-Gaucher France **9** 48.47N 3.18E
La Ferté-Macé France **9** 48.36N 0.22W
La Ferté-St. Aubin France **9** 47.43N 1.56E
Lafia Nigeria **38** 8.35N 8.34E
Lafiagi Nigeria **38** 8.50N 5.23E
La Flèche France **9** 47.42N 0.05W
Laforest Canada **55** 47.02N 81.13W
La Fregeneda Spain **10** 40.58N 6.54W
La Fuente de San Esteban Spain **10** 40.48N 6.15W
Lagan *r.* U.K. **7** 54.37N 5.44W
Lågen *r.* Akershus Norway **17** 60.10N 11.28E
Lågen *r.* Vestfold Norway **17** 59.03N 10.05E
Laghouat Algeria **34** 33.50N 2.59E
Lagos Mexico **56** 21.21N101.55W
Lagos Nigeria **38** 6.27N 3.28E
Lagos *d.* Nigeria **38** 6.32N 3.30E
Lagos Portugal **10** 37.05N 8.40W
La Grande U.S.A. **54** 45.20N118.05W
La Grande Résr. 3 Canada **51** 53.35N 74.55W
La Grande Résr. 2 Canada **51** 53.35N 77.10W
Lagrange Australia **42** 18.46S121.49E
La Grange U.S.A. **53** 33.02N 85.02W
La Guaira Venezuela **60** 10.38N 66.55W
La Guerche-de-Bretagne France **9** 47.56N 1.14W
Laguna Brazil **62** 28.29S 48.47W
Laguna Dam U.S.A. **54** 32.55N114.25W
Lagunas Chile **62** 20.59S 69.37W
Lagunas Peru **60** 5.10S 73.35W
La Habana Cuba **57** 23.07N 82.25W
Lahad Datu Malaysia **26** 5.05N118.20E
Lahat Indonesia **26** 3.46S103.32E
La Haye-du-Puits France **9** 49.18N 1.33W
Lāhījān Iran **31** 37.12N 50.00E
Lahn *r.* Germany **8** 50.18N 7.36E
Lahnstein Germany **8** 50.17N 7.38E
Laholm Sweden **17** 56.31N 13.02E
Lahore Pakistan **28** 31.34N 74.22E
Lahti Finland **17** 60.58N 25.40E
Laï Chad **34** 9.22N 16.14E
Laiagam P.N.G. **27** 5.31S143.39E
L'Aigle France **9** 48.45N 0.38E
Laignes France **9** 47.50N 4.22E
Laihia Finland **16** 62.58N 22.01E
Laingsburg R.S.A. **39** 33.11S 20.49E
Lainio *r.* Sweden **16** 67.28N 22.50E
Lairg U.K. **6** 58.01N 4.25W
Laisamis Kenya **37** 1.38N 37.47E
Laissac France **11** 44.23N 2.49E
Laitila Finland **17** 60.53N 21.41E
Laizhou Wan *b.* China **25** 37.30N119.30E
Lajes Brazil **59** 27.48S 50.20W
La Junta U.S.A. **52** 37.59N103.33W
Lak Bor *r.* Somali Rep. **37** 0.32N 42.05E
Lake Biddy *town* Australia **43** 33.01S118.51E
Lake Boga *town* Australia **46** 35.27S143.39E
Lake Bolac *town* Australia **46** 37.42S142.50E
Lake Brown *town* Australia **43** 30.57S118.19E
Lake Cargelligo *town* Australia **47** 33.19S146.23E
Lake Charles *town* U.S.A. **53** 30.13N 93.13W
Lake City U.S.A. **53** 30.05N 82.40W
Lake District *f.* U.K. **4** 54.30N 3.10W
Lake Grace *town* Australia **43** 33.06S118.28E
Lake Harbour *town* Canada **51** 62.50N 69.50W
Lake King *town* Australia **43** 33.05S119.40E
Lakeland *town* U.S.A. **53** 28.02N 81.59W
Lake Mead Nat. Recreation Area U.S.A. **54** 36.00N114.30W
Lake Nash *town* Australia **44** 21.00S137.55E
Lake Placid *town* U.S.A. **55** 44.17N 73.59W
Lakes Entrance *town* Australia **47** 37.53S147.59E
Lakeshore U.S.A. **54** 37.15N119.12W
Lakeside Utah U.S.A. **54** 41.13N112.54W
Lake Superior Prov. Park Canada **55** 47.43N 84.53W
Lakeview U.S.A. **54** 42.11N120.21W
Lakewood N.J. U.S.A. **55** 40.06N 74.12W
Lakewood Ohio U.S.A. **55** 41.29N 81.50W
Lakhpat India **28** 23.49N 68.47E
Lakonikós Kólpos *g.* Greece **13** 36.35N 22.42E
Lakota Ivory Coast **38** 5.50N 5.30W
Laksefjorden *est.* Norway **16** 70.58N 27.00E
Lakselv Norway **16** 70.03N 24.55E
Lakshadweep Is. Indian Oc. **28** 11.00N 72.00E
Lalaua Mozambique **37** 14.20S 38.30E
Lālehzār, Kūh-e *mtn.* Iran **31** 29.26N 56.48E
La Libertad El Salvador **57** 13.28N 89.20W
Lalín Spain **10** 42.40N 8.05W
La Línea Spain **10** 36.10N 5.21W
Lalitpur India **29** 24.42N 78.24E
La Loupe France **9** 48.28N 1.01E
La Louvière Belgium **8** 50.29N 4.11E
Lamar U.S.A. **52** 38.04N102.37W
Lambaréné Gabon **36** 0.41S 10.13E
Lambayeque Peru **60** 6.36S 79.50W
Lambay I. Rep. of Ire. **7** 53.29N 6.01W
Lambert's Bay *town* R.S.A. **39** 32.06S 18.16E
Lamé Chad **38** 9.14N 14.33E
Lame Nigeria **38** 10.27N 9.12E
Lamego Portugal **10** 41.05N 7.49W
Lameroo Australia **46** 35.20S140.33E
La Mesa Calif. U.S.A. **54** 32.46N117.01W
Lamía Greece **13** 38.53N 22.25E
Lammermuir Hills U.K. **6** 55.51N 2.40W
Lammhult Sweden **17** 57.09N 14.35E
Lamont U.S.A. **54** 42.12N107.28W
Lamotrek *i.* Federated States of Micronesia **27** 7.28N146.23E
Lamotte-Beuvron France **9** 47.37N 2.01E
Lampa Peru **60** 15.10S 70.30W
Lampazos Mexico **56** 27.01N100.31W
Lampedusa *i.* Italy **12** 35.30N 12.35E
Lampeter U.K. **5** 52.06N 4.06W
Lampione *i.* Italy **12** 35.33N 12.18E
Lamu Kenya **37** 2.20S 40.54E
La Mure France **11** 44.54N 5.47E
La Nao, Cabo de Spain **10** 38.42N 0.15E
Lanark U.K. **6** 55.41N 3.47W
Lancang Jiang *r.* China *see* Mekong *r.* Asia **24**
Lancashire *d.* U.K. **4** 53.53N 2.30W
Lancaster U.K. **4** 54.03N 2.48W
Lancaster Calif. U.S.A. **54** 34.42N118.08W
Lancaster Ohio U.S.A. **55** 39.43N 82.37W
Lancaster Penn. U.S.A. **55** 40.02N 76.19W
Lancaster Sd. Canada **51** 74.00N 85.00W
Lancelin Australia **43** 31.01S115.19E
Lanchow *see* Lanzhou China **24**
Landau Bayern Germany **14** 48.40N 12.43E
Landeck Austria **14** 47.09N 10.35E
Landen Belgium **8** 50.46N 5.04E
Lander *r.* Australia **44** 20.25S132.00E
Lander U.S.A. **54** 42.50N108.44W
Landerneau France **11** 48.27N 4.16W
Landor Australia **42** 25.06S116.50E
Landrecies France **8** 50.08N 3.40E
Land's End *c.* U.K. **5** 50.03N 5.45W
Landshut Germany **14** 48.31N 12.10E
Landskrona Sweden **17** 55.52N 12.50E
Langå Denmark **17** 56.23N 9.55E
Langadhás Greece **13** 40.45N 23.04E
Langanes *c.* Iceland **16** 66.30N 14.30W
Langao China **25** 33.22N109.04E
Langeais France **9** 47.20N 0.24E
Langeland *i.* Denmark **17** 55.00N 10.50E
Längelmävesi *l.* Finland **17** 61.32N 24.22E
Langeoog *i.* Germany **8** 53.46N 7.30E
Langesund Norway **17** 59.00N 9.45E
Langholm U.K. **6** 55.09N 3.00W
Langjökull *ice cap* Iceland **16** 63.43N 20.03W
Langkawi *i.* Malaysia **26** 6.20N 99.30E
Langlade Canada **55** 48.14N 75.59W
Langon France **11** 44.33N 0.14W
Langöy *i.* Norway **16** 68.45N 15.00E
Langres France **11** 47.53N 5.20E
Langsa Indonesia **26** 4.28N 97.59E
Lang Son Vietnam **26** 21.50N106.55E
Languedoc-Roussillon *d.* France **11** 43.50N 3.30E
Lannion France **11** 48.44N 3.27W
Lansing U.S.A. **55** 42.44N 84.34W
Lanslebourg France **9** 45.17N 6.52E
Lantewa Nigeria **38** 12.15N 11.45E
Lanzarote *i.* Canary Is. **34** 29.00N 13.55W
Lanzhou China **24** 36.01N103.45E
Lanzo Torinese Italy **9** 45.16N 7.28E
Laoag Phil. **27** 18.14N120.36E
Lào Cai Vietnam **26** 22.30N104.00E
Laois *d.* Rep. of Ire. **7** 53.00N 7.20W
Laon France **9** 49.34N 3.37E
La Oroya Peru **60** 11.36S 75.54W
Laos Asia **26** 19.00N104.00E
La Palma *i.* Canary Is. **34** 28.50N 18.00W
La Palma Spain **10** 37.23N 6.33W
La Pampa *d.* Argentina **63** 37.00S 66.00W
La Paragua Venezuela **60** 6.53N 63.22W
La Paz Entre Ríos Argentina **63** 30.45S 59.38W
La Paz Mendoza Argentina **63** 33.28S 67.34W
La Paz Bolivia **62** 16.30S 68.09W
La Paz *d.* Bolivia **62** 16.00S 68.10W
La Paz Mexico **56** 24.10N110.18W
La Pedrera Colombia **60** 1.18S 69.43W
Lapeer U.S.A. **55** 43.03N 83.09W
La Peña, Sierra de *mts.* Spain **10** 42.30N 0.50W
La Perouse Str. Russian Fed. **21** 45.50N142.30E
La Pine U.S.A. **54** 43.40N121.30W
Lapinjärvi Finland **17** 60.38N 26.13E
Lapland *f.* Sweden/Finland **16** 68.10N 24.10E
La Plata Argentina **63** 34.55S 57.57W
La Plata, Río de *est.* Argentina/Uruguay **63** 35.15S 56.45W
Lappajärvi *l.* Finland **16** 63.08N 23.40E
Lappeenranta Finland **18** 61.04N 28.05E
Lappi *d.* Finland **16** 67.20N 26.00E
Laptevykh, More *sea* Russian Fed. **21** 74.30N125.00E
Lapua Finland **16** 62.57N 23.00E
La Push U.S.A. **54** 47.55N124.38W
La Quiaca Argentina **62** 22.05S 65.36W
L'Aquila Italy **12** 42.22N 13.25E
Lār Iran **31** 27.37N 54.16E
Lara Australia **46** 38.01S144.26E
Larache Morocco **34** 35.12N 6.10W
Laramie U.S.A. **52** 41.19N105.35W
Lärbro Sweden **17** 57.47N 18.47E
Larche, Col de France/Italy **9** 44.25N 6.53E
Laredo U.S.A. **52** 27.32N 99.22W
Largeau Chad **34** 17.55N 19.07E
Largs U.K. **6** 55.48N 4.52W
Lariang Indonesia **26** 1.35S119.25E
La Rioja Argentina **62** 29.25S 66.50W
La Rioja *d.* Argentina **62** 29.00S 66.00W
La Rioja *d.* Spain **10** 42.15N 2.25W
Lárisa Greece **13** 39.36N 22.24E
Lark *r.* U.K. **5** 52.26N 0.20E
Lārkāna Pakistan **28** 27.32N 68.18E
Larnaca *see* Lárnax Cyprus **32**
Lárnax Cyprus **32** 34.54N 33.39E
Larne U.K. **7** 54.51N 5.49W
La Robla Spain **10** 42.50N 5.41W
La Roche Belgium **8** 50.11N 5.35E
La Rochelle France **11** 46.10N 1.10W
La Roche-sur-Yon France **11** 46.40N 1.25W
La Roda Spain **10** 39.13N 2.10W
La Romana Dom. Rep. **57** 18.27N 68.57W
La Ronge Canada **50** 55.07N105.18W
La Ronge, Lac *l.* Canada **50** 55.07N105.15W
Laroquebrou France **11** 44.58N 2.11E
Larrimah Australia **44** 15.35S133.12E
Larvik Norway **17** 59.04N 10.00E
La Sagra *mtn.* Spain **10** 37.58N 2.35W
La Sarre Canada **55** 48.49N 79.12W
Las Cruces U.S.A. **52** 32.23N106.29W
La Seine, Baie de France **11** 49.40N 0.30W
La Serena Chile **62** 29.54S 71.16W
La Seyne France **11** 43.06N 5.53E
Las Flores Argentina **63** 36.02S 59.07W
Lāsh-e Joveyn Afghan. **31** 31.43N 61.39E
Las Heras Argentina **63** 32.50S 68.50W
Lashio Burma **29** 22.58N 97.48E
Las Lomitas Argentina **62** 24.43S 60.35W
Las Marismas *f.* Spain **10** 37.00N 6.15W
Las Palmas Canary Is. **34** 28.08N 15.27W
Las Perlas, Archipelago de Panama **57** 8.45N 79.30W
La Spezia Italy **9** 44.07N 9.49E
Las Piedras Uruguay **63** 34.44S 56.13W
Las Plumas Argentina **63** 43.40S 67.15W
Lassay France **9** 48.26N 0.30W
Lassen Peak *mtn.* U.S.A. **54** 40.29N121.31W
Lastoursville Gabon **36** 0.50S 12.47E
Lastovo *i.* Croatia **13** 42.45N 16.52E
Lastrup Germany **8** 52.48N 7.55E
La Suze France **9** 47.54N 0.02E
Las Vegas Nev. U.S.A. **54** 36.11N115.08W
Las Vegas N.Mex. U.S.A. **52** 35.36N105.13W
Latacunga Ecuador **60** 0.58S 78.36W
La Tagua Colombia **60** 0.03S 74.40W
Latakia *see* Al Lādhiqīyah Syria **32**
La Teste-de-Buch France **11** 44.38N 1.09W
Lathen Germany **8** 52.54N 7.20E
Latina Italy **12** 41.28N 12.52E
Latisana Italy **9** 45.47N 13.00E
La Tortuga *i.* Venezuela **60** 11.00N 65.20W
La Trobe, Mt. Australia **47** 39.03S146.25E
La Tuque Canada **55** 47.26N 72.47W
Latvia Europe **18** 56.45N 25.00E
Lau Nigeria **38** 9.14N 11.15E
Lauchhammer Germany **14** 51.30N 13.48E
Lauenburg Germany **14** 53.22N 10.33E
Laughlen, Mt. Australia **44** 23.23S134.23E
Launceston Australia **45** 41.25S147.07E
Launceston U.K. **5** 50.38N 4.21W
La Unión Chile **63** 40.15S 73.02W
La Unión Spain **10** 37.38N 0.53W
Laura Australia **46** 33.08S138.19E
La Urbana Venezuela **60** 7.08N 66.56W
Laurel Miss. U.S.A. **53** 31.41N 89.09W
Laurel Mont. U.S.A. **54** 45.40N108.46W
Laurencekirk U.K. **6** 56.50N 2.29W
Laurentides Prov. Park Canada **55** 47.46N 71.40W
Laurieton Australia **47** 31.38S152.46E
Lausanne Switz. **14** 46.32N 6.39E
Laut *i.* Indonesia **26** 3.45S116.20E
Lautaro Chile **63** 38.31S 72.27W
Lauterecken Germany **8** 49.39N 7.36E
Lavagh More *mtn.* Rep. of Ire. **7** 54.45N 8.07W
Lava Hot Springs *town* U.S.A. **54** 42.37N112.01W
Laval France **9** 48.04N 0.45W
La Vega Dom. Rep. **57** 19.15N 70.33W
La Vela Venezuela **60** 11.27N 69.34W
La Vérendrye Prov. Park Canada **55** 47.29N 77.06W
Laverton Australia **43** 28.49S122.25E
Lavia Finland **17** 61.36N 22.36E
Lavik Norway **17** 61.06N 5.30E
Lavras Brazil **59** 21.15S 44.59W
Lávrion Greece **13** 37.44N 24.04E
Lawra Ghana **38** 10.40N 2.49W
Lawrence New Zealand **48** 45.55S169.42E
Lawrence Kans. U.S.A. **53** 38.58N 95.15W
Lawrence Mass. U.S.A. **55** 42.42N 71.09W
Lawton Okla. U.S.A. **52** 34.36N 98.25W
Lawz, Jabal al *mtn.* Saudi Arabia **32** 28.40N 35.20E
Laxå Sweden **17** 58.59N 14.37E
Laytonville U.S.A. **54** 39.41N123.29W
Lazio *d.* Italy **12** 42.20N 12.00E
Leadhills U.K. **6** 55.25N 3.46W
Leamington U.S.A. **54** 39.31N112.17W
Learmonth Australia **42** 22.13S114.04E
Leavenworth U.S.A. **53** 39.19N 94.55W
Lebak Phil. **27** 6.32N124.03E
Lebanon Asia **32** 34.00N 36.00E
Lebanon Ind. U.S.A. **55** 40.02N 87.28W
Lebanon Oreg. U.S.A. **54** 44.32N122.54W
Lebanon Penn. U.S.A. **55** 40.20N 76.25W
Lebanon Tenn. U.S.A. **53** 36.11N 86.19W
Lebec U.S.A. **54** 34.50N118.52W
Lebesby Norway **16** 70.34N 27.00E
Le Blanc France **11** 46.37N 1.03E
Lebork Poland **15** 54.33N 17.44E
Lebrija Spain **10** 36.55N 6.10W
Lebu Chile **63** 37.37S 73.39W
Le Bugue France **11** 44.55N 0.56E
Le Cateau France **8** 50.07N 3.33E
Le Catelet France **8** 50.00N 3.12E
Lecce Italy **13** 40.21N 18.11E
Lecco Italy **9** 45.51N 9.23E
Lech *r.* Germany **14** 48.45N 10.51E
Le Chesne France **8** 49.31N 4.46E
Lechiguanas, Islas de las *is.* Argentina **63** 33.26S 59.42W
Le Creusot France **11** 46.48N 4.27E
Lectoure France **11** 43.56N 0.38E
Ledbury U.K. **5** 52.03N 2.25W
Ledesma Spain **10** 41.05N 6.00W
Le Dorat France **11** 46.14N 1.05E
Leduc Canada **50** 53.16N113.33W
Lee *r.* Rep. of Ire. **7** 51.53N 8.25W
Leech L. U.S.A. **53** 47.10N 94.30W
Leeds U.K. **4** 53.48N 1.34W
Leek U.K. **4** 53.07N 2.02W
Leer Germany **8** 53.14N 7.27E
Leeston New Zealand **48** 43.46S172.18E
Leeton Australia **47** 34.33S146.24E
Leeuwarden Neth. **8** 53.12N 5.48E
Leeuwin, C. Australia **43** 34.22S115.08E
Leeward Is. C. America **57** 18.00N 61.00W
Lefroy, L. Australia **43** 31.15S121.40E
Legazpi Phil. **27** 13.10N123.45E
Legges Tor *mtn.* Australia **45** 41.32S147.40E
Legget U.S.A. **54** 39.52N123.34W
Leghorn *see* Livorno Italy **12**
Legion Mine Zimbabwe **39** 21.23S 28.33E
Legionowo Poland **15** 52.25N 20.56E
Legnago Italy **9** 45.11N 11.18E
Legnano Italy **9** 45.36N 8.54E
Legnica Poland **14** 51.12N 16.10E
Le Grand-Lucé France **9** 47.52N 0.28E
Le Grand-Quevilly France **9** 49.25N 1.02E
Leh Jammu & Kashmir **28** 34.09N 77.35E
Le Havre France **9** 49.30N 0.06E
Lehrte Germany **14** 52.22N 9.59E
Lehututu Botswana **39** 23.54S 21.52E
Leibnitz Austria **14** 46.48N 15.32E
Leicester U.K. **5** 52.39N 1.09W
Leicestershire *d.* U.K. **5** 52.29N 1.10W
Leichhardt *r.* Australia **44** 17.35S139.48E
Leiden Neth. **8** 52.10N 4.30E
Leie *r.* Belgium **8** 51.03N 3.44E
Leigh Creek *r.* Australia **46** 29.49S138.10E
Leigh Creek *town* Australia **46** 30.31S138.25E
Leighton Buzzard U.K. **5** 51.55N 0.39W
Leikanger Norway **17** 61.10N 6.52E
Leinster Australia **43** 27.59S120.30E
Leipzig Germany **14** 51.20N 12.20E
Leiria Portugal **10** 39.45N 8.48W
Leitrim *d.* Rep. of Ire. **7** 54.08N 8.00W
Leizhou Bandao *pen.* China **25** 20.40N109.30E
Lek *r.* Neth. **8** 51.55N 4.29E
Leksvik Norway **16** 63.40N 10.40E
Lelchitsy Belorussia **15** 51.48N 28.20E
Leleque Argentina **63** 42.24S 71.04W
Le Lion-d'Angers France **9** 47.38N 0.43W
Le Lude France **9** 47.39N 0.09E
Lelystad Neth. **8** 52.32N 5.29E
Léman, Lac *l.* Switz. **14** 46.30N 6.30E
Le Mans France **9** 48.01N 0.10E
Leme Brazil **59** 22.10S 47.23W
Le Merlerault France **9** 48.42N 0.18E
Lemesós Cyprus **32** 34.40N 33.03E
Lemgo Germany **14** 52.02N 8.54E
Lemhi Range *mts.* U.S.A. **54** 44.30N113.25W
Lemmer Neth. **8** 52.50N 5.43E
Lemmon U.S.A. **52** 45.56N102.10W
Lemvig Denmark **17** 56.32N 8.18E
Lena *r.* Russian Fed. **21** 72.00N127.10E
Lendery Russian Fed. **18** 63.24N 31.04E
Lendinara Italy **9** 45.05N 11.36E
Lengerich Germany **8** 52.12N 7.52E
Lenina, Kanal *canal* Russian Fed. **19** 43.46N 45.00E
Lenina, Pik *mtn.* Tajikistan **24** 40.14N 69.40E
Leninakan Armenia **31** 40.47N 43.49E
Leningrad *see* Sankt-Peterburg Russian Fed. **18**
Leninogorsk Kazakhstan **20** 50.23N 83.32E
Leninsk Russian Fed. **19** 48.42N 45.14E
Leninsk Kuznetskiy Russian Fed. **20** 54.44N 86.13E
Lenkoran Azerbaijan **31** 38.45N 48.50E
Lenmalu Indonesia **27** 1.58S130.00E
Lenne *r.* Germany **8** 51.24N 7.30E
Lens France **8** 50.26N 2.50E
Lentini Italy **12** 37.17N 15.00E
Lenvik Norway **16** 69.22N 18.10E
Léo Burkina **38** 11.05N 2.06W
Leoben Austria **14** 47.23N 15.06E
Leominster U.K. **5** 52.15N 2.43W
Leominster U.S.A. **55** 42.32N 71.45W
León Mexico **56** 21.10N101.42W
León Nicaragua **57** 12.24N 86.52W
León Spain **10** 42.35N 5.34W
Leonardville Namibia **39** 23.21S 18.47E
Leonárison Cyprus **32** 35.28N 34.08E
Leongatha Australia **47** 38.29S145.57E
Leonora Australia **43** 28.54S121.20E
Leopoldina Brazil **59** 21.30S 42.38W
Leopoldsburg Belgium **8** 51.08N 5.13E
Leovo Moldavia **15** 46.29N 28.12E
Lepel Russian Fed. **18** 54.48N 28.40E
Le Puy France **11** 45.03N 3.54E
Le Quesnoy France **8** 50.15N 3.39E
Lerbäck Sweden **17** 58.56N 15.02E
Léré Chad **38** 9.41N 14.17E
Lerici Italy **9** 44.04N 9.55E
Lérida Spain **10** 41.37N 0.38E
Lerma Spain **10** 42.02N 3.46W
Le Roy Mich. U.S.A. **55** 44.03N 85.29W
Lerwick U.K. **6** 60.09N 1.09W
Les Andelys France **9** 49.15N 1.25E
Les Cayes Haiti **57** 18.15N 73.46W
Leschenault, C. Australia **43** 31.50S115.23E
Les Ecrins *mtn.* France **11** 44.50N 6.20E
Leshan China **29** 29.34N103.42E
Leshukonskoye Russian Fed. **18** 64.55N 45.50E
Lesjaskog Norway **17** 62.15N 8.22E
Leskovac Yugo. **13** 43.00N 21.56E
Lesotho Africa **39** 29.00S 28.00E
Lesozavodsk Russian Fed. **25** 45.30N133.29E
Les Pieux France **9** 49.35N 1.50W
Les Riceys France **9** 47.59N 4.22E
Les Sables d'Olonne France **11** 46.30N 1.47W
Lessay France **9** 49.14N 1.30W
Lesser Antilles *is.* C. America **57** 13.00N 65.00W
Lesser Slave L. Canada **50** 55.30N115.00W
Lesser Sunda Is. *see* Nusa Tenggara *is.* Indonesia **26**
Lessines Belgium **8** 50.43N 3.50E
Lesti *r.* Finland **16** 64.04N 23.38E
Lésvos *i.* Greece **13** 39.10N 26.16E
Leszno Poland **14** 51.51N 16.35E
Letchworth U.K. **5** 51.58N 0.13W
Lethbridge Canada **50** 49.43N112.48W
Lethem Guyana **60** 3.18N 59.46W
Leti, Kepulauan *is.* Indonesia **27** 8.20S128.00E
Letiahau *r.* Botswana **39** 21.16S 24.00E
Leticia Colombia **60** 4.09S 69.57W

93

94

95

Mpika Zambia 37 11.52S 31.30E
Mponela Malaŵi 37 13.32S 33.43E
Mporokoso Zambia 37 9.22S 30.06E
Mpunde *mtn.* Tanzania 37 6.12S 33.48E
Mpwapwa Tanzania 37 6.23S 36.38E
Msaken Tunisia 34 35.44N 10.35E
Mseleni R.S.A. 39 27.21S 32.33E
Msingu Tanzania 37 4.52S 39.08E
Msta *r.* Russian Fed. 18 58.28N 31.20E
Mtakuja Tanzania 37 7.21S 30.37E
Mtama Tanzania 37 10.20S 39.19E
Mtito Andei Kenya 37 2.32S 38.10E
Mtsensk Russian Fed. 18 53.18N 36.35E
Mtwara Tanzania 37 10.17S 40.11E
Mtwara *d.* Tanzania 37 10.00S 38.30E
Muaná Brazil 61 1.32S 49.13W
Muang Chiang Rai Thailand 29 19.56N 99.51E
Muang Khammouan Laos 29 17.25N 104.45E
Muang Khon Kaen Thailand 29 16.25N 102.50E
Muang Lampang Thailand 29 18.16N 99.30E
Muang Nakhon Phanom Thailand 26 17.22N 104.45E
Muang Nakhon Sawan Thailand 29 15.35N 100.10E
Muang Nan Thailand 29 18.52N 100.42E
Muang Ngoy Laos 29 20.43N 102.41E
Muang Pak Lay Laos 29 18.12N 101.25E
Muang Phichit Thailand 29 16.29N 100.21E
Muang Phitsanulok Thailand 29 16.50N 100.15E
Muang Phrae Thailand 29 18.07N 100.09E
Muang Ubon Thailand 29 15.15N 104.50E
Muar Malaysia 26 2.01N 102.35E
Muara Brunei 26 5.01N 115.01E
Muara Indonesia 26 0.32S 101.20E
Muarakaman Indonesia 26 0.02S 116.45E
Muaratewe Indonesia 26 0.57S 114.53E
Mubende Uganda 37 0.30N 31.24E
Mubi Nigeria 38 10.16N 13.17E
Muchea Australia 43 31.36S 115.57E
Muchinga Mts. Zambia 37 12.15S 31.00E
Muck *i.* U.K. 6 56.50N 6.14W
Mucojo Mozambique 37 12.05S 40.26E
Mudanjiang China 25 44.36N 129.42E
Mudgee Australia 47 32.37S 149.36E
Mudyuga Russian Fed. 18 63.45N 39.29E
Muèda Mozambique 37 11.40S 39.31E
Mufulira Zambia 37 12.30S 28.12E
Muganskaya Ravnina *f.* Azerbaijan 31 39.40N 48.30E
Mugía Spain 10 43.06N 9.14W
Muğla Turkey 13 37.12N 28.22E
Muḥammad, Ra's *c.* Egypt 32 27.42N 34.13E
Muhola Finland 16 63.20N 25.05E
Muhos Finland 16 64.48N 25.59E
Muhu *i.* Estonia 17 58.32N 23.20E
Muhu Väin *str.* Estonia 17 58.45N 23.30E
Mui Ca Mau *c.* Vietnam 26 8.30N 104.35E
Muine Bheag *town* Rep. of Ire. 7 52.42N 6.58W
Muir, L. Australia 43 34.30S 116.30E
Mukachevo Ukraine 15 48.26N 22.45E
Mukah Malaysia 26 2.56N 112.02E
Mukawa P.N.G. 44 9.48S 150.00E
Mukinbudin Australia 43 30.52S 118.08E
Muko *r.* Japan 23 34.41N 135.23E
Mukwela Zambia 39 17.02S 26.39E
Mulanje Mts. Malaŵi 37 15.57S 35.33E
Mulchén Chile 63 37.43S 72.14W
Mulde *r.* Germany 14 51.10N 12.48E
Mulgathing Australia 46 30.15S 134.00E
Mulgrave Canada 51 45.37N 61.23W
Mulhacén *mtn.* Spain 10 37.04N 3.22W
Mulhouse France 11 47.45N 7.21E
Mull *i.* U.K. 6 56.28N 5.56W
Mull, Sd. of *str.* U.K. 6 56.32N 5.55W
Mullaghanattin *mtn.* Rep. of Ire. 7 51.56N 9.51W
Mullaghareirk Mts. Rep. of Ire. 7 52.19N 9.06W
Mullaghmore *mtn.* U.K. 7 54.51N 6.51W
Mullaley Australia 47 31.06S 149.55E
Mullengudgery Australia 47 31.40S 147.23E
Mullet Pen. Rep. of Ire. 7 54.12N 10.04W
Mullewa Australia 43 28.33S 115.31E
Mullingar Rep. of Ire. 7 53.31N 7.21W
Mull of Galloway *c.* U.K. 6 54.39N 4.52W
Mull of Kintyre *c.* U.K. 6 55.17N 5.45W
Mullovka Russian Fed. 18 54.12N 49.26E
Mullumbimby Australia 47 28.32S 153.30E
Mulobezi Zambia 39 16.49S 25.09E
Muloorina Australia 46 29.10S 137.51E
Multān Pakistan 28 30.10N 71.36E
Multyfarnham Rep. of Ire. 7 53.37N 7.25W
Mulyungarie Australia 46 31.30S 140.45E
Mumbai *see* Bombay India 28
Muna *i.* Indonesia 27 5.00S 122.30E
Munābāo India 28 25.45N 70.17E
Muncie U.S.A. 55 40.11N 85.23W
Mundaring Weir Australia 43 31.59S 116.13E
Mundiwindi Australia 42 23.50S 120.07E
Mundo *r.* Spain 10 38.20N 1.50W
Mungari Mozambique 39 17.12S 33.31E
Mungbere Zaïre 37 2.40N 28.25E
Mungeranie Australia 46 28.00S 138.36E
Mungindi Australia 47 28.58S 148.56E
Munich *see* München Germany 14
Muniz Freire Brazil 59 20.25S 41.23W
Munkfors Sweden 17 59.50N 13.32E
Munning *r.* Australia 47 31.50S 152.30E
Muntadgin Australia 43 31.41S 118.32E
Munyati *r.* Zimbabwe 39 17.32S 29.23E
Muonio Finland 16 67.57N 23.42E
Muonio *r.* Finland / Sweden 16 67.10N 23.40E
Mupa *r.* Mozambique 39 19.07S 35.50E
Muqdisho Somali Rep. 37 2.02N 45.21E
Mur *r.* Austria *see* Mura *r.* Croatia 14
Mura *r.* Croatia 14 46.18N 16.53E
Murallón *mtn.* Argentina / Chile 63 49.48S 73.25W
Muranga Kenya 37 0.43S 37.10E
Murashi Russian Fed. 18 59.20N 48.59E
Murchison Australia 47 36.36S 145.14E
Murchison *r.* Australia 42 27.30S 114.10E
Murchison *Ld* New Zealand 48 41.48S 172.20E
Murcia Spain 10 37.59N 1.08W
Murcia Spain 10 38.15N 1.50W
Mureş *r.* Romania 15 46.16N 20.10E
Muret France 11 43.28N 1.19E
Murewa Zimbabwe 39 17.40S 31.47E
Murgon Australia 44 26.15S 151.57E
Murguía Spain 10 42.57N 2.49W
Muriaé Brazil 59 21.08S 42.33W
Murjek Sweden 16 66.29N 20.50E
Murmansk Russian Fed. 18 68.59N 33.08E
Murom Russian Fed. 18 55.04N 42.04E
Muroran Japan 25 42.21N 140.59E
Murrah al Kubrá, Al Buḥayrah al *l.* Egypt 32 30.20N 32.20E
Murra Murra Australia 47 28.18S 146.48E
Murray *r.* S.A. Australia 46 35.23S 139.20E
Murray *r.* W.A. Australia 43 32.35S 115.46E
Murray Utah U.S.A. 54 40.40N 111.53W
Murray, L. P.N.G. 27 7.00S 141.30E
Murray Bridge *town* Australia 46 35.10S 139.17E
Murrayville Australia 46 35.16S 141.14E
Murringo Australia 47 34.19S 148.36E
Murrumbidgee *r.* Australia 46 34.38S 143.10E
Murrumburrah Australia 47 34.33S 148.21E
Murrurundi Australia 47 31.47S 150.51E
Murtoa Australia 46 36.40S 142.31E
Murud *mtn.* Malaysia 26 3.45N 115.30E
Murwāra India 29 23.49N 80.28E
Murwillumbah Australia 47 28.20S 153.24E
Mūsá, Jabal *mtn.* Egypt 32 28.31N 33.59E
Musala *mtn.* Bulgaria 13 42.11N 23.35E
Musay'īd Qatar 31 24.47N 51.36E
Muscat *see* Masqaṭ Oman 31
Musgrave Australia 44 14.47S 143.30E
Musgrave Ranges *mts.* Australia 42 26.10S 131.50E
Mushin Nigeria 38 6.33N 3.22E
Musi *r.* Indonesia 26 2.20S 104.57E
Muskegon U.S.A. 55 43.13N 86.15W
Muskegon *r.* U.S.A. 55 43.13N 86.16W
Muskegon Heights *town* U.S.A. 55 43.03N 86.16W
Muskogee U.S.A. 53 35.45N 95.21W
Muskoka, L. Canada 55 45.00N 79.25W
Musoma Tanzania 37 1.31S 33.48E
Musselburgh U.K. 6 55.57N 3.04W
Musselkanaal Neth. 8 52.57N 7.01E
Musselshell *r.* U.S.A. 54 47.21N 107.58W
Mustang Nepal 29 29.10N 83.55E
Mustjala Estonia 17 58.28N 22.14E
Muswellbrook Australia 47 32.17S 150.55E
Muş Turkey 30 38.45N 41.30E
Mut Turkey 30 36.38N 33.27E
Mutala Mozambique 37 15.54S 37.51E
Mutare Zimbabwe 39 18.59S 32.40E
Mutoko Zimbabwe 39 17.23S 32.13E
Mutooroo Australia 46 32.30S 140.58E
Mutoray Russian Fed. 21 61.20N 100.32E
Muwale Tanzania 37 6.22S 33.46E
Muya Russian Fed. 21 56.28N 115.50E
Muyinga Burundi 37 2.48S 30.21E
Muzaffarnagar India 28 29.28N 77.42E
Muzaffarpur India 29 26.07N 85.23E
Muzhi Russian Fed. 18 65.25N 64.40E
Muztag *mtn.* China 24 36.25N 87.25E
Mühldorf Germany 14 48.15N 12.32E
Mühlhausen Germany 14 51.12N 10.27E
Mühlig Hofmann fjella *mts.* Antarctica 64 72.30S 5.00E
Mülheim N.-Westfalen Germany 8 51.25N 6.50E
Mülheim N.-Westfalen Germany 8 50.58N 7.00E
Münchberg Germany 14 50.11N 11.47E
München Germany 14 48.08N 11.35E
Münden Germany 14 51.25N 9.39E
Münster N.-Westfalen Germany 8 51.58N 7.37E
Müritzsee *l.* Germany 14 52.25N 12.45E
Mvomero Tanzania 37 6.18S 37.26E
Mvuma Zimbabwe 39 19.16S 30.30E
Mwali *see* Mohèli *i.* Comoros 37
Mwanza Tanzania 37 2.30S 32.54E
Mwanza *d.* Tanzania 37 3.00S 32.30E
Mwaya Mbeya Tanzania 37 9.33S 33.56E
Mweka Zaïre 36 4.51S 21.34E
Mwene Ditu Zaïre 36 7.01S 23.27E
Mwenezi *r.* Mozambique 39 22.42S 31.45E
Mwenezi Zimbabwe 39 21.22S 30.45E
Mweru, L. Zaïre / Zambia 37 9.00S 28.40E
Mwingi Kenya 37 1.00S 38.04E
Mwinilunga Zambia 36 11.44S 24.24E
Myanaung Burma 29 18.25N 95.10E
Myanma *see* Burma Asia 29
Myingyan Burma 29 21.25N 95.20E
Myitkyinā Burma 29 25.24N 97.25E
Mymensingh Bangla. 29 24.45N 90.23E
Myrdal Norway 17 60.44N 7.08E
Myrdalsjökull *ice cap* Iceland 16 63.40N 19.06W
Myrtle Creek *town* U.S.A. 54 43.01N 123.17W
Myrtleford Australia 47 36.35S 146.44E
Myrtle Point *town* U.S.A. 54 43.04N 124.08W
Myślenice Poland 15 49.51N 19.56E
Mysore India 28 12.18N 76.37E
My Tho Vietnam 26 10.21N 106.21E
Mytishchi Russian Fed. 18 55.54N 37.47E
Mziha Tanzania 37 5.53S 37.48E
Mzimba Malaŵi 37 12.00S 33.39E

N

Naab *r.* Germany 14 49.01N 12.02E
Naantali Finland 17 60.27N 22.02E
Naas Rep. of Ire. 7 53.13N 6.41W
Näätämö *r.* Norway 16 69.40N 29.30E
Nababeep R.S.A. 39 29.36S 17.44E
Nabadwīp India 29 23.25N 88.22E
Nabari *r.* Japan 23 34.45N 136.01E
Naberezhnyye Chelny Russian Fed. 18 55.42N 52.20E
Nabingora Uganda 37 0.31N 31.11E
Naboomspruit R.S.A. 39 24.31S 28.24E
Nabq Egypt 32 28.04N 34.26E
Nābulus Jordan 32 32.13N 35.16E
Nacala Mozambique 37 14.34S 40.41E
Nachingwea Tanzania 37 10.21S 38.46E
Nadiād India 28 22.42N 72.55E
Nadūshan Iran 31 32.03N 53.33E
Nadvoitsy Russian Fed. 18 63.56N 34.20E
Nadvornaya Ukraine 15 48.37N 24.30E
Nadym Russian Fed. 20 65.25N 72.40E
Naeröy Norway 16 64.48N 11.17E
Naestved Denmark 17 55.14N 11.46E
Nafada Nigeria 38 11.08N 11.20E
Nafishah Egypt 32 30.34N 32.15E
Naft-e Safid Iran 31 31.38N 49.20E
Naga Phil. 27 13.36N 123.12E
Nāgāland *d.* India 29 26.10N 94.30E
Nagambie Australia 47 36.48S 145.12E
Nagano Japan 25 36.39N 138.10E
Nagano *d.* Japan 23 35.33N 137.50E
Nagaoka Japan 25 37.30N 138.50E
Nāgappattinam India 29 10.45N 79.50E
Nagara *r.* Japan 23 35.01N 136.43E
Nagasaki Japan 25 32.45N 129.52E
Nāgaur India 28 27.12N 73.44E
Nagele Neth. 8 52.39N 5.43E
Nāgercoil India 28 8.11N 77.30E
Nagles Mts. Rep. of Ire. 7 52.06N 8.26W
Nagorskoye Russian Fed. 18 58.18N 50.50E
Nagoya Japan 23 35.10N 136.55E
Nāgpur India 29 21.10N 79.12E
Nagqên China 29 32.15N 96.13E
Nagykanizsa Hungary 15 46.27N 17.01E
Naha Japan 25 26.10N 127.40E
Nahanni Butte *town* Canada 50 61.03N 123.31W
Nahariyya Israel 32 33.01N 35.05E
Nahāvand Iran 31 34.13N 48.23E
Nahe *r.* Germany 8 49.58N 7.54E
Nahr al Furāt *r.* Asia 31 31.00N 47.27E
Nain Canada 51 56.30N 61.45W
Nā'īn Iran 31 32.52N 53.05E
Nairn U.K. 6 57.35N 3.52W
Nairobi Kenya 37 1.17S 36.50E
Naivasha Kenya 37 0.44S 36.26E
Najd *f.* Saudi Arabia 30 25.00N 45.00E
Naj 'Hammādī Egypt 30 26.04N 32.13E
Nakambe *r.* Burkina *see* White Volta *r.* Ghana 38
Nakatsugawa Japan 23 35.29N 137.30E
Nakhichevan Azerbaijan 31 39.12N 45.24E
Nakhodka Russian Fed. 25 42.53N 132.54E
Nakhon Pathom Thailand 29 13.50N 100.01E
Nakhon Ratchasima Thailand 29 14.59N 102.12E
Nakhon Si Thammarat Thailand 29 8.29N 100.00E
Nakina Canada 55 50.11N 86.43W
Nakło Poland 15 53.08N 17.35E
Naknek U.S.A. 50 58.45N 157.00W
Nakop Namibia 39 28.05S 19.57E
Nakskov Denmark 17 54.50N 11.09E
Näkten *l.* Sweden 16 65.50N 14.35E
Nakuru Kenya 37 0.16S 36.04E
Nalchik Russian Fed. 19 43.31N 43.38E
Nalón *r.* Spain 10 43.35N 6.06W
Nālūt Libya 34 31.53N 10.59E
Namacurra Mozambique 37 17.35S 37.00E
Namakī *r.* Iran 31 31.02N 55.20E
Namanga Kenya 37 2.33S 36.48E
Namangan Uzbekistan 24 40.59N 71.41E
Namanyere Tanzania 37 7.34S 31.00E
Namapa Mozambique 37 13.48S 39.44E
Namaponda Mozambique 37 15.51S 39.52E
Namarroi Mozambique 37 15.58S 36.55E
Namatele Tanzania 37 10.01S 38.26E
Nambour Australia 45 26.36S 152.59E
Nambucca Heads *town* Australia 47 30.38S 152.59E
Nam Co *l.* China 24 30.40N 90.30E
Nam Dinh Vietnam 26 20.25N 106.12E
Namecala Mozambique 37 12.50S 39.38E
Nametil Mozambique 37 15.41S 39.30E
Namib Desert Namibia 39 23.00S 15.20E
Namibe Angola 36 15.10S 12.10E
Namibia Africa 36 21.30S 16.45E
Namīn Iran 31 38.25N 48.30E
Namlea Indonesia 27 3.15S 127.07E
Namoi *r.* Australia 47 30.14S 148.28E
Nampa U.S.A. 54 43.44N 116.34W
Nam Phong Thailand 29 16.45N 102.52E
Namp'o N. Korea 25 38.40N 125.30E
Nampula Mozambique 37 15.09S 39.14E
Nampula *d.* Mozambique 37 15.00S 39.00E
Namsen *r.* Norway 16 64.27N 12.19E
Namsos Norway 16 64.28N 11.30E
Namuchabawashan *mtn.* China 29 29.30N 95.10E
Namungua Mozambique 37 13.11S 40.30E
Namur Belgium 8 50.28N 4.52E
Namur *d.* Belgium 8 50.20N 4.45E
Namutoni Namibia 39 18.48S 16.58E
Nanaimo Canada 50 49.08N 123.58W
Nanango Australia 45 26.42S 151.58E
Nanchang China 25 28.38N 115.56E
Nanchong China 24 30.54N 106.06E
Nancy France 11 48.42N 6.12E
Nanda Devi *mtn.* India 29 30.21N 79.50E
Nānded India 28 19.11N 77.21E
Nandewar Range *mts.* Australia 47 30.20S 150.45E
Nandyāl India 29 15.29N 78.29E
Nanga Eboko Cameroon 38 4.41N 12.21E
Nānga Parbat *mtn.* Jammu & Kashmir 28 35.10N 74.35E
Nangapinoh Indonesia 26 0.20S 111.44E
Nangqên China 24 32.15N 96.13E
Nanjing China 25 32.00N 118.40E
Nan Ling *mts.* China 25 25.20N 110.30E
Nannine Australia 42 26.53S 118.20E
Nanning China 25 22.50N 108.19E
Nannup Australia 43 33.57S 115.42E
Nanortalik Greenland 51 60.09N 45.15W
Nanping Fujian China 25 26.40N 118.07E
Nansei shotō *is.* Japan 25 26.30N 125.00E
Nanshan *is.* S. China Sea 26 10.30N 116.00E
Nantes France 9 47.14N 1.35W
Nanteuil-le-Haudouin France 9 49.08N 2.48E
Nanticoke U.S.A. 55 41.12N 76.00W
Nantong China 25 32.05N 120.59E
Nantua France 14 46.09N 5.37E
Nantucket I. U.S.A. 55 41.16N 70.03W
Nantucket Sd. U.S.A. 55 41.30N 70.15W
Nantwich U.K. 4 53.05N 2.31W
Nanyang China 25 33.06N 112.31E
Nanyuki Kenya 37 0.01N 37.03E
Naococane, Lac *l.* Canada 51 52.52N 70.40W
Napa U.S.A. 54 38.18N 122.17W
Napadogan Canada 55 46.25N 67.01W
Napier New Zealand 48 39.29S 176.58E
Naples *see* Napoli Italy 12
Napo *r.* Peru 60 3.30S 73.10W
Napoleon U.S.A. 55 41.24N 84.09W
Napoli Italy 12 40.50N 14.14E
Napoli, Golfo di *g.* Italy 12 40.42N 14.15E
Naqb Ishtar Jordan 32 30.00N 35.30E
Nara Japan 23 34.41N 135.50E
Nara *d.* Japan 23 34.27N 135.55E
Nara Mali 34 15.13N 7.20W
Naracoorte Australia 46 36.58S 140.46E
Naradhan Australia 47 33.39S 146.20E
Naran Mongolia 25 45.20N 113.41E
Narathiwat Thailand 29 6.25N 101.48E
Nārāyanganj Bangla. 29 23.36N 90.28E
Narbada *r.* *see* Narmada *r.* India 28
Narbonne France 11 43.11N 3.00E
Nardò Italy 13 40.11N 18.02E
Narembeen Australia 43 32.04S 118.23E
Nares Str. Canada 51 78.30N 75.00W
Naretha Australia 43 31.01S 124.50E
Narita Japan 23 35.47N 140.19E
Narmada *r.* India 28 21.40N 73.00E
Narodichi Ukraine 15 51.11N 29.01E
Narodnaya *mtn.* Russian Fed. 18 65.00N 61.00E
Narok Kenya 37 1.04S 35.54E
Narooma Australia 47 36.15S 150.06E
Narrabri Australia 47 30.20S 149.49E
Narrabri West Australia 47 30.22S 149.47E
Narran *r.* Australia 47 29.45S 147.20E
Narrandera Australia 47 34.36S 146.34E
Narran L. Australia 47 29.40S 147.25E
Narrogin Australia 43 32.58S 117.10E
Narromine Australia 47 32.17S 148.20E
Narsimhapur India 29 22.58N 79.15E
Narubis Namibia 39 26.56S 18.36E
Narva Russian Fed. 18 59.22N 28.17E
Narvik Norway 16 68.26N 17.25E
Naryan Mar Russian Fed. 18 67.37N 53.02E
Naryilco Australia 46 28.41S 141.50E
Naryn Kyrgyzstan 20 41.24N 76.00E
Nasa *mtn.* Norway 16 66.29N 15.23E
Nasarawa Nigeria 38 8.35N 7.44E
Naseby New Zealand 48 45.01S 170.09E
Nashua Mont. U.S.A. 54 48.08N 106.22W
Nashua N.H. U.S.A. 55 42.46N 71.27W
Nashville U.S.A. 53 36.10N 86.50W
Našice Croatia 15 45.29N 18.06E
Näsijärvi *l.* Finland 17 61.37N 23.42E
Nāsik India 28 20.00N 73.52E
Nassau Bahamas 57 25.03N 77.20W
Nasser, L. *see* Nāṣir, Buḥayrat *l.* Egypt 30
Nassian Ivory Coast 38 8.33N 3.18W
Nässjö Sweden 17 57.39N 14.41E
Nāṣir, Buḥayrat *l.* Egypt 30 22.40N 32.00E
Naṣr Egypt 32 30.36N 30.23E
Nata Botswana 39 20.12S 26.12E
Natal Brazil 61 5.46S 35.15W
Natal Indonesia 26 0.35N 99.07E
Natal *d.* R.S.A. 39 28.30S 30.30E
Natanes Plateau *f.* U.S.A. 54 33.35N 110.15W
Naṭanz Iran 31 33.30N 51.57E
Natashquan Canada 51 50.12N 61.49W
Natchez U.S.A. 53 31.22N 91.24W
Nathalia Australia 47 36.02S 145.14E
National City U.S.A. 54 32.40N 117.06W
Natitingou Benin 38 10.17N 1.19E
Natron, L. Tanzania 37 2.18S 36.05E
Naṭrūn, Wādī an *f.* Egypt 32 30.25N 30.18E
Natuna Besar *i.* Indonesia 26 4.00N 108.20E
Natuna Selatan, Kepulauan *is.* Indonesia 26 3.00N 108.50E
Naturaliste, C. Australia 43 33.32S 115.01E
Naubinway U.S.A. 55 46.05N 85.27W
Naumburg Germany 14 51.09N 11.48E
Nā'ūr Jordan 32 31.53N 35.50E
Nauru Pacific Oc. 40 0.32S 166.55E
Naustdal Norway 17 61.31N 5.43E
Nauta Peru 60 4.30S 73.40W
Nautla Mexico 56 20.13N 96.47W
Navalmoral de la Mata Spain 10 39.54N 5.33W
Navan Rep. of Ire. 7 53.39N 6.42W
Navarra *d.* Spain 10 42.40N 1.45W
Navarre Australia 46 36.54S 143.09E
Navarro Argentina 63 35.00S 59.10W
Naver *r.* U.K. 6 58.32N 4.14W
Navlya Russian Fed. 18 52.51N 34.30E
Navoi Uzbekistan 20 40.04N 65.20E
Navojoa Mexico 56 27.06N 109.26W
Návpaktos Greece 13 38.24N 21.49E
Návplion Greece 13 37.33N 22.47E
Navrongo Ghana 38 10.51N 1.03W
Nawá Syria 32 32.53N 36.03E
Nawābshāh Pakistan 28 26.15N 68.26E
Náxos Greece 13 37.06N 25.23E
Náxos *i.* Greece 13 37.03N 25.30E
Nayarit *d.* Mexico 56 21.30N 104.00W
Nāy Band Iran 31 27.23N 52.38E
Nāy Band Iran 31 32.20N 57.34E
Nāy Band, Kūh-e *mtn.* Iran 31 32.25N 57.30E
Nazaré Brazil 61 13.00S 39.00W
Nazarovka Russian Fed. 18 54.19N 41.20E
Nazas *r.* Mexico 56 25.34N 103.25W
Nazca Peru 60 14.53S 74.54W
Nazerat Israel 32 32.41N 35.16E
Nazilli Turkey 30 37.55N 28.20E
Nazinon *r.* Burkina *see* Red Volta *r.* Ghana 38
Nchanga Zambia 37 12.30S 27.55E
Ncheu Malaŵi 37 14.50S 34.45E
Ndali Benin 38 9.53N 2.45E
Ndasegera *mtn.* Tanzania 37 1.58S 35.41E
Ndélé C.A.R. 35 8.24N 20.39E
Ndélélé Cameroon 38 4.03N 14.55E
N'Dendé Gabon 36 2.23S 11.23E
Ndikiniméki Cameroon 38 4.46N 10.49E
N'Djamena Chad 38 12.10N 14.59E
Ndola Zambia 37 12.58S 28.39E
Ndungu Tanzania 37 4.25S 38.04E
Nea *r.* Norway 16 63.15N 11.00E
Neagh, Lough U.K. 7 54.36N 6.25W
Neale, L. Australia 44 24.21S 130.04E
Néa Páfos Cyprus 32 34.45N 32.25E
Neápolis Greece 13 36.30N 23.04E
Neath U.K. 5 51.39N 3.49W
Nebit-Dag Turkmenistan 31 39.31N 54.24E
Nebraska *d.* U.S.A. 52 41.30N 100.00W
Nebraska City U.S.A. 53 40.41N 95.50W
Nebrodi, Monti *mts.* Italy 12 37.53N 14.32E
Neches *r.* U.S.A. 53 29.55N 93.50W
Neckar *r.* Germany 14 49.32N 8.26E
Necochea Argentina 63 38.31S 58.46W
Necuto Angola 36 4.55S 12.38E
Needles U.S.A. 54 34.51N 114.37W
Neerpelt Belgium 8 51.13N 5.28E
Neftegorsk Russian Fed. 19 44.21N 39.44E
Nefyn U.K. 4 52.55N 4.31W
Negaunee U.S.A. 55 46.31N 87.37W
Negele Ethiopia 35 5.20N 39.36E
Negev *des.* *see* HaNegev *des.* Israel 32
Negoiu *mtn.* Romania 15 45.36N 24.32E
Negomano Mozambique 37 11.26S 38.30E
Negombo Sri Lanka 29 7.13N 79.50E
Negotin Yugo. 15 44.14N 22.33E
Negrais, C. Burma 29 16.00N 94.30E
Negritos Peru 60 4.42S 81.18W
Negro *r.* Argentina 63 40.50S 63.00W
Negro *r.* Brazil 60 3.00S 59.55W
Negro *r.* Uruguay 63 33.27S 58.20W
Negros *i.* Phil. 27 10.00N 123.00E
Negru-Vodă Romania 15 43.50N 28.12E
Neijiang China 24 29.32N 105.03E
Nei Monggol *d.* China 25 41.60N 109.60E
Neisse *r.* Poland Germany 14 52.05N 14.42E
Neiva Colombia 60 2.58N 75.15W
Nekső Denmark 17 55.04N 15.09E
Nelidovo Russian Fed. 18 56.13N 32.46E
Nelkan Russian Fed. 21 57.40N 136.04E
Nelligen Australia 47 35.39S 150.06E
Nellore India 29 14.29N 80.00E
Nelson Australia 46 38.04S 141.05E
Nelson Canada 50 49.29N 117.17W
Nelson *r.* Canada 51 57.00N 93.20W
Nelson New Zealand 48 41.18S 173.17E
Nelson U.K. 4 53.50N 2.14W
Nelson U.S.A. 54 35.30N 113.16W
Nelson, C. Australia 46 38.27S 141.35E
Nelson, Estrecho *str.* Chile 63 51.33S 74.40W
Nelson Bay *town* Australia 47 32.43S 152.08E
Nelson-Marlborough *d.* New Zealand 48 41.40S 173.40E
Nelspoort R.S.A. 39 32.07S 23.00E
Nelspruit R.S.A. 39 25.27S 30.58E
Néma Mauritania 34 16.32N 7.12W
Nembe Nigeria 38 4.32N 6.25E
Nemours France 9 48.16N 2.41E
Nemunas *r.* Lithuania 17 55.18N 21.23E
Nenagh Rep. of Ire. 7 52.52N 8.13W
Nenana U.S.A. 50 64.35N 149.20W
Nene *r.* U.K. 4 52.49N 0.12E
Nenjiang China 25 49.10N 125.15E
Nepal Asia 29 28.00N 84.30E
Nephi U.S.A. 54 39.43N 111.50W
Nephin Beg *mtn.* Rep. of Ire. 7 54.02N 9.38W
Nephin Beg Range *mts.* Rep. of Ire. 7 54.00N 9.37W
Nera *r.* Italy 12 42.33N 12.43E
Nérac France 11 44.08N 0.20E
Nerekhta Russian Fed. 18 57.30N 40.40E
Neretva *r.* Bosnia-Herzegovina 13 43.02N 17.28E
Neriquinha Angola 36 15.50S 21.40E
Nero Deep Pacific Oc. 27 12.40N 145.50E
Néronde France 11 45.50N 4.14E
Nerva Spain 10 37.42N 6.30W
Nes Neth. 8 53.27N 5.46E
Nesbyen Norway 17 60.34N 9.09E
Nesle France 9 49.46N 2.51E
Nesna Norway 16 66.13N 13.04E
Nesöy *i.* Norway 16 66.35N 12.40E
Ness, Loch U.K. 6 57.16N 4.30W
Nestaocano *r.* Canada 55 48.40N 73.25W
Nesterov Ukraine 15 50.04N 24.00E
Néstos *r.* Greece 13 40.51N 24.48E
Nesttun Norway 17 60.19N 5.20E
Nesvizh Belorussia 15 53.16N 26.40E
Netanya Israel 32 32.20N 34.51E
Netherlands Europe 8 52.00N 5.30E
Netherlands Antilles S. America 57 12.30N 69.00W
Neto *r.* Italy 13 39.12N 17.08E
Nettilling L. Canada 51 66.30N 70.40W
Neubrandenburg Germany 14 53.33N 13.16E
Neuchâtel Switz. 14 47.00N 6.56E
Neuchâtel, Lac de *l.* Switz. 14 46.55N 6.55E
Neuenhaus Germany 8 52.30N 6.58E
Neufchâteau Belgium 8 49.51N 5.26E
Neufchâtel France 9 49.44N 1.26E
Neuillé-Pont-Pierre France 9 47.33N 0.33E
Neumarkt Germany 14 49.16N 11.28E
Neumünster Germany 14 54.06N 9.59E
Neuquén Argentina 63 39.00S 68.05W
Neuquén *d.* Argentina 63 38.30S 70.00W

Neuquén r. Argentina 63 39.02S 68.07W
Neuruppin Germany 14 52.55N 12.48E
Neuse r. U.S.A. 53 35.04N 77.04W
Neusiedler See l. Austria 14 47.52N 16.45E
Neuss Germany 8 51.12N 6.42E
Neustadt Bayern Germany 14 49.44N 12.11E
Neustrelitz Germany 14 53.22N 13.05E
Neuvic France 11 45.23N 2.16E
Neuwied Germany 8 50.26N 7.28E
Nevada d. U.S.A. 54 39.50N116.10W
Nevada, Sierra mts. Spain 10 37.04N 3.20W
Nevada, Sierra mts. U.S.A. 52 37.30N119.00W
Nevanka Russian Fed. 21 56.31N 98.57E
Nevel Russian Fed. 18 56.00N 29.59E
Nevers France 11 47.00N 3.09E
Nevertire Australia 47 31.52S147.47E
Nevinnomyssk Russian Fed. 19 44.38N 41.59E
Nevşehir Turkey 30 38.38N 34.43E
Newala Tanzania 37 10.56S 39.15E
New Albany Ind. U.S.A. 55 38.17N 85.50W
New Amsterdam Guyana 61 6.18N 57.30W
New Angledool Australia 47 29.06S147.57E
Newark N.J. U.S.A. 55 40.44N 74.11W
Newark N.Y. U.S.A. 55 43.03N 77.06W
Newark Ohio U.S.A. 55 40.03N 82.25W
Newark-on-Trent U.K. 4 53.06N 0.48E
New Bedford U.S.A. 55 41.38N 70.56W
Newberg U.S.A. 54 45.18N122.58W
New Bern U.S.A. 53 35.05N 77.04W
Newberry Mich. U.S.A. 55 46.22N 85.30W
Newbiggin-by-the-Sea U.K. 4 55.11N 1.30W
New Braunfels U.S.A. 52 29.43N 98.09W
New Britain i. P.N.G. 41 6.00S150.00E
New Brunswick d. Canada 55 46.30N 66.15W
New Brunswick U.S.A. 55 40.29N 74.27W
Newburgh U.S.A. 55 41.30N 74.00W
Newbury U.K. 5 51.24N 1.19W
New Bussa Nigeria 38 9.53N 4.29E
Newcastle Australia 47 32.55S151.46E
Newcastle N.B. Canada 55 47.01N 65.36W
Newcastle Ont. Canada 55 43.55N 78.35W
Newcastle R.S.A. 39 27.44S 29.55E
Newcastle U.K. 7 54.13N 5.53W
New Castle Penn. U.S.A. 55 41.00N 80.22W
Newcastle Wyo. U.S.A. 52 43.50N104.11W
Newcastle B. Australia 44 10.50S142.37E
Newcastle Emlyn U.K. 5 52.02N 4.29W
Newcastle-under-Lyme U.K. 4 53.02N 2.15W
Newcastle upon Tyne U.K. 4 54.58N 1.36W
Newcastle Waters town Australia 44 17.24S133.24E
Newcastle West Rep. of Ire. 7 52.26N 9.04W
Newdegate Australia 43 33.06S119.01E
New Delhi India 28 28.37N 77.13E
New England Range mts. Australia 47 30.30S151.50E
Newenham, C. U.S.A. 50 58.37N162.12W
Newent U.K. 5 51.56N 2.24W
New Forest f. U.K. 5 50.50N 1.35W
Newfoundland d. Canada 51 55.00N 60.00W
Newfoundland i. Canada 51 48.30N 56.00W
New Galloway U.K. 6 55.05N 4.09W
New Guinea i. Austa. 27 5.00S140.00E
New Hampshire d. U.S.A. 55 43.35N 71.40W
New Hanover i. Pacific Oc. 41 2.00S150.00E
Newhaven U.K. 5 50.47N 0.04E
New Haven U.S.A. 55 41.18N 72.55W
New Ireland i. P.N.G. 41 2.30S151.30E
New Jersey d. U.S.A. 55 40.15N 74.30W
New Liskeard Canada 55 47.30N 79.40W
New London Conn. U.S.A. 55 41.21N 72.06W
Newman Australia 42 23.22S119.43E
Newman, Mt. Australia 42 23.15S119.33E
Newmarket Rep. of Ire. 7 52.13N 9.00W
Newmarket U.K. 5 52.15N 0.23E
Newmarket on Fergus Rep. of Ire. 7 52.46N 8.55W
New Martinsville U.S.A. 55 39.39N 80.52W
New Meadows U.S.A. 54 44.58N116.32W
New Mexico d. U.S.A. 52 33.30N106.00W
New Norcia Australia 43 30.58S116.15E
New Norfolk Australia 45 42.46S147.02E
New Orleans U.S.A. 53 30.00N 90.03W
New Philadelphia U.S.A. 55 40.31N 81.28W
New Plymouth New Zealand 48 39.03S174.04E
Newport Mayo Rep. of Ire. 7 53.53N 9.34W
Newport Tipperary Rep. of Ire. 7 52.42N 8.25W
Newport Dyfed U.K. 5 52.01N 4.51W
Newport Essex U.K. 5 51.58N 0.13E
Newport Gwent U.K. 5 51.34N 2.59W
Newport Hants. U.K. 5 50.43N 1.18W
Newport Ark. U.S.A. 53 35.35N 91.16W
Newport Maine U.S.A. 55 44.50N 69.17W
Newport N.H. U.S.A. 55 43.21N 72.09W
Newport Oreg. U.S.A. 54 44.38N124.03W
Newport R.I. U.S.A. 55 41.13N 71.18W
Newport News U.S.A. 53 36.59N 76.26W
New Providence i. Bahamas 57 25.03N 77.25W
Newquay U.K. 5 50.24N 5.06W
New Quay U.K. 5 52.13N 4.22W
New Radnor U.K. 5 52.15N 3.10W
New Romney U.K. 5 50.59N 0.58E
New Ross Rep. of Ire. 7 52.24N 6.57W
Newry U.K. 7 54.11N 6.21W
New Scone U.K. 6 56.25N 3.25W
New South Wales d. Australia 47 32.40S147.40E
Newton Kans. U.S.A. 53 38.02N 97.22W
Newton Abbot U.K. 5 50.32N 3.37W
Newton Aycliffe U.K. 4 54.36N 1.34W
Newtonmore U.K. 6 57.04N 4.08W
Newton Stewart U.K. 6 54.57N 4.29W
Newtown U.K. 5 52.31N 3.19W
Newtownabbey U.K. 7 54.39N 5.57W
Newtownards U.K. 7 54.35N 5.41W
Newtown Butler U.K. 7 54.12N 7.22W
Newtown St. Boswells U.K. 6 55.35N 2.40W
Newtownstewart U.K. 7 54.43N 7.25W
New Westminster Canada 50 49.12N122.55W
New York U.S.A. 55 40.40N 73.50W
New York d. U.S.A. 55 43.00N 75.00W
New Zealand Austa. 48 41.00S175.00E
Neya Russian Fed. 18 58.18N 43.40E
Neyagawa Japan 23 34.46N135.38E
Neyrīz Iran 31 29.12N 54.17E
Neyshābūr Iran 31 36.13N 58.49E
Nezhin Ukraine 15 51.03N 31.54E
Ngala Nigeria 38 12.21N 14.10E
Ngami, L. Botswana 39 20.32S 22.38E
Ngamiland d. Botswana 39 19.40S 22.00E
Ngamiland f. Botswana 39 20.00S 22.30E
Ngangla Ringco l. China 29 31.40N 83.00E
Nganglong Kangri mtn. China 24 32.45N 81.12E
N'Gao Congo 36 2.28S 15.40E
Ngaoundéré Cameroon 38 7.20N 13.35E
Ngaruawahia New Zealand 48 37.40S175.09E
Ngaruroro r. New Zealand 48 39.34S176.54E
Ngauruhoe mtn. New Zealand 48 39.10S175.35E
Ng'iro, Mt. Kenya 37 2.06N 36.44E
N'Giva Angola 39 17.03S 15.47E
Ngomba Tanzania 37 8.16S 32.51E
Ngomeni Kenya 37 3.00S 40.11E
Ngong Kenya 37 1.22S 36.40E
Ngorongoro Crater f. Tanzania 37 3.13S 35.32E
Ngozi Burundi 37 2.52S 29.50E
Nguigmi Niger 38 14.00N 13.11E
Nguru Nigeria 38 12.53N 10.30E
Nguruka Tanzania 37 5.08S 30.58E
Ngwaketse d. Botswana 39 25.10S 25.00E
Ngwerere Zambia 37 15.18S 28.20E
Nhacongo Mozambique 39 24.18S 35.14E
Nhachengue Mozambique 39 22.52S 35.10E
Nhandugue r. Mozambique 39 18.47S 34.30E
Nha Trang Vietnam 26 12.15N109.10E
Nhill Australia 46 36.20S141.40E
Nhulunbuy Australia 44 12.11S136.46E
Niafounké Mali 38 15.56N 4.00W
Niagara Falls town U.S.A. 55 43.06N 79.02W
Niah Malaysia 26 3.52N113.44E
Niamey Niger 38 13.32N 2.05E
Niamey d. Niger 38 14.00N 1.40E
Nia-Nia Zaïre 37 1.30N 27.41E
Niapa, Gunung mtn. Indonesia 26 1.45N117.30E
Nias i. Indonesia 26 1.05N 97.30E
Niassa d. Mozambique 37 13.00S 36.30E
Nicaragua C. America 57 13.00N 85.00W
Nicaragua, Lago de l. Nicaragua 57 11.30N 85.30W
Nicastro Italy 12 38.58N 16.16E
Nice France 11 43.42N 7.16E
Nichelino Italy 9 44.59N 7.38E
Nicholson Australia 42 18.02S128.54E
Nicholson r. Australia 44 17.31S139.36E
Nicobar Is. India 29 8.00N 94.00E
Nicolls Town Bahamas 57 25.08N 78.00W
Nicosia see Levkosía Cyprus 32
Nicoya, Golfo de g. Costa Rica 57 9.30N 85.00W
Nicoya, Península de pen. Costa Rica 57 10.30N 85.30W
Nid r. Norway 17 58.24N 8.48E
Nida r. Poland 15 50.18N 20.52E
Nidzica Poland 15 53.22N 20.26E
Niederösterreich d. Austria 14 48.20N 15.50E
Niedersachsen d. Germany 8 52.55N 7.40E
Niekerkshoop R.S.A. 39 29.19S 22.48E
Niéllé Ivory Coast 38 10.05N 5.28W
Nienburg Germany 14 52.38N 9.13E
Niers r. Neth. 8 51.43N 5.56E
Nieuw Nickerie Surinam 61 5.57N 56.59W
Nieuwpoort Belgium 8 51.08N 2.45E
Nigde Turkey 30 37.58N 34.42E
Niger Africa 34 17.00N 9.30E
Niger d. Nigeria 38 9.50N 6.00E
Niger r. Nigeria 38 4.15N 6.05E
Niger Delta Nigeria 38 4.00N 6.10E
Nigeria Africa 38 9.00N 9.00E
Nightcaps New Zealand 48 45.58S168.02E
Niigata Japan 25 37.58N139.02E
Niiza Japan 23 35.48N139.34E
Nijmegen Neth. 8 51.50N 5.52E
Nikel Russian Fed. 16 69.20N 30.00E
Nikiniki Indonesia 42 9.49S124.29E
Nikki Benin 38 9.55N 3.18E
Nikolayev Ukraine 19 46.57N 32.00E
Nikolayevskiy Russian Fed. 19 50.05N 45.32E
Nikolayevsk-na-Amure Russian Fed. 21 53.20N140.44E
Nikolsk Russian Fed. 18 59.33N 45.30E
Nikopol Ukraine 19 47.34N 34.25E
Niksar Turkey 30 40.35N 36.59E
Nīkshahr Iran 31 26.14N 60.15E
Nikšić Yugo. 13 42.48N 18.56E
Nīl, An r. Egypt 32 31.30N 30.25E
Nila i. Indonesia 27 6.45S129.30E
Nile r. see Nīl, An r. Egypt 32
Nile Delta Egypt 32 31.00N 31.00E
Niles Mich. U.S.A. 55 41.51N 86.15W
Nilgiri Hills India 28 11.30N 77.30E
Nimbin Australia 47 28.35S153.12E
Nîmes France 11 43.50N 4.21E
Nindigully Australia 47 28.20S148.47E
Ninety Mile Beach f. Australia 47 38.07S147.30E
Ninety Mile Beach f. New Zealand 48 34.45S173.00E
Nineveh ruins Iraq 30 36.24N 43.08E
Ningbo China 25 29.54N121.33E
Ningde China 25 26.41N119.32E
Ningnan China 24 27.03N102.46E
Ningwu China 25 39.00N112.19E
Ningxia Huizu d. China 24 37.00N106.00E
Ninh Binh Vietnam 26 20.14N106.00E
Ninove Belgium 8 50.50N 4.02E
Niobrara r. U.S.A. 52 42.45N 98.10W
Nioro Mali 34 15.12N 9.35W
Niort France 11 46.19N 0.27W
Nipāni India 28 16.24N 74.23E
Nipigon Canada 55 49.00N 88.17W
Nipigon, L. Canada 55 49.50N 88.30W
Nipigon B. Canada 55 48.53N 87.50W
Nipissing, L. Canada 55 46.17N 80.00W
Niquelândia Brazil 59 14.27S 48.27W
Nirasaki Japan 23 35.42N138.27E
Niš Yugo. 13 43.20N 21.54E
Nisa Portugal 10 39.31N 7.39W
Nishinomiya Japan 23 34.43N135.20E
Nisko Poland 15 50.35N 22.07E
Nissedal Norway 17 59.10N 8.30E
Nisser l. Norway 17 59.10N 8.30E
Niṭā' Saudi Arabia 31 27.13N 48.25E
Niterói Brazil 59 22.54S 43.06W
Nith r. U.K. 6 55.00N 3.35W
Nitra Czech. 15 48.20N 18.05E
Niue i. Cook Is. 40 19.02S169.52W
Niut, Gunung mtn. Indonesia 26 1.00N110.00E
Nivala Finland 16 63.55N 24.58E
Nivelles Belgium 8 50.36N 4.20E
Nizāmābād India 29 18.40N 78.05E
Nizhneangarsk Russian Fed. 21 55.48N109.35E
Nizhnekamskoye Vodokhranilishche Russian Fed. 18 55.45N 53.50E
Nizhne Kolymsk Russian Fed. 21 68.34N160.58E
Nizhneudinsk Russian Fed. 21 54.55N 99.00E
Nizhnevartovsk Russian Fed. 20 60.57N 76.40E
Nizhniy Novgorod Russian Fed 18 56.20N 44.00E
Nizhniy Tagil Russian Fed. 18 58.00N 60.00E
Nizhnyaya Tunguska r. Russian Fed. 21 65.50N 88.00E
Nizhnyaya Tura Russian Fed. 18 58.40N 59.48E
Nizke Tatry mts. Czech. 15 48.54N 19.40E
Nizza Monferrato Italy 9 44.46N 8.21E
Njazīdja see Grande Comore i. Comoros 37
Njombe Tanzania 37 9.20S 34.47E
Njombe r. Tanzania 37 7.02S 35.55E
Njoro Tanzania 37 5.16S 36.30E
Nkalagu Nigeria 38 6.28N 7.46E
Nkawkaw Ghana 38 6.35N 0.47W
Nkayi Zimbabwe 39 19.00S 28.54E
Nkhata Bay town Malaŵi 37 11.37S 34.20E
Nkhotakota Malaŵi 37 12.55S 34.19E
Nkongsamba Cameroon 38 4.59N 9.53E
Nkungwe Mt. Tanzania 37 6.15S 29.54E
Noatak U.S.A. 50 67.34N162.59W
Noce r. Italy 9 46.09N 11.04E
Nogales Mexico 56 31.20N110.56W
Nogara Italy 9 45.11N 11.04E
Nogayskiye Step f. Russian Fed. 19 44.25N 45.30E
Nogent-le-Rotrou France 9 48.19N 0.50E
Nogent-sur-Seine France 9 48.29N 3.30E
Nogoyá Argentina 63 32.22S 59.49W
Noguera Ribagorçana r. Spain 10 41.27N 0.25E
Noirmoutier, Île de i. France 11 47.00N 2.15W
Nojima-zaki c. Japan 23 34.56N139.53E
Nokia Finland 17 61.28N 23.30E
Nok Kundi Pakistan 28 28.48N 62.46E
Nokomis Canada 50 51.30N105.00W
Nokou Chad 38 14.35N 14.47E
Nolinsk Russian Fed. 18 57.38N 49.52E
Noma Omuramba r. Botswana 39 19.14S 22.15E
Nome U.S.A. 50 64.30N165.30W
Nomgon Mongolia 24 42.50N105.13E
Nonancourt France 9 48.47N 1.11E
Nonburg Russian Fed. 18 65.32N 50.37E
Nong Khai Thailand 29 17.50N102.46E
Nongoma R.S.A. 39 27.58S 31.35E
Nonning Australia 46 32.30S136.30E
Nonthaburi Thailand 26 13.48N100.31E
Noojee Australia 47 37.57S146.00E
Noonamah Australia 42 12.35S131.03E
Noongaar Australia 43 31.21S118.55E
Noonkanbah Australia 42 18.30S124.50E
Noonthorangee Range mts. Australia 46 31.00S142.20E
Noorama Creek r. Australia 47 28.05S145.55E
Noord Beveland f. Neth. 8 51.35N 3.45E
Noord Brabant d. Neth. 8 51.37N 5.00E
Noord Holland d. Neth. 8 52.37N 4.50E
Noordoost-Polder f. Neth. 8 52.45N 5.45E
Noordwijk Neth. 8 52.16N 4.29E
Noorvik U.S.A. 50 66.50N161.14W
Noosa Heads town Australia 44 26.23S153.07E
Nora Sweden 17 59.31N 15.02E
Noranda Canada 55 48.18N 79.01W
Nord d. Burkina 38 13.50N 2.20W
Nord d. France 8 50.17N 3.14E
Nordaustlandet i. Arctic Oc. 64 79.55N 23.00E
Norddeich Germany 8 53.35N 7.10E
Norden Germany 8 53.34N 7.13E
Nordenham Germany 14 53.30N 8.29E
Norderney Germany 8 53.43N 7.09E
Norderney i. Germany 8 53.45N 7.15E
Nordfjord est. Norway 17 61.54N 5.12E
Nordfjordeid Norway 17 61.54N 6.00E
Nordfold Norway 16 67.48N 15.20E
Nordfriesische Inseln is. Germany 14 54.30N 8.00E
Nordhausen Germany 14 51.31N 10.48E
Nordhorn Germany 8 52.27N 7.05E
Nordkapp c. Norway 16 71.11N 25.48E
Nordkinnhalvöya pen. Norway 16 70.55N 27.45E
Nordland d. Norway 16 66.50N 14.50E
Nord-Ostsee-Kanal Germany 14 53.54N 9.12E
Nordreisa Norway 16 69.46N 21.00E
Nordrhein-Westfalen d. Germany 8 51.18N 6.32E
Nord Tröndelag d. Norway 16 64.20N 12.00E
Nordvik Russian Fed. 21 73.40N110.50E
Nore Norway 17 60.10N 9.01E
Nore r. Rep. of Ire. 7 52.25N 6.58W
Norfolk d. U.K. 5 52.39N 1.00E
Norfolk Va. U.S.A. 53 36.54N 76.18W
Norfolk Broads f. U.K. 4 52.43N 1.35E
Norheimsund Norway 17 60.22N 6.08E
Norilsk Russian Fed. 21 69.21N 88.02E
Norman r. Australia 44 17.28S140.49E
Normanby r. Australia 44 14.25S144.08E
Normanby New Zealand 48 39.32S174.16E
Normanby I. P.N.G. 44 10.05S151.05E
Normandie, Collines de hills France 9 48.50N 0.40W
Normanton Australia 44 17.40S141.05E
Norman Wells Canada 50 65.19N126.46W
Nornalup Australia 43 34.58S116.49E
Ñorquinco Argentina 63 41.50S 70.55W
Norrahammar Sweden 17 57.42N 14.06E
Norra Kvarken str. Sweden / Finland 16 63.36N 20.43E
Norra Storfjället mtn. Sweden 16 65.52N 15.18E
Norrbotten d. Sweden 16 67.00N 19.50E
Norris L. U.S.A. 53 36.20N 83.55W
Norristown U.S.A. 55 40.07N 75.20W
Norrköping Sweden 17 58.36N 16.11E
Norrsundet Sweden 17 60.56N 17.08E
Norrtälje Sweden 17 59.46N 18.42E
Norseman Australia 43 32.15S121.47E
Norsk Russian Fed. 21 52.22N129.57E
Norte, C. Brazil 61 1.40N 49.55W
Norte, Punta c. Argentina 63 36.17S 56.46W
Northallerton U.K. 4 54.20N 1.26W
Northam Australia 43 31.41S116.40E
Northampton Australia 43 28.21S114.37E
Northampton U.K. 5 52.14N 0.54W
Northamptonshire d. U.K. 5 52.18N 0.55W
North Battleford Canada 50 52.47N108.19W
North Bay town Canada 55 46.19N 79.28W
North Bend Oreg. U.S.A. 54 43.24N124.14W
North Berwick U.K. 6 56.04N 2.43W
North Bourke Australia 47 30.01S145.59E
North C. Antarctica 64 71.00S166.00E
North C. New Zealand 48 34.28S173.00E
North Canadian r. U.S.A. 53 35.30N 95.45W
North Carolina d. U.S.A. 53 35.30N 79.00W
North Channel str. Canada 55 46.02N 82.50W
North Channel U.K. 7 55.15N 5.52W
North China Plain f. see Huabei Pingyuan f. China 25
Northcliffe Australia 43 34.36S116.04E
North Dakota d. U.S.A. 52 47.00N100.00W
North Dorset Downs hills U.K. 5 50.46N 2.25W
North Downs hills U.K. 5 51.18N 0.40E
North East d. Botswana 39 20.45S 27.05E
North Eastern d. Kenya 37 1.00N 40.00E
Northern d. Ghana 38 9.00N 1.30W
Northern Ireland d. U.K. 7 54.40N 6.45W
Northern Marianas is. Pacific Oc. 40 15.00N145.00E
Northern Territory d. Australia 44 20.00S133.00E
North Esk r. U.K. 6 56.45N 2.25W
North Foreland c. U.K. 5 51.23N 1.26E
North French r. Canada 55 51.03N 80.52W
North Frisian Is. see Nordfriesische Inseln is. Germany 14
North Horr Kenya 37 3.19N 37.00E
North I. New Zealand 48 39.00S175.00E
Northiam U.K. 5 50.59N 0.39E
North Korea Asia 25 40.00N128.00E
Northland d. New Zealand 48 35.25S174.00E
North Las Vegas U.S.A. 54 36.12N115.07W
North Ogden U.S.A. 54 41.18N112.00W
North Platte U.S.A. 52 41.09N100.45W
North Platte r. U.S.A. 52 41.09N100.55W
North Powder U.S.A. 54 45.13N117.55W
North Ronaldsay i. U.K. 6 59.23N 2.26W
North Sea Europe 3 56.00N 5.00E
North Sporades see Vorίai Sporádhes is. Greece 13
North Taranaki Bight b. New Zealand 48 38.45S174.15E
North Tawton U.K. 5 50.48N 3.55W
North Tonawanda U.S.A. 55 43.02N 78.54W
North Uist i. U.K. 6 57.35N 7.20W
Northumberland d. U.K. 4 55.12N 2.00W
Northumberland, C. Australia 46 38.04S140.40E
Northumberland Is. Australia 44 21.40S150.00E
North Walsham U.K. 4 52.49N 1.22E
Northway U.S.A. 50 62.58N142.00W
North West C. Australia 42 21.48S114.10E
North West Highlands U.K. 6 57.30N 5.15W
North West River town Canada 51 53.30N 60.10W
Northwest Territories d. Canada 51 66.00N 95.00W
Northwich U.K. 4 53.16N 2.30W
North York Moors hills U.K. 4 54.21N 0.50W
North Yorkshire d. U.K. 4 54.14N 1.14W
Norton Sound b. U.S.A. 50 63.50N164.00W
Nort-sur-Erdre France 9 47.26N 1.30W
Norwalk Conn. U.S.A. 55 41.07N 73.25W
Norwalk Ohio U.S.A. 55 41.14N 82.37W
Norway Europe 16 65.00N 13.00E
Norway House town Canada 51 53.59N 97.50W
Norwegian Dependency Antarctica 64 77.00S 10.00E
Norwegian Sea Europe 64 65.00N 5.00E
Norwich U.K. 5 52.38N 1.17E
Norwood Ohio U.S.A. 55 39.12N 84.21W
Noshul Russian Fed. 18 60.04N 49.30E
Nosovka Ukraine 15 50.55N 31.37E
Noss Head U.K. 6 58.28N 3.03W
Nossob r. R.S.A. / Botswana 36 26.54S 20.39E
Noṣratābād Iran 31 29.54N 59.58E
Noteć r. Poland 14 52.44N 15.26E
Noto Italy 12 36.53N 15.05E
Notodden Norway 17 59.34N 9.17E
Notre Dame, Monts mts. Canada 55 48.00N 69.00W
Nottawasaga B. Canada 55 44.40N 80.30W
Nottaway r. Canada 55 51.25N 78.50W
Nottingham U.K. 4 52.57N 1.10W
Nottinghamshire d. U.K. 4 53.10N 1.00W
Notwani r. Botswana 39 23.46S 26.57E
Nouadhibou Mauritania 34 20.54N 17.01W
Nouakchott Mauritania 34 18.09N 15.58W
Nouméa New Caledonia 40 22.16S166.27E
Nouna Burkina 38 12.44N 3.54W
Noupoort R.S.A. 39 31.11S 24.56E
Nouvelle Calédonia is. Pacific Oc. 40 21.30S165.30E
Nouzonville France 9 49.49N 4.45E
Novafeltria Bagnodi Romagna Italy 9 43.53N 12.17E
Nova Friburgo Brazil 59 22.16S 42.32W
Nova Iguaçu Brazil 59 22.45S 43.27W
Nova Lima Brazil 59 19.59S 43.51W
Novara Italy 9 45.27N 8.37E
Nova Scotia d. Canada 51 45.00N 64.00W
Nova Sofala Mozambique 39 20.09S 34.24E
Novato U.S.A. 54 38.06N122.34W
Novaya Ladoga Russian Fed. 18 60.09N 32.15E
Novaya Lyalya Russian Fed. 20 59.02N 60.38E
Novaya Sibir, Ostrov i. Russian Fed. 21 75.20N148.00E
Novaya Ushitsa Ukraine 15 48.50N 27.12E
Novaya Zemlya i. Russian Fed. 20 74.00N 56.00E
Novelda Spain 10 38.24N 0.45W
Nové Zámky Czech. 15 47.59N 18.11E
Novgorod Russian Fed. 18 58.30N 31.20E
Novgorod Severskiy Belorussia 18 52.00N 33.15E
Novi di Modena Italy 9 44.54N 10.54E
Novigrad Croatia 14 45.19N 13.34E
Novi Ligure Italy 9 44.46N 8.47E
Novi Pazar Yugo. 13 43.08N 20.28E
Novi Sad Yugo. 15 45.16N 19.52E
Novoalekseyevka Ukraine 19 46.14N 34.36E
Novoanninskiy Russian Fed. 19 50.32N 42.42E
Novo Arkhangel'sk Ukraine 15 48.34N 30.50E
Novocherkassk Russian Fed. 19 47.25N 40.05E
Novofedorovka Ukraine 19 47.04N 35.18E
Novograd Volynskiy Ukraine 15 50.34N 27.32E
Novogrudok Belorussia 15 53.35N 25.50E
Novo Hamburgo Brazil 59 29.37S 51.07W
Novokazalinsk Kazakhstan 20 45.48N 62.06E
Novokuznetsk Russian Fed. 20 53.45N 87.12E
Novomoskovsk Russian Fed. 18 54.06N 38.15E
Novomoskovsk Ukraine 19 48.38N 35.15E
Novorossiysk Russian Fed. 19 44.44N 37.46E
Novoshakhtinsk Russian Fed. 19 47.46N 39.55E
Novosibirsk Russian Fed. 20 55.04N 82.55E
Novosibirskiye Ostrova is. Russian Fed. 21 76.00N144.00E
Novouzensk Russian Fed. 19 50.29N 48.08E
Novo-Vyatsk Russian Fed. 18 58.30N 49.40E
Novozybkov Russian Fed. 15 52.31N 31.58E
Novska Croatia 14 45.21N 16.59E
Nový Jičín Czech. 15 49.36N 18.00E
Novyy Bykhov Belorussia 15 53.20N 30.21E
Novyy Port Russian Fed. 20 67.38N 72.33E
Nowa Ruda Poland 14 50.34N 16.30E
Nowa Sól Poland 14 51.49N 15.41E
Nowendoc Australia 47 31.35S151.45E
Nowgong Assam India 29 26.20N 92.41E
Nowingi Australia 46 34.36S142.15E
Nowra Australia 47 35.54S150.36E
Nowy Dwór Mazowiecki Poland 15 52.26N 20.43E
Nowy Korczyn Poland 15 50.19N 20.48E
Nowy Sacz Poland 15 49.39N 20.40E
Nowy Targ Poland 15 49.29N 20.02E
Nowy Tomśyl Poland 14 52.20N 16.07E
Noxon U.S.A. 54 48.01N115.47W
Noyant France 9 47.31N 0.08E
Noyon France 9 49.35N 3.00E
Nozay France 9 47.34N 1.38W
Nörresundby Denmark 17 57.04N 9.56E
Nsanje Malaŵi 37 16.55S 35.12E
Nsawam Ghana 38 5.49N 0.20W
Nsombo Zambia 37 10.50S 29.56E
Nsukka Nigeria 38 6.51N 7.29E
Nuatja Togo 38 6.59N 1.11E
Nubian Desert Sudan 35 21.00N 34.00E
Nueces r. U.S.A. 53 27.55N 97.30W
Nueltin L. Canada 51 60.20N 99.50W
Nueva Gerona Cuba 57 21.53N 82.49W
Nueva Helvecia Uruguay 63 34.19S 57.13W
Nueva Palmira Uruguay 63 33.53S 58.25W
Nueva Rosita Mexico 56 27.57N101.13W
Nueve de Julio Argentina 63 35.30S 60.50W
Nuevitas Cuba 57 21.34N 77.18W
Nuevo, Golfo g. Argentina 63 42.42S 64.35W
Nuevo Berlín Uruguay 63 32.59S 58.03W
Nuevo Laredo Mexico 56 27.30N 99.30W
Nuevo León d. Mexico 56 26.00N 99.00W
Nuevo Rocafuerte Ecuador 60 0.56S 75.24W
Nu Jiang r. China see Salween r. Burma 29
Nukha Azerbaijan 31 41.12N 47.10E
Nuku'alofa Tonga 40 21.07S175.12W
Nulato U.S.A. 50 64.43N158.06W
Nullagine Australia 42 21.56S120.06E
Nullarbor Australia 43 31.26S130.55E
Nullarbor Plain f. Australia 43 31.30S128.00E
Numalla, L. Australia 46 28.45S144.21E
Numan Nigeria 38 9.30N 12.01E
Numazu Japan 23 35.06N138.52E
Numedal f. Norway 17 60.06N 9.06E
Numurkah Australia 47 36.05S145.26E
Nundle Australia 47 31.28S151.08E
Nuneaton U.K. 5 52.32N 1.29W
Nungo Mozambique 37 13.25S 37.45E
Nunivak I. U.S.A. 50 60.00N166.30W
Nuoro Italy 12 40.19N 9.20E
Nuqūb Yemen 35 14.59N 45.48E
Nure r. Italy 9 45.03N 9.49E
Nuriootpa Australia 46 34.27S139.02E
Nurri, Mt. Australia 47 31.44S146.04E
Nusa Tenggara is. Indonesia 26 8.30S118.00E
Nusa Tenggara Barat d. Indonesia 26 8.50S117.30E
Nusa Tenggara Timur d. Indonesia 27 9.30S122.00E
Nusaybin Turkey 30 37.05N 41.11E
Nutak Canada 51 57.30N 61.59W
Nuuk see Godthåb Greenland 51

Nuwaybi'al Muzayyinah Egypt 32 28.58N 34.38E
Nuweveldberge mts. R.S.A. 39 32.15S 21.50E
Nuyts, Pt. Australia 43 35.02S116.32E
Nuyts Archipelago is. Australia 45 32.35S133.17E
Nürburg Germany 8 50.20N 6.59E
Nürnberg Germany 14 49.27N 11.05E
Nxaunxau Botswana 39 18.19S 21.04E
Nyabing Australia 43 33.32S118.09E
Nyahua Tanzania 37 5.25S 33.16E
Nyahururu Falls town Kenya 37 0.04N 36.22E
Nyah West Australia 46 35.11S143.21E
Nyainqêntanglha Shan mts. China 24 30.10N 91.00E
Nyakanazi Tanzania 37 3.05S 31.16E
Nyaksimvol Russian Fed. 18 62.30N 60.52E
Nyala Sudan 35 12.01N 24.50E
Nyamandhlovu Zimbabwe 39 19.50S 28.15E
Nyamapanda Zimbabwe 39 16.59S 32.50E
Nyamtukusa Tanzania 37 3.03S 32.44E
Nyandoma Russian Fed. 18 61.33N 40.05E
Nyanza d. Kenya 37 0.30S 34.30E
Nyanza Rwanda 37 2.20S 29.42E
Nyashabozh Russian Fed. 18 65.28N 53.42E
Nyaunglebin Burma 29 17.57N 96.44E
Nyborg Denmark 17 55.19N 10.48E
Nybro Sweden 17 56.45N 15.54E
Nyda Russian Fed. 20 66.35N 72.58E
Nyeri Kenya 37 0.22S 36.56E
Nyhammar Sweden 17 60.17N 14.58E
Nyika Plateau f. Malaŵi 37 10.25S 33.50E
Nyimba Zambia 37 14.33S 30.49E
Nyíregyháza Hungary 15 47.59N 21.43E
Nyköbing Falster Denmark 17 54.46N 11.53E
Nyköbing Jylland Denmark 17 56.48N 8.52E
Nyköbing Sjaelland Denmark 17 55.55N 11.41E
Nyköping Sweden 17 58.45N 17.00E
Nylstroom R.S.A. 39 24.42S 28.24E
Nymagee Australia 47 32.05S146.20E
Nymboida Australia 47 29.57S152.32E
Nymboida r. Australia 47 29.39S152.30E
Nymburk Czech. 14 50.11N 15.03E
Nynäshamn Sweden 17 58.54N 17.57E
Nyngan Australia 47 31.34S147.14E
Nyngynderry Australia 46 32.16S143.22E
Nyong r. Cameroon 38 3.15N 9.55E
Nyons France 11 44.22N 5.08E
Nysa Poland 15 50.29N 17.20E
Nysa Klodzka r. Poland 15 50.49N 17.50E
Nyssa U.S.A. 54 43.53N117.00W
Nyuksenitsa Russian Fed. 18 60.24N 44.08E
Nyunzu Zaïre 37 5.55S 28.00E
Nyurba Russian Fed. 21 63.18N118.28E
Nzega Tanzania 37 4.13S 33.09E
N'zérékoré Guinea 34 7.49N 8.48W
N'zeto Angola 36 7.13S 12.56E
Nzwani see Anjouan i. Comoros 37

O

Oahe Resr. U.S.A. 52 45.45N100.20W
Oahu i. Hawaii U.S.A. 52 21.30N158.00W
Oakbank Australia 46 33.07S140.33E
Oakesdale U.S.A. 54 47.08N117.15W
Oakey Australia 45 27.26S151.43E
Oak Harbour U.S.A. 54 48.18N122.39W
Oakland Calif. U.S.A. 54 37.47N122.13W
Oakland Oreg. U.S.A. 54 43.25N123.18W
Oaklands Australia 47 35.25S146.15E
Oakley U.S.A. 54 42.15N113.53W
Oakover r. Australia 42 20.49S120.40E
Oakridge U.S.A. 54 43.45N122.28W
Oak Ridge town U.S.A. 53 36.02N 84.12W
Oakvale Australia 46 33.01S140.41E
Oakville Canada 55 43.27N 79.41W
Oamaru New Zealand 48 45.07S170.58E
Oates Land f. Antarctica 64 70.00S155.00E
Oaxaca Mexico 56 17.05N 96.41W
Oaxaca d. Mexico 56 17.30N 97.00W
Ob r. Russian Fed. 18 66.50N 69.00E
Oba Canada 55 49.04N 84.07W
Oban U.K. 6 56.26N 5.28W
Oberá Argentina 62 27.30S 55.07W
Oberhausen Germany 8 51.28N 6.51E
Oberon Australia 47 33.41S149.52E
Oberösterreich d. Austria 14 48.15N 14.00E
Obi i. Indonesia 27 1.45S127.30E
Obidos Brazil 61 1.55S 55.31W
Obitsu r. Japan 23 35.24N139.54E
Obo C.A.R. 35 5.18N 26.28E
Obodovka Ukraine 15 48.28N 29.10E
Oboyan Russian Fed. 19 51.13N 36.17E
Obozerskiy Russian Fed. 18 63.28N 40.29E
Obruk Platosu f. Turkey 30 38.00N 33.30E
Obskaya Guba g. Russian Fed. 20 68.30N 74.00E
Ôbu Japan 23 35.00N136.58E
Obuasi Ghana 38 6.15N 1.36W
Obudu Nigeria 38 6.42N 9.07E
Ocala U.S.A. 53 29.11N 82.09W
Ocaña Colombia 60 8.16N 73.21W
Ocaña Spain 10 39.57N 3.30W
Occidental, Cordillera mts. Colombia 60 5.00N 76.15W
Occidental, Cordillera mts. S. America 62 17.00S 69.00W
Oceanside Calif. U.S.A. 54 33.12N117.23W
Oceanside N.Y. U.S.A. 55 40.38N 73.38W
Ochamchire Georgia 19 42.44N 41.30E
Ochil Hills U.K. 6 56.16N 3.25W
Ochsenfurt Germany 14 49.40N 10.03E
Ockelbo Sweden 17 60.53N 16.43E
Ocotal Nicaragua 57 13.37N 86.31W
Ocotlán Mexico 56 20.21N102.42W
Octeville France 9 49.37N 1.39W
Ocua Mozambique 37 13.40S 39.46E
Oda Ghana 38 5.55N 0.56W
Odádhahraun mts. Iceland 16 65.00N 17.30W
Odawara Japan 23 35.15N139.10E
Odda Norway 17 60.04N 6.33E
Odemira Portugal 10 37.36N 8.38W
Odense Denmark 17 55.24N 10.23E
Odenwald mts. Germany 14 49.40N 9.20E
Oder r. Germany see Odra r. Poland 14
Oderzo Italy 9 45.47N 12.29E
Odessa Ukraine 15 46.30N 30.46E
Odessa Tex. U.S.A. 52 31.50N102.23W
Odorhei Romania 15 46.18N 25.18E
Odra r. Poland 14 53.30N 14.36E
Odžak Bosnia-Herzegovina 15 45.03N 18.18E
Odzi r. Zimbabwe 39 19.46S 32.22E
Oegstgeest Neth. 8 52.12N 4.31E
Oeiras Brazil 61 7.00S 42.07W
Ofanto r. Italy 12 41.22N 16.12E
Ofaqim Israel 32 31.19N 34.37E
Offa Nigeria 38 8.09N 4.44E
Offaly d. Rep. of Ire. 7 53.15N 7.30W
Offenbach Germany 14 50.06N 8.46E
Offenburg Germany 14 48.29N 7.57E
Offerdal Sweden 16 63.28N 14.03E
Offranville France 9 49.52N 1.03E
Ofir Portugal 10 41.31N 8.47W
Ofotfjorden est. Norway 16 68.25N 17.00E
Ōgaki Japan 23 35.21N136.37E
Ogbomosho Nigeria 38 8.05N 4.11E
Ogden Utah U.S.A. 54 41.14N111.58W
Ogeechee r. U.S.A. 53 32.54N 81.05W
Ogilvie Mts. Canada 50 65.00N139.30W
Oginskiy, Kanal canal Belorussia 15 52.25N 25.55E
Oglio r. Italy 9 45.02N 10.39E
Ognon r. France 11 47.20N 5.37E
Ogoja Nigeria 38 6.40N 8.45E
Ogoki r. Canada 55 51.38N 85.57W
Ogoki Resr. Canada 55 50.50N 88.26W
Ogooué r. Gabon 36 1.00S 9.05E
Ogosta r. Bulgaria 13 43.44N 23.51E
Ogulin Croatia 14 45.17N 15.14E
Ogun d. Nigeria 38 6.50N 3.20E
Ohai New Zealand 48 45.56S167.57E
Ohanet Algeria 34 28.45N 8.55E
Ohey Belgium 8 50.26N 5.06E
O'Higgins, L. Chile 63 48.03S 73.10W
Ohio d. U.S.A. 55 40.15N 82.45W
Ohio r. U.S.A. 55 36.59N 89.08W
Ōhito Japan 23 34.59N138.56E
Ohře r. Czech. 14 50.32N 14.08E
Ohrid Yugo. 13 41.06N 20.48E
Ohrid, L. Albania/Yugo. 13 41.00N 20.43E
Ōi r. Japan 23 34.45N138.18E
Oil City U.S.A. 55 41.26N 79.42W
Oise d. France 9 49.30N 2.30E
Oise r. France 9 49.00N 2.10E
Oisterwijk Neth. 8 51.34N 5.10E
Ojai U.S.A. 54 34.27N119.15W
Ojocaliente Mexico 56 22.35N102.18W
Ojo de Agua Argentina 62 29.30S 63.44W
Ojos del Salado mtn. Argentina/Chile 62 27.05S 68.05W
Oka Nigeria 38 7.28N 5.48E
Oka r. Russian Fed. 18 56.09N 43.00E
Okaba Indonesia 27 8.06S139.46E
Okahandja Namibia 39 21.58S 16.44E
Okanogan U.S.A. 54 48.39N120.41W
Okanogan r. U.S.A. 54 48.22N119.35W
Okaputa Namibia 39 20.08S 16.58E
Okarito New Zealand 48 43.14S 170.07
Okaukuejo Namibia 39 19.12S 15.56E
Okavango r. Botswana 39 18.30S 22.04E
Okavango Basin f. Botswana 39 19.30S 22.30E
Okayama Japan 25 34.40N133.54E
Okazaki Japan 23 34.57N137.10E
Okeechobee, L. U.S.A. 53 27.00N 80.45W
Okefenokee Swamp f. U.S.A. 53 30.40N 82.40W
Okehampton U.K. 5 50.44N 4.01W
Okere r. Uganda 37 1.37N 33.53E
Okha Russian Fed. 21 53.35N142.50E
Okhansk Russian Fed. 18 57.42N 55.20E
Okhotsk Russian Fed. 21 59.20N143.15E
Okhotsk, Sea of Russian Fed. 21 55.00N150.00E
Okhotskiy Perevoz Russian Fed. 21 61.55N135.40E
Okiep R.S.A. 39 29.36S 17.49E
Oki guntō is. Japan 25 36.30N133.20E
Okinawa jima i. Japan 25 26.30N128.00E
Okipoko r. Namibia 39 18.40S 16.03E
Okitipupa Nigeria 38 6.31N 4.50E
Oklahoma d. U.S.A. 53 35.00N 97.00W
Oklahoma City U.S.A. 53 35.28N 97.33W
Oknitsa Moldavia 15 48.22N 27.30E
Okola Cameroon 38 4.03N 11.23E
Oksskolten mtn. Norway 16 65.59N 14.15E
Oktyabr'sk Kazakhstan 19 49.30N 57.22E
Oktyabrskiy Belorussia 15 52.35N 28.45E
Oktyabrskiy Russian Fed. 18 54.30N 53.30E
Oktyabr'skoy Revolyutsii, Ostrov i. Russian Fed. 21 79.30N 96.00E
Okuru New Zealand 48 43.56S168.55E
Okuta Nigeria 38 9.13N 3.12E
Ólafsvík Iceland 16 64.53N 23.44W
Olancha U.S.A. 54 36.17N118.01W
Olary Australia 46 32.18S140.19E
Olascoaga Argentina 63 35.14S 60.37W
Olavarría Argentina 63 36.57S 60.20W
Oława Poland 15 50.57N 17.17E
Olbia Italy 12 40.55N 9.29E
Old Bar Australia 47 31.59S152.35E
Old Crow Canada 50 67.34N139.43W
Oldenburg Nschn. Germany 8 53.08N 8.13E
Oldenburg Sch.-Hol. Germany 14 54.17N 10.52E
Oldenzaal Neth. 8 52.19N 6.55E
Old Forge Penn. U.S.A. 55 41.22N 75.44W
Old Gumbiro Tanzania 37 10.00S 35.24E
Oldham U.K. 4 53.33N 2.08W
Old Head of Kinsale c. Rep. of Ire. 7 51.37N 8.33W
Old Moolawatana Australia 46 30.04S140.02E
Old Town U.S.A. 55 44.56N 68.39W
Olean U.S.A. 55 42.05N 78.26W
Olecko Poland 15 54.03N 22.30E
Olekma r. Russian Fed. 21 60.20N120.30E
Olekminsk Russian Fed. 21 60.25N120.00E
Olema Russian Fed. 18 64.25N 40.15E
Olenëk Russian Fed. 21 68.38N112.15E
Olenëk r. Russian Fed. 21 73.00N120.00E
Olenëkskiy Zaliv g. Russian Fed. 21 74.00N120.00E
Oléron, Île d' i. France 11 45.55N 1.16W
Oleśnica Poland 15 51.13N 17.23E
Olevsk Ukraine 15 51.12N 27.35E
Olga Russian Fed. 25 43.46N135.14E
Olga, Mt. Australia 44 25.18S130.44E
Olga L. Canada 55 49.37N 77.26W
Olgopol Ukraine 15 48.10N 29.30E
Olhão Portugal 10 37.01N 7.50W
Olifants r. Namibia 39 25.28S 19.23E
Olifants r. C.P. R.S.A. 39 31.42S 18.10E
Olifants r. Trans. R.S.A. 39 24.08S 32.39E
Ólimbos mtn. Cyprus 32 34.55N 32.52E
Ólimbos Greece 13 35.44N 27.11E
Ólimbos mtn. Greece 13 40.04N 22.20E
Olinda Brazil 61 8.00S 34.51W
Oliva Argentina 62 32.05S 63.35W
Oliva Spain 10 38.58N 0.15W
Olivares Spain 10 39.45N 2.21W
Oliveira Brazil 59 20.39S 44.47W
Olivenza Spain 10 38.41N 7.09W
Olney U.K. 5 52.09N 0.42W
Olofström Sweden 17 56.16N 14.30E
Olomouc Czech. 15 49.36N 17.16E
Olonets Russian Fed. 18 61.00N 32.59E
Oloron France 11 43.12N 0.35W
Olot Spain 10 42.11N 2.30E
Olovyannaya Russian Fed. 25 50.58N115.35E
Olpe Germany 8 51.02N 7.52E
Olsztyn Poland 15 53.48N 20.29E
Olsztynek Poland 15 53.36N 20.17E
Olt r. Romania 15 43.43N 24.51E
Oltenița Romania 15 44.05N 26.31E
Olteț r. Romania 15 44.13N 24.28E
Olympia U.S.A. 54 47.03N122.53W
Olympic Mts. U.S.A. 54 47.50N123.45W
Olympic Nat. Park U.S.A. 54 47.48N123.30W
Olympus mtn. see Ólimbos mtn. Greece 13
Olympus, Mt. U.S.A. 54 47.48N123.43W
Omae-zaki c. Japan 23 34.36N138.14E
Omagh U.K. 7 54.36N 7.20W
Omaha U.S.A. 53 41.15N 96.00W
Oman Asia 28 22.30N 57.30E
Oman, G. of Asia 31 25.00N 58.00E
Omarama New Zealand 48 44.29S169.58E
Omaruru Namibia 39 21.25S 15.57E
Omate Peru 62 16.40S 70.58W
Ombrone r. Italy 12 42.40N 11.00E
Omdurman see Umm Durmān Sudan 35
Omegna Italy 9 45.53N 8.24E
Omeo Australia 47 37.05S147.37E
Ometepec Mexico 56 16.41N 98.25W
Ōmi-hachiman Japan 23 35.08N136.06E
Omitara Namibia 39 22.18S 18.01E
Ōmiya Japan 23 35.54N139.38E
Ommen Neth. 8 52.32N 6.25E
Omolon r. Russian Fed. 21 68.50N158.30E
Omsk Russian Fed. 20 55.00N 73.22E
Omulew r. Poland 15 53.05N 21.32E
Omuramba Omatako r. Namibia 39 18.19S 19.52E
Ōmuta Japan 25 33.02N130.26E
Oña Spain 10 42.44N 3.25W
Onda Spain 10 39.58N 0.16W
Ondangua Namibia 39 17.59S 16.02E
Ondo d. Nigeria 38 7.10N 5.20E
Onega Russian Fed. 18 63.57N 38.11E
Onega r. Russian Fed. 18 63.59N 38.11E
Oneida U.S.A. 55 43.06N 75.39W
Onezhskaya Guba b. Russian Fed. 18 63.55N 37.30E
Onezhskoye Ozero l. Russian Fed. 18 62.00N 35.30E
Ongerup Australia 43 33.58S118.29E
Ongole India 29 15.31N 80.04E
Onitsha Nigeria 38 6.10N 6.47E
Onjiva Angola 36 17.03S 15.41E
Onslow Australia 42 21.41S115.12E
Onstwedde Neth. 8 53.04N 7.02E
Ontario d. Canada 51 52.00N 86.00W
Ontario Calif. U.S.A. 54 34.04N117.39W
Ontario Oreg. U.S.A. 54 44.02N116.58W
Ontario, L. Canada/U.S.A. 55 43.45N 78.00W
Ontonagon U.S.A. 55 46.52N 89.18W
Oodnadatta Australia 45 27.30S135.27E
Ooldea Australia 45 30.27S131.50E
Oostelijk-Flevoland f. Neth. 8 52.30N 5.40E
Oostende Belgium 8 51.13N 2.55E
Oosterhout Neth. 8 51.38N 4.50E
Oosterschelde est. Neth. 8 51.35N 3.57E
Oosthuizen Neth. 8 52.33N 5.00E
Oostmalle Belgium 8 51.18N 4.45E
Oost Vlaanderen d. Belgium 8 51.00N 3.45E
Oost Vlieland Neth. 8 53.18N 5.04E
Opaka Bulgaria 13 43.28N 26.10E
Opala Russian Fed. 21 51.58N156.30E
Oparino Russian Fed. 18 59.53N 48.10E
Opasatika Canada 55 49.32N 82.53W
Opasatika r. Canada 55 50.23N 82.26W
Opava Czech. 15 49.56N 17.54E
Opochka Russian Fed. 18 56.41N 28.42E
Opole Poland 15 50.40N 17.56E
Oporto see Porto Portugal 10
Opotiki New Zealand 48 38.00S177.18E
Oppdal Norway 16 62.36N 9.41E
Oppland d. Norway 17 61.30N 9.00E
Opportunity U.S.A. 54 47.39N117.15W
Opunake New Zealand 48 39.27S173.51E
Ora Italy 9 46.21N 11.18E
Ora Banda Australia 43 30.27S121.04E
Oradea Romania 15 47.03N 21.55E
Orai India 29 26.00N 79.26E
Oran Algeria 34 35.45N 0.38W
Orán Argentina 62 23.07S 64.16W
Orange Australia 47 33.19S149.10E
Orange France 11 44.08N 4.48E
Orange r. R.S.A. 39 28.38S 16.38E
Orange Tex. U.S.A. 53 30.05N 93.43W
Orange, C. Brazil 61 4.25N 51.32W
Orangeburg U.S.A. 53 33.28N 80.53W
Orange Free State d. R.S.A. 39 28.00S 28.00E
Orangevale U.S.A. 54 38.41N121.13W
Oranienburg Germany 14 52.45N 13.14E
Oranjefontein R.S.A. 39 23.27S 27.40E
Oranjemund Namibia 39 28.35S 16.26E
Oras Phil. 27 12.09N125.22E
Orbetello Italy 12 42.27N 11.13E
Orbost Australia 47 37.42S148.30E
Orchies France 8 50.28N 3.15E
Orchila i. Venezuela 57 11.52N 66.10W
Orco r. Italy 9 45.10N 7.52E
Ord r. Australia 42 15.30S128.30E
Ordu Turkey 30 41.00N 37.52E
Orduña Spain 10 43.00N 3.00W
Oregon d. U.S.A. 54 43.49N120.36W
Oregon City U.S.A. 54 45.21N122.36W
Orekhovo-Zuyevo Russian Fed. 18 55.47N 39.00E
Orel Russian Fed. 18 52.58N 36.04E
Orem U.S.A. 54 40.19N111.42W
Orenburg Russian Fed. 18 51.50N 55.00E
Orense Spain 10 42.20N 7.52W
Oressa r. Belorussia 15 52.33N 28.45E
Orestiás Greece 13 41.30N 26.33E
Orfanoú, Kólpos g. Greece 13 40.40N 24.00E
Orford U.S.A. 55 43.54N 72.10W
Orford Ness c. Australia 44 11.22S142.50E
Orford Ness c. U.K. 5 52.05N 1.36E
Orgeyev Moldavia 15 47.24N 28.50E
Orick U.S.A. 54 41.17N124.04W
Oriental, Cordillera mts. Bolivia 62 17.00S 65.00W
Oriental, Cordillera mts. Colombia 60 5.00N 74.30W
Origny France 9 49.54N 3.30E
Orihuela Spain 10 38.05N 0.56W
Orillia Canada 55 44.37N 79.25W
Orimattila Finland 17 60.48N 25.45E
Orinduik Guyana 60 4.42N 60.01W
Orinoco r. Venezuela 60 9.00N 61.30W
Orinoco, Delta del f. Venezuela 60 9.00N 61.00W
Orissa d. India 29 20.15N 84.00E
Oristano Italy 12 39.53N 8.36E
Oristano, Golfo di g. Italy 12 39.50N 8.30E
Orizaba Mexico 56 18.51N 97.08W
Orkanger Norway 16 63.17N 9.52E
Orkney Is. d. U.K. 6 59.00N 3.00W
Orlândia Brazil 59 20.55S 47.54W
Orlando U.S.A. 53 28.33N 81.21W
Orléans France 9 47.54N 1.54E
Orléans, Canal d' France 9 47.54N 1.55E
Ormāra Pakistan 28 25.12N 64.38E
Ormoc Phil. 27 11.00N124.37E
Ormond New Zealand 48 38.35S177.58E
Ormskirk U.K. 4 53.35N 2.53W
Orne d. France 9 48.40N 0.05E
Orne r. France 9 49.17N 0.10W
Orobie, Alpi mts. Italy 9 46.03N 10.00E
Orocué Colombia 60 4.48N 71.20W
Orodara Burkina 38 11.00N 4.54W
Oromocto Canada 55 45.50N 66.28W
Oron Israel 32 30.55N 35.01E
Oron Nigeria 38 4.49N 8.15E
Orono U.S.A. 55 44.53N 68.40W
Orosei Italy 12 40.23N 9.40E
Orosei, Golfo di g. Italy 12 40.15N 9.45E
Orosháza Hungary 15 46.34N 20.40E
Orotukan Russian Fed. 21 62.16N151.43E
Oroville Calif. U.S.A. 54 39.31N121.33W
Oroville Wash. U.S.A. 54 48.56N119.26W
Orroroo Australia 46 32.46S138.39E
Orsa Sweden 17 61.07N 14.37E
Orsha Belorussia 18 54.30N 30.23E
Orsières Switz. 9 46.02N 7.09E
Orsk Russian Fed. 18 51.13N 58.35E
Orşova Romania 15 44.42N 22.22E
Orta Nova Italy 12 41.19N 15.42E
Orthez France 11 43.29N 0.46W
Ortigueira Spain 10 43.41N 7.51W
Ortona Italy 12 42.21N 14.24E
Orūmīyeh Iran 31 37.32N 45.02E
Oruro Bolivia 62 17.59S 67.09W
Oruro d. Bolivia 62 18.00S 72.30W
Oryakhovo Bulgaria 13 43.42N 23.58E
Orzinuovi Italy 9 45.24N 9.55E
Os Norway 16 62.31N 11.11E
Osa, Península de pen. Costa Rica 57 8.20N 83.30W
Osage r. U.S.A. 53 38.35N 91.57W
Ōsaka Japan 23 34.40N135.30E
Ōsaka d. Japan 23 34.24N135.25E
Ōsaka-wan b. Japan 23 34.30N135.18E
Osby Sweden 17 56.22N 13.59E
Osen Norway 16 64.18N 10.32E
Osh Kyrgyzstan 20 40.37N 72.49E
Oshawa Canada 55 43.54N 78.51W
Ō shima i. Tosan Japan 23 34.43N139.24E
Oshmyany Belorussia 15 54.22N 25.52E
Oshnovīyeh Iran 31 37.03N 45.05E
Oshogbo Nigeria 38 7.50N 4.35E
Oshtorān, Kūh mtn. Iran 31 33.18N 49.15E
Oshvor Russian Fed. 18 66.59N 62.59E
Osijek Croatia 13 45.35N 18.43E
Osipovichi Belorussia 15 53.19N 28.36E
Oskarshamn Sweden 17 57.16N 16.26E
Oskol r. Ukraine 19 49.08N 37.10E
Oslo Norway 17 59.56N 10.45E
Oslofjorden est. Norway 17 59.20N 10.35E
Osmancik Turkey 30 40.58N 34.50E
Osmaniye Turkey 30 37.04N 36.15E
Osnabrück Germany 8 52.17N 8.03E
Osorno Chile 63 40.35S 73.14W
Osorno Spain 10 42.24N 4.22W
Osöyra Norway 17 60.11N 5.30E
Osprey Reef Australia 44 13.55S146.38E
Oss Neth. 8 51.46N 5.31E
Ossa mtn. Greece 13 39.47N 22.41E
Ossa, Mt. Australia 45 41.52S146.04E
Osse r. Nigeria 38 5.55N 5.15E
Ostashkov Russian Fed. 18 57.09N 33.10E
Ostend see Oostende Belgium 8
Oster Ukraine 15 50.55N 30.53E
Oster r. Ukraine 15 53.47N 31.46E
Osteröy i. Norway 17 60.33N 5.35E
Ostfriesische Inseln is. Germany 8 53.45N 7.00E
Ostrava Czech. 15 49.50N 18.15E
Ostróda Poland 15 53.43N 19.59E
Ostrog Ukraine 15 50.20N 26.29E
Ostrołeka Poland 15 53.06N 21.34E
Ostrov Russian Fed. 18 57.22N 28.22E
Ostrowiec-Świetokrzyski Poland 15 50.57N 21.23E
Ostrów Mazowiecka Poland 15 52.50N 21.51E
Ostrów Wielkopolski Poland 15 51.39N 17.49E
Ostuni Italy 13 40.44N 17.35E
Osŭm r. Bulgaria 13 43.41N 24.51E
Ōsumi shotō is. Japan 25 30.30N131.00E
Osun d. Nigeria 38 7.15N 4.30E
Osuna Spain 10 37.14N 5.06W
Oswego U.S.A. 55 43.27N 76.31W
Oswestry U.K. 4 52.52N 3.03W
Otago d. New Zealand 48 45.10S169.20E
Otago Pen. New Zealand 48 45.48S170.45E
Otaki New Zealand 48 40.45S175.08E
Otaru Japan 25 43.14N140.59E
Otavalo Ecuador 60 0.14N 78.16W
Otavi Namibia 39 19.37S 17.21E
Otelec Romania 15 45.36N 20.50E
Otematata New Zealand 48 44.37S170.11E
Oti r. Ghana 38 8.43N 0.10E
Otira New Zealand 48 42.51S171.33E
Otiwarongo Namibia 39 20.30S 16.39E
Otjiwarongo Namibia 36 20.29S 16.36E
Otjiwero Namibia 39 17.59S 13.22E
Otju Namibia 39 18.15S 13.18E
Otočac Croatia 14 44.52N 15.14E
Otra r. Norway 17 58.09N 8.00E
Otradnyy Russian Fed. 18 53.26N 51.30E
Otranto Italy 13 40.09N 18.30E
Otranto, Str. of Med. Sea 13 40.10N 19.00E
Otrokovice Czech. 15 49.13N 17.31E
Otsego U.S.A. 55 42.26N 85.42W
Otsego Lake town U.S.A. 55 44.55N 84.41W
Ōtsu Japan 23 35.02N135.52E
Ōtsuki Japan 23 35.36N138.57E
Otta Norway 17 61.46N 9.32E
Ottawa Canada 55 45.25N 75.43W
Ottawa r. Canada 55 45.20N 73.58W
Ottawa Kans. U.S.A. 53 38.35N 95.16W
Ottawa Is. Canada 51 59.50N 80.00W
Otter r. U.K. 5 50.38N 3.19W
Otterbäcken Sweden 17 58.57N 14.02E
Otterburn U.K. 4 55.14N 2.10W
Otterndorf Germany 14 53.48N 8.53E
Otteröy i. Norway 16 62.45N 6.50E
Ottosdal R.S.A. 39 26.48S 26.00E
Ottumwa U.S.A. 53 41.02N 92.26W
Oturkpo Nigeria 38 7.13N 8.10E
Otway, C. Australia 46 38.51S143.34E
Ouachita r. U.S.A. 53 33.10N 92.10W
Ouachita Mts. U.S.A. 53 34.40N 94.30W
Ouadda C.A.R. 35 8.04N 22.24E
Ouagadougou Burkina 38 12.20N 1.40W
Ouahigouya Burkina 38 13.31N 2.21W
Ouallam Niger 38 14.23N 2.09E
Ouallene Algeria 34 24.37N 1.14E
Ouargla Algeria 34 32.00N 5.16E
Ouarzazate Morocco 34 30.57N 6.50W
Ouassouas well Mali 38 16.01N 1.26E
Ouddorp Neth. 8 51.49N 3.57E
Oudenaarde Belgium 8 50.50N 3.37E
Oudenbosch Neth. 8 51.35N 4.30E
Oude Rijn r. Neth. 8 52.14N 4.26E
Oudon r. France 9 47.47N 1.02W
Oudtshoorn R.S.A. 39 33.35S 22.11E
Ouellé Ivory Coast 38 7.26N 4.01W
Ouessant, Île d' i. France 11 48.28N 5.05W
Ouezzane Morocco 34 34.52N 5.35W
Oughter, Lough Rep. of Ire. 7 54.01N 7.28W
Ouimet Canada 55 48.43N 88.35W
Ouistreham France 9 49.17N 0.15W
Oujda Morocco 34 34.41N 1.45W
Oulu Finland 16 65.01N 25.28E
Oulu d. Finland 16 65.00N 27.00E
Oulu r. Finland 16 65.01N 25.25E
Oulujärvi l. Finland 16 64.20N 27.15E
Oum Chalouba Chad 35 15.48N 20.46E
Oumé Ivory Coast 38 6.25N 5.23W
Ounas r. Finland 16 66.30N 25.45E
Oundle U.K. 5 52.28N 0.28W
Our r. Lux. 8 49.53N 6.16E
Ouray U.S.A. 54 40.06N109.40W
Ourcq r. France 9 49.01N 3.01E
Ourense see Orense Spain 10
Ourinhos Brazil 59 23.00S 49.54W
Ouro Fino Brazil 59 22.16S 46.25W
Ouro Prêto Brazil 59 20.54S 43.30W
Ourthe r. Belgium 8 50.38N 5.36E
Ouse r. Humber. U.K. 4 53.41N 0.42W
Outardes, Rivière aux r. Canada 55 49.04N 68.25W
Outer Hebrides is. U.K. 6 57.40N 7.35W
Outjo Namibia 39 20.07S 16.10E
Ouyen Australia 46 35.06S142.22E
Ouzouer-le-Marché France 9 47.55N 1.32E
Ovalle Chile 62 30.36S 71.12W
Ovamboland f. Namibia 39 17.45S 16.00E
Ovar Portugal 10 40.52N 8.38W
Ovens r. Australia 47 36.20S146.18E

Overath Germany **8** 50.56N 7.18E
Overflakkee *i.* Neth. **8** 51.45N 4.08E
Overijssel *d.* Neth. **8** 52.25N 6.30E
Overton U.S.A. **54** 36.33N114.27W
Ovidiopol Ukraine **15** 46.18N 30.28E
Oviedo Spain **10** 43.21N 5.50W
Ovinishche Russian Fed. **18** 58.20N 37.00E
Ovruch Ukraine **15** 51.20N 28.50E
Owaka New Zealand **48** 46.27S169.40E
Owando Congo **36** 0.30S 15.48E
Owel, Lough Rep. of Ire. **7** 53.34N 7.24W
Owen Falls Dam Uganda **37** 0.30N 33.07E
Owensboro U.S.A. **53** 37.45N 87.05W
Owens L. U.S.A. **54** 36.25N117.56W
Owen Sound *town* Canada **55** 44.34N 80.56W
Owen Stanley Range *mts.* P.N.G. **44** 9.30S148.00E
Owerri Nigeria **38** 5.29N 7.02E
Owo Nigeria **38** 7.10N 5.39E
Owosso U.S.A. **55** 43.00N 84.11W
Owyhee *r.* U.S.A. **54** 43.46N117.02W
Oxelösund Sweden **17** 58.40N 17.06E
Oxford U.K. **5** 51.45N 1.15W
Oxfordshire *d.* U.K. **5** 51.46N 1.10W
Oxley Australia **46** 34.11S144.10E
Oxnard U.S.A. **54** 34.12N119.11W
Oyapock *r.* Guiana **61** 4.10N 51.40W
Oyem Gabon **36** 1.34N 11.31E
Oykel *r.* U.K. **6** 57.53N 4.21W
Oymyakon Russian Fed. **21** 63.30N142.44E
Oyo Nigeria **38** 7.50N 3.55E
Oyo *d.* Nigeria **38** 8.10N 3.40E
Oyonnax France **11** 46.15N 5.40E
Ozamiz Phil. **27** 8.09N123.59E
Ozarichi Belorussia **15** 52.28N 29.12E
Ozark Plateau U.S.A. **53** 36.00N 93.35W
Ózd Hungary **15** 48.14N 20.18E
Ozernoye Russian Fed. **18** 51.45N 51.29E
Ozersk Russian Fed. **15** 54.26N 22.00E
Ozinki Russian Fed. **19** 51.11N 49.43E
Ödeborg Sweden **17** 58.33N 12.00E
Ödemiş Turkey **13** 38.12N 28.00E
Öland *i.* Sweden **17** 56.45N 16.38E
Ölgiy Mongolia **24** 48.54N 90.00E
Öraefajökull *mtn.* Iceland **16** 64.02N 16.39W
Örbyhus Sweden **17** 60.14N 17.42E
Örebro Sweden **17** 59.17N 15.13E
Örebro *d.* Sweden **17** 59.30N 15.00E
Öregrund Sweden **17** 60.20N 18.26E
Örnsköldsvik Sweden **16** 63.17N 18.50E
Österdal *r.* Sweden **17** 61.03N 14.30E
Østerdalen *f.* Norway **17** 61.15N 11.10E
Östergötland *d.* Sweden **17** 58.25N 15.35E
Osterö *i.* Faroe Is. **16** 62.10N 7.00W
Östersund Sweden **16** 63.10N 14.40E
Østfold *d.* Norway **17** 59.20N 11.10E
Östhammar Sweden **17** 60.16N 18.22E
Överkalix Sweden **16** 66.21N 22.56E
Övertorneå Sweden **16** 66.23N 23.40E
Øyer Norway **17** 61.12N 10.22E
Øyeren *l.* Norway **17** 59.48N 11.14E

P

Paamiut *see* Frederikshåb Greenland **51**
Paarl R.S.A. **39** 33.44S 18.58E
Pabianice Poland **15** 51.40N 19.22E
Pābna Bangla. **29** 24.00N 89.15E
Pacaraima, Sierra *mts.* Venezuela **60** 4.00N 62.30W
Pacasmayo Peru **60** 7.27S 79.33W
Pachuca Mexico **56** 20.10N 98.44W
Packsaddle Australia **46** 30.28S141.28E
Packwood U.S.A. **54** 46.36N121.40W
Pacy-sur-Eure France **9** 49.01N 1.23E
Padang Indonesia **26** 0.55S100.21E
Padangpanjang Indonesia **26** 0.30S100.26E
Padangsidempuan Indonesia **26** 1.20N 99.11E
Padany Russian Fed. **18** 63.12N 33.20E
Padauari *r.* Brazil **60** 0.15S 64.05W
Paderborn Germany **14** 51.43N 8.44E
Padilla Bolivia **62** 19.19S 64.20W
Padlei Canada **51** 62.00N 96.50W
Padloping Island *town* Canada **51** 67.00N 62.50W
Padova Italy **9** 45.27N 11.52E
Padre I. U.S.A. **53** 27.00N 97.20W
Padstow U.K. **5** 50.33N 4.57W
Padthaway Australia **46** 36.37S140.28E
Padua *see* Padova Italy **9**
Paducah U.S.A. **53** 37.03N 88.36W
Paeroa New Zealand **48** 37.23S175.41E
Pafúri Mozambique **39** 22.27S 31.21E
Pag *i.* Croatia **14** 44.28N 15.00E
Pagadian Phil. **27** 7.50N123.30E
Pagai Selatan *i.* Indonesia **26** 3.00S100.18E
Pagai Utara *i.* Indonesia **26** 2.42S100.05E
Page U.S.A. **54** 36.57N111.27W
Pager *r.* Uganda **37** 3.05N 32.28E
Pagwa River *town* Canada **55** 50.02N 85.14W
Pahala Hawaii U.S.A. **52** 19.12N155.28W
Pahiatua New Zealand **48** 40.26S175.49E
Paible U.K. **6** 57.35N 7.27W
Paide Estonia **17** 58.54N 25.33E
Paihia New Zealand **48** 35.16S174.05E
Päijänne *l.* Finland **17** 61.35N 25.30E
Paimboeuf France **11** 47.14N 2.01W
Painan Indonesia **26** 1.21S100.34E
Painesville U.S.A. **55** 41.43N 81.15W
Pains Brazil **59** 20.23S 45.38W
Paisley U.K. **6** 55.50N 4.26W
País Vasco *d.* Spain **10** 43.00N 2.30W
Pajala Sweden **16** 67.11N 23.22E
Pajule Uganda **37** 2.58N 32.53E
Pakaraima Mts. Guyana **60** 5.00N 60.00W
Paki Nigeria **38** 11.33N 8.08E
Pakistan Asia **28** 30.00N 70.00E
Paks Hungary **15** 46.39N 18.53E
Pakwach Uganda **37** 2.27N 31.18E
Pakxé Laos **26** 15.05N105.50E
Pala Chad **38** 9.25N 15.05E
Palaiokhóra Greece **13** 35.14N 23.41E
Palaiseau France **9** 48.43N 2.15E
Palamós Spain **10** 41.51N 3.08E
Palana Russian Fed. **21** 59.05N159.59E
Palangkaraya Indonesia **26** 2.16S113.56E
Palanguinos Spain **10** 42.27N 5.31W
Pālanpur India **28** 24.10N 72.26E
Palapye Botswana **39** 22.33S 27.07E
Palau *is.* Pacific Oc. **27** 7.00N134.25E
Palawan *i.* Phil. **26** 9.30N118.30E
Paldiski Estonia **17** 59.20N 24.06E
Paleleh Indonesia **27** 1.04N121.57E
Palembang Indonesia **26** 2.59S104.50E
Palencia Spain **10** 42.01N 4.34W
Palenque Mexico **56** 17.32N 91.59W
Palermo Italy **12** 38.09N 13.22E
Palimé Togo **38** 6.55N 0.38E
Palisades Resr. U.S.A. **54** 43.15N111.05W
Palizada Mexico **56** 18.15N 92.05W
Palk Str. India / Sri Lanka **29** 10.00N 79.40E
Pallës, Bishti i *c.* Albania **13** 41.24N 19.23E
Pallinup *r.* Australia **43** 34.29S118.54E
Palliser, C. New Zealand **48** 41.35S175.15E
Palma Mozambique **37** 10.48S 40.25E
Palma Spain **10** 39.36N 2.39E
Palma, Bahía de *b.* Spain **10** 39.30N 2.40E
Palma del Río Spain **10** 37.43N 5.17W
Palmanova Italy **9** 45.54N 13.19E
Palmares Brazil **61** 8.41S 35.36W
Palmas, C. Liberia **34** 4.30N 7.55W
Palmas, Golfo di *g.* Italy **12** 39.00N 8.30E
Palmeira dos Indios Brazil **61** 9.25S 36.38W
Palmer *r.* Australia **42** 24.46S133.25E
Palmer U.S.A. **50** 61.36N149.07W
Palmer Land Antarctica **64** 74.00S 61.00W
Palmerston New Zealand **48** 45.29S170.43E
Palmerston, C. Australia **44** 21.32S149.29E
Palmerston North New Zealand **48** 40.20S175.39E
Palmi Italy **12** 38.22N 15.50E
Palmira Colombia **60** 3.33N 76.17W
Palm Is. Australia **44** 18.48S146.37E
Palms U.S.A. **55** 43.37N 82.46W
Palm Springs *town* U.S.A. **54** 33.50N116.33W
Palmyras Pt. India **29** 20.40N 87.00E
Paloh Indonesia **26** 1.46N109.17E
Palojoensuu Finland **16** 68.17N 23.05E
Palomani *mtn.* Bolivia **62** 14.38S 69.14W
Palopo Indonesia **27** 3.01S120.12E
Palu Turkey **30** 38.43N 39.56E
Pama Burkina **38** 11.15N 0.44E
Pamekasan Indonesia **26** 7.11S113.50E
Pamiers France **11** 43.07N 1.36E
Pamir *mts.* Tajikistan **24** 37.50N 73.30E
Pampa U.S.A. **52** 35.32N100.58W
Pampas *f.* Argentina **63** 34.00S 64.00W
Pamplona Colombia **60** 7.24N 72.38W
Pamplona Spain **10** 42.49N 1.39W
Panaca U.S.A. **54** 37.47N114.23W
Panaji India **28** 15.29N 73.50E
Panama C. America **57** 9.00N 80.00W
Panamá *town* Panama **57** 8.57N 79.30W
Panama Sri Lanka **29** 6.46N 81.47E
Panamá, Golfo de *g.* Panama **57** 8.30N 79.00W
Panama City U.S.A. **53** 30.10N 85.41W
Panamint Range *mts.* U.S.A. **54** 36.30N117.20W
Panaro *r.* Italy **9** 44.55N 11.25E
Panay *i.* Phil. **27** 11.10N122.30E
Pandan Phil. **27** 11.45N122.10E
Pando *d.* Bolivia **62** 11.20S 67.40W
Pando Uruguay **63** 34.43S 55.57W
Panevežys Lithuania **17** 55.44N 24.21E
Panfilov Kazakhstan **24** 44.10N 80.01E
Panga Zaïre **36** 1.51N 26.25E
Pangani Tanga Tanzania **37** 5.21S 39.00E
Pangkalpinang Indonesia **26** 2.05S106.09E
Pang Long Burma **29** 23.11N 98.45E
Pangnirtung Canada **51** 66.05N 65.45W
Pankshin Nigeria **38** 9.22N 9.25E
Pannawonica Australia **42** 21.42S116.22E
Páno Lévkara Cyprus **32** 34.55N 33.10E
Páno Plátres Cyprus **32** 34.53N 32.52E
Pantano del Esla *l.* Spain **10** 41.40N 5.50W
Pantelleria *i.* Italy **12** 36.48N 12.00E
Panton *r.* Australia **42** 17.05S128.46E
Pánuco Mexico **56** 22.03N 98.10W
Paola Italy **12** 39.21N 16.03E
Pápa Hungary **15** 47.19N 17.28E
Papeete Tahiti **40** 17.32S149.34W
Papenburg Germany **8** 53.05N 7.25E
Paphos *see* Néa Páfos Cyprus **32**
Papua, G. of P.N.G. **44** 8.30S145.00E
Papua New Guinea Austa. **41** 6.00S144.00E
Papun Burma **29** 18.05N 97.26E
Papunya Australia **44** 23.15S131.53E
Para *d.* Brazil **61** 4.00S 53.00W
Paraburdoo Australia **42** 23.12S117.40E
Paracatu Brazil **59** 17.14S 46.52W
Paracatu *r.* Brazil **59** 16.30S 45.10W
Paracel Is. S. China Sea **26** 16.20N112.00E
Parachilna Australia **46** 31.09S138.24E
Paraćin Yugo. **15** 43.52N 21.24E
Pará de Minas Brazil **59** 19.53S 44.35W
Paradise Calif. U.S.A. **54** 39.46N121.37W
Paradise Nev. U.S.A. **54** 36.09N115.10W
Paragonah U.S.A. **54** 37.53N112.46W
Paragua *r.* Venezuela **60** 6.55N 62.55W
Paraguaçu *r.* Brazil **61** 12.35S 38.59W
Paraguaná, Península de *pen.* Venezuela **60** 11.50N 69.59W
Paraguarí Paraguay **59** 25.36S 57.06W
Paraguay *r.* Argentina **59** 27.30S 58.50W
Paraguay S. America **59** 23.00S 57.00W
Paraiba *d.* Brazil **61** 7.30S 36.30W
Paraíba *r.* Brazil **59** 21.45S 41.10W
Paraibuna Brazil **59** 23.29S 45.32W
Paraisópolis Brazil **59** 22.33S 45.48W
Parakou Benin **38** 9.23N 2.40E
Paramagudi India **29** 9.33N 78.36E
Paramaribo Surinam **61** 5.52N 55.14W
Paramonga Peru **60** 10.42S 77.50W
Paraná Argentina **63** 31.45S 60.30W
Paranã *r.* Argentina **63** 34.00S 58.30W
Paranã Brazil **61** 12.33S 47.48W
Paraná *d.* Brazil **59** 24.30S 52.00W
Paranã *r.* Brazil **61** 12.30S 48.10W
Paranaguá Brazil **59** 25.32S 48.36W
Paranaíba Brazil **59** 19.44S 51.12W
Paranaíba *r.* Brazil **59** 20.00S 51.00W
Paranapanema *r.* Brazil **59** 22.30S 53.03W
Paranapiacaba, Serra *mts.* Brazil **59** 24.30S 49.15W
Paranavaí Brazil **59** 23.02S 52.36W
Parangaba Brazil **61** 3.45S 38.33W
Paraparaumu New Zealand **48** 40.55S175.00E
Paratoo Australia **46** 32.46S139.40E
Paray-le-Monial France **11** 46.27N 4.07E
Parchim Germany **14** 53.25N 11.51E
Parczew Poland **15** 51.39N 22.54E
Pardo *r.* Bahia Brazil **59** 15.40S 39.38W
Pardo *r.* Mato Grosso Brazil **59** 21.56S 52.07W
Pardo *r.* São Paulo Brazil **59** 20.10S 48.36W
Pardubice Czech. **14** 50.03N 15.45E
Parecis, Serra dos *mts.* Brazil **60** 13.30S 58.30W
Parent Canada **55** 47.55N 74.36W
Parent, Lac *l.* Canada **55** 48.40N 77.00W
Parepare Indonesia **26** 4.03S119.40E
Párga Greece **13** 39.17N 20.23E
Pargas Finland **17** 60.18N 22.18E
Paria, Golfo de *g.* Venezuela **60** 10.30S 62.00W
Paria, Península de *pen.* Venezuela **60** 10.45N 62.30W
Pariaguán Venezuela **60** 8.51N 64.43W
Pariaman Indonesia **26** 0.36S100.09E
Parichi Belorussia **15** 52.48N 29.25E
Parigi Indonesia **27** 0.49S120.10E
Parika Guyana **60** 6.51N 58.25W
Parima, Sierra *mts.* Venezuela **60** 2.30N 64.00W
Parinari Peru **60** 4.35S 74.25W
Paringa Australia **46** 34.10S140.49E
Parintins Brazil **61** 2.36S 56.44W
Paris France **9** 48.52N 2.20E
Paris Ky. U.S.A. **55** 38.13N 84.15W
Paris Tex. U.S.A. **53** 33.41N 95.33W
Parisienne *d.* France **9** 48.50N 2.20E
Parkano Finland **17** 62.01N 23.01E
Parker Ariz. U.S.A. **54** 34.09N114.17W
Parker, C. Canada **51** 75.04N 79.40W
Parker Dam U.S.A. **54** 34.18N114.10W
Parkersburg U.S.A. **55** 39.17N 81.33W
Parkes Australia **47** 33.10S148.13E
Parkland U.S.A. **54** 47.09N122.26W
Parlākimidi India **29** 18.46N 84.05E
Parma Italy **9** 44.48N 10.18E
Parma *r.* Italy **9** 44.56N 10.26E
Parma U.S.A. **55** 41.24N 81.44W
Parnaguá Brazil **61** 10.17S 44.39W
Parnaíba Brazil **61** 2.58S 41.46W
Parnaíba *r.* Brazil **61** 2.58S 41.47W
Parnassós *mtn.* Greece **13** 38.33N 22.35E
Parndana Australia **46** 35.44S137.14E
Pärnu Estonia **17** 58.24N 24.32E
Pärnu *r.* Estonia **17** 58.23N 24.29E
Paroo *r.* Australia **46** 31.30S143.34E
Páros *i.* Greece **13** 37.04N 25.11E
Parrakie Australia **46** 35.18S140.12E
Parral Chile **63** 36.09S 71.50W
Parramatta Australia **47** 33.50S150.57E
Parras Mexico **56** 25.25N102.11W
Parrett *r.* U.K. **5** 51.10N 3.00W
Parry, Kap *c.* Greenland **51** 76.50N 71.00W
Parry Is. Canada **51** 76.00N102.00W
Parry Sound *town* Canada **55** 45.21N 80.02W
Parsęta *r.* Poland **14** 54.12N 15.33E
Parsons Kans. U.S.A. **53** 37.20N 95.17W
Parthenay France **11** 46.39N 0.14W
Partille Sweden **17** 57.44N 12.07E
Partinico Italy **12** 38.03N 13.07E
Partry Mts. Rep. of Ire. **7** 53.40N 9.30W
Paru *r.* Brazil **61** 1.33S 52.38W
Parys R.S.A. **39** 26.54S 27.26E
Pasadena Calif. U.S.A. **54** 34.09N118.09W
Pasadena Tex. U.S.A. **53** 29.42N 95.14W
Pasaje Ecuador **60** 3.23S 79.50W
Pasay Phil. **27** 14.33N121.00E
Pasco U.S.A. **54** 46.14N119.06W
Pasewalk Germany **14** 53.30N 14.00E
Pasinler Turkey **30** 39.59N 41.41E
Pasir Puteh Malaysia **26** 5.50N102.24E
Påskallavik Sweden **17** 57.10N 16.27E
Pasley, C. Australia **43** 33.55S123.30E
Pasmore *r.* Australia **46** 31.07S139.48E
Paso de los Libres *town* Argentina **63** 29.45S 57.05W
Paso de los Toros *town* Uruguay **63** 32.49S 56.31W
Paso Robles U.S.A. **54** 35.38N120.41W
Paspébiac Canada **55** 48.03N 65.17W
Passau Germany **14** 48.35N 13.28E
Passero, C. Italy **12** 36.40N 15.08E
Passo Fundo Brazil **59** 28.16S 52.20W
Passos Brazil **59** 20.45S 46.38W
Pastaza *r.* Peru **60** 4.50S 76.25W
Pasto Colombia **60** 1.12N 77.17W
Pasuruan Indonesia **26** 7.38S112.44E
Paşcani Romania **15** 47.15N 26.44E
Patagonia *f.* Argentina **63** 42.20S 67.00W
Patchewollock Australia **46** 35.25S142.14E
Patea New Zealand **48** 39.46S174.29E
Pategi Nigeria **38** 8.44N 5.47E
Pate I. Kenya **37** 2.08S 41.02E
Paternò Italy **12** 37.34N 14.54E
Paterson U.S.A. **55** 40.55N 74.10W
Pathānkot India **28** 32.17N 75.39E
Pathein *see* Bassein Burma **29**
Pathfinder Resr. U.S.A. **54** 42.30N106.50W
Patía *r.* Colombia **60** 1.54N 78.30W
Patiāla India **28** 30.21N 76.27E
Patkai Hills Burma **29** 26.30N 95.40E
Pátmos *i.* Greece **13** 37.20N 26.33E
Patna India **29** 25.37N 85.12E
Patos Brazil **61** 6.55S 37.15W
Patos, Lagoa dos *l.* Brazil **59** 31.00S 51.10W
Patos de Minas Brazil **59** 18.35S 46.32W
Patquía Argentina **62** 30.02S 66.55W
Pátrai Greece **13** 38.15N 21.45E
Patraïkós Kólpos *g.* Greece **13** 38.15N 21.35E
Patrasuy Russian Fed. **18** 63.35N 61.50E
Patrickswell Rep. of Ire. **7** 52.36N 8.43W
Pattani Thailand **29** 6.53N101.16E
Patuca *r.* Honduras **57** 15.50N 84.18W
Pau France **11** 43.18N 0.22W
Pauillac France **11** 45.12N 0.44W
Paulina U.S.A. **54** 44.09N119.58W
Paulistana Brazil **61** 8.09S 41.09W
Paulo Afonso Brazil **61** 9.25S 38.15W
Pavia Italy **9** 45.10N 9.10E
Pavilly France **9** 49.34N 0.58E
Pavlodar Kazakhstan **20** 52.21N 76.59E
Pavlograd Ukraine **19** 48.34N 35.50E
Pavlovo Russian Fed. **18** 55.58N 43.05E
Pavlovsk Russian Fed. **19** 50.28N 40.07E
Pavlovskaya Russian Fed. **19** 46.18N 39.48E
Pavullo nel Frignano Italy **9** 44.20N 10.50E
Paxoí *i.* Greece **13** 39.12N 20.12E
Payette U.S.A. **54** 44.05N116.56W
Payne, L. Canada **51** 59.25N 74.00W
Paynes Find Australia **43** 29.15S117.41E
Paysandú Uruguay **63** 32.19S 58.05W
Pays de Caux *f.* France **9** 49.40N 0.40E
Pays de la Loire *d.* France **11** 47.30N 1.00W
Pazardzhik Bulgaria **13** 42.10N 24.22E
Peace *r.* Canada **50** 59.00N111.26W
Peace River *town* Canada **50** 56.15N117.18W
Peach Springs *town* U.S.A. **54** 35.32N113.25W
Peacock Hills Canada **50** 66.05N110.45W
Peake Creek *r.* Australia **46** 28.05S136.07E
Peak Hill *town* N.S.W. Australia **47** 32.47S148.13E
Peak Range *mts.* Australia **44** 23.18S148.30E
Peale, Mt. U.S.A. **54** 38.26N109.14W
Pearl *r.* U.S.A. **53** 30.15N 89.25W
Peary Land *f.* Greenland **64** 82.00N 35.00W
Pebane Mozambique **37** 17.14S 38.10E
Pebas Peru **60** 3.17S 71.55W
Peć Yugo. **13** 42.40N 20.17E
Pechenga Russian Fed. **16** 69.28N 31.04E
Pechora Russian Fed. **18** 65.14N 57.18E
Pechora *r.* Russian Fed. **18** 68.10N 54.00E
Pechorskaya Guba *g.* Russian Fed. **18** 69.00N 56.00E
Pechorskoye More *sea* Russian Fed. **18** 69.00N 55.00E
Pecos U.S.A. **52** 31.25N103.30W
Pecos *r.* U.S.A. **52** 29.45N101.25W
Pécs Hungary **15** 46.05N 18.14E
Peddie R.S.A. **39** 33.12S 27.07E
Pedregulho Brazil **59** 20.15S 47.29W
Pedreiras Brazil **61** 4.32S 44.40W
Pedrinhas Brazil **61** 11.12S 37.41W
Pedro Afonso Brazil **61** 8.59S 48.11W
Pedro de Valdivia Chile **62** 22.36S 69.40W
Pedro Juan Caballero Paraguay **59** 22.30S 55.44W
Peebinga Australia **46** 34.55S140.57E
Peebles U.K. **6** 55.39N 3.12W
Peebles U.S.A. **55** 38.57N 83.14W
Peel *r.* Canada **50** 68.13N135.00W
Peel I.o.M Europe **4** 54.14N 4.42W
Peel Inlet Australia **43** 32.35S115.44E
Peel Pt. Canada **50** 73.22N114.35W
Peene *r.* Germany **14** 53.53N 13.49E
Peera Peera Poolanna L. Australia **44** 26.43S137.42E
Pegasus B. New Zealand **48** 43.15S173.00E
Pegu Burma **29** 17.18N 96.31E
Pegunungan Van Rees *mts.* Indonesia **27** 2.35S138.15E
Pegu Yoma *mts.* Burma **29** 18.40N 96.00E
Pehuajó Argentina **63** 35.50S 61.50W
Peipus, L. Estonia / Russian Fed. **18** 58.30N 27.30E
Peixe Brazil **61** 12.03S 48.32W
Pekalongan Indonesia **26** 6.54S109.37E
Pekanbaru Indonesia **26** 0.33N101.20E
Peking *see* Beijing China **25**
Pelat, Mont *mtn.* France **11** 44.17N 6.41E
Peleaga *mtn.* Romania **15** 45.22N 22.54E
Peleng *i.* Indonesia **27** 1.30S123.10E
Peleniya Moldavia **15** 47.58N 27.48E
Pelkum Germany **8** 51.38N 7.44E
Pello Finland **16** 66.47N 24.00E
Pelly *r.* Canada **50** 62.50N137.35W
Pelly Bay *town* Canada **51** 68.38N 89.45W
Pelly L. Canada **51** 65.59N101.12W
Pelotas Brazil **59** 31.45S 52.20W
Pematangsiantar Indonesia **26** 2.59N 99.01E
Pemba Mozambique **37** 13.02S 40.30E
Pemba I. Tanzania **37** 5.10S 39.45E
Pemberton Australia **43** 34.28S116.01E
Pembroke Canada **55** 45.49N 77.07W
Pembroke U.K. **5** 51.41N 4.57W
Penang *see* Pinang, Pulau *i.* Malaysia **26**
Peñaranda de Bracamonte Spain **10** 40.54N 5.13W
Penarth U.K. **5** 51.26N 3.11W
Peñas, Cabo de *c.* Spain **10** 43.42N 5.52W
Penas, Golfo de *g.* Chile **63** 47.20S 75.00W
Pendine U.K. **5** 51.44N 4.33W
Pendleton U.S.A. **54** 45.40N118.47W
Penedo Brazil **61** 10.16S 36.33W
Penetanguishene Canada **55** 44.47N 79.55W
Penganga *r.* India **29** 18.52N 79.56E
Pengshui China **25** 29.17N108.13E
Penicuik U.K. **6** 55.49N 3.13W
Peninsular Malaysia *d.* Malaysia **26** 5.00N102.00E
Penneshaw Australia **46** 35.42S137.55E
Pennines, Alpes *mts.* Switz. **9** 46.08N 7.34E
Pennsylvania *d.* U.S.A. **55** 40.45N 77.30W
Penn Yan U.S.A. **55** 42.41N 77.03W
Penny Highland *mtn.* Canada **51** 67.10N 66.50W
Penobscot *r.* U.S.A. **55** 44.30N 68.50W
Penola Australia **46** 37.23S140.21E
Penong Australia **43** 31.55S133.01E
Penonomé Panama **57** 8.30N 80.20W
Penrith Australia **47** 33.47S150.44E
Penrith U.K. **4** 54.40N 2.45W
Penryn U.K. **5** 50.10N 5.07W
Pensacola U.S.A. **53** 30.30N 87.12W
Pensacola Mts. Antarctica **64** 84.00S 45.00W
Penshurst Australia **46** 37.52S142.20E
Penticton Canada **50** 49.29N119.38W
Pentland Australia **44** 20.32S145.24E
Pentland Firth *str.* U.K. **6** 58.40N 3.00W
Pentland Hills U.K. **6** 55.50N 3.20W
Penza Russian Fed. **18** 53.11N 45.00E
Penzance U.K. **5** 50.07N 5.32W
Penzhinskaya Guba *g.* Russian Fed. **21** 61.00N163.00E
Peoria Ariz. U.S.A. **54** 33.35N112.14W
Peoria Ill. U.S.A. **53** 40.43N 89.38W
Perabumulih Indonesia **26** 3.29S104.14E
Perche, Collines du *hills* France **9** 48.30N 0.40E
Percival Lakes Australia **42** 21.25S125.00E
Pereira Colombia **60** 4.47N 75.46W
Perekop Ukraine **19** 46.10N 33.42E
Perené *r.* Peru **62** 11.02S 74.19W
Perevolotskiy Russian Fed. **18** 51.10N 54.15E
Pereyaslav-Khmelnitskiy Ukraine **15** 50.05N 31.28E
Pergamino Argentina **63** 33.53S 60.35W
Pergine Valsugana Italy **9** 46.04N 11.14E
Péribonca *r.* Canada **55** 48.45N 72.05W
Périers France **9** 49.11N 1.25W
Périgueux France **11** 45.12N 0.44E
Perija, Sierra de *mts.* Venezuela **60** 10.30N 72.30W
Peri L. Australia **46** 30.44S143.34E
Perm Russian Fed. **18** 58.01N 56.10E
Pernambuco *d.* Brazil **61** 8.00S 39.00W
Pernatty L. Australia **46** 31.31S137.14E
Pernik Bulgaria **13** 42.35N 23.03E
Perniö Finland **17** 60.12N 23.08E
Péronne France **8** 49.56N 2.57E
Perosa Argentina Italy **9** 44.58N 7.10E
Perpendicular, Pt. Australia **47** 35.03S150.50E
Perpignan France **11** 42.42N 2.54E
Perranporth U.K. **5** 50.21N 5.09W
Perryton U.S.A. **52** 36.23N100.48W
Persepolis *ruins* Iran **31** 29.55N 53.00E
Perth Australia **43** 31.58S115.49E
Perth Canada **55** 44.54N 76.15W
Perth U.K. **6** 56.24N 3.28W
Perth Amboy U.S.A. **55** 40.32N 74.17W
Peru S. America **60** 10.00S 75.00W
Perugia Italy **12** 43.06N 12.24E
Péruwelz Belgium **8** 50.32N 3.36E
Pervomaysk Ukraine **15** 48.03N 30.50E
Pervouralsk Russian Fed. **18** 56.59N 59.58E
Pesaro Italy **9** 43.54N 12.54E
Pescara Italy **12** 42.27N 14.13E
Pescara *r.* Italy **12** 42.28N 14.13E
Pescia Italy **9** 43.54N 10.41E
Peshāwar Pakistan **28** 34.01N 71.40E
Pesqueira Brazil **61** 8.24S 36.38W
Pessac France **11** 44.48N 0.38W
Peşteana Jiu Romania **15** 44.50N 23.15E
Pestovo Russian Fed. **18** 58.32N 35.42E
Petah Tiqwa Israel **32** 32.05N 34.53E
Petaluma U.S.A. **54** 38.14N122.39W
Pétange Lux. **8** 49.32N 5.56E
Petare Venezuela **60** 10.31N 66.50W
Petatlán Mexico **56** 17.31N101.16W
Petauke Zambia **37** 14.16S 31.21E
Petawawa Canada **55** 45.54N 77.17W
Peterborough S.A. Australia **46** 33.00S138.51E
Peterborough Vic. Australia **46** 38.36S142.55E
Peterborough Canada **55** 44.18N 78.19W
Peterborough U.K. **5** 52.35N 0.14W
Peterhead U.K. **6** 57.30N 1.46W
Peterlee U.K. **4** 54.45N 1.18W
Petermann Ranges *mts.* Australia **42** 25.00S129.46E
Petersburg W.Va. U.S.A. **55** 39.00N 79.07W
Petersfield U.K. **5** 51.00N 0.56W
Petitot *r.* Canada **50** 60.14N123.29W
Petit St. Bernard, Col du *pass* France / Italy **9** 45.40N 6.53E
Petoskey U.S.A. **55** 45.22N 84.59W
Petra *ruins* Jordan **32** 30.19N 35.26E
Petrich Bulgaria **13** 41.25N 23.13E
Petrikov Belorussia **15** 52.09N 28.30E
Petrodvorets Russian Fed. **18** 59.50N 29.57E
Petrolina Brazil **61** 9.22S 40.30W
Petropavlovsk Kazakhstan **20** 54.53N 69.13E
Petropavlovsk Kamchatskiy Russian Fed. **21** 53.03N158.43E
Petrópolis Brazil **59** 22.30S 43.06W
Petroşani Romania **15** 45.25N 23.22E
Petrovaradin Yugo. **15** 45.16N 19.55E
Petrovsk Russian Fed. **18** 52.20N 45.24E
Petrovsk Zabaykal'skiy Russian Fed. **21** 51.20N108.55E
Petrozavodsk Russian Fed. **18** 61.46N 34.19E
Petrus Steyn R.S.A. **39** 27.38S 28.08E
Peureulak Indonesia **26** 4.48N 97.45E
Pevek Russian Fed. **21** 69.41N170.19E
Pézenas France **11** 43.28N 3.25E
Pezinok Czech. **15** 48.18N 17.17E
Pezmog Russian Fed. **18** 61.50N 51.45E
Pfaffenhofen Germany **14** 48.31N 11.30E
Pfalzel Germany **8** 49.47N 6.41E
Pforzheim Germany **14** 48.53N 8.41E

Privolzhskaya Vozvyshennost f. Russian Fed. 18 53.15N 45.45E
Prizren Yugo. 13 42.13N 20.42E
Proddatūr India 29 14.44N 78.33E
Progreso Mexico 57 21.20N 89.40W
Prokopyevsk Russian Fed. 20 53.55N 86.45E
Prome Burma 29 18.50N 95.14E
Prome see Pyè Burma 29
Propriá Brazil 61 10.15S 36.51W
Proserpine Australia 44 20.24S148.34E
Prostějov Czech. 15 49.29N 17.07E
Provence-Côte d'Azur d. France 11 43.45N 6.00E
Providence U.S.A. 55 41.50N 71.25W
Providence Mts. U.S.A. 54 34.55N115.35W
Providencia, Isla de i. Colombia 57 13.21N 81.22W
Provins France 9 48.34N 3.18E
Provo U.S.A. 54 40.14N111.39W
Prozor Bosnia-Herzegovina 15 43.49N 17.37E
Prudhoe Bay town U.S.A. 50 70.20N148.25W
Pruszcz Gdański Poland 15 54.17N 18.40E
Pruszków Poland 15 52.11N 20.48E
Prut r. Romania / Ukraine 15 45.29N 28.14E
Pruzhany Belorussia 15 52.23N 24.28E
Prüm Germany 8 50.12N 6.25E
Prüm r. Germany 8 49.50N 6.29E
Prydz B. Antarctica 64 68.30S 74.00E
Przemyśl Poland 15 49.48N 22.48E
Przeworsk Poland 15 50.05N 22.29E
Przhevalsk Kyrgyzstan 24 42.31N 78.22E
Psará i. Greece 13 38.34N 25.35E
Psel Ukraine 19 49.00N 33.30E
Pskov Russian Fed. 18 57.48N 28.00E
Pskovskoye, Ozero l. Russian Fed. 18 58.00N 27.55E
Ptich Belorussia 15 52.15N 28.49E
Ptich r. Belorussia 15 52.09N 28.52E
Ptolemais Greece 13 40.31N 21.41E
Puán Argentina 63 37.30S 62.45W
Pucallpa Peru 60 8.21S 74.33W
Pucarani Bolivia 62 16.23S 68.30W
Pucheng China 25 27.55N118.31E
Pudasjärvi Finland 16 65.25N 26.50E
Pudozh Russian Fed. 18 61.50N 36.32E
Pudozhgora Russian Fed. 18 62.18N 35.54E
Puebla Mexico 56 19.03N 98.10W
Puebla d. Mexico 56 18.30N 98.00W
Pueblo U.S.A. 52 38.16N104.37W
Pueblo Hundido Chile 62 26.23S 70.03W
Puelches Argentina 63 38.09S 65.58W
Puelén Argentina 63 37.32S 67.38W
Puente Alta Chile 63 33.37S 70.35W
Puente-Genil Spain 10 37.24N 4.46W
Puerto Aisén Chile 63 45.27S 72.58W
Puerto Ángel Mexico 56 15.40N 96.29W
Puerto Armuelles Panama 57 8.19N 82.15W
Puerto Ayacucho Venezuela 60 5.39N 67.32W
Puerto Barrios Guatemala 57 15.41N 88.32W
Puerto Bermúdez Peru 60 10.20S 75.00W
Puerto Berrío Colombia 60 6.28N 74.28W
Puerto Cabello Venezuela 60 10.29N 68.02W
Puerto Cabezas Nicaragua 57 14.02N 83.24W
Puerto Carreño Colombia 60 6.08N 67.27W
Puerto Casado Paraguay 62 22.20S 57.55W
Puerto Coig Argentina 63 50.54S 69.15W
Puerto Cortés Costa Rica 57 8.58N 83.32W
Puerto Cortés Honduras 57 15.50N 87.55W
Puerto de Nutrias Venezuela 60 8.07N 69.18W
Puerto de Santa María Spain 10 36.36N 6.14W
Puerto Heath Bolivia 60 12.30S 68.40W
Puerto Juárez Mexico 57 21.26N 86.51W
Puerto La Cruz Venezuela 60 10.14N 64.40W
Puerto Leguízamo Colombia 60 0.12S 74.46W
Puertollano Spain 10 38.41N 4.07W
Puerto Lobos Argentina 63 42.01S 65.04W
Puerto Madryn Argentina 63 42.46S 65.02W
Puerto Maldonado Peru 60 12.37S 69.11W
Puerto Melendez Peru 60 4.30S 77.30W
Puerto Montt Chile 63 41.28S 73.00W
Puerto Natales Chile 63 51.44S 72.31W
Puerto Páez Venezuela 60 6.13N 67.28W
Puerto Peñasco Mexico 56 31.20N113.33W
Puerto Pinasco Paraguay 59 22.36S 57.53W
Puerto Plata Dom. Rep. 57 19.48N 70.41W
Puerto Princesa Phil. 26 9.46N118.45E
Puerto Quepos Costa Rica 57 9.28N 84.10W
Puerto Rey Colombia 60 8.48N 76.34W
Puerto Rico C. America 57 18.20N 66.30W
Puerto Rico Trench Atlantic Oc. 57 19.50N 66.00W
Puerto Saavedra Chile 63 38.47S 73.24W
Puerto Santa Cruz Argentina 63 50.03S 68.35W
Puerto Sastre Paraguay 59 22.02S 58.00W
Puerto Siles Bolivia 62 12.48S 65.05W
Puerto Tejado Colombia 60 3.16N 76.22W
Puerto Vallarta Mexico 56
Puerto Varas Chile 63 41.20S 73.00W
Pugachev Russian Fed. 18 52.02N 48.49E
Puglia d. Italy 13 41.00N 16.40E
Puisaye, Collines de la hills France 9 47.34N 3.28E
Pukaki, L. New Zealand 48 44.00S170.10E
Pukekohe New Zealand 48 37.12S174.56E
Pukeuri New Zealand 48 45.02S171.02E
Pukhovichi Belorussia 15 53.28N 28.18E
Pula Croatia 14 44.52N 13.53E
Pulacayo Bolivia 62 20.25S 66.41W
Pulawy Poland 15 51.25N 21.57E
Pulkkila Finland 16 64.16N 25.52E
Pullman U.S.A. 54 46.44N117.10W
Pulog mtn. Phil. 27 16.50N120.50E
Pulozero Russian Fed. 18 68.22N 33.15E
Pultusk Poland 15 52.42N 21.02E
Puma Tanzania 37 5.02S 34.46E
Puncak Jaya mtn. Indonesia 27 4.00S137.15E
Pune India 28 18.34N 73.58E
Punjab d. India 28 30.30N 75.15E
Puno Peru 60 15.53S 70.03W
Punta Alta town Argentina 63 38.50S 62.00W
Punta Arenas town Chile 63 53.10S 70.56W
Puntabie Australia 46 32.15S134.13E
Punta Delgada town Argentina 63 42.43S 63.38W
Punta Gorda town Belize 57 16.10N 88.45W
Puntarenas Costa Rica 57 10.00N 84.50W
Punto Fijo Venezuela 60 11.50N 70.16W
Puolanka Finland 16 64.52N 27.40E
Puquio Peru 60 14.44S 74.07W
Pur r. Russian Fed. 20 67.30N 75.30E
Purari r. P.N.G. 27 7.49S145.10E
Puri India 29 19.49N 85.54E
Purnea India 29 25.47N 87.28E
Purros Namibia 39 18.38S 12.59E
Purūlia India 29 23.20N 86.24E
Purus r. Brazil 60 3.58S 61.25W
Pusan S. Korea 25 35.05N129.02E
Pushkin Russian Fed. 18 59.43N 30.22E
Pushkino Russian Fed. 19 51.16N 47.09E
Pustoshka Russian Fed. 18 56.20N 29.20E
Putao Burma 29 27.22N 97.27E
Putaruru New Zealand 48 38.03S175.47E
Putian China 25 25.32N119.02E
Puting, Tanjung c. Indonesia 26 3.35S111.52E
Putorana, Gory mts. Russian Fed. 21 68.30N 96.00E
Putsonderwater R.S.A. 39 29.14S 21.50E
Puttalam Sri Lanka 29 8.02N 79.50E
Puttgarden Germany 14 54.30N 11.13E
Putumayo r. Brazil 60 3.05S 68.10W
Puulavesi l. Finland 17 61.50N 26.42E
Puyallup U.S.A. 54 47.11N122.18W
Puy de Dôme mtn. France 11 45.46N 2.56E
Puysegur Pt. New Zealand 48 46.10S166.35E
Püspökladány Hungary 15 47.19N 21.07E
Pwani d. Tanzania 37 7.00S 39.00E
Pweto Zaïre 37 8.27S 28.52E
Pwllheli U.K. 4 52.53N 4.25W
Pyaozero, Ozero l. Russian Fed. 18 66.00N 31.00E
Pyapon Burma 29 16.15N 95.40E
Pyasina r. Russian Fed. 21 73.10N 84.55E
Pyatigorsk Russian Fed. 19 44.04N 43.06E
Pyè Burma 29 18.50N 95.14E
Pyhä r. Finland 16 64.28N 24.13E
Pyhäjärvi l. Oulu Finland 16 63.35N 25.57E
Pyhäjärvi l. Turku-Pori Finland 17 61.00N 22.20E
Pyhäjoki Finland 16 64.28N 24.14E
Pyinmana Burma 29 19.45N 96.12E
Pyongyang N. Korea 25 39.00N125.47E
Pyramid U.S.A. 54 40.05N119.43W
Pyramid Hill town Australia 46 36.03S144.24E
Pyramid L. U.S.A. 54 40.00N119.35W
Pyrénées mts. France / Spain 11 42.40N 0.30E
Pyrzyce Poland 14 53.10N 14.55E
Pytteggja mtn. Norway 17 62.13N 7.42E

Q

Qaanaaq see Thule Greenland 51
Qā'emshahr Iran 31 36.28N 52.53E
Qagcaka China 29 32.32N 81.49E
Qahâ Egypt 32 30.17N 31.12E
Qalāt Afghan. 28 32.07N 66.54E
Qal'eh-ye Now Afghan 31 34.58N 63.04E
Qalyūb Egypt 32 30.11N 31.12E
Qamdo China 24 31.11N 97.18E
Qanâtir Muhammad 'Alī Egypt 32 30.12N 31.08E
Qandahār Afghan. 28 31.36N 65.47E
Qandala Somali Rep. 35 11.23N 49.53E
Qaqortoq see Julianehåb Greenland 51
Qārah Egypt 30 27.37N 26.30E
Qareh Sū Iran 31 34.52N 51.25E
Qareh Sū r. Iran 31 35.58N 56.25E
Qarqan He r. China 24 40.56N 86.27E
Qārūn, Birkat l. Egypt 32 29.30N 30.40E
Qasigiannguit see Christianshåb Greenland 51
Qaşr al Farāfirah Egypt 30 27.15N 28.10E
Qaşr-e Qand Iran 31 26.13N 60.37E
Qatanā Syria 32 33.27N 36.04E
Qatar Asia 31 25.20N 51.10E
Qattara Depression see Qaţţārah, Munkhafaḑ al mts. Egypt 32 29.40N 30.36E
Qattara Depression see Qaţţārah, Munkhafaḑ al f. Egypt 30
Qaţţārah, Munkhafaḑ al f. Egypt 30 29.40N 27.30E
Qāyen Iran 31 33.44N 59.07E
Qazvīn Iran 31 36.16N 50.00E
Qeqertarsuaq see Godhavn Greenland 51
Qeqertarsuatsiaat see Fiskenaesset Greenland 51
Qeshm Iran 31 26.58N 57.17E
Qeshm i. Iran 31 26.48N 55.48E
Qezel Owzan r. Iran 31 36.44N 49.27E
Qezi'ot Israel 32 30.52N 34.28E
Qianjiang China 25 29.31N108.46E
Qiemo China 24 38.08N 85.33E
Qilian Shan mts. China 24 38.30N 99.20E
Qimantag mts. China 24 37.45N 89.40E
Qinā Egypt 30 26.10N 32.43E
Qinā, Wādī r. Egypt 30 26.07N 32.42E
Qingdao China 25 36.04N120.22E
Qinghai d. China 24 36.15N 96.00E
Qinghai Hu l. China 24 36.40N100.00E
Qingjiang China 25 28.02N115.23E
Qingxu China 25 37.36N112.21E
Qingyang China 24 36.06N107.49E
Qing Zang Gaoyuan f. China 24 34.00N 84.30E
Qinhuangdao China 25 39.55N119.37E
Qin Ling mts. China 25 33.40N109.00E
Qinzhou China 25 21.57N108.37E
Qiqihar China 25 47.23N124.00E
Qira China 24 37.02N 80.53E
Qiryat Ata Israel 32 32.48N 35.06E
Qiryat Gat Israel 32 31.37N 34.47E
Qiryat Shemona Israel 32 33.13N 35.35E
Qishn Yemen 28 15.25N 51.40E
Qom Iran 31 34.40N 50.57E
Qornet'es Sauda mtn. Lebanon 32 34.17N 36.04E
Qoţūr Iran 31 38.28N 44.25E
Quairading Australia 43 32.00S117.22E
Quakenbrück Germany 8 52.41N 7.59E
Quambatook Australia 46 35.52S143.36E
Quambone Australia 47 30.54S147.55E
Quang Ngai Vietnam 26 15.09N108.50E
Quang Tri Vietnam 26 16.46N107.11E
Quan Long Vietnam 26 9.11N105.09E
Quanzhou Fujian China 25 24.57N118.36E
Qu'Appelle r. Canada 51 51.13N 98.05W
Quaqtaq Canada 51 61.05N 69.36W
Quaraí Brazil 63 30.23S 56.27W
Quaraí r. Brazil 63 30.12S 57.36W
Quartu Sant'Elena Italy 12 39.14N 9.11E
Quartzsite U.S.A. 54 33.40N114.13W
Qūchān Iran 31 37.04N 58.29E
Queanbeyan Australia 47 35.24S149.17E
Québec Canada 55 46.50N 71.15W
Québec d. Canada 51 52.00N 72.00W
Quebracho Uruguay 63 31.57S 57.53W
Quedlinburg Germany 14 51.48N 11.09E
Queen Charlotte Is. Canada 50 53.00N132.30W
Queen Charlotte Str. Canada 50 51.00N129.00W
Queen Elizabeth Is. Canada 51 78.30N 99.00W
Queen Maud G. Canada 51 68.30N 99.00W
Queen Maud Range mts. Antarctica 64 86.20S165.00W
Queens Channel Australia 42 14.46S129.24E
Queenscliff Australia 47 38.17S144.42E
Queensland d. Australia 44 23.30S144.00E
Queenstown Australia 45 42.07S145.33E
Queenstown New Zealand 48 45.03S168.41E
Queenstown R.S.A. 39 31.52S 26.51E
Queguay Grande r. Uruguay 63 32.09S 58.09W
Queimadas Brazil 61 10.58S 39.38W
Quela Angola 36 9.18S 17.05E
Quelimane Mozambique 37 17.53S 36.57E
Quemado U.S.A. 54 34.20N108.30W
Quequén Argentina 63 38.34S 58.42W
Querétaro Mexico 56 20.38N100.23W
Querétaro d. Mexico 56 21.03N100.00W
Quesnel Canada 50 53.03N122.31W
Quetta Pakistan 28 30.15N 67.00E
Quettehou France 9 49.36N 1.18W
Quevedo Ecuador 60 0.59S 79.27W
Quezaltenango Guatemala 56 14.50N 91.30W
Quezon City Phil. 27 14.39N121.01E
Quibdo Colombia 60 5.40N 76.38W
Quiberon France 11 47.29N 3.07W
Quilán, C. Chile 63 43.16S 74.27W
Quilengues Angola 36 14.09S 14.04E
Quillabamba Peru 60 12.50S 72.50W
Quillacollo Bolivia 62 17.26S 66.17W
Quillota Chile 63 32.53S 71.16W
Quilpie Australia 44 26.37S144.15E
Quilpué Chile 63 33.03S 71.27W
Quimilí Argentina 62 27.35S 62.25W
Quimper France 11 48.00N 4.06W
Quimperlé France 11 47.52N 3.33W
Quincy Ill. U.S.A. 53 39.55N 91.22W
Quincy Wash. U.S.A. 54 47.14N119.51W
Qui Nhon Vietnam 26 13.47N109.11E
Quintanar de la Orden Spain 10 39.36N 3.05W
Quintana Roo d. Mexico 57 19.00N 88.00W
Quinto Spain 10 41.25N 0.30W
Quionga Mozambique 37 10.37S 40.31E
Quiriguá ruins Guatemala 57 15.20N 89.25W
Quirindi Australia 47 31.30S150.42E
Quissanga Mozambique 37 12.24S 40.33E
Quissico Mozambique 39 24.42S 34.44E
Quiterajo Mozambique 37 11.46S 40.25E
Quito Ecuador 60 0.14S 78.30W
Quorn Australia 46 32.20S138.02E
Qurayyah, Wādī r. Egypt 32 30.26N 34.01E
Qurdud Sudan 35 10.17N 29.56E
Qurlurtuuq Canada 50 67.49N115.12W
Qu Xian China 25 28.57N118.52E

R

Raahe Finland 16 64.41N 24.29E
Raalte Neth. 8 52.22N 6.17E
Raasay i. U.K. 6 57.25N 6.05W
Raas Caseyr c. Somali Rep. 35 12.00N 51.30E
Rába r. Hungary 15 47.42N 17.38E
Raba Indonesia 26 8.27S118.45E
Rabat Morocco 34 34.02N 6.51W
Rabbit Flat town Australia 42 20.10S129.53E
Rābor Iran 31 29.18N 56.56E
Racconigi Italy 9 44.46N 9.46E
Race, C. Canada 51 46.40N 53.10W
Rach Gia Vietnam 26 10.02N105.05E
Racibórz Poland 15 50.06N 18.13E
Racine U.S.A. 53 42.42N 87.50W
Rădăuţi Romania 15 47.51N 25.55E
Radebeul Germany 14 51.06N 13.41E
Radekhov Ukraine 15 50.18N 24.35E
Radium Hill town Australia 46 32.30S140.32E
Radom Poland 15 51.26N 21.10E
Radomir Bulgaria 13 42.32N 22.56E
Radomsko Poland 15 51.05N 19.25E
Radomyshl Ukraine 15 50.30N 29.14E
Radöy i. Norway 17 60.38N 5.05E
Radstock U.K. 5 51.17N 2.25W
Radstock, C. Australia 46 33.11S134.21E
Radwā, Jabal mtn. Saudi Arabia 30 24.36N 38.18E
Rae Canada 50 62.50N116.03W
Raeren Germany 8 50.41N 6.07E
Raeside, L. Australia 43 29.30S122.00E
Rafaela Argentina 62 31.16S 61.44W
Rafah Egypt 32 31.18N 34.15E
Rafaï C.A.R. 35 4.56N 23.55E
Rafsanjān Iran 31 30.24N 56.00E
Rafsanjān Iran 28 30.24N 56.00E
Ragged, Mt. Australia 43 33.27S123.27E
Ragunda Sweden 16 63.06N 16.23E
Ragusa Italy 12 36.56N 14.44E
Raha Indonesia 27 4.50S122.43E
Raḩā, Ḩarrat ar f. Saudi Arabia 32 28.00N 36.35E
Rāichūr India 28 16.15N 77.20E
Raiganj India 29 25.38N 88.11E
Raigarh India 29 21.53N 83.28E
Rainbow Australia 46 35.56S142.01E
Rainier, Mt. U.S.A. 54 46.52N121.46W
Raipur India 29 21.16N 81.42E
Ra's Saudi Arabia 30 23.35N 38.36E
Rājahmundry India 29 17.01N 81.52E
Rajang r. Malaysia 26 2.10N112.45E
Rājapālaiyam India 28 9.26N 77.36E
Rājasthān d. India 28 27.00N 74.00E
Rājgarh Madhya P. India 28 23.56N 76.58E
Rājkot India 28 22.18N 70.53E
Rakaia New Zealand 48 43.45S172.01E
Rakaia r. New Zealand 48 43.52S172.13E
Rakhov Ukraine 15 48.02N 24.10E
Rakitnoye Ukraine 15 51.18N 27.10E
Rakops Botswana 39 21.00S 24.32E
Rakov Belorussia 15 53.58N 26.59E
Rakulka Russian Fed. 18 62.19N 46.52E
Rakvåg Norway 16 63.47N 10.10E
Rakvere Estonia 18 59.22N 26.28E
Raleigh U.S.A. 53 35.46N 78.39W
Rama Nicaragua 57 12.09N 84.15W
Rāmah Saudi Arabia 31 25.33N 47.08E
Rām Allāh Jordan 32 31.55N 35.12E
Ramallo Argentina 63 33.28S 60.02W
Ramat Gan Israel 32 32.05N 34.48E
Rambouillet France 9 48.39N 1.50E
Rame Head Australia 47 37.50S149.25E
Rame Head U.K. 5 50.18N 4.13W
Ramelton Rep. of Ire. 7 55.02N 7.40W
Rāmhormoz Iran 31 31.14N 49.37E
Ramillies Belgium 8 50.39N 4.56E
Ramingstein Austria 14 47.04N 13.50E
Ramla Israel 32 31.56N 34.52E
Ramlu mtn. Ethiopia 35 13.20N 41.45E
Ramona Calif. U.S.A. 54 33.08N116.52W
Ramore Canada 55 48.27N 80.20W
Ramos Arizpe Mexico 56 25.35N100.59W
Rāmpur Uttar P. India 29 28.48N 79.03E
Ramree I. Burma 29 19.10N 93.40E
Ramsey I.o.M. Europe 4 54.19N 4.23W
Ramsey England U.K. 5 52.27N 0.06W
Ramsey L. Canada 55 47.15N 82.16W
Ramsgate U.K. 5 51.20N 1.25E
Rāmshīr Iran 31 30.54N 49.24E
Ramsjö Sweden 17 62.11N 15.39E
Ramu r. P.N.G. 27 4.00S144.40E
Ranau Malaysia 26 5.58N116.41E
Rancagua Chile 63 34.10S 70.45W
Rānchī India 29 23.22N 85.20E
Rand Australia 47 35.34S146.35E
Randalstown U.K. 7 54.45N 6.20W
Randburg R.S.A. 39 26.07S 28.02E
Randers Denmark 17 56.28N 10.03E
Randsburg U.S.A. 54 35.22N117.39W
Randsfjorden l. Norway 17 60.25N 10.24E
Råne r. Sweden 16 65.52N 22.19E
Rånea Sweden 16 65.52N 22.18E
Ranfurly New Zealand 48 45.08S170.08E
Rangely U.S.A. 54 40.05N108.48W
Rangia India 29 26.28N 91.38E
Rangiora New Zealand 48 43.18S172.38E
Rangitaiki r. New Zealand 48 37.55S176.50E
Rangoon see Yangon Burma 29
Rankin Inlet town Canada 51 62.52N 92.00W
Rankins Springs town Australia 47 33.52S146.18E
Rannoch, Loch U.K. 6 56.41N 4.20W
Rann of Kachchh f. India 28 23.50N 69.50E
Ranong Thailand 29 9.59N 98.40E
Rantauprapat Indonesia 26 2.05N 99.46E
Rantekombola mtn. Indonesia 26 3.30S119.58E
Rapallo Italy 9 44.20N 9.14E
Rapid Bay town Australia 46 35.33S138.09E
Rapid City U.S.A. 52 44.05N103.14W
Raquette Lake town U.S.A. 55 43.49N 74.41W
Ra's al Ḩadd c. Oman 28 22.32N 59.49E
Ra's al Khaymah U.A.E. 31 25.48N 55.56E
Ra's an Nabq town Egypt 32 29.36N 34.51E
Ra's an Naqb town Jordan 32 30.30N 35.29E
Ra's Banās c. Egypt 35 23.54N 35.48E
Ras Dashen mtn. Ethiopia 35 13.20N 38.10E
Rås Ghârib Egypt 32 28.22N 33.04E
Rashid Egypt 32 31.25N 30.25E
Rasht Iran 31 37.18N 49.38E
Raška Yugo. 13 43.17N 20.37E
Rason L. Australia 43 28.46S124.20E
Ratangarh India 28 28.05N 74.36E
Rat Buri Thailand 26 13.30N 99.50E
Ratcatchers L. Australia 46 32.40S143.13E
Rathcormack Rep. of Ire. 7 52.05N 8.18W
Rathdrum Rep. of Ire. 7 52.56N 6.15W
Rathenow Germany 14 52.37N 12.21E
Rathlin I. U.K. 7 55.17N 6.15W
Rath Luirc Rep. of Ire. 7 52.21N 8.41W
Rathmullen Rep. of Ire. 7 55.06N 7.32W
Ratlām India 28 23.18N 75.06E
Ratnāgiri India 28 16.59N 73.18E
Ratno Ukraine 15 51.40N 24.32E
Raton U.S.A. 52 36.54N104.24W
Rattlesnake Range mts. U.S.A. 54 42.45N107.10W
Rattray Head U.K. 6 57.37N 1.50W
Rättvik Sweden 17 60.53N 15.06E
Rauch Argentina 63 36.47S 59.05W
Raufoss Norway 17 60.43N 10.37E
Raul Soares Brazil 59 20.04S 42.27W
Rauma Finland 17 61.08N 21.30E
Rauma r. Norway 16 62.32N 7.43E
Raurkela India 29 22.16N 85.01E
Rautas Sweden 16 68.00N 19.55E
Rāvar Iran 31 31.14N 56.51E
Rava-Russkaya Ukraine 15 50.15N 23.36E
Ravena U.S.A. 55 42.29N 73.49W
Ravenna Italy 9 44.25N 12.12E
Ravensburg Germany 14 47.47N 9.37E
Ravenshoe Australia 44 17.37S145.29E
Ravensthorpe Australia 43 33.35S120.02E
Ravi r. Pakistan 28 30.30N 72.13E
Rāwalpindi Pakistan 28 33.40N 73.08E
Rawāndūz Iraq 31 36.38N 44.32E
Rawene New Zealand 48 35.24S173.30E
Rawicz Poland 14 51.37N 16.52E
Rawlinna Australia 43 31.00S125.21E
Rawlins U.S.A. 54 41.47N107.14W
Rawson Argentina 63 34.40S 60.02W
Raya mtn. Indonesia 26 0.45S112.45E
Rāyen Iran 31 29.34N 57.26E
Raymond U.S.A. 54 46.41N123.44W
Raymond Terrace Australia 47 32.47S151.45E
Razan Iran 31 35.22N 49.02E
Razdelnaya Ukraine 15 46.50N 30.02E
Razgrad Bulgaria 15 43.32N 26.30E
Ré, Île de i. France 11 46.10N 1.26W
Reading U.K. 5 51.27N 0.57W
Reading U.S.A. 55 40.20N 75.56W
Realicó Argentina 63 35.02S 64.14W
Reay Forest f. U.K. 6 58.17N 4.48W
Rebecca, L. Australia 43 30.07S122.32E
Rebi Indonesia 27 6.24S134.07E
Reboly Russian Fed. 18 63.50N 30.49E
Recalde Argentina 63 36.39S 61.05W
Recherche, Archipelago of the is. Australia 43 34.05S122.45E
Rechitsa Belorussia 15 52.21N 30.24E
Recife Brazil 61 8.06S 34.53W
Recklinghausen Germany 8 51.36N 7.11E
Reconquista Argentina 62 29.08S 59.38W
Recreo Argentina 62 29.20S 65.04W
Red r. Canada 51 50.30N 96.50W
Red r. U.S.A. 53 31.10N 92.00W
Red r. see Hong Hà r. Vietnam 26
Red Bluff U.S.A. 54 40.11N122.15W
Redcar U.K. 4 54.37N 1.04W
Red Cliffs town Australia 46 34.22S142.13E
Red Deer Canada 50 52.15N113.48W
Redding U.S.A. 54 40.35N122.24W
Redditch U.K. 5 52.18N 1.57W
Rede r. U.K. 4 55.08N 2.13W
Redhill town Australia 46 33.34S138.12E
Red L. U.S.A. 53 48.00N 95.00W
Red Lake town Canada 51 50.59N 93.40W
Redlands U.S.A. 54 34.03N117.11W
Red Lodge U.S.A. 54 45.11N109.15W
Redmond U.S.A. 54 44.17N121.11W
Red Oak U.S.A. 53 41.01N 95.15W
Redondela Spain 10 42.15N 8.38W
Redondo Portugal 10 38.39N 7.33W
Redondo Beach town U.S.A. 54 33.51N118.23W
Redrock U.S.A. 54 32.35N111.19W
Redruth U.K. 5 50.14N 5.14W
Red Sea Africa / Asia 35 20.00N 39.00E
Red Volta r. Ghana 38 10.32N 0.31W
Redwood City U.S.A. 54 37.29N122.13W
Ree, Lough Rep. of Ire. 7 53.31N 7.58W
Reed City U.S.A. 55 43.54N 85.31W
Reedsport U.S.A. 54 43.42N124.06W
Reefton New Zealand 48 42.07S171.52E
Reese r. U.S.A. 54 40.39N116.54W
Reftele Sweden 17 57.11N 13.35E
Rega r. Poland 14 54.10N 15.18E
Regensburg Germany 14 49.01N 12.07E
Reggane Algeria 34 26.30N 0.30E
Reggio Calabria Italy 12 38.07N 15.38E
Reggio Emilia-Romagna Italy 9 44.40N 10.37E
Reghin Romania 15 46.47N 24.42E
Regina Canada 50 50.30N104.38W
Regnéville France 9 49.01N 1.33W
Rehoboth Namibia 39 23.19S 17.10E
Rehovot Israel 32 31.54N 34.46E
Reigate U.K. 5 51.14N 0.13W
Reims France 9 49.15N 4.02E
Reindeer L. Canada 50 57.00N102.20W
Reinosa Spain 10 43.01N 4.09W
Remanso Brazil 61 9.41S 42.04W
Remarkable, Mt. Australia 46 32.48S138.10E
Rembang Indonesia 26 6.45S111.22E
Remeshk Iran 31 26.52N 58.46E
Remich Lux. 8 49.34N 6.23E
Remiremont France 11 48.01N 6.35E
Remscheid Germany 8 51.10N 7.11E
Rena Norway 17 61.08N 11.22E
Rendsburg Germany 14 54.19N 9.39E
Renfrew Canada 55 45.28N 76.41W
Rengat Indonesia 26 0.26S102.35E
Rengo Chile 63 34.25S 70.52W
Renheji China 25 31.56N115.07E
Reni Ukraine 15 45.28N 28.17E
Renkum Neth. 8 51.59N 5.46E
Renmark Australia 46 34.10S140.45E
Renner Springs town Australia 44 18.20S133.48E
Rennes France 9 48.06N 1.40W
Reno r. Italy 9 44.36N 12.17E
Reno U.S.A. 54 39.31N119.48W
Renton U.S.A. 54 47.30N122.11W
Réo Burkina 38 12.20N 2.27W
Repki Ukraine 15 51.47N 31.06E
Republic Wash. U.S.A. 54 48.39N118.44W
Republican r. U.S.A. 53 39.05N 94.50W
Republic of Ireland Europe 7 53.00N 8.00W
Republic of South Africa Africa 39 28.30S 24.50E
Repulse B. Australia 44 20.36S148.43E
Repulse Bay town Canada 51 66.35N 86.20W
Requa U.S.A. 54 41.34N124.05W
Requena Peru 60 5.05S 73.52W
Requena Spain 10 39.29N 1.08W
Resistencia Argentina 62 27.28S 59.00W
Resolute Canada 51 74.40N 95.00W
Resolution I. Canada 51 61.30N 65.00W

St. Augustine U.S.A. **53** 29.54N 81.19W
St. Augustin Saguenay Canada **51** 51.14N 58.39W
St. Austell U.K. **5** 50.20N 4.48W
St. Barthélemy *i.* Leeward Is. **57** 17.55N 62.50W
St. Bees Head U.K. **4** 54.31N 3.39W
St. Boniface Canada **51** 49.54N 97.07W
St. Brides B. U.K. **5** 51.48N 5.03W
St. Brieuc France **11** 48.31N 2.45W
St. Calais France **9** 47.55N 0.45E
St. Catharines Canada **55** 43.10N 79.15W
St. Catherine's Pt. U.K. **5** 50.34N 1.18W
St. Céré France **11** 44.52N 1.53E
St. Cloud U.S.A. **53** 45.34N 94.10W
St. Croix *i.* U.S.V.Is. **57** 17.45N 64.35W
St. David's U.K. **5** 51.54N 5.16W
St. David's Head U.K. **5** 51.55N 5.19W
St. Denis France **9** 48.56N 2.21E
St. Dié France **11** 48.17N 6.57E
St. Dizier France **9** 48.38N 4.58E
Sainte-Agathe-des-Monts Canada **55** 46.03N 74.19W
Sainte Anne de Beaupré Canada **55** 47.02N 70.58W
St. Elias, Mt. U.S.A. **50** 60.20N139.00W
St. Éloi Canada **55** 48.03N 69.14W
Sainte Menehould France **14** 49.05N 4.54E
Sainte Menehould France **9** 49.05N 4.54E
Sainte Mère-Église France **9** 49.24N 1.19W
Saintes France **11** 45.44N 0.38W
Sainte-Thérèse-de-Blainville Canada **55** 45.38N 73.50W
St. Étienne France **11** 45.26N 4.26E
St. Fargeau France **9** 47.38N 3.04E
Saintfield U.K. **7** 54.28N 5.50W
St. Florent France **11** 42.41N 9.18E
St. Florentin France **9** 48.00N 3.44E
St. Flour France **11** 45.02N 3.05E
St. Gallen Switz. **14** 47.25N 9.23E
St. Gaudens France **11** 43.07N 0.44E
St. George Australia **45** 28.03S148.30E
St. George N.B. Canada **55** 45.08N 66.56W
St. George U.S.A. **54** 37.06N113.35W
St. Georges Belgium **8** 50.37N 5.20E
St. George's Grenada **57** 12.04N 61.44W
St. Georges Guiana **61** 3.54N 51.48W
St. George's Channel Rep. of Ire./U.K. **7** 51.30N 6.20W
St. Germain France **9** 48.53N 2.04E
St. Gheorghe's Mouth *est.* Romania **13** 44.51N 29.37E
St. Gilles-Croix-de-Vie France **11** 46.42N 1.56W
St. Girons France **11** 42.59N 1.08E
St. Gotthard Pass Switz. **11** 46.30N 8.55E
St. Govan's Head U.K. **5** 51.36N 4.55W
St. Helena B. R.S.A. **39** 32.35S 18.05E
St. Helens U.K. **4** 53.28N 2.43W
St. Helens U.S.A. **54** 45.52N122.48W
St. Helier U.K. **5** 49.12N 2.07W
St. Hilaire-du-Harcouët France **9** 48.35N 1.06W
St. Hubert Belgium **8** 50.02N 5.22E
St. Hyacinthe Canada **55** 45.38N 72.57W
St. Ignace U.S.A. **55** 45.53N 84.44W
St. Ives U.K. **5** 50.13N 5.29W
St. Jean Canada **55** 45.18N 73.16W
St. Jean France **11** 45.17N 6.21E
St. Jean, Lac *l.* Canada **55** 48.35N 72.00W
St. Jean de Matha Canada **55** 46.14N 73.33W
St. Jean Pied-de-Port France **11** 43.10N 1.14W
St. Jérôme Canada **55** 45.47N 74.01W
St. John Canada **55** 45.16N 66.03W
St. John *r.* Canada **55** 45.15N 66.04W
St. John's Antigua **57** 17.07N 61.51W
St. John's Canada **51** 47.34N 52.41W
St. Johns U.S.A. **54** 34.30N109.22W
St. Johnsbury U.S.A. **55** 44.25N 72.01W
St. John's Pt. U.K. **7** 54.14N 5.39W
St. Jordi, Golf de *g.* Spain **10** 40.50N 1.10E
St. Joseph Mich. U.S.A. **55** 42.05N 86.30W
St. Joseph Mo. U.S.A. **53** 39.45N 94.51W
St. Joseph, L. Canada **51** 51.05N 90.35W
St. Junien France **11** 45.53N 0.55E
St. Just-en-Chaussée France **9** 49.30N 2.26E
St. Kitts-Nevis Leeward Is. **57** 17.20N 62.45W
St. Laurent Que. Canada **55** 45.31N 73.42W
St. Laurent du Maroni Guiana **61** 5.30N 54.02W
St. Lawrence *r.* Canada **55** 48.45N 68.30W
St. Lawrence, G. of Canada **51** 48.00N 62.00W
St. Lawrence I. U.S.A. **50** 63.00N170.00W
St. Lô France **9** 49.07N 1.05W
St. Louis Senegal **34** 16.01N 16.30W
St. Louis U.S.A. **53** 38.40N 90.15W
St. Lucia Windward Is. **57** 14.05N 61.00W
St. Lucia, L. R.S.A. **39** 28.05S 32.26E
St. Maixent France **11** 46.25N 0.12W
St. Malo France **9** 48.39N 2.00W
St. Malo, Golfe de *g.* France **11** 49.20N 2.00W
St.-Marc Haiti **57** 19.08N 72.41W
St. Margaret's Hope U.K. **6** 58.49N 2.57W
St. Maries U.S.A. **54** 47.19N116.35W
St. Martin *i.* Leeward Is. **57** 18.05N 63.05W
St. Martin U.K. **5** 49.27N 2.34W
St. Martin's *i.* U.K. **5** 49.57N 6.16W
St. Mary U.K. **5** 49.14N 2.10W
St.Mary Peak Australia **46** 31.30S138.35E
St. Marys Australia **45** 41.33S148.12E
St. Mary's *i.* U.K. **5** 49.55N 6.16W
St. Matthew I. U.S.A. **50** 60.30N172.45W
St. Maur France **9** 48.48N 2.30E
St. Maurice *r.* Canada **55** 46.21N 72.31W
St. Moritz Switz. **14** 46.30N 9.51E
St. Nazaire France **11** 47.17N 2.12W
St. Neots U.K. **5** 52.14N 0.16W
St. Niklaas Belgium **8** 51.10N 4.09E
St. Omer France **11** 50.45N 2.15E
St. Pacôme Canada **55** 47.24N 69.58W
St. Pascal Canada **55** 47.32N 69.48W
St. Paul Pyr. Or. France **11** 42.49N 2.29E
St. Paul Minn. U.S.A. **53** 45.00N 93.10W
St. Paul du Nord Canada **55** 48.27N 69.16W
St. Peter Port U.K. **5** 49.27N 2.32W
St. Petersburg U.S.A. **53** 27.45N 82.40W
St. Pierre Char. Mar. France **11** 45.57N 1.19W
St. Pierre S. Mar. France **9** 49.48N 0.29E
St. Pierre and Miquelon *is.* N. America **51** 47.00N 56.15W
St. Pierre-Église France **9** 49.40N 1.24W
St. Pölten Austria **14** 48.13N 15.37E
St. Quentin France **9** 49.51N 3.17E
St. Seine-l'Abbaye France **9** 47.26N 4.47E
St. Siméon Canada **55** 47.56N 69.58W
St. Stephen Canada **55** 45.12N 67.18W
St. Thomas Canada **55** 42.47N 81.12W
St. Thomas *i.* U.S.V.Is. **57** 18.22N 64.57W
St. Tropez France **11** 43.16N 6.39E
St. Truiden Belgium **8** 50.49N 5.11E
St. Valéry France **9** 49.52N 0.43E
St. Vallier France **11** 45.11N 4.49E
St. Vincent, G. Australia **46** 35.00S138.05E
St. Vincent and the Grenadines Windward Is. **57** 13.00N 61.15W
St. Vith Belgium **8** 50.15N 6.08E
St. Wendel Germany **8** 49.27N 7.10E
St. Yrieix France **11** 45.31N 1.12E
Saitama *d.* Japan **23** 35.55N139.00E
Sajama *mtn.* Bolivia **62** 18.06S 69.00W
Saka Kenya **37** 0.09S 39.18E
Sakai Japan **23** 34.35N135.28E
Sakākah Saudi Arabia **30** 29.59N 40.12E
Sakania Zaïre **37** 12.44S 28.34E
Sakarya *r.* Turkey **30** 41.08N 30.36E
Sakété Benin **38** 6.45N 2.45E
Sakhalin *i.* Russian Fed. **25** 50.00N143.00E
Sakht-Sar Iran **31** 36.54N 50.41E
Sakivier R.S.A. **36** 30.50S 20.26E
Sakrivier R.S.A. **39** 30.53S 20.24E
Sakuma Japan **23** 35.05N137.48E
Sal *r.* Russian Fed. **19** 47.33N 40.40E
Sala Sweden **17** 59.55N 16.36E
Salaca *r.* Latvia **17** 57.45N 24.21E
Salacgriva Latvia **17** 57.45N 24.21E
Salado *r.* Buenos Aires Argentina **63** 35.44S 57.22W
Salado *r.* Santa Fé Argentina **63** 31.40S 60.41W
Salado *r.* La Pampa Argentina **63** 36.15S 66.55W
Salado *r.* Mexico **56** 26.46N 98.55W
Salaga Ghana **38** 8.36N 0.32W
Salālah Oman **28** 17.00N 54.04E
Salamanca Spain **10** 40.58N 5.40W
Salamina Colombia **60** 5.24N 75.31W
Salatiga Indonesia **26** 7.15S110.34E
Salbris France **9** 47.26N 2.03E
Salcombe U.K. **5** 50.14N 3.47W
Saldaña Spain **10** 42.32N 4.48W
Saldanha R.S.A. **39** 33.00S 17.56E
Saldanha B. R.S.A. **39** 33.05S 17.50E
Saldus Latvia **17** 56.40N 22.30E
Sale Australia **47** 38.06S147.06E
Salekhard Russian Fed. **18** 66.33N 66.35E
Salem India **29** 11.38N 78.08E
Salem Ind. U.S.A. **55** 38.38N 86.06W
Salem Oreg. U.S.A. **54** 44.57N123.01W
Sälen Sweden **17** 61.10N 13.16E
Salerno Italy **12** 40.41N 14.45E
Salerno, Golfo di *g.* Italy **12** 40.30N 14.45E
Salford U.K. **4** 53.30N 2.17W
Salgótarján Hungary **15** 48.07N 19.48E
Salgueiro Brazil **61** 8.04S 39.05W
Salima Malaŵi **37** 13.45S 34.29E
Salim's Tanzania **37** 10.37S 36.33E
Salina Cruz Mexico **56** 16.11N 95.12W
Salinas Ecuador **60** 2.13S 80.58W
Salinas U.S.A. **54** 36.40N121.38W
Salinas *r.* U.S.A. **52** 36.45N121.48W
Salinópolis Brazil **61** 0.37S 47.20W
Salins France **11** 46.56N 5.53E
Salisbury U.K. **5** 51.04N 1.48W
Salisbury Md. U.S.A. **55** 38.22N 75.36W
Salisbury Plain *f.* U.K. **5** 51.15N 1.55W
Salluit Canada **51** 62.10N 75.40W
Salmās Iran **31** 38.13N 44.50E
Salmi Russian Fed. **18** 61.19N 31.46E
Salmon U.S.A. **54** 45.11N113.55W
Salmon *r.* U.S.A. **54** 45.51N116.46W
Salmon Gums Australia **43** 32.59S121.39E
Salmon River Mts. U.S.A. **54** 44.45N115.30W
Salo Finland **17** 60.23N 23.08E
Salò Italy **9** 45.36N 10.31E
Salobreña Spain **10** 36.45N 3.35W
Salome U.S.A. **54** 33.47N113.37W
Salon France **11** 43.38N 5.06E
Salonta Romania **15** 46.48N 21.40E
Salsk Russian Fed. **19** 46.30N 41.33E
Salso *r.* Italy **12** 37.07N 13.57E
Salsomaggiore Terme Italy **9** 44.49N 9.59E
Salt *r.* U.S.A. **54** 33.23N112.18W
Salta Argentina **62** 24.47S 65.24W
Salta *d.* Argentina **62** 25.00S 65.00W
Saltdal Norway **16** 67.06N 15.25E
Saltee Is. Rep. of Ire. **7** 52.08N 6.36W
Saltfjorden *est.* Norway **16** 67.15N 14.10E
Saltfleet U.K. **4** 53.25N 0.11E
Salt Fork *r.* U.S.A. **53** 36.41N 97.05W
Saltillo Mexico **56** 25.30N101.00W
Salt Lake City U.S.A. **54** 40.46N111.53W
Salto Argentina **63** 34.17S 60.15W
Salto Brazil **59** 23.10S 47.16W
Salto *r.* Italy **12** 42.23N 12.54E
Salto Uruguay **63** 31.23S 57.58W
Salto da Divisa Brazil **61** 16.04S 40.00W
Salto Grande, Embalse de *resr.* Argentina/Uruguay **63** 31.00S 57.50W
Salton Sea *l.* U.S.A. **54** 33.19N115.50W
Saluzzo Italy **9** 44.39N 7.29E
Salvador Brazil **61** 12.58S 38.29W
Salween *r.* Burma **29** 16.30N 97.33E
Salyany Azerbaijan **31** 39.36N 48.59E
Salzbrunn Namibia **39** 24.23S 18.00E
Salzburg Austria **14** 47.54N 13.03E
Salzburg *d.* Austria **14** 47.25N 13.15E
Salzgitter Germany **14** 52.02N 10.22E
Salzwedel Germany **14** 52.51N 11.09E
Samālūt Egypt **32** 28.18N 30.43E
Samaná Dom. Rep. **57** 19.14N 69.20W
Samana Cay *i.* Bahamas **57** 23.05N 73.45W
Samanga Tanzania **37** 8.24S 39.18E
Samannūd Egypt **32** 30.58N 31.14E
Samar *i.* Phil. **27** 11.45N125.15E
Samara Russian Fed. **18** 53.10N 50.15E
Samara *r.* Russian Fed. **18** 53.17N 50.42E
Samarai P.N.G. **44** 10.37S150.40E
Samarinda Indonesia **26** 0.30S117.09E
Samarkand Uzbekistan **20** 39.40N 66.57E
Sāmarrā Iraq **31** 34.13N 43.52E
Sambalpur India **29** 21.28N 84.04E
Sambor Ukraine **15** 49.31N 23.10E
Samborombón, Bahía *b.* Argentina **63** 36.00S 57.00W
Sambre *r.* Belgium **8** 50.29N 4.52E
Samburu Kenya **37** 3.46S 39.17E
Samch'ŏk S. Korea **25** 37.30N129.10E
Same Tanzania **37** 4.10S 37.43E
Samobor Slovenia **14** 45.48N 15.43E
Samorogouan Burkina **38** 11.21N 4.57W
Sámos *i.* Greece **13** 37.44N 26.45E
Samothráki *i.* Greece **13** 40.26N 25.35E
Sampit Indonesia **26** 2.34S112.59E
Samsang China **29** 30.22N 82.50E
Samsun Turkey **30** 41.17N 36.22E
Samtredia Georgia **19** 42.10N 42.22E
Samui, Ko *i.* Thailand **29** 9.30N100.00E
Samur *r.* Russian Fed. **19** 42.00N 48.20E
Samut Sakhon Thailand **29** 13.32N100.17E
San Mali **38** 13.21N 4.57W
San *r.* Poland **15** 50.25N 22.20E
Sanaba Burkina **38** 12.25N 3.47W
Sanaga *r.* Cameroon **38** 3.35N 9.40E
Sanandaj Iran **31** 35.18N 47.01E
San Andreas U.S.A. **54** 38.12N120.41W
San Andrés, Isla de *i.* Colombia **57** 12.33N 81.42W
San Andrés Tuxtla Mexico **56** 18.27N 95.13W
San Angelo U.S.A. **52** 31.28N100.28W
San Antonio Chile **63** 33.35S 71.38W
San Antonio Tex. U.S.A. **52** 29.25N 98.30W
San Antonio, C. Cuba **57** 21.50N 84.57W
San Antonio, Cabo *c.* Argentina **63** 36.40S 56.42W
San Antonio, Punta *c.* Mexico **56** 29.45N115.41W
San Antonio Abad Spain **10** 38.58N 1.18E
San Antonio de Areco Argentina **63** 34.16S 59.30W
San Antonio Oeste Argentina **63** 40.44S 64.57W
San Benedetto Italy **12** 42.57N 13.53E
San Benedetto Po Italy **9** 45.02N 10.55E
San Benito Guatemala **57** 16.55N 89.54W
San Bernardino U.S.A. **54** 34.06N117.17W
San Bernardo Chile **63** 33.36S 70.43W
San Blas, C. U.S.A. **53** 29.40N 85.25W
San Bonifacio Italy **9** 45.24N 11.16E
San Carlos Chile **63** 36.25S 71.58W
San Carlos Mexico **56** 29.01N100.51W
San Carlos Nicaragua **57** 11.07N 84.47W
San Carlos Phil. **27** 15.59N120.22E
San Carlos Venezuela **60** 1.55N 67.04W
San Carlos Venezuela **60** 9.39N 68.35W
San Carlos de Bariloche Argentina **63** 41.08S 71.15W
San Carlos del Zulia Venezuela **60** 9.01N 71.55W
Sancerre France **9** 47.20N 2.51E
Sancerrois, Collines du *hills* France **9** 47.25N 2.45E
San Clemente U.S.A. **54** 33.26N117.37W
San Clemente *i.* U.S.A. **54** 32.54N118.29W
San Cristóbal Argentina **62** 30.20S 61.41W
San Cristóbal Dom. Rep. **57** 18.27N 70.07W
San Cristóbal Venezuela **60** 7.46N 72.15W
Sancti Spíritus Cuba **57** 21.55N 79.28W
Sand Norway **17** 59.29N 6.15E
Sanda *i.* U.K. **6** 55.17N 5.34W
Sandakan Malaysia **26** 5.52N118.04E
Sanday *i.* U.K. **6** 59.15N 2.33W
Sandbach U.K. **4** 53.09N 2.23W
Sandefjord Norway **17** 59.08N 10.14E
Sanders U.S.A. **54** 35.13N109.20W
Sandgate Australia **47** 27.18S153.00E
Sandhornöy *i.* Norway **16** 67.05N 14.10E
Sandia Peru **60** 14.14S 69.25W
San Diego U.S.A. **54** 32.43N117.09W
San Diego, C. Argentina **63** 54.38S 65.05W
Sand Lake *town* Canada **55** 47.46N 84.31W
Sandnes Norway **17** 58.51N 5.44E
Sandness U.K. **6** 60.18N 1.38W
Sandoa Zaïre **36** 9.41S 22.56E
Sandomierz Poland **15** 50.41N 21.45E
San Donà di Piave Italy **9** 45.38N 12.34E
Sandover *r.* Australia **44** 21.43S136.32E
Sandoway Burma **29** 18.28N 94.20E
Sandown U.K. **5** 50.39N 1.09W
Sandö *i.* Faroe Is. **16** 61.50N 6.45W
Sandpoint *town* U.S.A. **54** 48.17N116.34W
Sandringham U.K. **4** 52.50N 0.30E
Sandstone Australia **43** 27.59S119.17E
Sandusky Ohio U.S.A. **55** 41.27N 82.42W
Sandveld *f.* Namibia **39** 21.25S 20.00E
Sandviken Sweden **17** 60.37N 16.46E
Sandy U.S.A. **54** 40.35N111.53W
Sandy Bight *b.* Australia **43** 33.53S123.25E
Sandy C. Australia **44** 24.42S153.17E
Sandy Creek *town* U.S.A. **55** 43.39N 76.05W
Sandy L. Ont. Canada **51** 53.00N 93.07W
San Enrique Argentina **63** 35.47S 60.22W
San Felipe Chile **63** 32.45S 70.44W
San Felipe Colombia **60** 1.55N 67.06W
San Felipe Mexico **56** 31.00N114.52W
San Felipe Venezuela **60** 10.25N 68.40W
San Fernando Argentina **63** 34.26S 58.34W
San Fernando Chile **63** 34.35S 71.00W
San Fernando Phil. **27** 16.39N120.19E
San Fernando Spain **10** 36.28N 6.12W
San Fernando Trinidad **60** 10.16N 61.28W
San Fernando de Apure Venezuela **60** 7.35N 67.15W
San Fernando de Atabapo Venezuela **60** 4.03N 67.45W
Sanford *r.* Australia **42** 27.22S115.53E
Sanford Fla. U.S.A. **53** 28.49N 81.17W
San Francisco Argentina **62** 31.29S 62.06W
San Francisco U.S.A. **54** 37.48N122.24W
San Francisco *r.* U.S.A. **54** 32.59N109.22W
San Francisco, C. Ecuador **60** 0.50N 80.05W
San Francisco de Macorís Dom. Rep. **57** 19.19N 70.15W
Sanga-Tolon Russian Fed. **21** 61.44N149.30E
Sanggan He *r.* China **25** 40.23N115.18E
Sangha *r.* Congo **36** 1.10S 16.47E
Sangihe *i.* Indonesia **27** 3.30N125.30E
Sangihe, Kepulauan *is.* Indonesia **27** 2.45N125.20E
San Gil Colombia **60** 6.35N 73.08W
San Giovanni in Persiceto Italy **9** 44.38N 11.11E
Sangkulirang Indonesia **26** 1.00N117.58E
Sāngli India **28** 16.55N 74.37E
Sangmélima Cameroon **38** 2.55N 12.01E
Sangonera *r.* Spain **10** 37.58N 1.04W
San Gottardo, Passo del *pass* Switz. **14** 46.30N 8.55E
San Gregorio Uruguay **63** 32.37S 55.40W
Sangri China **24** 29.18N 92.05E
San Ignacio Bolivia **62** 16.23S 60.59W
San Ignacio Paraguay **62** 26.52S 57.03W
San Isidro Argentina **63** 34.29S 58.31W
Saniyah, Hawr as *l.* Iraq **31** 31.52N 46.50E
San Javier Argentina **63** 30.40S 59.55W
San Javier Bolivia **62** 16.22S 62.38W
San Javier Chile **63** 35.35S 71.45W
San Joaquin *r.* U.S.A. **54** 38.03N121.50W
San Jorge, Golfo *g.* Argentina **63** 46.00S 66.00W
San José Costa Rica **57** 9.59N 84.04W
San José Guatemala **56** 13.58N 90.50W
San Jose U.S.A. **54** 37.20N121.53W
San José de Chiquitos Bolivia **62** 17.53S 60.45W
San José de Feliciano Argentina **63** 30.25S 58.45W
San José de Guanipa Venezuela **60** 8.54N 64.09W
San José del Guaviare Colombia **60** 2.35N 72.38W
San José de Mayo Uruguay **63** 34.20S 56.42W
San José de Ocuné Colombia **60** 4.15N 70.20W
San Juan Argentina **62** 31.30S 68.30W
San Juan *d.* Argentina **62** 31.00S 68.30W
San Juan *r.* Costa Rica **57** 10.50N 83.40W
San Juan Dom. Rep. **57** 18.40N 71.05W
San Juan Peru **62** 15.20S 75.09W
San Juan Phil. **27** 8.25N126.22E
San Juan Puerto Rico **57** 18.29N 66.08W
San Juan *r.* U.S.A. **54** 37.18N110.28W
San Juan, C. Argentina **63** 54.45S 63.50W
San Juan Bautista Spain **10** 39.05N 1.30E
San Juan del Norte Nicaragua **57** 10.58N 83.40W
San Juan de los Morros Venezuela **60** 9.53N 67.23W
San Juan del Río Querétaro Mexico **56** 20.23N100.00W
San Juan Mts. U.S.A. **54** 37.35N107.10W
San Julián Argentina **63** 49.19S 67.40W
San Justo Argentina **63** 30.47S 60.35W
Sankt Niklaus Switz. **9** 46.11N 7.48E
Sankt-Peterburg Russian Fed. **18** 59.55N 30.25E
San Lázaro, Cabo *c.* Mexico **56** 24.50N112.18W
San Leonardo Spain **10** 41.49N 3.04W
Şanliurfa Turkey **30** 37.08N 38.45E
San Lorenzo Argentina **63** 32.45S 60.44W
San Lorenzo *mtn.* Chile **63** 47.37S 72.19W
San Lorenzo Ecuador **60** 1.17N 78.50W
San Lorenzo de El Escorial Spain **10** 40.34N 4.08W
Sanlúcar de Barrameda Spain **10** 36.46N 6.21W
Sanlúcar la Mayor Spain **10** 37.26N 6.18W
San Lucas Bolivia **62** 20.06S 65.07W
San Lucas, Cabo *c.* Mexico **56** 22.50N109.55W
San Luis Argentina **63** 33.20S 66.20W
San Luis *d.* Argentina **63** 34.00S 66.00W
San Luis Cuba **57** 20.13N 75.50W
San Luis Obispo U.S.A. **54** 35.17N120.40W
San Luis Potosí Mexico **56** 22.10N101.00W
San Luis Potosí *d.* Mexico **56** 23.00N100.00W
San Marcos U.S.A. **52** 29.54N 97.57W
San Marino Europe **9** 43.55N 12.27E
San Marino *town* San Marino **9** 43.55N 12.27E
San Martin *r.* Bolivia **62** 12.25S 64.25W
San Mateo U.S.A. **54** 37.35N122.19W
San Matías Bolivia **60** 16.22S 58.24W
San Matías, Golfo *g.* Argentina **63** 41.30S 64.00W
Sanmenxia China **25** 34.46N111.17E
San Miguel *r.* Bolivia **62** 12.25S 64.25W
San Miguel *r.* Bolivia **60** 13.52S 63.56W
San Miguel El Salvador **57** 13.28N 88.10W
San Miguel del Monte Argentina **63** 35.25S 58.49W
San Miguel de Tucumán Argentina **62** 26.49S 65.13W
San Miguelito Panama **57** 9.02N 79.30W
Sannār Sudan **35** 13.31N 33.38E
Sannicandro Italy **12** 41.50N 15.34E
San Nicolas Argentina **63** 33.20S 60.13W
Sanok Poland **15** 49.35N 22.10E
San Pablo Phil. **27** 13.58N121.10E
San Pedro Buenos Aires Argentina **63** 33.40S 59.41W
San Pedro Jujuy Argentina **62** 24.14S 64.50W
San Pedro Dom. Rep. **57** 18.30N 69.18W
San Pedro Paraguay **59** 24.08S 57.08W
San Pedro, Punta *c.* Costa Rica **57** 8.38N 83.45W
San Pedro, Sierra de *mts.* Spain **10** 39.20N 6.20W
San Pedro de las Colonias Mexico **56** 25.50N102.59W
San Pedro Sula Honduras **57** 15.26N 88.01W
San Pellegrino Terme Italy **9** 45.50N 9.40E
San Pietro *i.* Italy **12** 39.09N 8.16E
Sanquhar U.K. **6** 55.22N 3.56W
San Quintín Mexico **56** 30.28N115.58W
San Rafael U.S.A. **54** 37.59N122.31W
San Raphael Argentina **63** 34.40S 68.21W
San Remo Italy **9** 43.48N 7.46E
San Salvador Argentina **63** 31.37S 58.30W
San Salvador *i.* Bahamas **57** 24.00N 74.32W
San Salvador El Salvador **57** 13.40N 89.10W
San Salvador de Jujuy Argentina **62** 24.10S 65.20W
San Sebastián Argentina **63** 53.15S 68.30W
San Sebastián Spain **10** 43.19N 1.59W
San Severo Italy **12** 41.40N 15.24E
Santa *r.* Peru **60** 9.00S 78.35W
Santa Ana Argentina **62** 27.20S 65.35W
Santa Ana Bolivia **62** 13.45S 65.35W
Santa Ana El Salvador **57** 14.00N 89.31W
Santa Ana U.S.A. **54** 33.44N117.54W
Santa Bárbara Mexico **56** 26.48N105.49W
Santa Barbara U.S.A. **54** 34.25N119.42W
Santa Catarina *d.* Brazil **59** 27.00S 52.00W
Santa Clara Cuba **57** 22.25N 79.58W
Santa Clara Calif. U.S.A. **54** 37.21N121.57W
Santa Clara Utah U.S.A. **54** 37.08N113.39W
Santa Clotilde Peru **60** 2.25S 73.35W
Santa Comba Dão Portugal **10** 40.24N 8.08W
Santa Cruz *d.* Argentina **63** 48.00S 69.30W
Santa Cruz *r.* Argentina **63** 50.03S 68.35W
Santa Cruz Bolivia **62** 17.45S 63.14W
Santa Cruz *d.* Bolivia **62** 17.45S 62.00W
Santa Cruz Canary Is. **34** 28.27N 16.14W
Santa Cruz U.S.A. **54** 36.58N122.08W
Santa Cruz *i.* U.S.A. **54** 34.01N119.45W
Santa Cruz Is. Solomon Is. **40** 10.30S166.00E
Santa Domingo Mexico **54** 25.32N112.02W
Santa Elena Argentina **63** 31.00S 59.50W
Santa Elena, C. Costa Rica **57** 10.54N 85.56W
Santa Fé Argentina **63** 31.40S 60.40W
Santa Fé *d.* Argentina **62** 30.00S 61.00W
Santa Fe U.S.A. **52** 35.42N106.57W
Santa Filomena Brazil **61** 9.07S 45.56W
Santa Inés, Isla *i.* Chile **63** 53.40S 73.00W
Santa Isabel Argentina **63** 36.15S 66.55W
Santa Isabel do Morro Brazil **61** 11.36S 50.37W
Santa Lucía Uruguay **63** 34.27S 56.24W
Santa Lucía *r.* Uruguay **63** 34.48S 56.22W
Santa Lucia Range *mts.* U.S.A. **54** 36.00N121.20W
Santa Margherita Ligure Italy **9** 44.20N 9.12E
Santa Maria Brazil **59** 29.40S 53.47W
Santa Maria U.S.A. **54** 34.57N120.26W
Santa Maria di Leuca, Capo *c.* Italy **13** 39.47N 18.24E
Santa Maria Madalena Brazil **59** 21.58S 42.02W
Santa Marta Colombia **60** 11.18N 74.10W
Santa Marta, Sierra Nevada de *mts.* Colombia **60** 11.20N 73.00W
Santa Monica U.S.A. **54** 34.01N118.30W
Santana do Livramento Brazil **63** 30.53S 55.31W
Santander Colombia **60** 3.00N 76.25W
Santander Spain **10** 43.28N 3.48W
Santañy Spain **10** 39.20N 3.07E
Santarém Brazil **61** 2.26S 54.41W
Santarém Portugal **10** 39.14N 8.40W
Santa Rosa Argentina **63** 36.00S 64.40W
Santa Rosa Bolivia **60** 10.36S 67.25W
Santa Rosa Brazil **59** 27.52S 54.29W
Santa Rosa Honduras **57** 14.47N 88.46W
Santa Rosa *i.* U.S.A. **54** 33.58N120.06W
Santa Rosa Calif. U.S.A. **54** 38.26N122.34W
Santa Rosa de Cabal Colombia **60** 4.52N 75.37W
Santa Rosalía Mexico **56** 27.19N112.17W
Santa Rosa Range *mts.* U.S.A. **54** 41.00N117.40W
Santa Vitória do Palmar Brazil **59** 33.31S 53.21W
Sant Feliu de Guíxols Spain **10** 41.47N 3.02E
Santhià Italy **9** 45.22N 8.10E
Santiago Chile **63** 33.27S 70.40W
Santiago Dom. Rep. **57** 19.30N 70.42W
Santiago Panama **57** 8.08N 80.59W
Santiago *r.* Peru **60** 4.30S 77.48W
Santiago de Compostela Spain **10** 42.52N 8.33W
Santiago de Cuba Cuba **57** 20.00N 75.49W
Santiago del Estero Argentina **62** 27.50S 64.15W
Santiago del Estero *d.* Argentina **62** 27.40S 63.30W
Santiago Vázquez Uruguay **63** 34.48S 56.21W
Santo Amaro Brazil **61** 12.35S 38.41W
Santo André Brazil **59** 23.39S 46.29W
Santo Angelo Brazil **59** 28.18S 54.16W
Santo Antônio do Içá Brazil **60** 3.05S 67.57W
Santo Domingo Dom. Rep. **57** 18.30N 69.57W
Santoña Spain **10** 43.27N 3.26W
Santos Brazil **59** 23.56S 46.22W
Santos Dumont Brazil **59** 21.30S 43.34W
Santo Tomás Peru **60** 14.34S 72.30W
Santo Tomé Argentina **62** 28.31S 56.03W
Santpoort Neth. **8** 52.27N 4.38E
San Valentín, Cerro *mtn.* Chile **63** 46.40S 73.25W
San Vicente El Salvador **57** 13.38N 88.42W
San Vito al Tagliamento Italy **9** 45.54N 12.52E

Sanya China 25 18.20N109.31E
São Borja Brazil 59 28.35S 56.01W
São Caetano do Sul Brazil 59 23.36S 46.34W
São Carlos Brazil 59 22.01S 47.54W
São Francisco *r.* Brazil 61 10.20S 36.20W
São Francisco do Sol Brazil 59 26.17S 48.39W
São Gabriel Brazil 59 30.20S 54.19W
São Gonçalo do Sapucaí Brazil 59 21.54S 45.35W
Sao Hill *town* Tanzania 37 8.21S 35.10E
São João da Boa Vista Brazil 59 21.59S 46.45W
São João da Madeira Portugal 10 40.54N 8.30W
São João del Rei Brazil 59 21.08S 44.15W
São João do Piauí Brazil 61 8.21S 42.15W
São Joaquim da Barra Brazil 59 20.36S 47.51W
São José do Calçado Brazil 59 21.01S 41.37W
São José do Rio Prêto Brazil 59 20.50S 49.20W
São José dos Campos Brazil 59 23.07S 45.52W
São Leopoldo Brazil 59 29.46S 51.09W
São Lourenço Brazil 59 22.08S 45.05W
São Luís Brazil 61 2.34S 44.16W
São Manuel Brazil 59 22.40S 48.35W
São Manuel *r.* see Teles Pires *r.* Brazil 61
São Miguel d'Oeste Brazil 59 26.45S 53.34W
Saona *i.* Dom. Rep. 57 18.09N 68.42W
Saône *r.* France 14 45.46N 4.52E
São Paulo Brazil 59 23.33S 46.39W
São Paulo *d.* Brazil 59 22.05S 48.00W
São Paulo de Olivença Brazil 60 3.34S 68.55W
São Roque Brazil 59 23.31S 47.09W
São Sebastião Brazil 59 23.48S 45.26W
São Sebastião, Ilha de *i.* Brazil 59 23.53S 45.17W
São Sebastião do Paraíso Brazil 59 20.54S 46.59W
São Tiago Brazil 59 20.54S 44.30W
São Tomé *i.* São Tomé & Príncipe 34 0.19N 6.43E
São Tomé & Príncipe Africa 34 1.00N 7.00E
São Vicente Brazil 59 23.57S 46.23W
São Vicente, Cabo de *c.* Portugal 10 37.01N 8.59W
São Vicente de Minas Brazil 59 21.40S 44.26W
Sapé Brazil 61 7.06S 35.13W
Sapele Nigeria 38 5.53N 5.41E
Sapporo Japan 25 43.05N141.21E
Sapri Italy 12 40.04N 15.38E
Saqqârah Egypt 32 29.51N 31.13E
Saqqez Iran 31 36.14N 46.15E
Sarâb Iran 31 37.56N 47.35E
Sarâbiyûm Egypt 32 30.23N 32.17E
Sara Buri Thailand 29 14.32N100.53E
Sarajevo Bosnia-Herzegovina 15 43.52N 18.26E
Saranac Lake *town* U.S.A. 55 44.20N 74.08W
Sarandí del Yi Uruguay 63 33.21S 55.38W
Sarandí Grande Uruguay 63 33.44S 56.20W
Sârangarh India 29 21.38N 83.09E
Saranley Somali Rep. 37 2.19N 42.15E
Saranpaul Russian Fed. 18 64.15N 60.58E
Saransk Russian Fed. 18 54.12N 45.10E
Sarapul Russian Fed. 18 56.30N 53.49E
Sarasota U.S.A. 53 27.20N 82.32W
Sarata Ukraine 15 46.00N 29.40E
Saratoga U.S.A. 54 37.16N122.02W
Saratoga Springs U.S.A. 55 43.05N 73.47W
Saratov Russian Fed. 19 51.30N 45.55E
Sarawak *d.* Malaysia 26 2.00N113.00E
Saraychik Kazakhstan 19 47.29N 51.42E
Sarbâz Iran 31 26.39N 61.20E
Sarcelles France 9 49.00N 2.23E
Sardegna *d.* Italy 12 40.05N 9.00E
Sardegna *i.* Italy 12 40.00N 9.00E
Sardinia *i.* see Sardegna *i.* Italy 12
Sarek *mtn.* Sweden 16 67.25N 17.46E
Sareks Nat. Park Sweden 16 67.15N 17.30E
Sargodha Pakistan 28 32.01N 72.40E
Sarh Chad 34 9.08N 18.22E
Sarī Iran 31 36.33N 53.06E
Sarikamiş Turkey 30 40.19N 42.35E
Sarikei Malaysia 26 2.07N111.31E
Sarina Australia 44 21.26S149.13E
Sark *i.* U.K. 5 49.26N 2.22W
Sarlat France 11 44.53N 1.13E
Sărmasu Romania 15 46.46N 24.11E
Sarmi Indonesia 27 1.51S138.45E
Sarmiento Argentina 63 45.35S 69.05W
Särna Sweden 17 61.41N 13.08E
Sarnia Canada 55 42.58N 82.23W
Sarny Ukraine 15 51.21N 26.31E
Saronno Italy 9 45.38N 9.02E
Saros Körfezi *g.* Turkey 13 40.32N 26.25E
Sárospatak Hungary 15 48.19N 21.34E
Sarpsborg Norway 17 59.17N 11.07E
Sarrebourg France 11 48.43N 7.03E
Sarreguemines France 11 49.06N 7.03E
Sarria Spain 10 42.47N 7.25W
Sarro Mali 38 13.40N 5.05W
Sartène France 11 41.36N 8.59E
Sarthe *d.* France 9 48.00N 0.05E
Sarthe *r.* France 9 47.29N 0.30W
Sartilly France 9 48.45N 1.27W
Sartynya Russian Fed. 20 63.22N 63.11E
Sárvár Hungary 14 47.15N 16.57E
Saryshagan Kazakhstan 24 46.08N 73.32E
Sarzana Italy 9 44.07N 9.58E
Sasebo Japan 25 33.10N129.42E
Saser *mtn.* Jammu & Kashmir 28 34.50N 77.50E
Saskatchewan *d.* Canada 50 55.00N105.00W
Saskatchewan *r.* Canada 51 53.25N100.15W
Saskatoon Canada 50 52.10N106.40W
Sasovo Russian Fed. 18 54.21N 41.58E
Sassandra Ivory Coast 38 4.58N 6.08W
Sassari Italy 12 40.43N 8.33E
Sassnitz Germany 14 54.32N 13.40E
Sasso Marconi Italy 9 44.24N 11.15E
Sassuolo Italy 9 44.33N 10.47E
Sasyk, Ozero *l.* Ukraine 15 45.38N 29.38E
Sâtâra India 28 17.43N 74.05E
Satna India 29 24.33N 80.50E
Sátoraljaújhely Hungary 15 48.24N 21.39E
Sâtpura Range *mts.* India 28 21.50N 76.00E
Satu Mare Romania 15 47.48N 22.52E
Sauce Argentina 63 30.05S 58.45W
Sauda Norway 17 59.39N 6.20E
Saudi Arabia Asia 30 26.00N 44.00E
Saulieu France 9 47.17N 4.14E
Sault Sainte Marie Canada 55 46.31N 84.20W
Sault Sainte Marie U.S.A. 55 46.29N 84.22W
Saumarez Reef Australia 44 21.50S153.40E
Saumlaki Indonesia 44 7.59S131.22E
Saumur France 9 47.16N 0.05W
Saurimo Angola 36 9.38S 20.20E
Sava *r.* Bosnia-Herzegovina 15 44.50N 20.26E
Sava *r.* Croatia 14 45.03N 16.23E
Savalou Benin 38 7.55N 1.59E
Savannah *r.* U.S.A. 53 32.10N 81.00W
Savannah Ga. U.S.A. 53 32.09N 81.01W
Savannakhét Laos 26 16.34N104.55E
Savant L. Canada 55 50.48N 90.20W
Savant Lake *town* Canada 55 50.20N 90.40W
Savé Benin 38 8.04N 2.37E
Save *r.* Mozambique 39 20.59S 35.02E
Save *r.* Zimbabwe 39 21.16S 32.20E
Sâveh Iran 31 35.00N 50.25E
Savelugu Ghana 38 9.39N 0.48W
Saverdun France 11 43.14N 1.35E
Savigliano Italy 9 44.38N 7.40E
Savigny-sur-Braye France 9 47.53N 0.49E
Savona Italy 9 44.18N 8.28E
Savonlinna Finland 18 61.52N 28.51E
Savoonga U.S.A. 50 63.42N170.27W
Savu Sea *see* Sawu, Laut *sea* Pacific Oc. 27
Sawâkin Sudan 35 19.04N 37.22E
Sawbridgeworth U.K. 5 51.50N 0.09W
Sawdâ', Qurnat as *mtn.* Lebanon 32 34.17N 36.04E
Sawhâj Egypt 30 26.33N 31.42E
Sawston U.K. 5 52.07N 0.11E
Sawtell Australia 47 30.21S153.05E
Sawtooth Mts. U.S.A. 54 44.03N114.35W
Sawu *i.* Indonesia 27 10.30S121.50E
Sawu, Laut *sea* Pacific Oc. 27 9.30S122.30E
Saxmundham U.K. 5 52.13N 1.29E
Saxon Switz. 9 46.09N 7.11E
Say Mali 38 13.50N 4.57W
Say Niger 38 13.08N 2.22E
Sayama Japan 23 35.51N139.24E
Sayers Lake *town* Australia 46 32.46S143.20E
Saynshand Mongolia 25 44.58N110.10E
Sayula Mexico 56 19.52N103.36W
Sâzova *r.* Czech. 14 49.53N 14.21E
Scafell Pike *mtn.* U.K. 4 54.27N 3.12W
Scalea Italy 12 39.49N 15.48E
Scalloway U.K. 6 60.08N 1.17W
Scammon Bay *town* U.S.A. 50 61.50N165.35W
Scapa Flow *str.* U.K. 6 58.53N 3.05W
Scarborough Tobago 60 11.11N 60.45W
Scarborough U.K. 4 54.17N 0.24W
Schaerbeek Belgium 8 50.54N 4.20E
Schaffhausen Switz. 14 47.42N 8.38E
Schagen Neth. 8 52.47N 4.47E
Schefferville Canada 51 54.50N 67.00W
Schelde *r.* Belgium 8 51.13N 4.25E
Schell Creek Range *mts.* U.S.A. 54 39.10N114.40W
Schenectady U.S.A. 55 42.47N 73.53W
Scheveningen Neth. 8 52.07N 4.16E
Schiedam Neth. 8 51.55N 4.25E
Schiermonnikoog *i.* Neth. 8 53.28N 6.15E
Schio Italy 9 45.43N 11.21E
Schleiden Germany 8 50.32N 6.29E
Schleswig Germany 14 54.32N 9.34E
Schleswig-Holstein *d.* Germany 14 54.00N 10.30E
Schouten, Kepulauan *is.* Indonesia 27 0.45S135.50E
Schouwen *i.* Neth. 8 51.42N 3.45E
Schreiber Canada 55 48.48N 87.17W
Schwandorf Germany 14 49.20N 12.08E
Schwaner, Pegunungan *mts.* Indonesia 26 0.45S113.20E
Schwarzrand *mts.* Namibia 39 25.40S 16.53E
Schwarzwald *f.* Germany 14 48.00N 7.45E
Schwedt Germany 14 53.04N 14.17E
Schweich Germany 8 49.50N 6.47E
Schweinfurt Germany 14 50.03N 10.16E
Schwelm Germany 8 51.17N 7.18E
Schwerin Germany 14 53.38N 11.25E
Schwyz Switz. 14 47.02N 8.40E
Sciacca Italy 12 37.31N 13.05E
Scilla Italy 12 38.15N 15.44E
Scilly, Isles of U.K. 5 49.55N 6.20W
Scone Australia 47 32.01S150.53E
Scotia Calif. U.S.A. 54 40.26N123.31W
Scotland U.K. 6 55.30N 4.00W
Scottburgh R.S.A. 39 30.17S 30.45E
Scott Reef Australia 42 14.00S121.50E
Scottsbluff U.S.A. 52 41.52N103.40W
Scottsdale Australia 45 41.09S147.31E
Scottsdale U.S.A. 54 33.30N111.56W
Scranton U.S.A. 55 41.24N 75.40W
Scugog, L. Canada 55 44.10N 78.51W
Scunthorpe U.K. 4 53.35N 0.38W
Scutari, L. Yugo./Albania 13 42.10N 19.18E
Seabrook, L. Australia 43 30.56S119.40E
Seaford U.S.A. 55 38.39N 75.37W
Seahouses U.K. 4 55.35N 1.38W
Sea Isle City U.S.A. 55 39.09N 74.42W
Seal *r.* Canada 51 59.00N 95.00W
Sea Lake *town* Australia 46 35.31S142.54E
Searchlight U.S.A. 54 35.28N114.55W
Seascale U.K. 4 54.24N 3.29W
Seaside Calif. U.S.A. 54 36.37N121.50W
Seaside Oreg. U.S.A. 54 46.02N123.55W
Seaton U.K. 5 50.43N 3.05W
Seattle U.S.A. 54 47.36N122.20W
Seaview Range *mts.* Australia 44 18.56S146.00E
Sebastián Vizcaíno, Bahía *b.* Mexico 56 28.00N114.30W
Sebba Burkina 38 13.27N 0.33E
Sebeş Romania 15 45.58N 23.34E
Sebidiro P.N.G. 27 9.00S142.15E
Sebinkarahisar Turkey 30 40.19N 38.25E
Sechura, Desierto de *des.* Peru 60 6.00S 80.30W
Seclin France 8 50.34N 3.01E
Sêda *r.* Portugal 10 38.55N 7.30W
Sedalia U.S.A. 53 38.42N 93.15W
Sedan France 9 49.42N 4.57E
Seddon New Zealand 48 41.40S174.04E
Sédhiou Senegal 34 12.44N 15.30W
Sedom Israel 32 31.04N 35.23E
Seeheim Namibia 39 26.50S 17.45E
Sées France 9 48.38N 0.10E
Ségou Mali 38 13.28N 6.18W
Ségou *d.* Mali 38 13.55N 6.20W
Segovia Spain 10 40.57N 4.07W
Segozero, Ozero *l.* Russian Fed. 18 63.15N 33.40E
Segré France 9 47.41N 0.53W
Segre *r.* Spain 10 41.25N 0.21E
Séguédine Niger 34 20.12N 12.59E
Segura Portugal 10 39.50N 6.59W
Segura *r.* Spain 10 38.07N 0.14W
Segura, Sierra de *mts.* Spain 10 38.00N 2.50W
Seiches-sur-le-Loir France 9 47.35N 0.22W
Seiland *i.* Norway 16 70.25N 23.10E
Seinäjoki Finland 16 62.47N 22.50E
Seine *r.* France 9 49.28N 0.25E
Seine, Baie de la *b.* France 9 49.25N 0.15E
Seine-et-Marne *d.* France 9 48.30N 3.00E
Seine-Maritime *d.* France 9 49.45N 1.00E
Sekayu Indonesia 26 2.58S103.58E
Seki Japan 23 35.29N136.55E
Sekoma Botswana 39 24.41S 23.50E
Sekondi-Takoradi Ghana 38 4.57N 1.44W
Seküheh Iran 31 30.45N 61.29E
Selaru *i.* Indonesia 44 8.09S131.00E
Selatan, Tanjung *c.* Indonesia 26 4.20S114.45E
Selayar *i.* Indonesia 27 6.07S120.28E
Selbu Norway 16 63.14N 11.03E
Selby U.K. 4 53.47N 1.05W
Seldovia U.S.A. 50 59.27N151.43W
Sele *r.* Italy 12 40.30N 14.50E
Selebi-Pikwe Botswana 36 22.01S 27.50E
Selenga *r.* Russian Fed. 24 52.20N106.20E
Selenge Mörön *r.* see Selenga Mongolia 24
Sélestat France 14 48.16N 7.28E
Seligman U.S.A. 54 35.20N112.53W
Seljord Norway 17 59.29N 8.37E
Selkirk U.K. 6 55.33N 2.51W
Selkirk Mts. Canada/U.S.A. 50 49.00N116.00W
Selles-sur-Cher France 9 47.16N 1.33E
Selma Calif. U.S.A 54 36.34N119.37W
Selseleh ye Safid Kūh *mts.* Afghan 31 34.30N 63.30E
Selsey Bill *c.* U.K. 5 50.44N 0.47W
Selty Russian Fed. 18 57.19N 52.12E
Sélune *r.* France 9 48.35N 1.15W
Selva Argentina 59 29.50S 62.02W
Selvas *f.* Brazil 60 6.00S 65.00W
Selwyn Mts. Canada 50 63.00N130.00W
Selwyn Range *mts.* Australia 44 21.35S140.35E
Seman *r.* Albania 13 40.53N 19.25E
Semara W. Sahara 34 26.44N 11.41W
Semarang Indonesia 26 6.58S110.29E
Sembabule Uganda 37 0.08S 31.27E
Seminoe Resr. U.S.A. 54 42.00N106.50W
Semiozernoye Kazakhstan 20 52.22N 64.06E
Semipalatinsk Kazakhstan 20 50.26N 80.16E
Semirom Iran 31 31.31N 52.10E
Semiyarka Kazakhstan 20 50.52N 78.23E
Semliki *r.* Zaïre 37 1.12N 30.27E
Semmering Pass Austria 14 47.40N 16.00E
Semnân Iran 31 35.31N 53.24E
Semois *r.* France 8 49.53N 4.45E
Semporna Malaysia 26 4.27N118.36E
Semu *r.* Tanzania 37 3.57S 34.20E
Semur-en-Auxois France 9 47.29N 4.20E
Sena Mozambique 37 17.36S 35.00E
Senador Pompeu Brazil 61 5.30S 39.25W
Senaja Malaysia 26 6.49N117.02E
Sena Madureira Brazil 60 9.04S 68.40W
Sendai Tōhoku Japan 25 38.16N140.52E
Sendenhorst Germany 8 51.52N 7.50E
Seneca Oreg. U.S.A. 54 44.08N118.58W
Senegal Africa 34 14.30N 14.30W
Sénégal *r.* Senegal/Mauritania 34 16.00N 16.28W
Senekal R.S.A. 39 28.18S 27.37E
Senhor do Bonfim Brazil 61 10.28S 40.11W
Senica Czech. 15 48.41N 17.22E
Senigallia Italy 14 43.42N 13.14E
Senise Italy 12 40.09N 16.18E
Senj Croatia 14 45.00N 14.58E
Senja *i.* Norway 16 69.15N 17.20E
Senlis France 9 49.12N 2.35E
Sennan Japan 23 34.22N135.17E
Sennen U.K. 5 50.04N 5.42W
Senneterre Canada 55 48.24N 77.14W
Sens France 9 48.12N 3.18E
Senta Yugo. 15 45.56N 20.04E
Sentinel U.S.A. 54 32.53N113.12W
Seoni India 29 22.05N 79.32E
Seoul *see* Sŏul S. Korea 25
Sepik *r.* P.N.G. 27 3.54S144.30E
Sepopa Botswana 39 18.45S 22.11E
Sept Îles *town* Canada 55 50.13N 66.22W
Sepúlveda Spain 10 41.18N 3.45W
Seraing Belgium 8 50.37N 5.33E
Seram *i.* Indonesia 27 3.10S129.30E
Seram, Laut *sea* Pacific Oc. 27 2.50S128.00E
Serang Indonesia 26 6.07S106.09E
Serbia *d.* *see* Srbija *d.* Yugo. 15
Seremban Malaysia 26 2.42N101.54E
Serengeti Nat. Park Tanzania 37 2.30S 35.00E
Serengeti Plain *f.* Tanzania 37 3.00S 35.00E
Serenje Zambia 37 13.12S 30.50E
Sergach Russian Fed. 18 55.32N 45.27E
Sergipe *d.* Brazil 61 11.00S 37.00W
Sergiyevsk Russian Fed. 18 53.56N 50.01E
Seria Brunei 26 4.39N114.23E
Serian Malaysia 26 1.10N110.35E
Sericho Kenya 37 1.13N 39.06E
Sérifos *i.* Greece 13 37.11N 24.31E
Serle, Mt Australia 46 30.34S138.55E
Sermata *i.* Indonesia 27 8.30S129.00E
Serodino Argentina 63 32.37S 60.57W
Serov Russian Fed. 18 59.42N 60.32E
Serowe Botswana 39 22.25S 26.42E
Serpa Portugal 10 37.56N 7.36W
Serpentine *r.* Australia 43 32.33S115.46E
Serpent's Mouth *str.* Venezuela 60 9.50N 61.00W
Serpukhov Russian Fed. 18 54.53N 37.25E
Serra do Navio Brazil 61 0.59N 52.03W
Sérrai Greece 13 41.04N 23.32E
Serra Talhada Brazil 61 8.01S 38.17W
Serravalle Scrivia Italy 9 44.43N 8.51E
Serre *r.* France 8 49.40N 3.22E
Serrinha Brazil 61 11.38S 38.56W
Serui Indonesia 27 1.53S136.15E
Serule Botswana 39 21.54S 27.17E
Serviceton Australia 46 36.22S141.02E
Seseganaga L. Canada 55 50.02N 90.08W
Sese Is. Uganda 37 0.20S 32.30E
Sesepe Indonesia 27 1.30S127.59E
Sesheke Zambia 39 17.27S 24.19E
Sesia *r.* Italy 9 45.05N 8.37E
Sesimbra Portugal 10 38.26N 9.06W
Sestao Spain 10 43.18N 3.00W
Sestri Levante Italy 9 44.16N 9.24E
Sète France 11 43.25N 3.43E
Sete Lagoas Brazil 59 19.29S 44.15W
Sétif Algeria 34 36.09N 5.26E
Seto Japan 23 35.14N137.06E
Settat Morocco 34 33.04N 7.37W
Setté Cama Gabon 36 2.32S 9.46E
Settimo Torinese Italy 9 45.09N 7.46E
Settle U.K. 4 54.05N 2.18W
Setúbal Portugal 10 38.31N 8.54W
Setúbal, Baía de *b.* Portugal 10 38.20N 9.00W
Sevan, Ozero *l.* Armenia 31 40.22N 45.20E
Sevastopol' Ukraine 19 44.36N 33.31E
Sevenoaks U.K. 5 51.16N 0.12E
Sévérac France 11 44.20N 3.05E
Severn *r.* Australia 47 29.08S150.50E
Severn *r.* Canada 51 56.00N 87.40W
Severn *r.* U.K. 5 51.50N 2.21W
Severnaya Zemlya *is.* Russian Fed. 21 80.00N 96.00E
Severnyy Russian Fed. 18 69.55N 49.01E
Severnyy Donets *r.* Ukraine 19 49.08N 37.28E
Severnyy Dvina *r.* Russian Fed. 18 57.03N 24.00E
Severodvinsk Russian Fed. 18 64.35N 39.50E
Severomorsk Russian Fed. 18 69.05N 33.30E
Sevier *r.* U.S.A. 54 39.04N113.06W
Sevier L. U.S.A. 54 38.55N113.09W
Sevilla Spain 10 37.24N 5.59W
Sèvre-Nantaise *r.* France 11 47.12N 1.35W
Sèvre Niortaise *r.* France 11 46.35N 1.05W
Sevrey Mongolia 24 43.33N102.13E
Seward U.S.A. 50 60.05N149.34W
Seward Pen. U.S.A. 50 65.00N164.10W
Seydhisfjördhur *town* Iceland 16 65.16N 14.02W
Seylac Somali Rep. 35 11.21N 43.30E
Seym *r.* Ukraine 19 51.30N 32.30E
Seymour Australia 47 37.01S145.10E
Sézanne France 9 48.44N 3.44E
Sfax Tunisia 34 34.45N 10.43E
Sfintu-Gheorghe Romania 15 45.52N 25.50E
'sGravenhage Neth. 8 52.05N 4.16E
Shaanxi *d.* China 25 35.00N109.00E
Shaba *d.* Zaïre 37 8.00S 27.00E
Shabeelle *r.* Somali Rep. 37 0.30N 43.10E
Shache China 24 38.27N 77.16E
Shafter U.S.A. 54 35.30N119.16W
Shaftesbury U.K. 5 51.00N 2.12W
Shahbâ' Syria 32 32.51N 36.37E
Shahdâd Iran 31 30.27N 57.44E
Shâh Jahân, Kūh-e *mts.* Iran 31 37.00N 58.00E
Shâhjahânpur India 29 27.53N 79.55E
Shâh Kūh *mtn.* Iran 31 31.38N 59.16E
Shahr-e Bâbak Iran 31 30.08N 55.04E
Shahrezâ Iran 31 32.00N 51.52E
Shahr Kord Iran 31 32.40N 50.52E
Shahsavâr Iran 31 36.49N 50.54E
Sha'īb Abâ al Qūr *wadi* Saudi Arabia 30 31.02N 42.00E
Shakawe Botswana 39 18.22S 21.50E
Shaker Heights *town* U.S.A. 55 41.29N 81.36W
Shakhty Russian Fed. 19 47.43N 40.16E
Shakhunya Russian Fed. 18 57.41N 46.46E
Shaki Nigeria 38 8.41N 3.24E
Shakshûk Egypt 32 29.28N 30.42E
Shala Hâyk' *l.* Ethiopia 35 7.25N 38.30E
Shâm, Jabal ash *mtn.* Oman 31 23.14N 57.17E
Shâmat al Akbâd *des.* Saudi Arabia 30 28.15N 43.05E
Shamokin U.S.A. 55 40.47N 76.34W
Shamva Zimbabwe 37 17.20S 31.38E
Shandong *d.* China 25 35.45N117.30E
Shandong Bandao *pen.* China 25 37.00N121.30E
Shanghai China 25 31.13N121.25E
Shanghai *d.* China 25 31.14N121.28E
Shangrao China 25 28.28N117.54E
Shangshui China 25 33.33N114.38E
Shannon *r.* Rep. of Ire. 7 52.39N 8.43W
Shannon, Mouth of the *est.* Rep. of Ire. 7 52.29N 9.57W
Shanshan China 24 42.52N 90.10E
Shantarskiy Ostrova *is.* Russian Fed. 21 55.00N138.00E
Shantou China 25 23.23N116.39E
Shanwa Tanzania 37 3.09S 33.48E
Shanxi *d.* China 25 36.45N112.00E
Shaoguan China 25 24.54N113.33E
Shaoxing China 25 30.02N120.35E
Shaoyang China 25 27.43N111.24E
Shap U.K. 4 54.32N 2.40W
Shapinsay *i.* U.K. 6 59.03N 2.51W
Shapur *ruins* Iran 31 29.42N 51.30E
Shaqrâ' Saudi Arabia 31 25.17N 45.14E
Shaqrâ' Yemen 35 13.21N 45.42E
Shark B. Australia 42 25.30S113.30E
Sharlyk Russian Fed. 18 52.58N 54.46E
Sharm ash Shaykh Egypt 32 27.51N 34.16E
Sharon U.S.A. 55 41.16N 80.30W
Sharqī, Al Jabal ash *mts.* Lebanon 32 34.00N 36.25E
Sharqīyah, Aş Şaḩrā' ash *des.* Egypt 32 27.40N 32.00E
Sharya Russian Fed. 18 58.22N 45.50E
Shashi *r.* Botswana/Zimbabwe 39 22.10S 29.15E
Shashi China 25 30.16N112.20E
Shasta, Mt. U.S.A. 54 41.20N122.20W
Shatt al Arab *r.* Iraq 31 30.00N 48.30E
Shaunavon Canada 50 49.40N108.25W
Shaw I. Australia 44 20.29S149.05E
Shawinigan Canada 55 46.33N 72.45W
Shay Gap *town* Australia 42 20.28S120.05E
Shaykh, Jabal ash *mtn.* Lebanon 32 33.24N 35.52E
Shchara *r.* Belorussia 15 53.27N 24.45E
Shchelyayur Russian Fed. 18 65.16N 53.17E
Shchors Ukraine 15 51.50N 31.59E
Sheboygan U.S.A. 53 43.46N 87.44W
Shebshi Mts. Nigeria 38 8.30N 11.45E
Sheeffry Hills Rep. of Ire. 7 53.41N 9.42W
Sheelin, Lough Rep. of Ire. 7 53.48N 7.20W
Sheep Range *mts.* U.S.A. 54 36.45N115.05W
Sheffield U.K. 4 53.23N 1.28W
Shefford U.K. 5 52.02N 0.20W
Sheki Azerbaijan 19 41.12N 47.10E
Sheksna *r.* Russian Fed. 18 60.00N 37.49E
Shelburne N.S. Canada 51 43.46N 65.19W
Shelburne B. Australia 44 11.49S143.00E
Shelby Mich. U.S.A. 55 43.36N 86.22W
Shelby Mont. U.S.A. 54 48.30N111.51W
Shelbyville Ind. U.S.A. 55 39.31N 85.46W
Sheldrake Canada 55 50.18N 64.54W
Shelikof Str. U.S.A. 50 58.00N153.45W
Shelley U.S.A. 54 43.23N112.07W
Shellharbour Australia 47 34.35S150.52E
Shelton U.S.A. 54 47.13N123.06W
Shenandoah *r.* U.S.A. 55 39.19N 78.12W
Shenandoah Va. U.S.A. 55 38.29N 78.37W
Shëngjin Albania 13 41.49N 19.33E
Shengze China 25 30.55N120.39E
Shenkursk Russian Fed. 18 62.05N 42.58E
Shenyang China 25 41.50N123.26E
Shepetovka Ukraine 15 50.12N 27.01E
Shepparton Australia 47 36.25S145.26E
Sheppey, Isle of U.K. 5 51.24N 0.50E
Sherborne U.K. 5 50.56N 2.31W
Sherbrooke Canada 55 45.24N 71.54W
Sherburne U.S.A. 55 42.41N 75.30W
Sheridan U.S.A. 54 44.48N106.58W
Sheringa Australia 46 33.51S135.15E
Sheringham U.K. 4 52.56N 1.11E
Sherkin I. Rep. of Ire. 7 51.28N 9.25W
Sherman Tex. U.S.A. 53 33.39N 96.35W
Sherman Mills U.S.A. 55 45.52N 68.23W
Sherridon Canada 51 57.07N101.05W
'sHertogenbosch Neth. 8 51.42N 5.19E
Shetland Is. *d.* U.K. 6 60.20N 1.15W
Shetpe Kazakhstan 19 44.09N 52.06E
Shevchenko Kazakhstan 19 43.37N 51.11E
Shibīn al Kawm Egypt 32 30.33N 31.00E
Shibīn al Qanâţir Egypt 32 30.19N 31.19E
Shiel, Loch U.K. 6 56.48N 5.33W
Shiga *d.* Japan 23 34.55N136.00E
Shijiazhuang China 25 38.04N114.28E
Shikârpur Pakistan 28 27.58N 68.42E
Shikoku *i.* Japan 25 33.30N133.30E
Shilka Russian Fed. 25 51.55N116.01E
Shilka *r.* Russian Fed. 25 53.20N121.10E
Shillong India 29 25.34N 91.53E
Shima Japan 23 34.13N136.51E
Shimada Japan 23 34.49N138.11E
Shima-hantō *pen.* Japan 23 34.25N136.45E
Shimizu Japan 23 35.01N138.29E
Shimoda Japan 23 34.40N138.57E
Shimoga India 28 13.56N 75.31E
Shimonoseki Japan 25 33.59N130.58E
Shimpek Kazakhstan 24 44.50N 74.10E
Shin, Loch U.K. 6 58.06N 4.32W
Shindand Afghan. 28 33.18N 62.08E
Shingleton U.S.A. 55 46.21N 86.28W
Shinshâr Syria 32 34.36N 36.45E
Shinshiro Japan 23 34.54N137.30E
Shinyanga Tanzania 37 3.40S 33.20E
Shinyanga *d.* Tanzania 37 3.30S 33.00E
Shipka Pass Bulgaria 13 42.45N 25.25E
Shippensburg U.S.A. 55 40.03N 77.31W
Shiprock U.S.A. 54 36.47N108.41W
Shipston on Stour U.K. 5 52.04N 1.38W
Shiqian China 25 27.30N108.20E
Shirakskaya Step *f.* Georgia 31 41.40N 46.20E
Shirane san *mtn.* Japan 23 35.40N138.15E
Shirâz Iran 31 29.36N 52.33E
Shirbîn Egypt 32 31.13N 31.31E
Shire *r.* Mozambique 37 17.46S 35.20E
Shīr Kūh *mtn.* Iran 31 31.38N 54.07E
Shirvân Iran 31 37.24N 57.55E
Shivpuri India 28 25.26N 77.39E
Shiyan Hubei China 25 32.34N110.47E
Shizuishan China 24 39.17N106.52E
Shizuoka Japan 23 34.58N138.23E
Shizuoka *d.* Japan 23 35.00N138.00E
Shklov Belorussia 15 54.16N 30.16E
Shkodër Albania 13 42.03N 19.30E
Shkumbin *r.* Albania 13 41.01N 19.26E
Shoal C. Australia 43 33.51S121.10E
Shoalhaven *r.* Australia 47 34.51S150.40E

Sholāpur India 28 17.43N 75.56E
Shonai r. Japan 23 35.04N136.50E
Shoshone Calif. U.S.A. 54 35.58N116.17W
Shoshone Idaho U.S.A. 54 42.57N114.25W
Shoshone Mts. U.S.A. 54 39.25N117.15W
Shoshoni U.S.A. 54 43.14N108.07W
Shostka Belorussia 18 51.53N 33.30E
Show Low U.S.A. 54 34.15N110.02W
Shpola Ukraine 15 49.00N 31.25E
Shreveport U.S.A. 53 32.30N 93.46W
Shrewsbury U.K. 5 52.42N 2.45W
Shropshire d. U.K. 5 52.35N 2.40W
Shuangliao China 25 43.30N123.29E
Shuangyashan China 25 46.37N131.22E
Shubrā al Khaymah Egypt 32 30.06N 31.15E
Shuksan U.S.A. 54 48.55N121.43W
Shule China 24 39.25N 76.06E
Shumagin Is. U.S.A. 50 55.00N160.00W
Shumerlya Russian Fed. 18 55.30N 46.25E
Shumikha Russian Fed. 20 55.15N 63.14E
Shumyachi Russian Fed. 15 53.52N 32.25E
Shunde China 25 22.50N113.16E
Shur r. Khorāsān Iran 31 34.05N 60.22E
Shūr r. Kermān Iran 31 31.14N 55.29E
Shūr r. Khorāsān Iran 31 34.11N 60.07E
Shūrāb Iran 31 28.09N 60.18E
Shūrāb r. Iran 31 31.30N 55.18E
Shurugwi Zimbabwe 39 19.40S 30.00E
Shūshtar Iran 31 32.04N 48.53E
Shuwak Sudan 35 14.23N 35.52E
Shuya Russian Fed. 18 56.49N 41.23E
Shwebo Burma 29 22.35N 95.42E
Shyok Jammu & Kashmir 29 34.11N 78.08E
Siāhān Range mts. Pakistan 28 27.25N 64.30E
Siālkot Pakistan 28 32.29N 74.35E
Sian see Xi'an China 25
Siargao i. Phil. 27 9.55N126.05E
Siau i. Indonesia 27 2.42N125.24E
Siauliai Lithuania 17 55.56N 23.19E
Sibasa R.S.A. 39 22.56S 30.28E
Šibenik Croatia 12 43.45N 15.55E
Siberut i. Indonesia 26 1.30S 99.00E
Sibi Pakistan 28 29.31N 67.54E
Sibiti r. Tanzania 37 3.47S 34.45E
Sibiu Romania 13 45.47N 24.09E
Sibolga Indonesia 26 1.42N 98.48E
Sibu Malaysia 26 2.18N111.49E
Sibut C.A.R. 36 5.46N 19.06E
Sicasica Bolivia 62 17.22S 67.45W
Siccus r. Australia 46 31.26S139.30E
Sichuan d. China 24 30.30N103.00E
Sicilia d. Italy 12 37.30N 14.00E
Sicilia i. Italy 12 37.30N 14.00E
Sicily i. see Sicilia i. Italy 12
Sicuani Peru 60 14.21S 71.13W
Sidaouet Niger 38 18.34N 8.03E
Sīdī Barrānī Egypt 30 31.38N 25.58E
Sidi bel Abbès Algeria 34 35.15N 0.39W
Sidi Ifni Morocco 34 29.24N 10.12W
Sīdī Sālim Egypt 32 31.16N 30.47E
Sidlaw Hills U.K. 6 56.31N 3.10W
Sidley, Mt. Antarctica 64 77.30S125.00W
Sidmouth U.K. 5 50.40N 3.13W
Sidney Canada 54 48.39N123.24W
Sidney Nebr. U.S.A. 52 41.09N102.59W
Sidney Ohio U.S.A. 55 40.16N 84.10W
Sidon see Şaydā Lebanon 32
Sidra, G. of see Surt, Khalīj g. Libya 34
Siedlce Poland 15 52.10N 22.18E
Sieg r. Germany 8 50.49N 7.11E
Siegburg Germany 8 50.48N 7.13E
Siegen Germany 8 50.52N 8.02E
Siemiatycze Poland 15 52.26N 22.53E
Siena Italy 12 43.19N 11.20E
Sieradz Poland 15 51.36N 18.45E
Sierck-les-Bains France 8 49.28N 6.20E
Sierpc Poland 15 52.52N 19.41E
Sierra Colorada Argentina 63 40.35S 67.50W
Sierra Leone Africa 34 9.00N 12.00W
Sierra Mojada town Mexico 56 27.17N103.42W
Sierra Nevada mts. U.S.A. 54 37.45N119.30W
Sierre Switz. 9 46.18N 7.32E
Sífnos i. Greece 13 36.59N 24.60E
Sig Russian Fed. 18 65.31N 34.16E
Sighetul Marmaţiei Romania 15 47.56N 23.54E
Sighişoara Romania 15 46.13N 24.49E
Sigli Indonesia 26 5.23N 95.57E
Siglufjördhur Iceland 16 66.12N 18.55W
Signy France 9 49.42N 4.25E
Siguiri Guinea 34 11.28N 9.07W
Sigüenza Spain 10 41.04N 2.38W
Siika r. Finland 16 64.50N 24.44E
Siirt Turkey 30 37.56N 41.56E
Sīkar India 28 27.33N 75.12E
Sikasso Mali 38 11.18N 5.38W
Sikasso d. Mali 38 11.20N 6.05W
Sikhote Alin mts. Russian Fed. 25 44.00N135.00E
Síkinos i. Greece 13 36.39N 25.06E
Sikkim d. India 29 27.30N 88.30E
Sil r. Spain 10 42.24N 7.15W
Silchar India 29 24.49N 92.47E
Silgarhi-Doti Nepal 29 29.14N 80.58E
Silifke Turkey 30 36.22N 33.57E
Silīguri India 29 26.42N 88.30E
Siling Co l. China 29 31.40N 88.30E
Silistra Bulgaria 13 44.07N 27.17E
Siljan l. Sweden 17 60.50N 14.45E
Silkeborg Denmark 17 56.10N 9.34E
Sille-le-Guillaume France 9 48.12N 0.08E
Silloth U.K. 4 54.53N 3.25W
Silogui Indonesia 26 1.10S 98.46E
Silver Bow U.S.A. 54 46.00N112.40W
Silver City U.S.A. 54 32.46N108.17W
Silver Lake town U.S.A. 54 43.08N120.56W
Silverstone U.K. 5 52.05N 1.03W
Silverton Australia 46 31.53S141.13E
Silverton U.S.A. 54 45.01N122.47W
Silvi Italy 12 42.34N 14.05E
Simanggang Malaysia 26 1.10N111.32E
Simàrd, Lac l. Canada 55 47.38N 78.40W
Simav r. Turkey 13 40.24N 28.31E
Simba Kenya 37 2.10S 37.37E
Simcoe Canada 55 42.50N 80.18W
Simcoe, L. Canada 55 44.20N 79.20W
Simenga Russian Fed. 21 62.42N108.25E
Simeria Romania 13 45.51N 23.01E
Simeulue i. Indonesia 26 2.30N 96.00E
Simferopol' Ukraine 19 44.57N 34.05E
Simitli Bulgaria 13 41.51N 23.09E
Simiyu r. Tanzania 37 2.32S 33.25E
Simla India 28 31.07N 77.09E
Simleul Silvaniei Romania 15 47.14N 22.48E
Simmern Germany 8 49.59N 7.32E
Simo r. Finland 16 65.37N 25.03E
Simojärvo l. Finland 16 66.06N 27.03E
Simon's Town R.S.A. 39 34.12S 18.26E
Simoom Sound town Canada 50 50.45N126.45W
Simplon Pass Switz. 11 46.15N 8.03E
Simplon Tunnel Italy / Switz. 12 46.20N 8.05E
Simpson Desert Australia 44 25.00S136.50E
Simrishamn Sweden 17 55.33N 14.20E
Simuco Mozambique 37 14.00S 40.35E
Sinā', Shibh Jazīrat pen. Egypt 32 29.00N 34.00E
Sinai see Sīnā', Shibh Jazīrat pen. Egypt 32
Sinaloa d. Mexico 56 25.00N107.30W
Sinan China 25 27.56N108.22E
Sincelejo Colombia 60 9.17N 75.23W
Sinclair U.S.A. 54 41.47N107.07W
Sines Portugal 10 37.58N 8.52W
Sinfra Ivory Coast 38 6.35N 5.56W
Singapore Asia 26 1.20N103.45E
Singapore town Singapore 26 1.20N103.45E
Singaraja Indonesia 26 8.06S115.07E
Singida Tanzania 37 4.45S 34.42E
Singida d. Tanzania 37 6.00S 34.30E
Singing India 29 28.53N 94.47E
Singitikós Kólpos g. Greece 13 40.12N 24.00E
Singkaling Hkāmti Burma 29 26.00N 95.42E
Singkang Indonesia 27 4.09S120.02E
Singkawang Indonesia 26 0.57N108.57E
Singkep i. Indonesia 26 0.30S104.20E
Singleton Australia 47 32.33S151.11E
Singosan N. Korea 25 38.50N127.27E
Sinj Croatia 13 43.42N 16.38E
Sînnicolau Mare Romania 13 46.05N 20.38E
Sinnūris Egypt 32 29.25N 30.52E
Sinop Turkey 30 42.02N 35.09E
Sinsheim Germany 14 49.15N 8.53E
Sintang Indonesia 26 0.03N111.31E
Sint Eustatius i. Leeward Is. 57 17.33N 63.00W
Sint Maarten i. see St. Martin i. Leeward Is. 57
Sinŭiju N. Korea 25 40.04N124.25E
Sinyavka Belorussia 15 52.58N 26.30E
Sinyukha r. Ukraine 15 48.03N 30.51E
Siocon Phil. 27 7.42N122.08E
Siófok Hungary 15 46.54N 18.04E
Sion Switz. 9 46.14N 7.21E
Sioux City U.S.A. 53 42.30N 96.28W
Sioux Falls town U.S.A. 53 43.34N 96.42W
Sioux Lookout town Canada 51 50.07N 91.54W
Siphaqeni R.S.A. 39 31.05S 29.29E
Siping Jilin China 25 43.15N124.25E
Sipura i. Indonesia 26 2.10S 99.40E
Sira r. Norway 17 58.17N 6.24E
Siracusa Italy 12 37.05N 15.17E
Sirasso Ivory Coast 38 9.16N 6.06W
Sir Edward Pellew Group is. Australia 44 15.40S136.48E
Siret r. Romania 13 45.28N 27.56E
Sirḥān, Wādī as f. Saudi Arabia 30 31.00N 37.30E
Sir James MacBrien, Mt. Canada 50 62.07N127.41W
Sir Joseph Banks Group is. Australia 46 34.35S136.12E
Síros i. Greece 13 37.26N 24.56E
Sirrah, Wādī as r. Saudi Arabia 31 23.10N 44.22E
Sisak Croatia 12 45.30N 16.21E
Sishen R.S.A. 39 27.46S 22.59E
Sisimiut see Holsteinsborg Greenland 51
Sisŏphŏn Cambodia 26 13.37N102.58E
Sissonne France 9 49.34N 3.54E
Sisteron France 11 44.16N 5.56E
Sitka U.S.A. 50 57.05N135.20W
Sittang r. Burma 29 17.30N 96.53E
Sittard Neth. 8 51.00N 5.52E
Sittwe Burma 29 20.09N 92.55E
Siuruan r. Finland 16 65.20N 25.55E
Sīvan r. Iran 31 29.50N 52.47E
Sivas Turkey 30 39.44N 37.01E
Sivomaskinskiy Russian Fed. 18 66.45N 62.44E
Sivrihisar Turkey 30 39.29N 31.32E
Sīwah Egypt 30 29.12N 25.31E
Sīwah, Wāḥat oasis Egypt 30 29.10N 25.40E
Siwa Oasis see Sīwah, Wāḥat oasis Egypt 30
Sixmilecross U.K. 7 54.34N 7.08W
Siya Russian Fed. 18 63.38N 41.40E
Sjaelland i. Denmark 17 55.30N 11.45E
Sjötorp Sweden 17 58.50N 13.59E
Skagafjördhur est. Iceland 16 65.55N 19.35W
Skagen Denmark 17 57.44N 10.36E
Skagerrak str. Denmark / Norway 17 57.45N 8.55E
Skagway U.S.A. 50 59.23N135.20W
Skaill U.K. 6 58.56N 2.43W
Skála Oropoú Greece 13 38.20N 23.46E
Skala Podolskaya Ukraine 15 48.51N 26.11E
Skalat Ukraine 15 49.20N 25.59E
Skanderborg Denmark 17 56.02N 9.56E
Skånevik Norway 17 59.44N 5.59E
Skara Sweden 17 58.22N 13.25E
Skaraborg d. Sweden 17 58.20N 13.30E
Skarnes Norway 17 60.15N 11.41E
Skarżysko-Kamienna Poland 15 51.08N 20.53E
Skeena r. Canada 50 54.10N129.08W
Skegness U.K. 4 53.09N 0.20E
Skellefte r. Sweden 16 64.42N 21.06E
Skellefteå Sweden 16 64.46N 20.57E
Skelleftehamn Sweden 16 64.41N 21.14E
Skelmersdale U.K. 4 53.34N 2.49W
Skene Sweden 17 57.29N 12.38E
Skerries Rep. of Ire. 7 53.35N 6.07W
Skhíza i. Greece 13 36.42N 21.45E
Ski Norway 17 59.43N 10.50E
Skiddaw mtn. U.K. 4 54.40N 3.09W
Skidel Belorussia 15 53.37N 24.19E
Skien Norway 17 59.12N 9.36E
Skierniewice Poland 15 51.58N 20.08E
Skikda Algeria 34 36.50N 6.58E
Skipness U.K. 6 56.45N 5.22W
Skipton U.K. 4 53.57N 2.01W
Skiros Greece 13 38.53N 24.33E
Skíros i. Greece 13 38.50N 24.33E
Skive Denmark 17 56.34N 9.02E
Skjálfanda Fljót r. Iceland 16 65.55N 17.30W
Skjálfandi est. Iceland 16 66.08N 17.38W
Skjönsta Norway 16 67.12N 15.45E
Skoghall Sweden 17 59.19N 13.26E
Skole Ukraine 15 49.00N 23.30E
Skopje Yugo. 13 41.58N 21.27E
Skotterud Norway 17 59.59N 12.07E
Skovorodino Russian Fed. 21 54.00N123.53E
Skövde Sweden 17 58.24N 13.50E
Skreia Norway 17 60.39N 10.56E
Skull Rep. of Ire. 7 51.32N 9.33W
Skuodas Lithuania 17 56.16N 21.32E
Skutskär Sweden 17 60.38N 17.25E
Skvira Ukraine 15 49.42N 29.40E
Skye i. U.K. 6 57.20N 6.15W
Slagelse Denmark 17 55.24N 11.22E
Slalowa Wola Poland 15 50.40N 22.05E
Slamet mtn. Indonesia 26 7.10S109.10E
Slaney r. Rep. of Ire. 7 52.21N 6.30W
Slantsy Russian Fed. 18 59.09N 28.09E
Slatina Romania 13 44.26N 24.23E
Slave r. Canada 50 61.10N113.30W
Slavgorod Belorussia 15 53.25N 31.00E
Slavgorod Russian Fed. 20 53.01N 78.37E
Slavuta Ukraine 15 50.20N 26.58E
Slavyansk Ukraine 19 48.51N 37.36E
Slawno Poland 14 54.22N 16.40E
Sleaford U.K. 4 53.00N 0.22W
Sleaford B. Australia 46 35.00S136.50E
Sleat, Sd. of str. U.K. 6 57.05N 5.48W
Sledmere U.K. 4 54.04N 0.35W
Sleetmute U.S.A. 50 61.40N157.11W
Sliedrecht Neth. 8 51.48N 4.46E
Slieve Aughty Mts. Rep. of Ire. 7 53.05N 8.31W
Slieve Bloom Mts. Rep. of Ire. 7 53.03N 7.35W
Slieve Callan mtn. Rep. of Ire. 7 52.51N 9.18W
Slieve Donard mtn. U.K. 7 54.11N 5.56W
Slieve Gamph mts. Rep. of Ire. 7 54.06N 8.52W
Slievekimalta mtn. Rep. of Ire. 7 52.45N 8.17W
Slieve Mish mts. Rep. of Ire. 7 52.48N 9.48W
Slieve Miskish mts. Rep. of Ire. 7 51.41N 9.56W
Slievenamon mtn. Rep. of Ire. 7 52.25N 7.34W
Slieve Snaght mtn. Donegal Rep. of Ire. 7 55.12N 7.20W
Sligo Rep. of Ire. 7 54.17N 8.28W
Sligo d. Rep. of Ire. 7 54.10N 8.35W
Sligo B. Rep. of Ire. 7 54.18N 8.40W
Slite Sweden 17 57.43N 18.48E
Sliven Bulgaria 13 42.41N 26.19E
Slobodka Ukraine 15 47.56N 29.18E
Slobodskoy Russian Fed. 18 58.42N 50.10E
Slonim Belorussia 15 53.05N 25.21E
Slough U.K. 5 51.30N 0.35W
Slovechna r. Belorussia 15 51.41N 29.41E
Slovechno Ukraine 15 51.23N 28.20E
Slovenia Europe 12 46.10N 14.45E
Slovenjgradec Slovenia 12 46.31N 15.05E
Slovensko d. Czech. 15 48.25N 19.20E
Słubice Poland 14 52.20N 14.32E
Sluch r. Belorussia 15 52.08N 27.31E
Sluis Neth. 8 51.18N 3.23E
Slunj Croatia 14 45.07N 15.35E
Słupsk Poland 15 54.28N 17.01E
Slurry R.S.A. 39 25.48S 25.49E
Slutsk Belorussia 15 53.02N 27.31E
Slyne Head Rep. of Ire. 7 53.25N 10.12W
Slyudyanka Russian Fed. 24 51.40N103.40E
Smallwood Resr. Canada 51 54.00N 64.00W
Smederevo Yugo. 13 44.40N 20.56E
Smela Ukraine 19 49.15N 31.54E
Smilde Neth. 8 52.58N 6.28E
Smilovichi Belorussia 15 53.45N 28.00E
Smith Arm b. Canada 50 66.15N124.00W
Smithfield R.S.A. 39 30.11S 26.31E
Smiths Falls town Canada 55 44.54N 76.01W
Smithton Australia 45 40.52S145.07E
Smithtown Australia 47 31.03S152.53E
Smoky Bay town Australia 46 32.22S133.56E
Smoky C. Australia 47 30.55S153.05E
Smoky Hill r. U.S.A. 52 39.03N 96.48W
Smolensk Russian Fed. 18 54.49N 32.04E
Smolevichi Belorussia 15 54.00N 28.01E
Smólikas mtn. Greece 13 40.06N 20.55E
Smolyan Bulgaria 13 41.34N 24.45E
Smorgon Belorussia 15 54.28N 26.20E
Smöla i. Norway 16 63.20N 8.00E
Snaefell mtn. I.o.M Europe 4 54.16N 4.28W
Snaefell mtn. Iceland 16 64.48N 15.34W
Snake r. Idaho U.S.A. 52 43.50N117.05W
Snake r. Wash. U.S.A. 54 46.12N119.02W
Snake Range mts. U.S.A. 54 39.00N114.15W
Snake River town U.S.A. 54 44.10N110.40W
Snake River Plain f. U.S.A. 54 43.00N113.00W
Snåsa Norway 16 64.15N 12.23E
Snåsavatn l. Norway 16 64.05N 12.00E
Sneek Neth. 8 53.03N 5.40E
Sneem Rep. of Ire. 7 51.50N 9.54W
Sneeuwberg mtn. R.S.A. 39 32.30S 19.09E
Śniardwy, Jezioro l. Poland 15 53.46N 21.44E
Snina Czech. 15 48.59N 22.07E
Snizort, Loch U.K. 6 57.35N 6.30W
Snov r. Ukraine 15 51.45N 31.45E
Snowdon mtn. U.K. 4 53.05N 4.05W
Snowdrift Canada 50 62.23N110.47W
Snowflake U.S.A. 54 34.30N110.05W
Snowtown Australia 46 33.47S138.13E
Snowy r. Australia 47 37.49S148.30E
Snowy Mts. Australia 47 36.30S148.20E
Snöhetta mtn. Norway 17 62.20N 9.17E
Snyatyn Ukraine 15 48.30N 25.50E
Soacha Colombia 60 4.35N 74.13W
Soalala Madagascar 37 16.06S 45.20E
Soasiu Indonesia 27 0.40N127.25E
Sob r. Ukraine 15 48.42N 29.17E
Sobat r. Sudan / Ethiopia 35 9.30N 31.30E
Sobernheim Germany 8 49.47N 7.40E
Sobradinho, Represa de resr. Brazil 61 10.00S 42.30W
Sobral Brazil 61 3.45S 40.20W
Sochi Russian Fed. 19 43.35N 39.46E
Socorro Colombia 60 6.30N 73.16W
Socorro, Isla i. Mexico 56 18.45N110.58W
Socotra i. see Suquṭrá i. Indian Oc. 35
Socuéllamos Spain 10 39.16N 2.47W
Sodankylä Finland 16 67.29N 26.32E
Sodium R.S.A. 39 30.10S 23.08E
Sodo Ethiopia 35 6.52N 37.47E
Soest Germany 8 51.34N 8.06E
Sofala Australia 47 33.05S149.42E
Sofala d. Mozambique 39 19.00S 34.39E
Sofia see Sofiya Bulgaria 13
Sofiya Bulgaria 13 42.41N 23.19E
Sofiysk Russian Fed. 21 52.19N133.55E
Sofporog Russian Fed. 18 65.47N 31.30E
Sogamoso Colombia 60 5.43N 72.56W
Sognefjorden est. Norway 17 61.06N 5.10E
Sogn og Fjordane d. Norway 17 61.30N 6.50E
Soignies Belgium 8 50.35N 4.04E
Soissons France 9 49.23N 3.20E
Sokal Ukraine 15 50.30N 24.10E
Sokodé Togo 38 8.59N 1.11E
Sokol Russian Fed. 18 59.28N 40.04E
Sokółka Poland 15 53.25N 23.31E
Sokolo Mali 38 14.53N 6.11W
Sokolov Czech. 14 50.09N 12.40E
Sokoto Nigeria 38 13.02N 5.15E
Sokoto d. Nigeria 38 11.50N 5.05E
Sokoto r. Nigeria 38 13.05N 5.13E
Solbad Hall Austria 14 47.17N 11.31E
Solec Kujawski Poland 15 53.06N 18.14E
Soledad Venezuela 60 8.10N 63.34W
Solesmes France 8 50.12N 3.32E
Solginskiy Russian Fed. 18 61.07N 41.30E
Solheim Norway 17 60.53N 5.27E
Soligalich Russian Fed. 18 59.02N 42.15E
Solikamsk Russian Fed. 18 59.40N 56.45E
Sol-Iletsk Russian Fed. 18 51.09N 55.00E
Solingen Germany 8 51.10N 7.05E
Sollefteå Sweden 16 63.12N 17.20E
Sollentuna Sweden 17 59.28N 17.54E
Sóller Spain 10 39.47N 2.41E
Sollia Norway 17 61.47N 10.24E
Solola Somali Rep. 37 0.08N 41.30E
Solomon Is. Pacific Oc. 40 8.00S160.00E
Solomon Sea Pacific Oc. 41 7.00S150.00E
Solon U.S.A. 55 44.57N 69.52W
Solothurn Switz. 14 47.13N 7.32E
Solovetskiye, Ostrova is. Russian Fed. 18 65.05N 35.30E
Šolta i. Croatia 12 43.23N 16.17E
Solṭānābād Iran 31 36.25N 58.02E
Soltau Germany 14 52.59N 9.49E
Solway Firth est. U.K. 4 54.50N 3.30W
Solzach r. Austria 14 48.35N 13.30E
Soma Turkey 13 39.11N 27.36E
Somabhula Zimbabwe 39 19.40S 29.38E
Somali Republic Africa 35 5.30N 47.00E
Sombor Yugo. 13 45.48N 19.08E
Sombrerete Mexico 56 23.38N103.39W
Somerset d. U.K. 5 51.09N 3.00W
Somerset East R.S.A. 39 32.43S 25.33E
Somerset I. Canada 51 73.00N 93.30W
Somes r. Hungary 15 48.40N 22.30E
Somme r. France 11 50.01N 1.40E
Sommen l. Sweden 17 58.01N 15.15E
Sompuis France 9 48.41N 4.23E
Son r. India 29 25.55N 84.55E
Sonbong N. Korea 25 42.19N130.24E
Sondershausen Germany 14 51.22N 10.52E
Sondrio Italy 9 46.10N 9.52E
Songa r. Norway 17 59.45N 7.59E
Songea Tanzania 37 10.42S 35.39E
Songhua Jiang r. China 25 47.46N132.30E
Songkhla Thailand 29 7.13N100.37E
Song Xian China 25 34.02N111.48E
Son La Vietnam 26 21.20N103.55E
Sonneberg Germany 14 50.22N 11.10E
Sonora d. Mexico 56 29.30N110.40W
Sonora r. Mexico 56 28.50N111.33W
Sonsorol i. Pacific Ocean 27 5.20N132.13E
Son Tay Vietnam 26 21.06N105.32E
Sopi Indonesia 27 2.40N128.28E
Sopot Poland 15 54.28N 18.34E
Sopotskin Belorussia 15 53.49N 23.42E
Soppero Sweden 16 68.07N 21.40E
Sopron Hungary 14 47.41N 16.36E
Sorel Canada 55 46.03N 73.06W
Sorgono Italy 12 40.01N 9.06E
Soria Spain 10 41.46N 2.28W
Soriano Uruguay 63 33.24S 58.19W
Sor Kvalöy i. Norway 16 69.40N 18.30E
Sor Mertvyy Kultuk f. Kazakhstan 19 45.30N 54.00E
Sorocaba Brazil 59 23.29S 47.27W
Sorochinsk Russian Fed. 18 52.29N 53.15E
Soroki Moldavia 15 48.08N 28.12E
Sorol i. Federated States of Micronesia 27 8.09N140.25E
Sorong Indonesia 27 0.50S131.17E
Soroti Uganda 37 1.40N 33.37E
Sorraia r. Portugal 10 39.00N 8.51W
Sorrento Italy 12 40.37N 14.22E
Sorsele Sweden 16 65.30N 17.30E
Sortavala Russian Fed. 18 61.40N 30.40E
Sortland Norway 16 68.44N 15.25E
Sosnogorsk Russian Fed. 18 63.32N 53.55E
Sosnovo Russian Fed. 18 60.33N 30.11E
Sosnovyy Russian Fed. 18 66.01N 32.40E
Sosnowiec Poland 15 50.18N 19.08E
Sosva Russian Fed. 18 59.10N 61.50E
Sosyka Russian Fed. 19 46.11N 38.49E
Sotik Kenya 37 0.40S 35.08E
Sotra i. Norway 17 60.15N 5.10E
Sotteville France 9 49.25N 1.06E
Souflíon Greece 13 41.12N 26.18E
Sŏul S. Korea 25 37.30N127.00E
Sources, Mont-aux- mtn. Lesotho 39 28.44S 28.52E
Soure Portugal 10 40.04N 8.38W
Souris r. Canada 52 49.38N 99.35W
Sousa Brazil 61 6.41S 38.14W
Sousse Tunisia 34 35.48N 10.38E
Soustons France 11 43.45N 1.19W
South Alligator r. Australia 44 12.53S132.29E
Southampton Canada 55 44.29N 81.23W
Southampton U.K. 5 50.54N 1.23W
Southampton I. Canada 51 64.30N 84.00W
South Australia d. Australia 46 30.00S137.00E
South Bend Ind. U.S.A. 55 41.40N 86.15W
South Bend Wash. U.S.A. 54 46.40N123.48W
South Branch U.S.A. 55 44.29N 83.36W
South Carolina d. U.S.A. 53 34.00N 81.00W
South Cerney U.K. 5 51.40N 1.55W
South China Sea Asia 26 12.30N115.00E
South Dakota d. U.S.A. 52 44.30N100.00W
South Dorset Downs hills U.K. 5 50.40N 2.25W
South Downs hills U.K. 5 50.04N 0.34W
South East d. Botswana 39 25.00S 25.45E
South East C. Australia 45 43.38S146.48E
South East Is. Australia 43 34.23S123.30E
Southend-on-Sea U.K. 5 51.32N 0.43E
Southern Alps mts. New Zealand 48 43.20S170.45E
Southern Cross Australia 43 31.14S119.16E
Southern Indian L. Canada 51 57.10N 98.40W
Southern Ocean Pacific Oc. 40 50.00S135.00E
Southern Uplands hills U.K. 6 55.30N 3.30W
South Esk r. U.K. 6 56.43N 2.32W
South Esk Tablelands f. Australia 42 20.50S126.40E
South Glamorgan d. U.K. 5 51.27N 3.22W
South-haa U.K. 6 60.34N 1.17W
South Haven U.S.A. 55 42.25N 86.16W
South Horr Kenya 37 2.10N 36.45E
South I. Kenya 37 2.36N 36.38E
South I. New Zealand 48 43.00S171.00E
South Korea Asia 25 36.00N128.00E
South Lake Tahoe town U.S.A. 54 38.57N119.57W
Southland d. New Zealand 48 45.40S168.00E
South Molton U.K. 5 51.01N 3.50W
South Nahanni r. Canada 50 61.00N123.20W
Southport Qld. Australia 47 27.58S153.20E
Southport Tas. Australia 45 43.25S146.59E
Southport U.K. 4 53.38N 3.01W
South Ronaldsay i. U.K. 6 58.47N 2.56W
South Shields U.K. 4 55.00N 1.24W
South Tyne r. U.K. 6 54.59N 2.08W
South Uist i. U.K. 6 57.15N 7.20W
Southwest C. New Zealand 48 47.15S167.30E
South Windham U.S.A. 55 43.44N 70.26W
Southwold U.K. 5 52.19N 1.41E
South Yorkshire d. U.K. 4 53.28N 1.25W
Soutpansberg mts. R.S.A. 39 22.58S 29.50E
Sovetsk Lithuania 17 55.05N 21.53E
Sovetsk Russian Fed. 18 57.39N 48.59E
Sovetskaya Gavan Russian Fed. 21 48.57N140.16E
Soweto R.S.A. 39 26.16S 27.51E
Soyo Angola 36 6.12S 12.25E
Sozh r. Belorussia 15 51.57N 30.48E
Söderhamn Sweden 17 61.18N 17.03E
Söderköping Sweden 17 58.29N 16.18E
Södermanland d. Sweden 17 59.10N 16.35E
Södertälje Sweden 17 59.12N 17.37E
Södra Vi Sweden 17 57.45N 15.48E
Sögel Germany 8 52.51N 7.31E
Söğüt Turkey 30 40.02N 30.10E
Söke Turkey 13 37.46N 27.26E
Sölvesborg Sweden 17 56.03N 14.33E
Sönderborg Denmark 17 54.55N 9.47E
Söndreströmfjord Greenland 51 66.30N 50.52W
Sörfjorden Norway 16 66.29N 13.20E
Sörfold Norway 16 67.30N 15.30E
Sörli Norway 16 64.15N 13.50E
Söröya i. Norway 16 70.35N 22.30E
Sör-Rondane mts. Antarctica 64 72.30S 22.00E
Sör Tröndelag d. Norway 16 63.00N 10.20E
Spa Belgium 8 50.29N 5.52E
Spain Europe 10 40.00N 4.00W
Spalding Australia 46 33.29S138.40E
Spalding U.K. 4 52.47N 0.09W
Spandau Germany 14 52.32N 13.13E
Spanish Fork U.S.A. 54 40.07N111.39W
Sparks U.S.A. 54 39.32N119.45W
Spartanburg U.S.A. 53 34.56N 81.57W
Spárti Greece 13 37.04N 22.28E
Spartivento, Capo c. Calabria Italy 12 37.55N 16.04E
Spartivento, Capo c. Sardegna Italy 12 38.53N 8.50E
Spátha, Ákra c. Greece 13 35.42N 23.43E
Speculator U.S.A. 55 43.30N 74.17W
Speke G. Tanzania 37 2.20S 33.30E
Spence Bay town Canada 51 69.30N 93.20W
Spencer Idaho U.S.A. 54 44.21N112.11W
Spencer Iowa U.S.A. 53 43.08N 95.08W
Spencer, C. Australia 46 35.18S136.53E

T

107

Tindouf Algeria **34** 27.50N 8.04W
Tingha Australia **47** 29.58S151.16E
Tingo María Peru **60** 9.09S 75.56W
Tingréla Ivory Coast **38** 10.26N 6.20W
Tingsryd Sweden **17** 56.32N 14.59E
Tinguipaya Bolivia **62** 19.11S 65.51W
Tinne *r.* Norway **3** 59.05N 9.43E
Tinnenburra Australia **47** 28.40S145.30E
Tinnoset Norway **17** 59.43N 9.02E
Tínos *i.* Greece **13** 37.36N 25.08E
Tinsukia India **29** 27.30N 95.22E
Tintinara Australia **46** 35.52S140.04E
Tioman, Pulau *i.* Malaysia **26** 2.45N104.10E
Tionaga Canada **55** 48.05N 82.06W
Tione di Trento Italy **9** 46.02N 10.43E
Tipperary Rep. of Ire. **7** 52.29N 8.10W
Tipperary *d.* Rep. of Ire. **7** 52.37N 7.55W
Tirān, Jazīrat Saudi Arabia **32** 27.56N 34.34E
Tiranë Albania **13** 41.20N 19.48E
Tirano Italy **9** 46.12N 10.10E
Tiraspol Moldavia **15** 46.50N 29.38E
Tirat Karmel Israel **32** 32.46N 34.58E
Tirebolu Turkey **30** 41.02N 38.49E
Tiree *i.* U.K. **6** 56.30N 6.50W
Tîrgovişte Romania **15** 44.56N 25.27E
Tîrgu-Jiu Romania **15** 45.03N 23.17E
Tîrgu-Lăpuş Romania **15** 47.27N 23.52E
Tîrgu Mureş Romania **15** 46.33N 24.34E
Tîrgu-Neamţ Romania **15** 47.12N 26.22E
Tîrgu-Ocna Romania **15** 46.15N 26.37E
Tîrgu-Secuiesc Romania **15** 46.00N 26.08E
Tírnavos Greece **13** 39.45N 22.17E
Tirol *d.* Austria **14** 47.15N 11.20E
Tir Pol Afghan. **31** 34.38N 61.19E
Tirso *r.* Italy **12** 39.52N 8.33E
Tiruchchirāppalli India **29** 10.50N 78.43E
Tirunelveli India **28** 8.45N 77.43E
Tirupati India **29** 13.39N 79.25E
Tiruppur India **28** 11.05N 77.20E
Tisa *r.* Yugo. **15** 45.09N 20.16E
Tis'ah Egypt **32** 30.02N 32.35E
Tisdale Canada **50** 52.51N104.01W
Tisza *r.* Hungary *see* Tisa *r.* Yugo. **15**
Titicaca, L. Bolivia / Peru **62** 16.00S 69.00W
Titiwa Nigeria **38** 12.14N 12.53E
Titograd Yugo. **13** 42.30N 19.16E
Titov Veles Yugo. **13** 41.43N 21.49E
Titran Norway **16** 63.42N 8.22E
Ti Tree Australia **44** 22.06S133.17E
Titusville Penn. U.S.A. **55** 41.38N 79.41W
Tiverton U.K. **5** 50.54N 3.30W
Tivoli Italy **12** 41.58N 12.48E
Tizimín Mexico **57** 21.10N 88.09W
Tizi Ouzou Algeria **34** 36.44N 4.05E
Tiznit Morocco **34** 29.43N 9.44W
Tjeuke Meer *l.* Neth. **8** 52.55N 5.51E
Tjörn *i.* Sweden **17** 58.00N 11.38E
Tlaxcala *d.* Mexico **56** 19.45N 98.20W
Tlemcen Algeria **34** 34.53N 1.21W
Tmassah Libya **34** 26.22N 15.47E
Toab U.K. **6** 59.53N 1.16W
Toamasina Madagascar **36** 18.10S 49.23E
Toano Italy **9** 44.23N 10.34E
Toba Japan **23** 34.29N136.51E
Toba, Danau *l.* Indonesia **26** 2.45N 98.50E
Toba Kākar Range *mts.* Pakistan **28** 31.15N 68.00E
Tobar U.S.A. **54** 40.53N114.54W
Tobelo Indonesia **27** 1.45N127.59E
Tobermory Canada **55** 45.15N 81.39W
Tobermory U.K. **6** 56.37N 6.04W
Tobi *i.* Pacific Ocean **27** 3.01N131.10E
Toboali Indonesia **26** 3.00S106.30E
Tobol *r.* Russian Fed. **20** 58.15N 68.12E
Tobolsk Russian Fed. **20** 58.15N 68.12E
Tobseda Russian Fed. **18** 68.34N 52.16E
Tocantinópolis Brazil **61** 6.20S 47.25W
Tocantins *d.* Brazil **61** 10.15S 48.30W
Tocantins *r.* Brazil **61** 1.50S 49.15W
Tocopilla Chile **62** 22.05S 70.12W
Tocorpuri *mtn.* Bolivia / Chile **62** 22.26S 67.53W
Tocumwal Australia **47** 35.51S145.34E
Tocuyo *r.* Venezuela **60** 11.03N 68.23W
Todenyang Kenya **37** 4.34N 35.52E
Togian, Kepulauan *is.* Indonesia **27** 0.20S122.00E
Togo Africa **38** 8.00N 1.00E
Toijala Finland **17** 61.10N 23.52E
Toili Indonesia **27** 1.25S122.23E
Tokaj Hungary **15** 48.08N 21.27E
Tokala *mtn.* Indonesia **27** 1.36S121.41E
Tokat Turkey **30** 40.20N 36.35E
Tokelau Is. Pacific Oc. **40** 9.00S171.45W
Toki Japan **23** 35.21N137.11E
Toki *r.* Japan **23** 35.12N136.52E
Tokmak Kyrgyzstan **24** 42.49N 75.15E
Tokoname Japan **23** 34.53N136.51E
Tokoroa New Zealand **48** 38.13S175.53E
Tokuno shima *i.* Japan **25** 27.40N129.00E
Tōkyō Japan **23** 35.42N139.46E
Tōkyō-wan *b.* Japan **23** 35.25N139.45E
Tolaga Bay *town* New Zealand **48** 38.22S178.18E
Toledo Spain **10** 39.52N 4.02W
Toledo U.S.A. **55** 41.40N 83.35W
Toledo, Montes de *mts.* Spain **10** 39.35N 4.30W
Toliara Madagascar **36** 23.21S 43.40E
Tolmezzo Italy **9** 46.24N 13.01E
Tolo, Teluk *g.* Indonesia **27** 2.00S122.30E
Tolosa Spain **10** 43.09N 2.04W
Tolstyy-Les Ukraine **15** 51.24N 29.48E
Toluca Mexico **56** 19.20N 99.40W
Toluca *mtn.* Mexico **56** 19.10N 99.40W
Tol'yatti Russian Fed. **18** 53.32N 49.24E
Tomar Portugal **10** 39.36N 8.25W
Tomás Gomensoro Uruguay **63** 30.26S 57.26W
Tomaszów Lubelski Poland **15** 50.28N 23.25E
Tomaszów Mazowiecki Poland **15** 51.32N 20.01E
Tombigbee *r.* U.S.A. **53** 31.05N 87.55W
Tombos Brazil **59** 20.53S 42.03W
Tombouctou Mali **38** 16.49N 2.59W
Tombouctou *d.* Mali **38** 18.30N 3.40W
Tombua Angola **36** 15.55S 11.51E
Tomé Chile **63** 36.37S 72.57W
Tomelilla Sweden **17** 55.33N 13.57E
Tomelloso Spain **10** 39.09N 3.01W
Tomingley Australia **47** 32.06S148.15E
Tomini Indonesia **27** 0.31N120.30E
Tomini, Teluk *g.* Indonesia **27** 0.30S120.45E
Tominian Mali **38** 13.17N 4.35W
Tomintoul U.K. **6** 57.15N 3.24W
Tomkinson Ranges *mts.* Australia **42** 26.11S129.05E
Tom Price Australia **42** 22.49S117.51E
Tomra Norway **16** 62.34N 6.55E
Tomsk Russian Fed. **20** 56.30N 85.05E
Toms River *town* U.S.A. **55** 39.57N 74.12W
Tonalá Mexico **56** 16.08N 93.41W
Tonalea U.S.A. **54** 36.20N110.58W
Tonasket U.S.A. **54** 48.42N119.26W
Tonbridge U.K. **5** 51.12N 0.16E
Tondano Indonesia **27** 1.19N124.56E
Tondibi Mali **38** 16.39N 0.14W
Tondoro Namibia **39** 17.45S 18.50E
Tone *r.* Japan **23** 35.44N140.51E
Tonga Pacific Oc. **40** 20.00S175.00W
Tongaat R.S.A. **39** 29.34S 31.07E
Tongeren Belgium **8** 50.47N 5.28E
Tongguan Shaanxi China **25** 34.36N110.21E
Tonghai China **29** 24.07N102.45E
Tonghua China **25** 41.40N126.52E
Tongking, G. of Asia **26** 20.00N107.50E
Tongling China **25** 30.57N117.40E
Tongo Australia **46** 30.30S143.47E
Tongoy Chile **62** 30.15S 71.30W
Tongue U.K. **6** 58.28N 4.25W
Tongue *r.* U.S.A. **54** 46.24N105.25W
Tongyu China **25** 44.48N123.06E
Tonk India **28** 26.10N 75.50E
Tonkābon Iran **31** 36.49N 50.54E
Tônlé Sap *l.* Cambodia **26** 12.50N104.00E
Tonnerre France **9** 47.51N 3.59E
Tonopah U.S.A. **54** 38.04N117.14W
Tonota Botswana **39** 21.28S 27.24E
Tonstad Norway **17** 58.40N 6.43E
Tonto Basin *town* U.S.A. **54** 33.55N111.18W
Toobeah Australia **47** 28.22S149.50E
Toodyay Australia **43** 31.35S116.26E
Tooele U.S.A. **54** 40.32N112.18W
Toolondo Australia **46** 36.55S142.00E
Toowoomba Australia **45** 27.35S151.54E
Topeka U.S.A. **53** 39.03N 95.41W
Topko *mtn.* Russian Fed. **21** 57.20N138.10E
Topliţa Romania **15** 46.55N 25.21E
Topock U.S.A. **54** 34.44N114.27W
Topolovgrad Bulgaria **13** 42.05N 26.20E
Topozero, Ozero *l.* Russian Fed. **18** 65.45N 32.00E
Toppenish U.S.A. **54** 46.23N120.19W
Tora-Khem Russian Fed. **21** 52.31N 96.13E
Torbat-e Ḩeydarīyeh Iran **31** 35.16N 59.13E
Torbat-e Jām Iran **31** 35.15N 60.37E
Tordesillas Spain **10** 41.30N 5.00W
Torgau Germany **14** 51.34N 13.00E
Torhout Belgium **8** 51.04N 3.06E
Toride Japan **23** 35.53N140.04E
Torino Italy **9** 45.04N 7.40E
Tormes *r.* Spain **10** 41.18N 6.29W
Torne *r.* Sweden *see* Tornio *r.* Finland **16**
Torneträsk Sweden **16** 68.15N 19.30E
Torneträsk *l.* Sweden **16** 68.20N 19.10E
Tornio Finland **16** 65.52N 24.10E
Tornio *r.* Finland **16** 65.53N 24.07E
Tornquist Argentina **63** 38.06S 62.14W
Toro Spain **10** 41.31N 5.24W
Toronaíos Kólpos *g.* Greece **13** 40.05N 23.38E
Toronto Canada **55** 43.39N 79.23W
Toropets Russian Fed. **18** 56.30N 31.40E
Tororo Uganda **37** 0.42N 34.13E
Toros Dağlari *mts.* Turkey **30** 37.15N 34.15E
Torquay Australia **46** 38.20S144.20E
Torquay U.K. **5** 50.27N 3.31W
Torrance U.S.A. **54** 33.50N118.19W
Torreblanca Spain **10** 40.14N 0.12E
Torre de Moncorvo Portugal **10** 41.10N 7.03W
Torrelavega Spain **10** 43.21N 4.00W
Torremolinos Spain **10** 36.38N 4.30W
Torrens, L. Australia **46** 31.00S137.50E
Torrens Creek *r.* Australia **44** 22.22S145.09E
Torrens Creek *town* Australia **44** 20.50S145.00E
Torreón Mexico **56** 25.34N103.25W
Torre Pellice Italy **9** 44.49N 9.13E
Torres Str. Australia **44** 10.00S142.20E
Torres Vedras Portugal **10** 39.05N 9.15W
Torrevieja Spain **10** 37.59N 0.40W
Torrey U.S.A. **54** 38.18N111.25W
Torridge *r.* U.K. **5** 51.01N 4.12W
Torridon U.K. **6** 57.23N 5.31W
Torridon, Loch U.K. **6** 57.35N 5.45W
Torriglia Italy **9** 44.31N 9.10E
Torsby Sweden **17** 60.08N 13.00E
Tortola *i.* B.V.Is. **57** 18.28N 64.40W
Tortona Italy **9** 44.54N 8.52E
Tortosa Spain **10** 40.49N 0.31E
Tortue, Île de la *i.* Cuba **57** 20.05N 72.57W
Toruń Poland **15** 53.01N 18.35E
Tory I. Rep. of Ire. **7** 55.16N 8.13W
Tory Sd. Rep. of Ire. **7** 55.14N 8.15W
Torzhok Russian Fed. **18** 57.02N 34.51E
Toscana *d.* Italy **12** 43.35N 11.10E
Tosen Norway **16** 65.16N 12.50E
Tosno Russian Fed. **18** 59.38N 30.46E
Tostado Argentina **62** 29.15S 61.45W
Totana Spain **10** 37.46N 1.30W
Tôtes France **9** 49.41N 1.03E
Totma Russian Fed. **18** 59.59N 42.44E
Totora Bolivia **62** 17.42S 65.09W
Tottenham Australia **47** 32.14S147.24E
Tottori Japan **25** 35.32N134.12E
Toubkal *mtn.* Morocco **34** 31.03N 7.57W
Toucy France **9** 47.44N 3.18E
Tougan Burkina **38** 13.05N 3.04W
Touggourt Algeria **34** 33.08N 6.04E
Toul France **11** 48.41N 5.54E
Toulnustouc *r.* Canada **55** 49.35N 68.25W
Toulon France **11** 43.07N 5.53E
Toulouse France **11** 43.33N 1.24E
Toummo Niger **34** 22.45N 14.08E
Toungoo Burma **29** 19.00N 96.30E
Touques *r.* France **9** 49.22N 0.06E
Tourcoing France **8** 50.44N 3.09E
Tournai Belgium **8** 50.36N 3.23E
Tournon France **11** 45.04N 4.50E
Tournus France **11** 46.33N 4.55E
Tours France **9** 47.23N 0.42E
Toury France **9** 48.11N 1.56E
Touwsrivier *town* R.S.A. **39** 33.20S 20.02E
Towcester U.K. **5** 52.07N 0.56W
Townsend, Mt. Australia **47** 36.24S148.15E
Townshend I. Australia **44** 22.15S150.30E
Townsville Australia **44** 19.13S146.48E
Towson U.S.A. **55** 39.24N 76.36W
Towyn U.K. **5** 52.37N 4.08W
Toyama Japan **25** 36.42N137.14E
Toyo *r.* Japan **23** 34.47N137.20E
Toyohashi Japan **23** 34.46N137.23E
Toyokawa Japan **23** 34.49N137.24E
Toyota Japan **23** 35.05N137.09E
Tozeur Tunisia **34** 33.55N 8.08E
Töcksfors Sweden **17** 59.30N 11.50E
Tönder Denmark **17** 54.56N 8.54E
Tönsberg Norway **17** 59.17N 10.25E
Tördal Norway **17** 59.10N 8.45E
Töre Sweden **16** 65.54N 22.39E
Töreboda Sweden **17** 58.43N 14.08E
Traben-Trarbach Germany **8** 49.57N 7.07E
Trabzon Turkey **30** 41.00N 39.43E
Trafalgar, Cabo *c.* Spain **10** 36.11N 6.02W
Traiguén Chile **63** 38.15S 72.41W
Trail Canada **50** 49.04N117.39W
Trajanova Vrata *pass* Bulgaria **13** 42.13N 23.58E
Trakt Russian Fed. **18** 62.40N 51.26E
Tralee Rep. of Ire. **7** 52.16N 9.42W
Tralee B. Rep. of Ire. **7** 52.18N 9.55W
Tranås Sweden **17** 58.03N 14.59E
Trang Thailand **29** 7.35N 99.35E
Trangan *i.* Indonesia **27** 6.30S134.15E
Trangie Australia **47** 32.03S148.01E
Trani Italy **12** 41.17N 16.26E
Tranqueras Uruguay **63** 31.12S 55.45W
Transkei Africa **39** 31.30S 29.00E
Transkei *f.* R.S.A. **39** 32.12S 28.20E
Transylvanian Alps *see* Carpaţii Meridionalimts. *mts.* Romania **13**
Transylvanian Alps *See* Carpaţii Meridionalimts. *mts.* R.S.A. **39** 24.30S 29.30E
Trapani Italy **12** 38.02N 12.30E
Traralgon Australia **47** 38.12S146.32E
Traryd Sweden **17** 56.35N 13.45E
Trasimeno, Lago *l.* Italy **12** 43.09N 12.07E
Traunstein Germany **14** 47.52N 12.38E
Travellers L. Australia **46** 33.18S142.00E
Travers, Mt. New Zealand **48** 42.05S172.45E
Traverse City U.S.A. **55** 44.46N 85.38W
Travnik Bosnia-Herzegovina **13** 44.14N 17.40E
Trayning Australia **43** 31.09S117.46E
Trbovlje Slovenia **14** 46.10N 15.03E
Trebbia *r.* Italy **9** 45.04N 9.41E
Třebíč Czech. **14** 49.13N 15.55E
Trebinje Bosnia-Herzegovina **13** 42.43N 18.20E
Trebišov Czech. **15** 48.40N 21.47E
Třeboň Czech. **14** 49.01N 14.50E
Trecate Italy **9** 45.26N 8.44E
Tredegar U.K. **5** 51.47N 3.16W
Tregaron U.K. **5** 52.14N 3.56W
Tregosse Islets and Reefs Australia **44** 17.41S150.43E
Tréguier France **11** 48.47N 3.16W
Treinta-y-Tres Uruguay **59** 33.16S 54.17W
Treis Germany **8** 50.10N 7.20E
Trélazé France **9** 47.27N 0.28W
Trelew Argentina **63** 43.15S 65.20W
Trelleborg Sweden **17** 55.22N 13.10E
Trélon France **8** 50.04N 4.05E
Tremadog B. U.K. **4** 52.52N 4.14W
Tremp Spain **10** 42.10N 0.52E
Trenčín Czech. **15** 48.54N 18.04E
Trenque Lauquen Argentina **63** 35.56S 62.43W
Trent *r.* U.K. **4** 53.41N 0.41W
Trentino-Alto Adige *d.* Italy **9** 46.30N 11.20E
Trento Italy **9** 46.04N 11.08E
Trenton Canada **55** 44.06N 77.35W
Trenton N.J. U.S.A. **55** 40.15N 74.43W
Trepassey Canada **51** 46.44N 53.22W
Tres Árboles Uruguay **63** 32.24S 56.43W
Tres Arroyos Argentina **63** 38.26S 60.17W
Três Corações Brazil **59** 21.44S 45.15W
Três Lagoas Brazil **59** 20.46S 51.43W
Três Marias, Reprêsa *resr.* Brazil **59** 18.15S 45.15W
Três Pontas Brazil **59** 21.23S 45.29W
Três Rios Brazil **59** 22.07S 43.12W
Treuchtlingen Germany **14** 48.57N 10.55E
Treviglio Italy **9** 45.31N 9.35E
Treviso Italy **9** 45.40N 12.14E
Tribulation, C. Australia **44** 16.03S145.30E
Trida Australia **47** 33.00S145.01E
Trier Germany **8** 49.45N 6.39E
Trieste Italy **12** 45.40N 13.47E
Triglav *mtn.* Slovenia **12** 46.21N 13.50E
Tríkala Greece **13** 39.34N 21.46E
Tríkomon Cyprus **32** 35.17N 33.53E
Trincomalee Sri Lanka **29** 8.34N 81.13E
Trinidad Bolivia **62** 14.47S 64.47W
Trinidad Colombia **60** 5.25N 71.40W
Trinidad Cuba **57** 21.48N 80.00W
Trinidad Uruguay **63** 33.32S 56.54W
Trinidad U.S.A. **52** 37.10N104.31W
Trinidad & Tobago S. America **57** 10.30N 61.20W
Trinity *r.* U.S.A. **53** 29.55N 94.45W
Trinity B. Australia **44** 16.26S145.26E
Trinity Range *mts.* U.S.A. **54** 40.13N119.12W
Trino Italy **9** 45.12N 8.18E
Tripoli *see* Ţarābulus Lebanon **32**
Tripoli *see* Ţarābulus Libya **34**
Trípolis Greece **13** 37.31N 22.21E
Tripolitania *f.* *see* Ţarābulus *f.* Libya **34**
Tripura *d.* India **29** 23.45N 91.45E
Trivandrum *see* Thiruvananthapuram India **28**
Trnava Czech. **15** 48.23N 17.35E
Troarn France **9** 49.11N 0.11W
Trobriand Is. P.N.G. **44** 8.35S151.05E
Troglav *mtn.* Croatia **13** 43.57N 16.36E
Troisdorf Germany **8** 50.50N 7.07E
Trois-Rivières *town* Canada **55** 46.21N 72.33W
Troitsk Russian Fed. **20** 54.08N 61.33E
Troitsko-Pechorsk Russian Fed. **18** 62.40N 56.08E
Troitskoye Russian Fed. **18** 52.18N 56.26E
Troitskoye Ukraine **15** 47.38N 30.19E
Trollhättan Sweden **17** 58.16N 12.18E
Trollheimen *mts.* Norway **16** 62.50N 9.15E
Troms *d.* Norway **16** 69.20N 19.30E
Tromsö Norway **16** 69.42N 19.00E
Trondheim Norway **16** 63.36N 10.23E
Trondheimsfjorden *est.* Norway **16** 63.40N 10.30E
Troon U.K. **6** 55.33N 4.40W
Troödos *mts.* Cyprus **32** 34.57N 32.50E
Tropic U.S.A. **54** 37.37N112.05W
Trosh Russian Fed. **18** 66.24N 56.08E
Trostan *mtn.* U.K **7** 55.03N 6.10W
Trostyanets Ukraine **15** 48.35N 29.10E
Trout Creek *town* Canada **55** 45.59N 79.22W
Trouville France **9** 49.22N 0.55E
Trowbridge U.K. **5** 51.18N 2.12W
Troy Mont. U.S.A. **54** 48.28N115.53W
Troy N.Y. U.S.A. **55** 42.43N 73.40W
Troy Ohio U.S.A. **55** 40.02N 84.12W
Troyes France **9** 48.18N 4.05E
Troy Peak *mtn.* U.S.A. **54** 38.19N115.30W
Trölladyngja *mtn.* Iceland **16** 64.54N 17.16W
Trpanj Croatia **13** 43.00N 17.17E
Truchas Peak *mtn.* U.S.A. **52** 35.58N105.39W
Truckee U.S.A. **54** 39.20N120.11W
Trujillo Honduras **57** 15.55N 86.00W
Trujillo Peru **60** 8.06S 79.00W
Trujillo Spain **10** 39.28N 5.53W
Trujillo Venezuela **60** 9.20N 70.37W
Trundle Australia **47** 32.54S147.35E
Truro Australia **46** 34.23S139.09E
Truro Canada **51** 45.24N 63.18W
Truro U.K. **5** 50.17N 5.02W
Trustrup Denmark **17** 56.21N 10.47E
Trysil Norway **17** 61.19N 12.16E
Trysil *r.* Norway **17** 61.03N 12.30E
Trzemeszno Poland **15** 52.35N 17.50E
Tsaratanana, Massif de *mts.* Madagascar **36** 14.00S 49.00E
Tsau Botswana **39** 20.10S 22.29E
Tsavo Nat. Park Kenya **37** 2.45S 38.45E
Tselinograd Kazakhstan **20** 51.10N 71.28E
Tses Namibia **39** 25.58S 18.08E
Tsévié Togo **38** 6.28N 1.15E
Tshabong Botswana **39** 26.03S 22.25E
Tshane Botswana **39** 24.02S 21.54E
Tshesebe Botswana **39** 20.45S 27.31E
Tsimlyansk Russian Fed. **19** 47.40N 42.06E
Tsimlyanskoye Vodokhranilishche *resr.* Russian Fed. **19** 48.00N 43.00E
Tsingtao *see* Qingdao China **25**
Tsiribihina Madagascar **39** 19.42S 44.31E
Tsivilsk Russian Fed. **18** 55.50N 47.28E
Tskhinvali Georgia **19** 42.14N 43.58E
Tsna *r.* Belorussia **15** 52.10N 27.03E
Tsna *r.* Russian Fed. **18** 54.45N 41.54E
Tsobis Namibia **39** 19.27S 17.30E
Tsu Japan **23** 34.43N136.31E
Tsuchiura Japan **23** 36.05N140.12E
Tsudakhar Russian Fed. **19** 42.20N 47.11E
Tsumeb Namibia **39** 19.12S 17.43E
Tsuru Japan **23** 35.30N138.56E
Tsushima Japan **23** 35.10N136.43E
Tsushima *i.* Japan **25** 34.30N129.20E
Tuam Rep. of Ire. **7** 53.32N 8.52W
Tuamotu, Îles *is.* Pacific Oc. **40** 17.00S142.00W
Tuapse Russian Fed. **19** 44.06N 39.05E
Tuatapere New Zealand **48** 46.08S167.41E
Tuba City U.S.A. **54** 36.08N111.14W
Tubarão Brazil **59** 28.30S 49.01W
Ţubayq, Jabal aţ *mts.* Saudi Arabia **32** 29.30N 37.15E
Tubbercurry Rep. of Ire. **7** 54.03N 8.45W
Ţubjah, Wādī *r.* Saudi Arabia **30** 25.35N 38.22E
Ţubruq Libya **35** 32.06N 23.58E
Tucacas Venezuela **60** 10.48N 68.19W
Tuchola Poland **15** 53.35N 17.50E
Tucson U.S.A. **52** 32.13N110.58W
Tucumán *d.* Argentina **62** 26.30S 65.20W
Tucumcari U.S.A. **52** 35.10N103.44W
Tucupita Venezuela **60** 9.02N 62.04W
Tucuruí Brazil **61** 3.42S 49.44W
Tucuruí, Reprêsa de *resr.* Brazil **61** 4.35S 49.33W
Tudela Spain **10** 42.04N 1.37W
Tufi P.N.G. **44** 9.05S149.20E
Tugela R.S.A. **39** 29.10S 31.25E
Tuguegarao Phil. **27** 17.36N121.44E
Tugur Russian Fed. **21** 53.44N136.45E
Tukangbesi, Kepulauan *is.* Indonesia **27** 5.30S124.00E
Tukayyid *well* Iraq **31** 29.47N 45.36E
Ţūkh Egypt **32** 30.21N 31.12E
Tuktoyaktuk Canada **50** 69.27N133.00W
Tukums Latvia **17** 57.00N 23.10E
Tukuyu Tanzania **37** 9.20S 33.37E
Tula Mexico **56** 23.00N 99.43W
Tula Russian Fed. **18** 54.11N 37.38E
Tulare U.S.A. **54** 36.13N119.21W
Tulare L. *resr.* U.S.A. **54** 36.03N119.49W
Tulcan Ecuador **60** 0.50N 77.48W
Tulcea Romania **13** 45.10N 28.50E
Tulchin Ukraine **15** 48.40N 28.49E
Tuli Zimbabwe **39** 21.50S 29.15E
Tuli *r.* Zimbabwe **39** 21.49S 29.00E
Ţūlkarm Jordan **32** 32.19N 35.02E
Tullamore Australia **47** 32.39S147.39E
Tullamore Rep. of Ire. **7** 53.17N 7.31W
Tulle France **11** 45.16N 1.46E
Tullins France **11** 45.18N 5.29E
Tullow Rep. of Ire. **7** 52.49N 6.45W
Tully Australia **44** 17.55S145.59E
Tully U.S.A. **55** 42.47N 76.06W
Tuloma *r.* Russian Fed. **18** 68.56N 33.00E
Tulsa U.S.A. **53** 36.07N 95.58W
Tuluá Colombia **60** 4.05N 76.12W
Tulumbasy Russian Fed. **18** 57.27N 57.40E
Tulun Russian Fed. **21** 54.32N100.35E
Tulungagung Indonesia **26** 8.03S111.54E
Tum Indonesia **27** 3.28S130.21E
Tumaco Colombia **60** 1.51N 78.46W
Tumba Sweden **17** 59.12N 17.49E
Tumbarumba Australia **47** 35.49S148.01E
Tumbes Peru **60** 3.37S 80.27W
Tumby Bay *town* Australia **46** 34.20S136.05E
Tumeremo Venezuela **60** 7.18N 61.30W
Tummel, Loch U.K. **6** 56.43N 3.55W
Tump Pakistan **28** 26.06N 62.24E
Tumuc Humac Mts. S. America **61** 2.20N 54.50W
Tumut Australia **47** 35.20S148.14E
Tunari *mtn.* Bolivia **62** 17.18S 66.22W
Tūnat al Jabal Egypt **32** 27.46N 30.44E
Tunceli Turkey **30** 39.07N 39.34E
Tuncurry Australia **47** 32.17S152.29E
Tunduma Tanzania **37** 9.19S 32.47E
Tunduru Tanzania **37** 11.08S 37.21E
Tundzha *r.* Bulgaria **13** 41.40N 26.34E
Tungabhadra *r.* India **28** 16.00N 78.15E
Tungsten U.S.A. **54** 40.48N118.08W
Tunis Tunisia **34** 36.47N 10.10E
Tunisia Africa **34** 34.00N 9.00E
Tunja Colombia **60** 5.33N 73.23W
Tunnsjöen *l.* Norway **16** 64.45N 13.25E
Tunuyán *r.* Argentina **63** 33.33S 67.30W
Tuoy-Khaya Russian Fed. **21** 62.33N111.25E
Tupã Brazil **59** 21.57S 50.28W
Tupelo U.S.A. **53** 34.15N 88.43W
Tupinambaranas, Ilha *f.* Brazil **61** 3.00S 58.00W
Tupiza Bolivia **62** 21.27S 65.43W
Tuquan China **25** 45.22N121.41E
Túquerres Colombia **60** 1.06N 77.37W
Tura Russian Fed. **21** 64.05N100.00E
Tura Tanzania **37** 5.30S 33.50E
Turangi New Zealand **48** 38.59S175.48E
Turbaco Colombia **60** 10.20N 75.25W
Turbanovo Russian Fed. **18** 60.05N 50.46E
Turbo Colombia **60** 8.06N 76.44W
Turda Romania **15** 46.34N 23.47E
Turek Poland **15** 52.02N 18.30E
Turgeon *r.* Canada **55** 50.00N 78.54W
Tŭrgovishte Bulgaria **13** 43.14N 26.37E
Turgutlu Turkey **13** 38.30N 27.43E
Turhal Turkey **30** 40.23N 36.05E
Turia *r.* Spain **10** 39.27N 0.19W
Turiaçu Brazil **61** 1.41S 45.21W
Turiaçu *r.* Brazil **61** 1.36S 45.19W
Turin *see* Torino Italy **9**
Turka Ukraine **15** 49.10N 23.02E
Turkana, L. Kenya **37** 4.00N 36.00E
Turkestan Kazakhstan **24** 43.17N 68.16E
Turkey Asia **30** 39.00N 35.00E
Turkey Creek *town* Australia **42** 17.04S128.15E
Turkmenistan Asia **20** 40.00N 60.00E
Turks Is. Turks & Caicos Is. **57** 21.30N 71.10W
Turku Finland **17** 60.27N 22.17E
Turku-Pori *d.* Finland **17** 61.00N 22.35E
Turkwel *r.* Kenya **37** 3.08N 35.39E
Turneffe Is. Belize **57** 17.30N 87.45W
Turnhout Belgium **8** 51.19N 4.57E
Turnu Măgurele Romania **13** 43.43N 24.53E
Turnu Roşu, Pasul *pass* Romania **13** 45.37N 24.17E
Turnu-Severin Romania **13** 44.37N 22.39E
Turon *r.* Australia **47** 33.03S149.33E
Turov Belorussia **15** 52.04N 27.40E
Turpan China **24** 42.55N 89.06E
Turpan Pendi *f.* China **24** 43.40N 89.00E
Turquino *mtn.* Cuba **57** 20.05N 76.50W
Turriff U.K. **6** 57.32N 2.28W
Turtkul Uzbekistan **31** 41.30N 61.00E
Turukhansk Russian Fed. **21** 65.21N 88.05E
Turya *r.* Ukraine **15** 51.48N 24.52E
Tuscaloosa U.S.A. **53** 33.12N 87.33W
Tuscarora U.S.A. **54** 41.19N116.14W
Tutera *see* Tudela Spain **10**
Tuticorin India **29** 8.48N 78.10E
Tutóia Brazil **61** 2.45S 42.16W
Tutrakan Bulgaria **13** 44.02N 26.40E
Tuttlingen Germany **14** 47.59N 8.49E
Tutuala Indonesia **27** 8.24S127.15E
Tutubu Tanzania **37** 5.28S 32.43E
Tuţūn Egypt **32** 29.09N 30.46E
Tuul Gol *r.* Mongolia **24** 48.53N104.35E
Tuvalu Pacific Oc. **40** 8.00S178.00E
Tuxpan Mexico **56** 21.00N 97.23W
Tuxtla Gutiérrez Mexico **56** 16.45N 93.09W
Túy Spain **10** 42.03N 8.39W
Tuz Gölü *l.* Turkey **30** 38.45N 33.24E
Ţūz Khurmātū Iraq **31** 34.53N 44.38E
Tuzla Bosnia-Herzegovina **13** 44.33N 18.41E
Tübingen Germany **14** 48.32N 9.04E
Türi Estonia **17** 58.48N 25.26E
Tvedestrand Norway **17** 58.37N 8.55E

Tveitsund Norway 17 59.01N 8.32E
Tver' Russian Fed. 18 56.47N 35.57E
Tweed r. U.K. 6 55.46N 2.00W
Tweed Heads town Australia 47 28.13S153.33E
Twentynine Palms U.S.A. 54 34.08N116.03W
Twin Bridges town U.S.A. 54 45.33N112.20W
Twin Falls town U.S.A. 54 42.34N114.28W
Twins Creek r. Australia 46 29.10S139.27E
Twizel New Zealand 48 44.15S170.06E
Twofold B. Australia 47 37.06S149.55E
Twyford U.K. 5 51.01N 1.19W
Tyler Tex. U.S.A. 53 32.22N 95.18W
Tyndinskiy Russian Fed. 21 55.11N124.34E
Tyne r. U.K. 4 55.00N 1.25W
Tyne and Wear d. U.K. 4 54.57N 1.35W
Tynemouth U.K. 4 55.01N 1.24W
Tynset Norway 17 62.17N 10.47E
Tyre see Şūr Lebanon 32
Tyrifjorden l. Norway 17 60.02N 10.08E
Tyrone d. U.K. 7 54.35N 7.15W
Tyrone U.S.A. 55 40.40N 78.14W
Tyrrell r. Australia 46 35.28S142.55E
Tyrrell, L. Australia 46 35.22S142.50E
Tyrrhenian Sea Med. Sea 12 40.00N 12.00E
Tysnesöy i. Norway 17 60.00N 5.35E
Tyumen Russian Fed. 20 57.11N 65.29E
Tywi r. U.K. 5 51.46N 4.22W
Tzaneen R.S.A. 39 23.49S 30.10E

U

Uatumã r. Brazil 61 2.30S 57.40W
Uaupés Brazil 60 0.07S 67.05W
Uaupés r. Brazil 60 0.00S 67.10W
Ubá Brazil 59 21.08S 42.59W
Ubangi r. Congo / Zaïre 36 0.25S 17.50E
Ubatuba Brazil 59 23.26S 45.05W
Ubayyiḍ, Wādī al r. Iraq 30 32.04N 42.17E
Ubeda Spain 10 38.01N 3.22W
Uberaba Brazil 59 19.47S 47.57W
Uberlândia Brazil 59 18.57S 48.17W
Ubombo R.S.A. 39 27.35S 32.05E
Ubort r. Belorussia 15 52.06N 28.28E
Ubundu Zaïre 35 0.24S 25.28E
Ucayali r. Peru 60 4.40S 73.20W
Udaipur India 28 24.36N 73.47E
Udaquiola Argentina 63 36.35S 58.30W
Jddevalla Sweden 17 58.21N 11.55E
Jddjaur l. Sweden 16 65.55N 17.49E
Jdine Italy 9 46.03N 13.15E
Jdipi India 28 13.21N 74.45E
Jdon Thani Thailand 29 17.29N102.46E
Jele r. Zaïre 36 4.08N 22.25E
Jelzen Germany 14 52.58N 10.34E
Jeno Japan 23 34.45N136.08E
Jfa Russian Fed. 18 54.45N 55.58E
Jfa r. Russian Fed. 18 54.45N 56.00E
Jffculme U.K. 5 50.45N 3.19W
Jgab r. Namibia 39 21.12S 13.37E
Jgalla r. Tanzania 37 5.43S 31.10E
Iganda Africa 37 2.00N 33.00E
Igep Nigeria 38 5.48N 8.05E
Ighelli Nigeria 38 5.33N 6.00E
Iglegorsk Russian Fed. 21 49.01N142.04E
Iglovka Russian Fed. 18 58.13N 33.30E
Igoma mtn. Zaïre 37 4.00S 28.45E
Igra r. Russian Fed. 18 54.30N 36.10E
Iherske Hradiště Czech. 15 49.05N 17.28E
Iig U.K. 6 57.35N 6.22W
Iíge Angola 36 7.40S 15.09E
Iil Kazakhstan 19 49.08N 54.43E
Iil r. Kazakhstan 19 48.33N 52.25E
Iinta Mts. U.S.A. 54 40.45N110.05W
Iitenhage R.S.A. 39 33.46S 25.23E
Iithuizen Neth. 8 53.24N 6.41E
ivlleq see Nanortalik Greenland 51
ji r. Japan 23 34.53N135.48E
jiji Tanzania 37 4.55S 29.39E
jjain India 28 23.11N 75.50E
jpest Hungary 15 47.33N 19.05E
jście Poland 14 53.04N 16.43E
jung Pandang Indonesia 26 5.09S119.28E
ka Russian Fed. 21 57.50N162.02E
kerewe I. Tanzania 37 2.00S 33.00E
khta Russian Fed. 18 63.33N 53.44E
kiah U.S.A. 54 39.09N123.13W
kmerge Lithuania 18 55.14N 24.49E
kraine Europe 15 49.45N 27.00E
kwi Botswana 39 23.22S 20.30E
laanbaatar Mongolia 24 47.54N106.52E
laangom Mongolia 24 49.59N 92.00E
lan Bator see Ulaanbaatar Mongolia 24
lan-Ude Russian Fed. 24 51.55N107.40E
lan Ul Hu l. China 29 34.45N 90.25E
lcinj Yugo. 13 41.55N 19.11E
lenia, L. Australia 46 29.57S142.24E
lhāsnagar India 28 19.13N 73.07E
liastay Mongolia 24 47.42N 96.52E
la r. Spain 10 42.38N 8.45W
ladulla Australia 47 35.21S150.25E
långer Sweden 16 62.58N 18.16E
lapool U.K. 6 57.54N 5.10W
lswater l. U.K. 4 54.34N 2.52W
m Germany 14 48.24N 10.00E
ongwé Mozambique 37 14.34S 34.21E
ricehamn Sweden 17 57.47N 13.25E
san S. Korea 25 35.32N129.21E
sberg Norway 16 62.45N 9.59E
tima Australia 46 35.30S143.20E
úa r. Honduras 57 15.50N 87.38W
uguru Mts. Tanzania 37 7.05S 37.40E
uru mtn. Australia 44 25.20S131.01E
verston U.K. 4 54.13N 3.07W
verstone Australia 45 41.09S146.10E
yanovsk Russian Fed. 18 54.19N 48.22E
naisha Nigeria 38 8.01N 7.12E
nala Bolivia 62 17.21S 68.00W
nan Ukraine 15 48.45N 30.10E
nbria d. Italy 12 42.55N 12.10E
Ume r. Sweden 16 63.47N 20.16E
Ume r. Zimbabwe 39 17.00S 28.22E
Umeå Sweden 16 63.45N 20.20E
Umfors Sweden 16 65.56N 15.00E
Umfuli r. Zimbabwe 39 17.32S 29.23E
Umiat U.S.A. 50 69.25N152.20W
Umm-al-Qaywayn U.A.E. 31 25.32N 55.34E
Umm Durmân Sudan 35 15.37N 32.59E
Umm el Faḥm Israel 32 32.31N 35.09E
Umm Lajj Saudi Arabia 30 25.03N 37.17E
Umniati Zimbabwe 39 18.41S 29.45E
Umtata R.S.A. 39 31.35S 28.47E
Umuahia Nigeria 38 5.31N 7.26E
Umzimkulu R.S.A. 39 30.15S 29.56E
Umzimvubu R.S.A. 39 31.37S 29.32E
Una r. Bosnia-Herzegovina 13 45.16N 16.55E
Unalakleet U.S.A. 50 63.53N160.47W
'Unayzah Jordan 32 30.29N 35.48E
'Unayzah Saudi Arabia 31 26.05N 43.57E
'Unayzah, Jabal mtn. Iraq 30 32.15N 39.19E
Uncia Bolivia 62 18.27S 66.37W
Uncompahgre Peak U.S.A. 54 38.04N107.28W
Uncompahgre Plateau f. U.S.A. 54 38.30N108.25W
Underberg R.S.A. 39 29.46S 29.26E
Underbool Australia 46 35.10S141.50E
Unecha Russian Fed. 15 52.52N 32.42E
Ungarie Australia 47 33.38S147.00E
Ungava, Péninsule d' pen. Canada 51 60.00N 74.00W
Ungava B. Canada 51 59.00N 67.30W
União Brazil 61 4.35S 42.52W
União da Vitória Brazil 59 26.13S 51.05W
Unimak I. U.S.A. 50 54.50N164.00W
Unini Peru 60 10.41S 73.59W
Uniondale R.S.A. 39 33.39S 23.07E
Union Gap U.S.A. 54 46.34N120.34W
Uniontown U.S.A. 55 39.54N 79.44W
United Arab Emirates Asia 31 24.00N 54.00E
United Kingdom Europe 3 54.00N 2.00W
United States of America N. America 52 39.00N100.00W
Unna Germany 8 51.32N 7.41E
Unst i. U.K. 6 60.45N 0.55W
Upata Venezuela 60 8.02N 62.25W
Upernavik Greenland 51 72.50N 56.00W
Upington R.S.A. 39 28.26S 21.12E
Upper East d. Ghana 38 10.40N 0.20W
Upper Egypt see Aş Şa'īd f. Egypt 30
Upper Hutt New Zealand 48 41.07S175.04E
Upper Klamath L. U.S.A. 54 42.23N122.55W
Upper Lough Erne U.K 7 54.13N 7.32W
Upper Tean U.K. 4 52.57N 1.59W
Upper Volta see Burkina Africa 38
Upper West d. Ghana 38 10.25N 2.00W
Upper Yarra Resr. Australia 47 37.43S145.56E
Uppsala Sweden 17 59.52N 17.38E
Uppsala d. Sweden 17 60.10N 17.50E
Uqlat aş Şuqūr Saudi Arabia 30 25.50N 42.12E
Ur ruins Iraq 31 30.55N 46.07E
Uracoa Venezuela 60 9.03N 62.27W
Uraga-suido str. Japan 23 35.10N139.42E
Ural r. Kazakhstan 19 47.00N 52.00E
Uralla Australia 47 30.40S151.31E
Ural Mts. see Ural'skiye Gory mts. Russian Fed. 18
Ural'sk Kazakhstan 19 51.19N 51.20E
Ural'skiye Gory mts. Russian Fed. 18 60.00N 59.00E
Urana Australia 47 35.21S146.19E
Urana, L. Australia 47 35.21S146.19E
Urandangi Australia 44 21.36S138.18E
Uranium City Canada 50 59.32N108.43W
Urapunga Australia 44 14.41S134.34E
Uraricoera r. Brazil 60 3.10N 60.30W
Urawa Japan 23 35.51N139.39E
Uray Russian Fed. 20 60.11N 65.00E
Urbino Italy 12 43.43N 12.38E
Urcos Peru 60 13.40S 71.38W
Urda Kazakhstan 19 48.44N 47.30E
Urdzhar Kazakhstan 20 47.06N 81.33E
Ure r. U.K. 4 54.05N 1.20W
Urechye Belorussia 15 52.59N 27.50E
Uren Russian Fed. 18 57.30N 45.50E
Urengoy Russian Fed. 20 65.59N 78.30E
Ures Mexico 56 29.26N110.24W
Uribia Colombia 60 11.43N 72.16W
Urisino Australia 46 29.44S143.49E
Urjala Finland 17 61.05N 23.32E
Urk Neth. 8 52.40N 5.36E
Urlingford Rep. of Ire. 7 52.44N 7.35W
Urmia, L. see Daryācheh-ye Orūmīyeh l. Iran 31
Ursus Poland 15 52.12N 20.53E
Uruaçu Brazil 61 14.30S 49.10W
Uruapan Mexico 56 19.26N102.04W
Urubamba Peru 60 13.20S 72.07W
Urubamba r. Peru 60 10.43S 73.55W
Urucará Brazil 61 2.32S 57.45W
Uruçui Brazil 61 7.14S 44.33W
Uruguaiana Brazil 63 29.45S 57.05W
Uruguay r. Argentina / Uruguay 63 34.00S 58.30W
Uruguay S. America 59 33.15S 56.00W
Urun P.N.G. 44 8.36S147.15E
Urunga Australia 47 30.30S152.28E
Urup r. Russian Fed. 19 44.59N 41.12E
Urzhum Russian Fed. 18 57.08N 50.00E
Urziceni Romania 13 44.43N 26.38E
Usa r. Russian Fed. 18 65.58N 56.35E
Usakos Namibia 39 22.02S 15.35E
Usambara Mts. Tanzania 37 4.45S 38.25E
Ushant i. see Ouessant, Île d' i. France 11
Ush-Tobe Kazakhstan 24 45.15N 77.59E
Ushuaia Argentina 63 54.47S 68.20W
Ushumun Russian Fed. 21 52.48N126.27E
Usisya Malaŵi 37 11.10S 34.12E
Usk r. U.K. 5 51.34N 2.59W
Uskedal Norway 17 59.56N 5.52E
Usman Russian Fed. 19 52.02N 39.43E
Usovo Ukraine 15 51.20N 28.01E
Uspenskiy Kazakhstan 20 48.41N 72.43E
Ussuriysk Russian Fed. 25 43.48N131.59E
Ustaoset Norway 17 60.30N 8.04E
Ustica i. Italy 12 38.42N 13.11E
Ust'-Ilga Russian Fed. 21 54.59N105.00E
Ústí nad Labem Czech. 14 50.41N 14.00E
Ust Ishim Russian Fed. 20 57.45N 71.05E
Ustka Poland 14 54.35N 16.50E
Ust'kamchatsk Russian Fed. 21 56.14N162.28E
Ust-Kamenogorsk Kazakhstan 20 50.00N 82.40E
Ust Kulom Russian Fed. 18 61.34N 53.40E
Ust Kut Russian Fed. 21 56.40N105.50E
Ust Lyzha Russian Fed. 18 65.45N 56.38E
Ust'Maya Russian Fed. 21 60.25N134.28E
Ust Nem Russian Fed. 18 61.38N 54.50E
Ust Olenëk Russian Fed. 21 72.59N120.00E
Ust-Omchug Russian Fed. 21 61.08N149.38E
Ust Port Russian Fed. 20 69.44N 84.23E
Ust Tapsuy Russian Fed. 18 62.25N 61.42E
Ust'Tsilma Russian Fed. 18 65.28N 53.09E
Ust-Tungir Russian Fed. 21 55.25N120.15E
Ust Ura Russian Fed. 18 63.06N 44.41E
Ust Vaga Russian Fed. 18 62.42N 42.45E
Ust Vym Russian Fed. 18 62.15N 50.25E
Ustyurt, Plato f. Kazakhstan 19 43.30N 55.00E
Usu China 24 44.27N 84.37E
Usumacinta r. Mexico 56 18.22N 92.40W
U.S. Virgin Is. C. America 57 18.30N 65.00W
Uşak Turkey 30 38.42N 29.25E
Ut Belorussia 15 52.18N 31.10E
Utah d. U.S.A. 54 39.37N112.28W
Utah L. U.S.A. 54 40.13N111.49W
'Utaybah, Buḥayrat al l. Syria 32 33.31N 36.37E
Utengule Tanzania 37 8.55S 35.43E
Utete Tanzania 37 8.00S 38.49E
Utiariti Brazil 60 13.02S 58.17W
Utica N.Y. U.S.A. 55 43.05N 75.14W
Utiel Spain 10 39.33N 1.13W
Utopia Australia 44 22.14S134.33E
Utrecht Neth. 8 52.04N 5.07E
Utrecht d. Neth. 8 52.04N 5.10E
Utrecht R.S.A. 39 27.38S 30.19E
Utrera Spain 10 37.10N 5.47W
Utsjoki Finland 16 69.53N 27.00E
Utsunomiya Japan 25 36.33N139.52E
Utta Russian Fed. 19 46.24N 46.01E
Uttaradit Thailand 29 17.38N100.05E
Uttar Pradesh d. India 29 27.40N 80.00E
Uummanarsuaq see Farvel, Kap c. Greenland 51
Uusikaupunki Finland 17 60.48N 21.25E
Uusimaa d. Finland 17 60.30N 25.00E
Uvalde U.S.A. 52 29.14N 99.49W
Uvarovichi Belorussia 15 52.35N 30.44E
Uvat Russian Fed. 20 59.10N 68.49E
Uvinza Tanzania 37 5.08S 30.23E
Uvira Zaïre 37 3.22S 29.06E
Uvs Nuur l. Mongolia 24 50.30N 92.30E
Uwajima Japan 25 33.13N132.32E
Uwayl Sudan 35 8.46N 27.24E
Uyo Nigeria 38 5.01N 7.56E
Uyuni Bolivia 62 20.28S 66.50W
Uyuni, Salar de f. Bolivia 62 20.20S 67.42W
Uzbekistan Asia 20 42.00N 63.00E
Uzda Belorussia 15 53.28N 27.11E
Uzh r. Ukraine 15 51.15N 30.12E
Uzhgorod Ukraine 15 48.38N 22.15E
Užice Yugo. 15 43.52N 19.51E
Ünye Turkey 30 41.09N 37.15E
Ürgüp Turkey 30 38.39N 34.55E
Ürümqi China 24 43.43N 87.38E
Üsküdar Turkey 13 41.00N 29.03E

V

Vaagö i. Faroe Is. 16 62.03N 7.14W
Vaal r. R.S.A. 39 29.04S 23.37E
Vaala Finland 16 64.26N 26.48E
Vaal Dam R.S.A. 39 26.51S 28.08E
Vaasa Finland 16 63.06N 21.36E
Vaasa d. Finland 16 62.50N 22.50E
Vác Hungary 15 47.49N 19.10E
Vadodara India 28 22.19N 73.14E
Vado Ligure Italy 9 44.17N 8.27E
Vadsö Norway 16 70.05N 29.46E
Vaduz Liech. 14 47.08N 9.32E
Vaeröy i. Norway 16 67.40N 12.40E
Vaga r. Russian Fed. 18 62.45N 42.48E
Vågåmo Norway 17 61.53N 9.06E
Vaggeryd Sweden 17 57.30N 14.07E
Váh r. Czech. 15 47.40N 17.50E
Vahsel B. Antarctica 64 77.00S 38.00W
Vailly-sur-Aisne France 9 49.25N 3.31E
Vakarai Sri Lanka 29 8.08N 81.26E
Vålådalen Sweden 16 63.09N 13.00E
Valavsk Belorussia 15 51.40N 28.38E
Valcheta Argentina 63 40.40S 66.10W
Valdagno Italy 9 45.39N 11.18E
Valday Russian Fed. 18 57.59N 33.10E
Valdayskaya Vozvyshennost mts. Russian Fed. 18 57.10N 33.00E
Valdemārpils Latvia 17 57.22N 22.35E
Valdemarsvik Sweden 17 58.12N 16.36E
Valdepeñas Spain 10 38.46N 3.24W
Valdés, Pen. Argentina 63 42.30S 64.00W
Valdez U.S.A. 50 61.07N146.17W
Val d'Isère France 9 45.27N 6.59E
Valdivia Chile 63 39.46S 73.15W
Val d'Oise d. France 9 49.10N 2.10E
Val d'Or town Canada 55 48.07N 77.47W
Valence France 11 44.56N 4.54E
Valencia Spain 10 39.29N 0.24W
Valencia d. Spain 10 39.30N 0.40W
Valencia Venezuela 60 10.14N 67.59W
Valencia, Golfo de g. Spain 10 39.38N 0.20W
Valencia de Alcántara Spain 10 39.25N 7.14
Valenciennes France 8 50.22N 3.32E
Valença Bahia Brazil 61 13.22S 39.06W
Valença R. de Janeiro Brazil 59 22.14S 43.45W
Valença Portugal 10 42.02N 8.38W
Vale of Evesham f. U.K. 5 52.05N 1.55W
Vale of Pewsey f. U.K. 5 51.21N 1.45W
Vale of York f. U.K. 4 54.12N 1.25W
Valera Venezuela 60 9.21N 70.38W
Valga Estonia 18 57.44N 26.00E
Valinco, Golfe de g. France 11 41.40N 8.50E
Valjevo Yugo. 15 44.16N 19.56E
Valkeakoski Finland 17 61.16N 24.02E
Valkenswaard Neth. 8 51.21N 5.27E
Valladolid Mexico 57 20.41N 88.12W
Valladolid Spain 10 41.39N 4.45W
Vall de Uxó town Spain 10 39.49N 0.15W
Valle Norway 17 59.12N 7.32E
Valle d'Aosta d. Italy 9 45.45N 7.25E
Valle de la Pascua Venezuela 60 9.15N 66.00W
Valledupar Colombia 60 10.31N 73.16W
Valle Edén Uruguay 63 31.50S 56.09W
Vallegrande Bolivia 62 18.29S 64.06W
Vallenar Chile 62 28.35S 70.46W
Valletta Malta 12 35.53N 14.31E
Valley City U.S.A. 52 46.57N 97.58W
Valley Falls town U.S.A. 54 42.29N120.16W
Valleyfield Canada 55 45.15N 74.08W
Vallgrund i. Finland 16 63.12N 21.14E
Valls Spain 10 41.18N 1.15E
Valmiera Latvia 18 57.32N 25.29E
Valnera mtn. Spain 10 43.10N 3.40W
Valognes France 9 49.31N 1.28W
Valparaíso Chile 63 33.02S 71.38W
Valparaíso Mexico 56 22.46N103.34W
Vals, Tanjung c. Indonesia 27 8.30S137.30E
Valverde Dom. Rep. 57 19.37N 71.04W
Valverde del Camino Spain 10 37.35N 6.45W
Vammala Finland 17 61.20N 22.54E
Van Turkey 30 38.28N 43.20E
Van Blommestein Meer, W.J. resr. Surinam 61 4.45N 55.05W
Vancouver Canada 50 49.13N123.06W
Vancouver U.S.A. 54 45.39N122.40W
Vancouver I. Canada 50 50.00N126.00W
Vanderbilt U.S.A. 55 45.09N 84.39W
Vanderlin I. Australia 44 15.44S137.02E
Van Diemen, C. Australia 44 16.31S139.41E
Van Diemen G. Australia 44 11.50S132.00E
Vandry Canada 55 47.50N 73.34W
Vänern l. Sweden 17 59.00N 13.15E
Vänersborg Sweden 17 58.22N 12.19E
Vang Norway 17 61.10N 8.40E
Vanga Kenya 37 4.37S 39.13E
Van Gölü l. Turkey 30 38.35N 42.52E
Vanimo P.N.G. 27 2.40S141.17E
Vankarem Russian Fed. 21 67.50N175.51E
Vanna i. Norway 16 70.10N 19.40E
Vännäs Sweden 16 63.58N 19.48E
Vannes France 11 47.40N 2.44W
Vanrhynsdorp R.S.A. 39 31.37S 18.42E
Vansbro Sweden 17 60.31N 14.13E
Vantaa Finland 17 60.13N 25.01E
Vanua Levu i. Fiji 40 16.33S179.15E
Vanuatu Pacific Oc. 40 16.00S167.00E
Van Wert U.S.A. 55 40.53N 84.36W
Vanzylsrus R.S.A. 39 26.51S 22.03E
Vapnyarka Ukraine 15 48.31N 28.44E
Var r. France 14 43.39N 7.11E
Varades France 9 47.23N 1.02W
Varallo Italy 9 45.49N 8.15E
Varāmīn Iran 31 35.20N 51.39E
Vārānasi India 29 25.20N 83.00E
Varangerfjorden est. Norway 16 70.00N 30.00E
Varangerhalvöya pen. Norway 16 70.25N 29.30E
Varaždin Croatia 12 46.18N 16.20E
Varazze Italy 9 44.22N 8.34E
Varberg Sweden 17 57.06N 12.15E
Vardar r. Yugo. see Axiós r. Greece 13
Varde Denmark 17 55.38N 8.29E
Varel Germany 8 53.24N 8.08E
Varennes France 11 46.19N 3.24E
Varese Italy 9 45.48N 8.48E
Varese Ligure Italy 9 44.22N 9.37E
Varginha Brazil 59 21.33S 45.25W
Varley Australia 43 32.48S119.31E
Värmland d. Sweden 17 59.55N 13.00E
Varna Bulgaria 15 43.13N 27.57E
Värnamo Sweden 17 57.11N 14.02E
Várpalota Hungary 15 47.12N 18.09E
Vartofta Sweden 17 58.06N 13.40E
Varzo Italy 9 46.12N 8.15E
Varzy France 9 47.21N 3.23E
Vasa see Vaasa Finland 16
Vashka r. Russian Fed. 18 64.55N 45.50E
Vasilkov Ukraine 15 50.12N 30.15E
Vaslui Romania 15 46.38N 27.44E
Västerås Sweden 17 59.37N 16.33E
Västerbotten d. Sweden 16 64.50N 18.10E
Västerdal r. Sweden 17 60.33N 15.08E
Västernorrland d. Sweden 16 63.20N 17.30E
Västervik Sweden 17 57.45N 16.38E
Västmanland d. Sweden 17 59.50N 16.15E
Vasto Italy 12 42.07N 14.42E
Vatan France 11 47.05N 1.48E
Vatican City Italy 12 41.54N 12.27E
Vatiua Mozambique 37 14.15S 37.22E
Vatnajökull mts. Iceland 16 64.20N 17.00W
Vatneyri Iceland 16 65.36N 23.59W
Vatra Dornei Romania 15 47.21N 25.21E
Vättern l. Sweden 17 58.30N 14.30E
Vaughn Mont. U.S.A. 54 47.35N111.34W
Vaughn N.Mex. U.S.A. 52 34.36N105.13W
Vaupés r. Colombia 60 0.20N 69.00W
Vavuniya Sri Lanka 29 8.45N 80.30E
Växjö Sweden 17 56.52N 14.49E
Vaygach Russian Fed. 20 70.28N 58.59E
Vaygach, Ostrov i. Russian Fed. 18 70.00N 59.00E
Vecht r. Neth. 8 52.39N 6.01E
Vecsés Hungary 15 47.26N 19.19E
Veddige Sweden 17 57.16N 12.19E
Veendam Neth. 8 53.08N 6.52E
Veenendaal Neth. 8 52.03N 5.32E
Vega i. Norway 16 65.39N 11.50E
Veghel Neth. 8 51.37N 5.35E
Vegreville Canada 50 53.30N112.02W
Veinticinco de Mayo Argentina 63 35.25S 60.11W
Vejen Denmark 17 55.29N 9.09E
Vejer Spain 10 36.15N 5.59W
Vejle Denmark 17 55.42N 9.32E
Velddrif R.S.A. 39 32.47S 18.09E
Vélez Málaga Spain 10 36.48N 4.05W
Vélez Rubio Spain 10 37.41N 2.05W
Velhas r. Brazil 59 17.20S 44.55W
Velikiye-Luki Russian Fed. 18 56.19N 30.31E
Velikiy Ustyug Russian Fed. 18 60.48N 45.15E
Veliko Tŭrnovo Bulgaria 13 43.04N 25.39E
Velizh Russian Fed. 18 55.36N 31.13E
Velletri Italy 12 41.41N 12.47E
Vellore India 29 12.56N 79.09E
Velsen Neth. 8 52.28N 4.39E
Velsk Russian Fed. 18 61.05N 42.06E
Veluwe f. Neth. 8 52.17N 5.45E
Vemdalen Sweden 16 62.29N 13.55E
Venado Tuerto Argentina 63 33.45S 61.56W
Venaria Italy 9 45.08N 7.38E
Vence France 9 43.43N 7.07E
Venda Africa 39 22.40S 30.40E
Vendas Novas Portugal 10 38.41N 8.27W
Vendeuvre-sur-Barse France 9 48.14N 4.28E
Vendôme France 9 47.48N 1.04E
Veneto d. Italy 9 45.25N 11.50E
Venev Russian Fed. 18 54.22N 38.15E
Venezia Italy 9 45.26N 12.20E
Venezuela S. America 60 7.00N 65.20W
Venezuela, Golfo de g. Venezuela 60 11.30N 71.00W
Vengurla India 28 15.52N 73.38E
Veniaminof Mtn. U.S.A. 50 56.05N159.20W
Venice see Venezia Italy 9
Venice, G. of Med. Sea 14 45.20N 13.00E
Venlo Neth. 8 51.22N 6.10E
Venraij Neth. 8 51.32N 5.58E
Venta r. Latvia 17 57.24N 21.33E
Ventersdorp R.S.A. 39 26.19S 26.48E
Ventimiglia Italy 9 43.47N 7.36E
Ventnor U.K. 5 50.35N 1.12W
Ventspils Latvia 17 57.24N 21.36E
Ventuari r. Venezuela 60 4.00N 67.35W
Venus B. Australia 47 38.40S145.43E
Vera Argentina 59 29.31S 60.30W
Vera Spain 10 37.15N 1.51W
Veracruz Mexico 56 19.11N 96.10W
Veracruz d. Mexico 56 18.00N 95.00W
Verāval India 28 20.53N 70.28E
Verbania Italy 9 45.56N 8.33E
Vercelli Italy 9 45.19N 8.26E
Verde r. Argentina 63 42.10S 65.03W
Verde r. Brazil 62 19.11S 50.44W
Verden Germany 14 52.55N 9.13E
Verdon r. France 11 43.42N 5.39E
Verdun Canada 55 45.28N 73.35W
Verdun Meuse France 11 49.10N 5.24E
Vereeniging R.S.A. 39 26.40S 27.55E
Vergelee R.S.A. 39 25.46S 24.09E
Verín Spain 10 41.55N 7.26W
Verkhniy Baskunchak Russian Fed. 19 48.14N 46.44E
Verkhniy Lyulyukary Russian Fed. 18 65.45N 64.28E
Verkhniy Shar Russian Fed. 18 68.21N 50.45E
Verkhniy Ufaley Russian Fed. 18 56.05N 60.14E
Verkhnyaya Taymyra r. Russian Fed. 21 74.10N 99.50E
Verkhnyaya Tura Russian Fed. 18 58.22N 59.50E
Verkhovye Russian Fed. 18 52.49N 37.14E
Verkhoyansk Russian Fed. 21 67.25N133.25E
Verkhoyanskiy Khrebet mts. Russian Fed. 21 66.00N130.00E
Vermenton France 9 47.40N 3.42E
Vermilion Canada 50 53.21N110.52W
Vermilion U.S.A. 55 41.24N 82.21W
Vermont d. U.S.A. 55 43.50N 72.45W
Vernal U.S.A. 54 40.27N109.32W
Verneuil France 9 48.44N 0.56E
Vernon Canada 50 50.16N119.16W
Vernon France 9 49.05N 1.29E
Véroia Greece 13 40.31N 22.12E
Verona Italy 9 45.27N 10.59E
Verónica Argentina 63 35.24S 57.22W
Verrès Italy 9 45.40N 7.42E
Versailles France 9 48.48N 2.08E
Vert, Cap c. Senegal 34 14.45N 17.25W
Vertou France 11 47.10N 1.28W
Vertus France 9 48.54N 4.00E
Verviers Belgium 8 50.36N 5.52E
Vervins France 9 49.50N 3.54E
Vesanto Finland 16 62.56N 26.25E
Veselí nad Lužnicí Czech. 14 49.11N 14.43E
Vesle r. France 9 49.23N 3.38E
Vesoul France 14 47.38N 6.09E
Vest-Agder d. Norway 17 58.30N 7.10E
Vestfjorden est. Norway 16 68.10N 15.00E
Vestfold d. Norway 17 59.20N 10.10E
Vestmanhavn Faroe Is. 16 62.09N 7.11W
Vestmannaeyjar is. Iceland 16 63.30N 20.20W
Vestvågöy i. Norway 16 68.10N 13.50E
Vesuvio mtn. Italy 12 40.48N 14.25E
Vesyegonsk Russian Fed. 18 58.38N 37.19E
Veszprém Hungary 15 47.06N 17.55E
Vésztő Hungary 15 46.55N 21.16E
Vetka Belorussia 15 52.35N 31.13E
Vetlanda Sweden 17 57.26N 15.04E
Vetluga Russian Fed. 18 57.50N 45.42E
Vetluga r. Russian Fed. 18 56.18N 46.19E
Vettore, Monte mtn. Italy 12 42.50N 13.18E
Veurne Belgium 8 51.04N 2.40E
Vevelstad Norway 16 65.43N 12.30E
Vézelise France 11 48.29N 6.05E

Vézère *r.* France **11** 44.53N 0.55E
Vezhen *mtn.* Bulgaria **13** 42.45N 24.22E
Viacha Bolivia **60** 16.40S 68.17W
Viadana Italy **9** 44.56N 10.31E
Viana Brazil **61** 3.13S 45.00W
Viana Portugal **10** 38.20N 8.00W
Viana do Castelo Portugal **10** 41.41N 8.50W
Viangchan *see* Vientiane Laos **29**
Viar *r.* Spain **10** 37.45N 5.54W
Viareggio Italy **9** 43.52N 10.14E
Viborg Denmark **17** 56.26N 9.24E
Vibo Valentia Italy **12** 38.40N 16.06E
Vibraye France **9** 48.03N 0.44E
Vic *see* Vich Spain **10**
Vicente López Argentina **63** 34.32S 58.29W
Vicenza Italy **9** 45.33N 11.32E
Vich Spain **10** 41.56N 2.16E
Vichada *r.* Colombia **60** 4.58N 67.35W
Vichuga Russian Fed. **18** 57.12N 41.50E
Vichy France **11** 46.07N 3.25E
Vicksburg U.S.A. **53** 32.21N 90.51W
Victor Harbor Australia **46** 35.36S 138.35E
Victoria Argentina **63** 32.40S 60.10W
Victoria *d.* Australia **47** 37.20S 145.00E
Victoria *r.* Australia **42** 15.12S 129.43E
Victoria Canada **50** 48.26N 123.20W
Victoria Chile **63** 38.13S 72.20W
Victoria U.S.A. **53** 28.49N 97.01W
Victoria, L. Africa **37** 1.00S 33.00E
Victoria, L. Australia **46** 34.00S 141.15E
Victoria, Mt. P.N.G. **44** 8.55S 147.35E
Victoria Beach *town* Canada **51** 50.43N 96.33W
Victoria Falls *f.* Zimbabwe / Zambia **39** 17.58S 25.45E
Victoria I. Canada **50** 71.00N 110.00W
Victoria L. Australia **46** 32.29S 143.22E
Victoria Nile *r.* Uganda **37** 2.14N 31.20E
Victoria River *town* Australia **42** 15.36S 131.06E
Victoria River Downs *town* Australia **44** 16.24S 131.00E
Victoriaville Canada **55** 46.04N 71.57W
Victoria West R.S.A. **39** 31.24S 23.07E
Victorica Argentina **63** 36.15S 65.25W
Viçosa Alagoas Brazil **61** 9.22S 36.10W
Viçosa Minas Gerais Brazil **59** 20.45S 42.53W
Videle Romania **15** 44.16N 25.31E
Viderö *i.* Faroe Is. **16** 62.20N 6.30W
Vidin Bulgaria **15** 43.58N 22.51E
Viedma Argentina **63** 40.50S 63.00W
Viedma, L. Argentina **63** 49.40S 72.30W
Vienna *see* Wien Austria **14**
Vienne France **11** 45.32N 4.54E
Vienne *r.* France **11** 47.13N 0.05W
Vientiane Laos **29** 18.01N 102.48E
Vieques *i.* Puerto Rico **57** 18.08N 65.30W
Viersen Germany **8** 51.16N 6.22E
Vierwaldstätter See *l.* Switz. **14** 47.10N 8.50E
Vierzon France **9** 47.14N 2.03E
Vietnam Asia **26** 15.00N 108.00E
Vieux-Condé France **8** 50.29N 3.31E
Vigan Phil. **27** 17.35N 120.23E
Vigevano Italy **9** 45.19N 8.51E
Vignemale, Pic de *mtn.* France **11** 42.46N 0.08W
Vigo Spain **10** 42.15N 8.44W
Vigrestad Norway **17** 58.34N 5.42E
Vijayawāda India **29** 16.34N 80.40E
Vik Norway **16** 65.19N 12.10E
Vikajärvi Finland **16** 66.37N 26.12E
Vikeke Indonesia **27** 8.42S 126.30E
Vikersund Norway **17** 59.59N 10.02E
Vikna *i.* Norway **16** 64.52N 10.57E
Vikulovo Russian Fed. **20** 56.51N 70.30E
Vila Vanuatu **40** 17.44S 168.19E
Vila da Maganja Mozambique **37** 17.25S 37.32E
Vila Franca Portugal **10** 38.57N 8.59W
Vilaine *r.* France **11** 47.30N 2.25W
Vilanculos Mozambique **39** 21.59S 35.16E
Vilanova i la Geltrú *see* Villaneuva y Geltrú Spain **10**
Vila Real Portugal **10** 41.17N 7.45W
Vila Real de Santo António Portugal **10** 37.12N 7.25W
Vila Velha Brazil **59** 20.20S 40.17W
Vileyka Belorussia **15** 54.30N 26.50E
Vilhelmina Sweden **16** 64.37N 16.39E
Vilhena Brazil **60** 12.40S 60.08W
Viliga Kushka Russian Fed. **21** 61.35N 156.55E
Viljandi Estonia **18** 58.22N 25.30E
Vilkaviškis Lithuania **15** 54.39N 23.02E
Vil'kitskogo, Proliv *str.* Russian Fed. **21** 77.57N 102.30E
Vilkovo Ukraine **15** 45.28N 29.32E
Villa Angela Argentina **62** 27.34S 60.45W
Villa Bella Bolivia **62** 10.23S 65.24W
Villablino Spain **10** 42.57N 6.19W
Villacañas Spain **10** 39.38N 3.20W
Villach Austria **14** 46.37N 13.51E
Villa Clara Argentina **63** 31.46S 58.50W
Villa Constitución Argentina **63** 33.14S 60.21W
Villa Dolores Argentina **62** 31.58S 65.12W
Villafranca di Verona Italy **9** 45.21N 10.50E
Villagarcía Spain **10** 42.35N 8.45W
Villaguay Argentina **63** 31.55S 59.00W
Villahermosa Mexico **56** 18.00N 92.53W
Villa Hernandarias Argentina **63** 31.15S 59.58W
Villa Huidobro Argentina **63** 34.50S 64.34W
Villaines-la-Juhel France **9** 48.21N 0.17W
Villajoyosa Spain **10** 38.31N 0.14W
Villalba Spain **10** 43.18N 7.41W
Villa María Argentina **62** 32.25S 63.15W
Villa Montes Bolivia **62** 21.15S 63.30W
Villaneuva y Geltrú Spain **10** 41.13N 1.43E
Villanueva de la Serena Spain **10** 38.58N 5.48W
Villaputzu Italy **12** 39.28N 9.35E
Villarrica Chile **63** 39.15S 72.15W
Villarrica Paraguay **59** 25.45S 56.28W
Villarrobledo Spain **10** 39.16N 2.36W
Villa San José Argentina **63** 32.12S 58.15W
Villasayas Spain **10** 41.24N 2.39W
Villavicencio Colombia **60** 4.09N 73.38W
Villaviciosa Spain **10** 43.29N 5.26W
Villazón Bolivia **62** 22.06S 65.36W
Villedieu France **9** 48.50N 1.13W
Villefranche France **11** 46.00N 4.43E
Villena Spain **10** 38.39N 0.52W
Villenauxe-la-Grande France **9** 48.35N 3.33E
Villeneuve France **11** 44.25N 0.43E
Villeneuve d'Ascq France **8** 50.37N 3.10E
Villeneuve-St. Georges France **9** 48.44N 2.27E
Villeneuve-sur-Yonne France **9** 48.05N 3.18E
Villers-Bocage France **9** 49.05N 0.39W
Villers-Cotterêts France **9** 49.15N 3.04E
Villers-sur-Mer France **9** 49.21N 0.02W
Villeurbanne France **14** 45.46N 4.54E
Vilnius Lithuania **15** 54.40N 25.19E
Vilvoorde Belgium **8** 50.56N 4.25E
Vilyuy *r.* Russian Fed. **21** 64.20N 126.55E
Vilyuysk Russian Fed. **21** 63.46N 121.35E
Vimianzo Spain **10** 43.07N 9.02W
Vimmerby Sweden **17** 57.40N 15.51E
Vimoutiers France **9** 48.55N 0.12E
Vina *r.* Chad **38** 7.43N 15.30E
Viña del Mar Chile **63** 33.02S 71.34W
Vinaroz Spain **10** 40.30N 0.27E
Vincennes France **9** 48.51N 2.26E
Vincennes U.S.A. **55** 38.42N 87.30W
Vindel *r.* Sweden **16** 63.54N 19.52E
Vindeln Sweden **16** 64.12N 19.44E
Vinderup Denmark **17** 56.29N 8.47E
Vindhya Range *mts.* India **28** 22.55N 76.00E
Vineland U.S.A. **55** 39.29N 75.02W
Vingåker Sweden **17** 59.02N 15.52E
Vinh Vietnam **26** 18.42N 105.41E
Vînju Mare Romania **15** 44.26N 22.52E
Vinkovci Croatia **13** 45.17N 18.38E
Vinnitsa Ukraine **15** 49.11N 28.30E
Vinson Massif Antarctica **64** 78.00S 85.00W
Vioolsdrif R.S.A. **39** 28.45S 17.33E
Vipava Slovenia **14** 45.51N 13.58E
Virac Phil. **27** 13.35N 124.15E
Viranşehir Turkey **30** 37.13N 39.45E
Vire France **11** 48.50N 0.53W
Vire *r.* France **9** 49.20N 0.53W
Vírgenes, C. Argentina **63** 52.00S 68.50W
Virgin Gorda *i.* B.V.Is. **57** 18.30N 64.26W
Virginia U.S.A. **53** 47.30N 92.28W
Virginia *d.* U.S.A. **53** 37.30N 79.00W
Virginia City Mont. U.S.A. **54** 45.18N 111.56W
Virginia City Nev. U.S.A. **54** 39.19N 119.39W
Virovitica Croatia **15** 45.51N 17.23E
Virrat Finland **16** 62.14N 23.47E
Virserum Sweden **17** 57.19N 15.35E
Virton Belgium **8** 49.35N 5.32E
Virtsu Estonia **17** 58.34N 23.31E
Virunga Nat. Park Zaïre **37** 0.30S 29.15E
Vis Croatia **12** 43.03N 16.21E
Vis *i.* Croatia **12** 43.03N 16.10E
Visalia U.S.A. **54** 36.20N 119.18W
Visayan Sea Phil. **27** 11.35N 123.51E
Visby Sweden **17** 57.38N 18.18E
Visconde do Rio Branco Brazil **59** 21.00S 42.51W
Viscount Melville Sd. Canada **50** 74.30N 104.00W
Visé Belgium **8** 50.44N 5.42E
Višegrad Bosnia-Herzegovina **13** 43.47N 19.20E
Viseu Brazil **61** 1.12S 46.07W
Viseu Portugal **10** 40.40N 7.55W
Viseu de Sus Romania **15** 47.44N 24.22E
Vishākhapatnam India **29** 17.42N 83.24E
Viso, Monte *mtn.* Italy **9** 44.38N 7.05E
Visp Switz. **9** 46.18N 7.53E
Vista U.S.A. **54** 33.12N 117.15W
Vistula *r. see* Wisła *r.* Poland **15**
Vitarte Peru **60** 12.03S 76.51W
Vitebsk Belorussia **18** 55.10N 30.14E
Viterbo Italy **12** 42.26N 12.07E
Vitim Russian Fed. **21** 59.28N 112.35E
Vitim *r.* Russian Fed. **21** 59.30N 112.36E
Vitória Espírito Santo Brazil **59** 20.19S 40.21W
Vitoria Spain **10** 42.51N 2.40W
Vitória da Conquista Brazil **61** 14.53S 40.52W
Vitré France **9** 48.07N 1.12W
Vitry-le-François France **9** 48.44N 4.35E
Vitteaux France **9** 47.24N 4.30E
Vittoria Italy **12** 36.57N 14.21E
Vittorio Veneto Italy **9** 45.59N 12.18E
Viveiro *see* Vivero Spain **10**
Vivero Spain **10** 43.40N 7.24W
Vivonne Bay *town* Australia **46** 35.58S 137.10E
Vizcaíno, Desierto de *des.* Mexico **56** 27.40N 114.40W
Vizianagaram India **29** 18.07N 83.30E
Vizinga Russian Fed. **18** 61.06N 50.05E
Vjosë *r.* Albania **13** 40.39N 19.20E
Vlaardingen Neth. **8** 51.55N 4.20E
Vladikavkaz Russian Fed. **19** 43.02N 44.43E
Vladimir Russian Fed. **18** 56.08N 40.25E
Vladimirets Ukraine **15** 51.28N 26.03E
Vladimir Volynskiy Ukraine **15** 50.51N 24.19E
Vladivostok Russian Fed. **25** 43.09N 131.53E
Vlasenica Bosnia-Herzegovina **15** 44.11N 18.56E
Vlieland *i.* Neth. **8** 53.15N 5.00E
Vlissingen Neth. **8** 51.27N 3.35E
Vlorë Albania **13** 40.28N 19.27E
Vltava *r.* Czech. **14** 50.22N 14.28E
Voerde Germany **8** 51.37N 6.39E
Vogelkop *f. see* Jazirah Doberai *f.* Indonesia **27**
Voghera Italy **9** 44.59N 9.01E
Voi Kenya **37** 3.23S 38.35E
Voiron France **11** 45.22N 5.35E
Volborg U.S.A. **54** 45.50N 105.40W
Volda Norway **17** 62.09N 6.06E
Volga *r.* Russian Fed. **19** 45.45N 47.50E
Volgograd Russian Fed. **19** 48.45N 44.30E
Volgogradskoye Vodokhranilishche *resr.* Russian Fed. **19** 51.00N 46.05E
Volkhov Russian Fed. **18** 59.54N 32.47E
Volkhov *r.* Russian Fed. **18** 60.15N 32.15E
Volkovysk Belorussia **15** 53.10N 24.28E
Vollenhove Neth. **8** 52.41N 5.59E
Volnovakha Ukraine **19** 47.36N 37.32E
Volochanka Russian Fed. **21** 70.59N 94.18E
Volochisk Ukraine **15** 49.34N 26.10E
Volodarsk Russian Fed. **18** 56.14N 43.10E
Vologda Russian Fed. **18** 59.10N 39.55E
Volokolamsk Russian Fed. **18** 56.02N 35.56E
Vólos Greece **13** 39.22N 22.57E
Volovets Ukraine **15** 48.44N 23.14E
Volsk Russian Fed. **18** 52.04N 47.22E
Volta *d.* Ghana **38** 7.30N 0.25E
Volta *r.* Ghana **38** 5.50N 0.41E
Volta, L. Ghana **38** 7.00N 0.00
Volta-Noire *d.* Burkina **38** 12.30N 3.25W
Volta Redonda Brazil **59** 22.31S 44.05W
Volterra Italy **12** 43.24N 10.51E
Voltri Italy **9** 44.26N 8.45E
Volturno *r.* Italy **12** 41.02N 13.56E
Volzhskiy Russian Fed. **19** 48.48N 44.45E
Voorburg Neth. **8** 52.05N 4.22E
Vopnafjördhur *est.* Iceland **16** 65.50N 14.30W
Vopnafjördhur *town* Iceland **16** 65.46N 14.50W
Vorarlberg *d.* Austria **14** 47.15N 9.55E
Vordingborg Denmark **17** 55.01N 11.55E
Voríai Sporádhes *is.* Greece **13** 39.00N 24.00E
Vorkuta Russian Fed. **18** 67.27N 64.00E
Vormsi *i.* Estonia **17** 59.00N 23.20E
Voronezh Russian Fed. **19** 51.40N 39.13E
Voronovo Belorussia **15** 54.09N 25.19E
Vosges *mts.* France **14** 48.10N 7.00E
Voss Norway **17** 60.39N 6.26E
Vostochno Sibirskoye More *sea* Russian Fed. **21** 73.00N 160.00E
Vostochnyy Sayan *mts.* Russian Fed. **24** 51.30N 102.00E
Votkinsk Russian Fed. **18** 57.02N 53.59E
Votkinskoye Vodokhranilishche *resr.* Russian Fed. **18** 57.00N 55.00E
Votuporanga Brazil **62** 20.26S 49.53W
Vouga *r.* Portugal **10** 40.41N 8.38W
Vouillé France **11** 46.38N 0.10E
Vouziers France **9** 49.24N 4.42E
Voves France **9** 48.16N 1.37E
Voxna Sweden **17** 61.20N 15.30E
Voxna *r.* Sweden **17** 61.17N 16.26E
Voyvozh Russian Fed. **18** 64.19N 55.12E
Vozhega Russian Fed. **18** 60.25N 40.11E
Voznesensk Ukraine **19** 47.34N 31.21E
Völklingen Germany **14** 49.15N 6.50E
Vrangelya, Ostrov *i.* Russian Fed. **21** 71.00N 180.00
Vranje Yugo. **13** 42.34N 21.52E
Vratsa Bulgaria **13** 43.12N 23.33E
Vrbas *r.* Bosnia-Herzegovina **13** 45.06N 17.29E
Vrede R.S.A. **39** 27.24S 29.09E
Vredendal R.S.A. **39** 31.40S 18.28E
Vresse Belgium **8** 49.53N 4.57E
Vries Neth. **8** 53.06N 6.35E
Vrnograč Bosnia-Herzegovina **12** 45.10N 15.56E
Vršac Yugo. **15** 45.08N 21.18E
Vryburg R.S.A. **39** 26.57S 24.42E
Vught Neth. **8** 51.39N 5.18E
Vukovar Croatia **15** 45.21N 19.00E
Vung Tau Vietnam **26** 10.21N 107.04E
Vyatka *r.* Russian Fed. **20** 55.40N 51.40E
Vyatskiye Polyany Russian Fed. **18** 56.14N 51.08E
Vyazma Russian Fed. **18** 55.12N 34.17E
Vyazniki Russian Fed. **18** 56.14N 42.08E
Vyborg Russian Fed. **18** 60.45N 28.41E
Vychegda *r.* Russian Fed. **18** 61.15N 46.28E
Vychodné Beskydy *mts.* Europe **15** 49.30N 22.00E
Vygozero, Ozero *l.* Russian Fed. **18** 63.30N 34.30E
Vyrnwy, L. U.K. **4** 52.46N 3.30W
Vyshka Turkmenistan **31** 39.19N 54.10E
Vyshniy-Volochek Russian Fed. **18** 57.34N 34.23E
Vytegra Russian Fed. **18** 61.04N 36.27E

W

Wa Ghana **38** 10.07N 2.28W
Waal *r.* Neth. **8** 51.45N 4.40E
Waalwijk Neth. **8** 51.42N 5.04E
Wabag P.N.G. **27** 5.28S 143.40E
Wabash U.S.A. **55** 40.47N 85.48W
Wabash *r.* U.S.A. **53** 38.25N 87.45W
Wabrzeźno Poland **15** 53.17N 18.57E
Wabush City Canada **51** 53.00N 66.50W
Waco U.S.A. **53** 31.33N 97.10W
Wad Pakistan **28** 27.21N 66.30E
Waddeneilanden *is.* Neth. **8** 53.20N 5.00E
Waddenzee *b.* Neth. **8** 53.15N 5.05E
Waddikee Australia **46** 33.18S 136.12E
Waddington, Mt. Canada **50** 51.30N 125.00W
Wadhurst U.K. **5** 51.03N 0.21E
Wādī Ḥalfā' Sudan **30** 21.56N 31.20E
Wādī Mūsá *town* Jordan **32** 30.19N 35.29E
Wad Madanī Sudan **35** 14.24N 33.30E
Wafrah Kuwait **31** 28.39N 47.56E
Wageningen Neth. **8** 51.58N 5.39E
Wager B. Canada **51** 65.26N 88.40W
Wager Bay *town* Canada **51** 65.55N 90.40W
Wagga Wagga Australia **47** 35.07S 147.24E
Wagin Australia **43** 33.18S 117.21E
Wāh Pakistan **28** 33.50N 72.44E
Wahai Indonesia **27** 2.48S 129.30E
Wahiba Sands *des.* Oman **28** 21.56N 58.55E
Wahpeton U.S.A. **53** 46.16N 96.36W
Waiau New Zealand **48** 42.39S 173.03E
Waidhofen Austria **14** 47.58N 14.47E
Waigeo *i.* Indonesia **27** 0.05S 130.30E
Waihi New Zealand **48** 37.24S 175.50E
Waikato *d.* New Zealand **48** 38.15S 175.10E
Waikato *r.* New Zealand **48** 37.19S 174.50E
Waikerie Australia **46** 34.11S 139.59E
Waikokopu New Zealand **48** 39.05S 177.50E
Waikouaiti New Zealand **48** 45.36S 170.41E
Waimakariri *r.* New Zealand **48** 43.23S 172.40E
Waimate New Zealand **48** 44.45S 171.03E
Waingapu Indonesia **27** 9.30S 120.10E
Wainwright U.S.A. **50** 70.39N 160.00W
Waiouru New Zealand **48** 39.39S 175.40E
Waipara New Zealand **48** 43.03S 172.45E
Waipawa New Zealand **48** 39.56S 176.35E
Waipiro New Zealand **48** 38.02S 178.21E
Waipu New Zealand **48** 35.59S 174.26E
Waipukurau New Zealand **48** 40.00S 176.33E
Wairau *r.* New Zealand **48** 41.32S 174.08E
Wairoa New Zealand **48** 39.03S 177.25E
Waitaki *r.* New Zealand **48** 44.56S 171.10E
Waitara New Zealand **48** 38.59S 174.13E
Waiuku New Zealand **48** 37.15S 174.44E
Wajir Kenya **37** 1.46N 40.05E
Wakatipu, L. New Zealand **48** 45.10S 168.30E
Wakayama Japan **23** 34.13N 135.11E
Wakefield U.K. **4** 53.41N 1.31W
Wakkanai Japan **25** 45.26N 141.43E
Wakre Indonesia **27** 0.30S 131.05E
Walamba Zambia **37** 13.27S 28.44E
Wałbrzych Poland **14** 50.48N 16.19E
Walcha Australia **47** 31.00S 151.36E
Walcheren *f.* Neth. **8** 51.32N 3.35E
Wałcz Poland **14** 53.17N 16.28E
Waldbröl Germany **8** 50.52N 7.34E
Waldeck Germany **14** 51.12N 9.04E
Walden U.S.A. **54** 40.34N 106.11W
Waldorf U.S.A. **55** 38.37N 76.54W
Waldport U.S.A. **54** 44.26N 124.04W
Wales *d.* U.K. **5** 52.30N 3.45W
Walgett Australia **47** 30.03S 148.10E
Walikale Zaïre **37** 1.29S 28.05E
Walker L. U.S.A. **54** 38.44N 118.43W
Wallace Idaho U.S.A. **54** 47.28N 115.55W
Wallaceburg Canada **55** 42.36N 82.23W
Wallachia *f.* Romania **15** 44.35N 25.00E
Wallambin, L. Australia **43** 30.58S 117.30E
Wallangarra Australia **47** 28.51S 151.52E
Wallaroo Australia **46** 33.57S 137.36E
Walla Walla Australia **47** 35.48S 146.52E
Walla Walla U.S.A. **54** 46.08N 118.20W
Wallis, Îles *is.* Pacific Oc. **40** 13.16S 176.15W
Wallowa U.S.A. **54** 45.34N 117.32W
Wallowa Mts. U.S.A. **54** 45.10N 117.30W
Wallsend Australia **47** 32.55S 151.40E
Walpole Australia **43** 34.57S 116.44E
Walsall U.K. **5** 52.36N 1.59W
Walsenburg U.S.A. **52** 37.37N 104.47W
Walton on the Naze U.K. **5** 51.52N 1.17E
Walton on the Wolds U.K. **4** 52.49N 0.49W
Walvis B. R.S.A. **39** 22.55S 14.30E
Walvisbaai R.S.A. **39** 22.57S 14.30E
Walvis Bay *d.* R.S.A. **39** 22.56S 14.35E
Walvis Bay *town* R.S.A. **36** 22.50S 14.31E
Walvis Bay *town see* Walvisbaai R.S.A. **39**
Wamanfo Ghana **38** 7.16N 2.44W
Wamba Kenya **37** 0.58N 37.19E
Wamba Nigeria **38** 8.57N 8.42E
Wamba Zaïre **37** 2.10N 27.59E
Wami *r.* Tanzania **37** 6.10S 38.50E
Wamsasi Indonesia **27** 3.27S 126.07E
Wan Indonesia **44** 8.23S 137.55E
Wāna Pakistan **28** 32.20N 69.32E
Wanaaring Australia **46** 29.42S 144.14E
Wanaka New Zealand **48** 44.42S 169.08E
Wanaka, L. New Zealand **48** 44.30S 169.10E
Wan'an China **25** 26.27N 114.46E
Wanapiri Indonesia **27** 4.30S 135.50E
Wanapitei *r.* Canada **55** 46.02N 80.51W
Wanapitei L. Canada **55** 46.45N 80.45W
Wanbi Australia **46** 34.46S 140.19E
Wandana Australia **46** 32.04S 133.45E
Wandoan Australia **44** 26.09S 149.51E
Wanganella Australia **47** 35.13S 144.53E
Wanganui New Zealand **48** 39.56S 175.00E
Wangaratta Australia **47** 36.22S 146.20E
Wangary Australia **46** 34.30S 135.26E
Wangerooge *i.* Germany **8** 53.50N 7.50E
Wangianna Australia **46** 29.42S 137.32E
Wantage U.K. **5** 51.35N 1.25W
Wanxian China **29** 30.52N 108.20E
Wanyuan China **29** 32.04N 108.02E
Warangal India **29** 18.00N 79.35E
Waranga Resr. Australia **47** 36.32S 145.04E
Waratah B. Australia **45** 38.55S 146.04E
Warburton *r.* Australia **45** 27.55S 137.15E
Warburton Range *mts.* S.A. Australia **46** 30.30S 134.32E
Warburton Range *mts.* W.A. Australia **42** 26.09S 126.38E
Ward Rep. of Ire. **7** 53.26N 6.20W
Warden R.S.A. **39** 27.49S 28.57E
Wardenburg Germany **8** 53.04N 8.11E
Wardha India **29** 20.41N 78.40E
Waren Germany **14** 53.31N 12.40E
Warendorf Germany **8** 51.57N 8.00E
Warialda Australia **47** 29.33S 150.36E
Wark Forest *hills* U.K. **4** 55.06N 2.24W
Warkopi Indonesia **27** 1.12S 134.09E
Warkworth New Zealand **48** 36.24S 174.40E
Warley U.K. **5** 52.29N 2.02W
Warmbad Namibia **39** 28.26S 18.41E
Warminster U.K. **5** 51.12N 2.11W
Warm Springs *town* U.S.A. **54** 39.39N 114.49W
Waroona Australia **43** 32.51S 115.50E
Warracknabeal Australia **46** 36.15S 142.28E
Warragul Australia **47** 38.11S 145.55E
Warrakalanna, L. Australia **46** 28.13S 139.23E
Warrambool *r.* Australia **47** 30.04S 147.38E
Warrego *r.* Australia **47** 30.25S 145.18E
Warrego Range *mts.* Australia **44** 24.55S 146.20E
Warren Australia **47** 31.44S 147.53E
Warren Mich. U.S.A. **55** 42.28N 83.01W
Warren Ohio U.S.A. **55** 41.15N 80.49W
Warren Penn. U.S.A. **55** 41.51N 79.08W
Warrenpoint U.K. **7** 54.06N 6.15W
Warrenton R.S.A. **39** 28.07S 24.49E
Warri Nigeria **38** 5.36N 5.46E
Warrina Australia **46** 28.10S 135.49E
Warriner Creek *r.* Australia **46** 29.15S 137.03E
Warrington U.K. **4** 53.25N 2.38W
Warrnambool Australia **46** 38.23S 142.03E
Warrumbungle Range *mts.* Australia **47** 31.20S 149.00E
Warsaw *see* Warszawa Poland **15**
Warsaw Ind. U.S.A. **55** 41.13N 85.52W
Warszawa Poland **15** 52.15N 21.00E
Warta *r.* Poland **14** 52.45N 15.09E
Warwick Australia **47** 28.12S 152.00E
Warwick U.K. **5** 52.17N 1.36W
Warwickshire *d.* U.K. **5** 52.13N 1.30W
Wasatch Plateau *f.* U.S.A. **54** 39.20N 111.30W
Wasco Calif. U.S.A. **54** 35.36N 119.20W
Wasco Oreg. U.S.A. **54** 45.35N 120.42W
Washburn L. Canada **50** 70.03N 106.50W
Washington U.K. **4** 54.55N 1.30W
Washington *d.* U.S.A. **54** 47.43N 120.00W
Washington D.C. U.S.A. **55** 38.55N 77.00W
Washington Ind. U.S.A. **55** 38.40N 87.10W
Washington N.C. U.S.A. **53** 35.33N 77.04W
Washington Utah U.S.A. **54** 37.08N 113.30W
Washington Va. U.S.A. **55** 38.43N 78.10W
Wasian Indonesia **27** 1.51S 133.21E
Wasior Indonesia **27** 2.38S 134.27E
Wasiri Indonesia **27** 7.30S 126.30E
Waskaganish Canada **55** 51.29N 78.45W
Wassenaar Neth. **8** 52.10N 4.26E
Wassy France **9** 48.30N 4.59E
Waswanipi Lac *l.* Canada **55** 49.36N 76.39W
Watampone Indonesia **27** 4.33S 120.20E
Watchet U.K. **5** 51.10N 3.20W
Waterbury U.S.A. **55** 41.33N 73.03W
Waterford Rep. of Ire. **7** 52.16N 7.08W
Waterford *d.* Rep. of Ire. **7** 52.10N 7.40W
Waterford Harbour *est.* Rep. of Ire. **7** 52.12N 6.56W
Waterloo Belgium **8** 50.44N 4.24E
Waterloo Canada **55** 43.28N 80.31W
Waterloo Iowa U.S.A. **53** 42.30N 92.20W
Watertown N.Y. U.S.A. **55** 43.59N 75.55W
Watertown S.Dak. U.S.A. **53** 44.54N 97.08W
Watervale Australia **46** 33.58S 138.39E
Waterville Rep. of Ire. **7** 51.50N 10.11W
Waterville Maine U.S.A. **55** 44.33N 69.38W
Waterville Wash. U.S.A. **54** 47.39N 120.04W
Watford U.K. **5** 51.40N 0.25W
Watrous Canada **50** 51.40N 105.29W
Watsa Zaïre **37** 3.03N 29.29E
Watson Lake *town* Canada **50** 60.07N 128.49W
Watsonville U.S.A. **54** 36.55N 121.45W
Wattiwarriganna Creek *r.* Australia **46** 28.57S 136.10E
Wau P.N.G. **27** 7.22S 146.40E
Wauchope N.S.W. Australia **47** 31.27S 152.43E
Wauchope N.T. Australia **44** 20.39S 134.13E
Waukaringa Australia **46** 32.18S 139.27E
Wausau U.S.A. **53** 44.58N 89.40W
Wave Hill *town* Australia **42** 17.29S 130.57E
Waveney *r.* U.K. **5** 52.29N 1.46E
Wavre Belgium **8** 50.43N 4.37E
Wāw Sudan **35** 7.40N 28.04E
Waxweiler Germany **8** 50.08N 6.20E
Way, L. Australia **42** 26.47S 120.21E
Waycross U.S.A. **53** 31.08N 82.22W
Waynesboro Penn. U.S.A. **55** 39.45N 77.35W
Waziers France **8** 50.24N 3.05E
Wear *r.* U.K. **4** 54.55N 1.21W
Weda Indonesia **27** 0.30N 127.52E
Weddell Sea Antarctica **64** 70.00S 40.00W
Wedderburn Australia **46** 36.26S 143.39E
Wedgeport Canada **55** 43.44N 66.00W
Wedmore U.K. **5** 51.14N 2.50W
Wedza Zimbabwe **39** 18.37S 31.33E
Weelde Belgium **8** 51.25N 5.00E
Weemelah Australia **47** 29.02S 149.15E
Weert Neth. **8** 51.14N 5.40E
Wee Waa Australia **47** 30.34S 149.27E
Wegorzyno Poland **14** 53.32N 15.33E
Węgrów Poland **15** 52.25N 22.01E
Weichang China **25** 41.56N 117.34E
Weiden in der Oberpfalz Germany **14** 49.40N 12.10E
Weifang China **25** 36.44N 119.10E
Weihai China **25** 37.30N 122.04E
Weilmoringle Australia **47** 29.16S 146.55E
Weimar Germany **14** 50.59N 11.20E
Weipa Australia **44** 12.41S 141.52E
Weir *r.* Australia **47** 29.10S 149.06E
Weiser U.S.A. **54** 44.37N 116.58W
Weissenfels Germany **14** 51.12N 11.58E
Weiya China **24** 41.50N 94.24E
Wejherowo Poland **15** 54.37N 18.15E
Weldon U.S.A. **54** 35.40N 118.20W
Welkom R.S.A. **39** 27.59S 26.42E
Welland Canada **55** 42.59N 79.14W
Welland *r.* U.K. **4** 52.53N 0.00
Wellesley Is. Australia **44** 16.42S 139.30E
Wellin Belgium **8** 50.05N 5.07E
Wellingborough U.K. **5** 52.18N 0.41W
Wellington N.S.W. Australia **47** 32.33S 148.59E
Wellington S.A. Australia **46** 35.21S 139.23E
Wellington New Zealand **48** 41.17S 174.47E
Wellington *d.* New Zealand **48** 40.00S 175.30E
Wellington Shrops. U.K. **5** 52.42N 2.31W
Wellington Somerset U.K. **5** 50.58N 3.13W
Wellington Nev. U.S.A. **54** 38.45N 119.22W
Wellington, Isla *i.* Chile **63** 49.30S 75.00W
Wells U.K. **5** 51.12N 2.39W
Wells Nev. U.S.A. **54** 41.07N 114.58W
Wellsboro U.S.A. **55** 41.45N 77.18W
Wells-next-the-Sea U.K. **4** 52.57N 0.51E
Wellton U.S.A. **54** 32.40N 114.08W

Wels Austria 14 48.10N 14.02E
Welshpool U.K. 5 52.40N 3.09W
Welwyn Garden City U.K. 5 51.48N 0.13W
Wem U.K. 4 52.52N 2.45W
Wembere *r.* Tanzania 37 4.07S 34.15E
Wemindji Canada 51 53.00N 78.42W
Wenatchee U.S.A. 54 47.25N120.19W
Wenchi Ghana 38 7.40N 2.06W
Wendel U.S.A. 54 40.20N120.14W
Wendover U.S.A. 54 40.44N114.02W
Wenebegon L. Canada 55 47.24N 83.08W
Wenlock *r.* Australia 44 12.02S141.55E
Wenquan China 29 33.13N 91.50E
Wenshan China 29 23.25N104.15E
Wensleydale *f.* U.K. 4 54.19N 2.04W
Wentworth Australia 46 34.06S141.56E
Wenzhou China 25 28.02N120.40E
Weott U.S.A. 54 40.19N123.54W
Wepener R.S.A. 39 29.43S 27.01E
Werda Botswana 39 25.15S 23.16E
Werdohl Germany 8 51.16N 7.47E
Weri Indonesia 27 3.10S132.30E
Werne Germany 8 51.39N 7.36E
Werra *r.* Germany 14 51.26N 9.39E
Werribee Australia 47 37.54S144.40E
Werris Creek *town* Australia 47 31.20S150.41E
Wesel Germany 8 51.39N 6.37E
Weser *r.* Germany 14 53.15N 8.30E
Wessel, C. Australia 44 10.59S136.46E
Wessel Is. Australia 44 11.30S136.25E
West Bank Jordan 32 32.00N 35.25E
West Bengal *d.* India 29 23.00N 87.40E
West Bromwich U.K. 5 52.32N 2.01W
Westbrook U.S.A. 55 43.41N 70.21W
West Coast *d.* New Zealand 48 43.15S170.10E
Westende Belgium 8 51.10N 2.46E
Western *d.* Ghana 38 6.00N 2.40W
Western *d.* Kenya 37 0.30N 34.30E
Western Australia *d.* Australia 42 24.20S122.30E
Western Ghâts *mts.* India 28 15.30N 74.30E
Western Isles *d.* U.K. 6 57.40N 7.10W
Western Sahara Africa 34 25.00N 13.30W
Western Samoa Pacific Oc. 40 13.55S172.00W
Westerschelde *est.* Neth. 8 51.25N 3.40E
Westerstede Germany 8 53.15N 7.56E
Westerwald *f.* Germany 8 50.40N 8.00E
West Falkland *i.* Falkland Is. 63 51.40W 60.00W
West Felton U.K. 4 52.49N 2.58W
Westfield Mass. U.S.A. 55 42.07N 72.45W
Westfield Penn. U.S.A. 55 41.55N 77.32W
West Frisian Is. *see* Waddeneilanden Neth. 14
West Glamorgan *d.* U.K. 5 51.42N 3.47W
West Lafayette U.S.A. 55 40.26N 86.56W
West Linton U.K. 6 55.45N 3.21W
Westmeath *d.* Rep. of Ire. 7 53.30N 7.30W
West Midlands *d.* U.K. 5 52.28N 1.50W
Westmoreland Australia 44 17.18S138.12E
West Nicholson Zimbabwe 39 21.06S 29.25E
Weston Malaysia 26 5.14N115.35E
Weston-Super-Mare U.K. 5 51.20N 2.59W
West Palm Beach *town* U.S.A. 53 26.42N 80.05W
Westport New Zealand 48 41.46S171.38E
Westport Rep. of Ire. 7 53.48N 9.32W
Westport Wash. U.S.A. 54 46.53N124.06W
Westray *i.* U.K. 6 59.18N 2.58W
West Siberian Plain *f.* *see* Zapadno-Sibirskaya Ravnina Russian Fed. 20
West Sussex *d.* U.K. 5 50.58N 0.30W
West Terschelling Neth. 8 53.22N 5.13E
West Virginia *d.* U.S.A. 53 38.45N 80.30W
West Vlaanderen *d.* Belgium 8 51.00N 3.00E
West Wyalong Australia 47 33.54S147.12E
West Yellowstone U.S.A. 54 44.30N111.05W
West Yorkshire *d.* U.K. 4 53.45N 1.40W
Wetar *i.* Indonesia 27 7.45S126.00E
Wetaskiwin Canada 50 52.57N113.20W
Wetteren Belgium 8 51.00N 3.51E
Wetzlar Germany 14 50.33N 8.30E
Wewak P.N.G. 27 3.35S143.35E
Wexford Rep. of Ire. 7 52.20N 6.28W
Wexford *d.* Rep. of Ire. 7 52.20N 6.25W
Wexford B. Rep. of Ire. 7 52.27N 6.18W
Weyburn Canada 50 49.41N103.52W
Weymouth U.K. 5 50.36N 2.28W
Weymouth, C. Australia 44 12.32S143.36E
Whakatane New Zealand 48 37.56S177.00E
Whalan *r.* Australia 47 29.10S148.42E
Whale Cove *town* Canada 51 62.30N 93.00W
Whalsay *i.* U.K. 6 60.22N 0.59W
Whangarei New Zealand 48 35.43S174.20E
Wharfe *r.* U.K. 4 53.50N 1.07W
Wharfedale *f.* U.K. 4 54.00N 1.55W
Whataroa New Zealand 48 43.16S170.22E
Wheeler Peak *mtn.* Nev. U.S.A. 54 38.59N114.19W
Wheeler Peak *mtn.* N.Mex. U.S.A. 52 36.34N105.25W
Wheeler Ridge *town* U.S.A. 54 35.06N119.01W
Wheeler Springs *town* U.S.A. 54 34.30N119.18W
Wheeling U.S.A. 55 40.05N 80.43W
Whernside *mtn.* U.K. 4 54.14N 2.25W
Whidbey Is. Australia 46 34.50S135.00E
Whitburn U.K. 6 55.52N 3.41W
Whitby Canada 55 43.52N 78.56W
Whitby U.K. 4 54.29N 0.37W
Whitchurch Shrops. U.K. 4 52.58N 2.42W
White *r.* Ark. U.S.A. 53 33.53N 91.10W
White *r.* Ind. U.S.A. 55 38.29N 87.45W
White *r.* S.Dak. U.S.A. 52 43.40N 99.30W
White *r.* Utah U.S.A. 52 40.04N109.41W
White, L. Australia 42 21.05S129.00E
White Cliffs *town* Australia 46 30.51S143.05E
Whitefish U.S.A. 54 48.25N114.20W
Whitefish B. U.S.A. 55 46.32N 84.45W
Whitehall Mont. U.S.A. 54 45.52N112.06W
Whitehaven U.K. 4 54.33N 3.35W
Whitehorse Canada 50 60.41N135.08W
Whitemark Australia 45 40.07S148.00E
White Mountain Peak U.S.A. 54 37.38N118.15W
White Mts. Calif. U.S.A. 54 37.30N118.15W
White Plains *town* U.S.A. 55 41.02N 73.46W
White Sea *see* Beloye More *sea* Russian Fed. 18
White Volta *r.* Ghana 38 9.13N 1.15W
Whitewater Baldy *mtn.* U.S.A. 54 33.20N108.39W
Whitfield Australia 47 36.49S146.22E
Whithorn U.K. 6 54.44N 4.25W
Whitianga New Zealand 48 36.50S175.42E
Whitley Bay *town* U.K. 4 55.03N 1.25W
Whitney Canada 55 45.30N 78.14W
Whitney, Mt. U.S.A. 54 36.35N118.18W
Whitstable U.K. 5 51.21N 1.02E
Whitsunday I. Australia 44 20.17S148.59E
Whittier U.S.A. 50 60.46N148.41W
Whittlesea Australia 47 37.31S145.08E
Whitton U.K. 4 53.42N 0.39W
Wholdaia L. Canada 50 60.43N104.10W
Whyalla Australia 46 33.02S137.35E
Wichita U.S.A. 53 37.43N 97.20W
Wichita Falls *town* U.S.A. 52 33.55N 98.30W
Wick U.K. 6 58.26N 3.06W
Wickenburg U.S.A. 54 33.58N112.44W
Wickepin Australia 43 32.45S117.31E
Wicklow Rep. of Ire. 7 52.59N 6.03W
Wicklow *d.* Rep. of Ire. 7 52.59N 6.25W
Wicklow Head Rep. of Ire. 7 52.58N 6.00W
Wicklow Mts. Rep. of Ire. 7 53.06N 6.20W
Widgiemooltha Australia 43 31.30S121.34E
Widnes U.K. 4 53.22N 2.44W
Wiehl Germany 8 50.57N 7.32E
Wieluń Poland 15 51.14N 18.34E
Wien Austria 14 48.13N 16.22E
Wiener Neustadt Austria 14 47.49N 16.15E
Wieprz *r.* Poland 15 51.34N 21.49E
Wiesbaden Germany 14 50.05N 8.15E
Wigan U.K. 4 53.33N 2.38W
Wight, Isle of U.K. 3 50.40N 1.17W
Wigton U.K. 4 54.50N 3.09W
Wigtown U.K. 6 54.47N 4.26W
Wigtown B. U.K. 6 54.47N 4.15W
Wilcannia Australia 46 31.33S143.24E
Wildhorn *mtn.* Switz. 11 46.22N 7.22E
Wildon Austria 14 46.53N 15.31E
Wildspitze *mtn.* Austria 14 46.55N 10.55E
Wildwood U.S.A. 55 38.59N 74.49W
Wilgena Australia 46 30.46S134.44E
Wilhelm, Mt. P.N.G. 27 6.00S144.55E
Wilhelm II Land Antarctica 64 68.00S 89.00E
Wilhelmshaven Germany 8 53.32N 8.07E
Wilkes-Barre U.S.A. 55 41.15N 75.50W
Wilkes Land *f.* Antarctica 64 69.00S120.00E
Wilkie Canada 50 52.27N108.42W
Wilkinsburg U.S.A. 55 40.27N 79.53W
Wilkinson Lakes Australia 45 29.40S132.39E
Willandra Billabong *r.* Australia 46 33.08S144.06E
Willemstad Neth. Antilles 60 12.12N 68.56W
Willeroo Australia 42 15.17S131.35E
William, Mt. Australia 46 37.20S142.41E
William Creek *town* Australia 46 28.52S136.18E
Williams Australia 43 33.01S116.45E
Williams *r.* Australia 43 32.59S116.24E
Williams Lake *town* Canada 50 52.08N122.09W
Williamsport Penn. U.S.A. 55 41.14N 77.00W
Willis Group *is.* Australia 44 16.18S150.00E
Williston R.S.A. 39 31.21S 20.53E
Williston U.S.A. 52 48.09N103.37W
Williston L. Canada 50 55.00N126.00W
Willits U.S.A. 54 39.25N123.21W
Willmar U.S.A. 53 45.06N 95.00W
Willochra Australia 46 32.12S138.10E
Willochra *r.* Australia 46 31.57S137.52E
Willow U.S.A. 50 61.42N150.08W
Willowmore R.S.A. 39 33.18S 23.28E
Willow Ranch U.S.A. 54 41.55N120.21W
Willunga Australia 46 35.18S138.33E
Wilmington Del. U.S.A. 55 39.44N 75.33W
Wilmington N.C. U.S.A. 53 34.14N 77.55W
Wilmslow U.K. 4 53.19N 2.14W
Wilpena *r.* Australia 46 31.13S139.25E
Wilson's Promontory *c.* Australia 47 39.06S146.23E
Wilton *r.* Australia 44 14.45S134.33E
Wilton U.K. 5 51.05N 1.52W
Wiltshire *d.* U.K. 5 51.20N 0.34W
Wiltz Lux. 8 49.59N 5.53E
Wiluna Australia 42 26.36S120.13E
Wimmera *r.* Australia 46 36.05S141.56E
Winam *b.* Kenya 37 0.15S 34.30E
Winburg R.S.A. 39 28.30S 27.01E
Wincanton U.K. 5 51.03N 2.24W
Winchester U.K. 5 51.04N 1.19W
Winchester Va. U.S.A. 55 39.11N 78.10W
Winchester Wyo. U.S.A. 54 43.51N108.10W
Windermere *l.* U.K. 4 54.20N 2.56W
Windhoek Namibia 39 22.34S 17.06E
Windorah Australia 44 25.26S142.39E
Wind River Range *mts.* U.S.A. 54 43.05N109.25W
Windsor Australia 47 33.38S150.47E
Windsor Ont. Canada 55 42.18N 83.01W
Windsor Que. Canada 55 45.35N 72.01W
Windsor U.K. 5 51.29N 0.38W
Windward Is. C. America 57 13.00N 60.00W
Windward Passage *str.* Carib. Sea 57 20.00N 74.00W
Wingen Australia 47 31.43S150.54E
Wingham Australia 47 31.50S152.20E
Wingham Canada 55 43.53N 81.19W
Winifred U.S.A. 54 47.34N109.23W
Winisk Canada 51 55.15N 85.12W
Winisk *r.* Canada 51 55.20N 85.20W
Winisk L. Canada 51 52.55N 87.22W
Winneba Ghana 38 5.22N 0.38W
Winnebago, L. U.S.A. 53 44.00N 88.25W
Winnemucca U.S.A. 52 40.58N117.45W
Winnemucca L. U.S.A. 54 40.09N119.20W
Winnipeg Canada 51 49.53N 97.10W
Winnipeg, L. Canada 51 52.45N 98.00W
Winnipegosis, L. Canada 51 52.00N100.00W
Winona Minn. U.S.A. 53 44.02N 91.37W
Winooski U.S.A. 55 44.29N 73.11W
Winschoten Neth. 8 53.07N 7.02E
Winsford U.K. 4 53.12N 2.31W
Winslow Ariz. U.S.A. 54 35.01N110.42W
Winslow Maine U.S.A. 55 44.32N 69.38W
Winston U.S.A. 54 46.28N111.38W
Winston-Salem U.S.A. 53 36.05N 80.05W
Winsum Neth. 8 53.20N 6.31E
Winterswijk Neth. 8 51.58N 6.44E
Winterthur Switz. 14 47.30N 8.45E
Winthrop Wash. U.S.A. 54 48.29N120.11W
Winton Australia 44 22.22S143.00E
Winton New Zealand 48 46.10S168.20E
Winton U.S.A. 54 41.45N109.10W
Wirrabara Australia 46 33.03S138.18E
Wirraminna Australia 46 31.11S136.04E
Wirrappa Australia 46 31.28S137.00E
Wirrega Australia 46 36.11S140.37E
Wirrida, L. Australia 46 29.45S134.39E
Wirulla Australia 46 32.24S134.33E
Wisbech U.K. 5 52.39N 0.10E
Wisconsin *d.* U.S.A. 53 45.00N 90.00W
Wisconsin Rapids *town* U.S.A. 53 44.24N 89.55W
Wisdom U.S.A. 54 45.37N113.27W
Wisla *r.* Poland 15 54.23N 18.52E
Wismar Germany 14 53.54N 11.28E
Wisznice Poland 15 51.48N 23.12E
Witham *r.* U.K. 4 52.56N 0.04E
Withernsea U.K. 4 53.43N 0.02E
Witkowo Poland 15 52.27N 17.47E
Witney U.K. 5 51.47N 1.29W
Witsand R.S.A. 39 34.23S 20.49E
Witten Germany 8 51.26N 7.19E
Wittenberg Germany 14 51.53N 12.39E
Wittenberge Germany 14 52.59N 11.45E
Wittenoom Australia 42 22.19S118.21E
Wittlich Germany 8 49.59N 6.54E
Witu Kenya 37 2.22S 40.20E
Witvlei Namibia 39 22.25S 18.29E
Wiveliscombe U.K. 5 51.02N 3.20W
Wkra *r.* Poland 15 52.27N 20.44E
Władysławowo Poland 15 54.49N 18.25E
Włocławek Poland 15 52.39N 19.01E
Włodawa Poland 15 51.33N 23.31E
Wodonga Australia 47 36.08S146.09E
Woerden Neth. 8 52.07N 4.55E
Wokam *i.* Indonesia 27 5.45S134.30E
Woking U.K. 5 51.20N 0.34W
Wolf Creek *town* U.S.A. 54 46.50N112.20W
Wolfenbüttel Germany 14 52.10N 10.33E
Wolf Point *town* U.S.A. 54 48.05N105.39W
Wolfsberg Austria 14 46.51N 14.51E
Wolfsburg Germany 14 52.27N 10.49E
Wolin Poland 14 53.51N 14.38E
Wollaston L. Canada 50 58.15N103.30W
Wollaston Pen. Canada 50 70.00N115.00W
Wollongong Australia 47 34.25S150.52E
Wolmaransstad R.S.A. 39 27.11S 25.58E
Wołomin Poland 15 52.21N 21.14E
Wolseley Australia 46 36.21S140.55E
Wolvega Neth. 8 52.53N 6.00E
Wolverhampton U.K. 5 52.35N 2.06W
Wondai Australia 44 26.19S151.52E
Wongan Hills *town* Australia 43 30.55S116.41E
Wŏnsan N. Korea 25 39.07N127.26E
Wonthaggi Australia 47 38.38S145.37E
Woocalla Australia 46 31.44S137.10E
Woodbridge U.K. 5 52.06N 1.19E
Woodbridge U.S.A. 55 38.39N 77.15W
Woodburn Australia 47 29.04S153.21E
Wooded Bluff *f.* Australia 47 29.22S153.22E
Woodenbong Australia 47 28.28S152.35E
Woodland U.S.A. 54 38.41N121.46W
Woodlark I. P.N.G. 44 9.05S152.50E
Woodroffe, Mt. Australia 44 26.20S131.45E
Woods, L. Australia 44 17.50S133.30E
Woods, L. of the Canada/U.S.A. 51 49.15N 94.45W
Woodside Australia 47 38.31S146.52E
Woodstock Canada 55 43.08N 80.45W
Woodstock U.K. 5 51.51N 1.20W
Woodville New Zealand 48 40.20S175.52E
Wooler U.K. 4 55.33N 2.01W
Woolgoolga Australia 47 30.07S153.12E
Wooltana Australia 46 30.28S139.26E
Woomera Australia 46 31.11S136.54E
Woonsocket U.S.A. 55 42.00N 71.31W
Wooramel Australia 42 25.42S114.20E
Wooramel *r.* Australia 42 25.47S114.10E
Woorong, L. Australia 46 29.24S134.06E
Worcester R.S.A. 39 33.39S 19.25E
Worcester U.K. 5 52.12N 2.12W
Worcester U.S.A. 55 42.16N 71.48W
Workington U.K. 4 54.39N 3.34W
Worksop U.K. 4 53.19N 1.09W
Workum Neth. 8 53.00N 5.26E
Worland U.S.A. 54 44.01N107.57W
Worms Germany 14 49.38N 8.23E
Worthing U.K. 5 50.49N 0.21W
Worthington Minn. U.S.A. 53 43.37N 95.36W
Worthington Ohio U.S.A. 55 40.03N 83.03W
Worthville U.S.A. 55 38.38N 85.05W
Wosi Indonesia 27 0.15S128.00E
Woutchaba Cameroon 38 5.13N 13.05E
Wowoni *i.* Indonesia 27 4.10S123.10E
Wragby U.K. 4 53.17N 0.18E
Wrangel I. *see* Vrangelya, Ostrov *i.* Russian Fed. 21
Wrangell U.S.A. 50 56.28N132.23W
Wrangell Mts. U.S.A. 50 62.00N143.00W
Wrangle U.K. 4 53.03N 0.09E
Wrath, C. U.K. 6 58.37N 5.01W
Wrexham U.K. 4 53.05N 3.00W
Wrigley Canada 50 63.16N123.39W
Wrocław Poland 15 51.05N 17.00E
Wronki Poland 14 52.43N 16.23E
Września Poland 15 52.20N 17.34E
Wubin Australia 43 30.06S116.38E
Wuchang China 25 30.32N114.18E
Wudham 'Alwā' Oman 31 23.48N 57.33E
Wudinna Australia 46 33.03S135.28E
Wuhan China 25 30.35N114.19E
Wuhu China 25 31.23N118.25E
Wu Jiang *r.* China 24 30.10N107.26E
Wukari Nigeria 38 7.57N 9.42E
Wuliang Shan *mts.* China 24 24.27N100.43E
Wum Cameroon 38 6.25N 10.03E
Wumbulgal Australia 47 34.25S146.16E
Wuppertal Germany 8 51.15N 7.10E
Wuppertal R.S.A. 39 32.16S 19.12E
Wurno Nigeria 38 13.20N 5.28E
Wutongqiao China 24 29.21N103.48E
Wuwei China 24 38.00N102.54E
Wuxi Jiangsu China 25 31.35N120.19E
Wuzhan China 25 50.14N125.18E
Wuzhou China 25 23.30N111.21E
Würzburg Germany 14 49.48N 9.57E
Wyalkatchem Australia 43 31.21S117.22E
Wyalong Australia 47 33.55S147.17E
Wyandotte U.S.A. 55 42.11N 83.10W
Wyandra Australia 45 27.15S146.00E
Wyangala Resr. Australia 47 33.58S148.55E
Wyara, L. Australia 46 28.42S144.16E
Wycheproof Australia 46 36.04S143.14E
Wye U.K. 5 51.11N 0.56E
Wye *r.* U.K. 5 51.37N 2.40W
Wymondham U.K. 5 52.34N 1.07E
Wynbring Australia 45 30.33S133.32E
Wyndham Australia 42 15.29S128.05E
Wyoming *d.* U.S.A. 52 43.10N107.36W
Wyong Australia 47 33.17S151.25E
Wyszków Poland 15 52.36N 21.28E

X

Xainza China 24 30.56N 88.38E
Xai-Xai Mozambique 39 25.05S 33.38E
Xam Nua Laos 29 20.25N104.04E
Xangongo Angola 36 16.43S 15.01E
Xanten Germany 8 51.40N 6.29E
Xánthi Greece 13 41.07N 24.55E
Xau, L. Botswana 39 21.15S 24.50E
Xenia U.S.A. 55 39.41N 83.56W
Xhora R.S.A. 39 31.58S 28.40E
Xiaguan *see* Dali China 24
Xiamen China 25 24.26N118.07E
Xi'an China 25 34.16N108.54E
Xiangfan China 25 32.20N112.05E
Xiangkhoang Laos 29 19.11N103.23E
Xiangtan China 25 27.55N112.47E
Xiangyin China 25 28.40N112.53E
Xianyang China 25 34.23N108.40E
Xiao Hinggan Ling *mts.* China 25 48.40N128.30E
Xichang China 24 27.53N102.18E
Xigazê China 24 29.18N 88.50E
Xi Jiang *r.* China 25 22.23N113.20E
Xilin China 29 24.30N105.03E
Ximeng China 29 22.45N 99.29E
Xinfeng Jiangxi China 25 25.27N114.58E
Xing'an China 25 25.37N110.40E
Xingkai Hu *l.* *see* Khanka, Ozero China/Russian Fed. 25
Xingtai China 25 37.08N114.29E
Xingu *r.* Brazil 61 1.40S 52.15W
Xinhe Xin. Uygur China 24 41.34N 82.38E
Xining China 24 36.35N101.55E
Xinjiang-Uygur *d.* China 24 41.15N 87.00E
Xinjin Liaoning China 25 39.25N121.58E
Xin Xian China 25 38.24N112.47E
Xinxiang China 25 35.16N113.51E
Xinyu China 25 27.48N114.56E
Xinzhu Taiwan 25 24.48N120.59E
Xique Xique Brazil 61 10.47S 42.44W
Xixabangma Feng *mtn.* China 29 28.21N 85.47E
Xizang *d.* China 29 32.20N 86.00E
Xorkol China 24 39.04N 91.05E
Xuanhua China 25 40.36N115.01E
Xuchang China 25 34.03N113.48E
Xueshuiwen China 25 49.15N129.39E
Xugou China 25 34.42N119.28E
Xuyong China 24 28.10N105.24E
Xuzhou China 25 34.17N117.18E

Y

Ya'an China 29 30.00N102.59E
Yaapeet Australia 46 35.48S142.07E
Yabassi Cameroon 38 4.30N 9.55E
Yablonovyy Khrebet *mts.* Russian Fed. 21 53.20N115.00E
Yabrūd Syria 32 33.58N 36.40E
Yacheng China 25 18.30N109.12E
Yacuiba Bolivia 62 22.00S 63.25W
Yādgīr India 28 16.46N 77.08E
Yagaba Ghana 38 10.13N 1.14W
Yagoua Cameroon 38 10.23N 15.13E
Yahagi *r.* Japan 23 34.50N136.59E
Yaizu Japan 23 34.52N138.20E
Yajua Nigeria 38 11.27N 12.49E
Yakima U.S.A. 54 46.36N120.31W
Yaksha Russian Fed. 18 61.51N 56.59E
Yakutat U.S.A. 50 59.33N139.44W
Yakutsk Russian Fed. 21 62.10N129.20E
Yala Thailand 29 6.32N101.19E
Yalgoo Australia 43 28.20S116.41E
Yalinga C.A.R. 35 6.31N 23.15E
Yallourn Australia 47 38.09S146.22E
Yalong Jiang *r.* China 24 26.35N101.44E
Yalta Ukraine 19 44.30N 34.09E
Yalutorovsk Russian Fed. 20 56.41N 66.12E
Yamal, Poluostrov *pen.* Russian Fed. 20 70.20N 70.00E
Yamanashi Japan 23 35.40N138.40E
Yamanashi *d.* Japan 23 35.30N138.35E
Yaman Tau *mtn.* Russian Fed. 19 54.20N 58.10E
Yamato Japan 23 35.29N139.29E
Yamato-takada Japan 23 34.31N135.45E
Yamba N.S.W. Australia 47 29.26S153.22E
Yamba S.A. Australia 46 34.15S140.54E
Yambio Sudan 35 4.34N 28.23E
Yambol Bulgaria 13 42.28N 26.30E
Yamdena *i.* Indonesia 27 7.30S131.00E
Yamethin Burma 29 20.24N 96.08E
Yam Kinneret *l.* Israel 32 32.49N 35.36E
Yamma Yamma, L. Australia 44 26.20S141.25E
Yamoussoukro Ivory Coast 38 6.51N 5.18W
Yampi Sound Australia 42 16.11S123.30E
Yampol Ukraine 15 48.13N 28.12E
Yamuna *r.* India 29 25.20N 81.49E
Yan Nigeria 38 10.05N 12.11E
Yana *r.* Russian Fed. 21 71.30N135.00E
Yanac Australia 46 36.09S141.29E
Yanbu'al Baḩr Saudi Arabia 30 24.07N 38.04E
Yancannia Australia 46 30.16S142.50E
Yancheng China 25 33.23N120.10E
Yanchep Australia 43 31.32S115.33E
Yanchuan China 25 36.55N110.04E
Yanco Australia 47 34.36S146.25E
Yanco Glen *town* Australia 46 31.43S141.39E
Yanda *r.* Australia 47 30.22S145.38E
Yangarey Russian Fed. 18 68.46N 61.29E
Yangjiang China 25 21.51N111.58E
Yangon Burma 29 16.45N 96.20E
Yangon *see* Rangoon Burma 29
Yangquan China 25 37.52N113.29E
Yangtze *r.* *see* Chang Jiang *r.* China 25
Yanji China 25 42.45N129.25E
Yanko Creek *r.* Australia 47 35.25S145.27E
Yanqi China 24 42.00N 86.30E
Yanshan China 29 23.36N104.20E
Yanskiy Zaliv *g.* Russian Fed. 21 72.00N136.10E
Yantabulla Australia 47 29.13S145.01E
Yantai China 25 37.30N121.22E
Yao Chad 34 12.52N 17.34E
Yao Japan 23 34.37N135.36E
Yaoundé Cameroon 38 3.51N 11.31E
Yap *i.* Federated States of Micronesia 27 9.30N138.09E
Yapen *i.* Indonesia 27 1.45S136.10E
Yaqui *r.* Mexico 56 27.37N110.39W
Yar Russian Fed. 18 58.13N 52.08E
Yaraka Australia 44 24.53S144.04E
Yaransk Russian Fed. 18 57.22N 47.49E
Yardea Australia 46 32.23S135.32E
Yare *r.* U.K. 5 52.34N 1.45E
Yaremcha Ukraine 15 48.26N 24.29E
Yarensk Russian Fed. 18 62.10N 49.07E
Yargora Moldavia 15 46.25N 28.20E
Yaritagua Venezuela 60 10.05N 69.07W
Yarkant He *r.* China 24 40.30N 80.55E
Yarlung Zangbo Jiang *r.* *see* Brahmaputra *r.* Asia 29
Yarmouth Canada 55 43.50N 66.08W
Yaroslavl Russian Fed. 18 57.34N 39.52E
Yarra *r.* Australia 47 37.51S144.54E
Yarram Australia 47 38.30S146.41E
Yarrawonga Australia 47 36.02S145.59E
Yarrow *r.* U.K. 6 55.32N 2.51W
Yar Sale Russian Fed. 20 66.50N 70.48E
Yartsevo Russian Fed. 18 55.06N 32.43E
Yartsevo Russian Fed. 21 60.17N 90.02E
Yarumal Colombia 60 6.59N 75.25W
Yaselda *r.* Belorussia 15 52.07N 26.28E
Yasen Belorussia 15 53.10N 28.55E
Yashi Nigeria 38 12.23N 7.54E
Yashkul Russian Fed. 19 46.10N 45.20E
Yasinya Ukraine 15 48.12N 24.20E
Yasothon Thailand 29 15.46N104.12E
Yass Australia 47 34.51S148.55E
Yatakala Niger 38 14.52N 0.22E
Yaví, Cerro *mtn.* Venezuela 60 5.32N 65.59W
Yavorov Ukraine 15 49.59N 23.20E
Ya Xian *see* Sanya China 25
Yazd Iran 31 31.54N 54.22E
Ybbs Austria 14 48.11N 15.05E
Ye Burma 29 15.15N 97.50E
Yea Australia 47 37.12S145.25E
Yecla Spain 10 38.35N 1.05W
Yedintsy Moldavia 19 48.09N 27.18E
Yeeda Australia 42 17.36S123.39E
Yefremov Russian Fed. 18 53.08N 38.08E
Yegorlyk *r.* Russian Fed. 19 46.30N 41.52E
Yegoryevsk Russian Fed. 18 55.21N 39.01E
Yegros Paraguay 59 26.24S 56.25W
Yei Sudan 35 4.05N 30.40E
Yei *r.* Sudan 35 7.40N 30.13E
Yekaterinburg Russian Fed. 18 56.52N 60.35E
Yelets Russian Fed. 18 52.36N 38.30E
Yeletskiy Russian Fed. 18 67.04N 64.00E
Yell *i.* U.K. 6 60.35N 1.05W
Yellowdine Australia 43 31.19S119.36E
Yellowhead Pass Canada 50 52.53N118.28W
Yellowknife Canada 50 62.30N114.29W
Yellow Mt. Australia 47 32.19S146.50E
Yellowstone *r.* U.S.A. 54 47.58N103.59W
Yellowstone *r.* U.S.A. 52 47.55N103.45W
Yellowstone L. U.S.A. 54 44.25N110.38W
Yellowstone Nat. Park U.S.A. 54 44.30N110.35W
Yell Sd. U.K. 6 60.30N 1.11W
Yelma Australia 42 26.30S121.40E
Yelsk Belorussia 15 51.50N 29.10E
Yelwa Nigeria 38 10.48N 4.42E
Yemen Asia 35 14.20N 45.10E
Yemilchino Ukraine 15 50.58N 27.40E
Yenagoa Nigeria 38 4.59N 6.15E
Yenda Australia 47 34.15S146.13E
Yendi Ghana 38 9.29N 0.01W
Yenisey *r.* Russian Fed. 21 69.00N 86.00E

THE WORLD : Physical

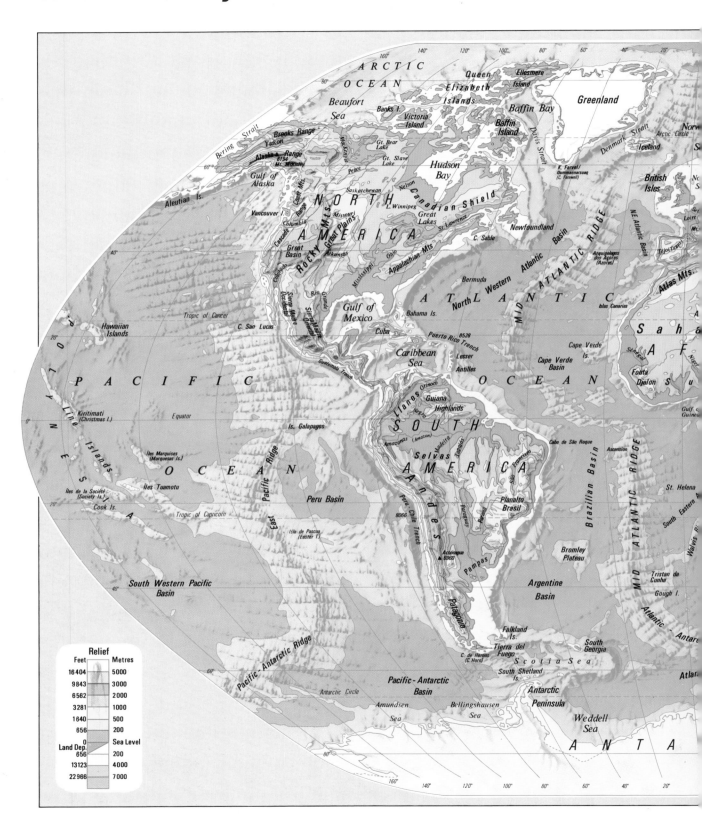

ARCTIC OCEAN

Beaufort Sea
Banks I.
Victoria Island
Queen Elizabeth Islands
Ellesmere Island
Greenland
Baffin Bay
Baffin Island
Davis Strait
Denmark Strait
Arctic Circle
Iceland
Norw

Bering Strait
Brooks Range
Yukon
Alaska Range
Mt. McKinley 6194
Gt. Bear Lake
Gt. Slave Lake
MacKenzie
Peace
Hudson Bay
K. Farvel Uummannarsuaq (C. Farewell)
British Isles
No S

Gulf of Alaska
Aleutian Is.
Vancouver I.
East Mts
Coast Range
Cascade Range
Columbia
NORTH AMERICA
Rocky Mts
Saskatchewan
L. Winnipeg
Great Lakes
Nelson
Canadian Shield
St. Lawrence
Newfoundland
C. Sable
North Western Atlantic Basin
MID ATLANTIC RIDGE
NE Atlantic Basin
Loire

Great Basin
Missouri
Great Plains
Arkansas
Ohio
Mississippi
Appalachian Mts
A T L A N T I C
Bermuda
Arquipelagos dos Açores (Azores)
Atlas Mts

Tropic of Cancer
Sierra Madre Occidental
Rio Grande
Sierra Madre Oriental
C. San Lucas
Gulf of Mexico
Bahama Is.
Cuba
Puerto Rico Trench 8528
Islas Canarias
Saha
A F

Hawaiian Islands
P A C I F I C
Guatemala Trench
Caribbean Sea
Lesser Antilles
Cape Verde
Cape Verde Basin
O C E A N
Senegal
Fouta Djalon
Niger
Su

Kiritimati (Christmas I.)
Equator
Is. Galapagos
Llanos
Orinoco
Guiana Highlands
SOUTH
Gulf of Guinea

Iles Marquises (Marquesas Is.)
Pacific Ridge
Amazonas (Amazon)
Selvas
AMERICA
Madeira
Cabo de São Roque
Ascension

Iles de la Société (Society Is.)
Iles Tuamotu
East
Peru Basin
São Francisco
Brazilian Basin
St. Helena

Cook Is.
Tropic of Capricorn
Isle de Pascoa (Easter I.)
Andes
Peru Chile Trench 8066
Tocantins
Paraguay
Paraná
Planalto Brasil
MID ATLANTIC RIDGE
South Eastern
Walvis R

South Western Pacific Basin
Aconcagua 6960
Pampas
Argentine Basin
Bromley Plateau
Tristan da Cunha
Gough I.
Atlantic Antar

Pacific-Antarctic Ridge
Patagonia
Falkland Is.
Tierra del Fuego
C. de Hornos (C. Horn)
South Georgia
Scotia Sea
South Shetland Is.
Antarctic Peninsula
Atlan

Antarctic Circle
Pacific-Antarctic Basin
Amundsen Sea
Bellingshausen Sea
Weddell Sea

A N T A

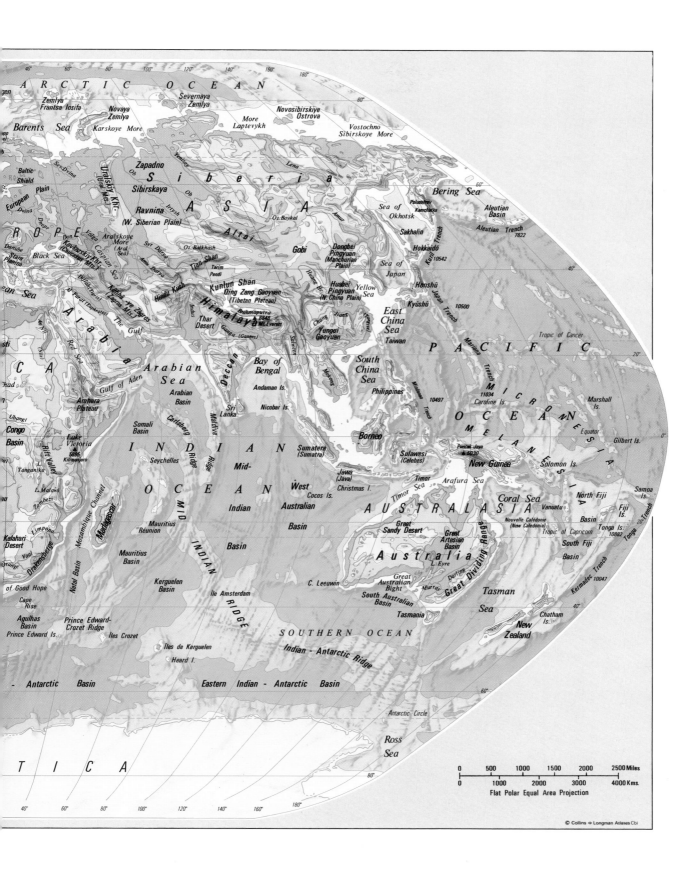

ARCTIC OCEAN

Zemlya Frantsa Iosifa
Severnaya Zemlya
Novosibirskiye Ostrova

Barents Sea
Novaya Zemlya
Karskoye More
More Laptevykh
Vostochno Sibirskoye More

Bering Sea

Baltic Shield
Zapadno Sibirskaya
Ravnina (W. Siberian Plain)
Siberia
ASIA
Peluostrov Kamchatka
Sea of Okhotsk
Aleutian Basin
Aleutian Trench 7822

European Plain
Uralskiy Kh. (Ural Mts.)
Ob
Sev. Dvina
Irtysh
Ob
Oz. Baykal
Amur
Altai
Sakhalin
Hokkaidō
Kuril Trench 10542

Dvina
Volga
Aralskoye More (Aral Sea)
Syr Darya
Oz. Balkhash
Gobi
Dongbei Pingyuan (Manchurian Plain)
Sea of Japan
Honshū
Japan Trench

Danube
Don
Caspian Sea
Kavkaskiy Kh. (Caucasus Mts.)
Amu Darya
Tian Shan
Tarim Pendi
Kunlun Shan
Qing Zang Gaoyuan (Tibetan Plateau)
Huabei Pingyuan (N. China Plain)
Yellow Sea
Kyūshū
10500

Black Sea
Stara Planina
Hindu Kush
Kettha ye Zagros (Zagros Mts.)
Himalaya
8848 Mt. Everest
Brahmaputra
Chang Yang
East China Sea
PACIFIC
Tropic of Cancer

Sea
Al Furat (Euphrates)
Dijla (Tigris)
The Gulf
Indus
Thar Desert
Ganga (Ganges)
Yungui Gaoyuan
Taiwan
20°

Arabia
Red Sea
Nile
Gulf of Aden
Arabian Sea
Deccan
Bay of Bengal
Mekong
Salween
South China Sea
40°

CA
Chad
Amhara Plateau
Somali Basin
Arabian Basin
Carlsberg
Sri Lanka
Andaman Is.
Nicobar Is.
Philippines
Mindanao Trench
10497
11034
Caroline Is.
MICRONESIA
Marshall Is.

Congo Basin
Ubangi
Lake Victoria
5895 Kilimanjaro
Seychelles
Maldive Ridge
Ridge
INDIAN
Mid-
Indian
Basin
Sumatera (Sumatra)
Borneo
Sulawesi (Celebes)
Puncak Jaya 5030
New Guinea
MELANESIA
Solomon Is.
OCEANIA
Equator
Gilbert Is.

Rift Valley
L. Malawi
Tanganika
Zambezi
Mozambique Channel
Madagascar
Mauritius
Réunion
West Australian
Cocos Is.
Jawa (Java)
Christmas I.
Timor
Timor Sea
Arafura Sea
AUSTRALASIA
Coral Sea
Vanuatu
Nouvelle Calédonie (New Caledonia)
North Fiji Basin
Samoa Is.
Fiji Is.

Kalahari Desert
Orange
Vaal
Drakensberg
Natal Basin
Mauritius Basin
Basin
Great Sandy Desert
Great Artesian Basin
L. Eyre
Australia
Great Dividing Range
Tropic of Capricorn
South Fiji Basin
Tonga Is. 10882
Tonga Trench

of Good Hope
Cape Rise
Agulhas Basin
Prince Edward-Crozet Ridge
Kerguelen Basin
Ile Amsterdam
MID
INDIAN
RIDGE
C. Leeuwin
Great Australian Bight
Murray
South Australian Basin
Darling
Tasman Sea
Chatham Is.
Kermadec Trench 10047
40°

Prince Edward Is.
Îles Crozet
Îles de Kerguelen
Heard I.
Tasmania
New Zealand

SOUTHERN OCEAN
Indian - Antarctic Ridge

Antarctic Basin
Eastern Indian - Antarctic Basin
Antarctic Circle
Ross Sea
60°

TICA
80°

0	500	1000	1500	2000	2500 Miles
0	1000	2000	3000	4000 Kms.	

Flat Polar Equal Area Projection

40° 60° 80° 100° 120° 140° 160° 180°
40° 60° 100° 120° 140° 160° 180°
80° 60° 40° 20°